The American
Immigration Collection

The Italians in Chicago

CARROLL D. WRIGHT

Arno Press and The New York Times

NEW YORK 1970

Reprint Edition 1970 by Arno Press Inc.

Reprinted from a copy in
The Kansas State University Library

LC# 72-129420
ISBN 0-405-00574-1

The American Immigration Collection—Series II
ISBN for complete set 0-405-00543-1

Manufactured in the United States of America

NINTH SPECIAL REPORT

OF THE

COMMISSIONER OF LABOR.

THE ITALIANS IN CHICAGO.

A SOCIAL AND ECONOMIC STUDY.

PREPARED UNDER THE DIRECTION OF

CARROLL D. WRIGHT,

COMMISSIONER OF LABOR.

WASHINGTON:

GOVERNMENT PRINTING OFFICE.

1897.

CONTENTS.

3

MESSAGE OF THE PRESIDENT.

To the Senate and House of Representatives:

I transmit herewith the Ninth Special Report of the Commissioner of Labor, which report relates to the social and economic condition of the Italians in Chicago.

WILLIAM McKINLEY.

EXECUTIVE MANSION,
     Washington, D. C., June 4, 1897.

5

LETTER OF TRANSMITTAL.

DEPARTMENT OF LABOR,
Washington, D. C., June 4, 1897.

SIR: I have the honor to transmit herewith the Ninth Special Report emanating from this Department. This report deals with the social and economic condition of the Italians in Chicago, and in it will be found valuable material for use in the consideration of the question of immigration. At the time of the Eleventh Census (1890) there were 5,685 persons of Italian birth residing in the city of Chicago. The report now submitted, covering portions of the years 1895 and 1896, shows the social and economic condition of 4,493 persons who were born in Italy, but embraces the facts for 6,773 persons in all, this number including those who were born in Italy and some who were born in this and other countries. The positive representative value of the report is thus seen to be established. The facts were collected entirely by Miss Caroline L. Hunt, in accordance with carefully prepared schedules. The tabulations have been under the charge of Mr. G. Wallace W. Hanger, while Mr. Oren W. Weaver, the chief clerk of the Department, has rendered most valuable services in revising the schedules and shaping the tables for the report. To Mr. Weaver, Mr. Hanger, and Miss Hunt I desire to express my acknowledgments for their services.

I am, very respectfully, your obedient servant,

CARROLL D. WRIGHT,
Commissioner.

The PRESIDENT.

CHAPTER I.

ANALYSIS OF TABLES.

CHAPTER I.

ANALYSIS OF TABLES.

This report is the result of an investigation commenced in April, 1896, by an agent of the Department into the social and economic condition of Italian families residing in the slum districts of Chicago. The questions pertaining to statistics covering a year are for the year preceding the date of the visit by the agent to the respective families. In all, 1,348 families of this character were visited and information secured for the 6,773 persons embraced therein. Of this number 4,493 were born in Italy. According to the United States census of 1890 there were 5,685 persons of Italian birth in the city of Chicago at that time. The limited time and force available for this investigation made it impossible to secure these individual reports from the whole Italian population of Chicago, and, indeed, such an extensive canvass was not deemed necessary. It is believed that the data secured for the 1,348 families visited is entirely representative of the conditions existing in all Italian families of a similar character in that city. The canvass was not confined to any particular portion of the city, but represents families from all sections. The following streets and avenues were canvassed, and each is represented by a number of families in the tables: Armour, Austin, Canal, Carpenter, Clark, De Koven, Desplaines, Erie, Ewing, Fay, Fifth, Forquer, Grand, Green, Halsted, Huron, Illinois, Indiana, Jefferson, Johnson, Kensington, Kenzie, Larrabee, La Salle, Law, Lincoln, Market, Morgan, Nineteenth, Ohio, One hundred and sixteenth, Pacific, Page, Peoria, Philip, Polk, Purple, Rockwell, Sangamon, Sebor, Sherman, Sixty-ninth, Taylor, Tilden, Twelfth, Twentieth, Twenty fifth, Union, Wentworth, Wood.

The general tables which relate to these families and form the basis of the analyses contained in this chapter are twenty in number, and are as follows:

TABLE I.—General social and economic condition, by families and individuals.

TABLE II.—General condition as to literacy and illiteracy, by families and individuals.

TABLE III.—School attendance, by families and individuals.

TABLE IV.— Conjugal condition, by sex, nativity, and age.

TABLE V.—Place of birth, by sex.

TABLE VI.—Number and size of families, by kind of family.

TABLE VII.—Nativity of parents.

11

TABLE VIII.—Relationship to head of family, by nativity and sex.

TABLE IX.—Foreign-born voters and aliens, by years in the United States.

TABLE X.—Weekly earnings and hours of work, by occupation and sex.

TABLE XI.—Persons unemployed, by months unemployed, sex, and age.

TABLE XII.—Illiterates, by sex, age periods, and degree of illiteracy.

TABLE XIII.—Literates, by sex, age periods, and language.

TABLE XIV.—Literates and illiterates, by sex.

TABLE XV.—School attendance, by nativity, age, kind of school, and sex.

TABLE XVI.—Condition of all children from 5 to 14 years of age, inclusive, by nativity and sex.

TABLE XVII.—Married women having a specified number of Italian-born children living, by number of children born to each in Italy and years of married life in Italy.

TABLE XVIII.—Married women having a specified number of native-born children living, by number of children born to each in the United States and years of married life in the United States.

TABLE XIX.—Married women having a specified number of children living, by number of children born to each and years of married life.

TABLE XX.—Persons sick or physically defective, by kind of ailment or defect and sex.

In the analysis of these tables comparisons have been made with the facts given in the Seventh Special Report of the Commissioner of Labor relating to the slums of great cities. That investigation was conducted along the same general lines as this, and embraced data for the year ending March 31, 1893, for all families, of whatever nationality, living within certain boundaries, which were designed to include the typical slum element of the four cities of Baltimore, Chicago, New York, and Philadelphia.

The first three tables in the above list show facts for individual persons and families, while the remaining tables are almost wholly compiled from them and bring the information given therein into a more concrete form. The analyses follow:

Table I.—General social and economic condition, by families and individuals, pp. 52 to 273.—In this table each family and individual is represented. The families are numbered from 1 to 1,348, inclusive, and a line given to each individual embraced in them. The various columns of the table give, for each individual, information as to the general social and economic condition. Information is first given as to the relationship to the head of the family, whether the head, or the wife, daughter, son, father, etc., of the head. The next column shows the sex of each individual, that being followed by the age in years, or fraction of a year, if less than 1 year old, and by conjugal condition—that is, whether single, married, or widowed. The name of the province where born follows, and the place of birth of the father and mother. The next column shows the years each individual has been in the United States if not born here, and the inquiry as to whether naturalized or not is then answered for each foreign-born male person 21 years of age or over. Following these inquiries, the economic condition is taken up, the next four columns showing the name of the principal profession, trade, or occupation at which each individual worked during the year, together with the hours of work per week, average weekly earnings, and weeks employed at the same during the year. In cases where persons were engaged in some other profession, trade, or occupation during the year, a footnote has been made, showing the name of such profession, trade, or occupation, together with the average weekly earnings and weeks employed at the same. The column showing profession, trade, or occupation is also used to describe the conditions pertaining to persons who, by reason of age, nonemployment, or their relation to the family, are not engaged in a gainful occupation. Persons 9 years of age or under, who have not been employed the whole year and were not at school during the year, have been designated as "at home." Wives engaged at housework have been designated "housewives" and persons having other relationships to the head of the family and employed in housework without pay have been designated as at "housework." Persons who have been at school during any part of the year are set down as "scholars." Persons 10 years of age or over who have been unemployed twelve months and have not been at school during the year are classed as having "no occupation." This designation includes those who are too old to work and those not capable. Persons of all gainful occupations who have retired from business are entered as "retired." The column immediately following those just described relating to occupations and earnings shows the total earnings during the past year of each wage earner, while the last column of the table answers the inquiry, Sick during the year, defective, maimed, or deformed, by giving the name of the ailment, defect, etc.

Each family is taken up in order in this table, the information relating to the head of the family being tabulated on the first line, while the remainder of the family follows, the facts for each individual member being given a line.

Turning to the table, and taking up family numbered 1, it is seen to consist of a male head, 35 years of age; his wife, 28 years of age; a daughter of 5 years, and two sons of 3 years and 3 months respectively. The next columns show that both the head of this family and his wife were born in the province of Calabria, that their parents were also born in that province, that they have been in the United States seven years, and that the head of the family has been naturalized. The three children were born in the United States. The columns following show that the head of the family worked forty-eight weeks during the year as porter in a bakery, his average weekly earnings being $7, and his hours of work per week sixty. Having worked at no other occupation during the year, his earnings for that period were $336. No other member of the family was a wage earner. The wife was occupied with the household duties and the care of the three children, all of whom as has been seen, were young, and have been classed as "at home." The final column of the table shows that the head of the family suffered from bronchitis at some time during the year, which probably accounts for the four weeks lost from work. A previous column showed the youngest child to have been 3 months old at the time the canvass was made, and the consequent illness of the wife is shown in the last column. The son 3 years of age is shown to have suffered from rickets during the year, while the daughter and younger son were not sick during that period. The other families embraced in this table may be analyzed in a similar manner.

Table II.—General condition as to literacy and illiteracy, by families and individuals, pp. 274 to 351.—In this table individuals under 10 years of age are not included, but the family numbers correspond to those in Table I, and the relationship to the head of the family, sex, and age are given in like order, that a comparison of the facts shown in both tables may be made for each individual.

Table II answers the inquiries as to the ability of all persons in these families 10 years of age or over to read and write their native language and to read, write, and speak the English language. As has been indicated, these questions are not answered for children under 10 years of age. Taking up the table and looking at the data for family numbered 1, which corresponds with family numbered 1 in Tables I and III, we notice that the head of this family is unable to read or write his native language (Italian), and, although he speaks English, is unable either to read or write that language. The wife can both read and write Italian, but can neither read nor write English, although she speaks that language. Both of these persons have been in the United States seven years. The other families follow in numerical order.

Table III.—School attendance, by families and individuals, pp. 352 to 369.—This table embraces all persons from 5 to 17 years of age, inclusive, as well as a few persons below or above these ages reported as scholars, showing for each the months of school attendance during the year and the kind of school. The family numbers are the same as for Tables I and II. In family numbered 1 but one member comes within the age limit, the daughter, 5 years old. It is shown that she did not attend school during the year. In the next family, numbered 2, a daughter 9 years old attended a public school ten months during the year. In family numbered 4, three persons come within the age limit, two sons and a nephew of the head of the family. The son 15 years old attended a public night school three months during the year, and the son 6 years old attended a public school seven months, while the nephew of 7 years did not attend school during the year.

Table IV.—Conjugal condition, by sex, nativity, and age, pp. 369 to 372.—This and the remaining tables of the report are largely in the nature of summaries of the facts already set forth in detail in the three preceding tables. Table IV deals with the conjugal condition of the persons embraced in the investigation, showing the number of single, married, and widowed, by sex, nativity, and age.

The following tables show the substantial facts to be drawn from Table IV:

PERSONS OF EACH CONJUGAL CONDITION, BY SEX AND NATIVITY.

Conjugal condition.	Males.			Females.			Males and females.		
	Native born.	Foreign born.	Total.	Native born.	Foreign born.	Total.	Native born.	Foreign born.	Total.
Single..............	1,141	1,012	2,153	1,089	382	1,471	2,230	1,394	3,624
Married............	3	1,726	1,729	16	1,255	1,271	19	2,981	3,000
Widowed...........	....	49	49	....	100	100	....	149	149
Total..........	1,144	2,787	3,931	·1,105	1,737	2,842	2,249	4,524	6,773

PER CENT OF PERSONS OF EACH CONJUGAL CONDITION, BY SEX AND NATIVITY.

Conjugal condition.	Males.			Females.			Males and females.		
	Native born.	Foreign born.	Total.	Native born.	Foreign born.	Total.	Native born.	Foreign born.	Total.
Single..............	99.74	36.31	54.77	98.55	21.99	51.76	99.16	30.81	53.51
Married............	.26	61.93	43.98	1.45	72.25	44.72	.84	65.89	44.29
Widowed...........	....	1.76	1.25	....	5.76	3.52	....	3.30	2.20
Total..........	100.00	100.00	100.00	100.00	100.00	100.00	100.00	100.00	100.00

It is here seen that 54.77 per cent of all males and 51.76 per cent of all females were single, and of all persons 53.51 per cent were single. Married males constituted 43.98 per cent of all males, while married females constituted 44.72 per cent of all females. The aggregate of married persons was 44.29 per cent of all persons. A small per cent of all persons were widowed, while it is shown that no divorced persons were found among these people.

The following table, reproduced from the Seventh Special Report of the Commissioner of Labor, shows the number and per cent of persons of each conjugal condition, by sex, found in the canvass of persons of all nationalities living in typical slum sections of the four cities of Baltimore, Chicago, New York, and Philadelphia:

NUMBER AND PER CENT OF PERSONS OF EACH CONJUGAL CONDITION, BY SEX, IN CERTAIN SLUM DISTRICTS OF BALTIMORE, CHICAGO, NEW YORK, AND PHIL-ADELPHIA.

[From the Seventh Special Report of the Commissioner of Labor.]

Conjugal condition.	Males.		Females.		Total.	
	Number.	Per cent.	Number.	Per cent.	Number.	Per cent.
BALTIMORE.						
Single	5,283	58.73	4,826	53.31	10,109	56.01
Married	3,437	38.21	3,425	37.84	6,862	38.02
Widowed	245	2.72	788	8.71	1,033	5.73
Divorced	12	.13	10	.11	22	.12
Not reported.........	19	.21	3	.03	22	.12
Total	8,996	100.00	9,052	100.00	18,048	100.00
CHICAGO.						
Single	6,359	59.70	4,859	53.41	11,218	56.81
Married	3,827	35.93	3,579	39.34	7,406	37.50
Widowed	193	1.81	570	6.27	763	3.86
Divorced	23	.22	51	.56	74	.38
Not reported.........	249	2.34	38	.42	287	1.45
Total	10,651	100.00	9,097	100.00	19,748	100.00

NUMBER AND PER CENT OF PERSONS OF EACH CONJUGAL CONDITION, BY SEX, IN CERTAIN SLUM DISTRICTS OF BALTIMORE, CHICAGO, NEW YORK, AND PHILA-DELPHIA—Concluded.

Conjugal condition.	Males.		Females.		Total.	
	Number.	Per cent.	Number.	Per cent.	Number.	Per cent.
NEW YORK.						
Single	8,614	54.40	6,785	51.55	15,399	53.11
Married	6,044	38.17	5,411	41.11	11,455	39.51
Widowed	278	1.75	947	7.20	1,225	4.22
Divorced	1	.01	3	.02	4	.01
Not reported	898	5.67	15	.12	913	3.15
Total	15,835	100.00	13,161	100.00	28,996	100.00
PHILADELPHIA.						
Single	5,207	57.07	4,264	53.72	9,471	55.52
Married	3,512	38.50	3,152	39.71	6,664	39.06
Widowed	154	1.69	508	6.40	662	3.88
Divorced	2	.02	2	.03	4	.02
Not reported	248	2.72	11	.14	259	1.52
Total	9,123	100.00	7,937	100.00	17,060	100.00

As has been stated, these figures refer to persons of all nationalities, while the figures drawn from Table IV of this report refer to persons of Italian nativity or extraction only, although the environment is very much the same in both cases. A comparison of the figures for these two classes shows a larger per cent of married persons among the families of Italian birth, whether compared with the figures for Chicago or with those for the other cities embraced in the Seventh Special Report. It is seen that of all persons included in the present report 44.29 per cent were married, while of all persons in the Seventh Special Report, Baltimore shows but 38.02 per cent, Chicago but 37.50 per cent, New York but 39.51 per cent, and Philadelphia but 39.06 per cent married.

The following table, taken from the Eleventh Census of the United States (1890), shows the number and per cent of persons of each conjugal condition, by sex, of the total population of Chicago:

NUMBER AND PER CENT OF PERSONS OF EACH CONJUGAL CONDITION, BY SEX, FOR THE CITY OF CHICAGO.

[From the Eleventh Census of the United States.]

Conjugal condition.	Males.		Females.		Total.	
	Number.	Per cent.	Number.	Per cent.	Number.	Per cent.
Single	349,795	61.54	292,515	55.04	642,310	58.40
Married	205,254	36.11	203.069	38.21	408,323	37.12
Widowed	10,752	1.89	34,629	6.52	45,381	4.13
Divorced	567	.10	1,073	.20	1,640	.15
Not reported	2,034	.36	162	.03	2,196	.20
Total	568,402	100.00	531,448	100.00	1,099.850	100.00

This table shows that of the entire male population of Chicago at the Eleventh Census 61.54 per cent were single and 36.11 per cent were married, while for the males embraced in the present report a much smaller per cent of single persons and a much larger per cent of married persons were found, the per cent being 54.77 and 43.98, respectively. The same condition was found to exist for the female population. Of the whole female population of Chicago, 55.04 per cent were single and 38.21 per cent were married. Of the persons included in this report, 51.76 per cent of the females were single and 44.72 per cent were married. Taking the total population of Chicago into consideration, the Eleventh Census shows 58.40 per cent single and 37.12 per cent married. Of those included in this report, persons of Italian birth or extraction, but 53.51 per cent were single, while 44.29 per cent were married.

As we have seen by the table on page 15, the Italians covered by the present report show for those born in this country 99.16 per cent of single persons and for those born abroad 30.81 per cent single. A similar disproportion was found to exist in the figures shown in the Seventh Special Report, and was there accounted for by the fact that "foreign-born persons coming to this country are usually married or of marriageable age, while the native born include a great number of children who have necessarily been classed as single." Reference to the table on page 15 shows this very clearly.

The following summary, drawn from Table IV, shows the ages, by periods of years, subdivided by sex and nativity, of the persons embraced in this investigation:

NUMBER AND PER CENT OF PERSONS OF EACH AGE PERIOD, BY SEX AND NATIVITY.

Age periods.	Males.				Females.				Total.			
	Native born.		Foreign born.		Native born.		Foreign born.		Native born.		Foreign born.	
	Number.	Per cent.	Number.	Per cent.	Number.	Per cent.	Number.	Per cent.	Number.	Per cent.	Number.	Per cent.
Under 5 years	648	56.64	14	0.50	631	57.11	20	1.15	1,279	56.87	34	0.75
5 to 9 years	344	30.07	113	4.05	326	29.50	124	7.14	670	29.79	237	5.24
10 to 14 years	115	10.05	185	6.64	106	9.59	150	8.64	221	9.83	335	7.41
15 to 19 years	20	1.75	234	8.40	24	2.17	146	8.40	44	1.96	380	8.40
20 to 24 years	10	.87	275	9.87	9	.82	185	10.65	19	.84	460	10.17
25 to 29 years	5	.44	384	13.78	5	.45	219	12.61	10	.44	603	13.33
30 to 34 years	2	.18	438	15.72	2	.18	234	13.47	4	.18	672	14.85
35 to 39 years			327	11.73	2	.18	210	12.09	2	.09	537	11.87
40 to 44 years			326	11.70			156	8.98			482	10.65
45 to 49 years			215	7.71			107	6.16			322	7.12
50 to 54 years			136	4.88			80	4.61			216	4.78
55 to 59 years			47	1.69			25	1.44			72	1.59
60 to 64 years			48	1.72			44	2.53			92	2.03
65 years or over			34	1.22			34	1.96			68	1.50
Age not reported			11	.39			3	.17			14	.31
Total	1,144	100.00	2,787	100.00	1,105	100.00	1,737	100.00	2,249	100.00	4,524	100.00

Taking up the total number of persons in these Italian families as shown in the total columns of the preceding table, it is seen that a very large proportion of native-born persons, 56.87 per cent, were under 5 years of age and 29.79 per cent were between 5 and 9 years of age, making 86.66 per cent under 10 years of age. This becomes more noticeable when compared with the following table, showing similar information for the inhabitants of the slum districts embraced in the

Seventh Special Report, where the proportion of native-born persons under 5 years of age was but 21.73 per cent in Baltimore, 29.42 per cent in Chicago, 35.80 per cent in New York, and 35.92 per cent in Philadelphia, and the proportion of those from 5 to 9 years of age but 17.72 per cent in Baltimore, 17.30 per cent in Chicago, 20.69 per cent in New York, and 18.08 per cent in Philadelphia. The largest proportion of foreign-born persons in these Italian families, 14.85 per cent, was found between 30 and 34 years of age, 60.87 per cent of all having been between 20 and 44 years of age. Of the slum population embraced in the Seventh Special Report the largest proportion of foreign-born persons was found in each of the cities between 25 and 29 years of age, while the proportion between 20 and 44 years, though not so large as that found in the Italian families embraced in this report, was quite large, amounting to 48.12 per cent in Baltimore, 55 per cent in Chicago, 54.96 per cent in New York, and 51.78 per cent in Philadelphia.

The table from the Seventh Special Report follows:

NUMBER AND PER CENT OF PERSONS OF EACH AGE PERIOD, BY SEX AND NATIV-
ITY, IN CERTAIN SLUM DISTRICTS OF BALTIMORE, CHICAGO, NEW YORK, AND
PHILADELPHIA.

[From the Seventh Special Report of the Commissioner of Labor.]

Age periods.	Males.				Females.				Total.			
	Native born.		Foreign born.		Native born.		Foreign born.		Native born.		Foreign born.	
	Number.	Per cent.	Number.	Per cent.	Number.	Per cent.	Number.	Per cent.	Number.	Per cent.	Number.	Per cent.
BALTIMORE.												
Under 5 years	1,134	21.17	64	1.76	1,211	22.29	51	1.41	2,345	21.73	115	1.59
5 to 9 years	917	17.12	172	4.73	995	18.31	169	4.67	1,912	17.72	341	4.70
10 to 14 years	598	11.16	244	6.70	634	11.67	204	5.64	1,232	11.42	448	6.17
15 to 19 years	558	10.42	275	7.56	548	10.09	359	9.92	1,106	10.25	634	8.74
20 to 24 years	495	9.24	313	8.60	536	9.87	404	11.16	1,031	9.56	717	9.88
25 to 29 years	443	8.27	404	11.10	386	7.10	403	11.14	829	7.68	807	11.12
30 to 34 years	386	7.21	423	11.62	366	6.74	345	9.53	752	6.97	768	10.58
35 to 39 years	299	5.58	311	8.55	300	5.52	259	7.16	599	5.55	570	7.85
40 to 44 years	207	3.86	331	9.10	185	3.41	300	8.29	392	3.63	631	8.69
45 to 49 years	133	2.48	269	7.39	105	1.93	237	6.55	238	2.21	506	6.97
50 to 54 years	86	1.61	259	7.12	65	1.20	253	6.99	151	1.40	512	7.05
55 to 59 years	30	.56	185	5.08	38	.70	167	4.61	68	.63	352	4.85
60 to 64 years	36	.67	156	4.29	22	.40	173	4.78	58	.54	329	4.53
65 years or over	31	.58	211	5.80	35	.64	292	8.07	66	.61	503	6.93
Age not reported	4	.07	22	.60	7	.13	3	.08	11	.10	25	.35
Total	5,357	100.00	3,639	100.00	5,433	100.00	3,619	100.00	10,790	100.00	7,258	100.00
CHICAGO.												
Under 5 years	1,202	28.07	157	2.46	1,267	30.83	139	2.79	2,469	29.42	296	2.61
5 to 9 years	735	17.17	366	5.75	717	17.45	318	6.38	1,452	17.30	684	6.02
10 to 14 years	454	10.60	422	6.63	452	11.00	407	8.16	906	10.80	829	7 30
15 to 19 years	383	8.94	512	8.04	442	10.76	551	11.05	825	9.83	1,063	9.36
20 to 24 years	456	10.65	719	11.29	432	10.51	608	12.19	888	10.58	1,327	11.68
25 to 29 years	333	7.78	949	14.90	296	7.20	690	13.83	629	7.50	1,639	14.43
30 to 34 years	256	5.98	799	12.54	185	4.50	495	9.92	441	5.26	1,294	11.39
35 to 39 years	189	4.41	615	9.66	136	3.31	449	9.00	325	3.87	1,064	9.37
40 to 44 years	91	2.13	541	8.49	69	1.68	382	7.66	160	1.91	923	8.13
45 to 49 years	42	.98	351	5.51	41	1.00	279	5.59	83	.99	630	5.55
50 to 54 years	29	.68	266	4.18	22	.54	220	4.41	51	.61	486	4.28
55 to 59 years	11	.26	135	2.12	4	.10	127	2.55	15	.18	262	2.31
60 to 64 years	13	.30	112	1.76	9	.22	108	2.16	22	.26	220	1.94
65 years or over	4	.09	155	2.43	6	.15	158	3.17	10	.12	313	2.75
Age not reported	84	1.96	270	4.24	31	.75	57	1.14	115	1.37	327	2.88
Total	4,282	100.00	6,369	100.00	4,109	100.00	4,988	100.00	8,391	100.00	11,357	100.00

NUMBER AND PER CENT OF PERSONS OF EACH AGE PERIOD, BY SEX AND NATIVITY, IN CERTAIN SLUM DISTRICTS OF BALTIMORE, CHICAGO, NEW YORK, AND PHILADELPHIA—Concluded.

Age periods.	Males.				Females.				Total.			
	Native born.		Foreign born.		Native born.		Foreign born.		Native born.		Foreign born.	
	Number.	Per cent.	Number.	Per cent.	Number.	Per cent.	Number.	Per cent.	Number.	Per cent.	Number.	Per cent.
NEW YORK.												
Under 5 years......	1,902	33.49	209	2.06	1,982	38.34	192	2.40	3,884	35.80	401	2.21
5 to 9 years.........	1,117	19.67	441	4.34	1,128	21.82	441	5.52	2,245	20.69	882	4.86
10 to 14 years.......	626	11.02	616	6.07	604	11.68	573	7.17	1,230	11.34	1,189	6.55
15 to 19 years.......	431	7.59	748	7.37	529	10.23	776	9.71	960	8.85	1,524	8.40
20 to 24 years.......	356	6.27	950	9.35	317	6.13	942	11.79	673	6.20	1,892	10.43
25 to 29 years.......	284	5.00	1,307	12.87	216	4.18	960	12.01	500	4.61	2,267	12.49
30 to 34 years.......	174	3.06	1,333	13.13	147	2.84	908	11.36	321	2.96	2,241	12.35
35 to 39 years.......	116	2.04	1,141	11.24	102	1.97	792	9.91	218	2.01	1,933	10.65
40 to 44 years.......	65	1.14	983	9.68	64	1.24	658	8.23	129	1.19	1,641	9.04
45 to 49 years.......	30	.53	581	5.72	27	.52	503	6.30	57	.52	1,084	5.98
50 to 54 years.......	23	.40	508	5.00	18	.35	408	5.11	41	.38	916	5.05
55 to 59 years.......	10	.18	246	2.42	10	.19	279	3.49	20	.18	525	2.89
60 to 64 years.......	9	.16	230	2.26	8	.16	263	3.29	17	.16	493	2.72
65 years or over....	7	.12	213	2.10	5	.10	225	2.82	12	.11	438	2.41
Age not reported...	530	9.33	649	6.39	13	.25	71	.89	543	5.00	720	3.97
Total	5,680	100.00	10,155	100.00	5,170	100.00	7,991	100.00	10,850	100.00	18,146	100.00
PHILADELPHIA.												
Under 5 years......	1,192	35.92	137	2.36	1,232	35.93	139	3.08	2,424	35.92	276	2.68
5 to 9 years.........	618	18.62	374	6.44	602	17.56	350	7.76	1,220	18.08	724	7.02
10 to 14 years.......	322	9.70	448	7.72	329	9.59	410	9.10	651	9.65	858	8.32
15 to 19 years.......	263	7.92	487	8.39	258	7.52	525	11.65	521	7.72	1,012	9.81
20 to 24 years.......	232	6.99	629	10.84	272	7.93	568	12.60	504	7.47	1,197	11.61
25 to 29 years.......	172	5.18	760	13.09	187	5.45	545	12.09	359	5.32	1,305	12.65
30 to 34 years.......	152	4.58	698	12.03	153	4.46	437	9.69	305	4.52	1,135	11.01
35 to 39 years.......	136	4.10	547	9.42	125	3.65	385	8.54	261	3.87	932	9.04
40 to 44 years.......	71	2.14	467	8.05	71	2.07	303	6.72	142	2.10	770	7.47
45 to 49 years.......	40	1.21	287	4.95	53	1.55	233	5.17	93	1.38	520	5.04
50 to 54 years.......	33	1.00	280	4.82	31	.90	194	4.30	64	.95	474	4.60
55 to 59 years.......	21	.63	138	2.38	24	.70	106	2.35	45	.67	244	2.37
60 to 64 years.......	14	.42	118	2.03	17	.50	128	2.84	31	.46	246	2.38
65 years or over....	26	.78	126	2.17	35	1.02	141	3.13	61	.90	267	2.59
Age not reported...	27	.81	308	5.31	40	1.17	44	.98	67	.99	352	3.41
Total	3,319	100.00	5,804	100.00	3,429	100.00	4,508	100.00	6,748	100.00	10,312	100.00

The following table, compiled from the Eleventh Census of the United States, shows similar facts for the total population of Chicago:

NUMBER AND PER CENT OF PERSONS OF EACH AGE PERIOD, BY SEX AND NATIVITY, OF THE TOTAL POPULATION OF CHICAGO.

[From the Eleventh Census of the United States.]

Age periods.	Males.				Females.				Total.			
	Native born.		Foreign born.		Native born.		Foreign born.		Native born.		Foreign born.	
	Number.	Per cent.	Number.	Per cent.	Number.	Per cent.	Number.	Per cent.	Number.	Per cent.	Number.	Per cent.
Under 5 years......	68,619	20.74	2,571	1.08	67,187	21.04	2,406	1.14	135,806	20.89	4,977	1.11
5 to 9 years	50,908	15.39	7,489	3.15	50,848	15.92	7,401	3.49	101,756	15.65	14,890	3.31
10 to 14 years.......	36,645	11.07	11,876	5.00	37,357	11.70	11,946	5.63	74,002	11.38	23,822	5.30
15 to 19 years.......	34,376	10.39	13,643	5.74	37,063	11.61	15,390	7.26	71,439	10.99	29,033	6.46
20 to 24 years.......	34,830	10.53	26,216	11.04	35,620	11.15	28,364	13.37	70,450	10.83	54,580	12.14
25 to 29 years.......	30,937	9.35	35,891	15.11	28,916	9.05	30,997	14.61	59,853	9.21	66,888	14.87
30 to 34 years.......	25,562	7.73	33,643	14.16	21,289	6.67	24,951	11.76	46,851	7.21	58,594	13.03
35 to 39 years.......	16,253	4.91	26,732	11.25	13,352	4.18	20,825	9.82	29,605	4.55	47,557	10.58
40 to 44 years.......	10,354	3.13	22,726	9.57	8,518	2.67	18,437	8.69	18,872	2.90	41,163	9.15
45 to 49 years.......	7,308	2.21	18,745	7.89	6,092	1.91	14,983	7.06	13,400	2.06	33,728	7.50
50 to 54 years.......	5,192	1.57	14,269	6.01	4,465	1.40	12,336	5.82	9,657	1.49	26,605	5.92
55 to 59 years.......	3,056	.92	8,516	3.59	2,693	.84	8,112	3.83	5,749	.88	16,628	3.70
60 to 64 years.......	2,214	.67	6,900	2.91	2,139	.67	6,993	3.30	4,353	.67	13,893	3.09
65 years or over....	2,761	.83	7,806	3.29	3,178	.99	8,726	4.11	5,939	.91	16,532	3.68
Age not reported...	1,864	.56	500	.21	626	.20	238	.11	2,490	.38	738	.16
Total	330,879	100.00	237,523	100.00	319,343	100.00	212,105	100.00	650,222	100.00	449,628	100.00

Table V.—Place of birth, by sex, p. 372.—This table shows the province or country where born for all persons embraced in the investigation. A very few of the foreign-born persons (less than one-half of 1 per cent) found in these families were of other than Italian origin. According to the Eleventh Census of the United States, there were 5,685 persons of Italian birth in the city of Chicago. As many as 4,493 persons of Italian birth were found in the families embraced in this report; 2,249 were born in the United States, while 31 were born in other countries. Of the 66.33 per cent of persons of both sexes born in Italy, the largest proportion, 18.28 per cent, were born in the province of Campania. Basilicata follows with 17.78 per cent, Calabria with 12.68 per cent, Sicily with 7.83 per cent, Abruzzo with 5.18 per cent, etc. Those born in the United States, mainly children, constituted 33.20 per cent of all persons found in these families.

Table VI.—Number and size of families, by kind of family, p. 372.—Three classes or kinds of families were found in gathering the data which form the basis of this report, viz, private families, cooperative families, and boarding and lodging houses. Every group of individuals living under one roof and bearing some relation to one head, whether of kin or not, has, according to the usual custom, been termed a family. In addition to the private or normal family, in which all or most of its members are related by ties of blood, and the boarding and lodging house, there has been found, among these Italians, the cooperative family. The cooperative family is composed of a number of persons, usually males, living together and sharing the household expenses. Very frequently they do their own cooking and housework. Table VI shows the number and per cent of families of each size, from one to eighteen persons, subdivided as to the kind of family, as described above. Reference to the table shows that of the 1,348 families investigated, 1,265, or 93.84 per cent, were private, 68, or 5.05 per cent, were cooperative, and 15, or 1.11 per cent, were boarding and lodging houses. Taking into consideration all families of whatever kind, it was found that those consisting of 4 persons predominated, embracing 20.55 per cent of all families; those of 5 persons follow, embracing 19.51 per cent, while those of 6 persons embraced 13.43 per cent, and those of 3 persons, 12.02 per cent.

The average size of all families in the present report is 5.02 persons. In the Seventh Special Report, in which slum families of various nationalities were included, the average size of the family was, in Baltimore, 4.48 persons; in Chicago, 5.09 persons; in New York, 4.90 persons, and in Philadelphia, 5.15 persons. The average size of all families in Chicago, according to the Eleventh Census of the United States, was 4.99 persons. The figures for the Italian families included in the present report do not, then, differ materially in respect to size of family from what has been shown in the Seventh Special Report and in the Eleventh Census.

*Table VII.—Nativity of parents, p. 373.—*This table classifies the native-born and foreign-born persons included in this investigation according to parent nativity, with specified place of birth. The following table, showing the number and per cent of persons of each parent nativity, brings the figures into more convenient form for comparison:

NUMBER AND PER CENT OF PERSONS OF EACH PARENT NATIVITY.

Birthplace of—		Native born.		Foreign born.		Total.	
Father.	Mother.	Number.	Per cent.	Number.	Per cent.	Number.	Per cent.
United States	United States	3	0. 14			3	0. 05
United States	Basilicata	1	. 04			1	. 01
United States	Liguria	4	. 18			4	. 06
Abruzzo	Abruzzo	117	5. 20	365	8. 07	482	7. 12
Abruzzo	Basilicata	2	. 09			2	. 03
Abruzzo	Campania			1	. 02	1	. 01
Apulia	Apulia	4	. 18	12	. 27	16	. 24
Basilicata	Abruzzo	4	. 18			4	. 06
Basilicata	Basilicata	715	31. 79	1, 195	26. 41	1, 910	28. 20
Basilicata	Campania	8	. 36			8	. 12
Basilicata	Lombardy	5	. 22			5	. 07
Basilicata	Sicily	5	. 22	1	. 02	6	. 09
Basilicata	Germany	2	. 09			2	. 03
Basilicata	Ireland	1	. 04			1	. 01
Basilicata	Sweden	1	. 04			1	. 01
Calabria	United States	2	. 09			2	. 03
Calabria	Abruzzo	2	. 09			2	. 03
Calabria	Basilicata	14	. 62			14	. 21
Calabria	Calabria	200	8. 89	859	18. 99	1, 059	15. 64
Calabria	Campania	1	. 04	1	. 02	2	. 03
Campagna di Roma.	United States	1	. 04			1	. 01
Campagna di Roma.	Campagna di Roma	3	. 14	6	. 13	9	. 13
Campania	United States	3	. 14			3	. 05
Campania	Abruzzo	2	. 09			2	. 03
Campania	Basilicata	52	2. 31	8	. 18	60	. 89
Campania	Calabria	6	. 27	1	. 02	7	. 10
Campania	Campagna di Roma	2	. 09			2	. 03
Campania	Campania	678	30. 15	1, 238	27. 36	1, 916	28. 29
Campania	Sicily	7	. 31			7	. 10
Campania	Ireland	4	. 18			4	. 06
Emilia	Emilia	14	. 62	32	. 71	46	. 68
Liguria	United States	6	. 27			6	. 09
Liguria	Basilicata	3	. 14			3	. 05
Liguria	Liguria	73	3. 25	105	2. 32	178	2. 63
Liguria	Scotland	1	. 04			1	. 01
Lombardy	Basilicata	9	. 40	1	. 02	10	. 15
Lombardy	Emilia	1	. 04			1	. 01
Lombardy	Liguria	2	. 09			2	. 03
Lombardy	Lombardy	17	. 76	36	. 80	53	. 78
Lombardy	Piedmont	3	. 14			3	. 05
Marches	Basilicata	1	. 04	2	. 05	3	. 05
Marches	Marches			4	. 09	4	. 06
Piedmont	Piedmont	1	. 04	7	. 15	8	. 12
Sicily	Basilicata	2	. 09			2	. 03
Sicily	Sicily	213	9. 47	530	11. 72	743	10. 97
Tuscany	Liguria	4	. 18			4	. 06
Tuscany	Tuscany	29	1. 29	80	1. 77	109	1. 61
Tuscany	France	3	. 14	4	. 09	7	. 10
Tuscany	Not specified			1	. 02	1	. 01
Venetia	United States	2	. 09			2	. 03
Venetia	Liguria	1	. 04			1	. 01
Venetia	Venetia	10	. 44	29	. 64	39	. 58
France	France			3	. 07	3	. 05
Germany	Germany	2	. 09	1	. 02	3	. 05
Ireland	United States	1	. 04			1	. 01
Ireland	Ireland			1	. 02	1	. 01
Sweden	Sweden			1	. 02	1	. 01
Not specified	Campania	1	. 04			1	. 01
Not specified	Not specified	1	. 04			1	. 01
Total		2, 249	100. 00	4, 524	100. 00	6, 773	100. 00

In Table V, showing the place of birth of persons included in the investigation, it was seen that the largest proportion were born in Campania, that province being followed by Basilicata, Calabria, Sicily, Abruzzo, etc. In this table, giving the birthplace of the parents of those shown in Table V, it is seen that Campania also shows the largest proportion, 28.29 per cent, and is followed by Basilicata with 28.20 per cent, Calabria with 15.64 per cent, Sicily with 10.97 per cent, Abruzzo with 7.12 per cent, etc.

Table VIII.—Relationship to head of family, by nativity and sex, p. 374.—Native-born persons, foreign-born persons, and native and foreign born persons combined are in this table classified according to their relationship to the head of the family in which they reside, and further classified by sex. It is seen from the table that of the native-born persons living in these Italian families 95.02 per cent were children of the heads of their respective families. This is accounted for in the same manner as the disproportion existing between the number of native and foreign born single and married persons in the analysis to Table IV. It was stated there that foreign-born persons coming to this country are usually married or of marriageable age, while the native born include a great number of children. Native-born heads of families and their wives constituted less than 1 per cent of all native-born persons living in these families. Of foreign-born persons, however, 54.07 per cent were heads of families and their wives, while sons and daughters of the head constituted but 20.07 per cent of all foreign born. Taking the third division of the table, which combines the facts for both native and foreign born persons, heads of families and their wives constituted 36.35 per cent of all persons, their sons and daughters 44.96 per cent, the remainder being fathers and mothers, brothers and sisters, uncles and aunts, nephews and nieces, cousins, boarders, lodgers, persons belonging to cooperative families, etc.

Table IX.—Foreign-born voters and aliens, by years in the United States, p. 375.—This table classifies all foreign-born males 21 years of age or over embraced in these families as voters or as aliens, and gives the number of years they have been in the United States. All males of foreign birth 21 years of age or over, not naturalized, have been considered aliens. A residence of five years in the United States is necessary for a person to become a voter in the State of Illinois. Of the foreign-born males 21 years of age or over who had been in the United States five years, 45 per cent were voters. Of those who had been in the United States a greater number of years, the proportion of voters was considerably larger, and taking into consideration all persons included in the table, 53.81 per cent were voters and 46.19 per cent were aliens. According to the Eleventh Census of the United States, 31.27 per cent of all foreign-born males 21 years of age or over in Chicago were aliens. The considerably larger proportion of aliens among the

Italians embraced in this investigation, 46.19 per cent, shows that persons of this class to quite a large extent have not taken advantage of the privilege of becoming naturalized citizens of this country. An even larger proportion, 52.51 per cent, of the foreign-born persons 21 years of age or over included in the Seventh Special Report were classed as aliens in Chicago.

Of the 1,012 aliens included in these Italian families a partial report was secured as to whether naturalization papers had been taken out. Of a total of 939 persons reporting as to this fact, 132, or 14.06 per cent, reported that they had taken out such papers preliminary to becoming citizens of the United States, while 807, or 85.94 per cent, reported that they had not taken out naturalization papers.

Table X.— Weekly earnings and hours of work, by occupation and sex, pp. 376 to 380.—This table shows the various occupations engaged in by the persons composing the Italian families canvassed, arranged under the following general industry heads: Agriculture, fisheries, and mining; professional; domestic and personal service; trade and transportation; manufactures and mechanical industries; nonproductive; housewives and at work, and scholars and at work. The number and sex of persons working at each occupation are shown, together with their average hours of work per week and their highest, lowest, and average weekly earnings while employed. It is unfortunate that the information as to working hours and earnings were so often impossible to secure, and are, consequently, not reported in the table. It is believed, however, that the data given on these points are representative and afford a very fair idea of the conditions that exist. It is interesting to note the occupations most frequently followed by the persons composing these families: Under the general industry heading of agriculture, fisheries, and mining, 28 worked as quarrymen; under professional, musicians and organ grinders numbered 62; under domestic and personal service were found 797 laborers, 126 street sweepers, 73 bootblacks, 45 barbers, 32 sewer diggers, 23 pavers, 22 saloon keepers, and 18 scissors grinders; under trade and transportation, 186 worked as rag and paper pickers, sorters, etc., 154 as small peddlers, 119 as railroad laborers, 78 as newsboys, news dealers, etc., 32 as small merchants or dealers in various lines, 20 as salesmen, 15 as teamsters, and 14 as wood pickers; under manufactures were found 60 hod carriers, 38 candy makers and candy factory employees, 26 pants makers and finishers, 22 mosaic layers, 19 tailors and tailoresses, 16 shoemakers, and 14 tinkers; under the head of nonproductive (by far the largest), 1,689 were classed as at home, which in this table means all persons 9 years of age or under who were not at school and unemployed during the year; 1,044 were housewives and 113 were engaged in housework without pay; 361 were classed as having no occupation, and include those 10 years of age or over who were unemployed twelve months and who were not at school during the year, and 876 were scholars. Under the division of housewives and at work, which includes those performing their household duties and, in addition, engaging in work for pay, were found 188 persons; the occupations most common to them were the making and finishing of pants and other garments, dressmaking, washing, and wood, coal, and rag picking. Under the division of scholars and at work were 112 persons who, in addition to attendance at school, were engaged in selling papers, blacking shoes, peddling, etc. It is seen that the occupations in which these persons were engaged are generally those requiring but a low grade of intelligence and little skill or muscular strength.

The following table, drawn from Table X, shows the number and per cent of persons of each industrial group:

NUMBER AND PER CENT OF PERSONS OF EACH INDUSTRIAL GROUP.

Groups of occupations.	Males.		Females.		Total.		Per cent under each group.
	Number.	Per cent.	Number.	Per cent.	Number.	Per cent.	
Agriculture, fisheries, and mining..........	32	100.00	....	....	32	100.00	0.47
Professional...............................	63	95.45	3	4.55	66	100.00	.98
Domestic and personal service..............	1,194	99.17	10	.83	1,204	100.00	17.78
Trade and transportation...................	655	95.34	32	4.66	687	100.00	10.14
Manufactures and mechanical industries...	306	81.82	68	18.18	374	100.00	5.52
Nonproductive.............................	1,581	38.47	2,529	61.53	4,110	100.00	60.68
Housewives and at work....................	....	....	188	100.00	188	100.00	2.78
Scholars and at work.......................	100	89.29	12	10.71	112	100.00	1.65
Total......................	3,931	58.04	2,842	41.96	6,773	100.00	100.00

According to this table, the nonproductive class included 60.68 per cent of all the persons in the families canvassed. Less than 1 per cent of all were engaged in agriculture, fisheries, and mining or in professional work. Those engaged in domestic and personal service constituted 17.78 per cent of all, those engaged in trade and transportation 10.14 per cent, those engaged in manufactures and mechanical industries 5.52 per cent, while those who were engaged in some work in addition to their household duties constituted 2.78 per cent, and those engaged in some work besides going to school, 1.65 per cent.

This table also shows the distribution of the sexes under each industrial group. The small proportion of women at work at gainful occupations is quite noticeable. In the largest group, domestic and personal service, less than 1 per cent were females; in the next largest group, trade and transportation, but 4.66 per cent of all embraced under that head were females, and in manufactures and mechanical industries, 18.18 per cent were females.

The following table, taken from the Seventh Special Report of the Commissioner of Labor, relating to the population of typical slum sections of four cities, is reproduced for comparison with the immediately preceding table relating to the Italian families embraced in the present report:

NUMBER AND PER CENT OF PERSONS OF EACH INDUSTRIAL GROUP IN CERTAIN SLUM DISTRICTS OF BALTIMORE, CHICAGO, NEW YORK, AND PHILADELPHIA.

[From the Seventh Special Report of the Commissioner of Labor.]

Groups of occupations.	Males.		Females.		Total.		Per cent under each group.
	Number.	Per cent.	Number.	Per cent.	Number.	Per cent.	
BALTIMORE.							
Agriculture, fisheries, and mining	63	82.89	13	17.11	76	100.00	0.42
Professional	95	84.82	17	15.18	112	100.00	.62
Domestic and personal service	1,685	82.92	347	17.08	2,032	100.00	11.26
Trade and transportation	1,668	90.11	183	9.89	1,851	100.00	10.26
Manufactures and mechanical industries	2,109	70.72	873	29.28	2,982	100.00	16.52
Nonproductive (not gainful)	3,373	31.80	7,234	68.20	10,607	100.00	58.77
Housewives and at work			384	100.00	384	100.00	2.13
Scholars and at work	3	75.00	1	25.00	4	100.00	.02
Total	8,996	49.84	9,052	50.16	18,048	100.00	100.00
CHICAGO.							
Agriculture, fisheries, and mining	10	100.00			10	100.00	.05
Professional	169	89.42	20	10.58	189	100.00	.96
Domestic and personal service	2,376	84.23	445	15.77	2,821	100.00	14.29
Trade and transportation	2,014	90.31	216	9.69	2,230	100.00	11.29
Manufactures and mechanical industries	2,235	77.04	666	22.96	2,901	100.00	14.69
Nonproductive (not gainful)	3,753	33.32	7,512	66.68	11,265	100.00	57.04
Housewives and at work			176	100.00	176	100.00	.89
Scholars and at work	94	60.26	62	39.74	156	100.00	.79
Total	10,651	53.93	9,097	46.07	19,748	100.00	100.00
NEW YORK.							
Agriculture, fisheries, and mining	27	96.43	1	3.57	28	100.00	.10
Professional	237	90.80	24	9.20	261	100.00	.90
Domestic and personal service	3,454	88.52	448	11.48	3,902	100.00	13.46
Trade and transportation	2,878	90.93	287	9.07	3,165	100.00	10.91
Manufactures and mechanical industries	2,930	67.17	1,432	32.83	4,362	100.00	15.04
Nonproductive (not gainful)	6,266	37.83	10,296	62.17	16,562	100.00	57.12
Housewives and at work			634	100.00	634	100.00	2.19
Scholars and at work	43	52.44	39	47.56	82	100.00	.28
Total	15,835	54.61	13,161	45.39	28,996	100.00	100.00
PHILADELPHIA.							
Agriculture, fisheries, and mining	13	92.86	1	7.14	14	100.00	.08
Professional	135	88.82	17	11.18	152	100.00	.89
Domestic and personal service	1,625	82.40	347	17.60	1,972	100.00	11.56
Trade and transportation	1,740	91.48	162	8.52	1,902	100.00	11.15
Manufactures and mechanical industries	2,286	77.60	660	22.40	2,946	100.00	17.27
Nonproductive (not gainful)	3,305	33.71	6,498	66.29	9,803	100.00	57.46
Housewives and at work			242	100.00	242	100.00	1.42
Scholars and at work	19	65.52	10	34.48	29	100.00	.17
Total	9,123	53.48	7,937	46.52	17,060	100.00	100.00

A comparison of these two classes of slum residents shows a uniformly smaller proportion of women at work among the families of Italian origin embraced in this report. As regards the distribution of these two classes among the various industrial groups, it is noticed that from 11.26 per cent to 14.29 per cent of the persons embraced in the Seventh Special Report were employed in domestic and personal service, the largest per cent, 14.29, being for Chicago, while 17.78 per cent of the persons included in the present report were employed under this industrial group. The proportions engaged in trade and transportation do not differ greatly, but while the Seventh Special Report shows 16.52 per cent engaged in manufactures and mechanical industries in Baltimore, 14.69 per cent in Chicago, 15.04 per cent in New York, and 17.27 per cent in Philadelphia, but 5.52 per cent of the persons in these Italian families fall in this group. The proportion of nonproductive persons is seen to be uniformly smaller for the persons embraced in the Seventh Special Report.

The following two summaries, taken from Table X, show for each industrial class the average weekly earnings and average hours of work per week of persons engaged in remunerative occupations. As Table X shows, a large number of persons engaged in productive or remunerative occupations did not report earnings or hours of work. The following summaries, of course, deal only with those who reported. Out of a total of 2,663 persons engaged in remunerative occupations, 2,420, or 90.87 per cent, reported as to earnings and 1,820, or 68.34 per cent, reported as to hours of work:

AVERAGE WEEKLY EARNINGS OF PERSONS ENGAGED IN REMUNERATIVE OCCUPATIONS.

Groups of occupations.	Males.		Females.		Total.	
	Number reporting.	Average weekly earnings.	Number reporting.	Average weekly earnings.	Number reporting.	Average weekly earnings.
Agriculture, fisheries, and mining	32	$7.64½	....	....	32	$7.64½
Professional	52	5.09½	3	$3.00	55	4.98
Domestic and personal service..........	1,115	7.27½	8	2.28½	1,123	7.23½
Trade and transportation...............	562	4.47	26	2.15	588	4.37
Manufactures and mechanical industries	297	8.25½	64	3.02	361	7.33
Housewives and at work	....	....	153	1.72	153	1.72
Scholars and at work	96	2.29	12	1.95	108	2.25
Total	2,154	6.41	266	2.11½	2,420	5.93½

AVERAGE HOURS OF WORK PER WEEK OF PERSONS ENGAGED IN REMUNERATIVE OCCUPATIONS.

Groups of occupations.	Males.		Females.		Total.	
	Number reporting.	Average hours of work per week.	Number reporting.	Average hours of work per week.	Number reporting.	Average hours of work per week.
Agriculture, fisheries, and mining......	26	59.8	....	....	26	59.8
Professional	24	52.0	....	....	24	52.0
Domestic and personal service..........	1,024	62.1	2	39.0	1,026	62.1
Trade and transportation...............	333	56.2	15	46.1	348	55.8
Manufactures and mechanical industries	248	55.5	34	54.6	282	55.3
Housewives and at work................	....	....	40	52.1	40	52.1
Scholars and at work	66	51.1	8	44.9	74	50.4
Total	1,721	59.4	99	51.2	1,820	59.0

It is seen that the highest earnings, $7.64½ per week, were made by those engaged in agriculture, fisheries, and mining, although but 32 persons reported under this class. In manufactures and mechanical industries, with 361 persons reporting, the average earnings were $7.33 per week; in domestic and personal service, with 1,123 persons reporting, they were $7.23½ per week. The average earnings for the 2,420 persons reporting in all industrial groups were $5.93½ per week. The average hours of work in the seven groups are shown to have varied from 50.4 to 62.1 per week, the average for all groups being 59 hours per week.

The following summaries, taken from the Seventh Special Report, relating to typical slum sections of Baltimore, Chicago, New York, and Philadelphia, and showing information similar to that given in the two summaries immediately preceding, enable us to institute a comparison as to earnings and hours of work between the Italian families just mentioned and slum residents of various nationalities:

AVERAGE WEEKLY EARNINGS OF PERSONS ENGAGED IN REMUNERATIVE OCCU-PATIONS IN CERTAIN SLUM DISTRICTS OF BALTIMORE, CHICAGO, NEW YORK, AND PHILADELPHIA.

[From the Seventh Special Report of the Commissioner of Labor.]

Groups of occupations.	Males.		Females.		Total.	
	Number reporting.	Average weekly earnings.	Number reporting.	Average weekly earnings.	Number reporting.	Average weekly earnings.
BALTIMORE.						
Agriculture, fisheries, and mining	61	$5. 49	13	$3. 73	74	$5. 18
Professional	78	15. 57	17	9. 02	95	14. 40
Domestic and personal service	1, 654	9. 00	332	4. 41½	1, 986	8. 23½
Trade and transportation	1, 592	11. 58½	176	7. 11½	1, 768	11. 14
Manufactures and mechanical industries	2, 037	9. 27½	854	4. 49	2, 891	7. 86
Housewives and at work			378	4. 62½	378	4. 62½
Scholars and at work	3	3. 00	1	3. 00	4	3. 00
Total	5, 425	9. 91½	1, 771	4. 80	7, 196	8. 65½
CHICAGO.						
Agriculture, fisheries, and mining	8	10. 93½			8	10. 93½
Professional	117	15. 30½	15	14. 09½	132	15. 16½
Domestic and personal service	2, 060	9. 93	355	5. 97	2, 415	9. 35
Trade and transportation	1, 578	11. 03	186	5. 90	1, 764	10. 49
Manufactures and mechanical industries	2, 043	11. 79½	636	5. 53	2, 679	10. 31
Housewives and at work			142	4. 71	142	4. 71
Scholars and at work	85	4. 06	58	3. 15	143	3. 69
Total	5, 891	10. 89½	1, 392	5. 60	7, 283	9. 88½
NEW YORK.						
Agriculture, fisheries, and mining	25	9. 44	1	4. 00	26	9. 23
Professional	142	13. 77½	12	11. 80	154	13. 62
Domestic and personal service	3, 080	8. 65½	343	4. 74½	3, 423	8. 26½
Trade and transportation	2, 168	10. 16½	218	4. 82	2, 386	9. 67½
Manufactures and mechanical industries	2, 441	10. 26½	1, 299	4. 56½	3, 740	8. 28½
Housewives and at work			579	3. 13	579	3. 13
Scholars and at work	35	3. 13½	33	3. 14	68	3. 13½
Total	7, 891	9. 64	2, 485	4. 29½	10, 376	8. 36
PHILADELPHIA.						
Agriculture, fisheries, and mining	6	9. 71	1	6. 00	7	9. 18
Professional	79	13. 70½	15	13. 79	94	13. 72
Domestic and personal service	1, 284	8. 63½	270	3. 93	1, 554	7. 82
Trade and transportation	1, 157	9. 83	102	5. 82½	1, 259	9. 50½
Manufactures and mechanical industries	1, 892	10. 16½	597	5. 02½	2, 489	8. 93
Housewives and at work			158	4. 41	158	4. 41
Scholars and at work	15	3. 10½	7	3. 21½	22	3. 14
Total	4, 433	9. 67½	1, 150	4. 86	5, 583	8. 68

AVERAGE HOURS OF WORK PER WEEK OF PERSONS ENGAGED IN REMUNERATIVE OCCUPATIONS IN CERTAIN SLUM DISTRICTS OF BALTIMORE, CHICAGO, NEW YORK, AND PHILADELPHIA.

[From the Seventh Special Report of the Commissioner of Labor.]

Groups of occupations.	Males.		Females.		Total.	
	Number reporting.	Average hours of work per week.	Number reporting.	Average hours of work per week.	Number reporting.	Average hours of work per week.
BALTIMORE.						
Agriculture, fisheries, and mining......	60	73. 97	8	66. 00	68	73. 03
Professional..........................	81	54. 33	16	33. 06	97	50. 82
Domestic and personal service..........	1, 624	64. 51	290	72. 81	1, 914	65. 77
Trade and transportation...............	1, 608	67. 60	176	67. 41	1, 784	67. 58
Manufactures and mechanical industries	2, 067	61. 40	850	61. 16	2, 917	61. 33
Housewives and at work.................	....	....	225	64. 48	225	64. 48
Scholars and at work...................	3	64. 51	1	72. 00.	4	66. 38
Total	5, 443	64. 19	1, 566	64. 24	7, 009	64. 21
CHICAGO.						
Agriculture, fisheries, and mining......	8	65. 50	....	....	8	65. 50
Professional..........................	113	50. 77	15	39. 00	128	49. 39
Domestic and personal service..........	2, 170	64. 84	336	71. 30	2, 506	65. 71
Trade and transportation...............	1, 801	61. 93	205	58. 34	2, 006	61. 56
Manufactures and mechanical industries	2, 178	57. 25	643	57. 19	2, 821	57. 24
Housewives and at work.................	....	....	123	57. 78	123	57. 78
Scholars and at work...................	80	53. 75	59	55. 81	139	54. 62
Total	6, 350	61. 02	1, 381	60. 59*	7, 731	60. 94
NEW YORK.						
Agriculture, fisheries, and mining	27	61. 52	1	60. 00	28	61. 47
Professional..........................	173	53. 69	21	43. 10	194	52. 54
Domestic and personal service..........	3, 201	66. 99	304	66. 68	3, 505	66. 96
Trade and transportation...............	2, 500	64. 86	259	60. 16	2, 759	64. 42
Manufactures and mechanical industries	2, 717	59. 34	1, 366	58. 34	4, 083	59. 01
Housewives and at work	....	....	560	55. 99	560	55. 99
Scholars and at work	37	57. 47	35	56. 96	72	57. 22
Total	8, 655	63. 65	2, 546	58. 86	11, 201	62. 55
PHILADELPHIA.						
Agriculture, fisheries, and mining	11	66. 55	1	66. 00	12	66. 50
Professional..........................	81	46. 59	17	31. 12	98	43. 91
Domestic and personal service..........	1, 323	64. 32	255	75. 40	1, 578	66. 11
Trade and transportation	1, 450	65. 65	133	64. 78	1, 583	65. 58
Manufactures and mechanical industries	2, 123	59. 78	624	58. 38	2, 747	59. 46
Housewives and at work	....	....	181	60. 30	181	60. 30
Scholars and at work...................	16	52. 69	5	52. 80	21	52. 72
Total	5, 004	62. 46	1, 216	62. 54	6, 220	62. 47

The very considerably smaller earnings of the persons belonging to the Italian families dealt with in the present report is noticed. Their average earnings for all the classes of work engaged in, as has been shown, were $5.93½ per week. For the general slum population shown in the tables just given the average weekly earnings for the group were, in Baltimore, $8.65½; in Chicago, $9.88½; in New York, $8.36, and in Philadelphia, $8.68. This difference is doubtless due to the fact that the persons embraced in these exclusively Italian families, as has been previously shown, were employed as a rule at occupations of the lowest grade, requiring no skill and but little manual dexterity or strength. The average hours of work per week were shorter for the members of these Italian families than for the general slum population.

Table XI.—Persons unemployed, by months unemployed, sex, and age, pp. 381, 382.—This table includes all persons 15 years of age or over engaged in remunerative occupations who reported that they were unemployed during any part of the year, and shows for each sex and age the months unemployed. It is proper to state that 90 males and 42 females, making a total of 132 persons, did not report whether employed or not, and have consequently been omitted from this table. In the previous table and the analysis, it was shown that of a total of 6,773 persons embraced in this investigation, 4,110, or 60.68 per cent, were not engaged in any remunerative or productive occupation. These persons were classed as nonproductive, and consisted of those too young to work, those who were unemployed during the whole year, housewives and persons engaged in housework without pay, those who had no occupation, retired persons, and scholars. In this table those who were unemployed fractional parts of months during the year have been classed under the nearest whole month, while those employed less than half a month have been excluded. Of the 2,663 persons employed in remunerative occupations, 1,517, or 56.97 per cent, were unemployed some part of the year. Of this number, 40 were unemployed one month, 56 two months, 49 three months, 66 four months, 102 five months, 250 six months, 183 seven months, 232 eight months, 310 nine months, 161 ten months, and 68 eleven months during the year. The average time unemployed for these 1,517 persons was, therefore, over seven months.

The following table, reproduced from the Seventh Special Report of the Commissioner of Labor, shows the results of the investigation of typical slum sections of Baltimore, Chicago, New York, and Philadelphia so far as it relates to nonemployment. The figures are for the year ending March 31, 1893:

PERSONS UNEMPLOYED AND AVERAGE MONTHS UNEMPLOYED IN CERTAIN SLUM DISTRICTS OF BALTIMORE, CHICAGO, NEW YORK, AND PHILADELPHIA.

[From the Seventh Special Report of the Commissioner of Labor.]

City.	Total population of the slum districts canvassed.	Slum population unemployed.		Months unemployed.	
		Number.	Per cent.	Total.	Average.
Baltimore	18,048	1,564	8.67	a 5,255	a 3.6
Chicago	19,748	3,135	15.88	a 7,327	a 3.1
New York	28,996	2,615	9.02	a 6,116	a 3.1
Philadelphia	17,060	2,591	15.19	a 5,132	a 2.9

a Not including those for whom the months unemployed were not reported.

It is seen from this table that of the total persons included in that investigation, both productive and nonproductive, 8.67 per cent in Baltimore were unemployed some part of the year, 15.88 per cent in Chicago, 9.02 per cent in New York, and 15.19 per cent in Philadelphia. Of the total persons in the Italian families included in the present report the very large proportion of 22.40 per cent were unemployed some part of the year. The average time unemployed of those who were shown to have been unemployed in the Seventh Special Report was 3.6 months in Baltimore, 3.1 months in Chicago and New York, and 2.9 months in Philadelphia. The present investigation shows that the average time of nonemployment of the unemployed in the Italian families was 7.2 months, or double the highest average of the unemployed slum population shown in the Seventh Special Report.

As has been stated, 1,517 persons engaged in productive occupations in these Italian families were unemployed during some portion of the year. The question as to the means of subsistence when unemployed was answered by 1,486 of these persons. It was stated by 717, or 48.25 per cent, that they lived on their savings while unemployed; 287, or 19.31 per cent, had credit and went into debt for the means of subsistence; 233, or 15.68 per cent, lived on their savings until they had exhausted them and then resorted to credit; 96, or 6.46 per cent, lived wholly on charity while unemployed; 26, or 1.75 per cent, lived on their children's earnings, while 127, or 8.55 per cent, subsisted in various ways, the most common being stated as on savings and charity, relatives' support, credit and charity, rents, wife's earnings, savings and wife's earnings, etc.

Table XII.—Illiterates, by sex, age periods, and degree of illiteracy, p. 383.—This table includes all illiterate persons 10 years of age or over embraced in the investigation. Those who can neither read nor write and those who can read but can not write, the two classes of illiterates, are shown by sex and nativity for each specified age period. The great majority of native-born persons in these families, as has been shown, were children under 10 years of age, and therefore do not appear in this table. Of the 2,752 illiterate persons found in these families, but 32 were native born, and of these 30 were under 21 years of age. Dealing with persons, therefore, almost entirely foreign born, no comparison of native and foreign born illiterate persons is possible or desirable.

As regards the degree of illiteracy, it is seen that 2,684, or 97.53 per cent, of the 2,752 illiterate persons could neither read nor write, while 68, or 2.47 per cent, could read but could not write any language. Similar data for the persons embraced in the Seventh Special Report are shown in the following table:

NUMBER AND PER CENT OF ILLITERATES OF EACH DEGREE OF ILLITERACY IN CERTAIN SLUM DISTRICTS OF BALTIMORE, CHICAGO, NEW YORK, AND PHILADELPHIA.

[From the Seventh Special Report of the Commissioner of Labor.]

Degree of illiteracy.	Baltimore.		Chicago.		New York.		Philadelphia.	
	Number.	Per cent.	Number.	Per cent.	Number.	Per cent.	Number.	Per cent.
Unable to read and write..	2,411	92.23	3,609	95.83	9,870	98.03	4,485	97.46
Unable to write.............	203	7.77	157	4.17	198	1.97	117	2.54
Total	2,614	100.00	3,766	100.00	10,068	100.00	4,602	100.00

Of a total of 2,752 illiterate persons embraced in the present report, 1,373, or 49.89 per cent, were from 31 to 50 years of age; 748, or 27.18 per cent, were from 21 to 30 years; 342, or 12.43 per cent, were from 10 to 20 years; 278, or 10.10 per cent, were 51 years of age or over, while 11, or 0.40 per cent, did not report as to age.

The following table, taken from the Seventh Special Report, shows the distribution as to age of the residents of the typical slum sections embraced in that report:

NUMBER AND PER CENT OF ILLITERATES OF EACH AGE PERIOD IN CERTAIN SLUM DISTRICTS OF BALTIMORE, CHICAGO, NEW YORK, AND PHILADELPHIA.

[From the Seventh Special Report of the Commissioner of Labor.]

Age periods.	Baltimore.		Chicago.		New York.		Philadelphia.	
	Number.	Per cent.	Number.	Per cent.	Number.	Per cent.	Number.	Per cent.
10 to 14 years	160	6.12	253	6.72	610	6.06	241	5.24
15 to 20 years	250	9.57	364	9.66	897	8.91	463	10.06
21 to 30 years	646	24.71	1,103	29.29	2,674	26.56	1,376	29.90
31 to 50 years	1,070	40.93	1,431	38.00	4,157	41.29	1,716	37.29
51 years or over..........	469	17.94	348	9.24	1,269	12.60	525	11.41
Age not reported	19	.73	267	7.09	461	4.58	281	6.10
Total	2,614	100.00	3,766	100.00	10,068	100.00	4,602	100.00

Table XIII.—Literates, by sex, age periods, and language, p. 383.— This table deals with the literate persons 10 years of age or over embraced in the families included in this report. The number of male and female native and foreign born persons falling under each age period is shown and further classified as to whether they read and write the English language only, Italian only, or both English and Italian. Of the native-born literates, 265 could read and write English only and 3 could read and write Italian only. No native-born persons in these families were found who could read and write both English and Italian. Of the 1,533 foreign-born literates, 221 could read and write English only, showing that the ability to read and write was probably acquired after their arrival in this country; 984 could read and write Italian only, while 328 were able to read and write both English and Italian.

*Table XIV.—Literates and illiterates, by sex, p. 383.—*This table brings into comparison the information given in the two previous tables relating to illiterates and literates. It is shown that of the 2,812 males 10 years of age or over included in this report, 48.04 per cent were literate and 51.96 per cent were illiterate. Of the 1,741 females 10 years of age or over, 25.85 per cent were literate and 74.15 per cent were illiterate. Comparing the literate males and females, it is seen that 19.32 per cent of the literate males could read and write English only, while 50 per cent of the literate females were in this class; 60.55 per cent of the males and 37.56 per cent of the females could read and write Italian only, and 20.13 per cent of the males and 12.44 per cent of the females were able to read and write both English and Italian. Taking into consideration persons of both sexes, it is seen that of a total of 4,553 persons 10 years of age or over 2,752, or 60.44 per cent, were illiterate, while 1,801, or 39.56 per cent, were literate. The proportion of illiterate persons (60.44 per cent) is thus seen to be very high in the families included in this investigation. It is shown in Table XII that but 32 of the 2,752 illiterates were native born, a proportion too small to be considered. A comparison as to illiteracy is, therefore, possible between these Italian families and the foreign-born population of the typical slum sections of Baltimore, Chicago, New York, and Philadelphia, as presented in the Seventh Special Report of the Commissioner of Labor. The following table, drawn from that report, shows the per cent of literates and illiterates of each foreign nationality as given there:

PER CENT OF LITERATES AND ILLITERATES BORN IN EACH SPECIFIED FOREIGN COUNTRY IN CERTAIN SLUM DISTRICTS OF BALTIMORE, CHICAGO, NEW YORK, AND PHILADELPHIA.

[From the Seventh Special Report of the Commissioner of Labor.]

Place of birth.	Baltimore.		Chicago.		New York.		Philadelphia.	
	Liter-ates.	Illiter-ates.	Liter-ates.	Illiter-ates.	Liter-ates.	Illiter-ates.	Liter-ates.	Illiter-ates.
Austria-Hungary	63.55	36.45	90.37	9.63	73.63	26.37	69.16	30.84
British America	72.73	27.27	87.01	12.99	100.00	....	80.00	20.00
China	66.67	33.33	93.94	6.06	81.91	18.09	81.25	18.75
France	90.00	10.00	90.48	9.52	83.33	16.67	100.00	....
Germany	72.50	27.50	87.62	12.38	92.02	7.98	85.26	14.74
Great Britain	94.93	5.07	93.42	6.58	92.23	7.77	91.41	8.59
Ireland	75.73	24.27	84.71	15.29	60.68	39.32	74.21	25.79
Italy	47.52	52.48	30.14	69.86	33.16	66.84	36.37	63.63
Netherlands	100.00	....	91.67	8.33	100.00	....	59.09	40.91
Norway and Sweden	92.50	7.50	91.67	8.33	100.00	....	100.00	....
Poland	52.69	47.31	69.80	30.20	49.76	50.24	59.73	40.27
Russia	70.30	29.70	71.31	28.69	45.65	54.35	58.08	41.92
Spain and Portugal	33.33	66.67	100.00	....	57.14	42.86	66.67	33.33
Other foreign and foreign not specified	74.42	25.58	56.39	43.61	66.61	33.39	57.35	42.65
Total	69.38	30.62	66.14	33.86	42.31	57.69	53.39	46.61

This table shows that those of Italian birth were to an even larger extent illiterate in the families included in the Seventh Special Report than is shown by the present report, and that in each of the four cities, with the exception of Baltimore, the proportion of illiterates among persons of that nationality was greater than among those of any other country.

Taking up again Table XIV, and considering the literates only, it is seen that 26.99 per cent of all the literates could read and write English only; 54.80 per cent could read and write Italian only, while 18.21 per cent were able to read and write both English and Italian.

The following table, showing the number and per cent of persons able and not able to speak English, by years in the United States, while not bearing directly on illiteracy, is thought to be of interest in this connection:

NUMBER AND PER CENT OF PERSONS ABLE AND NOT ABLE TO SPEAK ENGLISH, BY YEARS IN THE UNITED STATES.

[This table includes all persons 10 years of age or over.]

Years in the United States.	Able to speak English.			Not able to speak English.			Per cent.	
	Males.	Females.	Total.	Males.	Females.	Total.	Able to speak English.	Not able to speak English.
Total native born	152	146	298	....	2	2	99.33	0.67
Foreign born:								
Under 1 year..................	2	....	2	60	49	109	1.80	98.20
1 year......................	11	4	15	33	29	62	19.48	80.52
2 years.....................	26	7	33	38	43	81	28.95	71.05
3 years.....................	110	30	140	107	107	214	39.55	60.45
4 years.....................	147	35	182	105	126	231	44.07	55.93
5 years.....................	178	42	220	78	121	199	52.51	47.49
6 years.....................	163	44	207	63	98	161	56.25	43.75
7 years.....................	133	43	176	30	49	79	69.02	30.98
8 years.....................	166	57	223	43	75	118	65.40	34.60
9 years.....................	128	57	185	31	69	100	64.91	35.09
10 years or over............	828	264	1,092	163	238	401	73.14	26.86
Not reported...............	14	4	18	3	2	5	78.26	21.74
Total foreign born	1,906	587	2,493	754	1,006	1,760	58.62	41.38
Aggregate...............	2,058	733	2,791	754	1,008	1,762	61.30	38.70

Of native-born persons, practically all were able to speak English. Of the total foreign-born persons, 58.62 per cent were able to speak English, while 41.38 per cent were unable to do so. Of all the persons in these families 10 years of age or over, both native and foreign born, 61.30 per cent were able to speak English, while 38.70 per cent were not able to do so. The proportion of persons able and not able to speak English who have been in the United States each specified number of years is shown in the table. The proportion able to speak English of those who have been in the United States less than one year is shown to be but 1.80 per cent. This proportion gradually increases as the years of residence in the United States increase, until 73.14 per cent of those who had been in the United States ten years or over were able to speak the English language with reasonable clearness.

Table XV.—School attendance, by nativity, age, kind of school, and sex, p. 384.—This table shows the native and foreign born males and females of each age attending public and private schools. Of a total of 988 persons in these families who attended school during some portion of the year, 582, or 58.91 per cent, were native born, and 406, or 41.09 per cent, were foreign born. No comparison as to the proportion of native and foreign born persons attending school can be made between these families and those embraced in the Seventh Special Report, owing to the fact that these families are exclusively Italian or of foreign extraction, while those embraced in the Seventh Special Report are to a large extent native, and would naturally show a larger proportion of native-born persons at school.

The following table classifies all scholars according to sex and age:

NUMBER AND PER CENT OF SCHOLARS OF EACH AGE.

Age.	Males.		Females.		Total.	
	Number.	Per cent.	Number.	Per cent.	Number.	Per cent.
Under 5 years	1	0.18	2	0.48	3	0.30
5 years	14	2.45	9	2.16	23	2.33
6 years	39	6.83	45	10.79	84	8.50
7 years	91	15.94	64	15.35	155	15.69
8 years	78	13.66	57	13.67	135	13.67
9 years	64	11.21	66	15.83	130	13.16
10 years	67	11.73	49	11.75	116	11.74
11 years	44	7.70	25	5.99	69	6.98
12 years	44	7.70	45	10.79	89	9.01
13 years	39	6.83	18	4.32	57	5.77
14 years	26	4.55	23	5.51	49	4.96
15 years	30	5.25	11	2.64	41	4.15
16 years	10	1.75	3	.72	13	1.32
17 years	14	2.45	....	....	14	1.42
18 years	3	.53	....	....	3	.30
19 years	1	.18	....	....	1	.10
20 years	2	.35	....	....	2	.20
21 years	2	.35	....	....	2	.20
24 years	1	.18	....	....	1	.10
25 years	1	.18	....	....	1	.10
Total	571	100.00	417	100.00	988	100.00

The largest proportion of scholars were 7 years of age, the per cent for males being 15.94, for females, 15.35, and for both males and females, 15.69. Over one-half of all scholars were from 7 to 10 years of age, inclusive, the proportion being 52.54 per cent of males, 56.60 per cent of females, and 54.26 per cent of both males and females.

The following table, taken from the Seventh Special Report and embracing the scholars in families residing in typical slum sections of Baltimore, Chicago, New York, and Philadelphia, shows the number and per cent of scholars classified according to age periods:

NUMBER AND PER CENT OF SCHOLARS OF EACH AGE PERIOD IN CERTAIN SLUM DISTRICTS OF BALTIMORE, CHICAGO, NEW YORK, AND PHILADELPHIA.

[From the Seventh Special Report of the Commissioner of Labor.]

Age periods.	Baltimore.		Chicago.		New York.		Philadelphia.	
	Number.	Per cent.	Number.	Per cent.	Number.	Per cent.	Number.	Per cent.
Under 5 years	....	....	7	0.25	25	0.58	16	0.61
5 to 9 years	1,201	45.68	1,197	42.58	2,313	53.29	1,356	51.85
10 to 13 years	1,166	44.35	1,183	42.08	1,613	37.16	995	38.05
14 to 19 years	259	9.85	419	14.91	384	8.85	243	9.29
20 years or over	3	.12	5	.18	3	.07	2	.08
Age not reported	....	....	....	....	2	.05	3	.12
Total	2,629	100.00	2,811	100.00	4,340	100.00	2,615	100.00

A similar classification of the scholars included in the present report shows that 3, or 0.30 per cent, were under 5 years of age; 527, or 53.35 per cent, were from 5 to 9 years; 331, or 33.50 per cent, were from 10 to

13 years; 121, or 12.25 per cent, were from 14 to 19 years; while 6, or 0.60 per cent, were 20 years of age or over.

The following table classifies the scholars in these Italian families according to the kind of school which they attended, whether public or private:

NUMBER AND PER CENT OF SCHOLARS ATTENDING PUBLIC AND PRIVATE SCHOOLS.

Kind of school.	Males.		Females.		Total.	
	Number.	Per cent.	Number.	Per cent.	Number.	Per cent.
Public	503	88.09	382	91.61	885	89.57
Private	68	11.91	35	8.39	103	10.43
Total	571	100.00	417	100.00	988	100.00

Of all male scholars 88.09 per cent attended public schools; of all female scholars 91.61 per cent attended public schools, while the proportion of all scholars of both sexes attending public schools was 89.57 per cent. In Table XV and the summaries drawn therefrom the term private school has been made to include schools variously designated as parochial schools, kindergartens, Italian private schools, and private night schools as well as those termed simply private schools. Table III of the general tables in this report shows in detail the specific kind of schools attended by the scholars in each of these Italian families.

The following table, taken from the Seventh Special Report, shows the distribution of the scholars included in that report, by kind of school:

NUMBER AND PER CENT OF SCHOLARS IN CERTAIN SLUM DISTRICTS OF BALTIMORE, CHICAGO, NEW YORK, AND PHILADELPHIA ATTENDING PUBLIC AND PRIVATE SCHOOLS.

[From the Seventh Special Report of the Commissioner of Labor.]

Kind of school.	Baltimore.		Chicago.		New York.		Philadelphia.	
	Number.	Per cent.	Number.	Per cent.	Number.	Per cent.	Number.	Per cent.
Public	1,703	64.78	2,181	77.59	2,743	63.20	2,241	85.70
Private	926	35.22	630	22.41	1,597	36.80	374	14.30
Total	2,629	100.00	2,811	100.00	4,340	100.00	2,615	100.00

This table shows that but 64.78 per cent of the scholars in the typical slum families of Baltimore attended public schools and 35.22 per cent private schools; in Chicago 77.59 per cent attended public and 22.41 per cent private schools; in New York 63.20 per cent attended public and 36.80 per cent private schools, and in Philadelphia 85.70 per cent attended public and 14.30 per cent private schools. As has been shown, 89.57 per cent of the scholars included in the present report attended public while but 10.43 per cent attended private schools.

In this connection the following table is given showing the months of school attendance during the year, by sex and kind of school:

MONTHS IN SCHOOL DURING YEAR, BY SEX AND KIND OF SCHOOL.

Months in school during year.	Males.		Females.		Total.	
	Number.	Per cent.	Number.	Per cent.	Number.	Per cent.
PUBLIC.						
1 month	2	0.40	3	0.79	5	0.57
2 months........	4	.80	10	2.62	14	1.58
3 months........	17	3.38	13	3.40	30	3.39
4 months........	18	3.58	17	4.45	35	3.96
5 months........	8	1.59	6	1.57	14	1.58
6 months........	39	7.75	12	3.14	51	5.76
7 months........	34	6.76	21	5.49	55	6.21
8 months........	6	1.19	10	2.62	16	1.81
9 months........	14	2.78	3	.79	17	1.92
10 months...	358	71.17	284	74.34	642	72.54
Not specified........	3	.60	3	.79	6	.68
Total	503	100.00	382	100.00	885	100.00
Average number of months in school...	....	8.80	....	8.78	....	8.79
PRIVATE.						
1 month....	1	1.47	....	....	1	.97
2 months........	....	....	1	2.86	1	.97
3 months........	1	1.47	1	2.86	2	1.95
4 months........	3	4.41	1	2.86	4	3.88
5 months........	1	1.47	....	....	1	.97
6 months........	3	4.41	1	2.86	4	3.88
7 months........	4	5.89	....	....	4	3.88
8 months........	3	4.41	1	2.86	4	3.88
9 months........	2	2.94	1	2.86	3	2.92
10 months........	50	73.53	29	82.84	79	76.70
Not specified	....	....	....	....	....	....
Total	68	100.00	35	100.00	103	100.00
Average number of months in school...	....	8.96	....	9.20	....	9.04
PUBLIC AND PRIVATE.						
1 month........	3	.53	3	.72	6	.61
2 months........	4	.70	11	2.64	15	1.52
3 months........	18	3.15	14	3.36	32	3.24
4 months........	21	3.68	18	4.31	39	3.95
5 months........	9	1.58	6	1.44	15	1.52
6 months........	42	7.35	13	3.12	55	5.57
7 months........	38	6.65	21	5.03	59	5.97
8 months........	9	1.58	11	2.64	20	2.02
9 months........	16	2.80	4	.96	20	2.02
10 months........	408	71.45	313	75.06	721	72.97
Not specified	3	.53	3	.72	6	.61
Total	571	100.00	417	100.00	988	100.00
Average number of months in school...	....	8.82	....	8.81	....	8.81

The first section of this table deals with those attending public schools, the second section with those attending private schools, while the third combines the data for both public and private schools. Of those attending public schools 72.54 per cent were in school ten months, the full school year, the average months in school of all attending public schools being 8.79. Of those attending private schools 76.70 per cent were in school ten months, the average months in school of all attending private schools being 9.04. Taking into consideration the data for both public and private schools, it is seen that 72.97 per cent were in school ten months during the year, the average months of school attendance for all scholars being 8.81.

These figures show very interesting results, taken in connection with Table XVI and its summary, which latter gives the per cent of persons from 5 to 14 years of age at home, at work, at school, and both at work and at school.

Table XVI.—Condition of all children from 5 to 14 years of age, inclusive, by nativity and sex, p. 385.—This table deals with the condition of all children from 5 to 14 years of age, inclusive, showing the number of males and females of each age and nativity who are at home, at work, at school, and both at work and at school. The following table, drawn from Table XVI, shows the number and per cent of each condition, by sex:

NUMBER AND PER CENT OF CHILDREN OF EACH CONDITION, BY SEX.

Sex.	At home.		At work.		At school.		At work and at school.		All children.	
	Number.	Per cent.	Number.	Per cent.	Number.	Per cent.	Number.	Per cent.	Number.	Per cent.
Male...............	199	26.29	52	6.87	450	59.44	56	7.40	757	100.00
Female	271	38.38	34	4.82	394	55.81	7	.99	706	100.00
Total.......	470	32.12	86	5.88	844	57.69	63	4.31	1,463	100.00

Of the males from 5 to 14 years of age, 26.29 per cent were at home. This designation includes all persons 5 to 14 years of age, inclusive, who were not at school during the year and who had no occupation. Of the females, a larger proportion, 38.38 per cent, were at home. The greatest proportion of children, however, of both sexes were at school; the per cent of males at school being 59.44 and of females 55.81. Of the males, 6.87 per cent were at work and 7.40 per cent both at work and at school, while of the females, 4.82 per cent were at work and 0.99 per cent both at work and at school. Taking up the totals for both males and females, it is seen that of the 1,463 children from 5 to 14 years of age, inclusive, in these Italian families, 844, or 57.69 per cent, were at school during some part of the year; 470, or 32.12 per cent, were at home during the year; 86, or 5.88 per cent, were at work during the whole or some part of the year, while 63, or 4.31 per cent, were both at work and at school.

The following summary, drawn from the Seventh Special Report, relating to the slums of large cities, shows similar figures for the children from 5 to 14 years of age in families residing in typical slum sections of Baltimore, Chicago, New York, and Philadelphia.

NUMBER AND PER CENT OF CHILDREN OF EACH CONDITION, BY SEX, IN CERTAIN SLUM DISTRICTS OF BALTIMORE, CHICAGO, NEW YORK, AND PHILADELPHIA.

[From the Seventh Special Report of the Commissioner of Labor.]

Cities and sex.	At home.		At work.		At school.		At work and at school.		All children.	
	Number.	Per cent.	Number.	Per cent.	Number.	Per cent.	Number.	Per cent.	Number.	Per cent.
BALTIMORE.										
Male	545	28.22	124	6.42	1,259	65.20	3	0.16	1,931	100.00
Female	651	32.52	97	4.84	1,253	62.59	1	.05	2,002	100.00
Total	1,196	30.41	221	5.62	2,512	63.87	4	.10	3,933	100.00
CHICAGO.										
Male	554	28.02	117	5.92	1,257	63.58	49	2.48	1,977	100.00
Female	531	28.04	73	3.85	1,254	66.21	36	1.90	1,894	100.00
Total	1,085	28.03	190	4.91	2,511	64.87	85	2.19	3,871	100.00
NEW YORK.										
Male	445	15.89	209	7.46	2,117	75.61	29	1.04	2,800	100.00
Female	569	20.72	204	7.43	1,948	70.94	25	.91	2,746	100.00
Total	1,014	18.28	413	7.45	4,065	73.30	54	.97	5,546	100.00
PHILADELPHIA.										
Male	379	21.51	175	9.93	1,192	67.65	16	.91	1,762	100.00
Female	309	18.27	109	6.45	1,264	74.75	9	.53	1,691	100.00
Total	688	19.92	284	8.23	2,456	71.13	25	.72	3,453	100.00

As just stated, 57.69 per cent of the children in the Italian families included in this report were at school during some part of the year. The table given above for the children in typical slum families shows the proportion of children at school was much larger, being 63.87 per cent in Baltimore, 64.87 per cent in Chicago, 73.30 per cent in New York, and 71.13 per cent in Philadelphia. The proportion of children at home in the typical slum families was, on the contrary, universally smaller than in these Italian families. In the latter 32.12 per cent were classed as at home; in the former 30.41 per cent were at home in Baltimore, 28.03 per cent in Chicago, 18.28 per cent in New York, and 19.92 per cent in Philadelphia. The proportion of children at work in typical slum families was 5.62 per cent in Baltimore, 4.91 per cent in Chicago, 7.45 per cent in New York, and 8.23 per cent in Philadelphia, while in the Italian families included in the present report it was 5.88 per cent. The proportion of children who were both at work and at school during some part of the year was greater in the Italian families.

Table XVII.—Married women having a specified number of Italian-born children living, by number of children born to each in Italy and years of married life in Italy, pp. 386 to 391.—This table is the first of a series of three tables relating to married women and their children. As the title indicates, this table deals with conditions in Italy, showing the number of children born in Italy and living, by years of married life in Italy.

Table XVIII.—Married women having a specified number of native-born children living, by number of children born to each in the United States and years of married life in the United States, pp. 392 to 395.—This table, the second relating to married women, etc., deals with conditions in the United States, showing facts similar to those given in the preceding table for Italy.

Table XIX.—Married women having a specified number of children living, by number of children born to each and years of married life, pp. 396 to 401.—In this table the facts are shown for married women, children born and living, and years of married life, regardless of locality.

The following table, drawn from Table XIX, shows the number and per cent of married women who have had no children and who have had children of total married women, by years married:

NUMBER AND PER CENT OF MARRIED WOMEN WHO HAVE HAD NO CHILDREN AND WHO HAVE HAD CHILDREN OF TOTAL MARRIED WOMEN, BY YEARS MARRIED.

Years married.	Married women who have had no children.		Married women who have had children.		Total married women.	
	Number.	Per cent.	Number.	Per cent.	Number.	Per cent.
Under 1 year	31	100.00	....	....	31	100.00
1 year	21	70.00	9	30.00	30	100.00
2 years	9	20.45	35	79.55	44	100.00
3 years	7	12.28	50	87.72	57	100.00
4 years	6	9.84	55	90.16	61	100.00
5 years	3	4.41	65	95.59	68	100.00
6 years	5	9.43	48	90.57	53	100.00
7 years	4	8.16	45	91.84	49	100.00
8 years	5	8.77	52	91.23	57	100.00
9 years	4	6.35	59	93.65	63	100.00
10 years	4	6.06	62	93.94	66	100.00
11 years	1	2.08	47	97.92	48	100.00
12 years	1	1.82	54	98.18	55	100.00
13 years	1	2.33	42	97.67	43	100.00
14 years	....	....	49	100.00	49	100.00
15 years	3	5.88	48	94.12	51	100.00
16 years	....	....	38	100.00	38	100.00
17 years	1	2.08	47	97.92	48	100.00
18 years	1	2.70	36	97.30	37	100.00
19 years	1	2.86	34	97.14	35	100.00
20 years	2	3.57	54	96.43	56	100.00
21 years	1	6.25	15	93.75	16	100.00
22 years	1	2.70	36	97.30	37	100.00
23 years	....	....	25	100.00	25	100.00
24 years	3	12.00	22	88.00	25	100.00
25 years	....	....	23	100.00	23	100.00
Over 25 years	4	2.99	130	97.01	134	100.00
Not reported	3	4.17	69	95.83	72	100.00
Total	122	8.90	1,249	91.10	1,371	100.00

Of the 1,371 women embraced in this table, including widowed as well as married women, 122, or 8.90 per cent, have had no children, while 1,249, or 91.10 per cent, have had children. Similar ratios are given for those married each specified number of years. It will be seen that it is stated in this and the following summary that no women who have been married under 1 year have had children. That it was so reported is probably due to the fact that some of those women who have been married less than but nearly one year reported themselves as married 1 year and have been so tabulated.

In the table immediately following is shown the number and per cent of married women who have had no children, by number of years married. A similar distribution according to years married is shown for married women who have had children and for total married women:

NUMBER AND PER CENT OF MARRIED WOMEN WHO HAVE HAD NO CHILDREN AND WHO HAVE HAD CHILDREN, BY YEARS MARRIED.

Years married.	Married women who have had no children.		Married women who have had children.		Total married women.	
	Number.	Per cent.	Number.	Per cent.	Number.	Per cent.
Under 1 year	31	25.41			31	2.26
1 year	21	17.21	9	0.72	30	2.19
2 years	9	7.37	35	2.80	44	3.21
3 years	7	5.73	50	4.00	57	4.16
4 years	6	4.92	55	4.41	61	4.45
5 years	3	2.46	65	5.21	68	4.96
6 years	5	4.10	48	3.84	53	3.87
7 years	4	2.28	45	3.60	49	3.57
8 years	5	4.10	52	4.16	57	4.16
9 years	4	3.28	59	4.73	63	4.60
10 years	4	3.28	62	4.97	66	4.81
11 years	1	.82	47	3.76	48	3.50
12 years	1	.82	54	4.33	55	4.01
13 years	1	.82	42	3.36	43	3.14
14 years			49	3.92	49	3.57
15 years	3	2.46	48	3.84	51	3.72
16 years			38	3.04	38	2.77
17 years	1	.82	47	3.76	48	3.50
18 years	1	.82	36	2.88	37	2.70
19 years	1	.82	34	2.72	35	2.55
20 years	2	1.64	54	4.33	56	4.09
21 years	1	.82	15	1.20	16	1.17
22 years	1	.82	36	2.88	37	2.70
23 years			25	2.00	25	1.82
24 years	3	2.46	22	1.76	25	1.82
25 years			23	1.84	23	1.68
Over 25 years	4	3.28	130	10.41	134	9.77
Not reported	3	2.46	69	5.53	72	5.25
Total	122	100.00	1,249	100.00	1,371	100.00

Of the married women who have had no children 25.41 per cent were married less than one year, 17.21 per cent were married one year, 7.37 per cent were married two years, etc. Of the married women who have had children 0.72 per cent were married one year, 2.80 per cent two years, 4 per cent three years, 4.41 per cent four years, etc.

The following table summarizes the results of Tables XVII, XVIII, and XIX, showing the number and per cent of married women who bore each specified number of children during their married life in Italy, in the United States, and in both countries. Looking at the table it will be seen that 96 married women bore no children during their married life in Italy, 331 none during their married life in the United States, and 122 none during their married life in both countries. This last number, it will be noted, is not the sum of those who bore no children in Italy and those who bore none in the United States, as many women who had no children in one country had children in the other. The figures for one child, two children, etc., should be read in like manner.

NUMBER AND PER CENT OF MARRIED WOMEN WHO HAVE BORNE EACH SPECIFIED NUMBER OF CHILDREN.

Number of children born.	In Italy.		In the United States.		In both Italy and the United States.	
	Number.	Per cent.	Number.	Per cent.	Number.	Per cent.
No children	96	10.95	331	24.61	122	8.90
1 child	175	19.96	174	12.94	108	7.88
2 children	155	17.67	236	17.55	148	10.80
3 children	117	13.34	181	13.46	166	12.11
4 children	93	10.61	144	10.71	166	12.11
5 children	63	7.18	95	7.06	161	11.74
6 children	37	4.22	67	4.98	137	9.99
7 children	39	4.45	44	3.27	95	6.93
8 children	28	3.19	23	1.71	90	6.56
9 children	20	2.28	14	1.04	71	5.18
10 children	11	1.26	5	.37	34	2.48
11 children	8	.91	4	.30	24	1.75
12 children	2	.23	1	.07	11	.80
13 children	1	.11			5	.37
14 children	4	.46			6	.44
15 children	1	.11				
17 children	1	.11			1	.07
18 children					1	.07
19 children	1	.11			1	.07
Not specified	25	2.85	26	1.93	24	1.75
Total	877	100.00	1,345	100.00	1,371	100.00

Of the 877 married women who spent a portion of their married life in Italy, 10.95 per cent had no children born in Italy, 19.96 per cent had one child, 17.67 per cent had two children, 13.34 per cent had three children, 10.61 per cent had four children, etc. Of the 1,345 married women who spent the whole or a portion of their married life in the United States, 24.61 per cent had no children born in the United States, 12.94 per cent had one child, 17.55 per cent had two children, 13.46 per cent had three children, 10.71 per cent had four children, etc. Considering the number of children born either in Italy or the United States, of the 1,371 married women embraced in the table, 7.88 per cent had one child, 10.80 per cent had two children, 12.11 per cent had three children, 12.11 per cent had four children, 11.74 per cent had five children, etc.

So far as conditions in Italy were concerned, 799 married women who had spent a portion of their married life in Italy before coming to the United States showed an aggregate of 8,455 years of married life spent there. During this time there were born to them 2,505 children. It is thus seen that while in Italy a child was born to each of these married women every 3.38 years. The conditions in the United States show that 1,280 married women who had spent the whole or a portion of their married life in the United States aggregated 8,997 years of married life in the United States and had borne during that time 3,329 children—that is, while in the United States a child was born to each of these married women every 2.70 years. Taking into consideration the results for both Italy and the United States, 1,296 married women in these families aggregated 17,466 years married and had 5,860 children, a child for every 2.98 years of married life. These figures necessarily include only those married women who reported both years married and children born.

Table XX.—Persons sick or physically defective, by kind of ailment or defect and sex, pp. 402, 403.—This table shows the various ailments and defective physical conditions from which the members of these Italian families suffered during the year. Out of a total of 6,773 persons 1,448, or 21.38 per cent, were reported as sick during the year or physically defective. Excluding childbirth from consideration, the number of persons otherwise sick and physically defective was 1,185, or 17.50 per cent; excluding childbirth, the proportions for the four cities canvassed in the slum investigation were 1.85 per cent for Baltimore, 3.90 per cent for Chicago, 2.35 per cent for New York, and 2.03 per cent for Philadelphia. The exceedingly small proportion of sick and physically defective persons found among the general slum population embraced in the Seventh Special Report was noticeable, the highest being 3.90 per cent for Chicago. In the present investigation the proportion of sick and defective, excluding childbirth, as has been shown, reached 17.50 per cent.

Referring to the table and noting the specific diseases or ailments, it is seen that of the 1,448 persons reported as sick or defective during the year, 301, or 20.79 per cent, of these persons suffered from childbirth, or childbirth and some other ailment; 203, or 14.02 per cent, suffered from fevers, malarial, typhoid, etc., or fever and some other ailment; 112, or 7.73 per cent, suffered from rickets, or rickets and some other ailment; 114, or 7.87 per cent, suffered from bronchitis, or bronchitis and some other ailment, while 100, or 6.91 per cent, suffered from rheumatism, or rheumatism and some other ailment. Over one-half (55.52 per cent) of all persons reporting ailments or defects suffered during the year from childbirth; fevers, rickets, bronchitis, and rheumatism. Going further and taking up the other ailments most frequently reported, 80, or 5.52 per cent of all ailing and defective persons, suffered from accidental injuries, etc.; 73, or 5.04 per cent, suffered from female complaint, etc.; 42, or 2.90 per cent, from pneumonia, etc.; 41, or 2.83 per cent, from measles, etc.; 28, or 1.93 per cent, from diphtheria; 26, or 1.80 per cent, from inflammation of the eyes; 23, or 1.59 per cent, from dyspepsia, etc.; 19, or 1.31 per cent, from consumption, etc.; 18, or 1.24 per cent, from miscarriage, etc., while the proportion of those suffering from any other ailment or defect ranged from 1.24 to 0.07 per cent.

DOMESTIC CONDITIONS, COST OF FOOD, ETC.

In connection with this investigation partial reports were secured from the families and individuals involved relating to their domestic conditions; their customs in the United States and in Italy as regards baking bread, spinning, sewing, knitting, etc.; their food and the cost of the same, and the padrone system, the commissions paid padrones, and the prices of food bought from padrones as compared with market prices, etc. These points are taken up and such data given as were secured.

BAKING, SPINNING, SEWING, ETC., IN ITALY AND IN THE UNITED STATES.

In answer to the inquiry, Do you bake your bread in this country? out of 965 families reporting 675, or 69.95 per cent, stated that they baked their bread, the remainder buying bread. The number of families answering the inquiry, Did you bake your bread in Italy? was 851. Of this number 777, or 91.30 per cent, answered in the affirmative, as against 69.95 per cent just shown as baking their bread in the United States.

In answer to the inquiry, Do you spin in this country? out of 895 families reporting only 7, or less than 1 per cent, answered in the affirmative, while in answer to the inquiry, Did you spin in Italy? out of 834 families reporting 636, or 76.26 per cent, answered in the affirmative.

In answer to the inquiry, Do you sew in this country? 770, or 86.32 per cent, of the 892 families reporting answered in the affirmative; of the 848 families answering the inquiry, Did you sew in Italy? 779, or 91.86 per cent, answered in the affirmative. Of those families reporting as to whether or not they did sewing in this country, 892 in number, the additional question, Do you sew for a boss? was asked, and an affirmative answer given in 88 cases.

In answer to the inquiry, Do you knit stockings in this country? 156, or 17.73 per cent, of the 880 families reporting answered in the affirmative, while of the 842 families reporting as to whether or not they knitted stockings in Italy 721, or 85.63 per cent, answered in the affirmative.

Of 849 families reporting, 633, or 74.56 per cent, stated they worked in the fields in Italy. In answer to the inquiry, Did you use kerosene lamps in Italy? 846 families reported, 571, or 67.49 per cent, of which answered in the affirmative. Of the 850 families reporting, but 27, or 3.18 per cent, had stoves in Italy. Coal is almost universally reported as the fuel used for cooking in this country, 969, or 98.48 per cent, out of a total of 984 families using that kind of fuel, the remaining 15 families, with the exception of one which used wood and one which used coke, using coal in connection with some other fuel.

In these families 305 persons were found who reported that they had sent money to bring relatives from Italy. The aggregate amount involved was $19,384.75, or an average of $63.56 for each of the 305 persons reporting.

But 9 persons reported that they had invested in land in Italy. The total amount was $2,440, or an average of $271.11 per individual. Seventy-six persons reported that they had invested in land in the United States. The aggregate amount of their investments was $260,665, or an average of $3,429.80 per individual.

Of the 271 male members of these families who were found to have visited Italy since their arrival in this country, 245 had returned to Italy once, 16 had returned twice, 8 had returned three times, 1 had returned four times, and 1 had returned five times. Of the 39 females who had visited Italy, 32 had returned to Italy once, 1 had returned twice, 5 had returned three times, and 1 had returned five times.

FOOD.

The following general report from the agent of the Department who canvassed these families and secured the data which form the basis of the tables included in this report relates to the food of these people and embodies the result of careful inquiry on this subject:

Three facts led to this inquiry concerning the food of the Italian working people:

1. Italians are considered fitted for the lighter kinds of manual labor only. In Chicago they are thought best fitted for street sweeping and not strong enough for work in the waterworks extension department and for sewer digging.

2. It is difficult to persuade an Italian to go to a hospital. He says he starves in places where the food is known to be abundant and well prepared. His absence from work is thus protracted by the unscientific care which he receives at home, and if he is suffering from a contagious disease his reluctance often leads to concealment which imperils other lives.

3. Rickets, a disease due to malnutrition, is exceedingly prevalent among the children of Italian working people.

Considering the large number of causes which may have resulted in this state of things—hereditary weakness, unhealthful housing, and utter ignorance of all the laws of hygiene—it would be presumptuous to attribute all these facts to the quality of food used. Indeed, one great cause of the antipathy to hospitals is probably ignorance of the English language. It may not, however, be entirely profitless to look to the food as one of the possible causes. Possibly the errors of diet common among Italian workingmen are just as common among workingmen of other nationalities. Investigations show that the Russian Jews and Bohemians market more judiciously and cook their food more wisely than do the Italians. It may be for this reason—probably for this and other reasons—that the workingmen of these nationalities are in better physical condition than are the Italians.

It must be borne in mind that the following statements are true only of Italians of the poorer class—not of the richer classes nor of the very poorest class. The food of the last named is obtained to a large extent from garbage boxes. Reference here is made to the laborer who works for $1.25 per day and to the fruit peddler or organ grinder with an income of about the same amount.

As is the case with the poor of other nationalities in this country, there is probably no fault to be found with the food from a purely quantitative standpoint. It is probable that there are exceedingly few Italian persons in the city of Chicago who do not spend enough money upon their food to buy sufficient nutriment to keep their bodies in good condition, providing only the money is judiciously spent and the food properly prepared. Except in rare cases, the Italians certainly eat enough. Immediately following this statement will be found brief dietaries of Italian workingmen at hard labor. The fact that the quantities are not generally given does not seem to render them valueless, for the reasons just given.

In connection with the first of the three points mentioned above, viz, the bearing of the food upon the capacity for labor, it must be remembered that the condition of the Italian laborer in this country, and particularly during the last two or three years, is peculiar. Having only the most unskilled labor to offer, he is the first to be thrown out of employment during seasons of industrial depression. The result has been that in the city of Chicago during the past two years the Italian has worked on an average but little more than four months out of the twelve. The other eight months were spent in idleness and almost absolute inactivity in poorly ventilated rooms. During these months the laborer, helpless because of his ignorance of the English language, hardly ventures farther than the nearest saloon. The food to which he has been accustomed in his native land and to which he clings is peculiarly ill adapted for this inactive period. In theory these eight months of idleness should be a preparation for the season of hard work. The man having little outdoor life and no immediate necessity for exertion has no need for large amounts of starches and fats, but he has the greatest need for the proteids or nitrogenous substances which create muscle and give powers of endurance. The food of the Italian fails to meet this requirement.

It must be mentioned, first, that the large expenditure for beer, which takes the place in this country of the light wines of Italy, seriously curtails the amount of money available for food. Were it not for this large outlay for beer, beef, which the Italian looks upon as a luxury, might be substituted more often for pork. Another thing to be noted is that the money available for food, after this unfortunately large sum has been deducted, is not expended in such a way as to accomplish the most good. Pork, with its large amount of fat and small amount of proteids, as compared with beef, is used much more than the latter. Lard is tried out in large quantities in the fall for use in winter, and enters into the preparation of almost every dish. The beef used is generally from the round. Wheat flour is used in very large quantities and is made into bread and macaroni. It is not uncommon for a family of five or six to use a barrel every six weeks. Oatmeal and other prepared cereals, whole wheat, graham and rye flours, are almost unknown. Beans, eggs, chickens, and cheese are the other more solid kinds of food. Green vegetables are used in very large quantities, but unfortunately are seldom obtained in fresh condition. With the exception of dandelion greens, which are cut by the Italians themselves, the vegetables reach them only after rejection from the better markets. Red peppers and tomatoes are in the greatest favor, and are dried for winter use. A paste, made by drying in the sun the pulp and juice of the tomato, is a characteristic Italian dish. Vegetables are used not as an accompaniment of meat, but as a substitute for it. It will be seen by reference to the dietaries that the Italian laborer frequently takes for his lunch only bread and peppers. The Italians use little butter and milk. Cases could be cited almost without number of these people who have 15 or 20 cents per day to spend for beer and only 3 cents for milk.

With reference to the methods of cooking, meats are generally fried. The Italian fries his round steak in lard, thus reducing it to its most indigestible and innutritious form. He might well take a lesson from his neighbor, the Russian Jew, who by long, slow cooking makes a most palatable, nutrious dish of his chuck beef, an even lower-priced cut of meat. Eggs, an excellent though not an economical food even when well prepared, are largely deprived of their food value by being fried hard in lard. They are usually mixed with potatoes before frying. Cabbage, peppers, and tomatoes are cooked in the same way with potatoes. Macaroni is boiled in water, covered with a sauce of lard flavored with onions, garlic, peppers, or parsley, and is served with cheese. Beans are boiled with potatoes and served with lard sauce or are used for salad.

The conclusion is that the amount of fat and starch taken in this diet is enough for a man at hardest labor and far in excess of the needs of an idle man, and that in the absence to so large an extent of beef, oatmeal, and other foods having large proportions of nitrogenous food principles, there is a deficiency of muscle-forming materials. Foods, such as eggs and beef, having the greatest value for giving strength of muscle and endurance, have their usefulness impaired by pernicious methods of cooking. In view of these facts it seems fair to infer that after a winter of inactivity, in bad air and on such a diet, the system of the Italian laborer is in such a debilitated condition as to make him entirely unprepared for the return of the working season. To this physical unfitness may be attributed his unwillingness to make any exertion to get work—a matter of surprise to his would-be benefactors who consider only his poverty and indebtedness, and not his physical condition.

As to the second point, the aversion to hospitals, there is no doubt that an Italian, taken from his food fried in lard, which attains and retains a much higher temperature than food cooked in milk or water, and which is highly spiced with peppers and highly flavored with garlic and onions, really suffers when the plain, nutritious, and well-prepared food of a hospital is set before him. We can learn more from the instinctive action of a little child than from the protests of scores of grown people. Italian children, when first taken to the hospitals, turn with disgust from such foods as bread and milk or milk toast. It is doubtless true that this change in diet is not only distasteful, but so radical as frequently to disorder the digestive system. Perhaps the treatment of an Italian during this period of change should be studied much as the treatment of an inebriate being won from his strong drink is studied. The sudden change certainly produces an abnormal physical condition. A little more attention to this subject by hospital authorities and a few harmless concessions to the taste of the Italians during the first few days of their stay in the hospital might result in their greater willingness to go to hospitals and in their greater tractableness while there. Many an Italian workingman, from pure aversion to American food, lies sick in his own home for months, while unhealthful surroundings and bad food conspire against his recovery, who might speedily return to health if taken to a hospital.

The third point, concerning the children, is of interest, because it bears upon the condition of the future workingman. A sick child may outgrow his diseases, but can hardly be expected to attain the greatest vigor of manhood. The great prevalence of rickets among Italian children may be seen by reference to the general tables. Rickets never proves fatal, but a child affected with this disease is especially subject to lung, bronchial, throat, and other troubles. The frequent acute troubles of the children, traceable to rickets, produce great drains upon the purse of the Italian laborer. The seeds of this disease are often sown before birth. A poorly nourished mother often nurses one child almost up to the time of the birth of her second child. The second child, weak at birth, is nursed until the mother's milk is entirely unfitted for the demands of its system. The weakness thus engendered is aggravated by giving the child the same unwholesome food that its parents eat, and in addition large quantities of fruit in a more or less decayed condition. Milk is used in very small quantities. The question, Do you give your children milk? is usually answered in the affirmative by the Italian mother, but further inquiry usually brings out the information that she buys only about 3 cents' worth per day and gives it to the children in form of "milk and tea" or "milk and coffee." Beer is given to the very youngest children. Oatmeal and other prepared cereals, whôle wheat and graham flours, with their wealth of mineral matters for the formation of bone, are as unfamiliar to the child as to the father, to whom, as previously stated, they are an unknown food. The food of the Italian, therefore, with its insufficiency of proteids and its excess of the most indigestible of fats, has an added fault, when considered as a diet for children, because of the exclusion to so large an extent of milk, oatmeal, and other foods rich in mineral matters.

DIETARIES OF ITALIAN LABORING MEN.

[Time, August, 1896. Sunday bills of fare not taken.]

No. 1. Age, 29; married; sewer digger. Breakfast and lunch: One pound round steak (beef), three times per week, one-half for breakfast and one-half for lunch; red peppers instead of the round steak, three times per week; every morning 5 cents' worth of beer; bread with all these meals. Supper: Macaroni and beans, or round steak fried with potatoes; always bread and 5 cents' worth of beer.

No. 2. Age, 19; single; sewer digger. Breakfast and lunch: One pound round steak, three times per week; peppers, three times per week; always bread and 5 cents' worth of beer. Supper: Fried potatoes and eggs, or boiled potatoes and macaroni; bread and 5 cents' worth of beer.

No. 3. Age, 35; married; sewer digger. Breakfast and lunch: One pound round steak; bread; 5 cents' worth of beer for lunch. Supper: Round steak fried with potatoes; macaroni and beans; potatoes and peppers fried together.

Nos. 4, 5, 6, 7. Day laborers. Food for each, breakfast and lunch: Five cents' worth of summer sausage; 1 pound bread. Supper: Three boiled eggs or head cheese; bread.

No. 8. Age, 29; single; sewer digger. Breakfast and lunch: Coffee, bread, 10 cents' worth of beer; pork chops, four times per week; fried eggs, twice a week. Supper: Beef fried with potatoes, or peppers fried with potatoes, or macaroni; bread and 5 cents' worth of beer.

No. 9. Age, 31; single; sewer digger. Breakfast and lunch: Bread; 10 cents' worth of beer; fried eggs, or potatoes fried with peppers or cheese. Supper: Macaroni with beans, or peppers fried with potatoes or sausage; bread; 5 cents' worth of beer.

No. 10. Age, 33; single; sewer digger. Breakfast: Coffee or tea and bread. Lunch: Five cents' worth of beer; bread; pork chops twice a week; other days fried eggs, ham, sausage, peppers, or cheese (always beer and bread, with choice of the other articles named). Supper: Potatoes fried with eggs, or sausage fried with peppers.

No. 11. Age, 34; single; sewer digger. Breakfast and lunch: Five cents' worth of pork chops; 15 cents' worth of beer; bread. Supper: Macaroni and beefsteak, or peppers fried with potatoes, or cabbage fried with potatoes, or beans and macaroni; bread and 5 cents' worth of beer.

No. 12. Age, 21; single; day laborer. Breakfast: One pound round steak, fried, three times per week; peppers, three times per week. Supper: Macaroni only, four times per week; fried potatoes with peppers, twice a week; beer unknown.

No. 13. Age, 24; single; day laborer. Breakfast and lunch: One pound pork chops every morning, one-half for breakfast and one-half for lunch; peppers three times per week; bread and 5 cents' worth of beer daily. Supper: Macaroni and beans, or peppers and potatoes, or beef and potatoes (beef three times per week); 5 cents' worth of beer.

No. 14. Age, 23; single. Eats no breakfast. Lunch: Ham or sausage with bread and peppers. Supper: Occasionally, round steak; usually, macaroni only, or potatoes and cabbage; beer unknown.

Inquiry was made as to the actual cost of food and milk among these people, and replies were secured as to food from 742 families, embracing 3,711 persons, while 782 families, embracing 3,914 individuals, reported as to the cost of milk. The result of this inquiry is embodied in the table which follows:

COST OF FOOD AND MILK, BY SIZE OF FAMILY.

Size of family.	Cost of food per week.		Cost of milk per day.	
	Per family.	Per individual.	Per family.	Per individual.
1 person	$1.88½	$1.88½	$0.003	$0.003
2 persons	2.65½	1.33	.017	.009
3 persons	3.18½	1.06	.023	.008
4 persons	3.60	.90	.024	.006
5 persons	3.97	.79½	.027	.005
6 persons	4.28	.71½	.028	.005
7 persons	4.73½	.67½	.039	.006
8 persons	5.77	.72	.036	.004
9 persons	6.82½	.76	.024	.003
10 persons	8.37½	.83½	.046	.005
11 persons	10.22½	.93	.038	.003
12 persons	10.90	.91	.060	.005
13 persons	17.87½	1.37½	.045	.003
Average	4.11	.82	.027	.005

In this table is shown the cost of food per week and the cost of milk per day, according to the size of the family. These costs are given for the family and for the individual. In families of one person the average cost of food per week was $1.88½ and the average cost of milk per day about one-third of a cent. In families of two persons the average cost of food per week per family was $2.65½ and per individual $1.33; the cost of milk per day in these families was 1.7 cents per family, or less than 1 cent per individual. The cost of food and of milk per family naturally increases as the size of family increases, while the cost per individual decreases. The average cost of food per week per individual for the 3,711 individuals in the 742 families reporting as to the cost of food was 82 cents; the average cost of milk per day per individual for the 3,914 individuals in the 782 families reporting as to cost of milk was one-half of 1 cent. The average cost of milk per day for each family reporting was 2.7 cents. Reports were secured from 726 families as to the amounts expended for beer per day. Of this number of families 533, or 73.42 per cent, reported that they used beer and that the average cost of beer per day per family was 11.1 cents. The average cost of milk per day per family was, as just stated, but 2.7 cents. In answer to the inquiry, Do you give your children milk? 573, or 82.09 per cent, of the 698 families reporting answered in the affirmative. In answer to the inquiry, Do you give your children beer? 498, or 71.65 per cent, of the 695 families reporting answered in the affirmative. The inquiry as to whether or not these families ate beefsteak was answered in the affirmative in 858, or 89.84 per cent, of the 955 families reporting as to this fact.

PADRONE SYSTEM.

The inquiry, Do you work for a padrone? was asked of 1,860 persons connected with these families, and 403, or 21.67 per cent, answered in the affirmative. Of this number 24, or 5.96 per cent, reported that they paid no commission to the padrone for securing the job, while 379, or 94.04 per cent, reported that they paid a commission. It was not found possible to ascertain the amount of commission paid by each of these 379 persons, but quite a large proportion of them were able to report the exact amount of commission paid for their last job and the length of time said job lasted. An aggregate of $1,650.50 was paid to padrones by the 341 persons reporting, or an average of $4.84 per individual, for the last job at which they worked, and the aggregate time worked on these jobs was 3,958⅜ weeks, or an average of 11 weeks and 4 days per individual. The average amount paid per week to padrones for employment at the last job at which the 341 persons worked, as shown by these figures, was 42 cents each. This commission to padrones is a matter of no small moment to the workmen when the very low wages at which they work is taken into consideration. This investigation has not shown that any large proportion of the workmen were fed by the padrones, but it is known that in many cases where they were taken out of the city to work they were compelled to purchase the whole or part of their food from the padrones. A number of reports were secured from workmen who were taken out of the city to work and a comparison made between the prices paid for the food which the workmen were compelled to purchase from the padrones and Chicago market prices. The following table shows the results of these reports:

PRICES PAID FOR CERTAIN ARTICLES OF FOOD TO THE PADRONE AND IN THE CHICAGO MARKETS.

Workman number.	Bread (per loaf).		Macaroni (per pound).		Macaroni (per box).		Cheese (per pound).		Sausage (per pound).		Bacon (per pound).	
	Padrone's price.	Chicago price.	Padrone's price.	Chicago price.	Padrone's price.	Chicago price.	Padrone's price.	Chicago price.	Padrone's price.	Chicago price.	Padrone's price.	Chicago price.
1	$0.07	$0.04			$1.50	$1.00	$0.14	$0.07	$0.22	$0.06	$0.16	$0.05
2			$0.09	$0.05					.15	.10		
3	.07	.04	.07	.05	1.60	1.00			.21	.12	.16	.10
4	.06	.04	.07	.04			.40	.25	.20	.10	.18	.08
5	.08	.04	.10	.06							.15	.12
6	.06	.04	.06	.05					.16	.10		
7	.06	.04			1.30	1.05	.30	.28				
8	.08	.04			1.75	1.00	.15	.08	.15	.08	.15	.08
9	.07	.03			1.50	1.00			.18	.12	.16	.10
10	.06	.04	.07	.05					.12	.08		
11	.10	.03	.12	.04							.15	.07
12	.07	.03	.08	.04					.22	.15	.13	.11
13			.06	.04					.18	.15	.13	.11
14	.06	.04	.07	.04			.35	.28	.18	.12	.18	.10
15	.07	.04			1.60	1.25	.35	.15	.20	.11	.13	.08
16	.07	.03	.07	.05			.35	.25	.22	.08	.14	.08
17	.08	.05	.10	.07			.35	.27	.17	.09	.12	.10
18	.07	.04			2.10	1.25	.36	.25	.20	.14	.16	.08
19	.06	.04	.07	.05			.20	.10	.20	.10		
20	.06	.04	.06	.04			.35	.28	.15	.10		
21	.08	.04	.07	.05					.20	.12	.15	.08

PRICES PAID FOR CERTAIN ARTICLES OF FOOD TO THE PADRONE AND IN THE CHICAGO MARKETS—Concluded.

Workman number.	Lard (per pound).		Sugar (per pound).		Coffee (per pound).		Tea (per pound).		Beans (per pound).		Tomatoes (per can).	
	Padrone's price.	Chicago price.	Padrone's price.	Chicago price.	Padrone's price.	Chicago price.	Padrone's price.	Chicago price.	Padrone's price.	Chicago price.	Padrone's price.	Chicago price.
1												
2			$0.09	$0.05½	$0.40	$0.25					$0.15	$0.09
3	$0.13	$0.08	.06	.05								
4	.15	.08	.08	.05			$0.50	$0.25				
5	.15	.08	.10	.06	.40	.20	.40	.20	$0.06	$0.03	.15	.07
6			.07	.05								
7									.03	.02½		
8	.15	.08							.07	.04		
9	.12	.06										
10			.07	.05	.35	.20	.30	.20				
11												
12	.14	.08							.08	.05		
13	.11	.08							.05	.04		
14	.10	.05										
15	.10	.07	.06	.05			.40	.20			.12½	.10
16	.14	.07									.12	.08
17	.17	.10										
18	.15	.09									.10	.05
19									.09	.05		
20												
21	.12½	.06	.07	.05	.30	.18	.20	.15				

The prices are given in this table, by each workman reporting, for such articles of food as were for sale by the padrones. The quality of the food for sale by the padrones was frequently reported as good, although in the majority of cases it was reported as of unknown or of bad quality. In each instance the prices of articles of food sold by the padrones are compared with Chicago prices for the same quality of food. Reports were secured from 21 workmen. Of this number 15 stated that they were compelled to purchase from the padrones such food as they kept for sale; 2 reported that they were practically compelled to patronize the padrones because they had no money to purchase elsewhere; 2 reported themselves helpless to do otherwise because of their distance from any other place where food could be purchased, while 1 did not report, and 1 reported that he was not compelled to patronize the padrones. All of these workmen were taken from the city to work on railroads, probably at track repairing or construction.

As will be seen from this table, the prices charged by padrones are frequently double those charged in Chicago markets for similar articles of food of the same quality. Considering each article embraced in the table, and all combined, it is seen that the padrone's prices show an average increase over Chicago prices as follows: For bread, 82.19 per cent; for macaroni by the pound, 61.11 per cent; for macaroni by the box, 50.33 per cent; for cheese, 46.02 per cent; for sausage, 72.40 per cent; for bacon, 67.91 per cent; for lard, 77.04 per cent; for sugar, 44.58 per cent; for coffee, 74.70 per cent; for tea, 80 per cent; for beans, 61.70 per cent; for tomatoes, 65.38 per cent; and for all articles of food combined, 59.55 per cent.

CHAPTER II.

GENERAL TABLES.

TABLE **I.**—GENERAL SOCIAL AND ECONOMIC CONDITION, BY FAMILIES AND INDIVIDUALS.

Family number.	Relationship to head of family.	Sex.	Age.	Conjugal condition.	Birthplace.	Birthplace of—	
						Father.	Mother.
1	Head	M.	35	Married...	Calabria	Calabria	Calabria
	Wife	F.	28	Married...	Calabria	Calabria	Calabria
	Daughter	F.	5	Single	United States	Calabria	Calabria
	Son	M.	3	Single	United States	Calabria	Calabria
	Son	M.	$\frac{7}{12}$	Single	United States	Calabria	Calabria
2	Head	M.	37	Married...	Basilicata	Basilicata	Basilicata
	Wife	F.	40	Married...	Basilicata	Basilicata	Basilicata
	Daughter	F.	9	Single	United States	Basilicata	Basilicata
	Mother	F.	70	Widowed	Basilicata	Basilicata	Basilicata
3	Head	M.	38	Married...	Campania	Campania	Campania
	Wife	F.	25	Married...	Campania	Campania	Campania
	Daughter	F.	3	Single	United States	Campania	Campania
	Cousin	M.	45	Married...	Campania	Campania	Campania
	Cousin	M.	15	Single	Campania	Campania	Campania
	Boarder	M.	24	Single	Apulia	Apulia	Apulia
4	Head	M.	50	Married...	Campania	Campania	Campania
	Wife	F.	48	Married...	Campania	Campania	Campania
	Son	M.	18	Single	Campania	Campania	Campania
	Son	M.	15	Single	Campania	Campania	Campania
	Son	M.	6	Single	United States	Campania	Campania
	Daughter	F.	2	Single	United States	Campania	Campania
	Sister	F.	29	Married...	Campania	Campania	Campania
	Brother-in-law	M.	30	Married...	Campania	Campania	Campania
	Nephew	M.	7	Single	Campania	Campania	Campania
	Niece	F.	1	Single	United States	Campania	Campania
5	Cooperative	M.	42	Married...	Calabria	Calabria	Calabria
	Cooperative	M.	30	Married...	Calabria	Calabria	Calabria
	Cooperative	M.	34	Married...	Calabria	Calabria	Calabria
	Cooperative	M.	43	Married...	Calabria	Calabria	Calabria
	Cooperative	M.	41	Married...	Calabria	Calabria	Calabria
	Cooperative	M.	40	Single	Calabria	Calabria	Calabria
	Cooperative	M.	40	Married...	Calabria	Calabria	Calabria
6	Head	M.	25	Married...	Basilicata	Basilicata	Basilicata
	Wife	F.	20	Married...	Basilicata	Basilicata	Basilicata
	Mother	F.	55	Widowed	Basilicata	Basilicata	Basilicata
7	Head	M.	28	Married...	Calabria	Calabria	Calabria
	Wife	F.	30	Married...	Calabria	Calabria	Calabria
	Daughter	F.	9	Single	Calabria	Calabria	Calabria
	Son	M.	2	Single	United States	Calabria	Calabria
	Son	M.	$\frac{5}{12}$	Single	United States	Calabria	Calabria
	Boarder	M.	30	Married...	Calabria	Calabria	Calabria
8	Head	M.	42	Married...	Calabria	Calabria	Calabria
	Wife	F.	34	Married...	Calabria	Calabria	Calabria
	Son	M.	9	Single	Calabria	Calabria	Calabria
	Daughter	F.	8	Single	United States	Calabria	Calabria
	Son	M.	4	Single	United States	Calabria	Calabria
	Daughter	F.	2	Single	United States	Calabria	Calabria
	Son	M.	$\frac{7}{12}$	Single	United States	Calabria	Calabria
9	Head	M.	52	Married...	Sicily	Sicily	Sicily
	Wife	F.	49	Married...	Sicily	Sicily	Sicily
	Son	M.	19	Single	Sicily	Sicily	Sicily
	Son	M.	9	Single	Sicily	Sicily	Sicily
10	Head	M.	44	Married...	Sicily	Sicily	Sicily
	Wife	F.	34	Married...	Sicily	Sicily	Sicily
	Daughter	F.	9	Single	Sicily	Sicily	Sicily
	Daughter	F.	7	Single	United States	Sicily	Sicily
	Son	M.	6	Single	United States	Sicily	Sicily
	Daughter	F.	3	Single	United States	Sicily	Sicily
	Daughter	F.	2	Single	United States	Sicily	Sicily
11	Head	M.	34	Married...	Sicily	Sicily	Sicily
	Wife	F.	29	Married...	Sicily	Sicily	Sicily
	Daughter	F.	5	Single	United States	Sicily	Sicily
	Son	M.	2	Single	United States	Sicily	Sicily
	Daughter	F.	$\frac{7}{12}$	Single	United States	Sicily	Sicily

a Not reported.   b Also worked as laborer nine weeks, at $8 per week.

TABLE **I.**—GENERAL SOCIAL AND ECONOMIC CONDITION, BY FAMILIES AND INDIVIDUALS.

Years in U.S.	Naturalized.	Profession, trade, or occupation.	Hours of work per week.	Average weekly earnings.	Weeks employed.	Total yearly earnings.	Sick during year, defective, maimed, or deformed.
7	Yes..	Porter, bakery	60	$7.00	48	$336	Bronchitis.
7	......	Housewife..................	......	......	......	......	Childbirth.
......	......	At home	......	......	......	......	No.
......	......	At home	......	......	......	......	Rickets.
......	......	At home	......	......	......	......	No.
11	Yes..	Packer, rags	60	3.50	52	182	No.
10	......	Ragpicker	60	2.50	52	130	No.
......	......	Scholar	......	......	......	......	No.
10	......	Housework	......	......	......	......	Dyspepsia.
13	Yes..	Street sweeper............	60	7.50	12	90	Rheumatism.
6	......	Housewife and merchant, groceries.	(a)	3.50	52	182	No.
......	......	At home	......	......	......	......	No.
9	Yes..	Street sweeper............	60	7.50	26	195	No.
7½	......	No occupation	......	......	......	......	No.
6	Yes..	Street sweeper............	60	7.50	13	98	No.
13	Yes..	Drayman	(a)	2.00	52	104	No.
8	......	Housewife.................	......	......	......	......	No.
8	......	Newsboy	72	2.00	52	104	No.
8	......	Scholar	......	......	......	......	Bronchitis.
......	......	Scholar	......	......	......	......	No.
......	......	At home	......	......	......	......	Debility, general.
7	......	Saleswoman, bakery	72	(a)	52	(a)	No.
8	No...	Baker.....................	72	(a)	52	(a)	No.
7	......	At home	......	......	......	......	Bronchitis.
......	......	At home	......	......	......	......	No.
13	No...	Laborer...................	60	6.00	18	108	No.
4	No...	Laborer...................	60	6.00	18	108	No.
4	No...	Laborer...................	60	6.00	18	108	No.
6	No...	Laborer...................	60	6.00	18	108	No.
5	No...	Laborer...................	60	6.00	18	108	No.
4	No...	Laborer...................	60	6.00	18	108	No.
7	Yes..	Laborer...................	60	7.50	13	98	No.
13	Yes..	Ragpicker (b).............	(a)	1.00	b 12	84	No.
12	......	Housewife.................	......	......	......	......	No.
4	......	No occupation	......	......	......	......	Catarrh, chronic.
9	Yes..	Laborer...................	60	5.00	13	65	No.
7	......	Housewife.................	......	......	......	......	Childbirth.
7	......	Scholar	......	......	......	......	No.
......	......	At home	......	......	......	......	Rickets.
......	......	At home	......	......	......	......	No.
7	Yes..	No occupation	......	......	......	......	No.
13	Yes..	Laborer...................	60	7.50	26	195	No.
9	......	Housewife.................	......	......	......	......	Childbirth.
9	......	Scholar	......	......	......	......	No.
......	......	Scholar	......	......	......	......	Fever, malarial.
......	......	At home	......	......	......	......	Rickets.
......	......	At home	......	......	......	......	No.
......	......	At home	......	......	......	......	No.
⁷⁄₁₂	No...	Peddler, fruit (c)..........	42	2.00	c 8	(a)	No.
⁷⁄₁₂	......	Housewife.................	......	......	......	......	No.
⁷⁄₁₂	......	Peddler, fruit (c)..........	42	2.00	c 8	(a)	No.
⁷⁄₁₂	......	At home	......	......	......	......	No.
10	No...	Peddler, fruit..............	(a)	10.00	52	520	No.
9	......	Housewife.................	......	......	......	......	No.
9	......	Scholar	......	......	......	......	No.
......	......	Scholar	......	......	......	......	No.
......	......	Scholar	......	......	......	......	No.
......	......	At home	......	......	......	......	No.
......	......	At home	......	......	......	......	No.
8	No...	Peddler, fruit..............	60	10.00	52	520	No.
8	......	Housewife.................	......	......	......	......	Childbirth.
......	......	At home	......	......	......	......	No.
......	......	At home	......	......	......	......	No.
......	......	At home	......	......	......	......	No.

c Also worked at another occupation, details not reported.

TABLE **I**—GENERAL SOCIAL AND ECONOMIC CONDITION, BY FAMILIES AND INDIVIDUALS—Continued.

Family number.	Relationship to head of family.	Sex.	Age.	Conjugal condition.	Birthplace.	Birthplace of—	
						Father.	Mother.
12	Head	M.	60	Married...	Sicily	Sicily	Sicily
	Wife	F.	50	Married...	Sicily	Sicily	Sicily
	Son	M.	15	Single.....	Sicily	Sicily	Sicily
13	Head	M.	47	Married...	Calabria	Calabria	Calabria
	Wife	F.	36	Married...	Calabria	Calabria	Calabria
	Daughter	F.	15	Single.....	Calabria	Calabria	Calabria
	Son	M.	3	Single.....	United States	Calabria	Calabria
	Son	M.	1	Single.....	United States	Calabria	Calabria
	Son-in-law	M.	20	Married...	Calabria	Calabria	Calabria
	Cousin	M.	29	Single.....	Calabria	Calabria	Calabria
	Boarder	M.	26	Married...	Calabria	Calabria	Calabria
14	Head	M.	40	Married.	Calabria	Calabria	Calabria
	Wife	F.	30	Married...	Calabria	Calabria	Calabria
	Daughter	F.	9	Single.....	Calabria	Calabria	Calabria
	Daughter	F.	6/12	Single....	United States	Calabria	Calabria
	Brother-in-law	M.	25	Married...	Calabria	Calabria	Calabria
	Sister-in-law	F.	21	Married...	Calabria	Calabria	Calabria
	Boarder	M.	37	Married...	Calabria	Calabria	Calabria
15	Head	M.	51	Married...	Calabria	Calabria	Calabria
	Wife	F.	42	Married...	Calabria	Calabria	Calabria
	Son	M.	22	Single.....	Calabria	Calabria	Calabria
	Son	M.	17	Single.....	Calabria	Calabria	Calabria
16	Head	M.	20	Married...	Marches	Marches	Marches
	Wife	F.	19	Married...	Marches	Marches	Marches
	Brother	M.	17	Single....	Marches	Marches	Marches
17	Head	M.	40	Married...	Venetia	Venetia	Venetia
	Wife	F.	25	Married...	United States	Liguria	Liguria
	Daughter	F.	5	Single.....	United States	Venetia	United States
	Son	M.	2	Single.....	United States	Venetia	United States
18	Head	M.	25	Married...	Campania	Campania	Campania
	Wife	F.	20	Married...	Campania	Campania	Campania
	Lodger	M.	40	Married...	Campania	Campania	Campania
	Lodger	M.	20	Single.....	Campania	Campania	Campania
	Lodger	M.	32	Married...	Campania	Campania	Campania
19	Head	M.	37	Married...	Campania	Campania	Campania
	Wife	F.	40	Married...	Campania	Campania	Campania
20	Head	M.	30	Married...	Calabria	Calabria	Calabria
	Wife	F.	29	Married...	Calabria	Calabria	Calabria
	Son	M.	1	Single.....	United States	Calabria	Calabria
	Boarder	M.	18	Single.....	Calabria	Calabria	Calabria
	Boarder	M.	28	Married...	Calabria	Calabria	Calabria
21	Head	M.	48	Married...	Calabria	Calabria	Calabria
	Wife	F.	40	Married...	Calabria	Calabria	Calabria
	Son	M.	18	Single.....	Calabria	Calabria	Calabria
	Nephew	M.	23	Single.....	Calabria	Calabria	Calabria
	Nephew	M.	15	Single.....	Calabria	Calabria	Calabria
	Lodger	M.	40	Married...	Calabria	Calabria	Calabria
22	Head	M.	39	Married...	Campania	Campania	Campania
	Wife	F.	32	Married...	Basilicata	Basilicata	Basilicata
	Son	M.	12	Single.....	United States	Campania	Basilicata
	Daughter	F.	8	Single.....	United States	Campania	Basilicata
	Son	M.	5	Single.....	United States	Campania	Basilicata
	Daughter	F.	2	Single.....	United States	Campania	Basilicata
23	Head	M.	31	Married...	Campania	Campania	Campania
	Wife	F.	34	Married...	United States	Ireland	United States
	Son	M.	1	Single.....	United States	Campania	United States
24	Head	M.	40	Married...	Campania	Campania	Campania
	Wife	F.	40	Married...	Campania	Campania	Campania
	Son	M.	18	Single....	Campania	Campania	Campania
	Son	M.	15	Single....	Campania	Campania	Campania
	Daughter	F.	14	Single....	United States	Campania	Campania
	Daughter	F.	12	Single....	United States	Campania	Campania
	Daughter	F.	9	Single....	United States	Campania	Campania
	Brother-in-law	M.	34	Married...	Campania	Campania	Campania
	Nephew	M.	14	Single....	Campania	Campania	Campania

a Also worked as laborer fifteen weeks, at $7.20 per week.   *b* Not reported.

TABLE **I.**—GENERAL SOCIAL AND ECONOMIC CONDITION, BY FAMILIES AND INDIVIDUALS—Continued.

Years in U. S.	Naturalized.	Profession, trade, or occupation.	Hours of work per week.	Average weekly earnings.	Weeks employed.	Total yearly earnings.	Sick during year, defective, maimed, or deformed.
12	No...	Peddler, fruit	60	$5.00	52	$260	No.
2		Housewife					No.
3		Scholar and peddler, fruit.	60	1.50	52	78	No.
4	No...	Laborer	60	7.50	18	135	No.
4		Housewife					No.
4		Housework					No.
		At home					Rickets.
		At home					No.
7		Peddler, fruit	60	6.00	39	234	No.
14	Yes.	Scrubber(a)	(b)	6.00	a 37	330	No.
2	No...	Laborer	60	7.50	18	135	No.
12	Yes..	Laborer	60	7.50	26	195	No.
3		Housewife					Childbirth.
3		At home					No.
		At home					Fever, not specified.
9	Yes..	Laborer	60	7.50	26	195	Rheumatism.
4		Housework					No.
4	No...	Laborer	60	7.50	21	158	No.
11	No...	Scissors grinder	48	3.00	52	156	No.
4		Housewife					Epilepsy.
7	Yes..	(b)					No.
4		(b)					Rheumatism.
2		Musician	(b)	5.50	52	286	No.
2		Housewife					No.
2		Musician	(b)	5.50	52	286	No.
11	No...	Watchmaker	(b)	9.00	52	468	No.
		Housewife					No.
		Scholar					No.
		At home					Diarrhea.
12	Yes..	Watchman	(b)	14.00	15	210	No.
10		Housewife and wet nurse	(b)	1.50	(b)	(b)	No.
12	No...	No occupation					No.
4		Laborer	60	7.50	13	98	No.
8	No...	Laborer	60	7.50	13	98	No.
11	Yes..	Laborer	60	7.50	22	165	No.
9		Housewife					Female complaint.
4	No...	Laborer	60	7.50	18	135	No.
3		Housewife					No.
		At home					Bronchitis.
3		Laborer	60	7.50	9	68	No.
3	No...	Laborer	60	7.50	35	263	No.
10	No...	Laborer	48	7.20	15	108	Kidneys, disease of.
4		Housewife					No.
4		Laborer	(b)	8.00	18	144	No.
5	No...	Laborer	60	7.50	30	225	No.
4		Bootblack and newsboy	54	1.75	52	91	No.
8	No...	Laborer	60	7.50	13	98	No.
13	Yes..	No occupation					No.
13		Housewife					Kidneys, disease of.
		Scholar and newsboy	40	1.00	52	52	No.
		Scholar					No.
		At home					Rickets.
		At home					No.
7	No...	Ragpicker (c)	48	2.75	c 37	231	No.
		Housewife					No.
		At home					Bronchitis.
14	Yes..	Laborer	60	6.00	21	126	No.
14		Housewife					No.
14		Barber	(b)	5.50	52	286	No.
14		Barber's apprentice	(b)	2.00	52	104	No.
		Scholar					No.
		Scholar					No.
		Scholar					No.
(b)	Yes..	No occupation					No.
(b)		No occupation					No.

c Also worked as laborer fifteen weeks, at $0.60 per week.

TABLE I.—GENERAL SOCIAL AND ECONOMIC CONDITION, BY FAMILIES AND INDIVIDUALS—Continued.

Family number.	Relationship to head of family.	Sex.	Age.	Conjugal condition.	Birthplace.	Birthplace of—	
						Father.	Mother.
25	Head	M.	34	Married	Campania	Campania	Campania
	Wife	F.	39	Married	Basilicata	Basilicata	Basilicata
	Daughter	F.	9	Single	United States	Campania	Basilicata
	Daughter	F.	4	Single	United States	Campania	Basilicata
	Son	M.	2	Single	United States	Campania	Basilicata
26	Head	M.	52	Married	Campania	Campania	Campania
	Wife	F.	38	Married	Campania	Campania	Campania
	Daughter	F.	15	Single	Campania	Campania	Campania
	Son	M.	12	Single	Campania	Campania	Campania
	Son	M.	10	Single	Campania	Campania	Campania
	Daughter	F.	3	Single	United States	Campania	Campania
	Son	M.	2	Single	United States	Campania	Campania
27	Head	M.	44	Married	Basilicata	Basilicata	Basilicata
	Wife	F.	32	Married	Basilicata	Basilicata	Basilicata
	Son	M.	14	Single	United States	Basilicata	Basilicata
	Son	M.	12	Single	Basilicata	Basilicata	Basilicata
	Daughter	F.	9	Single	United States	Basilicata	Basilicata
	Son	M.	5	Single	United States	Basilicata	Basilicata
	Daughter	F.	2	Single	United States	Basilicata	Basilicata
28	Head	M.	36	Married	Abruzzo	Abruzzo	Abruzzo
	Wife	F.	31	Married	Abruzzo	Abruzzo	Abruzzo
	Daughter	F.	7	Single	France	Abruzzo	Abruzzo
	Son	M.	$\frac{1}{12}$	Single	United States	Abruzzo	Abruzzo
29	Head	F.	44	Widowed	Basilicata	Basilicata	Basilicata
	Son	M.	9	Single	United States	Basilicata	Basilicata
	Son	M.	7	Single	United States	Basilicata	Basilicata
	Daughter	F.	6	Single	United States	Basilicata	Basilicata
	Daughter	F.	5	Single	United States	Basilicata	Basilicata
30	Head	M.	33	Married	Calabria	Calabria	Calabria
	Wife	F.	29	Married	Calabria	Calabria	Calabria
	Son	M.	7	Single	Calabria	Calabria	Calabria
	Son	M.	$\frac{1}{12}$	Single	United States	Calabria	Calabria
	Boarder	M.	38	Widowed	Calabria	Calabria	Calabria
31	Head	M.	26	Married	Calabria	Calabria	Calabria
	Wife	F.	29	Married	United States	United States	United States
	Son	M.	5	Single	United States	Calabria	United States
	Daughter	F.	2	Single	United States	Calabria	United States
	Brother	M.	24	Married	Calabria	Calabria	Calabria
32	Head	M.	44	Widowed	Campania	Campania	Campania
33	Head	M.	49	Married	Abruzzo	Abruzzo	Abruzzo
	Wife	F.	30	Married	Abruzzo	Abruzzo	Abruzzo
	Son	M.	5	Single	United States	Abruzzo	Abruzzo
	Daughter	F.	4	Single	United States	Abruzzo	Abruzzo
	Daughter	F.	2	Single	United States	Abruzzo	Abruzzo
34	Head	M.	31	Married	Calabria	Calabria	Calabria
	Wife	F.	32	Married	Calabria	Calabria	Calabria
	Son	M.	2	Single	United States	Calabria	Calabria
	Cousin	M.	29	Married	Calabria	Calabria	Calabria
	Cousin	M.	35	Married	Calabria	Calabria	Calabria
	Cousin	M.	36	Married	Calabria	Calabria	Calabria
35	Head	M.	30	Married	Calabria	Calabria	Calabria
	Wife	F.	29	Married	Calabria	Calabria	Calabria
	Daughter	F.	7	Single	Calabria	Calabria	Calabria
	Son	M.	1	Single	United States	Calabria	Calabria
	Boarder	M.	24	Single	Tuscany	Tuscany	Tuscany
36	Head	M.	37	Married	Campania	Campania	Campania
	Wife	F.	23	Married	Campania	Campania	Campania

a Also worked as laborer thirteen weeks, at $6.50 per week.
b Not reported.
c Also worked as peddler, ice cream, at $1 per week, number of weeks not reported.

TABLE **I.**—GENERAL SOCIAL AND ECONOMIC CONDITION, BY FAMILIES
AND INDIVIDUALS—Continued.

Years in U.S.	Naturalized.	Profession, trade, or occupation.	Hours of work per week.	Average weekly earnings.	Weeks employed.	Total yearly earnings.	Sick during year, defective, maimed, or deformed.
10	Yes...	Ragpicker(a)	(b)	$1.75	a 39	$153	No.
10	......	Housewife..................					No.
......	......	Scholar				......	No.
......	......	At home					No.
......	......	At home					No.
10	No...	No occupation					Eye, loss of one.
10	......	Housewife..................				......	No.
10	......	Housework.................					No.
10	......	Bootblack	18	1.00	52	52	No.
10	......	Scholar....................					No.
......	......	At home					Rickets.
......	......	At home					No.
23	Yes..	No occupation				......	Epilepsy.
12	......	Housewife and washerwoman.	48	2.00	52	104	No.
......	......	Scholar and newsboy	72	1.50	52	78	No.
12	......	No occupation				......	No.
......	......	Scholar					No.
......	......	At home					Erysipelas.
......	......	At home					No.
6	Yes..	Laborer (c)	48	9.00	c 18	(b)	No.
6	......	Housewife..................					Childbirth.
6	......	At home					No.
......	......	At home					No.
13	......	Housewife and washerwoman.	(b)	1.75	52	91	No.
......	......	Scholar					No.
......	......	Scholar					No.
......	......	At home					No.
......	......	At home					No.
6	Yes..	Laborer....................	60	7.50	18	135	No.
1	......	Housewife..................					Childbirth.
1	......	Scholar					No.
......	......	At home					No.
16	Yes..	Laborer....................	60	7.50	18	135	No.
15	Yes..	Foreman, sewer diggers(d)	48	11.00	d 6	106	No.
......	......	Housewife and waist finisher.	(b)	.40	18	7	No.
......	......	At home...................					Rickets.
......	......	At home				......	No.
5	Yes..	Sewer digger (e)	(b)	(b)	e 23	(b)	No.
10	Yes..	Mason, stone	48	24.00	6	144	No.
6	Yes..	Organ grinder	48	(b)	52	(b)	Leg, loss of one.
5	......	Housewife..................					No.
......	......	At home...................					Rickets.
......	......	At home...................					No.
......	......	At home...................					Rickets.
6	Yes..	Laborer....................	(b)	9.00	13	117	No.
5	......	Housewife..................					Bronchitis.
......	......	At home...................				......	No.
2	No...	Laborer....................	60	9.00	13	117	No.
3	No...	Laborer....................	(b)	9.00	13	117	No.
7	No...	Laborer....................	(b)	9.00	22	198	No.
5	Yes..	Laborer....................	54	5.00	52	260	No.
4	......	Housewife..................					No.
4	......	Scholar					Bronchitis.
......	......	At home...................					No.
8	No...	Tailor	(b)	15.00	12	180	No.
15	Yes..	Laborer....................	60	9.00	18	162	No.
8	......	Housewife..................					No.

d Also worked as car cleaner four weeks, at $10 per week.
e Also worked as car cleaner twenty-two weeks, at $6.90 per week.

TABLE **I.**—GENERAL SOCIAL AND ECONOMIC CONDITION, BY FAMILIES
AND INDIVIDUALS—Continued.

Family number.	Relationship to head of family.	Sex.	Age.	Conjugal condition.	Birthplace.	Birthplace of—	
						Father.	Mother.
37	Head	M.	34	Married	Campania	Campania	Campania
	Wife	F.	27	Married	Campania	Campania	Campania
	Daughter	F.	3	Single	United States	Campania	Campania
	Daughter	F.	2	Single	United States	Campania	Campania
38	Head	M.	30	Married	Campania	Campania	Campania
	Wife	F.	20	Married	Campania	Campania	Campania
	Daughter	F.	3	Single	United States	Campania	Campania
	Son	M.	2	Single	United States	Campania	Campania
39	Head	M.	24	Married	Calabria	Calabria	Calabria
	Wife	F.	15	Married	Calabria	Calabria	Calabria
	Boarder	M.	40	Married	Calabria	Calabria	Calabria
40	Head	M.	47	Married	Basilicata	Basilicata	Basilicata
	Wife	F.	35	Married	Basilicata	Basilicata	Basilicata
	Son	M.	13	Single	Basilicata	Basilicata	Basilicata
	Son	M.	7	Single	United States	Basilicata	Basilicata
	Son	M.	7	Single	United States	Basilicata	Basilicata
	Son	M.	2	Single	United States	Basilicata	Basilicata
	Mother	F.	69	Widowed	Basilicata	Basilicata	Basilicata
41	Head	M.	36	Married	Calabria	Calabria	Calabria
	Wife	F.	30	Married	Calabria	Calabria	Calabria
	Daughter	F.	1	Single	United States	Calabria	Calabria
	Son	M.	$\frac{1}{12}$	Single	United States	Calabria	Calabria
42	Head	M.	45	Married	Calabria	Calabria	Calabria
	Wife	F.	45	Married	Calabria	Calabria	Calabria
	Daughter	F.	4	Single	United States	Calabria	Calabria
43	Head	M.	34	Married	Calabria	Calabria	Calabria
	Wife	F.	38	Married	Calabria	Calabria	Calabria
	Daughter	F.	8	Single	Calabria	Calabria	Calabria
	Daughter	F.	$\frac{2}{3}$	Single	United States	Calabria	Calabria
	Lodger	M.	30	Married	Calabria	Calabria	Calabria
44	Head	M.	50	Married	Campania	Campania	Campania
	Wife	F.	51	Married	Campania	Campania	Campania
	Daughter	F.	21	Widowed	Campania	Campania	Campania
	Son	M.	18	Single	Campania	Campania	Campania
	Grandson	M.	6	Single	United States	Campania	Campania
	Granddaughter	F.	2	Single	United States	Campania	Campania
45	Head	M.	33	Married	Campania	Campania	Campania
	Wife	F.	29	Married	Campania	Campania	Campania
	Son	M.	5	Single	United States	Campania	Campania
	Son	M.	2	Single	United States	Campania	Campania
	Son	M.	1	Single	United States	Campania	Campania
	Brother	M.	30	Single	Campania	Campania	Campania
46	Head	M.	36	Married	Campania	Campania	Campania
	Wife	F.	33	Married	Campania	Campania	Campania
	Son	M.	8	Single	United States	Campania	Campania
	Son	M.	5	Single	United States	Campania	Campania
	Daughter	F.	3	Single	United States	Campania	Campania
47	Head	M.	45	Married	Calabria	Calabria	Calabria
	Son	M.	22	Single	Calabria	Calabria	Calabria
	Cousin	M.	50	Widowed	Calabria	Calabria	Calabria
	Lodger	M.	45	Married	Calabria	Calabria	Calabria
	Lodger	M.	30	Married	Calabria	Calabria	Calabria
48	Head	M.	47	Married	Calabria	Calabria	Calabria
	Wife	F.	50	Married	Calabria	Calabria	Calabria
	Son	M.	16	Single	Calabria	Calabria	Calabria
49	Head	M.	29	Married	Calabria	Calabria	Calabria
	Wife	F.	27	Married	Calabria	Calabria	Calabria
	Daughter	F.	5	Single	Calabria	Calabria	Calabria
	Son	M.	3	Single	United States	Calabria	Calabria
	Daughter	F.	1	Single	United States	Calabria	Calabria

a Not reported.

TABLE **I.**—GENERAL SOCIAL AND ECONOMIC CONDITION, BY FAMILIES
AND INDIVIDUALS—Continued.

Years in U. S.	Naturalized.	Profession, trade, or occupation.	Hours of work per week.	Average weekly earnings.	Weeks employed.	Total yearly earnings.	Sick during year, defective, maimed, or deformed.
15	No...	Scissors grinder	60	$9.00	52	$468	No.
5	....	Housewife..............	....	....	....	....	No.
....	....	At home................	....	....	....	....	No.
....	....	At home................	....	....	....	....	No.
17	Yes..	Scissors grinder	60	9.00	52	468	No.
18	....	Housewife..............	....	....	....	....	No.
....	....	At home................	....	....	....	....	No.
....	....	At home................	....	....	....	....	No.
8	Yes..	Candy maker	(a)	3.00	48	144	No.
3	....	Housewife..............	....	....	....	....	No.
7	Yes..	Laborer................	48	7.50	52	390	No.
13	Yes..	Laborer................	60	8.75	9	79	No.
9	....	Housewife and wood picker	(a)	.55	(a)	(a)	No.
9	....	Scholar and bootblack	36	.50	52	26	No.
....	....	At home................	....	....	....	....	Rickets.
....	....	At home................	....	....	....	....	No.
....	....	At home................	....	....	....	....	Bronchitis.
4	....	Housework	....	....	....	....	No.
13	Yes..	Laborer................	60	7.50	13	98	Injury by accident.
3	....	Housewife..............	....	....	....	....	Childbirth
....	....	At home................	....	....	....	....	No.
....	....	At home................	....	....	....	....	No.
14	Yes..	Laborer................	60	7.50	13	98	No.
8	....	Housewife..............	....	....	....	....	Rheumatism.
....	....	At home................	....	....	....	....	Ear (middle), inflammation of
8	Yes..	Laborer................	60	3.75	13	49	No
6	....	Housewife..............	....	....	....	....	Childbirth.
6	....	Scholar	....	....	....	....	Erysipelas.
....	....	At home................	....	....	....	....	No.
4	No...	Laborer................	60	3.75	13	49	No.
18	Yes..	Barber.................	80	14.00	52	728	No.
14	....	Housewife..............	....	....	....	....	Bronchitis.
14	....	Cloak maker.............	(a)	9.00	26	234	No.
14	....	Barber.................	80	3.00	52	156	No.
....	....	At home................	....	....	....	....	No.
....	....	At home................	....	....	....	....	No.
14	Yes..	Saloon keeper	(a)	(a)	52	(a)	No.
5	....	Housewife..............	....	....	....	....	Neuralgia.
....	....	At home................	....	....	....	....	No.
....	....	At home................	....	....	....	....	No.
....	....	At home................	....	....	....	....	Bronchitis.
15	Yes..	Helper in saloon (b).......	(a)	(a)	b 34	(a)	No.
14	Yes..	Laborer................	(a)	7.50	17	128	No.
9	....	Housewife..............	....	....	....	....	No.
....	....	Scholar	....	....	....	....	No.
....	....	At home................	....	....	....	....	No.
....	....	At home................	....	....	....	....	No.
12	No...	Boarding-house keeper...	(a)	(a)	52	(a)	Rheumatism.
1¾	No...	No occupation	....	....	....	....	No.
14	No...	No occupation	....	....	....	....	Debility, general; deformity of one hand.
14	No...	Laborer....	(a)	7.70	21	162	No.
4	No...	Street sweeper	48	4.50	9	41	No.
15	Yes..	Laborer................	60	7.50	17	128	Bronchitis.
4	....	Housewife..............	....	....	....	....	Female complaint.
4	....	Scholar and newsboy	38	1.50	52	78	No.
8	Yes..	Laborer................	60	7.50	22	165	No.
4	....	Housewife..............	....	....	....	....	No.
4	....	At home................	....	....	....	....	No.
....	....	At home................	....	....	....	....	Rickets.
....	....	At home................	....	....	....	....	No.

b Also worked as laborer eighteen weeks, at $8.40 per week.

TABLE **I.**—GENERAL SOCIAL AND ECONOMIC CONDITION, BY FAMILIES AND INDIVIDUALS—Continued.

Family number.	Relationship to head of family.	Sex.	Age.	Conjugal condition.	Birthplace.	Birthplace of— Father.	Birthplace of— Mother.
50	Head	M.	40	Married	Basilicata	Basilicata	Basilicata
	Wife	F.	50	Married	Basilicata	Basilicata	Basilicata
	Stepson	M.	23	Single	United States	Basilicata	Basilicata
	Boarder	M.	29	Single	Sicily	Sicily	Sicily
	Boarder	M.	23	Single	Sicily	Sicily	Sicily
	Boarder	M.	25	Single	Sicily	Sicily	Sicily
51	Head	M.	44	Married	Calabria	Calabria	Calabria
	Wife	F.	42	Married	Calabria	Calabria	Calabria
	Son	M.	5	Single	United States	Calabria	Calabria
	Daughter	F.	2	Single	United States	Calabria	Calabria
	Boarder	M.	23	Single	Calabria	Calabria	Calabria
	Boarder	M.	27	Married	Calabria	Calabria	Calabria
	Boarder	M.	30	Married	Calabria	Calabria	Calabria
52	Head	M.	39	Married	Campagna di Roma.	Campagna di Roma.	Campagna di Roma.
	Wife	F.	35	Married	United States	Germany	Germany
	Daughter	F.	11	Single	United States	Campagna di Roma.	United States
53	Head	M.	45	Married	Campania	Campania	Campania
	Wife	F.	36	Married	Campania	Campania	Campania
	Son	M.	6	Single	United States	Campania	Campania
54	Head	F.	29	Married	Campania	Campania	Campania
	Son	M.	5	Single	United States	Campania	Campania
	Daughter	F.	3	Single	United States	Campania	Campania
	Son	M.	1½	Single	United States	Campania	Campania
	Cousin	F.	11	Single	Campania	Campania	Campania
55	Head	M.	32	Married	Basilicata	Basilicata	Basilicata
	Wife	F.	45	Married	Campania	Campania	Campania
56	Head	M.	36	Married	Campania	Campania	Campania
	Wife	F.	39	Married	Campania	Campania	Campania
	Son	M.	12	Single	Campania	Campania	Campania
	Son	M.	11	Single	Campania	Campania	Campania
	Son	M.	7	Single	United States	Campania	Campania
	Daughter	F.	3	Single	United States	Campania	Campania
57	Head	M.	45	Married	Basilicata	Basilicata	Basilicata
	Wife	F.	34	Married	Basilicata	Basilicata	Basilicata
	Son	M.	15	Single	Basilicata	Basilicata	Basilicata
	Daughter	F.	7	Single	United States	Basilicata	Basilicata
	Daughter	F.	5	Single	United States	Basilicata	Basilicata
	Son	M.	3	Single	United States	Basilicata	Basilicata
58	Head	M.	46	Married	Basilicata	Basilicata	Basilicata
	Wife	F.	37	Married	Basilicata	Basilicata	Basilicata
	Daughter	F.	14	Single	Basilicata	Basilicata	Basilicata
	Daughter	F.	12	Single	Basilicata	Basilicata	Basilicata
	Daughter	F.	7	Single	United States	Basilicata	Basilicata
	Daughter	F.	5	Single	United States	Basilicata	Basilicata
	Son	M.	3	Single	United States	Basilicata	Basilicata
	Son	M.	9⁄12	Single	United States	Basilicata	Basilicata
59	Head	M.	35	Married	Campania	Campania	Campania
	Wife	F.	25	Married	Campania	Campania	Campania
	Daughter	F.	8	Single	United States	Campania	Campania
	Daughter	F.	6	Single	United States	Campania	Campania
	Son	M.	5	Single	United States	Campania	Campania
60	Head	M	48	Married	Basilicata	Basilicata	Basilicata
	Wife	F.	46	Married	Basilicata	Basilicata	Basilicata
	Daughter	F.	20	Married	Basilicata	Basilicata	Basilicata
	Son	M.	13	Single	United States	Basilicata	Basilicata
	Daughter	F.	11	Single	United States	Basilicata	Basilicata
	Daughter	F.	9	Single	United States	Basilicata	Basilicata
	Son-in-law	M.	25	Married	Campania	Campania	Campania

a Not reported.
b Also worked as ragpicker thirteen weeks, at $1 per week.

TABLE I.—GENERAL SOCIAL AND ECONOMIC CONDITION, BY FAMILIES AND INDIVIDUALS—Continued.

Years in U. S.	Naturalized.	Profession, trade, or occupation.	Hours of work per week.	Average weekly earnings.	Weeks employed.	Total yearly earnings.	Sick during year, defective, maimed, or deformed.
16	Yes..	Driver, rag shop..........	60	(a)	52	(a)	No.
23	....	Housewife and boarding-house keeper.	(a)	$4.00	52	$208	No.
		Musician	(a)	4.00	(a)	(a)	Consumption.
11	No...	Laborer...................	(a)	9.00	52	468	No.
7	No...	Laborer...................	60	6.60	15	99	No.
3	No...	Laborer...................	60	6.60	18	119	No.
15	Yes..	Laborer...................	60	6.00	18	108	No.
10	....	Housewife................					No.
	....	Scholar					No.
	....	At home..................					No.
6	Yes..	Laborer..................	60	7.50	26	195	Eye, loss of one.
3	No...	Laborer..................	60	7.50	26	195	No.
5	Yes..	No occupation...........					Dyspepsia.
12	Yes..	Plasterer	48	9.00	22	198	No.
		Housewife and laundress..	84	(a)	6	(a)	No.
		Scholar					No.
12	Yes..	Umbrella mender.........	72	3.00	52	156	Syphilis.
9	......	Housewife................					Syphilis.
	......	At home..................					No.
7	......	Washerwoman............	30	3.00	(a)	(a)	Childbirth.
	......	Scholar					No.
	......	At home..................					No.
	......	At home..................					No.
7	......	No occupation...........					No.
13	No...	Laborer (b)	60	3.75	b 13	62	No.
9	......	Housewife................					Injury by accident.
10	No...	Stonebreaker	60	8.00	39	312	Fever, typhoid.
10	......	Housewife and wood picker	24	1.80	34	61	Female complaint.
10	......	Scholar					No.
10	......	Scholar					Fever, not specified.
	......	Scholar					Fever, typhoid.
	......	At home					Fever, typhoid.
20	Yes..	Merchant, rags	96	(a)	50	(a)	Throat, inflammation of.
8	......	Housewife................					No.
8	......	Scholar					Bronchitis.
	......	Scholar					No..
	......	At home					No.
	......	At home					No.
12	Yes..	Tinker (c)	(a)	3.50	c 43	188	No.
9	......	Housewife................					Childbirth; rheumatism.
9	......	Cash girl.................	57	2.00	52	104	No.
9	......	Scholar					Measles.
	....	Scholar					No.
	......	At home					No.
	......	At home					No.
	......	At home					No.
19	Yes..	Saloon keeper and interpreter.	(a)	11.25	52	585	No.
19	......	Housewife................					No.
	......	Scholar					No.
	......	Scholar					No.
	......	At home					No.
14	No...	Laborer...................	60	3.75	35	131	No.
14	......	Housewife................					No.
14	......	Housework					No.
	......	Scholar					No.
	......	Scholar					No.
	......	Scholar					No.
14	Yes..	Street car conductor (d)...	63	16.00	d 30	624	No.

c Also worked as laborer nine weeks, at $4.20 per week.
d Also worked as foreman, railroad laborers, twelve weeks, at $12 per week.

TABLE **I.**—GENERAL SOCIAL AND ECONOMIC CONDITION, BY FAMILIES AND INDIVIDUALS—Continued.

Family number.	Relationship to head of family.	Sex.	Age.	Conjugal condition.	Birthplace.	Birthplace of—	
						Father.	Mother.
61	Head	M.	37	Married	Basilicata	Basilicata	Basilicata
	Wife	F.	37	Married	Basilicata	Basilicata	Basilicata
	Daughter	F.	4	Single	United States	Basilicata	Basilicata
	Brother	M.	34	Married	Basilicata	Basilicata	Basilicata
	Cousin	M.	39	Single	Basilicata	Basilicata	Basilicata
62	Head	M.	50	Married	Calabria	Calabria	Calabria
	Son	M.	18	Single	Calabria	Calabria	Calabria
63	Head	M.	37	Married	Abruzzo	Abruzzo	Abruzzo
	Wife	F.	37	Married	Abruzzo	Abruzzo	Abruzzo
	Daughter	F.	10	Single	Abruzzo	Abruzzo	Abruzzo
	Daughter	F.	6	Single	Abruzzo	Abruzzo	Abruzzo
	Son	M.	4	Single	United States	Abruzzo	Abruzzo
	Daughter	F.	2	Single	United States	Abruzzo	Abruzzo
64	Head	M.	34	Married	Abruzzo	Abruzzo	Abruzzo
	Wife	F.	24	Married	Abruzzo	Abruzzo	Abruzzo
65	Head	M.	36	Married	Basilicata	Basilicata	Basilicata
	Wife	F.	34	Married	Basilicata	Basilicata	Basilicata
	Daughter	F.	7	Single	United States	Basilicata	Basilicata
	Son	M.	4	Single	United States	Basilicata	Basilicata
	Son	M.	$\frac{1}{12}$	Single	United States	Basilicata	Basilicata
66	Head	M.	40	Married	Calabria	Calabria	Calabria
	Wife	F.	38	Married	Calabria	Calabria	Calabria
	Daughter	F.	9	Single	Calabria	Calabria	Calabria
	Son	M.	6	Single	Calabria	Calabria	Calabria
	Son	M.	1	Single	United States	Calabria	Calabria
	Son	M.	$\frac{3}{12}$	Single	United States	Calabria	Calabria
67	Head	F.	51	Widowed	Calabria	Calabria	Calabria
	Son	M.	27	Single	Calabria	Calabria	Calabria
	Son	M.	21	Single	Calabria	Calabria	Calabria
	Daughter	F.	10	Single	Calabria	Calabria	Calabria
	Son	M.	9	Single	Calabria	Calabria	Calabria
68	Head	M.	42	Married	Calabria	Calabria	Calabria
	Wife	F.	35	Married	Calabria	Calabria	Calabria
	Son	M.	13	Single	Calabria	Calabria	Calabria
	Daughter	F.	11	Single	Calabria	Calabria	Calabria
	Daughter	F.	7	Single	United States	Calabria	Calabria
	Daughter	F.	5	Single	United States	Calabria	Calabria
	Son	M.	4	Single	United States	Calabria	Calabria
	Son	M.	2	Single	United States	Calabria	Calabria
69	Head	M.	52	Married	Calabria	Calabria	Calabria
	Wife	F.	45	Married	Calabria	Calabria	Calabria
	Son	M.	19	Single	Calabria	Calabria	Calabria
	Son	M.	16	Single	Calabria	Calabria	Calabria
	Son	M.	14	Single	Calabria	Calabria	Calabria
	Daughter	F.	12	Single	Calabria	Calabria	Calabria
	Daughter	F.	10	Single	Calabria	Calabria	Calabria
	Boarder	M.	26	Married	Calabria	Calabria	Calabria
	Boarder	M.	23	Single	Calabria	Calabria	Calabria
	Boarder	M.	46	Married	Calabria	Calabria	Calabria
	Boarder	M.	30	Married	Calabria	Calabria	Calabria
	Boarder	M.	31	Married	Calabria	Calabria	Calabria
	Boarder	M.	30	Married	Calabria	Calabria	Calabria
	Boarder	M.	28	Married	Calabria	Calabria	Calabria
	Boarder	M.	29	Single	Calabria	Calabria	Calabria
	Boarder	M.	34	Married	Calabria	Calabria	Calabria
	Boarder	M.	23	Single	Calabria	Calabria	Calabria
70	Head	M.	39	Married	Basilicata	Basilicata	Basilicata
	Wife	F.	37	Married	Basilicata	Basilicata	Basilicata
	Son	M.	12	Single	Basilicata	Basilicata	Basilicata
	Daughter	F.	6	Single	Canada	Basilicata	Basilicata
	Daughter	F.	2	Single	United States	Basilicata	Basilicata
	Daughter	F.	$\frac{2}{12}$	Single	United States	Basilicata	Basilicata
	Boarder	M.	27	Married	Basilicata	Basilicata	Basilicata
	Lodger	M.	44	Married	Calabria	Calabria	Calabria
	Lodger	M.	32	Single	Calabria	Calabria	Calabria

a Not reported.
b Sick, disease not specified.
c Also worked as laborer nine weeks, at $7.50 per week.

TABLE I.—GENERAL SOCIAL AND ECONOMIC CONDITION, BY FAMILIES AND INDIVIDUALS—Continued.

Years in U. S.	Naturalized.	Profession, trade, or occupation.	Hours of work per week.	Average weekly earnings.	Weeks employed.	Total yearly earnings.	Sick during year, defective, maimed, or deformed.
5	Yes..	Laborer	(a)	$3.75	18	$68	No.
5	....	Housewife and pants finisher.	30	.60	48	29	No.
....	No...	At home					No.
2	No...	Laborer	(a)	3.75	18	68	No.
8	Yes..	Laborer	(a)	3.75	18	68	No.
10	No...	Ragpicker	48	.90	52	47	No.
6	....	Ragpicker	48	.90	52	47	No.
4	No...	Laborer	(a)	6.00	17	102	No.
4	....	Housewife					(b)
4	....	Scholar					No.
4	....	At home					No.
....	....	At home					No.
....	....	At home					Fever, not specified.
3	No...	Laborer	48	7.50	9	68	No.
3	....	Housewife					No.
12	Yes..	Ragpicker	72	3.00	52	156	No.
9	....	Housewife					Childbirth; puerperal fever.
....	....	At home					No.
....	....	At home					(b)
....	....	At home					No.
10	Yes..	Ragpicker (c)	(a)	.50	c43	89	No.
5	....	Housewife					Childbirth.
(a)	....	Scholar					No.
(a)	....	Scholar					No.
....	....	At home					No.
....	....	At home					No.
5	....	Housewife					No.
3	No...	No occupation					Fingers, loss of three.
5	No...	No occupation					No.
5	....	Macaroni maker (d)	(a)	3.50	d13	61	No.
5	....	Scholar					No.
11	Yes..	Laborer	60	7.50	13	98	Kidneys, disease of.
8	....	Housewife					No.
8	....	Scholar					No.
8	....	Scholar					No.
....	....	At home					Idiot.
....	....	At home					No.
....	....	At home					No.
....	....	At home					No.
8	No...	No occupation					No.
1½	....	Housewife and boarding-house keeper. (e)	(a)	10.00	e17	(a)	No.
8	....	Salesman, groceries	72	7.50	39	293	No.
4½	....	No occupation					No.
1½	....	No occupation					No.
1½	....	Scholar					Eye, loss of one.
1½	....	Scholar					No.
8	No...	Laborer	60	7.50	9	68	No.
3	No...	Laborer	60	7.50	9	68	Injury by accident.
3	No...	Laborer	60	(a)	9	(a)	No.
6	No...	Laborer	60	5.00	9	45	Fever, not specified.
8	No...	Laborer	60	5.00	9	45	Injury by accident.
7	No...	Laborer	60	7.50	3	23	Eyes, weakness of.
7	No...	Laborer	(a)	(a)	(a)	(a)	No.
8	No...	Laborer	60	5.00	9	45	No.
8	No...	Laborer	60	5.00	9	45	No.
7	No...	Painter	60	7.00	52	364	No.
12	Yes..	Laborer	60	7.50	13	98	No.
7	....	Housewife					Childbirth.
7	....	Bootblack and newsboy..	(a)	.90	(a)	(a)	No.
6	....	Scholar					No.
....	....	At home					Rickets.
....	No...	At home					No.
4	No...	Laborer	60	6.60	15	99	No.
6	No...	Laborer	60	(a)	9	(a)	No.
8	No...	Laborer	60	(a)	9	(a)	No.

d Also worked as feather-duster factory employee six weeks, at $2.50 per week.
e Also worked at another occupation, details not reported.

TABLE **I.**—GENERAL SOCIAL AND ECONOMIC CONDITION, BY FAMILIES AND INDIVIDUALS—Continued.

Family number.	Relationship to head of family.	Sex.	Age.	Conjugal condition.	Birthplace.	Birthplace of— Father.	Birthplace of— Mother.
71	Head	M.	40	Married...	Basilicata	Basilicata	Basilicata
	Wife	F.	30	Married...	Basilicata	Basilicata	Basilicata
	Son	M.	18	Single	Basilicata	Basilicata	Basilicata
	Son	M.	11	Single	Basilicata	Basilicata.:...	Basilicata
	Son	M.	9	Single	Basilicata	Basilicata	Basilicata
	Daughter	F.	4	Single	United States	Basilicata	Basilicata
	Daughter	F.	2	Single	United States	Basilicata	Basilicata
72	Head	M.	23	Married...	Basilicata	Basilicata	Basilicata
	Wife	F.	37	Married...	Basilicata	Basilicata	Basilicata
73	Head	M.	42	Married...	Campania	Campania	Campania
	Wife	F.	40	Married...	Campania	Campania	Campania
	Daughter	F.	18	Single	Campania	Campania	Campania
	Daughter	F.	14	Single	Campania	Campania	Campania
	Son	M.	11	Single	Campania	Campania	Campania
	Daughter	F.	3	Single	United States	Campania	Campania
74	Head	M.	41	Married...	Campania	Campania	Campania
	Wife	F.	41	Married...	Campania	Campania	Campania
	Son	M.	20	Single	Campania	Campania	Campania
	Son	M.	17	Single	Campania	Campania	Campania
	Daughter	F.	15	Single	Campania	Campania	Campania
	Daughter	F.	13	Single	Campania	Campania	Campania
	Daughter	F.	10	Single	United States	Campania	Campania
	Daughter	F.	8	Single	United States	Campania	Campania
	Daughter	F.	4	Single	United States	Campania	Campania
	Son	M.	2	Single	United States	Campania	Campania
75	Head	M.	40	Married...	Calabria	Calabria	Calabria
	Wife	F.	21	Married...	Campania	Campania	Campania
76	Head	M.	28	Married...	Abruzzo	Abruzzo	Abruzzo
	Wife	F.	28	Married...	Abruzzo	Abruzzo	Abruzzo
	Son	M.	2	Single	United States	Abruzzo	Abruzzo
	Daughter	F.	$\frac{7}{12}$	Single	United States	Abruzzo	Abruzzo
	Father-in-law	M.	73	Widowed	Abruzzo	Abruzzo	Abruzzo
	Brother-in-law	M.	33	Widowed	Abruzzo	Abruzzo	Abruzzo
77	Head	M.	33	Married...	Campania	Campania	Campania
	Wife	F.	25	Married...	Campania	Campania	Campania
78	Head	M.	46	Married...	Abruzzo	Abruzzo	Abruzzo
	Wife	F.	50	Married...	Abruzzo	Abruzzo	Abruzzo
	Son	M.	21	Single	Abruzzo	Abruzzo	Abruzzo
	Son	M.	20	Single	Abruzzo	Abruzzo	Abruzzo
	Nephew	M.	20	Single	Abruzzo	Abruzzo	Abruzzo
79	Head	M.	40	Single	Campania	Campania	Campania
80	Head	M.	30	Married...	Calabria	Calabria	Calabria
	Wife	F.	30	Married...	Calabria	Calabria	Calabria
	Son	M.	3	Single	United States	Calabria	Calabria
	Son	M.	1	Single	United States	Calabria	Calabria
	Cousin	M.	16	Single	Calabria	Calabria	Calabria
	Cousin	M.	25	Single	Calabria	Calabria	Calabria
81	Head	M.	40	Married...	Campania	Campania	Campania
	Wife	F.	40	Married...	Campania	Campania	Campania
	Son	M.	17	Single	Campania	Campania	Campania
	Son	M.	15	Single	Campania	Campania	Campania
	Daughter	F.	2	Single	United States	Campania	Campania
	Daughter	F.	1	Single	United States	Campania	Campania
82	Head	M.	39	Married	Campania	Campania	Campania
	Wife	F.	36	Married...	Campania	Campania	Campania
	Daughter	F.	12	Single	Campania	Campania	Campania
	Daughter	F.	2	Single	United States	Campania	Campania

a Not reported.   b Also worked as sewer digger seven weeks, at $8.40 per week.

TABLE **I.**—GENERAL SOCIAL AND ECONOMIC CONDITION, BY FAMILIES AND INDIVIDUALS—Continued.

Years in U.S.	Natu- ral- ized.	Profession, trade, or occupation.	Hours of work per week.	Average weekly earn- ings.	Weeks em- ploy- ed.	Total yearly earn- ings.	Sick during year, defective, maimed, or deformed.
11	Yes..	Tinker	54	$1.50	49	$74	Pleurisy.
6	......	Housewife					Miscarriage.
6	......	Water carrier	60	3.00	7	21	No.
6	......	Scholar					No.
6	......	Scholar					No.
......	......	At home					No.
......	......	At home					No.
4	No...	Tinker	54	2.70	52	140	No.
7	......	Housewife					Female complaint.
10	Yes..	Laborer	48	5.60	18	101	No.
10	......	Housewife and paper sorter.	48	1.00	52	52	No.
10	......	Paper sorter	48	3.00	52	156	No.
10	......	No occupation					Hip-joint disease.
10	......	Scholar					No.
......	......	At home					No.
10	No...	Barber	81	(a)	52	(a)	No.
10	......	Housewife					No.
10	......	Barber	81	(a)	52	(a)	No.
10	......	Scholar					Erysipelas; loss of one leg.
10	......	Housework					No.
10	......	Housework					No.
......	......	Scholar					No.
......	......	Scholar					No.
......	......	At home					No.
......	......	At home					No.
12	Yes..	Organ grinder (b)	72	6.00	b 39	293	No.
16	......	Housework and dress- maker.	(a)	(a)	(a)	(a)	No.
13	Yes..	Laborer	54	7.50	52	390	No.
4	......	Housewife					Childbirth.
......	......	At home					No.
......	......	At home					No.
4	No...	No occupation					No.
13	Yes..	Barber	80	(a)	52	(a)	No.
11	Yes..	Shoemaker (c)	(a)	6.00	c 22	230	No.
4	......	Housewife					No.
6	No...	Laborer	48	3.75	22	83	Fever, typhoid.
6	......	Housewife					No.
6	Yes..	Laborer	48	3.75	22	83	No.
6	......	Laborer	48	3.75	22	83	No.
6	......	Laborer	48	3.75	22	83	No.
21	Yes..	Barber	(a)	5.00	52	260	No.
5	No...	Laborer	(a)	7.50	52	390	No.
5	......	Housewife					No.
......	......	At home					No.
......	......	At home					No.
......	......	No occupation					No.
$\frac{1}{5}$	No...	Bootblack	77	4.00	52	208	Leg, loss of one.
14	Yes..	Driver, brewery	(a)	9.00	52	468	No.
6	......	Housewife					No.
6	......	Scholar and picture-frame joiner.	60	4.00	26	104	No.
6	......	Scholar and picture-frame joiner.	60	3.50	22	77	Injury by accident.
......	......	At home					Bronchitis.
......	......	At home					No.
12	No...	Pants finisher	96	(a)	52	(a)	Leg, loss of one.
4	......	Housewife and pants fin- isher.	96	(a)	52	(a)	No.
4	......	Scholar					No.
......	......	At home					No.

c Also worked as laborer thirteen weeks, at $7.50 per week.

TABLE **I**—GENERAL SOCIAL AND ECONOMIC CONDITION, BY FAMILIES
AND INDIVIDUALS—Continued.

Family number.	Relationship to head of family.	Sex.	Age.	Conjugal condition.	Birthplace.	Birthplace of— Father.	Birthplace of— Mother.
83	Head	M.	53	Married...	Campania.......	Campania......	Campania......
	Wife	F.	45	Married...	Campania.......	Campania......	Campania......
	Son	M.	5	Single.....	United States...	Campania.......	Campania......
84	Head	M.	34	Married...	Campania.......	Campania......	Campania......
	Wife	F.	34	Married...	Campania.......	Campania......	Campania......
	Son	M.	11	Single.....	United States...	Campania......	Campania......
	Daughter	F.	9	Single.....	United States...	Campania......	Campania......
	Son	M.	8	Single.....	United States...	Campania......	Campania......
	Son	M.	6	Single.....	United States...	Campania......	Campania......
	Son	M.	4	Single.....	United States...	Campania......	Campania......
	Daughter	F.	1	Single.....	United States...	Campania......	Campania......
85	Head	M.	46	Married...	Sicily	Sicily	Sicily ....
	Wife	F.	36	Married...	Sicily	Sicily	Sicily ....
	Daughter	F.	16	Married...	Sicily	Sicily	Sicily ....
	Son	M.	7	Single.....	Sicily	Sicily	Sicily ....
	Daughter	F.	2	Single.....	United States...	Sicily	Sicily ....
86	Head	M.	35	Married...	Calabria	Calabria	Calabria ....
	Wife	F.	34	Married...	Calabria	Calabria	Calabria ....
	Son	M.	18	Single.....	Calabria	Calabria	Calabria ....
	Son	M.	13	Single.....	Calabria	Calabria	Calabria ....
	Brother	M.	24	Single.....	Calabria	Calabria	Calabria ....
87	Head	M.	30	Married...	Campania.......	Campania.:.....	Campania......
	Wife	F.	29	Married...	Abruzzo	Abruzzo	Abruzzo.......
	Daughter	F.	3	Single.....	United States...	Campania......	Abruzzo.......
	Daughter	F.	1	Single.....	United States...	Campania......	Abruzzo.......
88	Head	M.	32	Married...	Campania.......	Campania......	Campania......
	Wife	F.	32	Married...	Campania.......	Campania......	Campania......
	Son	M.	7	Single.....	Campania.......	Campania......	Campania......
	Daughter	F.	3	Single.....	United States...	Campania......	Campania......
	Son	M.	1	Single.....	United States...	Campania......	Campania......
	Boarder	M.	40	Married...	Campania.......	Campania......	Campania......
	Boarder	M.	26	Single.....	Campania.......	Campania......	Campania......
	Lodger	M.	42	Single.....	Campania.......	Campania......	Campania......
	Lodger	M.	40	Married...	Campania.......	Campania......	Campania......
89	Head	M.	40	Married...	Campania.......	Campania......	Campania......
	Wife	F.	28	Married...	Campania.......	Campania......	Campania......
	Daughter	F.	15	Single.....	Campania.......	Campania......	Campania......
	Son	M.	12	Single.....	Campania.......	Campania......	Campania......
	Daughter	F.	2	Single.....	United States...	Campania......	Campania......
	Brother	M.	35	Married...	Campania.......	Campania......	Campania......
	Lodger	M.	42	Married...	Campania.......	Campania......	Campania......
	Lodger	M.	28	Married...	Campania.......	Campania......	Campania......
	Lodger	M.	27	Single.....	Campania.......	Campania......	Campania......
	Lodger	M.	51	Single.....	Campania.......	Campania......	Campania......
90	Head	M.	34	Married...	Abruzzo........	Abruzzo.......	Abruzzo.......
	Wife	F.	34	Married...	Abruzzo..........	Abruzzo.......	Abruzzo.......
	Daughter	F.	7	Single.....	Abruzzo........	Abruzzo.......	Abruzzo.......
	Daughter	F.	3	Single.....	United States...	Abruzzo.......	Abruzzo.......
	Daughter	F.	1	Single.....	United States...	Abruzzo.......	Abruzzo.......
	Father	M.	60	Married...	Abruzzo........	Abruzzo.......	Abruzzo.......
	Mother	F.	60	Married...	Abruzzo........	Abruzzo.......	Abruzzo.......
91	Head	M.	48	Married...	Campania.......	Campania......	Campania......
	Wife	F.	37	Married...	Campania.......	Campania......	Campania......
	Cousin	M.	29	Single.....	Campania.......	Campania......	Campania......
92	Head	M.	35	Married...	Campania.......	Campania......	Campania......
	Wife	F.	35	Married...	Campania.......	Campania......	Campania......
	Daughter	F.	12	Single.....	Campania.......	Campania......	Campania......
	Mother	F.	82	Widowed .	Campania.......	Campania......	Campania......

a Not reported.
b Also worked as ragpicker twenty weeks, at $1.50 per week.
c Also worked as laborer nine weeks, at $9 per week.

TABLE **I.**—GENERAL SOCIAL AND ECONOMIC CONDITION, BY FAMILIES AND INDIVIDUALS—Continued.

Years in U. S.	Naturalized.	Profession, trade, or occupation.	Hours of work per week.	Average weekly earnings.	Weeks employed.	Total yearly earnings.	Sick during year, defective, maimed, or deformed.
13	Yes..	Street sweeper	48	$7.25	18	$131	No.
12	....	Housewife					Heart, disease of.
......	....	At home					No.
24	Yes..	Musician	56	14.00	52	728	No.
12	....	Housewife					No.
......	....	Scholar					Fever, typhoid.
......	....	Scholar					Fever, typhoid.
......	....	Scholar					Fever, typhoid.
......	....	At home					Fever, typhoid.
......	....	At home					Fever, typhoid.
......	....	At home					No.
7	Yes..	Mason, stone	48	22.50	22	495	No.
4	....	Housewife and dressmaker.	(a)	.80	30	24	No.
4	....	No occupation					No.
7	....	Scholar					No.
......	....	At home					No.
11	Yes..	Saloon keeper	(a)	(a)	26	(a)	No.
8	....	Housewife					No.
8	....	Candy maker	60	6.00	46	276	No.
8	....	Scholar and bootblack	24	2.40	52	125	No.
3	No...	Scholar and laborer	60	7.50	19	143	No.
12	Yes..	Laborer	(a)	8.10	26	211	No.
5	....	Housewife					No.
......	....	At home					No.
......	....	At home					No.
12	Yes..	Street sweeper (b)	78	9.00	b 26	264	No.
4	....	Housewife					No.
4	....	Scholar					No.
......	....	At home					Erysipelas.
......	....	At home					No.
20	Yes..	Ragpicker	60	1.50	52	78	No.
18	Yes..	Ragpicker (c)	(a)	1.50	c 43	146	No.
18	Yes..	Ragpicker (d)	(a)	1.50	d 43	132	No.
6	No...	Laborer	77	8.75	52	455	No.
13	Yes..	Ragpicker	(a)	2.00	43	86	No.
3	....	Housewife					No.
3	....	Scholar and pants finisher.	36	1.50	(a)	(a)	No.
3	....	Bootblack	54	1.50	(a)	(a)	No.
......	....	At home					No.
5	No...	Ragpicker	(a)	2.00	52	104	No.
5	No...	Ragpicker	(a)	2 00	52	104	No.
7	Yes..	No occupation					Leg, loss of one.
7	No...	Laborer	(a)	7.50	9	68	No.
6	No...	Ragpicker	(a)	2.00	52	104	Fever, typhoid.
8	Yes..	Laborer	48	7.50	4	30	No.
4	....	Housewife and pants finisher.	(a)	(a)	(a)	(a)	Female complaint.
4	....	Scholar					No.
......	....	At home					Rickets.
......	....	At home					No.
5	No...	No occupation					Bronchitis.
5	....	No occupation					No.
13	No...	Laborer	60	6.00	13	78	Rheumatism.
13	....	Housewife					Lame.
9	No...	Laborer	60	6.00	13	78	No.
16	Yes..	Cigar maker (e)	36	6.00	e 43	(a)	No.
12	....	Housewife and cigar maker.	(a)	(a)	(a)	(a)	No.
12	....	No occupation					Epilepsy.
16	....	No occupation					No.

d Also worked as laborer nine weeks, at $7.50 per week.
e Also worked as notary public, time and wages not reported.

TABLE **I.**—GENERAL SOCIAL AND ECONOMIC CONDITION, BY FAMILIES AND INDIVIDUALS—Continued.

Family number.	Relationship to head of family.	Sex.	Age.	Conjugal condition.	Birthplace.	Birthplace of—	
						Father.	Mother.
93	Head	M.	30	Married	Basilicata	Basilicata	Basilicata
	Wife	F.	25	Married	Basilicata	Basilicata	Basilicata
	Lodger	M.	35	Married	Basilicata	Basilicata	Basilicata
	Lodger	M.	35	Married	Basilicata	Basilicata	Basilicata
	Lodger	M.	35	Married	Basilicata	Basilicata	Basilicata
94	Head	M.	44	Married	Basilicata	Basilicata	Basilicata
	Wife	F.	40	Married	Basilicata	Basilicata	Basilicata
	Daughter	F.	17	Married	Basilicata	Basilicata	Basilicata
	Daughter	F.	4	Single	United States	Basilicata	Basilicata
	Son-in-law	M.	22	Married	Campania	Campania	Campania
	Granddaughter	F.	$\frac{4}{12}$	Single	United States	Campania	Basilicata
95	Head	M.	37	Married	Basilicata	Basilicata	Basilicata
	Wife	F.	30	Married	Basilicata	Basilicata	Basilicata
	Son	M.	14	Single	United States	Basilicata	Basilicata
	Son	M.	7	Single	United States	Basilicata	Basilicata
	Daughter	F.	3	Single	United States	Basilicata	Basilicata
	Son	M.	1	Single	United States	Basilicata	Basilicata
	Mother	F.	62	Widowed	Basilicata	Basilicata	Basilicata
	Brother	M.	50	Married	Basilicata	Basilicata	Basilicata
96	Head	M.	36	Married	Calabria	Calabria	Calabria
	Wife	F.	36	Married	Calabria	Calabria	Calabria
	Son	M.	10	Single	Calabria	Calabria	Calabria
	Son	M.	7	Single	Calabria	Calabria	Calabria
97	Head	M.	46	Married	Campania	Campania	Campania
	Wife	F.	49	Married	Campania	Campania	Campania
98	Head	M.	47	Married	Campania	Campania	Campania
	Wife	F.	40	Married	Campania	Campania	Campania
	Son	M.	18	Single	Campania	Campania	Campania
	Son	M.	16	Single	Campania	Campania	Campania
	Daughter	F.	14	Single	Campania	Campania	Campania
	Boarder	M.	30	Single	Calabria	Calabria	Calabria
99	Head	M.	34	Married	Basilicata	Basilicata	Basilicata
	Wife	F.	30	Married	Basilicata	Basilicata	Basilicata
	Daughter	F.	13	Single	Basilicata	Basilicata	Basilicata
	Brother	M.	33	Married	Basilicata	Basilicata	Basilicata
	Boarder	M.	23	Single	Basilicata	Basilicata	Basilicata
	Boarder	M.	25	Single	Basilicata	Basilicata	Basilicata
100	Head	M.	37	Married	Campania	Campania	Campania
	Wife	F.	38	Married	Campania	Campania	Campania
	Daughter	F.	7	Single	United States	Campania	Campania
	Son	M.	1	Single	United States	Campania	Campania
101	Head	M.	43	Widowed	Basilicata	Basilicata	Basilicata
102	Head	M.	34	Married	Campania	Campania	Campania
	Wife	F.	37	Married	Calabria	Calabria	Calabria
	Stepson	M.	18	Single	Calabria	Calabria	Calabria
	Stepdaughter	F.	16	Married	Calabria	Calabria	Calabria
	Son-in-law	M.	23	Married	Campania	Campania	Campania
103	Head	M.	44	Married	Campania	Campania	Campania
	Wife	F.	33	Married	Calabria	Calabria	Calabria
	Son	M.	18	Single	Campania	Campania	Calabria
	Daughter	F.	9	Single	United States	Campania	Calabria
	Daughter	F.	4	Single	United States	Campania	Calabria
	Daughter	F.	$\frac{6}{12}$	Single	United States	Campania	Calabria
104	Head	M.	60	Married	Calabria	Calabria	Calabria
	Wife	F.	60	Married	Calabria	Calabria	Calabria
	Son	M.	29	Single	Calabria	Calabria	Calabria
	Son	M.	19	Single	Calabria	Calabria	Calabria
	Nephew	M.	22	Single	Calabria	Calabria	Calabria
	Lodger	M.	41	Married	Calabria	Calabria	Calabria

a Not reported
b Also worked as street sweeper four weeks, at $7.50 per week.
c Also worked as laborer nine weeks, at $7.50 per week.
d Also worked as street sweeper eighteen weeks, at $7.50 per week.

TABLE **I.**—GENERAL SOCIAL AND ECONOMIC CONDITION, BY FAMILIES AND INDIVIDUALS—Continued.

Years in U.S.	Naturalized.	Profession, trade, or occupation.	Hours of work per week.	Average weekly earnings.	Weeks employed.	Total yearly earnings.	Sick during year, defective, maimed, or deformed.
8	Yes..	Laborer	60	$9.00	19	$171	No.
2		Housewife					No.
3	No...	Laborer	60	7.50	18	135	No.
8	Yes..	Laborer	60	7.50	26	195	No.
3	No...	Laborer	60	7.50	18	135	No.
10	Yes..	Laborer	53	13.50	13	176	No.
5		Housewife and cloak finisher.	(a)	.75	30	23	No.
5		Housework					Childbirth.
....		At home					No.
7	Yes..	Laborer	60	7.20	52	374	No.
....		At home					No.
17	Yes..	Merchant, rags	72	(a)	22	(a)	Bronchitis.
18		Housewife					No.
....		Scholar					No.
....		Scholar					No.
....		At home					No.
....		At home					No.
18		No occupation					Heart, disease of.
22	Yes..	Packer, rags	72	(a)	52	(a)	No.
6	No...	Laborer	60	7.50	22	165	No.
1/12		Housewife					No.
1/12		No occupation					No.
1/12		At home					No.
8	Yes..	Laborer (b)	60	3.75	b 4	45	No.
14		Housewife					Insane.
13	Yes..	Porter	60	9.00	52	468	No.
4		Housewife and pants finisher.	72	.90	18	16	Injury by accident.
4		Compositor	72	4.75	52	247	No.
4		Scholar and compositor	72	2.75	30	83	No.
4		Scholar					Diphtheria.
6	No...	Janitor	65	10.00	43	430	Kidneys, disease of.
4	No...	Tinker	(a)	2.40	13	31	Rheumatism.
3		Housewife and pants finisher.	72	1.20	52	62	No.
3		Scholar					No.
3	No...	Laborer	60	8.20	4	33	No.
3	No...	Tinker (c)	42	2.40	c 26	130	Diphtheria.
2	No...	Ragpicker	42	1.20	52	62	No.
15	Yes..	Laborer	(a)	6.00	13	78	Diphtheria.
15		Housewife					No.
....		Scholar					No.
....		At home					No.
14	Yes..	Ragpicker (d)	(a)	1.20	d 34	176	No.
14	Yes..	Janitor	36	4.25	52	221	No.
12		Housewife					No.
6		Baker's helper	60	5.00	52	260	No.
12		Housework					No.
3	No...	Laborer (e)	(a)	6.72	e 13	132	No.
14	Yes..	Peddler, cottage cheese (f)	(a)	5.25	f 48	276	No.
16		Housewife					Childbirth.
3		Newsboy (g)	(a)	2.80	g 26	(a)	No.
....		Scholar					No.
....		At home					No.
....		At home					Fever, not specified.
15	Yes..	No occupation					Eyes, weakness of.
5		Housewife					Rheumatism.
5	Yes..	No occupation					Epilepsy.
5		Tailor	60	9.00	43	387	No.
7/12	No...	Tailor (h)	60	3.00	h 13	(a)	No.
8/12	No...	Laborer (h)	60	7.50	h 9	(a)	Boils.

e Also worked as shoemaker nine weeks, at $5 per week.
f Also worked as laborer four weeks, at $6 per week.
g Also worked as painter's apprentice twenty-six weeks, wages not reported.
h Also worked at another occupation, details not reported.

TABLE I.—GENERAL SOCIAL AND ECONOMIC CONDITION, BY FAMILIES AND INDIVIDUALS—Continued.

Family number.	Relationship to head of family.	Sex.	Age.	Conjugal condition.	Birthplace.	Birthplace of—	
						Father.	Mother.
105	Head	M.	30	Married...	Basilicata.......	Basilicata......	Basilicata.....
	Wife..............	F.	26	Married...	Basilicata.......	Basilicata.......	Basilicata.....
	Son	M.	7	Single.....	Basilicata.......	Basilicata......	Basilicata......
	Daughter	F.	2	Single.....	United States...	Basilicata......	Basilicata......
	Daughter	F.	7/12	Single.....	United States...	Basilicata......	Basilicata......
	Father-in-law.....	M.	65	Married...	Basilicata.......	Basilicata......	Basilicata......
106	Head	M.	60	Widowed .	Campania........	Campania......	Campania.....
	Son	M.	18	Single.....	Campania........	Campania......	Campania.....
	Daughter	F.	16	Single.....	Campania........	Campania......	Campania.....
	Daughter	F.	14	Single.....	Campania........	Campania......	Campania.....
	Daughter	F.	12	Single.....	Campania........	Campania......	Campania.....
	Lodger.............	M.	57	Married...	Campania........	Campania......	Campania.....
107	Head	M.	40	Married...	Calabria	Calabria	Calabria ......
	Wife..............	F.	28	Married...	Calabria	Calabria	Calabria ......
	Son	M.	17	Single.....	Calabria	Calabria	Calabria ......
	Daughter	F.	1	Single.....	United States...	Calabria	Calabria ......
	Brother...........	M.	38	Married...	Calabria	Calabria	Calabria ......
	Brother...........	M.	30	Married...	Calabria	Calabria	Calabria ......
108	Head	M.	38	Married...	Campania.......	Campania......	Campania.....
	Wife..............	F.	32	Married...	Campania.......	Campania......	Campania.....
	Daughter	F.	14	Single.....	Campania.......	Campania......	Campania.....
	Daughter	F.	8	Single.....	United States...	Campania......	Campania.....
	Daughter	F.	7	Single.....	United States...	Campania......	Campania.....
	Daughter	F.	5	Single.....	United States...	Campania......	Campania.....
	Son	M.	4	Single.....	United States...	Campania......	Campania.....
	Son	M.	1	Single.....	United States...	Campania......	Campania.....
109	Head	M.	20	Married...	Campania........	Campania......	Campania.....
	Wife..............	F.	18	Married...	Calabria	Calabria	Calabria ......
110	Head	M.	22	Married...	Campania........	Campania......	Campania.....
	Wife..............	F.	18	Married...	Campania........	Campania......	Campania.....
	Son	M.	3/12	Single.....	United States...	Campania......	Campania.....
	Mother	F.	64	Widowed .	Campania........	Campania......	Campania.....
111	Head	M.	55	Married...	Calabria	Calabria	Calabria ......
	Wife..............	F.	42	Married...	Calabria	Calabria	Calabria ......
	Son	M.	12	Single.....	United States...	Calabria	Calabria ......
	Daughter	F.	9	Single.....	Calabria	Calabria	Calabria ......
	Daughter	F.	7	Single.....	United States...	Calabria	Calabria ......
	Son	M.	3	Single.....	United States...	Calabria	Calabria ......
	Son	M.	1	Single.....	United States...	Calabria	Calabria ......
112	Head	M.	53	Married...	Campania........	Campania......	Campania.....
	Wife..............	F.	43	Married...	Campania........	Campania......	Campania.....
	Son	M.	22	Single.....	Campania........	Campania......	Campania.....
	Daughter	F.	18	Single.....	Campania........	Campania......	Campania.....
	Son	M.	16	Single.....	Campania........	Campania......	Campania.....
	Son	M.	12	Single.....	Campania........	Campania......	Campania.....
	Daughter	F.	9	Single.....	Campania........	Campania......	Campania.....
	Son	M.	6	Single.....	United States...	Campania......	Campania.....
	Son	M.	3	Single.....	United States...	Campania......	Campania.....
	Daughter	F.	1/12	Single.....	United States...	Campania......	Campania.....
113	Head	M.	30	Married...	Sicily	Sicily	Sicily ....
	Wife..............	F.	25	Married...	Sicily	Sicily	Sicily ....
	Daughter	F.	4	Single.....	Sicily	Sicily	Sicily ....
	Daughter	F.	2	Single.....	Sicily	Sicily	Sicily ....
114	Cooperative........	M.	47	Married...	Campania........	Campania........	Campania......
	Cooperative........	M.	32	Married...	Campania........	Campania......	Campania......
	Cooperative........	M.	31	Married...	Campania........	Campania......	Campania......
	Cooperative........	M.	29	Single.....	Campania........	Campania......	Campania......
115	Cooperative........	M.	25	Single.....	Sicily	Sicily	Sicily ....
	Cooperative........	M.	40	Single.....	Sicily	Sicily	Sicily ....
	Cooperative........	M.	46	Married...	Sicily	Sicily	Sicily ....
	Cooperative........	M.	54	Married...	Sicily	Sicily	Sicily ....
	Cooperative........	M.	16	Single.....	Sicily	Sicily	Sicily ....
	Cooperative........	M.	45	Married...	Sicily	Sicily	Sicily ....
	Cooperative........	M.	40	Married...	Sicily	Sicily	Sicily ....
	Cooperative........	M.	35	Married...	Campania........	Campania......	Campania......

a Also worked as laborer thirteen weeks, at $7.50 per week.   b Not reported.

TABLE I.—GENERAL SOCIAL AND ECONOMIC CONDITION, BY FAMILIES AND INDIVIDUALS—Continued.

Years in U.S.	Natu- ral- ized.	Profession, trade, or occupation.	Hours of work per week.	Average weekly earn- ings.	Weeks em- ploy- ed.	Total yearly earn- ings.	Sick during year, defective, maimed, or deformed.
5	Yes..	Pants finisher (a).........	(b)	$1.80	a 39	$168	No.
4	......	Housewife and pants fin- isher.	48	1.80	52	94	Childbirth.
4	......	Scholar..................					No.
......	......	At home.................					No.
......	......	At home.................					No.
3	No...	Ragpicker	30	1.50	52	78	Lame.
6	No...	Merchant, groceries......	(b)	(b)	52	(b)	No.
6	......	Barber's apprentice......	81	2.00	39	78	No.
6	......	Ragsorter...............	60	3.00	52	156	No.
6	......	Scholar.................					No.
6	......	Scholar.................					No.
17	No...	Laborer.................	60	7.20	9	65	No.
15	No...	Laborer.................	60	8.40	13	109	Fever, not specified.
6	......	Housewife..............					No.
10	......	Baker's helper..........	60	4.00	52	208	No.
......	......	At home................					No.
17	Yes..	Laborer.................	60	8.40	26	218	No.
10	Yes..	Laborer.................	60	8.40	22	185	No.
14	Yes..	No occupation..........					Asthma.
14	......	Housewife..............					No.
14	......	Scholar and packer, knife factory.	60	2.50	52	130	No.
......	......	Scholar.................					No.
......	......	Scholar.................					No.
......	......	At home................					No.
......	......	At home................					No.
......	......	At home................					No.
14	......	Newsboy...............	48	5.50	52	286	No.
13	......	Housewife..............					No.
12	No...	Newsboy...............	48	7.50	52	390	No.
10	......	Housewife..............					Childbirth.
......	......	At home................					No.
10	......	Housework					No.
20	Yes..	Laborer.................	60	7.50	9	68	Injury by accident.
28	......	Housewife..............					No.
......	......	No occupation..........					No.
8	......	At home................					No.
......	......	At home................					Lame.
......	......	At home................					No.
......	......	At home................					No.
9	Yes..	No occupation..........					No.
9	......	Housewife..............					Childbirth.
9	Yes..	Janitor	63	10.00	52	520	No.
9	......	Housework					No.
9	......	Furniture polisher (c).....	60	4.00	c 13	68	No.
9	......	Scholar					No.
9	......	Scholar					No.
9	......	Scholar					No.
......	......	At home................					No.
......	......	At home................					No.
8	Yes..	Laborer.................	(b)	3.60	26	94	Pneumonia.
2	......	Housewife..............					No.
2	......	At home................					No.
2	......	At home................					Skin, disease of.
6	Yes..	Stonecutter.............	54	19.50	9	176	Fever, not specified.
4	No...	No occupation..........					Consumption.
5	Yes..	Laborer.................	60	7.05	18	127	No.
7	Yes..	Laborer.................	60	6.80	13	88	No.
4	No...	Laborer.................	72	2.00	52	104	No.
5	No...	Laborer.................	68	3.90	35	137	No.
7	No...	Laborer.................	68	3.90	35	137	No.
5	No...	Laborer.................	68	6.30	19	120	No.
6	......	Laborer.................	72	3.60	9	32	Fever, malarial.
8	Yes..	Laborer.................	68	6.75	18	122	No.
4	No...	Laborer.................	72	3.00	26	78	No.
6	Yes..	Laborer.................	60	6.60	9	59	No.

c Also worked as candy factory employee four weeks, at $4 per week.

TABLE I.—GENERAL SOCIAL AND ECONOMIC CONDITION, BY FAMILIES AND INDIVIDUALS—Continued.

Family number.	Relationship to head of family.	Sex.	Age.	Conjugal condition.	Birthplace.	Birthplace of— Father.	Birthplace of— Mother.
116	Head	M.	50	Married	Basilicata	Basilicata	Basilicata
	Wife	F.	32	Married	Basilicata	Basilicata	Basilicata
	Son	M.	8	Single	United States	Basilicata	Basilicata
	Son	M.	6	Single	United States	Basilicata	Basilicata
	Son	M.	4	Single	United States	Basilicata	Basilicata
	Daughter	F.	3	Single	United States	Basilicata	Basilicata
117	Head	M.	30	Married	Campania	Campania	Campania
	Wife	F.	27	Married	Campania	Campania	Campania
	Daughter	F.	5	Single	Campania	Campania	Campania
	Daughter	F.	3	Single	United States	Campania	Campania
	Daughter	F.	1	Single	United States	Campania	Campania
	Brother	M.	16	Single	Campania	Campania	Campania
	Brother	M.	36	Married	Campania	Campania	Campania
	Brother	M.	46	Married	Campania	Campania	Campania
118	Head	M.	48	Married	Basilicata	Basilicata	Basilicata
	Wife	F.	47	Married	Basilicata	Basilicata	Basilicata
	Son	M.	23	Single	Basilicata	Basilicata	Basilicata
	Son	M.	12	Single	Basilicata	Basilicata	Basilicata
	Daughter	F.	8	Single	United States	Basilicata	Basilicata
	Daughter	F.	6	Single	United States	Basilicata	Basilicata
	Son	M.	4	Single	United States	Basilicata	Basilicata
119	Head	M.	40	Married	Campania	Campania	Campania
	Wife	F.	36	Married	Campania	Campania	Campania
	Son	M.	7	Single	England	Campania	Campania
	Son	M.	4	Single	United States	Campania	Campania
	Daughter	F.	2	Single	United States	Campania	Campania
	Daughter	F.	$\frac{6}{12}$	Single	United States	Campania	Campania
120	Head	M.	46	Married	Campania	Campania	Campania
	Wife	F.	36	Married	Basilicata	Campania	Basilicata
	Daughter	F.	18	Married	United States	Campania	Basilicata
	Son	M.	10	Single	United States	Campania	Basilicata
	Daughter	F.	10	Single	United States	Campania	Basilicata
	Son	M.	5	Single	United States	Campania	Basilicata
	Son	M.	2	Single	United States	Campania	Basilicata
	Son-in-law	M.	28	Married	Basilicata	Basilicata	Basilicata
121	Head	M.	45	Married	Sicily	Sicily	Sicily
	Wife	F.	45	Married	Sicily	Sicily	Sicily
	Daughter	F.	13	Single	United States	Sicily	Sicily
	Daughter	F.	9	Single	United States	Sicily	Sicily
122	Head	M.	53	Married	Basilicata	Basilicata	Basilicata
	Wife	F.	51	Married	Basilicata	Basilicata	Basilicata
	Son	M.	22	Single	Basilicata	Basilicata	Basilicata
	Daughter	F.	13	Single	United States	Basilicata	Basilicata
	Son	M.	12	Single	United States	Basilicata	Basilicata
	Daughter	F.	8	Single	United States	Basilicata	Basilicata
123	Head	M.	32	Married	Calabria	Calabria	Calabria
	Wife	F.	32	Married	Basilicata	Basilicata	Basilicata
	Daughter	F.	3	Single	United States	Calabria	Basilicata
	Son	M.	1	Single	United States	Calabria	Basilicata
124	Head	M.	50	Married	Basilicata	Basilicata	Basilicata
	Wife	F.	42	Married	Basilicata	Basilicata	Basilicata
	Son	M.	22	Single	Basilicata	Basilicata	Basilicata
	Son	M.	18	Single	Basilicata	Basilicata	Basilicata
	Son	M.	9	Single	United States	Basilicata	Basilicata
	Son	M.	4	Single	United States	Basilicata	Basilicata
	Daughter	F.	2	Single	United States	Basilicata	Basilicata
125	Head	M.	30	Married	Basilicata	Basilicata	Basilicata
	Wife	F.	21	Married	Basilicata	Basilicata	Basilicata
	Daughter	F.	1	Single	United States	Basilicata	Basilicata
	Boarder	M.	30	Single	Basilicata	Basilicata	Basilicata
126	Head	M.	30	Married	Basilicata	Basilicata	Basilicata
	Wife	F.	32	Married	Basilicata	Basilicata	Basilicata
	Boarder	M.	39	Married	Basilicata	Basilicata	Basilicata

a Also worked as merchant, rags, thirteen weeks, wages not reported.
b Not reported.
c Also worked as laborer two weeks, at $7.50 per week.

TABLE I.—GENERAL SOCIAL AND ECONOMIC CONDITION, BY FAMILIES AND INDIVIDUALS—Continued.

Years in U. S.	Natu-ral-ized.	Profession, trade, or occupation.	Hours of work per week.	Average weekly earn-ings.	Weeks em-ploy-ed.	Total yearly earn-ings.	Sick during year, defective, maimed, or deformed.
8	Yes..	Ragpicker (a).............	(b)	$7.00	a 39	(b)	No.
6 12		Housewife............					No.
		Scholar					No.
		At home............					No.
		At home............					Rickets.
		At home............					No.
3	No...	Organ grinder	90	4.50	52	$234	No.
3		Housewife............					No.
3		At home............					No.
		At home............					No.
		At home............					No.
2		Organ grinder	90	4.50	22	99	No.
4	No...	Organ grinder (c)	90	4.50	c 22	114	No.
5	No..	Organ grinder	90	4.50	22	99	No.
13	Yes..	Laborer..............	60	3.75	26	98	Injury by accident.
9		Housewife............					No.
9	No...	Driver milk wagon (d)	52	3.00	d 13	69	Injury by accident.
9		Scholar					No.
		Scholar					No.
		Scholar					Rickets.
		Scholar					No.
6	Yes..	Organ grinder.............	60	(b)	22	(b)	No.
6		Housewife and organ grinder.	60	(b)	22	(b)	Childbirth.
6		At home............					No.
		At home............					Rickets.
		At home............					Dyspepsia.
		At home............					No.
18	Yes..	Street sweeper.............	64	8.40	44	370	Rheumatism.
18		Housewife............					No.
		Housework............					No.
		Scholar					No.
		Scholar					No.
		Scholar					No.
		At home............					No.
10	Yes..	Laborer..............	60	7.50	46	345	No.
15	No...	Furniture polisher........	48	6.00	43	258	La grippe.
21		Housewife and dressmaker	(b)	(b)	(b)	(b)	No.
		Scholar					Idiot; malarial fever.
		At home............					No.
16	Yes..	Laborer..............	60	7.50	5	38	No.
15		Housewife............					No.
15	Yes..	Musician	(b)	(b)	52	(b)	No.
		Candy factory employee...	60	2.00	52	104	No.
		Scholar					No.
		Scholar					No.
16	Yes..	Laborer..............	60	9.00	26	234	No.
9		Housewife............					No.
		At home............					No.
		At home............					No.
14	Yes..	Laborer.............	(b)	7.50	4	30	Harelip.
11		Housewife............					No.
11	Yes..	Stonecutter.............	44	6.00	43	258	No.
11		Press feeder	59	6.25	47	294	No.
		Scholar					No.
		At home............					Skin, disease of.
		At home............					
9	Yes..	Tinker (e)..............	(b)	2.50	e 39	176	No.
5		Housewife............					Fever, not specified.
		At home............					Rupture.
4	No...	Tinker (f).............	(b)	2.50	f 22	78	Debility, general.
9	Yes..	Laborer..............	60	7.50	26	195	No.
9		Housewife and tailoress....	(b)	1.75	4	7	No.
7	Yes..	Laborer..............	60	7.50	18	135	No.

d Also worked as laborer four weeks, at $7.50 per week.
e Also worked as laborer thirteen weeks, at $6 per week.
f Also worked as laborer three weeks, at $7.50 per week.

TABLE **I.**—GENERAL SOCIAL AND ECONOMIC CONDITION, BY FAMILIES AND INDIVIDUALS—Continued.

Family number.	Relationship to head of family.	Sex.	Age.	Conjugal condition.	Birthplace.	Birthplace of—	
						Father.	Mother.
127	Head	M.	33	Married	Sicily	Sicily	Sicily
	Wife	F.	27	Married	Sicily	Sicily	Sicily
	Son	M.	10	Single	Sicily	Sicily	Sicily
	Daughter	F.	8	Single	Sicily	Sicily	Sicily
	Son	M.	4	Single	Sicily	Sicily	Sicily
	Son	M.	3	Single	United States	Sicily	Sicily
	Lodger	M.	33	Married	Campania	Campania	Campania
	Lodger	F.	28	Married	Sicily	Sicily	Sicily
	Lodger	F.	4	Single	United States	Campania	Sicily
	Lodger	F.	3	Single	United States	Campania	Sicily
	Lodger	F.	2	Single	United States	Campania	Sicily
	Lodger	M.	3/12	Single	United States	Campania	Sicily
128	Head	M.	40	Married	Abruzzo	Abruzzo	Abruzzo
	Wife	F.	28	Married	Abruzzo	Abruzzo	Abruzzo
	Son	M.	7	Single	Abruzzo	Abruzzo	Abruzzo
	Son	M.	6	Single	Abruzzo	Abruzzo	Abruzzo
	Son	M.	5	Single	Abruzzo	Abruzzo	Abruzzo
	Son	M.	2	Single	United States	Abruzzo	Abruzzo
	Son	M.	3/12	Single	United States	Abruzzo	Abruzzo
	Brother	M.	23	Single	Abruzzo	Abruzzo	Abruzzo
	Uncle	M.	45	Married	Abruzzo	Abruzzo	Abruzzo
	Cousin	M.	22	Single	Abruzzo	Abruzzo	Abruzzo
	Cousin	M.	17	Single	Abruzzo	Abruzzo	Abruzzo
129	Head	M.	42	Married	Sicily	Sicily	Sicily
	Wife	F.	46	Married	Sicily	Sicily	Sicily
	Stepson	M.	11	Single	United States	Sicily	Sicily
	Lodger	M.	30	Single	Sicily	Sicily	Sicily
130	Head	M.	28	Married	Campania	Campania	Campania
	Wife	F.	28	Married	Campania	Campania	Campania
	Son	M.	1	Single	United States	Campania	Campania
131	Head	M.	31	Married	Basilicata	Basilicata	Basilicata
	Wife	F.	26	Married	Basilicata	Basilicata	Basilicata
	Son	M.	2	Single	United States	Basilicata	Basilicata
	Son	M.	1	Single	United States	Basilicata	Basilicata
	Lodger	M.	60	Married	Basilicata	Basilicata	Basilicata
	Lodger	M.	26	Single	Basilicata	Basilicata	Basilicata
132	Cooperative	M.	34	Married	Calabria	Calabria	Calabria
	Cooperative	M.	34	Married	Calabria	Calabria	Calabria
	Cooperative	M.	23	Single	Calabria	Calabria	Calabria
	Cooperative	M.	34	Married	Calabria	Calabria	Calabria
	Cooperative	M.	30	Single	Calabria	Calabria	Calabria
	Cooperative	M.	40	Married	Calabria	Calabria	Calabria
	Cooperative	M.	35	Married	Calabria	Calabria	Calabria
133	Head	M.	41	Married	Sicily	Sicily	Sicily
	Wife	F.	40	Married	Sicily	Sicily	Sicily
	Son	M.	17	Single	Sicily	Sicily	Sicily
	Son	M.	15	Single	Sicily	Sicily	Sicily
	Daughter	F.	12	Single	Sicily	Sicily	Sicily
	Son	M.	5	Single	United States	Sicily	Sicily
	Son	M.	3	Single	United States	Sicily	Sicily
	Son	M.	1	Single	United States	Sicily	Sicily
	Brother	M.	32	Married	Sicily	Sicily	Sicily
	Cousin	M.	44	Married	Sicily	Sicily	Sicily
134	Head	M.	30	Married	Calabria	Calabria	Calabria
	Wife	F.	16	Married	Calabria	Calabria	Calabria
135	Head	M.	35	Married	Basilicata	Basilicata	Basilicata
	Wife	F.	28	Married	Basilicata	Basilicata	Basilicata
	Son	M.	12	Single	United States	Basilicata	Basilicata
	Son	M.	10	Single	United States	Basilicata	Basilicata
	Son	M.	9	Single	United States	Basilicata	Basilicata
	Daughter	F.	7	Single	United States	Basilicata	Basilicata
	Daughter	F.	4	Single	United States	Basilicata	Basilicata
136	Head	M.	28	Married	Campania	Campania	Campania
	Wife	F.	29	Married	Calabria	Calabria	Calabria
	Son	M.	4	Single	United States	Campania	Calabria
	Brother	M.	26	Single	Campania	Campania	Campania

a Also worked as laborer thirteen weeks, at $7.50 per week.
b Also worked as ragpicker twelve weeks, at $1.80 per week.
c Also worked as bartender fifteen weeks, wages not reported.

TABLE I.—GENERAL SOCIAL AND ECONOMIC CONDITION, BY FAMILIES AND INDIVIDUALS—Continued.

Years in U. S.	Naturalized.	Profession, trade, or occupation.	Hours of work per week.	Average weekly earnings.	Weeks employed.	Total yearly earnings.	Sick during year, defective, maimed, or deformed.
4	No...	Tailor	72	$5.00	52	$260	No.
4		Housewife					No.
4		Scholar					No.
4		Scholar					No.
4		At home					No.
		At home					No.
12	No...	Baker	66	11.00	52	572	Childbirth.
5		Housework					No.
		At home					No.
		At home					No.
		At home					No.
		At home					No.
5	No...	Accordion maker	60	5.00	52	260	No.
3		Housewife					Childbirth.
3		Scholar					Fever, not specified.
3		At home					No.
3		At home					No.
		At home					Bronchitis.
		At home					No.
6	Yes..	Laborer	48	6.75	9	61	Bronchitis.
6	Yes..	Street sweeper (a)	48	7.50	a 13	195	No.
5	Yes..	Carpenter	60	10.50	13	137	No.
3		Scholar and laborer	60	7.50	18	135	No.
8	No...	Laborer	60	7.50	11	83	No.
29		Housewife		1.05			Fever, not specified.
		Scholar and newsboy	40	1.05	52	55	No.
6	No...	Laborer	60	7.50	9	68	No.
6	Yes..	No occupation					Rheumatism.
1		Housewife					Goitre.
		At home					No.
7	Yes..	Laborer (b)	60	7.25	b 26	210	No.
4		Housewife					No.
		At home					Rickets; bronchitis.
		At home					No.
20	Yes..	Laborer	60	7.50	11	83	No.
20	Yes..	Laborer	60	7.50	11	83	No.
12	Yes..	Laborer	60	7.50	15	113	No.
8	No...	No occupation					No.
5	No...	No occupation					No.
5	Yes..	Laborer	60	7.50	6	45	No.
12	Yes..	Laborer (c)	60	7.50	c 24	(d)	No.
15	Yes..	Laborer	60	7.50	15	113	No.
5	No...	Laborer	60	7.50	(d)	(d)	No.
9	No...	Peddler, fruit and vegetables. (e)	60	1.50	e 51	84	Elbow joint, immobility of one.
6		Housewife					No.
6		Candy factory employee	60	3.00	26	78	No.
6		Scholar and peddler	(d)	1.25	(d)	(d)	No.
6		No occupation					Rickets; convulsions.
		At home					No.
		At home					No.
		At home					No.
3	No...	Laborer	60	7.50	7	53	No.
3	No...	Laborer	60	7.50	7	53	No.
15	Yes..	Saloon keeper	119	(d)	52	(d)	No.
4		Housewife and seamstress.	(d)	.40	52	21	No.
23	Yes..	Musician	24	10.00	52	520	No.
14		Housewife					No.
		Scholar					No.
		Scholar					No.
		Scholar					No.
		At home					No.
		At home					No.
7	No...	Laborer	(d)	7.50	24	180	No.
5		Housewife					Blood poisoning.
		At home					No.
7	Yes..	Laborer	(d)	12.00	52	624	No.

d Not reported.
e Also worked as laborer one week, at $7.50 per week.

TABLE **I.**—GENERAL SOCIAL AND ECONOMIC CONDITION, BY FAMILIES AND INDIVIDUALS—Continued.

Family number.	Relationship to head of family.	Sex.	Age.	Conjugal condition.	Birthplace.	Birthplace of— Father.	Birthplace of— Mother.
137	Head	M.	44	Married...	Basilicata	Basilicata	Basilicata
	Wife	F.	42	Married...	Basilicata	Basilicata	Basilicata
	Daughter	F.	16	Single	Basilicata	Basilicata	Basilicata
	Son	M.	13	Single	Basilicata	Basilicata	Basilicata
	Son	M.	7	Single	United States...	Basilicata	Basilicata
	Daughter	F.	2	Single	United States...	Basilicata	Basilicata
138	Head	M.	43	Married...	Basilicata	Basilicata	Basilicata
	Wife	F.	40	Married...	Basilicata	Basilicata	Basilicata
	Son	M.	21	Single	Basilicata	Basilicata	Basilicata
	Daughter	F.	6	Single	United States...	Basilicata	Basilicata
	Daughter	F.	4	Single	United States...	Basilicata	Basilicata
	Daughter	F.	1	Single	United States...	Basilicata	Basilicata
139	Head	M.	35	Married ..	Sicily	Sicily	Sicily
	Wife	F.	22	Married...	Sicily	Sicily	Sicily
	Son	M.	4	Single	Sicily	Sicily	Sicily
	Daughter	F.	1	Single	United States...	Sicily	Sicily
	Brother	M.	23	Single	Sicily	Sicily	Sicily
140	Head	M.	31	Married...	Calabria	Calabria	Calabria
	Wife	F.	21	Married...	Basilicata	Basilicata	Basilicata
	Brother-in-law	M.	37	Married...	Calabria	Calabria	Calabria
	Boarder	M.	37	Married...	Calabria	Calabria	Calabria
141	Head	M.	38	Married...	Campania	Campania	Campania
	Wife	F.	29	Married...	Basilicata	Basilicata	Basilicata
	Nephew	M.	7	Single	United States...	Basilicata	Basilicata
	Nephew	M.	5	Single	United States...	Basilicata	Basilicata
142	Head	M.	30	Married...	Abruzzo	Abruzzo	Abruzzo
	Wife	F.	30	Married...	Abruzzo	Abruzzo	Abruzzo
	Daughter	F.	11	Single	Abruzzo	Abruzzo	Abruzzo
	Lodger	M.	40	Married...	Abruzzo	Abruzzo	Abruzzo
143	Head	M.	39	Married...	Campania	Campania	Campania
	Wife	F.	37	Married...	Campania	Campania	Campania
	Son	M.	7	Single	United States...	Campania	Campania
	Daughter	F.	$\frac{1}{12}$	Single	United States...	Campania	Campania
144	Head	M.	30	Married...	Basilicata	Basilicata	Basilicata
	Wife	F.	25	Married...	Basilicata	Basilicata	Basilicata
	Son	M.	11	Single	Basilicata	Basilicata	Basilicata
	Son	M.	4	Single	United States...	Basilicata	Basilicata
	Son	M.	3	Single	United States...	Basilicata	Basilicata
	Son	M.	1	Single	United States...	Basilicata	Basilicata
	Sister	F.	14	Single	Basilicata	Basilicata	Basilicata
145	Head	M.	60	Widowed .	Campania	Campania	Campania
	Son	M.	27	Married...	Campania	Campania	Campania
	Son	M.	24	Married...	Campania	Campania	Campania
	Son	M.	22	Single	Campania	Campania	Campania
	Son	M.	20	Single	Campania	Campania	Campania
	Daughter-in-law ..	F.	20	Married...	Campania	Campania	Campania
	Daughter-in-law ..	F.	20	Married...	Basilicata	Basilicata	Basilicata
	Granddaughter ...	F.	2	Single	United States...	Campania	Basilicata
	Grandson	M.	1	Single	United States...	Campania	Campania
146	Head	M.	47	Married...	Calabria	Calabria	Calabria
	Wife	F.	42	Married...	Calabria	Calabria	Calabria
	Son	M.	$\frac{1}{2}$	Single	United States...	Calabria	Calabria
	Son-in-law	M.	23	Married...	Calabria	Calabria	Calabria
	Nephew	M.	20	Single	Calabria	Calabria	Calabria
147	Cooperative	M.	40	Married...	Calabria	Calabria	Calabria
	Cooperative	M.	30	Single	Calabria	Calabria	Calabria
	Cooperative	M.	24	Single	Calabria	Calabria	Calabria
	Cooperative	M.	30	Married...	Calabria	Calabria	Calabria
148	Cooperative	M.	25	Married...	Calabria	Calabria	Calabria
	Cooperative	M.	26	Married...	Calabria	Calabria	Calabria

a Not reported.

TABLE I.—GENERAL SOCIAL AND ECONOMIC CONDITION, BY FAMILIES AND INDIVIDUALS—Continued.

Years in U. S.	Naturalized.	Profession, trade, or occupation.	Hours of work per week.	Average weekly earnings.	Weeks employed.	Total yearly earnings.	Sick during year, defective, maimed, or deformed.
11	Yes..	Street sweeper............	60	$7.50	28	$210	No.
10	......	Housewife and seamstress.	18	2.00	52	104	Asthma.
10	......	Seamstress	24	2.00	52	104	No.
10	......	Scholar	......	......	......	......	Fever, typhoid.
......	......	Scholar	......	......	......	......	No.
......	......	At home	......	......	......	......	Whooping cough.
16	Yes..	Laborer..................	60	7.50	26	195	No.
8	......	Housewife	......	......	......	......	No.
8	Yes..	Elevator tender...........	(a)	9.00	52	468	No.
......	......	Scholar	......	......	......	......	No.
......	......	At home	......	......	......	......	No.
......	......	At home	......	......	......	......	No.
4	No...	Candy factory employee...	60	6.00	32	192	Hay fever.
4	......	Housewife...............	......	......	......	......	Fever, typhoid.
4	......	At home	......	......	......	......	Measles.
4	......	At home	......	......	......	......	Measles.
3	No...	Candy factory employee...	60	7.00	32	224	No.
8	Yes..	Laborer..................	(a)	9.00	15	135	Eyes, inflammation of both.
9	......	Housewife and button sewer,	60	.40	52	21	No.
2	No...	Laborer..................	(a)	6.72	26	175	No.
9	Yes..	Laborer..................	(a)	7.50	36	270	No.
14	Yes..	Laborer..................	60	7.50	23	173	No.
10	......	Housewife and seamstress.	6	.25	4	1	No.
......	......	Scholar	......	......	......	......	No.
......	......	Scholar	......	......	......	......	Rickets; fever, not specified.
8	Yes..	Laborer..................	60	7.50	(a)	(a)	Fever, not specified.
1	......	Housewife	......	......	......	......	No.
1	......	No occupation	......	......	......	......	No.
5	No...	Laborer..................	60	7.50	(a)	(a)	No.
10	Yes..	Laborer (b)...............	60	3.75	b 30	(a)	No.
9	......	Housewife...............	......	......	......	......	Childbirth; syphilis.
......	......	Scholar	......	......	......	......	No.
......	......	At home	......	......	......	......	No.
8	No...	Laborer..................	60	7.50	52	390	Fever, gastric.
5	......	Housewife	......	......	......	......	No.
8	......	Newsboy	(a)	(a)	52	(a)	No.
......	......	At home	......	......	......	......	No.
......	......	At home	......	......	......	......	No.
......	......	At home	......	......	......	......	No.
8	......	Peddler, wood	36	1.80	52	94	No.
14	Yes..	Retired	......	......	......	......	No.
4	No...	Bootblack................	(a)	.90	52	47	No.
14	Yes..	Newsboy	126	7.00	52	364	No.
14	Yes..	Bootblack................	105	5.00	52	260	No.
14	......	Newsboy	70	1.40	52	73	No.
4	......	Housewife...............	......	......	......	......	No.
12	......	Housework	......	......	......	......	No.
......	......	At home	......	......	......	......	No.
......	......	At home	......	......	......	......	No.
13	Yes..	Laborer..................	60	6.90	26	179	No.
4	......	Housewife...............	......	......	......	......	Childbirth.
......	......	At home	......	......	......	......	No.
2	No...	Laborer..................	(a)	7.50	9	68	No.
6	......	Laborer..................	(a)	7.50	22	165	No.
5	No...	No occupation	......	......	......	......	Injury by accident.
5	No...	Laborer..................	60	6.60	9	59	No.
6	Yes..	Laborer..................	60	7.50	13	98	No.
4	No...	Laborer..................	60	7.50	9	68	No.
3	No...	Laborer..................	60	7.50	13	98	No.
4	No...	Laborer..................	60	7.50	9	68	No.

b Also worked as shoemaker, time and wages not reported.

TABLE I.—GENERAL SOCIAL AND ECONOMIC CONDITION, BY FAMILIES AND INDIVIDUALS—Continued.

Family number.	Relationship to head of family.	Sex.	Age.	Conjugal condition.	Birthplace.	Birthplace of— Father.	Birthplace of— Mother.
149	Head	M.	43	Married	Sicily	Sicily	Sicily
	Wife	F.	33	Married	Sicily	Sicily	Sicily
	Daughter	F.	14	Single	Sicily	Sicily	Sicily
	Son	M.	9	Single	United States	Sicily	Sicily
	Daughter	F.	7	Single	United States	Sicily	Sicily
	Daughter	F.	3	Single	United States	Sicily	Sicily
	Daughter	F.	$\frac{7}{12}$	Single	United States	Sicily	Sicily
150	Cooperative	M.	47	Married	Calabria	Calabria	Calabria
	Cooperative	M.	40	Married	Calabria	Calabria	Calabria
	Cooperative	M.	20	Single	Calabria	Calabria	Calabria
	Cooperative	M.	32	Single	Calabria	Calabria	Calabria
	Cooperative	M.	50	Single	Calabria	Calabria	Calabria
151	Head	M.	40	Married	Abruzzo	Abruzzo	Abruzzo
	Wife	F.	38	Married	Abruzzo	Abruzzo	Abruzzo
	Son	M.	16	Single	Abruzzo	Abruzzo	Abruzzo
	Son	M.	8	Single	United States	Abruzzo	Abruzzo
	Son	M.	7	Single	United States	Abruzzo	Abruzzo
	Daughter	F.	4	Single	United States	Abruzzo	Abruzzo
	Daughter	F.	3	Single	United States	Abruzzo	Abruzzo
	Son	M.	$\frac{7}{12}$	Single	United States	Abruzzo	Abruzzo
152	Head	F.	60	Widowed	Emilia	Emilia	Emilia
	Daughter	F.	26	Widowed	Emilia	Emilia	Emilia
	Son	M.	24	Single	Emilia	Emilia	Emilia
	Grandson	M.	7	Single	United States	Emilia	Emilia
153	Head	M.	50	Married	Sicily	Sicily	Sicily
	Wife	F.	48	Married	Sicily	Sicily	Sicily
	Son	M.	27	Married	Sicily	Sicily	Sicily
	Son	M.	24	Married	Sicily	Sicily	Sicily
	Son	M.	20	Single	Sicily	Sicily	Sicily
	Daughter	F.	18	Single	Sicily	Sicily	Sicily
	Son	M.	12	Single	Sicily	Sicily	Sicily
	Daughter	F.	8	Single	Sicily	Sicily	Sicily
	Son	M.	1	Single	United States	Sicily	Sicily
	Daughter-in-law	F.	24	Married	Sicily	Sicily	Sicily
	Grandson	M.	1	Single	United States	Sicily	Sicily
154	Head	M.	43	Married	Campania	Campania	Campania
	Wife	F.	45	Married	Campania	Campania	Campania
	Daughter	F.	17	Married	Campania	Campania	Campania
	Daughter	F.	3	Single	United States	Campania	Campania
	Grandson	M.	$\frac{5}{12}$	Single	United States	Campania	Campania
	Son-in-law	M.	21	Married	Campania	Campania	Campania
	Boarder	M.	12	Single	Campania	Campania	Campania
155	Head	M.	30	Married	Calabria	Calabria	Calabria
	Wife	F.	23	Married	Calabria	Calabria	Calabria
	Daughter	F.	$\frac{7}{12}$	Single	United States	Calabria	Calabria
	Lodger	M.	25	Single	Calabria	Calabria	Calabria
156	Head	M.	29	Married	Campania	Campania	Campania
	Wife	F.	28	Married	Calabria	Calabria	Calabria
	Son	M.	2	Single	United States	Campania	Calabria
	Daughter	F.	$\frac{8}{12}$	Single	United States	Campania	Calabria
157	Head	M.	65	Married	Liguria	Liguria	Liguria
	Wife	F.	35	Married	Liguria	Liguria	Liguria
	Son	M.	17	Single	United States	Liguria	Liguria
	Daughter	F.	15	Single	United States	Liguria	Liguria
	Daughter	F.	8	Single	United States	Liguria	Liguria
	Son	M.	2	Single	United States	Liguria	Liguria

a Sick, disease not specified.
b Not reported.

TABLE **I.**—GENERAL SOCIAL AND ECONOMIC CONDITION, BY FAMILIES
AND INDIVIDUALS—Continued.

Years in U. S.	Naturalized.	Profession, trade, or occupation.	Hours of work per week.	Average weekly earnings.	Weeks employed.	Total yearly earnings.	Sick during year, defective, maimed, or deformed.
10	No...	Laborer....................	60	$4.00	35	$140	No.
9	......	Housewife.................					Childbirth.
9	......	Housework.................					No.
......	......	Scholar...................					No.
......	......	Scholar...................					No.
......	......	At home....................					No.
......	......	At home....................					No.
4	No...	Laborer....................	60	6.60	13	86	No.
3	No...	Laborer....................	60	6.60	13	86	No.
3	......	Laborer....................	60	6.60	13	86	No.
3	No...	Laborer....................	60	6.60	13	86	No.
10	No...	Laborer....................	60	6.60	13	86	Pneumonia.
15	No...	Scissors grinder..........	60	5.50	52	286	No.
9	......	Housewife.................					Childbirth; female complaint.
9	......	Scholar and salesman, groceries.	72	2.00	48	96	No.
......	......	Scholar...................					No.
......	......	Scholar...................					No.
......	......	At home....................					No.
......	......	At home....................					No.
......	......	At home....................					No.
10	......	Housewife.................					No.
10	......	Housework.................					(a)
10	Yes..	Macaroni maker...........	(b)	8.00	52	416	No.
......	......	Scholar...................					No.
4	No...	Peddler, fruit.............	(b)	3.30	52	172	No.
4	......	Housewife and jacket finisher.	72	3.00	22	66	No.
5	No...	Peddler, fruit.............	(b)	3.30	43	142	Eyes, inflammation of both.
6	Yes..	Packer, fruit..............	60	7.50	52	390	No.
5	......	Laborer (c)	60	7.50	c 26	231	No.
4	......	Housework.................					No.
4	......	Scholar and peddler, fruit.	(b)	3.00	52	156	No.
4	......	Scholar...................					No.
......	......	At home....................					No.
4	......	Housework.................					No.
......	......	At home....................					No.
14	Yes..	Fireman...................	60	4.20	26	109	No.
10	......	Housewife.................					No.
10	......	Housework.................					Childbirth.
......	......	At home....................					No.
......	......	At home....................					No.
5	No...	Newsboy	(b)	(b)	50	(b)	No.
3/12	......	Newsboy (d)	42	1.50	d 13	(b)	No.
16	Yes..	Boiler washer.............	70	10.50	10	105	No.
3	......	Housewife.................					Childbirth.
......	......	At home....................					No.
5	Yes..	Cracker-factory employee.	60	6.00	30	180	No.
15	No...	No occupation					No.
4	......	Housewife.................					Childbirth.
......	......	At home....................					No.
......	......	At home....................					No.
18	Yes..	Organ grinder	(b)	3.00	52	156	No.
18	......	Housewife.................					No.
......	......	Porter....................	(b)	6.00	26	156	No.
......	......	Scholar and saleswoman, dry goods.	18	3.50	18	63	No.
......	......	Scholar...................					No.
......	......	At home....................					Rickets.

c Also worked as peddler, fruit, twenty-six weeks, at $1.40 per week.
d Also worked at another occupation, details not reported.

TABLE I.—GENERAL SOCIAL AND ECONOMIC CONDITION, BY FAMILIES AND INDIVIDUALS—Continued.

Family number.	Relationship to head of family.	Sex.	Age.	Conjugal condition.	Birthplace.	Birthplace of—	
						Father.	Mother.
158	Head	M.	40	Married	Campania	Campania	Campania
	Wife	F.	43	Married	Campania	Campania	Campania
	Son	M.	21	Single	Campania	Campania	Campania
	Daughter	F.	16	Single	Campania	Campania	Campania
	Son	M.	13	Single	United States	Campania	Campania
	Son	M.	10	Single	United States	Campania	Campania
	Son	M.	8	Single	United States	Campania	Campania
	Daughter	F.	6	Single	United States	Campania	Campania
	Son	M.	4	Single	United States	Campania	Campania
	Cousin	M.	21	Single	Campania	Campania	Campania
159	Head	M.	39	Married	Calabria	Calabria	Calabria
	Wife	F.	39	Married	Calabria	Calabria	Calabria
	Son	M.	15	Single	Calabria	Calabria	Calabria
	Son	M.	13	Single	Calabria	Calabria	Calabria
	Son	M.	4	Single	United States	Calabria	Calabria
	Daughter	F.	2	Single	United States	Calabria	Calabria
	Daughter	F.	$\frac{6}{12}$	Single	United States	Calabria	Calabria
160	Head	M.	27	Married	Calabria	Calabria	Calabria
	Wife	F.	20	Married	Calabria	Calabria	Calabria
	Son	M.	2	Single	United States	Calabria	Calabria
161	Head	M.	40	Married	Calabria	Calabria	Calabria
	Wife	F.	35	Married	Calabria	Calabria	Calabria
	Daughter	F.	7	Single	United States	Calabria	Calabria
	Daughter	F.	6	Single	United States	Calabria	Calabria
	Son	M.	$\frac{1}{12}$	Single	United States	Calabria	Calabria
162	Head	M.	52	Married	Campania	Campania	Campania
	Wife	F.	46	Married	Campania	Campania	Campania
	Son	M.	13	Single	Campania	Campania	Campania
	Daughter, adopted	F.	5	Single	Campania	Campania	Campania
163	Head	M.	36	Married	Campania	Campania	Campania
	Wife	F.	39	Married	Campania	Campania	Campania
	Son	M.	13	Single	Campania	Campania	Campania
	Son	M.	7	Single	Campania	Campania	Campania
	Son	M.	4	Single	United States	Campania	Campania
	Daughter	F.	1	Single	United States	Campania	Campania
	Nephew	M.	33	Married	Campania	Campania	Campania
164	Head	M.	40	Married	Campania	Campania	Campania
	Wife	F.	35	Married	Campania	Campania	Campania
	Son	M.	13	Single	Campania	Campania	Campania
	Daughter	F.	9	Single	Campania	Campania	Campania
	Daughter	F.	6	Single	Campania	Campania	Campania
	Son	M.	2	Single	United States	Campania	Campania
165	Head	M.	25	Married	Campania	Campania	Campania
	Wife	F.	20	Married	Campania	Campania	Campania
	Daughter	F.	$\frac{1}{12}$	Single	United States	Campania	Campania
166	Head	M.	34	Married	Campania	Campania	Campania
	Wife	F.	24	Married	Basilicata	Basilicata	Basilicata
	Son	M.	8	Single	United States	Campania	Basilicata
	Son	M.	6	Single	United States	Campania	Basilicata
	Daughter	F.	4	Single	United States	Campania	Basilicata
	Daughter	F.	2	Single	United States	Campania	Basilicata
	Daughter	F.	$\frac{1}{12}$	Single	United States	Campania	Basilicata
167	Head	M.	43	Married	Campania	Campania	Campania
	Wife	F.	33	Married	Campania	Campania	Campania
168	Head	M.	45	Married	Campania	Campania	Campania
	Wife	F.	40	Married	Campania	Campania	Campania
	Daughter	F.	6	Single	Campania	Campania	Campania
	Daughter	F.	2	Single	United States	Campania	Campania
	Boarder	M.	27	Married	Campania	Campania	Campania
	Lodger	M.	33	Single	Campania	Campania	Campania
	Lodger	M.	33	Married	Campania	Campania	Campania

a Not reported.

TABLE **I.**—GENERAL SOCIAL AND ECONOMIC CONDITION, BY FAMILIES AND INDIVIDUALS—Continued.

Years in U. S.	Naturalized.	Profession, trade, or occupation.	Hours of work per week.	Average weekly earnings.	Weeks employed.	Total yearly earnings	Sick during year, defective, maimed, or deformed.
16	Yes..	Barber	81	$17.50	52	$910	No.
11		Housewife					No.
16	Yes..	Barber	81	(a)	52	(a)	No.
16		Housework					No.
		Scholar					No.
		Scholar					No.
		Scholar					Fingers, loss of two.
		Scholar					No.
		At home					No.
1¹⁄₁₂	No...	Mason, stone, apprentice; no pay.					No.
12	Yes..	Laborer	70	7.76	26	200	No.
5		Housewife					Childbirth.
5		Bootblack and newsboy...	84	3.00	52	156	No.
5		Bootblack and newsboy...	84	3.00	52	156	No.
		At home					No.
		At home					No.
		At home					No.
6	Yes..	Laborer	60	7.50	17	128	No.
3		Housewife					No.
		At home					Glands, scrofulous.
8	Yes..	Laborer	60	7.50	15	113	No.
8		Housewife					Childbirth.
		Scholar					No.
		Scholar					No.
		At home					No.
11	Yes..	Retired					Leg, loss of one.
8		Housewife					No.
8		Scholar and newsboy	24	.60	52	31	No.
4		At home					No.
13	Yes..	Laborer (b)	60	9.00	b17	177	No.
5		Housewife					No.
5		Newsboy	72	1.40	52	73	No.
5		Scholar					No.
		At home					No.
		At home					No.
3	No...	Railroad laborer	60	9.00	30	270	No.
6	Yes..	Railroad laborer	60	9.00	17	153	Lame.
3		Housewife					No.
1		Scholar					No.
1		At home					No.
3		At home					No.
		At home					Rickets.
11	Yes..	Bootblack	72	3.00	52	156	No.
8		Housewife					Childbirth.
		At home					No.
20	Yes..	Laborer	60	9.00	9	81	No.
11		Housewife					Childbirth.
		At home					Idiot.
		Scholar					No.
		At home					No.
		At home					No.
		At home					No.
5	No...	Laborer	60	6.60	17	112	No.
1¹⁄₁₂		Housewife					No.
10	Yes..	Laborer	60	3.75	13	49	Pneumonia.
4		Housewife					Fever, typhoid.
4		Scholar					No.
		At home					No.
3	No...	Laborer	60	6.60	13	86	No.
10	No...	Laborer	60	8.40	17	143	No.
6	No...	Laborer	60	7.50	43	323	No.

b Also worked as ragpicker seventeen weeks, at $1.40 per week.

S. Doc. 138——6

TABLE I.—GENERAL SOCIAL AND ECONOMIC CONDITION, BY FAMILIES
AND INDIVIDUALS—Continued.

Family number.	Relationship to head of family.	Sex.	Age.	Conjugal condition.	Birthplace.	Birthplace of—	
						Father.	Mother.
169	Head	M.	50	Married...	Campania	Campania	Campania
	Wife	F.	41	Married...	Campania	Campania	Campania
	Daughter	F.	15	Single	Campania	Campania	Campania
	Son	M.	9	Single	Campania	Campania	Campania
	Daughter	F.	4	Single	Campania	Campania	Campania
	Son	M.	1	Single	United States	Campania	Campania
170	Head	M.	27	Married...	Campania	Campania	Campania
	Wife	F.	20	Married...	Campania	Campania	Campania
	Lodger	M.	32	Single	Abruzzo	Abruzzo	Abruzzo
171	Head	M.	27	Married...	Campania	Campania	Campania
	Wife	F.	25	Married...	Campania	Campania	Campania
	Son. adopted	M.	2	Single	United States	Campania	Campania
	Brother	M.	22	Single	Campania	Campania	Campania
172	Head	M.	42	Married...	Campania	Campania	Campania
	Wife	F.	35	Married...	Campania	Campania	Campania
	Son	M.	14	Single	United States	Campania	Campania
	Daughter	F.	10	Single	United States	Campania	Campania
	Daughter	F.	7	Single	United States	Campania	Campania
	Daughter	F.	1	Single	United States	Campania	Campania
173	Head	M.	37	Married...	Basilicata	Basilicata	Basilicata
	Wife	F.	34	Married...	Basilicata	Basilicata	Basilicata
	Son	M.	6	Single	United States	Basilicata	Basilicata
	Daughter	F.	4	Single	United States	Basilicata	Basilicata
	Daughter	F.	2	Single	United States	Basilicata	Basilicata
	Daughter	F.	2/12	Single	United States	Basilicata	Basilicata
174	Head	M.	20	Married...	Calabria	Calabria	Calabria
	Wife	F.	16	Married...	Calabria	Calabria	Calabria
	Cousin	M.	27	Single	Calabria	Calabria	Calabria
	Boarder	M.	26	Single	Calabria	Calabria	Calabria
175	Head	M.	38	Married...	Calabria	Calabria	Calabria
	Wife	F.	20	Married...	Calabria	Calabria	Calabria
	Nephew	M.	16	Single	Calabria	Calabria	Calabria
	Boarder	M.	26	Married...	Calabria	Calabria	Calabria
176	Head	M.	35	Married...	Campania	Campania	Campania
	Wife	F.	32	Married...	Campania	Campania	Campania
	Daughter	F.	9	Single	United States	Campania	Campania
	Son	M.	5	Single	United States	Campania	Campania
	Son	M.	3	Single	United States	Campania	Campania
	Son	M.	1	Single	United States	Campania	Campania
177	Head	M.	39	Married...	Basilicata	Basilicata	Basilicata
	Wife	F.	37	Married...	Basilicata	Basilicata	Basilicata
	Daughter	F.	14	Single	Basilicata	Basilicata	Basilicata
	Lodger	M.	58	Married...	Basilicata	Basilicata	Basilicata
178	Head	M.	36	Married...	Campania	Campania	Campania
	Wife	F.	30	Married...	Campania	Campania	Campania
	Daughter	F.	10	Single	United States	Campania	Campania
	Daughter	F.	8	Single	United States	Campania	Campania
	Son	M.	6	Single	United States	Campania	Campania
	Son	M.	4	Single	United States	Campania	Campania
	Son	M.	1	Single	United States	Campania	Campania
	Stepmother	F.	60	Widowed	Campania	Campania	Campania
179	Head	M.	31	Married...	Basilicata	Basilicata	Basilicata
	Wife	F.	42	Married...	Basilicata	Basilicata	Basilicata
	Son	M.	9	Single	United States	Basilicata	Basilicata
	Daughter	F.	5	Single	United States	Basilicata	Basilicata
	Son	M.	2	Single	United States	Basilicata	Basilicata
180	Head	M.	29	Married...	Campania	Campania	Campania
	Wife	F.	20	Married...	Campania	Campania	Campania
181	Head	M.	35	Married...	Campania	Campania	Campania
	Wife	F.	27	Married...	Campania	Campania	Campania
	Son	M.	7	Single	United States	Campania	Campania
	Son	M.	5	Single	United States	Campania	Campania
	Daughter	F.	2	Single	United States	Campania	Campania

a Not reported.   b Sick, disease not specified.

TABLE I.—GENERAL SOCIAL AND ECONOMIC CONDITION, BY FAMILIES AND INDIVIDUALS—Continued.

Years in U. S.	Natu- ral- ized.	Profession, trade, or occupation.	Hours of work per week.	Average weekly earn- ings.	Weeks em- ploy- ed.	Total yearly earn- ings.	Sick during year, defective, maimed, or deformed.
13	Yes..	Laborer.....................	60	$7.50	9	$68	No.
3	......	Housewife...................	......	......	......	......	No.
3	......	Housework..................	......	......	......	......	No.
3	......	Scholar.....................	......	......	......	......	No.
3	......	At home....................	......	......	......	......	No.
......	......	At home....................	......	......	......	......	No.
8	Yes..	Laborer.....................	60	6.90	26	179	No.
10	......	Housewife...................	......	......	......	......	No.
4	No...	Laborer.....................	60	7.50	22	165	No.
10	Yes..	Laborer.....................	60	7.50	26	195	No.
3	......	Housewife and nurse.....	(a)	.75	(a)	(a)	No.
......	......	At home....................	......	......	......	......	No.
6	Yes..	Laborer.....................	70	9.45	26	246	No.
15	Yes..	Merchant, groceries........	(a)	(a)	52	(a)	No.
15	......	Housewife...................	......	......	......	......	No.
......	......	Scholar	......	......	......	......	No.
......	......	Scholar.....................	......	......	......	......	No.
......	......	Scholar.....................	......	......	......	......	No.
......	......	At home....................	......	......	......	......	No.
14	Yes..	Laborer.....................	60	7.50	17	128	No.
10	......	Housewife...................	......	......	......	......	Childbirth.
......	......	At home....................	......	......	......	......	No.
......	......	At home....................	......	......	......	......	Cross-eyed.
......	......	At home....................	......	......	......	......	(b)
......	......	At home....................	......	......	......	......	No.
$\frac{7}{2}$	......	Laborer.....................	60	5.00	(a)	(a)	No.
$1\frac{1}{7}$	......	Housewife...................	......	......	......	......	No.
4	No...	Laborer.....................	60	6.60	9	59	No.
3	No...	Laborer.....................	60	6.90	13	90	No.
14	Yes..	Laborer.....................	60	9.00	7	63	No.
4	......	Housewife...................	......	......	......	......	No.
$1\frac{1}{2}$	......	No occupation	......	......	......	......	No.
4	No...	Laborer.....................	60	7.50	4	30	Diphtheria.
11	Yes..	Laborer.....................	70	8.40	39	328	No.
9	......	Housewife and merchant, wood.	(a)	1.20	(a)	(a)	No.
......	......	At home....................	......	......	......	......	No.
......	......	At home....................	......	......	......	......	No.
......	......	At home....................	......	......	......	......	Rickets.
......	......	At home....................	......	......	......	......	No.
14	Yes..	Street sweeper (c)	(a)	7.50	c 26	(a)	No.
9	......	Housewife...................	......	......	......	......	No.
9	......	Scholar	......	......	......	......	No.
14	Yes..	Street sweeper.............	(a)	7.50	26	195	No.
11	No...	Laborer.....................	60	7.50	13	98	No.
11	......	Ragpicker..................	12	1.20	36	43	No.
......	......	Scholar	......	......	......	......	No.
......	......	At home....................	......	......	......	......	Rickets.
......	......	Scholar	......	......	......	......	No.
......	......	At home....................	......	......	......	......	No.
......	......	At home....................	......	......	......	......	No.
11	......	Housewife...................	......	......	......	......	No.
13	Yes..	Street sweeper.............	60	9.00	52	468	No.
10	......	Housewife...................	......	......	......	......	Rheumatism.
......	......	Scholar	......	......	......	......	No.
......	......	At home....................	......	......	......	......	Rickets.
......	......	At home....................	......	......	......	......	Rickets.
6	No...	Organ grinder	72	3.00	(a)	(a)	No.
17	......	Housewife...................	......	......	......	......	No.
15	Yes..	Stonebreaker	68	6.50	52	338	No.
11	......	Housewife...................	......	......	......	......	No.
......	......	Scholar	......	......	......	......	No.
......	......	At home....................	......	......	......	......	No.
......	......	At home....................	......	......	......	......	No.

c Also worked as ragpicker twenty-six weeks, wages not reported.

TABLE **I.**—GENERAL SOCIAL AND ECONOMIC CONDITION, BY FAMILIES
AND INDIVIDUALS—Continued.

Family number.	Relationship to head of family.	Sex.	Age.	Conjugal condition.	Birthplace.	Birthplace of—	
						Father.	Mother.
182	Head	M.	26	Married...	Calabria	Calabria	Calabria
	Wife	F.	33	Married...	Calabria	Calabria	Calabria
	Stepson	M.	13	Single	Calabria	Calabria	Calabria
	Stepson	M.	10	Single	Calabria	Calabria	Calabria
	Son	M.	$\frac{7}{12}$	Single	United States	Calabria	Calabria
	Father	M.	56	Married...	Calabria	Calabria	Calabria
183	Head	M.	32	Married...	Calabria	Calabria	Calabria
	Wife	F.	30	Married...	Calabria	Calabria	Calabria
	Daughter	F.	9	Single	Calabria	Calabria	Calabria
	Son	M.	6	Single	Calabria	Calabria	Calabria
	Son	M.	6	Single	Calabria	Calabria	Calabria
	Son	M.	2	Single	United States	Calabria	Calabria
	Daughter	F.	1	Single	United States	Calabria	Calabria
	Boarder	M.	26	Single	Calabria	Calabria	Calabria
184	Head	M.	48	Married...	Campania	Campania	Campania
	Wife	F.	46	Married...	Campania	Campania	Campania
	Son	M.	24	Single	Campania	Campania	Campania
	Son	M.	19	Single	Campania	Campania	Campania
	Daughter	F.	16	Single	Campania	Campania	Campania
	Son	M.	13	Single	United States	Campania	Campania
	Daughter	F.	12	Single	United States	Campania	Campania
	Daughter	F.	7	Single	United States	Campania	Campania
185	Head	M.	30	Married...	Campania	Campania	Campania
	Wife	F.	28	Married...	Campania	Campania	Campania
	Daughter	F.	8	Single	United States	Campania	Campania
	Daughter	F.	5	Single	United States	Campania	Campania
	Daughter	F.	3	Single	United States	Campania	Campania
	Nephew	M.	15	Single	Campania	Campania	Campania
186	Head	M.	47	Married...	Campania	Campania	Campania
	Wife	F.	45	Married...	Campania	Campania	Campania
	Son	M.	23	Married...	Campania	Campania	Campania
	Son	M.	16	Single	Campania	Campania	Campania
	Son	M.	12	Single	United States	Campania	Campania
	Son	M.	10	Single	United States	Campania	Campania
	Daughter-in-law	F.	21	Married...	Campania	Campania	Campania
	Grandson	M.	5	Single	United States	Campania	Campania
	Granddaughter	F.	2	Single	United States	Campania	Campania
	Granddaughter	F.	$\frac{1}{12}$	Single	United States	Campania	Campania
187	Head	M.	38	Married...	Campania	Campania	Campania
	Wife	F.	33	Married...	Campania	Campania	Campania
	Son	M.	9	Single	United States	Campania	Campania
	Son	M.	5	Single	United States	Campania	Campania
	Son	M.	2	Single	United States	Campania	Campania
188	Head	M.	30	Married...	Campania	Campania	Campania
	Wife	F.	28	Married...	Campania	Campania	Campania
	Son	M.	5	Single	United States	Campania	Campania
	Daughter	F.	3	Single	United States	Campania	Campania
189	Head	M.	32	Married...	Campania	Campania	Campania
	Wife	F.	36	Married...	Campania	Campania	Campania
	Daughter	F.	1	Single	United States	Campania	Campania
190	Head	M.	25	Married...	Calabria	Calabria	Calabria
	Wife	F.	19	Married...	Calabria	Calabria	Calabria
	Daughter	F.	$\frac{7}{12}$	Single	United States	Calabria	Calabria
191	Head	M.	40	Married...	Campania	Campania	Campania
	Wife	F.	35	Married...	Campania	Campania	Campania
	Son	M.	13	Single	Campania	Campania	Campania
	Son	M.	11	Single	Campania	Campania	Campania
	Son	M.	8	Single	United States	Campania	Campania
	Son	M.	$\frac{4}{12}$	Single	United States	Campania	Campania
	Nephew	M.	13	Single	Campania	Campania	Campania
	Cousin	M.	19	Single	Campania	Campania	Campania

a Not reported.

TABLE **I.**—GENERAL SOCIAL AND ECONOMIC CONDITION, BY FAMILIES AND INDIVIDUALS—Continued.

Years in U. S.	Naturalized.	Profession, trade, or occupation.	Hours of work per week.	Average weekly earnings.	Weeks employed.	Total yearly earnings.	Sick during year, defective, maimed, or deformed.
7	Yes..	Laborer.....................	60	$7.50	22	$165	No.
2	....	Housewife.................	....	....	....	....	Childbirth; female complaint.
4	....	No occupation	....	....	....	....	No.
2	....	No occupation	....	....	....	....	No.
....	....	At home...................	....	....	....	....	No.
4	No..	Laborer.....................	60	7.50	17	128	No.
8	Yes..	Ragpicker	48	3.60	39	140	Injury by accident.
3	....	Housewife............	....	....	....	....	No.
3	....	Scholar.....................	....	....	....	....	No.
3	....	At home...................	....	....	....	....	No.*
3	.. ....	At home...................	....	....	....	....	No.
....	....	At home...................	....	....	....	....	No.
7	Yes..	Laborer.....................	60	6.60	(a)	(a)	No.
17	Yes..	Laborer.....................	60	9.00	26	234	No.
15	....	Housewife and ragpicker.	(a)	2.40	52	125	No.
15	Yes..	Bootblack	84	4.75	4	19	No.
15	....	Bootblack	84	3.00	22	66	No.
15	....	No occupation	....	....	....	....	Blind.
....	....	Newsboy	24	.60	(a)	(a)	No.
....	....	Wood picker...............	24	.90	(a)	(a)	No.
....	....	Scholar.....................	....	....	....	....	No.
10	Yes..	Bootblack	78	8.00	52	416	No.
10	....	Housewife.................	....	....	....	....	No.
....	....	Scholar.....................	....	....	....	....	No.
....	....	At home...................	....	....	....	....	No.
....	....	At home...................	....	....	....	....	No.
8	....	Scholar and bootblack	78	5.00	52	260	No.
14	Yes..	Laborer.....................	68	7.50	13	98	No.
12	....	Housewife and ragpicker.	24	2.25	35	79	No.
12	Yes..	Laborer.....................	60	9.00	52	468	No.
12	....	Scholar.....................	....	....	....	....	No.
....	....	Scholar and newsboy (b) ..	77	.60	b 26	19	No.
....	....	Scholar.....................	....	....	....	....	No.
13	....	Housework	....	....	....	....	Childbirth.
....	....	At home...................	....	....	....	....	No.
....	....	At home...................	....	....	....	....	No.
....	....	At home...................	....	....	....	....	No.
10	Yes..	Street sweeper.............	60	7.50	22	165	No.
10	....	Housewife.................	....	....	....	....	No.
....	....	Scholar	....	....	....	....	No.
....	....	At home...................	....	....	....	....	No.
....	....	At home...................	....	....	....	....	No.
11	No...	Laborer.....................	(a)	8.00	30	240	No.
6	....	Housewife and merchant, groceries.	(a)	(a)	52	(a)	No.
....	....	At home...................	....	....	....	....	No.
....	....	At home...................	....	....	....	....	No.
6	No...	Laborer.....................	60	7.50	13	98	No.
2	....	Housewife.................	....	....	....	....	No.
....	....	At home...................	....	....	....	....	No.
5	Yes..	Baker's helper.............	72	5.50	52	286	No.
3	....	Housewife..................	....	....	....	....	Childbirth.
....	....	At home...................	....	....	....	....	No.
15	Yes..	Laborer.....................	60	9.00	9	81	No.
10	....	Housewife..................	....	....	....	....	Childbirth.
10	....	Newsboy	49	1.75	52	91	No.
10	....	No occupation	....	....	....	....	Idiot.
....	....	Scholar	....	....	....	....	No.
....	....	At home...................	....	....	....	....	No.
4	....	Newsboy	49	1.75	52	91	No.
1	....	Newsboy	49	1.75	52	91	No.

b Also worked as water carrier, theater, two weeks, at $1.50 per week.

TABLE I.—GENERAL SOCIAL AND ECONOMIC CONDITION, BY FAMILIES AND INDIVIDUALS—Continued.

Family number	Relationship to head of family.	Sex.	Age.	Conjugal condition.	Birthplace.	Birthplace of— Father.	Birthplace of— Mother.
192	Head	M.	27	Married ..	Calabria	Calabria	Calabria
	Wife	F.	15	Married	Calabria	Calabria	Calabria
	Father	M.	54	Married	Calabria	Calabria	Calabria
	Brother	M.	20	Single	Calabria	Calabria	Calabria
	Lodger	M.	51	Married	Calabria	Calabria	Calabria
	Lodger	M.	21	Single	Calabria	Calabria	Calabria
	Lodger	M.	52	Married	Calabria	Calabria	Calabria
	Lodger	M.	22	Single	Calabria	Calabria	Calabria
	Lodger	M.	20	Single	Calabria	Calabria	Calabria
	Lodger	M.	40	Widowed	Calabria	Calabria	Calabria
	Lodger	M.	24	Single	Calabria	Calabria	Calabria
	Lodger	M.	26	Single	Calabria	Calabria	Calabria
	Lodger	M.	9	Single	United States	Calabria	Calabria
193	Head	M.	30	Married	Basilicata	Basilicata	Basilicata
	Wife	F.	27	Married	Basilicata	Basilicata	Basilicata
	Son	M.	$\frac{1}{12}$	Single	United States	Basilicata	Basilicata
194	Head	M.	32	Married	Campania	Campania	Campania
	Wife	F.	31	Married	Campania	Campania	Campania
	Daughter	F.	8	Single	Campania	Campania	Campania
	Son	M.	2	Single	United States	Campania	Campania
195	Head	M.	30	Married	Campania	Campania	Campania
	Wife	F.	32	Married	Campania	Campania	Campania
	Daughter	F.	5	Single	United States	Campania	Campania
	Daughter	F.	3	Single	United States	Campania	Campania
	Daughter	F.	$\frac{5}{12}$	Single	United States	Campania	Campania
196	Head	M.	40	Married	Basilicata	Basilicata	Basilicata
	Wife	F.	30	Married	Basilicata	Basilicata	Basilicata
	Daughter	F.	10	Single	Basilicata	Basilicata	Basilicata
197	Head	M.	29	Married	Basilicata	Basilicata	Basilicata
	Wife	F.	20	Married	Basilicata	Basilicata	Basilicata
	Son	M.	1	Single	United States	Basilicata	Basilicata
	Daughter	F.	$\frac{1}{12}$	Single	United States	Basilicata	Basilicata
	Father	M.	64	Widowed	Basilicata	Basilicata	Basilicata
198	Head	M.	45	Married	Basilicata	Basilicata	Basilicata
	Wife	F.	44	Married	Basilicata	Basilicata	Basilicata
	Son	M.	15	Single	Basilicata	Basilicata	Basilicata
199	Head	M.	28	Married	Campania	Campania	Campania
	Wife	F.	19	Married	Campania	Campania	Campania
	Daughter	F.	1	Single	United States	Campania	Campania
	Lodger	M.	28	Single	Campania	Campania	Campania
200	Head	M.	36	Married	Basilicata	Basilicata	Basilicata
	Wife	F.	36	Married	Basilicata	Basilicata	Basilicata
	Son	M.	11	Single	Basilicata	Basilicata	Basilicata
	Son	M.	8	Single	United States	Basilicata	Basilicata
	Daughter	F.	4	Single	United States	Basilicata	Basilicata
	Son	M.	1	Single	United States	Basilicata	Basilicata
201	Head	M.	31	Married	Abruzzo	Abruzzo	Abruzzo
	Wife	F.	35	Married	Abruzzo	Abruzzo	Abruzzo
	Stepdaughter	F.	10	Single	Abruzzo	Abruzzo	Abruzzo
202	Head	M.	65	Married	Basilicata	Basilicata	Basilicata
	Wife	F.	58	Married	Basilicata	Basilicata	Basilicata
	Son	M.	20	Single	Basilicata	Basilicata	Basilicata
203	Head	M.	43	Married	Campania	Campania	Campania
	Wife	F.	48	Married	Campania	Campania	Campania
	Son	M.	8	Single	United States	Campania	Campania
	Son	M.	5	Single	United States	Campania	Campania
	Son	M.	$\frac{1}{12}$	Single	United States	Campania	Campania
204	Head	M.	38	Married	Basilicata	Basilicata	Basilicata
	Wife	F.	48	Married	Basilicata	Basilicata	Basilicata
	Son	M.	13	Single	Basilicata	Basilicata	Basilicata
	Daughter	F.	8	Single	United States	Basilicata	Basilicata

a Also worked at another occupation, details not reported.
b Not reported.
c Also worked as laborer seven weeks, at $7.50 per week.

TABLE **I.**—GENERAL SOCIAL AND ECONOMIC CONDITION, BY FAMILIES AND INDIVIDUALS—Continued.

Years in U.S.	Natu- ral- ized.	Profession, trade, or occupation.	Hours of work per week.	Average weekly earn- ings.	Weeks em- ploy- ed.	Total yearly earn- ings.	Sick during year, defective, maimed, or deformed.
3	No...	Laborer	60	$7.50	9	$68	No.
7	......	Housewife					No.
3	No...	Laborer	60	7.50	9	68	No.
3	......	Laborer	60	7.50	9	68	No.
4	No...	Laborer	60	6.60	13	86	No.
4	No...	Laborer	60	6.60	13	86	No.
4	No...	Laborer	60	6.60	13	86	No.
4	No...	Laborer	60	6.60	13	86	No.
4	......	Laborer	60	6.60	13	86	No.
14	Yes..	Laborer	60	6.60	13	86	No.
1½	No...	Frame factory employee (a)	60	4.00	a 1	(b)	No.
¼	No...	Laborer	60	6.60	13	86	No.
......	......	Scholar					No.
6	Yes:	Laborer	60	7.50	4	30	No.
4	......	Housewife					Childbirth.
......	......	At home					No.
3	No...	Street sweeper	(b)	6.75	52	351	No.
3	......	Housewife					No.
3	......	Scholar					No.
......	......	At home					No.
9	No...	Ragpicker (c)	60	2.00	c 45	143	No.
8	......	Housewife					Childbirth.
......	......	At home					No.
......	......	At home					No.
......	......	At home					No.
6	Yes..	Street sweeper	42	8.25	52	429	No.
4	......	Housewife					Neuralgia.
6	......	Scholar					No.
10	Yes..	Laborer	60	7.50	13	98	No.
15	......	Housewife					Childbirth.
......	......	At home					No.
......	......	At home					No.
5	No...	No occupation					Consumption.
7	Yes..	Laborer	60	7.50	13	98	No.
5	......	Housewife and dress fin- isher.	36	1.50	52	78	No.
5	......	Scholar					No.
7	Yes..	Laborer	60	9.00	22	198	Dyspepsia.
5	......	Housewife					No.
......	......	At home					No.
4	No...	Laborer	60	7.50	22	165	No.
12	Yes..	Street sweeper	60	7.50	26	195	No.
9	......	Housewife					No.
9	......	Scholar					No.
......	......	Scholar					No.
......	......	At home					Rickets; bronchitis.
......	......	At home					No.
11	Yes..	Dressmaker	(b)	.75	52	39	Eyes, inflammation of both.
6	......	Housewife and seamstress	(b)	.50	52	26	No.
6	......	Seamstress	(b)	.25	44	11	Fever, not specified.
14	No...	No occupation					No.
10	......	Housewife					No.
10	......	Candy factory employee	60	6.00	52	312	No.
12	No...	Peddler (d)	(b)	2.40	d 33	279	No.
8	......	Housewife					Childbirth; varicose veins.
......	......	Scholar					No.
......	......	At home					No.
......	......	At home					No.
10	Yes..	Street sweeper (e)	60	9.00	e 37	351	No.
8	......	Housewife					No.
10	......	Scholar					No.
......	......	Scholar					No.

d Also worked as laborer nineteen weeks, at $10.50 per week.
e Also worked as ragpicker twelve weeks, at $1.50 per week.

TABLE **I.**—GENERAL SOCIAL AND ECONOMIC CONDITION, BY FAMILIES AND INDIVIDUALS—Continued.

Family number.	Relationship to head of family.	Sex.	Age.	Conjugal condition.	Birthplace.	Birthplace of—	
						Father.	Mother.
205	Head	M.	41	Married...	Basilicata.......	Basilicata......	Basilicata......
	Wife..............	F.	40	Married...	Basilicata.......	Basilicata......	Basilicata......
	Daughter.........	F.	6	Single.....	Basilicata.......	Basilicata......	Basilicata......
	Stepdaughter.....	F.	5	Single.....	United States...	Basilicata......	Basilicata......
206	Head	M.	46	Married...	Basilicata.......	Basilicata......	Basilicata......
	Wife..............	F.	45	Married...	Basilicata.......	Basilicata......	Basilicata......
	Son	M.	14	Single.....	Basilicata.......	Basilicata......	Basilicata......
	Son	M.	9	Single.....	United States...	Basilicata......	Basilicata......
207	Head	M.	29	Married...	Abruzzo	Abruzzo	Abruzzo ....
	Wife..............	F.	20	Married...	Basilicata.......	Basilicata......	Basilicata......
	Daughter.........	F.	3	Single.....	United States...	Abruzzo	Basilicata......
208	Head	M.	37	Married...	Abruzzo	Abruzzo	Abruzzo ......
	Wife..............	F.	30	Married...	Campania.......	Campania.......	Campania......
	Son	M.	7	Single.....	Campania.......	Abruzzo	Campania......
209	Head	M.	35	Married...	Calabria	Calabria	Calabria ....
	Wife..............	F.	30	Married...	Calabria	Calabria	Calabria ....
	Son	M.	14	Single.....	Calabria	Calabria	Calabria ....
	Son	M.	3	Single.....	United States...	Calabria	Calabria ....
	Son	M.	1	Single.....	United States...	Calabria	Calabria ....
210	Head	M.	30	Married...	Calabria	Calabria	Calabria ....
	Wife..............	F.	23	Married...	Calabria	Calabria	Calabria ....
211	Head	M.	46	Married...	Campania.......	Campania.......	Campania......
	Wife..............	F.	36	Married...	Campania.......	Campania.......	Campania......
	Son	M.	12	Single.....	Campania.......	Campania.......	Campania......
	Daughter.........	F.	8	Single.....	United States...	Campania.......	Campania......
	Son	M.	7	Single.....	United States...	Campania.......	Campania......
	Daughter.........	F.	4	Single.....	United States...	Campania.......	Campania......
	Son	M.	1	Single.....	United States...	Campania.......	Campania......
	Lodger	M.	26	Married...	Campania.......	Campania.......	Campania......
212	Head	M.	33	Married...	Calabria	Calabria	Calabria ....
	Wife..............	F.	34	Married...	Calabria	Calabria	Calabria ....
	Son	M.	8	Single.....	Calabria	Calabria	Calabria ....
	Son	M.	4	Single.....	United States...	Calabria	Calabria ....
213	Head	M.	28	Married...	Basilicata.......	Basilicata......	Basilicata......
	Wife..............	F.	24	Married...	Basilicata.......	Basilicata......	Basilicata......
	Daughter.........	F.	3	Single.....	United States...	Basilicata......	Basilicata......
	Son	M.	2	Single.....	United States...	Basilicata......	Basilicata......
214	Head	M.	47	Married...	Basilicata.......	Basilicata......	Basilicata......
	Wife..............	F.	46	Married...	Basilicata.......	Basilicata......	Basilicata......
	Daughter.........	F.	8	Single.....	United States...	Basilicata......	Basilicata......
	Son	M.	6	Single.....	United States...	Basilicata......	Basilicata......
	Mother-in-law.....	F.	80	Widowed .	Basilicata.......	Basilicata......	Basilicata......
215	Head	M.	38	Married...	Basilicata.......	Basilicata......	Basilicata......
	Wife..............	F.	30	Married...	Basilicata.......	Basilicata......	Basilicata......
	Son	M.	4	Single.....	United States...	Basilicata......	Basilicata......
	Son	M.	1	Single.....	United States...	Basilicata......	Basilicata......
216	Head	M.	33	Married...	Sicily	Sicily	Sicily ....
	Wife..............	F.	37	Married...	Sicily	Sicily	Sicily ....
	Daughter.........	F.	13	Single.....	Sicily	Sicily	Sicily ....
	Son	M.	9	Single.....	Sicily	Sicily	Sicily ....
217	Head	M.	40	Married...	Campania.......	Campania.......	Campania......
	Wife..............	F.	26	Married...	Campania.......	Campania.......	Campania......
	Son	M.	11	Single.....	United States...	Campania.......	Campania......
	Son	M.	10	Single.....	United States...	Campania.......	Campania......
	Daughter.........	F.	8	Single.....	United States...	Campania.......	Campania......
	Son	M.	3	Single.....	United States...	Campania.......	Campania......
	Son	M.	*a*	Single.....	United States...	Campania.......	Campania......

a Not reported.
b Also worked as washerwoman four weeks, at $1 per week.
c Also worked as ragpicker three weeks, at $1.50 per week.
d Sick, disease not specified.

TABLE **I.**—GENERAL SOCIAL AND ECONOMIC CONDITION, BY FAMILIES AND INDIVIDUALS—Continued.

Years in U. S.	Natu- ral- ized.	Profession, trade, or occupation.	Hours of work per week.	Average weekly earn- ings.	Weeks em- ploy- ed.	Total yearly earn- ings.	Sick during year, defective, maimed, or deformed.
10	No...	Pants finisher	(a)	$0.75	4	$3	Foot, loss of one.
5	....	Housewife and pants fin- isher. (b)	66	.30	b 48	18	No.
5	....	At home					No.
....	....	At home					Rickets; bronchitis.
15	Yes..	Street sweeper (c)	60	7.50	c 25	192	(d)
10	....	Housewife					No.
10	....	Bootblack	(a)	.60	(a)	(a)	No.
....	....	Scholar					Injury by accident.
8	Yes..	Laborer	60	6.11	28	171	No.
11	....	Housewife and seamstress	78	1.20	26	31	No.
....	....	At home					Bronchitis.
8	Yes..	Laborer	60	7.50	10	75	No.
3	....	Housewife and seamstress	54	1.20	52	62	No.
3	....	At home					Fever, typhoid.
13	Yes..	Street sweeper (e)	60	7.50	e 19	155	No.
9	....	Housewife					No.
9	....	Scholar and bootblack	(a)	1.50	52	78	No.
....	....	At home					No.
....	....	At home					No.
12	Yes..	No occupation					Bronchitis; fever, not speci- fied.
3	....	Housewife					No.
11	Yes..	Street sweeper (f)	60	7.50	f 26	228	No.
11	....	Housewife					No.
11	. .....	Newsboy	36	1.00	47	47	Injury by accident.
....	....	Scholar					No.
....	....	Scholar					Fever, not specified.
....	....	At home					Fever, not specified.
....	....	At home					No.
3	No...	Laborer	54	6.90	(a)	(a)	No.
5	No...	Ragpicker (g)	(a)	1.50	g 26	107	Fever, typhoid.
6	....	Housewife					No.
5	....	Scholar					Rickets.
....	....	At home					Rickets; bronchitis.
8	Yes..	Ragpicker (g)	(a)	.90	g 17	83	No.
6	....	Housewife					No.
....	....	At home					Fever, not specified.
....	....	At home					Rickets.
14	Yes..	Street sweeper (h)	60	7.50	h 15	152	Fever, typhoid; consump- tion.
2	....	Housewife					Fever, typhoid.
....	....	Scholar					Rickets.
....	....	Scholar					No.
3	....	No occupation					Fever, typhoid.
8	Yes..	Merchant, rags	72	4.00	48	192	Fever, typhoid.
7	....	Housewife					Injury by accident.
....	....	At home					Injury by accident; rickets.
....	....	At home					No.
6	No...	Laborer	(a)	7.50	17	128	No.
6	....	Housewife and pants fin- isher.	(a)	.90	26	23	No.
6	....	Housework					Idiot.
6	....	Scholar					No.
16	Yes..	No occupation					Insane; dropsy.
20	....	Housewife					Childbirth.
....	....	Scholar and newsboy	30	.60	4	2	No.
....	....	Scholar and newsboy	30	.60	4	2	No.
....	....	Scholar					No.
....	....	At home					No.
....	....	At home					No.

e Also worked as ragpicker twelve weeks, at $1 per week.
f Also worked as ragpicker twenty-six weeks, at $1.25 per week.
g Also worked as laborer nine weeks, at $7.50 per week.
h Also worked as ragpicker thirteen weeks, at $3 per week.

TABLE **I.**—GENERAL SOCIAL AND ECONOMIC CONDITION, BY FAMILIES AND INDIVIDUALS—Continued.

Family number.	Relationship to head of family.	Sex.	Age.	Conjugal condition.	Birthplace.	Birthplace of—	
						Father.	Mother.
218	Cooperative	M.	33	Single	Campania	Campania	Campania
	Cooperative	M.	40	Single	Campania	Campania	Campania
	Cooperative	M.	29	Married	Campania	Campania	Campania
219	Head	M.	39	Married	Campania	Campania	Campania
	Wife	F.	37	Married	Campania	Campania	Campania
	Daughter	F.	13	Single	Campania	Campania	Campania
	Daughter	F.	6	Single	United States	Campania	Campania
	Son	M.	4	Single	United States	Campania	Campania
	Son	M.	3	Single	United States	Campania	Campania
	Daughter, adopted	F.	$\frac{5}{12}$	Single	United States	(a)	Campania
220	Head	M.	32	Married	Campania	Campania	Campania
	Wife	F.	33	Married	Campania	Campania	Campania
	Son	M.	11	Single	Campania	Campania	Campania
	Daughter	F.	8	Single	Campania	Campania	Campania
	Daughter	F.	4	Single	United States	Campania	Campania
	Son	M.	2	Single	United States	Campania	Campania
221	Head	M.	50	Married	Campania	Campania	Campania
	Wife	F.	45	Married	Campania	Campania	Campania
	Son	M.	22	Single	Campania	Campania	Campania
	Son	M.	21	Single	Campania	Campania	Campania
	Son	M.	14	Single	United States	Campania	Campania
	Daughter	F.	12	Single	United States	Campania	Campania
	Daughter	F.	10	Single	United States	Campania	Campania
222	Head	M.	29	Married	Campania	Campania	Campania
	Wife	F.	29	Married	Campania	Campania	Campania
	Daughter	F.	4	Single	United States	Campania	Campania
	Daughter	F.	2	Single	United States	Campania	Campania
	Son	M.	$\frac{7}{12}$	Single	United States	Campania	Campania
	Brother-in-law	M.	34	Single	Campania	Campania	Campania
223	Head	M.	28	Married	Campania	Campania	Campania
	Wife	F.	28	Married	Campania	Campania	Campania
	Son	M.	2	Single	United States	Campania	Campania
	Son	M.	1	Single	United States	Campania	Campania
224	Head	M.	30	Married	Basilicata	Basilicata	Basilicata
	Wife	F.	27	Married	Basilicata	Basilicata	Basilicata
	Son	M.	3	Single	United States	Basilicata	Basilicata
	Daughter	F.	$\frac{7}{12}$	Single	United States	Basilicata	Basilicata
	Boarder	M.	30	Single	Calabria	Calabria	Calabria
225	Head	M.	50	Married	Basilicata	Basilicata	Basilicata
	Wife	F.	44	Married	Basilicata	Basilicata	Basilicata
	Son	M.	15	Single	Basilicata	Basilicata	Basilicata
	Son	M.	13	Single	Basilicata	Basilicata	Basilicata
	Daughter	F.	8	Single	Basilicata	Basilicata	Basilicata
	Son	M.	7	Single	Basilicata	Basilicata	Basilicata
226	Head	M.	25	Married	Campania	Campania	Campania
	Wife	F.	22	Married	Basilicata	Basilicata	Basilicata
	Son	M.	6	Single	United States	Campania	Basilicata
	Daughter	F.	4	Single	United States	Campania	Basilicata
	Son	M.	$\frac{1}{12}$	Single	United States	Campania	Basilicata
227	Head	M.	26	Married	Sicily	Sicily	Sicily
	Wife	F.	21	Married	Sicily	Sicily	Sicily
	Daughter	F.	2	Single	United States	Sicily	Sicily
	Daughter	F.	1	Single	United States	Sicily	Sicily
	Brother-in-law	M.	28	Married	Sicily	Sicily	Sicily
	Sister-in-law	F.	26	Married	Sicily	Sicily	Sicily
	Niece	F.	2	Single	United States	Sicily	Sicily
228	Head	M.	24	Married	Sicily	Sicily	Sicily
	Wife	F.	20	Married	Sicily	Sicily	Sicily
	Son	M.	2	Single	United States	Sicily	Sicily
	Father-in-law	M.	50	Married	Sicily	Sicily	Sicily
	Brother-in-law	M.	17	Single	Sicily	Sicily	Sicily

a Not reported.

TABLE **I.**—GENERAL SOCIAL AND ECONOMIC CONDITION, BY FAMILIES AND INDIVIDUALS—Continued.

Years in U. S.	Naturalized.	Profession, trade, or occupation.	Hours of work per week.	Average weekly earnings.	Weeks employed.	Total yearly earnings.	Sick during year, defective, maimed, or deformed.
13	Yes..	Laborer....................	60	$8.00	13	$104	Pneumonia.
5	No...	Laborer....................	60	8.00	13	104	No.
4	No...	Laborer....................	60	7.50	13	98	Injury by accident.
11	No...	Mason, stone.............	48	20.00	9	180	Pneumonia.
6	......	Housewife and nurse.....	(a)	2.25	(a)	(a)	No.
6	......	Scholar					No.
......	......	Scholar					No.
......	......	At home.................					No.
......	......	At home.................					No.
......	......	At home.................					No.
8	Yes..	Laborer....................	48	9.00	13	117	No.
4	......	Housewife................					No.
4	......	Scholar					No.
4	......	Scholar					No.
......	......	At home.................					No.
......	......	At home.................					No.
20	Yes..	Retired					No.
20	......	Housewife................					No.
20	No...	Plaster cast maker.......	54	9.00	17	153	No.
20	No...	Baker's helper...........	48	4.00	52	208	No.
......	......	Scholar					No.
......	......	Scholar					No.
......	......	Scholar					No.
4	No...	Laborer....................	60	7.50	13	98	No.
.4	......	Housewife................					Childbirth.
......	......	At home.................					No.
......	......	At home.................					No.
......	......	At home.................					No.
14	Yes..	Laborer....................	60	7.50	17	128	No.
9	Yes..	Laborer....................	60	9.00	35	315	Rheumatism.
4	......	Housewife................					No.
......	......	At home.................					No.
......	......	At home.................					No.
8	Yes..	Tinker...................	60	3.00	52	156	No.
5	......	Housewife................					Childbirth.
......	......	At home.................					No.
13	Yes..	Laborer....................	60	7.50	22	165	No.
3	No...	Ragpicker	(a)	(a)	52	(a)	No.
2	......	Housewife................					No.
2	......	Scholar and knife factory employee.	60	3.00	52	156	No.
2	......	Scholar and knife factory employee. (b)	60	3.00	b17	(a)	No.
2	......	Scholar					No.
2	......	Scholar					No.
10	No...	Laborer....................	48	10.50	52	546	No.
7	......	Housewife................					Childbirth.
......	......	Scholar					No.
......	......	At home.................					No.
......	......	At home.................					No.
7	No...	Peddler, fruit............	66	1.50	52	78	No.
3	......	Housewife................					Cross-eyed.
......	......	At home.................					No.
......	......	At home.................					No.
5	No...	Peddler, fruit............	66	1.50	52	78	No.
5	......	Housework					No.
......	......	At home.................					No.
3	No...	Peddler, fruit............	(a)	2.40	52	125	No.
3	......	Housewife................					No.
......	......	At home.................					No.
4	No...	Peddler, fruit............	(a)	2.40	52	125	No.
½	......	No occupation...........					No.

b Also worked as ragpicker thirty-five weeks, wages not reported.

TABLE **I.**—GENERAL SOCIAL AND ECONOMIC CONDITION, BY FAMILIES AND INDIVIDUALS—Continued.

Family number.	Relationship to head of family.	Sex.	Age.	Conjugal condition.	Birthplace.	Birthplace of—	
						Father.	Mother.
229	Head	M.	28	Married	Sicily	Sicily	Sicily
	Wife	F.	21	Married	Sicily	Sicily	Sicily
	Son	M.	3	Single	United States	Sicily	Sicily
	Son	M.	2	Single	United States	Sicily	Sicily
	Daughter	F.	$\frac{1}{12}$	Single	United States	Sicily	Sicily
230	Head	M.	55	Married	Sicily	Sicily	Sicily
	Wife	F.	35	Married	Sicily	Sicily	Sicily
	Brother	M.	41	Married	Sicily	Sicily	Sicily
	Sister-in-law	F.	23	Married	Sicily	Sicily	Sicily
	Niece	F.	5	Single	United States	Sicily	Sicily
	Niece	F.	3	Single	United States	Sicily	Sicily
	Nephew	M.	1	Single	United States	Sicily	Sicily
231	Head	M.	41	Married	Sicily	Sicily	Sicily
	Wife	F.	35	Married	Sicily	Sicily	Sicily
	Son	M.	11	Single	Sicily	Sicily	Sicily
	Daughter	F.	9	Single	Sicily	Sicily	Sicily
	Daughter	F.	6	Single	United States	Sicily	Sicily
	Daughter	F.	4	Single	United States	Sicily	Sicily
	Daughter	F.	2	Single	United States	Sicily	Sicily
	Nephew	M.	34	Married	Sicily	Sicily	Sicily
	Niece	F.	23	Married	Sicily	Sicily	Sicily
	Uncle	M.	55	Widowed	Sicily	Sicily	Sicily
232	Head	M.	39	Married	Basilicata	Basilicata	Basilicata
	Wife	F.	38	Married	Basilicata	Basilicata	Basilicata
	Son	M.	15	Single	Basilicata	Basilicata	Basilicata
	Daughter	F.	10	Single	Basilicata	Basilicata	Basilicata
	Son	M.	8	Single	Basilicata	Basilicata	Basilicata
	Son	M.	5	Single	United States	Basilicata	Basilicata
	Daughter	F.	3	Single	United States	Basilicata	Basilicata
	Daughter	F.	$\frac{7}{12}$	Single	United States	Basilicata	Basilicata
233	Head	M.	25	Married	Basilicata	Basilicata	Basilicata
	Wife	F.	23	Married	Basilicata	Basilicata	Basilicata
	Stepdaughter	F.	8	Single	United States	Basilicata	Basilicata
	Father-in-law	M.	52	Married	Basilicata	Basilicata	Basilicata
234	Head	F.	45	Married	Campania	Campania	Campania
	Son-in-law	M.	32	Married	Campania	Campania	Campania
	Lodger	M.	38	Married	Abruzzo	Abruzzo	Abruzzo
	Lodger	M.	25	Single	Abruzzo	Abruzzo	Abruzzo
	Lodger	M.	52	Single	Campania	Campania	Campania
235	Head	M.	32	Married	Basilicata	Basilicata	Basilicata
	Wife	F.	32	Married	Basilicata	Basilicata	Basilicata
	Son	M.	10	Single	United States	Basilicata	Basilicata
	Son	M.	7	Single	United States	Basilicata	Basilicata
	Daughter	F.	5	Single	United States	Basilicata	Basilicata
	Son	M.	2	Single	United States	Basilicata	Basilicata
236	Head	M.	38	Married	Basilicata	Basilicata	Basilicata
	Wife	F.	28	Married	Basilicata	Basilicata	Basilicata
	Daughter	F.	5	Single	Basilicata	Basilicata	Basilicata
	Son	M.	$\frac{7}{12}$	Single	United States	Basilicata	Basilicata
237	Head	M.	28	Married	Calabria	Calabria	Calabria
	Wife	F.	24	Married	Calabria	Calabria	Calabria
238	Head	M.	39	Married	Basilicata	Basilicata	Basilicata
	Wife	F.	30	Married	Basilicata	Basilicata	Basilicata
	Son	M.	7	Single	United States	Basilicata	Basilicata
	Son	M.	2	Single	United States	Basilicata	Basilicata
239	Head	M.	27	Married	Calabria	Calabria	Calabria
	Wife	F.	24	Married	Calabria	Calabria	Calabria
	Son	M.	3	Single	United States	Calabria	Calabria
	Son	M.	$\frac{2}{12}$	Single	United States	Calabria	Calabria

a Also worked as foreman, laborers, nine weeks, at $12 per week.

TABLE **I.**—GENERAL SOCIAL AND ECONOMIC CONDITION, BY FAMILIES AND INDIVIDUALS—Continued.

Years in U. S.	Naturalized.	Profession, trade, or occupation.	Hours of work per week.	Average weekly earnings.	Weeks employed.	Total yearly earnings.	Sick during year, defective, maimed, or deformed.
9	Yes..	Peddler, fruit and vegetables. (a)	(b)	$9.00	a 43	$495	No.
13	......	Housewife.................					Childbirth
......	......	At home..............					No.
......	......	At home..............					No.
......	......	At home..............					No.
8	Yes..	Peddler, fruit..............	66	5.00	(b)	(b)	No.
8	......	Housewife............					No.
12	No...	Peddler, fruit..............	66	5.00	(b)	(b)	No.
6	......	Housework.................					No.
......	......	At home..............					No.
......	......	At home..............					No.
......	......	At home..............					No.
9	No...	Laborer..................	60	7.50	13	98	No.
7	......	Housewife and coat finisher.	60	2.40	52	125	No.
7	......	Scholar					No.
7	......	Scholar					No.
......	......	At home..............					No.
......	......	At home..............					Rickets.
......	......	At home..............					No.
9	No...	Laborer..................	60	7.50	13	98	No.
3	......	Housework.................					No.
8	No...	No occupation.............					Palsy.
8	Yes..	Street sweeper..........	60	7.50	22	165	No.
8	......	Housewife............					Childbirth.
8	......	Scholar and bartender....	72	3.00	52	156	No.
8	......	Scholar					No.
8	......	Scholar					Rickets.
......	......	At home..............					Rickets.
......	......	At home..............					No.
......	......	At home..............					No.
7	Yes..	Musician	(b)	(b)	52	(b)	No.
10	......	Housewife and dress finisher.	(b)	.75	52	39	No.
......	......	Scholar					No.
10	Yes..	No occupation					No.
15	......	Housewife and dress finisher.	(b)	.45	22	10	Bronchitis.
10	Yes..	Padrone	60	15.75	3	47	Rheumatism.
14	Yes..	Laborer..................	60	7.50	17	128	No.
12	Yes..	Laborer..................	60	7.50	22	165	No.
9	Yes..	No occupation					No.
27	Yes..	Packing-house employee..	(b)	9.00	52	468	Rheumatism.
11	......	Housewife............					Asthma.
......	......	Scholar					Bronchitis.
......	......	Scholar					Bronchitis.
......	......	Scholar					Bronchitis.
......	......	At home..............					Dyspepsia.
25	Yes..	Laborer..................	60	6.00	26	156	No.
4	......	Housewife............					Childbirth; abscess.
4	......	At home..............					Rickets.
......	......	At home..............					No.
9	Yes..	Marble polisher...........	(b)	(b)	46	(b)	Injury by accident.
7	......	Housewife and dressmaker.	(b)	(b)	52	(b)	No.
10	Yes..	Ragpicker	90	2.00	52	104	No.
8	......	Housewife............					Female complaint.
......	......	Scholar					Pneumonia.
......	......	At home..............					Rickets.
5	Yes..	Barber..................	75	4.00	13	52	No.
5	......	Housewife and macaroni maker.	60	3.00	13	39	Childbirth.
......	......	At home..............					No.
......	......	At home..............					No.

b Not reported.

TABLE **I.**—GENERAL SOCIAL AND ECONOMIC CONDITION, BY FAMILIES AND INDIVIDUALS—Continued.

Family number	Relationship to head of family.	Sex.	Age.	Conjugal condition.	Birthplace.	Birthplace of— Father.	Birthplace of— Mother.
240	Head	M.	36	Married...	Calabria	Calabria	Calabria
	Wife	F.	24	Married...	Calabria	Calabria	Calabria
	Son	M.	2	Single.....	United States...	Calabria	Calabria
	Son	M.	$\frac{3}{12}$	Single.....	United States...	Calabria	Calabria
241	Head	M.	33	Married...	Calabria	Calabria	Calabria
	Wife	F.	33	Married...	Calabria	Calabria	Calabria
	Son	M.	9	Single.....	Calabria	Calabria	Calabria
	Daughter	F.	8	Single.....	Calabria	Calabria	Calabria
	Son	M.	2	Single.....	United States...	Calabria	Calabria
	Daughter	F.	$\frac{7}{12}$	Single.....	United States...	Calabria	Calabria
242	Head	M.	51	Married...	Calabria	Calabria	Calabria
	Wife	F.	43	Married...	Calabria	Calabria	Calabria
243	Head	M.	48	Married...	Calabria	Calabria	Calabria
	Wife	F.	33	Married...	Calabria	Calabria	Calabria
	Son	M.	12	Single.....	Calabria	Calabria	Calabria
	Son	M.	3	Single.....	United States...	Calabria	Calabria
	Son	M.	$\frac{10}{12}$	Single.....	United States...	Calabria	Calabria
244	Head	M.	27	Married...	Calabria	Calabria	Calabria
	Wife	F.	19	Married...	Calabria	Calabria	Calabria
245	Head	M.	40	Married...	Calabria	Calabria	Calabria
	Wife	F.	35	Married...	Calabria	Calabria	Calabria
	Son	M.	14	Single.....	Calabria	Calabria	Calabria
	Daughter	F.	7	Single.....	United States	Calabria	Calabria
	Son	M.	3	Single.....	United States...	Calabria	Calabria
	Daughter	F.	$\frac{1}{12}$	Single.....	United States...	Calabria	Calabria
246	Head	M.	23	Married...	Abruzzo	Abruzzo	Abruzzo
	Wife	F.	18	Married...	Abruzzo	Abruzzo	Abruzzo
247	Head	M.	60	Married...	Abruzzo	Abruzzo	Abruzzo
	Wife	F.	60	Married...	Abruzzo	Abruzzo	Abruzzo
	Son	M.	27	Married...	Abruzzo	Abruzzo	Abruzzo
	Son	M.	15	Single.....	Abruzzo	Abruzzo	Abruzzo
	Daughter-in-law ..	F.	27	Married...	Abruzzo	Abruzzo	Abruzzo
248	Cooperative	M.	24	Married...	Calabria	Calabria	Calabria
	Cooperative	M.	25	Married...	Calabria	Calabria	Calabria
	Cooperative	M.	27	Married...	Calabria	Calabria	Calabria
	Cooperative	M.	31	Married...	Calabria	Calabria	Calabria
249	Head	M.	38	Married...	Calabria	Calabria	Calabria
	Wife	F.	36	Married...	Calabria	Calabria	Calabria
	Daughter	F.	13	Single.....	Calabria	Calabria	Calabria
	Son	M.	8	Single.....	United States...	Calabria	Calabria
	Son	M.	$\frac{3}{12}$	Single.....	United States...	Calabria	Calabria
250	Head	M.	30	Married...	Sicily	Sicily	Sicily
	Wife	F.	27	Married...	Sicily	Sicily	Sicily
	Daughter	F.	5	Single.....	United States...	Sicily	Sicily
	Son	M.	$\frac{1}{12}$	Single.....	United States...	Sicily	Sicily
251	Head	M.	24	Married...	Basilicata	Basilicata	Basilicata
	Wife	F.	17	Married...	Basilicata	Basilicata	Basilicata
252	Head	M.	50	Married...	Basilicata	Basilicata	Basilicata
	Wife	F.	54	Married...	Basilicata	Basilicata	Basilicata
	Son	M.	22	Single.....	Basilicata	Basilicata	Basilicata
	Daughter	F.	20	Single.....	Basilicata	Basilicata	Basilicata
253	Head	M.	42	Married...	Basilicata	Basilicata	Basilicata
	Wife	F.	38	Married...	Basilicata	Basilicata	Basilicata
	Son	M.	16	Single.....	Basilicata	Basilicata	Basilicata
	Daughter	F.	6	Single.....	United States...	Basilicata	Basilicata
	Daughter	F.	4	Single.....	United States...	Basilicata	Basilicata
	Daughter	F.	2	Single.....	United States...	Basilicata	Basilicata
	Son	M.	$\frac{1}{12}$	Single.....	United States...	Basilicata	Basilicata

a Not reported.
b Also worked as laborer nine weeks, at $7.50 per week.
c Also worked as pants finisher, time and wages not reported.

TABLE **I.**—GENERAL SOCIAL AND ECONOMIC CONDITION, BY FAMILIES
AND INDIVIDUALS—Continued.

Years in U. S.	Naturalized.	Profession, trade, or occupation.	Hours of work per week.	Average weekly earnings.	Weeks employed.	Total yearly earnings.	Sick during year, defective, maimed, or deformed.
13	Yes..	Saloon keeper.............	(a)	(a)	22	(a)	Dyspepsia.
7	......	Housewife................	......	......	......	......	Childbirth.
......	......	At home.................	......	......	......	......	No.
......	......	At home.................	......	......	......	......	No.
6	No...	Ragpicker (b).............	(a)	$1.80	b 13	$91	No.
3	......	Housewife and pants finisher.	(a)	.75	26	20	Childbirth.
3	......	Scholar..................	......	......	......	......	No.
3	......	At home.................	......	......	......	......	No.
......	......	At home.................	......	......	......	......	No.
......	......	At home.................	......	......	......	......	No.
22	No...	Grain elevator laborer (c).	60	9.00	c 13	(a)	No.
7	......	Housewife and pants finisher.	(a)	(a)	(a)	(a)	No.
11	No...	Laborer (d)...............	60	7.50	d 26	257	No.
6	......	Housewife and pants finisher.	(a)	.75	52	39	Childbirth.
6	......	Scholar..................	......	......	......	......	No.
......	......	At home.................	......	......	......	......	No.
......	......	At home.................	......	......	......	......	No.
14	Yes..	Padrone	60	(a)	17	(a)	No.
5	......	Housewife................	......	......	......	......	No.
16	Yes..	Laborer..................	(a)	8.25	13	107	No.
11	......	Housewife................	......	......	......	......	Childbirth.
11	......	Scholar and newsboy	28	1.75	52	91	No.
......	......	Scholar..................	......	......	......	......	No.
......	......	At home.................	......	......	......	......	No.
......	......	At home.................	......	......	......	......	No.
13	Yes..	Street sweeper...........	60	7.50	30	225	No.
3	......	Housewife................	......	......	......	......	Pneumonia.
3	No...	Laborer..................	70	8.75	13	114	No.
3	......	Housewife................	......	......	......	......	No.
7	Yes..	Laborer..................	70	7.70	26	200	No.
3	......	Bootblack	105	2.80	3	8	No.
3	......	Housework	......	......	......	......	No.
3	No...	Laborer (e)..............	60	7.20	e 11	(a)	No.
3	No...	Laborer (e)..............	60	7.20	e 11	(a)	No.
3	No...	Laborer (e)..............	60	7.20	e 11	(a)	No.
5	Yes..	Street sweeper...........	48	9.00	4	36	Skin, disease of.
12	Yes..	Barber..................	91	7.00	52	364	No.
9	......	Housewife................	......	......	......	......	Childbirth; rheumatism.
9	......	Scholar..................	......	......	......	......	No.
......	......	Scholar..................	......	......	......	......	No.
......	......	At home.................	......	......	......	......	No.
9	No...	Peddler, fruit............	90	14.00	52	728	No.
14	......	Housewife................	......	......	......	......	Childbirth.
......	......	At home.................	......	......	......	......	No.
......	......	At home.................	......	......	......	......	No.
(a)	Yes..	Carpenter	48	12.00	37	444	No.
10	......	Housewife................	......	.	......	......	Bladder, inflammation of.
16	Yes..	No occupation	......	......	......	......	No.
8	......	Housewife and skirt finisher.	(a)	1.25	52	65	No.
8	No...	Tailor	48	3.50	30	105	Bronchitis.
8	......	Skirt finisher	(a)	1.25	52	65	No.
11	Yes..	Shoemaker	(a)	2.00	52	104	Eye, loss of one.
11	......	Housewife................	......	......	......	......	Childbirth.
11	......	Messenger	42	3.00	52	156	No.
......	......	Scholar..................	......	......	......	......	No.
......	......	At home.................	......	......	......	......	No.
......	......	At home.................	......	......	......	......	No.
......	......	At home.................	......	......	......	......	No.

d Also worked as ragpicker twenty-six weeks, at $2.40 per **week.**
e Also worked at another occupation, details not reported.

TABLE **I.**—GENERAL SOCIAL AND ECONOMIC CONDITION, BY FAMILIES AND INDIVIDUALS—Continued.

Family number.	Relationship to head of family.	Sex.	Age.	Conjugal condition.	Birthplace.	Birthplace of— Father.	Birthplace of— Mother.
254	Head	M.	25	Married	Campania	Campania	Campania
	Wife	F.	25	Married	Campania	Campania	Campania
	Daughter	F.	3	Single	United States	Campania	Campania
	Daughter	F.	1½	Single	United States	Campania	Campania
255	Head	M.	49	Married	Basilicata	Basilicata	Basilicata
	Wife	F.	39	Married	Basilicata	Basilicata	Basilicata
	Son	M.	18	Single	Basilicata	Basilicata	Basilicata
	Daughter	F.	14	Single	United States	Basilicata	Basilicata
	Daughter	F.	10	Single	United States	Basilicata	Basilicata
	Son	M.	8	Single	United States	Basilicata	Basilicata
	Son	M.	7	Single	United States	Basilicata	Basilicata
	Daughter	F.	3	Single	United States	Basilicata	Basilicata
	Son	M.	1	Single	United States	Basilicata	Basilicata
256	Head	M.	47	Married	Calabria	Calabria	Calabria
	Wife	F.	47	Married	Calabria	Calabria	Calabria
	Daughter	F.	4	Single	United States	Calabria	Calabria
	Daughter	F.	2	Single	United States	Calabria	Calabria
	Nephew	M.	22	Single	Calabria	Calabria	Calabria
257	Head	M.	27	Married	Basilicata	Basilicata	Basilicata
	Wife	F.	20	Married	Basilicata	Basilicata	Basilicata
	Son	M.	4	Single	United States	Basilicata	Basilicata
	Daughter	F.	2	Single	United States	Basilicata	Basilicata
258	Head	M.	42	Married	Basilicata	Basilicata	Basilicata
	Wife	F.	32	Married	Basilicata	Basilicata	Basilicata
	Son	M.	6	Single	United States	Basilicata	Basilicata
	Son	M.	3	Single	United States	Basilicata	Basilicata
259	Head	M.	39	Married	Calabria	Calabria	Calabria
	Wife	F.	30	Married	Calabria	Calabria	Calabria
	Son	M.	12	Single	Calabria	Calabria	Calabria
	Daughter	F.	9	Single	United States	Calabria	Calabria
	Son	M.	6	Single	United States	Calabria	Calabria
	Son	M.	2	Single	United States	Calabria	Calabria
260	Head	M.	30	Married	Campania	Campania	Campania
	Wife	F.	31	Married	Campania	Campania	Campania
	Son	M.	5	Single	United States	Campania	Campania
	Son	M.	4	Single	United States	Campania	Campania
	Daughter	F.	3	Single	United States	Campania	Campania
	Son	M.	1	Single	United States	Campania	Campania
	Father	M.	60	Married	Campania	Campania	Campania
	Mother	F.	60	Married	Campania	Campania	Campania
	Brother	M.	21	Single	Campania	Campania	Campania
261	Head	M.	39	Married	Abruzzo	Abruzzo	Abruzzo
	Wife	F.	32	Married	Abruzzo	Abruzzo	Abruzzo
	Son	M.	10	Single	Abruzzo	Abruzzo	Abruzzo
	Daughter	F.	1	Single	United States	Abruzzo	Abruzzo
	Sister	F.	24	Married	Abruzzo	Abruzzo	Abruzzo
	Brother	M.	32	Married	Abruzzo	Abruzzo	Abruzzo
	Brother	M.	37	Married	Abruzzo	Abruzzo	Abruzzo
	Brother-in-law	M.	36	Married	Abruzzo	Abruzzo	Abruzzo
	Lodger	M.	26	Single	Abruzzo	Abruzzo	Abruzzo
262	Head	M.	45	Married	Sicily	Sicily	Sicily
	Wife	F.	35	Married	Sicily	Sicily	Sicily
	Son	M.	17	Single	Sicily	Sicily	Sicily
	Son	M.	11	Single	Sicily	Sicily	Sicily
	Son	M.	5	Single	Sicily	Sicily	Sicily
	Daughter	F.	2	Single	United States	Sicily	Sicily
	Daughter	F.	¾	Single	United States	Sicily	Sicily
	Sister	F.	33	Married	Sicily	Sicily	Sicily
	Brother-in-law	M.	28	Married	Sicily	Sicily	Sicily
	Niece	F.	6	Single	Sicily	Sicily	Sicily
	Niece	F.	2	Single	United States	Sicily	Sicily
263	Head	M.	38	Married	Campania	Campania	Campania
	Wife	F.	34	Married	Campania	Campania	Campania
	Daughter	F.	8	Single	Campania	Campania	Campania
	Daughter	F.	5	Single	Campania	Campania	Campania

a Not reported.

TABLE I.—GENERAL SOCIAL AND ECONOMIC CONDITION, BY FAMILIES AND INDIVIDUALS—Continued.

Years in U.S.	Natu-ral-ized.	Profession, trade, or occupation.	Hours of work per week.	Average weekly earn-ings.	Weeks em-ploy-ed.	Total yearly earn-ings.	Sick during year, defective, maimed, or deformed.
8	Yes..	Laborer....................	48	$5.25	43	$226	Injury by accident.
6	......	Housewife.................					Childbirth.
......	......	At home...................					No.
......	......	At home...................					No.
17	Yes..	Ragpicker.................	48	1.50	52	78	Rheumatism.
15	......	Housewife.................					No.
15	......	No occupation.............					No.
......	......	Housework.................					No.
......	......	Scholar...................					No.
......	......	Scholar...................					Deafness, partial.
......	......	Scholar...................					Deafness, partial.
......	......	At home...................					No.
......	......	At home...................					No.
5	No...	Laborer....................	(a)	6.60	22	145	Toe, loss of one.
5	......	Housewife.................					No.
......	......	At home...................					Rickets.
......	......	At home...................					Rickets.
4	No...	Laborer....................	60	9.00	13	117	No.
8	Yes..	Laborer....................	60	7.50	26	195	No.
8	......	Housewife.................					No.
......	......	At home...................					No.
......	......	At home...................					No.
21	Yes..	No occupation.............					Injury by accident.
8	......	Housewife.................					No.
......	......	At home...................					No.
......	......	At home...................					No.
14	Yes..	Laborer....................	60	7.50	9	68	No.
11	......	Housewife and mer-chant, groceries.	(a)	(a)	52	(a)	Female complaint.
11	......	Scholar and newsboy.....	12	.60	52	31	No.
—	......	Scholar...................					No.
......	......	Scholar...................					No.
......	......	At home...................					No.
6	Yes..	Laborer....................	60	7.50	26	195	No.
6	......	Housewife.................					No.
......	......	At home...................					No.
......	......	At home...................					No.
......	......	At home...................					Rickets.
......	......	At home...................					No.
4	No...	Wood picker..............	(a)	6.00	52	312	No.
4	......	Housewife.................					No.
6	Yes..	Barber....................	82	5.00	52	260	No.
9	Yes..	Laborer....................	60	9.00	7	63	Injury by accident.
4	......	Housewife.................					No.
4	......	Scholar...................					Feeble-minded.
......	......	At home...................					Bronchitis.
5	......	Housework................					Rheumatism.
8	Yes..	Laborer....................	60	9.00	30	270	No.
8	Yes..	Laborer....................	60	9.00	30	270	No.
9	No...	Laborer....................	60	9.00	26	234	No.
4	No...	Laborer....................	60	9.00	30	270	Diphtheria.
6	No...	Laborer....................	55	3.30	30	99	No.
5	......	Housewife.................					Childbirth.
5	......	Barber....................	93	3.50	52	182	No.
5	......	No occupation.............					No.
5	......	At home...................					No.
......	......	At home...................					No.
......	......	At home...................					No.
3	......	Housework................					No.
6	No...	Laborer....................	55	3.30	30	99	No.
3	......	At home...................					No.
......	......	At home...................					No.
6	Yes..	Ragpicker (b).............	(a)	2.40	b 39	191	No.
4	......	Housewife.................					No.
4	......	At home...................					No.
4	......	At home...................					No.

b Also worked as laborer thirteen weeks, at $7.50 per week.

TABLE I.—GENERAL SOCIAL AND ECONOMIC CONDITION, BY FAMILIES AND INDIVIDUALS—Continued.

Family number.	Relationship to head of family.	Sex.	Age.	Conjugal condition.	Birthplace.	Birthplace of—	
						Father.	Mother.
263	Daughter	F.	4	Single	United States	Campania	Campania
	Son	M.	2	Single	United States	Campania	Campania
	Lodger	M.	28	Married	Calabria	Calabria	Calabria
	Lodger	F.	17	Married	Campania	Campania	Campania
	Lodger	M.	₇⁄₁₂	Single	United States	Calabria	Campania
264	Head	M.	43	Married	Calabria	Calabria	Calabria
	Wife	F.	38	Married	Calabria	Calabria	Calabria
	Son	M.	6	Single	United States	Calabria	Calabria
	Daughter	F.	5	Single	United States	Calabria	Calabria
	Nephew	M.	24	Married	Calabria	Calabria	Calabria
	Lodger	M.	41	Married	Calabria	Calabria	Calabria
	Lodger	M.	28	Married	Calabria	Calabria	Calabria
265	Head	M.	23	Married	Campania	Campania	Campania
	Wife	F.	16	Married	Campania	Campania	Campania
266	Head	M.	26	Married	Calabria	Calabria	Calabria
	Wife	F.	20	Married	Calabria	Calabria	Calabria
	Cousin	M.	30	Married	Calabria	Calabria	Calabria
	Cousin	M.	28	Single	Calabria	Calabria	Calabria
	Boarder	M.	32	Widowed	Calabria	Calabria	Calabria
267	Head	M.	40	Married	Calabria	Calabria	Calabria
	Wife	F.	35	Married	Calabria	Calabria	Calabria
	Son	M.	13	Single	Calabria	Calabria	Calabria
	Daughter	F.	7	Single	United States	Calabria	Calabria
	Daughter	F.	3	Single	United States	Calabria	Calabria
	Brother	M.	45	Married	Calabria	Calabria	Calabria
	Nephew	M.	25	Single	Calabria	Calabria	Calabria
268	Head	M.	45	Married	Calabria	Calabria	Calabria
	Wife	F.	24	Married	Calabria	Calabria	Calabria
	Father-in-law	M.	50	Married	Calabria	Calabria	Calabria
	Stepmother-in-law	F.	60	Married	Calabria	Calabria	Calabria
	Brother	M.	30	Single	Calabria	Calabria	Calabria
	Brother-in-law	M.	40	Single	Calabria	Calabria	Calabria
	Lodger	M.	42	Widowed	Calabria	Calabria	Calabria
	Lodger	M.	27	Married	Calabria	Calabria	Calabria
269	Head	M.	33	Married	Calabria	Calabria	Calabria
	Wife	F.	38	Married	Calabria	Calabria	Calabria
	Son	M.	14	Single	Calabria	Calabria	Calabria
	Daughter	F.	9	Single	Calabria	Calabria	Calabria
270	Head	M.	40	Married	Abruzzo	Abruzzo	Abruzzo
	Wife	F.	41	Married	Abruzzo	Abruzzo	Abruzzo
	Daughter	F.	13	Single	Abruzzo	Abruzzo	Abruzzo
	Son	M.	10	Single	Abruzzo	Abruzzo	Abruzzo
	Son	M.	6	Single	Abruzzo	Abruzzo	Abruzzo
	Son	M.	3	Single	United States	Abruzzo	Abruzzo
	Daughter	F.	1	Single	United States	Abruzzo	Abruzzo
	Brother-in-law	M.	28	Married	Abruzzo	Abruzzo	Abruzzo
	Lodger	M.	28	Single	Abruzzo	Abruzzo	Abruzzo
	Lodger	M.	45	Married	Abruzzo	Abruzzo	Abruzzo
271	Head	M.	45	Married	Calabria	Calabria	Calabria
	Wife	F.	43	Married	Calabria	Calabria	Calabria
	Son	M.	17	Single	Calabria	Calabria	Calabria
	Daughter	F.	5	Single	United States	Calabria	Calabria
	Son	M.	4	Single	United States	Calabria	Calabria
	Daughter	F.	2	Single	United States	Calabria	Calabria
	Brother-in-law	M.	25	Single	Calabria	Calabria	Calabria
272	Head	M.	40	Married	Basilicata	Basilicata	Basilicata
	Wife	F.	38	Married	Basilicata	Basilicata	Basilicata
	Son	M.	8	Single	United States	Basilicata	Basilicata
	Daughter	F.	6	Single	United States	Basilicata	Basilicata
	Daughter	F.	2	Single	United States	Basilicata	Basilicata
	Son	M.	₃⁄₁₂	Single	United States	Basilicata	Basilicata
273	Head	M.	23	Married	Campania	Campania	Campania
	Wife	F.	22	Married	Campania	Campania	Campania
	Mother	F.	60	Widowed	Campania	Campania	Campania

a Also worked as laborer seven weeks, at $7.50 per week.
b Not reported.
c Also worked as laborer three weeks, at $6.90 per week.

TABLE I.—GENERAL SOCIAL AND ECONOMIC CONDITION, BY FAMILIES AND INDIVIDUALS—Continued.

Years in U.S.	Naturalized.	Profession, trade, or occupation.	Hours of work per week	Average weekly earnings.	Weeks employed.	Total yearly earnings.	Sick during year, defective, maimed, or deformed.
		At home					No.
		At home					Bronchitis.
5	Yes..	Laborer	70	$8.15	22	$179	No.
8		Housework					Childbirth.
		At home					No.
15	Yes..	Laborer	60	7.50	17	128	Boils.
7		Housewife					Pneumonia.
		Scholar					Diphtheria.
		At home					No.
5	Yes..	No occupation					Bronchitis.
13	Yes..	Laborer	60	4.80	7	34	No.
3	No...	Railroad laborer	70	8.15	26	212	No.
12	Yes..	Lumber shover	60	7.50	52	390	No.
8		Housewife					No.
6	Yes..	Laborer	60	7.50	13	98	No.
1½		Housewife					No.
4	No...	Laborer	60	7.00	13	91	No.
6	Yes..	Laborer	60	7.50	13	98	No.
6	Yes..	Laborer	60	7.50	13	98	No.
10	No...	Ragpicker (a)	(b)	2.00	a 45	143	No.
9		Housewife					No.
9		Scholar and ragpicker	(b)	(b)	26	(b)	No.
		Scholar					No.
		At home					No.
9	Yes..	Laborer	60	6.00	13	78	No.
5	Yes..	Laborer	60	6.00	13	78	No.
6	No...	Ragpicker (c)	(b)	1.20	c 45	75	No.
6		Housewife and pants finisher.	(b)	.72	9	6	No.
8	No...	Ragpicker (c)	(b)	1.20	c 45	75	No.
4	No...	Pants finisher	(b)	.72	9	6	No.
8	No...	No occupation					Fever, not specified.
10	No...	Laborer	(b)	(b)	(b)	(b)	No.
5	No...	Ragpicker (d)	(b)	1.20	d 40	120	No.
1	No...	Ragpicker (c)	(b)	1.20	c 45	75	No.
4	No...	Laborer	60	7.20	6	43	No.
3		Housewife					No.
3		Scholar					No.
3		Scholar					No.
5	Yes..	Laborer	60	9.00	11	99	Injury by accident.
5		Housewife					No.
5		Scholar and musician	(b)	1.20	17	20	Fever, not specified; lame.
5		Scholar					No.
5		Scholar					No.
		At home					No.
		At home					No.
5	Yes..	Laborer	48	9.00	9	81	Kidneys, disease of.
5	No...	Laborer	60	10.50	17	179	No.
4	No...	Laborer	60	9.00	11	99	No.
13	Yes..	Ragpicker (e)	(b)	2.00	e 38	181	No.
8		Housewife					No.
8		Newsboy	18	.90	17	15	No.
		At home					Rickets.
		At home					Rickets.
		At home					Rickets.
7	Yes..	Laborer	60	8.10	13	105	No.
13	Yes..	Ragpicker (f)	(b)	1.50	f 17	93	Fever, not specified.
9		Housewife					Childbirth.
		Scholar					No.
		Scholar					Rickets.
		At home					No.
		At home					No.
3	No..	Ragpicker	54	3.00	52	156	No.
2		Housewife					No.
5		No occupation					No.

d Also worked as laborer nine weeks, at $8.00 per week.
e Also worked as laborer thirteen weeks, at $8.10 per week.
f Also worked as laborer nine weeks, at $7.50 per week.

TABLE **I.**—GENERAL SOCIAL AND ECONOMIC CONDITION, BY FAMILIES AND INDIVIDUALS—Continued.

Family number.	Relationship to head of family.	Sex.	Age.	Conjugal condition.	Birthplace.	Birthplace of— Father.	Birthplace of— Mother.
274	Head	M.	48	Married...	Sicily	Sicily	Sicily
	Wife	F.	40	Married...	Sicily	Sicily	Sicily
	Daughter	F.	15	Single....	Sicily	Sicily	Sicily
	Daughter	F.	12	Single....	Sicily	Sicily	Sicily
	Daughter	F.	9	Single....	Sicily	Sicily	Sicily
	Daughter	F.	6	Single....	Sicily	Sicily	Sicily
	Son	M.	5	Single....	United States...	Sicily	Sicily
	Daughter	F.	3	Single....	United States...	Sicily	Sicily
	Daughter	F.	$\frac{1}{2}$	Single....	United States...	Sicily	Sicily
275	Head	M.	38	Married...	Basilicata	Basilicata	Basilicata
	Wife	F.	22	Married...	Basilicata	Basilicata	Basilicata
	Daughter	F.	6	Single....	United States...	Basilicata	Basilicata
	Daughter	F.	3	Single....	United States...	Basilicata	Basilicata
	Son	M.	$1\frac{1}{2}$	Single....	United States...	Basilicata	Basilicata
	Cousin	M.	30	Single....	Calabria	Calabria	Calabria
276	Head	M.	34	Married...	Abruzzo	Abruzzo	Abruzzo
	Wife	F.	28	Married...	Abruzzo	Abruzzo	Abruzzo
	Son	M.	9	Single....	Belgium	Abruzzo	Abruzzo
	Son	M.	3	Single....	United States...	Abruzzo	Abruzzo
	Son	M.	$\frac{1}{12}$	Single....	United States...	Abruzzo	Abruzzo
277	Head	M.	33	Married...	Abruzzo	Abruzzo	Abruzzo
	Wife	F.	28	Married...	Abruzzo	Abruzzo	Abruzzo
	Daughter	F.	8	Single....	Abruzzo	Abruzzo	Abruzzo
	Son	M.	$1\frac{1}{2}$	Single....	United States...	Abruzzo	Abruzzo
278	Head	M.	47	Married...	Basilicata	Basilicata	Basilicata
	Wife	F.	41	Married...	Basilicata	Basilicata	Basilicata
	Son	M.	4	Single....	United States...	Basilicata	Basilicata
	Daughter	F.	2	Single....	United States...	Basilicata	Basilicata
279	Head	M.	34	Married...	Basilicata	Basilicata	Basilicata
	Wife	F.	39	Married...	Basilicata	Basilicata	Basilicata
	Daughter	F.	2	Single....	United States...	Basilicata	Basilicata
280	Head	M.	31	Married...	Calabria	Calabria	Calabria
	Wife	F.	20	Married...	Calabria	Calabria	Calabria
	Daughter	F.	1	Single....	United States...	Calabria	Calabria
281	Head	M.	50	Married...	Calabria	Calabria	Calabria
	Wife	F.	30	Married...	Calabria	Calabria	Calabria
	Daughter	F.	15	Single....	Calabria	Calabria	Calabria
	Son	M.	3	Single....	United States...	Calabria	Calabria
	Mother-in-law	F.	48	Married...	Calabria	Calabria	Calabria
	Lodger	M.	40	Married...	Calabria	Calabria	Calabria
282	Head	M.	23	Married...	Basilicata	Basilicata	Basilicata
	Wife	F.	26	Married...	Basilicata	Basilicata	Basilicata
	Son	M.	2	Single....	United States...	Basilicata	Basilicata
	Son	M.	$\frac{1}{12}$	Single....	United States...	Basilicata	Basilicata
283	Head	M.	45	Married...	Campania	Campania	Campania
	Wife	F.	32	Married...	Campania	Campania	Campania
	Daughter	F.	14	Single....	Campania	Campania	Campania
	Daughter	F.	8	Single....	Campania	Campania	Campania
	Daughter	F.	$\frac{1}{12}$	Single....	United States...	Campania	Campania
284	Head	M.	60	Married...	Basilicata	Basilicata	Basilicata
	Wife	F.	52	Married...	Basilicata	Basilicata	Basilicata
285	Head	M.	50	Married...	Basilicata	Basilicata	Basilicata
	Wife	F.	40	Married...	Basilicata	Basilicata	Basilicata
	Son	M.	1	Single....	United States...	Basilicata	Basilicata
286	Cooperative	M.	41	Married...	Sicily	Sicily	Sicily
	Cooperative	M.	48	Married...	Sicily	Sicily	Sicily
287	Head	M.	29	Married...	Calabria	Calabria	Calabria
	Wife	F.	26	Married...	Basilicata	Basilicata	Basilicata
	Cousin	M.	33	Married...	Calabria	Calabria	Calabria
	Cousin	M.	27	Single....	Calabria	Calabria	Calabria

a Not reported.

TABLE **I.**—GENERAL SOCIAL AND ECONOMIC CONDITION, BY FAMILIES AND INDIVIDUALS—Continued.

Years in U.S.	Naturalized.	Profession, trade, or occupation.	Hours of work per week.	Average weekly earnings.	Weeks employed.	Total yearly earnings.	Sick during year, defective, maimed, or deformed.
6	No...	Peddler, fruit..............	(a)	$2.40	52	$125	No.
5	....	Housewife.................					Childbirth.
5	....	Housework.................					No.
5	....	No occupation.............					No.
5	....	Scholar...................					Eye, loss of one.
5	....	At home..................					No.
....	....	Scholar...................					No.
....	....	At home..................					No.
....	....	At home..................					No.
15	Yes..	Hod carrier..............	60	9.00	13	117	No.
15	....	Housewife.................					Childbirth.
....	....	Scholar...................					No.
....	....	At home..................					No.
....	....	At home..................					No.
7	Yes..	Laborer..................	60	6.60	13	86	No.
6	No...	Laborer..................	60	7.50	13	98	Consumption.
6	....	Housewife.................					Childbirth.
6	....	Scholar...................					No.
....	....	At home..................					No.
....	....	At home..................					No.
4	No...	Laborer (b)...............	60	5.00	b 42	228	No.
4	....	Housewife.................					Childbirth; congestion of liver.
4	....	Scholar...................					No.
....	....	At home..................					No.
14	No...	Ragpicker...............	(a)	3.00	52	156	No.
6	....	Housewife.................					Fever, malarial.
....	....	At home..................					No.
....	....	At home...................					No.
13	Yes..	Laborer..................	60	7.50	26	195	No.
8	....	Housewife.................					No.
....	....	At home..................					No.
5	No...	Laborer..................	60	7.50	22	165	No.
3	....	Housewife.................					No.
....	....	At home..................					Fever, malarial.
10	No...	Tailor	(a)	4.50	52	234	No.
6	....	Housewife and seamstress	(a)	2.00	40	80	No.
6	....	Scholar and seamstress ...	47½	2.50	26	65	No.
....	....	At home..................					Convulsions.
3	....	Housework.................					No.
9	No...	Bootblack	(a)	2.50	9	23	No.'
16	Yes..	Laborer..................	(a)	(a)	52	(a)	Eye, loss of one.
3	....	Housewife.................					Childbirth.
....	....	At home..................					No.
....	....	At home..................					No.
8	Yes..	Furniture finisher	60	5.00	46	230	No.
4	....	Housewife and dressmaker	(a)	.60	(a)	(a)	Childbirth.
4	....	Scholar............. ..					No.
4	....	Scholar..................					No.
....	....	At home..................					No.
10	No...	No occupation					Feeble-minded.
10	....	Housewife.................					Lame.
20	Yes..	Street sweeper............	60	7.50	26	195	No.
16	....	Housewife.................					Bronchitis.
....	....	At home..................					Rickets; bronchitis.
1	No...	Laborer...................	55	3.00	7	21	Rheumatism.
6	No...	Laborer...................	55	3.00	14	42	Bowels, inflammation of.
10	No..	Shoemaker................	72	3.00	52	156	No.
7	....	Housewife.................					Bowels, inflammation of
6	No..	Shoemaker	84	4.00	52	208	No.
4	No..	Shoemaker	90	6.00	52	312	No.

b Also worked as peddler, ice cream, nine weeks, at $2 per **week.**

TABLE **I.**—GENERAL SOCIAL AND ECONOMIC CONDITION, BY FAMILIES AND INDIVIDUALS—Continued.

Family number.	Relationship to head of family.	Sex.	Age.	Conjugal condition.	Birthplace.	Birthplace of— Father.	Birthplace of— Mother.
288	Head	M.	31	Married	Basilicata	Basilicata	Basilicata
	Wife	F.	28	Married	Basilicata	Basilicata	Basilicata
	Daughter	F.	6	Single	Basilicata	Basilicata	Basilicata
	Daughter	F.	2	Single	United States	Basilicata	Basilicata
	Son	M.	$\frac{5}{12}$	Single	United States	Basilicata	Basilicata
	Brother-in-law	M.	26	Married	Basilicata	Basilicata	Basilicata
	Lodger	M.	34	Married	Basilicata	Basilicata	Basilicata
289	Head	M.	44	Married	Calabria	Calabria	Calabria
	Wife	F.	36	Married	Calabria	Calabria	Calabria
	Son	M.	18	Single	Calabria	Calabria	Calabria
	Daughter	F.	16	Single	Calabria	Calabria	Calabria
	Nephew	M.	21	Single	Calabria	Calabria	Calabria
	Boarder	M.	44	Married	Calabria	Calabria	Calabria
290	Head	M.	50	Married	Calabria	Calabria	Calabria
	Wife	F.	46	Married	Calabria	Calabria	Calabria
	Son	M.	21	Single	Calabria	Calabria	Calabria
291	Head	M.	30	Married	Calabria	Calabria	Calabria
	Wife	F.	28	Married	Calabria	Calabria	Calabria
	Daughter	F.	6	Single	Calabria	Calabria	Calabria
	Brother-in-law	M.	44	Single	Calabria	Calabria	Calabria
292	Cooperative	M.	28	Single	Calabria	Calabria	Calabria
	Cooperative	M.	40	Married	Calabria	Calabria	Calabria
293	Cooperative	M.	35	Married	Calabria	Calabria	Calabria
	Cooperative	M.	27	Single	Calabria	Calabria	Calabria
	Cooperative	M.	21	Single	Calabria	Calabria	Calabria
	Cooperative	M.	39	Married	Calabria	Calabria	Calabria
294	Head	M.	35	Married	Basilicata	Basilicata	Basilicata
	Wife	F.	35	Married	Basilicata	Basilicata	Basilicata
	Daughter	F.	12	Single	Basilicata	Basilicata	Basilicata
	Daughter	F.	7	Single	United States	Basilicata	Basilicata
	Son	M.	4	Single	United States	Basilicata	Basilicata
	Daughter	F.	1	Single	United States	Basilicata	Basilicata
295	Cooperative	M.	30	Married	Calabria	Calabria	Calabria
	Cooperative	M.	26	Married	Calabria	Calabria	Calabria
	Cooperative	M.	38	Married	Calabria	Calabria	Calabria
	Cooperative	M.	27	Married	Calabria	Calabria	Calabria
296	Head	M.	38	Married	Campania	Campania	Campania
	Wife	F.	27	Married	Campania	Campania	Campania
	Daughter	F.	5	Single	United States	Campania	Campania
	Son	M.	1	Single	United States	Campania	Campania
297	Head	M.	40	Single	Calabria	Calabria	Calabria
	Mother	F.	64	Widowed	Calabria	Calabria	Calabria
298	Head	M.	37	Married	Campania	Campania	Campania
	Wife	F.	40	Married	Campania	Campania	Campania
	Daughter	F.	3	Single	United States	Campania	Campania
	Son	M.	$\frac{8}{12}$	Single	United States	Campania	Campania
299	Head	M.	45	Married	Campania	Campania	Campania
	Wife	F.	38	Married	Campania	Campania	Campania
	Son	M.	7	Single	United States	Campania	Campania
	Daughter	F.	4	Single	United States	Campania	Campania
300	Head	M.	40	Married	Campagna di Roma.	Campagna di Roma.	Campagna di Roma.
	Wife	F.	36	Married	Campagna di Roma.	Campagna di Roma.	Campagna di Roma.
	Son	M.	13	Single	United States	Campagna di Roma.	Campagna di Roma.
	Son	M.	12	Single	United States	Campagna di Roma.	Campagna di Roma.

a Not reported.
b Also worked as bartender seventeen weeks, at $6 per week.
c Also worked as pants finisher eight weeks, at $0.75 per week.

TABLE **I.**—GENERAL SOCIAL AND ECONOMIC CONDITION, BY FAMILIES AND INDIVIDUALS—Continued.

Years in U. S.	Naturalized.	Profession, trade, or occupation.	Hours of work per week.	Average weekly earnings.	Weeks employed.	Total yearly earnings.	Sick during year, defective, maimed, or deformed.
6	Yes..	Laborer	60	$7.50	13	$98	No.
4		Housewife					Childbirth.
4		At home					No.
		At home					No.
		At home					No.
1/12	No...	No occupation					No.
1/4	No...	Laborer	60	9.00	41	369	Injury by accident.
15	Yes..	Baker	60	5.00	52	260	No.
9		Housewife and pants finisher.	(a)	1.60	52	83	No.
9		Baker	60	5.00	52	260	No.
9		Pants finisher	(a)	(a)	(a)	(a)	No.
5	No...	Bootblack and newsboy (b)	(a)	6.00	b 35	312	No.
15	Yes..	Baker	60	5.00	52	260	No.
8	Yes..	Laborer (c)	(a)	7.50	c 16	126	No.
5		Housewife and seamstress	60	.75	11	8	No.
4	No...	Laborer (d)	60	8.10	d 11	(a)	No.
6	Yes..	Laborer	60	7.50	19	143	No.
2/12		Housewife					No.
3/12		At home					No.
13	Yes..	Foreman, laborers	60	10.50	13	137	No.
7	Yes..	Laborer (e)	(a)	8.10	e 17	178	No.
7	No...	Laborer	(a)	7.50	22	165	No.
7	Yes..	Laborer	60	8.40	19	160	Indigestion.
6	Yes..	Laborer	60	8.40	24	202	No.
5	Yes..	Laborer	60	7.50	24	180	No.
5	Yes..	Laborer	60	7.50	24	180	No.
13	Yes..	Wood sawyer (f)	(a)	.75	f 37	127	No.
9		Housewife					No.
9		Wood picker	15	.75	52	39	No.
		At home					No.
		At home					Rickets; bronchitis.
		At home					No.
6	Yes..	Laborer	(a)	8.00	15	120	No.
3	No...	Laborer	60	6.60	15	99	No.
5	No...	Laborer	(a)	8.00	15	120	No.
5	Yes..	Laborer	60	6.10	15	92	No.
14	Yes..	Laborer	48	7.50	15	113	No.
5		Housewife					Female complaint.
		At home					No.
		At home					Bronchitis.
13	Yes..	Mason's helper	48	7.50	23	173	Asthma.
10		Housewife					Fever, not specified.
9	Yes..	Street sweeper	54	9.00	52	468	No.
6		Housewife					Childbirth.
		At home					No.
		At home					No.
15	Yes..	Street sweeper	60	7.50	26	195	No.
8		Housewife and cloak finisher.	42	1.19	9	11	No.
		Scholar					No.
		At home					No.
18	Yes..	Laborer	60	8.40	23	193	Rheumatism.
16		Housewife and coat finisher.	60	1.50	13	20	No.
		Scholar					Bowlegs.
		Scholar					No.

d Also worked as pants finisher, time and wages not reported.
e Also worked as bartender eight weeks, at $5 per week.
f Also worked as laborer fifteen weeks, at $6.60 per week.

TABLE I.—GENERAL SOCIAL AND ECONOMIC CONDITION, BY FAMILIES AND INDIVIDUALS—Continued.

Family number.	Relationship to head of family.	Sex.	Age.	Conjugal condition.	Birthplace.	Birthplace of—	
						Father.	Mother.
301	Head	M.	46	Married...	Basilicata	Basilicata	Basilicata
	Wife	F.	46	Married...	Basilicata	Basilicata	Basilicata
	Son	M.	10	Single	United States	Basilicata	Basilicata
	Son	M.	9	Single	United States	Basilicata	Basilicata
	Son	M.	3	Single	United States	Basilicata	Basilicata
	Son	M.	2	Single	United States	Basilicata	Basilicata
	Son	M.	7/12	Single	United States	Basilicata	Basilicata
302	Head	M.	46	Married...	Campania	Campania	Campania
	Wife	F.	36	Married...	Campania	Campania	Campania
	Son	M.	11	Single	United States	Campania	Campania
	Son	M.	8	Single	United States	Campania	Campania
	Daughter	F.	6	Single	United States	Campania	Campania
	Son	M.	4	Single	United States	Campania	Campania
	Son	M.	2	Single	United States	Campania	Campania
303	Cooperative	M.	41	Married...	Campania	Campania	Campania
	Cooperative	M.	33	Married...	Campania	Campania	Campania
	Cooperative	M.	32	Married...	Campania	Campania	Campania
	Cooperative	M.	41	Married...	Campania	Campania	Campania
	Cooperative	M.	33	Married...	Campania	Campania	Campania
	Cooperative	M.	22	Married...	Campania	Campania	Campania
304	Head	M.	36	Married...	Abruzzo	Abruzzo	Abruzzo
	Wife	F.	36	Married...	Abruzzo	Abruzzo	Abruzzo
	Daughter	F.	18	Married...	Abruzzo	Abruzzo	Abruzzo
	Son	M.	8/12	Single	United States	Abruzzo	Abruzzo
	Son-in-law	M.	28	Married...	Abruzzo	Abruzzo	Abruzzo
	Grandson	M.	8/12	Single	United States	Abruzzo	Abruzzo
	Boarder	M.	16	Single	Abruzzo	Abruzzo	Abruzzo
305	Head	M.	63	Married...	Campania	Campania	Campania
	Wife	F.	30	Married...	Campania	Campania	Campania
	Son	M.	7	Single	Campania	Campania	Campania
	Daughter	F.	1	Single	United States	Campania	Campania
	Lodger	M.	25	Single	Campania	Campania	Campania
	Lodger	M.	60	Married...	Abruzzo	Abruzzo	Abruzzo
	Lodger	M.	25	Single	Abruzzo	Abruzzo	Abruzzo
306	Head	M.	44	Married...	Campania	Campania	Campania
	Daughter	F.	18	Married.	Campania	Campania	Campania
	Son-in-law	M.	24	Married...	Campania	Campania	Campania
307	Head	M.	34	Married...	Basilicata	Basilicata	Basilicata
	Wife	F.	24	Married...	Basilicata	Basilicata	Basilicata
	Daughter	F.	7	Single	United States	Basilicata	Basilicata
	Son	M.	5	Single	United States	Basilicata	Basilicata
	Daughter	F.	3	Single	United States	Basilicata	Basilicata
	Son	M.	7/12	Single	United States	Basilicata	Basilicata
	Lodger	F.	48	Married...	Basilicata	Basilicata	Basilicata
308	Head	M.	45	Married...	Basilicata	Basilicata	Basilicata
	Wife	F.	35	Married...	Basilicata	Basilicata	Basilicata
	Son	M.	18	Single	Basilicata	Basilicata	Basilicata
	Son	M.	15	Single	Basilicata	Basilicata	Basilicata
	Son	M.	11	Single	Basilicata	Basilicata	Basilicata
	Lodger	M.	27	Single	Basilicata	Basilicata	Basilicata
	Lodger	M.	40	Married...	Basilicata	Basilicata	Basilicata
	Lodger	M.	42	Married...	Basilicata	Basilicata	Basilicata
309	Head	M.	38	Married...	Abruzzo	Abruzzo	Abruzzo
	Wife	F.	38	Married...	Abruzzo	Abruzzo	Abruzzo
	Daughter	F.	11	Single	Abruzzo	Abruzzo	Abruzzo
310	Head	M.	32	Married...	Abruzzo	Abruzzo	Abruzzo
	Wife	F.	31	Married...	Abruzzo	Abruzzo	Abruzzo
311	Cooperative	M.	48	Single	Campania	Campania	Campania
	Cooperative	M.	47	Widowed.	Basilicata	Basilicata	Basilicata
312	Cooperative	M.	30	Single	Basilicata	Basilicata	Basilicata
	Cooperative	M.	45	Single	Basilicata	Basilicata	Basilicata
	Cooperative	M.	34	Single	Basilicata	Basilicata	Basilicata
	Cooperative	M.	38	Single	Basilicata	Basilicata	Basilicata

a Not reported.
b Also worked as laborer six weeks, at $7.50 per week.

TABLE **I.**—GENERAL SOCIAL AND ECONOMIC CONDITION, BY FAMILIES AND INDIVIDUALS—Continued.

Years in U.S.	Naturalized.	Profession, trade, or occupation.	Hours of work per week.	Average weekly earnings.	Weeks employed.	Total yearly earnings.	Sick during year, defective, maimed, or deformed.
12	Yes..	Ragpicker	36	$1.80	52	$94	Rheumatism.
11	......	Housewife.................	......	......	......	......	Childbirth.
......	......	Scholar	......	......	......	......	No.
......	......	Scholar	......	......	......	......	No.
......	......	At home..................	......	......	......	......	No.
......	......	At home..................	......	......	......	......	No.
......	......	At home..................	......	......	......	......	No.
16	Yes..	Laborer...................	54	7.50	30	225	No.
16	......	Housewife.................	......	......	......	......	No.
......	......	Scholar	......	......	......	......	No.
......	......	Scholar	......	......	......	......	Bronchitis.
......	......	Scholar	......	......	......	......	Bronchitis.
......	......	At home..................	......	......	......	......	Bronchitis.
......	......	At home..................	......	......	......	......	Bronchitis.
7	Yes .	Laborer...................	60	13.50	13	176	No.
8	Yes..	Laborer...................	60	9.00	17	153	Fever, typhoid.
6	Yes..	Railroad laborer	60	6.60	13	86	No.
8	Yes..	Laborer...................	60	7.50	13	98	No.
8	Yes..	Laborer...................	60	7.50	13	98	No.
$\frac{1}{12}$	No...	No occupation	......	......	......	......	No.
9	Yes..	Laborer...................	48	9.60	9	86	No.
3	......	Housewife	......	......	......	......	Childbirth.
3	......	Housework	......	......	......	......	Childbirth.
......	......	At home..................	......	......	......	......	No.
9	Yes..	Laborer...................	48	9.60	9	86	No.
......	......	At home..................	......	......	......	......	No.
$\frac{1}{12}$	......	No occupation	......	......	......	......	No.
6	No...	Laborer...................	60	7.50	11	83	No.
3	......	Housewife	......	......	......	......	Syphilis.
3	......	Scholar	......	......	......	......	No.
......	......	At home..................	......	......	......	......	Syphilis.
3	No...	Laborer...................	60	6.00	9	54	No.
(a)	No...	Laborer...................	(a)	(a)	(a)	(a)	No.
(a)	No...	Laborer...................	(a)	(a)	(a)	(a)	Humpback.
4	No...	Tailor....................	60	7.00	26	182	No.
4	......	Housewife and tailoress...	60	6.00	26	156	No.
4	No...	Laborer...................	60	6.72	52	349	No.
10	Yes..	Laborer...................	60	6.72	22	148	No.
8	......	Housewife.................	......	......	......	......	Childbirth.
......	......	Scholar	......	......	......	......	No.
......	......	Scholar	......	......	......	......	No.
......	......	At home..................	......	......	......	......	No.
......	......	At home..................	......	......	......	......	No.
10	......	Washerwoman	(a)	1.00	(a)	(a)	No.
9	No...	Laborer...................	60	9.00	13	117	No.
3	......	Housewife.................	......	......	......	......	No.
5	......	Bootblack	(a)	(a)	(a)	(a)	No.
3	......	Scholar	......	......	......	......	No.
3	......	Scholar	......	......	......	......	No.
5	No...	Laborer...................	60	8.25	26	215	No.
7	No...	Laborer...................	60	9.00	13	117	No.
9	Yes..	Laborer...................	60	9.00	6	54	No.
9	Yes..	No occupation	......	......	......	......	Diphtheria.
$\frac{5}{12}$	......	Housewife.................	......	......	......	......	No.
$\frac{5}{12}$	......	Housework	......	......	......	......	No.
6	No...	Laborer...................	60	6.00	17	102	No.
$\frac{5}{12}$	......	Housewife.................	......	......	......	......	Syphilis; loss of one eye.
6	Yes..	Street sweeper (b).........	(a)	9.00	b 29	306	No.
14	No...	Laborer...................	60	7.50	9	68	No.
5	Yes..	Laborer...................	60	7.50	11	83	No.
5	Yes..	Laborer...................	60	7.50	11	83	No.
14	Yes..	Tinker (c).................	(a)	3.00	c 41	206	No.
10	Yes..	Scissors grinder (d).......	(a)	2.40	d 35	237	No.

c Also worked as laborer eleven weeks, at $7.50 per week.
d Also worked as street sweeper seventeen weeks, at $9 per week.

TABLE I.—GENERAL SOCIAL AND ECONOMIC CONDITION, BY FAMILIES AND INDIVIDUALS—Continued.

Family number.	Relationship to head of family.	Sex.	Age.	Conjugal condition.	Birthplace.	Birthplace of— Father.	Birthplace of— Mother.
313	Head	M.	40	Married	Basilicata	Basilicata	Basilicata
	Wife	F.	49	Married	Basilicata	Basilicata	Basilicata
	Son	M.	5	Single	Basilicata	Basilicata	Basilicata
	Daughter	F.	1/12	Single	United States	Basilicata	Basilicata
314	Cooperative	M.	73	Widowed	Basilicata	Basilicata	Basilicata
	Cooperative	M.	52	Widowed	Basilicata	Basilicata	Basilicata
	Cooperative	M.	45	Married	Abruzzo	Abruzzo	Abruzzo
	Cooperative	M.	48	Married	Basilicata	Basilicata	Basilicata
	Cooperative	M.	30	Married	Sicily	Sicily	Sicily
315	Head	M.	38	Married	Basilicata	Basilicata	Basilicata
	Wife	F.	37	Married	Basilicata	Basilicata	Basilicata
	Son	M.	14	Single	Basilicata	Basilicata	Basilicata
	Son	M.	5	Single	United States	Basilicata	Basilicata
	Son	M.	3	Single	United States	Basilicata	Basilicata
316	Head	M.	50	Married	Campania	Campania	Campania
	Wife	F.	40	Married	Campania	Campania	Campania
	Son	M.	19	Single	Campania	Campania	Campania
	Daughter	F.	9	Single	Campania	Campania	Campania
	Boarder	M.	50	Married	Campania	Campania	Campania
317	Head	M.	32	Married	Campania	Campania	Campania
	Wife	F.	32	Married	Campania	Campania	Campania
	Son	M.	10	Single	Campania	Campania	Campania
	Daughter	F.	7	Single	Campania	Campania	Campania
	Son	M.	2	Single	United States	Campania	Campania
318	Head	M.	40	Married	Basilicata	Basilicata	Basilicata
	Wife	F.	27	Married	Basilicata	Basilicata	Basilicata
	Son	M.	1	Single	United States	Basilicata	Basilicata
319	Head	M.	35	Married	Abruzzo	Abruzzo	Abruzzo
	Wife	F.	25	Married	Abruzzo	Abruzzo	Abruzzo
	Son	M.	5	Single	United States	Abruzzo	Abruzzo
	Daughter	F.	1/12	Single	United States	Abruzzo	Abruzzo
320	Head	M.	26	Married	Campania	Campania	Campania
	Wife	F.	17	Married	Campania	Campania	Campania
	Son	M.	1/12	Single	United States	Campania	Campania
	Father	M.	52	Married	Campania	Campania	Campania
	Mother	F.	50	Married	Campania	Campania	Campania
321	Head	M.	30	Married	Abruzzo	Abruzzo	Abruzzo
322	Cooperative	M.	23	Single	Campania	Campania	Campania
	Cooperative	M.	26	Single	Campania	Campania	Campania
323	Cooperative	M.	32	Married	Abruzzo	Abruzzo	Abruzzo
	Cooperative	M.	36	Married	Abruzzo	Abruzzo	Abruzzo
	Cooperative	M.	37	Single	Abruzzo	Abruzzo	Abruzzo
	Cooperative	M.	32	Single	Abruzzo	Abruzzo	Abruzzo
324	Head	M.	41	Married	Campania	Campania	Campania
325	Head	F.	40	Widowed	Sicily	Sicily	Sicily
	Daughter	F.	17	Single	Sicily	Sicily	Sicily
	Daughter	F.	12	Single	Sicily	Sicily	Sicily
	Son	M.	9	Single	United States	Sicily	Sicily
	Son	M.	4	Single	United States	Sicily	Sicily
	Son	M.	1	Single	United States	Sicily	Sicily
326	Head	M.	45	Married	Sicily	Sicily	Sicily
	Wife	F.	41	Married	Sicily	Sicily	Sicily
	Son	M.	16	Single	Sicily	Sicily	Sicily
	Daughter	F.	7	Single	Sicily	Sicily	Sicily
	Son	M.	5	Single	Sicily	Sicily	Sicily
	Son	M.	3	Single	United States	Sicily	Sicily
	Daughter	F.	1	Single	United States	Sicily	Sicily
327	Head	M.	28	Married	Campania	Campania	Campania
	Wife	F.	24	Married	Campania	Campania	Campania
	Son	M.	4	Single	Campania	Campania	Campania
	Daughter	F.	2	Single	United States	Campania	Campania
	Daughter	F.	1/12	Single	United States	Campania	Campania

a Not reported.   b Also worked as cigar maker twenty-six weeks, wages not reported.

TABLE **I.**—GENERAL SOCIAL AND ECONOMIC CONDITION, BY FAMILIES
AND INDIVIDUALS—Continued.

Years in U.S.	Naturalized.	Profession, trade, or occupation.	Hours of work per week.	Average weekly earnings.	Weeks employed.	Total yearly earnings.	Sick during year, defective, maimed, or deformed.
5	No...	No occupation					Epilepsy.
4		Housewife					Childbirth.
4		Scholar					Rickets.
		At home					Debility, general.
10	No...	Merchant, groceries	(a)	(a)	(a)	(a)	Consumption.
10	No...	Laborer	60	$7.50	11	$83	No.
15	Yes..	Laborer	48	9.00	15	135	Rheumatism.
5	No...	Tinker	48	1.40	9	13	Rheumatism.
4	No...	Peddler, fruit	72	(a)	52	(a)	No.
12	Yes..	Railroad laborer	60	7.00	52	364	No.
10		Housewife					No.
10		Scholar and water carrier	60	6.00	4	24	No.
		Scholar					No.
		At home					No.
7	Yes..	Laborer	60	7.50	17	128	Injury by accident.
12½		Housewife					No.
7		Laborer	60	7.50	22	165	Diphtheria.
12½		At home					No.
3	No...	Laborer	60	7.50	13	98	Rheumatism.
7	Yes..	Laborer (b)	(a)	9.00	b 26	(a)	No.
3		Housewife					No.
3		Scholar					No.
3		Scholar					No.
		At home					No.
14	Yes..	Peddler, eggs	30	1.50	52	78	No.
2		Housewife					No.
		At home					No.
8	No...	Laborer	60	6.72	39	262	Bronchitis.
6		Housewife					Childbirth; female complaint.
		At home					Rickets; typhoid fever.
		At home					No.
12	Yes..	Street sweeper	48	9.00	17	153	No.
15		Housewife					Childbirth.
		At home					No.
12	No...	No occupation					No.
8		Housework					No.
4	No...	Laborer	60	9.00	9	81	Dyspepsia.
6	Yes..	Hospital employee	(a)	(a)	32	(a)	No.
6	Yes..	Laborer	60	7.50	13	98	Fever, malarial.
7	Yes..	Laborer	48	13.50	35	473	No.
17	Yes..	Laborer	60	9.00	22	198	No.
7	Yes..	Laborer	60	9.00	9	81	No.
5	Yes..	No occupation					Dyspepsia.
7	Yes..	Laborer	60	(a)	14	(a)	No.
10		Housewife and pants finisher.	(a)	1.92	30	58	No.
10		Pants finisher	(a)	1.92	30	58	No.
10		Housework					No.
		Scholar					No.
		At home					No.
		At home					No.
5	No...	Laborer	60	7.50	17	128	Fever, malarial.
5		Housewife					No.
5		Newsboy	90	1.80	26	47	Arm, loss of one.
5		Scholar					No.
5		At home					Rickets.
		At home					Rickets.
		At home					No.
4	No...	Ragpicker (c)	(a)	1.25	c 30	185	No.
3		Housewife					Childbirth.
3		At home					No.
		At home					Diarrhea, chronic.
		At home					No.

c Also worked as laborer twenty-two weeks, at $6.72 per week.

TABLE I.—GENERAL SOCIAL AND ECONOMIC CONDITION, BY FAMILIES AND INDIVIDUALS—Continued.

Family number.	Relationship to head of family.	Sex.	Age.	Conjugal condition.	Birthplace.	Birthplace of—	
						Father.	Mother.
328	Head	M.	35	Married...	Basilicata	Basilicata	Basilicata
	Wife	F.	20	Married...	Basilicata	Basilicata	Basilicata
	Daughter	F.	2	Single	United States	Basilicata	Basilicata
	Lodger	M.	30	Single	Basilicata	Basilicata	Basilicata
	Lodger	M.	(b)	Single	Basilicata	Basilicata	Basilicata
329	Head	M.	50	Married...	Basilicata	Basilicata	Basilicata
	Wife	F.	40	Married...	Basilicata	Basilicata	Basilicata
	Son	M.	16	Single	Basilicata	Basilicata	Basilicata
	Daughter	F.	14	Single	Basilicata	Basilicata	Basilicata
	Son	M.	8	Single	United States	Basilicata	Basilicata
	Daughter	F.	5	Single	United States	Basilicata	Basilicata
	Son	M.	$\frac{1}{12}$	Single	United States	Basilicata	Basilicata
330	Cooperative	M.	48	Married...	Calabria	Calabria	Calabria
	Cooperative	M.	48	Married...	Calabria	Calabria	Calabria
331	Head	M.	49	Married...	Basilicata	Basilicata	Basilicata
	Wife	F.	45	Married...	Basilicata	Basilicata	Basilicata
	Son	M.	19	Single	Basilicata	Basilicata	Basilicata
	Daughter	F.	14	Single	United States	Basilicata	Basilicata
	Daughter	F.	12	Single	United States	Basilicata	Basilicata
	Daughter	F.	9	Single	United States	Basilicata	Basilicata
	Daughter	F.	7	Single	United States	Basilicata	Basilicata
332	Head	M.	35	Married...	Calabria	Calabria	Calabria
	Wife	F.	21	Married...	Calabria	Calabria	Calabria
	Daughter	F.	4	Single	United States	Calabria	Calabria
	Son	M.	2	Single	United States	Calabria	Calabria
	Daughter	F.	$\frac{1}{12}$	Single	United States	Calabria	Calabria
333	Head	M.	33	Married...	Campania	Campania	Campania
	Wife	F.	30	Married...	Campania	Campania	Campania
	Son	M.	8	Single	Campania	Campania	Campania
	Daughter	F.	1	Single	United States	Campania	Campania
	Son	M.	1	Single	United States	Campania	Campania
334	Head	M.	33	Married...	Campania	Campania	Campania
	Wife	F.	33	Married...	Campania	Campania	Campania
	Son	M.	11	Single	United States	Campania	Campania
	Daughter	F.	7	Single	United States	Campania	Campania
	Daughter	F.	5	Single	United States	Campania	Campania
	Son	M.	3	Single	United States	Campania	Campania
	Son	M.	1	Single	United States	Campania	Campania
335	Head	F.	34	Widowed	Basilicata	Basilicata	Basilicata
	Son	M.	16	Single	Basilicata	Basilicata	Basilicata
	Daughter	F.	12	Single	United States	Basilicata	Basilicata
	Son	M.	10	Single	United States	Basilicata	Basilicata
	Son	M.	7	Single	United States	Basilicata	Basilicata
336	Head	M.	30	Married...	Basilicata	Basilicata	Basilicata
	Wife	F.	32	Married...	Basilicata	Basilicata	Basilicata
	Daughter	F.	2	Single	United States	Basilicata	Basilicata
337	Head	M.	60	Married...	Campania	Campania	Campania
	Wife	F.	37	Married...	Campania	Campania	Campania
	Son	M.	15	Single	Campania	Campania	Campania
	Daughter	F.	6	Single	United States	Campania	Campania
	Son	M.	4	Single	United States	Campania	Campania
	Daughter	F.	2	Single	United States	Campania	Campania
	Nephew	M.	17	Single	Campania	Campania	Campania
	Boarder	M.	(b)	Married...	Abruzzo	Abruzzo	Abruzzo
338	Head	M.	60	Married...	Campania	Campania	Campania
	Wife	F.	56	Married...	Campania	Campania	Campania
	Son	M.	22	Single	Campania	Campania	Campania
	Daughter	F.	16	Single	Campania	Campania	Campania
339	Cooperative	M.	50	Married...	Calabria	Calabria	Calabria
	Cooperative	M.	45	Married...	Calabria	Calabria	Calabria
	Cooperative	M.	35	Married...	Calabria	Calabria	Calabria
	Cooperative	M.	35	Married...	Calabria	Calabria	Calabria

a Also worked as laborer thirteen weeks, at $7.50 per week.

TABLE **I.**—GENERAL SOCIAL AND ECONOMIC CONDITION, BY FAMILIES AND INDIVIDUALS—Continued.

Years in U.S.	Naturalized.	Profession, trade, or occupation.	Hours of work per week.	Average weekly earnings.	Weeks employed.	Total yearly earnings.	Sick during year, defective, maimed, or deformed.
5	No...	Newsboy (a)	(b)	$1.50	a 39	$156	No.
7	......	Housewife	......	......	......	......	Cross-eyed.
......	......	At home	......	......	......	......	No.
6	Yes..	Hill boy	70	7.50	52	390	No.
2	No...	No occupation	......	......	......	......	No.
15	Yes..	Laborer	48	13.50	26	351	No.
9	......	Housewife	......	......	......	......	Childbirth.
9	......	No occupation	......	......	......	......	No.
9	......	Macaroni maker	60	3.00	52	156	No.
......	......	Scholar	......	......	......	......	No.
......	......	At home	......	......	......	......	No.
......	......	At home	......	......	......	......	No.
3	No...	Railroad laborer	60	6.60	9	59	No.
3	No...	Laborer	60	6.60	15	99	No.
15	Yes..	Laborer	60	6.60	17	112	No.
15	......	Housewife and saloon keeper.	(b)	(b)	(b)	(b)	No.
15	......	Bartender	(b)	(b)	(b)	(b)	No.
......	......	Housework	......	......	......	......	Feeble-minded.
......	......	Scholar	......	......	......	......	No.
......	......	At home	......	......	......	......	No.
......	......	Scholar	......	......	......	......	No.
17	Yes..	Laborer	60	6.72	26	175	Eyes, inflammation of both.
6	......	Housewife	......	......	......	......	Childbirth.
......	......	At home	......	......	......	......	No.
......	......	At home	......	......	......	......	Injury by accident.
......	......	At home	......	......	......	......	No.
7	No...	Laborer	60	7.00	52	364	No.
6	......	Housewife	......	......	......	......	No.
6	......	Scholar	......	......	......	......	No.
......	......	At home	......	......	......	......	No.
......	......	At home	......	......	......	......	No.
15	Yes..	Street sweeper	48	9.00	4	36	Injury by accident.
15	......	Housewife	......	......	......	......	No.
......	......	Scholar	......	......	......	......	Fever, typhoid.
......	......	Scholar	......	......	......	......	No.
......	......	At home	......	......	......	......	No.
......	......	At home	......	......	......	......	Fever, typhoid.
......	......	At home	......	......	......	......	No.
16	......	Housewife and ragpicker	(b)	.90	52	47	No.
16	......	Bootblack	105	2.00	52	104	No.
......	......	Scholar and macaroni maker.	60	1.50	9	14	No.
......	......	Scholar	......	......	......	......	No.
......	......	Scholar	......	......	......	......	No.
12	Yes..	Laborer	60	9.00	13	117	Pneumonia.
3	......	Housewife	......	......	......	......	No.
......	......	At home	......	......	......	......	No.
12	Yes..	Laborer	60	9.00	4	36	Injury by accident.
12	......	Housewife	......	......	......	......	No.
12	......	Newsboy	71	2.00	52	104	No.
......	......	Scholar	......	......	......	......	No.
......	......	At home	......	......	......	......	No.
......	......	At home	......	......	......	......	No.
5	......	Newsboy	71	2.00	52	104	No.
(b)	Yes..	Street sweeper	48	9.00	26	234	No.
12	Yes..	Laborer	60	7.50	9	68	No.
4	......	Housewife	......	......	......	......	No.
6	Yes..	Newsboy	78	(b)	52	(b)	No.
4	......	Macaroni maker	60	3.00	52	156	No.
3	No...	Laborer	(b)	7.15	13	93	No.
5	Yes..	Laborer	60	8.10	22	178	No.
5	Yes..	Laborer	60	7.50	6	45	Fever, typhoid.
3	No...	Laborer	60	7.50	26	195	No.

b Not reported.

TABLE **I.**—GENERAL SOCIAL AND ECONOMIC CONDITION, BY FAMILIES AND INDIVIDUALS—Continued.

Family number.	Relationship to head of family.	Sex.	Age.	Conjugal condition.	Birthplace.	Birthplace of— Father.	Mother.
339	Cooperative	M.	45	Married...	Calabria	Calabria	Calabria ....
	Cooperative	M.	40	Married...	Calabria	Calabria	Calabria ....
	Cooperative	M.	15	Single.....	Calabria	Calabria	Calabria ....
	Cooperative	M.	15	Single.....	Calabria	Calabria	Calabria ....
340	Head	M.	35	Married...	Campania.......	Campania......	Campania......
	Wife..............	F.	25	Married...	Campania.......	Campania......	Campania......
	Daughter.........	F.	4	Single.....	United States...	Campania......	Campania......
	Daughter.........	F.	2	Single.....	United States...	Campania......	Campania......
	Son	M.	$\frac{1}{12}$	Single.....	United States...	Campania......	Campania......
341	Head	M.	40	Married...	Campania........	Campania......	Campania......
	Wife..............	F.	30	Married...	Campania.......	Campania......	Campania......
	Son	M.	14	Single.....	Campania.......	Campania......	Campania......
	Son	M.	11	Single.....	Campania.......	Campania......	Campania......
	Son	M.	5	Single.....	United States...	Campania......	Campania......
	Son	M.	3	Single.....	United States...	Campania......	Campania......
	Daughter.........	F.	2	Single.....	United States...	Campania......	Campania......
342	Head	M.	45	Married...	Basilicata.......	Basilicata......	Basilicata.......
	Wife..............	F.	36	Married...	Basilicata	Basilicata......	Basilicata......
	Daughter.........	F.	11	Single.....	Basilicata.......	Basilicata......	Basilicata......
	Son	M.	7	Single.....	United States...	Basilicata......	Basilicata......
	Daughter.........	F.	5	Single.....	United States...	Basilicata......	Basilicata......
	Son	M.	$\frac{9}{12}$	Single.....	United States...	Basilicata......	Basilicata......
343	Head	M.	30	Married...	Sicily............	Sicily	Sicily ....
	Wife..............	F.	17	Married...	Sicily............	Sicily	Sicily ....
344	Head	M.	28	Married...	Sicily............	Sicily	Sicily ....
	Wife..............	F.	18	Married...	Basilicata.......	Basilicata......	Basilicata......
	Daughter.........	F.	3	Single.....	United States...	Sicily	Basilicata......
	Son	M.	$\frac{4}{12}$	Single.....	United States...	Sicily	Basilicata......
345	Head	M.	30	Married...	Basilicata.......	Basilicata......	Basilicata......
	Wife..............	F.	27	Married...	Basilicata.......	Basilicata......	Basilicata......
	Son	M.	8	Single.....	United States...	Basilicata......	Basilicata......
	Daughter.........	F.	6	Single.....	United States...	Basilicata......	Basilicata......
	Daughter.........	F.	5	Single.....	United States...	Basilicata......	Basilicata......
	Son	M.	3	Single.....	United States...	Basilicata......	Basilicata......
	Son	M.	1	Single.....	United States...	Basilicata......	Basilicata......
346	Head	M.	39	Married...	Basilicata.......	Basilicata......	Basilicata......
	Wife..............	F.	38	Married...	Basilicata.......	Basilicata......	Basilicata......
	Son	M.	10	Single.....	United States...	Basilicata......	Basilicata......
	Daughter.........	F.	4	Single.....	United States...	Basilicata......	Basilicata......
	Daughter.........	F.	$\frac{3}{12}$	Single.....	United States...	Basilicata......	Basilicata......
347	Head	M.	26	Married...	Calabria	Calabria	Calabria ....
	Wife..............	F.	20	Married...	Calabria	Calabria	Calabria ....
	Daughter.........	F.	3	Single.....	United States...	Calabria	Calabria ....
	Daughter.........	F.	2	Single.....	United States...	Calabria	Calabria ....
348	Head	M.	60	Married...	Basilicata.......	Basilicata......	Basilicata......
	Wife..............	F.	45	Married...	Basilicata.......	Basilicata......	Basilicata......
	Daughter.........	F.	13	Single.....	United States...	Basilicata......	Basilicata......
	Daughter.........	F.	9	Single.....	United States...	Basilicata......	Basilicata......
	Daughter.........	F.	6	Single.....	United States...	Basilicata......	Basilicata......
349	Cooperative	M.	56	Married...	Calabria	Calabria	Calabria ....
	Cooperative	M.	33	Married...	Calabria	Calabria	Calabria ....
	Cooperative	M.	39	Married...	Calabria	Calabria	Calabria ....
	Cooperative	M.	24	Single.....	Calabria	Calabria	Calabria ....
	Cooperative	M.	33	Married...	Calabria	Calabria	Calabria ....
350	Head	M.	29	Married...	Basilicata.......	Basilicata......	Basilicata......
	Wife..............	F.	22	Married...	Basilicata.......	Basilicata......	Basilicata......
	Son	M.	5	Single.....	United States...	Basilicata......	Basilicata......
	Mother	F.	60	Widowed .	Basilicata.......	Basilicata......	Basilicata......

a Also worked as peddler, fruit, nine weeks, at $4.50 per week.

TABLE **I.**—GENERAL SOCIAL AND ECONOMIC CONDITION, BY FAMILIES AND INDIVIDUALS—Continued.

Years in U.S.	Naturalized.	Profession, trade, or occupation.	Hours of work per week.	Average weekly earnings.	Weeks employed.	Total yearly earnings.	Sick during year, defective, maimed, or deformed.
6	Yes..	Laborer..................	60	$7.50	26	$195	No.
5	Yes..	Laborer..................	60	7.50	22	165	No.
5	....	Scholar and newsboy	97	2.10	52	109	No.
6	....	Scholar and newsboy	97	2.10	52	109	Fever. typhoid.
15	No...	Laborer..................	60	7.50	17	128	Pneumonia.
5	....	Housewife...............					Childbirth.
.....	....	At home.................					Rickets.
.....	....	At home.................					No.
.....	....	At home.................					No.
13	No...	No occupation					Injury by accident; loss of one eye.
7	....	Housewife...............					No.
7	....	Bootblack and newsboy...	60	1.75	52	91	No.
7	....	No occupation					Paralysis.
.....	....	At home					No.
.....	....	At home					Rickets.
.....	....	At home					No.
10	Yes..	Laborer..................	60	7.50	9	68	Fever, typhoid.
8	....	Housewife...............					Childbirth.
8	....	Scholar					No.
.....	....	Scholar					No.
.....	....	At home					No.
.....	....	At home					No.
10	Yes..	Furniture polisher (a)	60	6.00	a 43	299	No.
8	....	Housewife...............					No.
8	Yes..	Bricklayer................	48	12.00	17	204	No.
12	....	Housewife...............					Childbirth.
.....	....	At home					No.
.....	....	At home					No.
10	Yes..	Musician	(b)	3.00	52	156	No.
16	....	Housewife...............					Cross-eyed.
.....	....	Scholar					No.
.....	....	At home					No.
.....	....	At home					No.
.....	....	At home					No.
.....	....	At home					No.
13	Yes..	Street sweeper............	72	7.50	17	128	No.
12	....	Housewife...............					Childbirth.
.....	....	Scholar					No.
.....	....	At home					No.
.....	....	At home					No.
15	Yes..	Candy maker	60	7.00	39	273	No.
12	....	Housewife...............					No.
.....	....	At home					Rickets.
.....	....	At home					No.
25	No...	No occupation					Rheumatism.
24	....	Housewife and pants finisher.	(b)	1.50	(b)	(b)	No.
.....	....	Scholar					No.
.....	....	Scholar					No.
.....	....	At home					Hip-joint disease.
3	No...	Laborer..................	60	5.94	10	59	No.
4	No...	Laborer..................	60	7.50	13	98	No.
4	No...	Laborer..................	60	7.50	13	98	No.
3	No...	Laborer..................	60	5.94	10	59	No.
5	No...	Laborer..................	60	5.94	10	59	No.
25	Yes..	Stonecutter..............	48	24.00	22	528	No.
6	....	Housewife...............					No.
.....	....	At home.................					No.
(b)	....	Housework...............					No.

b Not reported.

TABLE **I.**—GENERAL SOCIAL AND ECONOMIC CONDITION, BY FAMILIES AND INDIVIDUALS—Continued.

Family number.	Relationship to head of family.	Sex.	Age.	Conjugal condition.	Birthplace.	Birthplace of—	
						Father.	Mother.
351	Head	M.	40	Married	Basilicata	Basilicata	Basilicata
	Wife	F.	32	Married	Campania	Campania	Campania
	Son	M.	15	Single	United States	Basilicata	Campania
	Son	M.	13	Single	United States	Basilicata	Campania
	Son	M.	11	Single	United States	Basilicata	Campania
	Son	M.	8	Single	United States	Basilicata	Campania
	Son	M.	6	Single	United States	Basilicata	Campania
	Son	M.	4	Single	United States	Basilicata	Campania
	Son	M.	2	Single	United States	Basilicata	Campania
	Boarder	F.	19	Married	Campania	Campania	Campania
352	Head	M.	31	Married	Calabria	Calabria	Calabria
	Wife	F.	31	Married	Calabria	Calabria	Calabria
	Son	M.	13	Single	Calabria	Calabria	Calabria
	Son	M.	8	Single	Calabria	Calabria	Calabria
	Son	M.	4	Single	United States	Calabria	Calabria
	Son	M.	2	Single	United States	Calabria	Calabria
	Daughter	F.	1	Single	United States	Calabria	Calabria
353	Head	M.	29	Married	Campania	Campania	Campania
	Wife	F.	25	Married	Campania	Campania	Campania
	Son	M.	1	Single	United States	Campania	Campania
354	Head	M.	32	Married	Calabria	Calabria	Calabria
	Wife	F.	32	Married	Calabria	Calabria	Calabria
	Daughter	F.	6	Single	Calabria	Calabria	Calabria
	Son	M.	2	Single	United States	Calabria	Calabria
355	Head	M.	28	Married	Campania	Campania	Campania
	Wife	F.	25	Married	Campania	Campania	Campania
	Daughter	F.	2	Single	United States	Campania	Campania
	Lodger	M.	27	Single	Campania	Campania	Campania
356	Head	F.	24	Widowed	Basilicata	Basilicata	Basilicata
	Son	M.	3	Single	United States	Basilicata	Basilicata
	Son	M.	$\frac{1}{12}$	Single	United States	Basilicata	Basilicata
357	Head	M.	45	Married	Calabria	Calabria	Calabria
	Brother	M.	42	Married	Calabria	Calabria	Calabria
	Nephew	M.	20	Single	Calabria	Calabria	Calabria
	Nephew	M.	15	Single	Calabria	Calabria	Calabria
358	Head	M.	25	Married	Calabria	Calabria	Calabria
	Wife	F.	23	Married	Calabria	Calabria	Calabria
	Brother	M.	47	Married	Calabria	Calabria	Calabria
	Brother	M.	23	Single	Calabria	Calabria	Calabria
	Sister-in-law	F.	37	Married	Calabria	Calabria	Calabria
	Niece	F.	3	Single	United States	Calabria	Calabria
	Nephew	M.	1	Single	United States	Calabria	Calabria
359	Head	M.	28	Married	Calabria	Calabria	Calabria
	Wife	F.	23	Married	Calabria	Calabria	Calabria
	Son	M.	3	Single	Calabria	Calabria	Calabria
	Brother-in-law	M.	32	Married	Calabria	Calabria	Calabria
	Brother-in-law	M.	26	Single	Calabria	Calabria	Calabria
360	Cooperative	M.	35	Married	Calabria	Calabria	Calabria
	Cooperative	M.	50	Married	Calabria	Calabria	Calabria
	Cooperative	M.	50	Married	Calabria	Calabria	Calabria
	Cooperative	M.	50	Married	Calabria	Calabria	Calabria
	Cooperative	M.	25	Single	Calabria	Calabria	Calabria
	Cooperative	M.	44	Married	Calabria	Calabria	Calabria
	Cooperative	M.	35	Single	Calabria	Calabria	Calabria
361	Head	M.	30	Married	Campania	Campania	Campania
	Wife	F.	20	Married	Campania	Campania	Campania
	Daughter	F.	4	Single	United States	Campania	Campania
	Son	M.	2	Single	United States	Campania	Campania
	Daughter	F.	$\frac{1}{12}$	Single	United States	Campania	Campania
362	Head	M.	50	Married	Abruzzo	Abruzzo	Abruzzo
	Wife	F.	42	Married	Abruzzo	Abruzzo	Abruzzo
	Daughter	F.	17	Married	Abruzzo	Abruzzo	Abruzzo
	Son	M.	2	Single	United States	Abruzzo	Abruzzo
	Son-in-law	M.	29	Married	Abruzzo	Abruzzo	Abruzzo
	Lodger	M.	45	Married	Abruzzo	Abruzzo	Abruzzo

a Not reported.

TABLE I.—GENERAL SOCIAL AND ECONOMIC CONDITION, BY FAMILIES
AND INDIVIDUALS—Continued.

Years in U. S.	Natu-ral-ized.	Profession, trade, or occupation.	Hours of work per week.	Average weekly earn-ings.	Weeks em-ploy-ed.	Total yearly earn-ings.	Sick during year, defective, maimed, or deformed.
25	Yes..	Musician	49	(a)	52	(a)	No.
22		Housewife					No.
		Scholar					Feeble-minded.
		Scholar					No.
		Scholar					No.
		At home					Idiot.
		Scholar					No.
		At home					No.
		At home					No.
7		Housework					No.
8	Yes..	Janitor	60	$8.00	52	$416	No.
4		Housewife					No.
4		Scholar					No.
4		Scholar					No.
		At home					No.
		At home					No.
		At home					No.
11	Yes..	Street sweeper	60	9.00	30	270	No.
4		Housewife					No.
		At home					Measles.
7	Yes..	Laborer	60	7.50	9	68	No.
4		Housewife					Fever, puerperal.
4		Scholar					No.
		At home					No.
9	Yes..	Laborer (b)	(a)	7.50	b 22	179	No.
4		Housewife					No.
		At home					Fever, not specified.
5	No...	Laborer	(a)	7.50	32	240	No.
6		Housewife					Childbirth.
		At home					No.
		At home					No.
3	No...	Laborer	60	6.60	13	86	Rheumatism.
4	No...	Laborer	60	7.50	13	98	No.
4		Scholar and laborer	60	7.50	13	98	No.
4		Scholar and newsboy	73	1.75	52	91	No.
15	Yes..	Merchant, rags	54	6.00	52	312	No.
8		Housewife					No.
17	No...	Saloon keeper	126	(a)	52	(a)	No.
7/12	No...	No occupation					Neuralgia.
4		Housework					No.
		At home					Fever, typhoid; bronchitis.
		At home					No.
3	No...	Laborer	60	7.50	26	195	No.
1		Housewife					No.
1		At home					No.
3	No...	Laborer	60	7.50	26	195	No.
3	No...	Laborer	60	7.50	26	195	No.
3	No...	Laborer	60	7.50	11	83	No.
1	No...	Laborer	60	6.60	11	73	No.
2	No...	Laborer	(a)	7.50	26	195	No.
9	No...	Laborer	60	7.50	11	83	No.
7	Yes..	Laborer	60	7.50	17	128	No.
14	No...	Laborer	60	7.50	13	98	No.
4	No...	Laborer	60	7.50	14	105	No.
10	Yes..	Laborer	60	7.50	48	360	Injury by accident.
6		Housewife					Childbirth.
		At home					No.
		At home					No.
		At home					No.
10	Yes..	Laborer	60	9.00	27	243	No.
5		Housewife					No.
5		Housework					No.
		At home					No.
8	Yes..	Laborer	60	6.75	30	203	No.
13	Yes..	Scissors grinder	(a)	3.00	52	156	No.

b Also worked as ragpicker nine weeks, at $1.50 per week.

TABLE I.—GENERAL SOCIAL AND ECONOMIC CONDITION, BY FAMILIES AND INDIVIDUALS—Continued.

Family number.	Relationship to head of family.	Sex.	Age.	Conjugal condition.	Birthplace.	Birthplace of—	
						Father.	Mother.
363	Cooperative	M.	28	Single	Campania	Campania	Campania
	Cooperative	M.	57	Widowed	Campania	Campania	Campania
	Cooperative	M.	41	Married	Campania	Campania	Campania
	Cooperative	M.	30	Married	Apulia	Apulia	Apulia
	Cooperative	M.	28	Single	Apulia	Apulia	Apulia
364	Head	M.	30	Married	Campania	Campania	Campania
	Wife	F.	23	Married	Campania	Campania	Campania
	Son	M.	3	Single	Campania	Campania	Campania
	Brother	M.	18	Single	Campania	Campania	Campania
	Cousin	M.	23	Married	Campania	Campania	Campania
365	Head	M.	25	Married	Basilicata	Basilicata	Basilicata
	Wife	F.	17	Married	Basilicata	Basilicata	Basilicata
366	Head	M.	46	Married	Campania	Campania	Campania
	Wife	F.	48	Married	Campania	Campania	Campania
	Son	M.	16	Single	Campania	Campania	Campania
	Son	M.	13	Single	Campania	Campania	Campania
	Son	M.	5	Single	United States	Campania	Campania
	Son	M.	3	Single	United States	Campania	Campania
367	Head	M.	38	Married	Campania	Campania	Campania
	Wife	F.	32	Married	Campania	Campania	Campania
	Daughter	F.	4	Single	Campania	Campania	Campania
	Boarder	M.	30	Married	Campania	Campania	Campania
	Boarder	M.	40	Married	Campania	Campania	Campania
	Boarder	M.	18	Single	Campania	Campania	Campania
368	Head	M.	32	Married	Campania	Campania	Campania
	Wife	F.	28	Married	Campania	Campania	Campania
	Son	M.	11	Single	Campania	Campania	Campania
	Daughter	F.	3	Single	United States	Campania	Campania
	Daughter	F.	1	Single	United States	Campania	Campania
	Brother-in-law	M.	20	Single	Campania	Campania	Campania
369	Head	M.	44	Married	Basilicata	Basilicata	Basilicata
	Wife	F.	45	Married	Basilicata	Basilicata	Basilicata
	Son	M.	16	Single	Basilicata	Basilicata	Basilicata
	Son	M.	8	Single	United States	Basilicata	Basilicata
	Son	M.	3	Single	United States	Basilicata	Basilicata
370	Head	M.	28	Married	Basilicata	Basilicata	Basilicata
	Wife	F.	22	Married	Basilicata	Basilicata	Basilicata
371	Head	M.	48	Married	Campania	Campania	Campania
	Wife	F.	38	Married	Campania	Campania	Campania
	Son	M.	17	Single	Campania	Campania	Campania
	Son	M.	7	Single	United States	Campania	Campania
	Son	M.	5	Single	United States	Campania	Campania
	Daughter	F.	2	Single	United States	Campania	Campania
	Daughter	F.	$\frac{1}{12}$	Single	United States	Campania	Campania
372	Head	M.	54	Married	Campania	Campania	Campania
	Wife	F.	44	Married	Campania	Campania	Campania
	Son	M.	22	Single	Campania	Campania	Campania
	Daughter	F.	10	Single	United States	Campania	Campania
	Son	M.	9	Single	United States	Campania	Campania
	Son	M.	6	Single	United States	Campania	Campania
	Son	M.	2	Single	United States	Campania	Campania
373	Head	M.	35	Married	Campania	Campania	Campania
	Wife	F.	31	Married	Campania	Campania	Campania
	Daughter	F.	5	Single	United States	Campania	Campania
	Son	M.	$\frac{1}{12}$	Single	United States	Campania	Campania
374	Head	M.	22	Married	Campania	Campania	Campania
	Wife	F.	16	Married	United States	Campania	Campania
375	Head	M.	42	Married	Campania	Campania	Campania
	Wife	F.	22	Married	Campania	Campania	Campania
	Daughter	F.	2	Single	United States	Campania	Campania
	Son	M.	$\frac{1}{12}$	Single	United States	Campania	Campania

a Not reported.　　　　b Also worked as laborer nine weeks, at $7.50 per week.

TABLE **I.**—GENERAL SOCIAL AND ECONOMIC CONDITION, BY FAMILIES
AND INDIVIDUALS—Continued.

Years in U. S.	Naturalized.	Profession, trade, or occupation.	Hours of work per week.	Average weekly earnings.	Weeks employed.	Total yearly earnings.	Sick during year, defective, maimed, or deformed.
11	Yes..	Railroad laborer	60	$7.50	21	$158	No.
12	Yes..	Railroad laborer	60	7.50	21	158	No.
8	Yes..	Laborer.....................	60	7.50	17	128	No.
6	Yes..	Laborer.....................	60	7.50	19	143	No.
6	Yes..	Stone breaker..............	57	7.50	26	195	Eye, loss of one.
3	No...	Newsboy	56	1.25	52	65	Arm, loss of one.
1	....	Housewife..................					No.
1	....	At home....................					No.
3	....	Laborer.....................	60	7.50	26	195	No.
1	No...	Laborer.....................	60	7.50	21	158	No.
3	No...	Hod carrier	54	14	35	490	No.
9	....	Housewife..................					No.
10	Yes..	Laborer.....................	60	7.50	23	173	No.
6	....	Housewife..................					No.
6	....	Scholar and newsboy	42	.20	26	5	No.
6	....	Scholar and newsboy	42	.15	36	5	No.
....	....	At home....................					No.
....	....	At home....................					No.
10	Yes..	Laborer.....................	(a)	9.75	17	166	No.
1	....	Housewife..................					No.
1	....	At home....................					No.
10	Yes..	Laborer.....................	(a)	9.00	9	81	No.
8	Yes..	No occupation					No.
1	....	No occupation					No.
12	Yes .	Newsboy (b)	(a)	1.75	b 43	143	No.
5	....	Housewife..................					No.
5	....	Scholar and newsboy	40	1.05	4	4	No.
....	....	At home....................					No.
....	....	At home....................					No.
3	....	Newsboy	56	1.75	52	91	No.
9	Yes..	Street sweeper.............	(a)	9.00	26	234	No.
9	....	Housewife..................					No.
9	....	No occupation					No.
....	....	Scholar					No.
....	....	At home....................					No.
(a)	Yes..	Street sweeper.............	(a)	9.00	30	270	No.
4	....	Housewife..................					(c)
12	Yes..	Laborer.....................	60	7.50	13	98	Deaf.
8	....	Housewife and pants finisher.	(a)	1.50	(a)	(a)	Childbirth.
8	....	Bootblack	84	1.75	52	91	Leg, loss of one.
....	....	At home....................					Idiot.
....	....	At home....................					No.
....	....	At home....................					No.
....	....	At home....................					No.
15	Yes..	No occupation					Injury by accident.
15	....	Housewife..................					No.
15	Yes..	Electrician.................	48	(a)	52	(a)	No.
....	....	Scholar					No.
....	....	Scholar					No.
....	....	Scholar					No.
....	....	At home....................					Rickets.
8	No...	Laborer.....................	60	7.50	19	143	No.
7	....	Housewife..................					Childbirth.
....	....	Scholar					Bronchitis.
....	....	At home....................					No.
4	No...	Bootblack	78	13.00	52	676	No.
....	....	Housewife..................					No.
12	Yes..	Laborer.....................	70	8.25	26	215	No.
3	....	Housewife..................					Childbirth.
....	....	At home....................					No.
....	....	At home....................					No.

c Sick, disease not specified.

TABLE I.—GENERAL SOCIAL AND ECONOMIC CONDITION, BY FAMILIES AND INDIVIDUALS—Continued.

Family number.	Relationship to head of family.	Sex.	Age.	Conjugal condition.	Birthplace.	Birthplace of—	
						Father.	Mother.
376	Head	M.	36	Married	Campania	Campania	Campania
	Wife	F.	27	Married	Campania	Campania	Campania
	Son	M.	7	Single	Campania	Campania	Campania
	Son	M.	3	Single	United States	Campania	Campania
	Son	M.	1	Single	United States	Campania	Campania
377	Head	M.	42	Married	Campania	Campania	Campania
	Wife	F.	38	Married	Campania	Campania	Campania
	Son	M.	18	Single	Campania	Campania	Campania
	Son	M.	16	Single	Campania	Campania	Campania
	Son	M.	11	Single	United States	Campania	Campania
	Daughter	F.	9	Single	United States	Campania	Campania
	Son	M.	7	Single	United States	Campania	Campania
	Daughter	F.	4	Single	United States	Campania	Campania
	Son	M.	2	Single	United States	Campania	Campania
	Father	M.	87	Widowed	Campania	Campania	Campania
378	Head	M.	31	Married	Abruzzo	Abruzzo	Abruzzo
	Wife	F.	31	Married	Abruzzo	Abruzzo	Abruzzo
	Daughter	F.	7	Single	Abruzzo	Abruzzo	Abruzzo
	Daughter	F.	2	Single	United States	Abruzzo	Abruzzo
	Son	M.	$\frac{8}{12}$	Single	United States	Abruzzo	Abruzzo
379	Head	M.	40	Married	Abruzzo	Abruzzo	Abruzzo
	Wife	F.	40	Married	Abruzzo	Abruzzo	Abruzzo
	Son	M.	5	Single	United States	Abruzzo	Abruzzo
	Daughter	F.	1	Single	United States	Abruzzo	Abruzzo
	Mother-in-law	F.	70	Widowed	Abruzzo	Abruzzo	Abruzzo
380	Head	M.	57	Married	Abruzzo	Abruzzo	Abruzzo
	Wife	F.	54	Married	Abruzzo	Abruzzo	Abruzzo
	Son	M.	18	Single	Abruzzo	Abruzzo	Abruzzo
	Son	M.	12	Single	France	Abruzzo	Abruzzo
381	Head	M.	60	Married	Campania	Campania	Campania
	Wife	F.	45	Married	Campania	Campania	Campania
	Son	M.	17	Single	United States	Campania	Campania
	Son	M.	15	Single	United States	Campania	Campania
	Son	M.	13	Single	United States	Campania	Campania
382	Head	M.	33	Married	Campania	Campania	Campania
	Wife	F.	20	Married	Campania	Campania	Campania
	Daughter	F.	2	Single	United States	Campania	Campania
	Daughter	F.	$\frac{1}{12}$	Single	United States	Campania	Campania
383	Head	M.	30	Married	Campania	Campania	Campania
	Wife	F.	28	Married	Campania	Campania	Campania
	Daughter	F.	3	Single	United States	Campania	Campania
	Son	M.	1	Single	United States	Campania	Campania
384	Head	M.	50	Married	Basilicata	Basilicata	Basilicata
	Wife	F.	45	Married	Basilicata	Basilicata	Basilicata
	Son	M.	23	Single	Basilicata	Basilicata	Basilicata
	Son	M.	14	Single	Basilicata	Basilicata	Basilicata
	Boarder	M.	35	Married	Basilicata	Basilicata	Basilicata
385	Head	M.	54	Married	Campania	Campania	Campania
	Wife	F.	47	Married	Campania	Campania	Campania
	Son	M.	23	Married	Campania	Campania	Campania
	Daughter	F.	14	Single	United States	Campania	Campania
	Daughter	F.	11	Single	United States	Campania	Campania
	Son	M.	8	Single	United States	Campania	Campania
	Daughter	F.	8	Single	United States	Campania	Campania
	Daughter	F.	5	Single	United States	Campania	Campania
	Daughter-in-law	F.	17	Married	Campania	Campania	Campania
	Grandson	M.	$\frac{3}{12}$	Single	United States	Campania	Campania
386	Head	M.	35	Married	Abruzzo	Abruzzo	Abruzzo
	Wife	F.	60	Married	Abruzzo	Abruzzo	Abruzzo
	Mother	F.	96	Widowed	Abruzzo	Abruzzo	Abruzzo
387	Head	M.	50	Married	Campania	Campania	Campania

a Not reported.

TABLE **I.**—GENERAL SOCIAL AND ECONOMIC CONDITION, BY FAMILIES AND INDIVIDUALS—Continued.

Years in U.S.	Natu- ral- ized.	Profession, trade, or occupation.	Hours of work per week.	Average weekly earn- ings.	Weeks em- ploy- ed.	Total yearly earn- ings.	Sick during year, defective, maimed, or deformed.
12	No...	Barber	(a)	(a)	52	(a)	No.
4		Housewife					Female complaint.
4		Scholar					No.
		At home					No.
		At home					Measles.
16	Yes..	No occupation					No.
16		Housewife					No.
16		Trunk-factory employee (b)	48	$4.00	b 49	$211	No.
16		Scholar					No.
		Scholar					No.
		Scholar					No.
		Scholar					No.
		At home					No.
		At home					No.
9	Yes..	No occupation					No.
5	Yes .	Laborer	60	7.50	17	128	No.
5		Housewife					Childbirth.
5		Scholar					No.
		At home					Rickets.
		At home					No.
11	Yes..	Laborer	60	6.60	4	26	Abscesses, scrofulous.
6		Housewife					No.
		At home					Lame.
		At home					Skin, disease of.
6		No occupation					No.
5	Yes..	Laborer	60	9.00	17	153	No.
5		Housewife					No.
5		No occupation					No.
5		Scholar					Injury by accident.
18	No...	Ragpicker	(a)	2.50	52	130	No.
18		Housewife					No.
		Scholar and bootblack	(a)	2.10	13	27	No.
		Scholar and newsboy	30	1.05	52	55	No.
		Scholar and bootblack	(a)	2.10	13	27	Lame.
14	Yes..	Laborer	48	7.50	30	225	No.
18		Housewife					Childbirth; cross-eyed.
		At home					No.
		At home					No.
12	Yes..	Bootblack	91	(a)	52	(a)	Leg, loss of one.
4		Housewife					No.
		At home					Rickets.
		At home					No.
14	Yes..	No occupation					No.
4		Housewife					No.
14	Yes..	Street sweeper	66	8.25	17	140	No.
4		Scholar and newsboy	78	1.75	42	74	No.
(a)	Yes..	Laborer	60	7.50	13	98	No.
16	No...	Wood sawyer	(a)	(a)	(a)	(a)	No.
14		Housewife and ragpicker	(a)	1.20	52	62	No.
14	Yes..	Bootblack	84	2.10	52	109	No.
		Wood picker	(a)	3.50	52	182	No.
		Wood picker	(a)	3.50	52	182	No.
		Scholar					No.
		Scholar					No.
		At home					No.
15		Housework					Childbirth.
		At home					No.
10	No...	No occupation					No.
10		Beggar					No.
10		Beggar					Blind.
15	No...	Laborer	60	7.50	9	68	No.

b Also worked as paint-shop employee three weeks, at $5 per week.

TABLE **I.**—GENERAL SOCIAL AND ECONOMIC CONDITION, BY FAMILIES AND INDIVIDUALS—Continued.

Family number.	Relationship to head of family.	Sex.	Age.	Conjugal condition.	Birthplace.	Birthplace of—	
						Father.	Mother.
388	Head	M.	26	Married	Basilicata	Basilicata	Basilicata
	Wife	F.	17	Married	Basilicata	Basilicata.:	Basilicata
	Daughter	F.	1	Single	United States	Basilicata	Basilicata
	Father	M.	55	Married	Basilicata	Basilicata	Basilicata
	Mother	F.	54	Married	Basilicata	Basilicata	Basilicata
	Sister	F.	22	Married	Basilicata	Basilicata	Basilicata
	Sister	F.	14	Single	Basilicata	Basilicata	Basilicata
	Brother	M.	12	Single	Basilicata	Basilicata	Basilicata
	Sister	F.	9	Single	United States	Basilicata	Basilicata
	Brother-in-law	M.	32	Married	Basilicata	Basilicata	Basilicata
	Niece	F.	$\frac{1}{12}$	Single	United States	Basilicata	Basilicata
389	Head	M.	55	Married	Campania	Campania	Campania
	Wife	F.	45	Married	Campania	Campania	Campania
	Son	M.	18	Single	Campania	Campania	Campania
	Daughter	F.	12	Single	United States	Campania	Campania
	Lodger	M.	32	Single	Abruzzo	Abruzzo	Abruzzo
	Lodger	M.	37	Married	Abruzzo	Abruzzo	Abruzzo
	Lodger	M.	28	Single	Basilicata	Basilicata	Basilicata
390	Head	M.	65	Married	Calabria	Calabria	Calabria
	Wife	F.	60	Married	Calabria	Calabria	Calabria
	Son	M.	15	Single	United States	Calabria	Calabria
	Lodger	M.	(b)	Single	Abruzzo	Abruzzo	Abruzzo
	Lodger	M.	40	Married	Calabria	Calabria	Calabria
391	Head	M.	39	Married	Basilicata	Basilicata	Basilicata
	Wife	F.	40	Married	Basilicata	Basilicata	Basilicata
	Daughter	F.	17	Single	Basilicata	Basilicata	Basilicata
	Daughter	F.	13	Single	Basilicata	Basilicata	Basilicata
	Son	M.	7	Single	Basilicata	Basilicata	Basilicata
	Son	M.	1	Single	United States	Basilicata	Basilicata
392	Head	M.	45	Married	Abruzzo	Abruzzo	Abruzzo
	Wife	F.	40	Married	Abruzzo	Abruzzo	Abruzzo
	Son	M.	15	Single	Abruzzo	Abruzzo	Abruzzo
	Daughter	F.	7	Single	United States	Abruzzo	Abruzzo
	Daughter	F.	2	Single	United States	Abruzzo	Abruzzo
	Daughter	F.	$\frac{3}{12}$	Single	United States	Abruzzo	Abruzzo
393	Head	M.	41	Married	Campania	Campania	Campania
	Wife	F.	40	Married	Campania	Campania	Campania
	Daughter	F.	14	Single	Campania	Campania	Campania
	Daughter	F.	10	Single	United States	Campania	Campania
	Daughter	F.	5	Single	United States	Campania	Campania
	Lodger	M.	27	Married	Campania	Campania	Campania
	Lodger	M.	25	Married	Campania	Campania	Campania
394	Head	M.	36	Married	Campania	Campania	Campania
	Wife	F.	21	Married	Campania	Campania	Campania
	Daughter	F.	5	Single	United States	Campania	Campania
	Daughter	F.	3	Single	United States	Campania	Campania
	Daughter	F.	$\frac{10}{12}$	Single	United States	Campania	Campania
395	Head	M.	34	Married	Campania	Campania	Campania
	Wife	F.	21	Married	Campania	Campania	Campania
	Son	M.	1	Single	United States	Campania	Campania
	Boarder	M.	37	Single	Campania	Campania	Campania
396	Head	M.	30	Married	Campania	Campania	Campania
	Wife	F.	28	Married	Campania	Campania	Campania
	Daughter	F.	$\frac{4}{12}$	Single	United States	Campania	Campania
	Lodger	M.	40	Married	Abruzzo	Abruzzo	Abruzzo
	Lodger	M.	40	Married	Campania	Campania	Campania
397	Head	M.	38	Married	Calabria	Calabria	Calabria
	Wife	F.	31	Married	Calabria	Calabria	Calabria
	Son	M.	13	Single	Calabria	Calabria	Calabria
	Daughter	F.	3	Single	United States	Calabria	Calabria
	Daughter	F.	1	Single	United States	Calabria	Calabria
398	Head	M.	50	Married	Calabria	Calabria	Calabria
	Wife	F.	47	Married	Calabria	Calabria	Calabria
	Son	M.	19	Single	Calabria	Calabria	Calabria

a Also worked as laborer thirteen weeks, at $4.50 per week.   *b* Not reported.

TABLE **I.**—GENERAL SOCIAL AND ECONOMIC CONDITION, BY FAMILIES AND INDIVIDUALS—Continued.

Years in U. S.	Natural ized.	Profession, trade, or occupation.	Hours of work per week.	Average weekly earnings.	Weeks employed.	Total yearly earnings.	Sick during year, defective, maimed, or deformed.
10	Yes..	Driver	72	$8.00	30	$240	No.
12		Housewife					No.
		At home					No.
9	No...	No occupation					No.
9		Housework					No.
9		Housework					Childbirth.
9		Housework					No.
9		Scholar					Leg, one broken.
		Scholar					No.
8	Yes..	Laborer	60	7.50	22	165	No.
		At home					No.
17	Yes..	Street sweeper	60	9.00	13	117	No.
16		Housewife					Bronchitis.
16		Newsboy (a)	(b)	7.00	a 15	164	No.
		No occupation					No.
13	Yes..	Laborer	60	9.00	22	198	No.
14	No...	Laborer	60	9.00	7	63	No.
6	Yes..	Laborer	60	9.00	17	153	No.
22	Yes..	No occupation					Consumption.
16		Housewife					Consumption.
		Scholar and newsboy	35	.70	52	36	No.
6	Yes..	No occupation					No.
8	No...	No occupation					No.
14	No...	Scissors grinder	72	4.50	30	135	Fever, malarial.
3		Housewife					No.
3		Tailoress	60	3.60	52	187	No.
3		Scholar					No.
3		Scholar					No.
		At home					No.
13	Yes..	Scissors grinder (c)	(b)	1.80	c 35	195	No.
7		Housewife					Childbirth.
7		Scholar and bootblack	10	.30	52	16	Hand, one crippled.
		Scholar					Fever, typhoid.
		At home					Fever, typhoid.
		At home					No.
12	Yes..	Wood picker	(b)	1.20	52	62	No.
10		Housewife					No.
10		Scholar					No.
		Scholar					Fever, typhoid.
		At home					No.
4	No...	No occupation					No.
1⁄2	No...	No occupation					No.
15	Yes..	No occupation					No.
10		Housewife					Childbirth.
		At home					No.
		At home					No.
		At home					No.
10	No...	Laborer	60	7.20	19	137	No.
6		Housewife					Measles.
		At home					Measles.
13	Yes..	No occupation					No.
6	Yes..	Laborer	60	8.52	13	111	No.
3		Housewife					Childbirth.
		At home					No.
6	Yes..	Laborer	54	12.00	13	156	No.
5	No...	Laborer	60	8.52	13	111	No.
14	Yes..	Street sweeper	48	9.00	13	117	No.
8		Housewife					No.
8		Scholar					No.
		At home					Diphtheria.
		At home					No.
13	Yes..	Laborer	60	7.50	9	68	No.
7		Housewife					Leg, loss of one.
7		Tailor	60	3.00	13	39	No.

c Also worked as laborer seventeen weeks, at $7.75 per week.

TABLE **I.**—GENERAL SOCIAL AND ECONOMIC CONDITION, BY FAMILIES
AND INDIVIDUALS—Continued.

Family number.	Relationship to head of family.	Sex.	Age.	Conjugal condition.	Birthplace.	Birthplace of— Father.	Birthplace of— Mother.
398	Son	M.	4	Single	United States	Calabria	Calabria
	Daughter	F.	2	Single	United States	Calabria	Calabria
	Lodger	M.	47	Married	Calabria	Calabria	Calabria
	Lodger	M.	23	Single	Calabria	Calabria	Calabria
399	Head	M.	37	Married	Calabria	Calabria	Calabria
	Lodger	M.	37	Married	Calabria	Calabria	Calabria
	Lodger	M.	37	Single	Calabria	Calabria	Calabria
	Lodger	M.	50	Married	Calabria	Calabria	Calabria
	Lodger	M.	16	Single	Calabria	Calabria	Calabria
	Lodger	M.	54	Widowed	Calabria	Calabria	Calabria
	Lodger	M.	45	Married	Calabria	Calabria	Calabria
400	Head	M.	28	Married	Calabria	Calabria	Calabria
	Wife	F.	27	Married	Calabria	Calabria	Calabria
	Son	M.	11	Single	Calabria	Calabria	Calabria
	Son	M.	6	Single	United States	Calabria	Calabria
	Daughter	F.	3	Single	United States	Calabria	Calabria
	Son	M.	$\frac{4}{12}$	Single	United States	Calabria	Calabria
	Lodger	M.	37	Married	Calabria	Calabria	Calabria
	Lodger	M.	45	Married	Calabria	Calabria	Calabria
	Lodger	M.	33	Married	Calabria	Calabria	Calabria
	Lodger	M.	23	Married	Calabria	Calabria	Calabria
	Lodger	M.	30	Single	Calabria	Calabria	Calabria
401	Head	M.	31	Married	Calabria	Calabria	Calabria
	Wife	F.	31	Married	Calabria	Calabria	Calabria
	Son	M.	3	Single	United States	Calabria	Calabria
	Boarder	M.	28	Single	Basilicata	Basilicata	Basilicata
402	Head	M.	48	Married	Calabria	Calabria	Calabria
	Wife	F.	44	Married	Calabria	Calabria	Calabria
	Son	M.	11	Single	Calabria	Calabria	Calabria
	Daughter	F.	10	Single	Calabria	Calabria	Calabria
403	Head	M.	40	Married	Calabria	Calabria	Calabria
	Wife	F.	40	Married	Calabria	Calabria	Calabria
	Son	M.	14	Single	Calabria	Calabria	Calabria
	Brother-in-law	M.	33	Single	Calabria	Calabria	Calabria
404	Head	M.	50	Married	Campania	Campania	Campania
	Wife	F.	45	Married	Campania	Campania	Campania
	Son	M.	21	Single	Campania	Campania	Campania
	Son	M.	17	Single	Campania	Campania	Campania
405	Head	M.	48	Married	Calabria	Calabria	Calabria
	Son	M.	21	Single	Calabria	Calabria	Calabria
	Cousin	M.	22	Single	Calabria	Calabria	Calabria
	Cousin	M.	21	Single	Calabria	Calabria	Calabria
	Lodger	M.	45	Married	Calabria	Calabria	Calabria
	Lodger	M.	45	Married	Calabria	Calabria	Calabria
	Lodger	M.	20	Single	Calabria	Calabria	Calabria
	Lodger	M.	24	Single	Calabria	Calabria	Calabria
406	Head	M.	55	Married	Calabria	Calabria	Calabria
	Son	M.	17	Single	Calabria	Calabria	Calabria
	Brother	M.	44	Married	Calabria	Calabria	Calabria
	Brother	M.	51	Married	Calabria	Calabria	Calabria
	Nephew	M.	14	Single	Calabria	Calabria	Calabria
	Lodger	M.	36	Married	Calabria	Calabria	Calabria
407	Head	M.	33	Married	Basilicata	Basilicata	Basilicata
	Wife	F.	28	Married	Basilicata	Basilicata	Basilicata
	Daughter	F.	10	Single	United States	Basilicata	Basilicata
	Daughter	F.	6	Single	United States	Basilicata	Basilicata
	Daughter	F.	4	Single	United States	Basilicata	Basilicata
	Daughter	F.	2	Single	United States	Basilicata	Basilicata
408	Head	M.	28	Married	Sicily	Sicily	Sicily
	Lodger	M.	25	Married	Sicily	Sicily	Sicily
	Lodger	M.	40	Single	Sicily	Sicily	Sicily
	Lodger	M.	20	Single	Sicily	Sicily	Sicily
	Lodger	M.	22	Single	Sicily	Sicily	Sicily

a Not reported.
b Also worked as laborer seven weeks, at $9 per week.
c Also worked as bootblack seventeen weeks, at $6 per week.

TABLE **I.**—GENERAL SOCIAL AND ECONOMIC CONDITION, BY FAMILIES AND INDIVIDUALS—Continued.

Years in U.S.	Naturalized.	Profession, trade, or occupation.	Hours of work per week.	Average weekly earnings.	Weeks employed.	Total yearly earnings.	Sick during year, defective, maimed, or deformed.
		At home					No.
	Yes..	At home					No.
6	Yes..	Laborer	60	$7.50	13	$98	No.
4	No...	Laborer	60	7.50	13	98	No.
13	Yes..	Laborer	60	7.50	13	98	No.
5	No...	Laborer	60	5.50	11	61	No.
13	Yes..	Laborer	60	5.50	11	61	No.
4	No...	Laborer	60	5.50	11	61	Fever, malarial.
4		Bootblack	91	1.20	52	62	No.
8	Yes..	Laborer	60	5.50	11	61	No.
9	Yes..	Laborer	60	5.50	11	61	No.
10	Yes..	Laborer	60	8.40	35	294	Rheumatism.
6		Housewife					Childbirth.
6		Scholar					No.
		Scholar					No.
		At home					Skin, disease of.
		At home					Bronchitis.
9	Yes..	Laborer	(a)	11.55	13	150	No.
14	Yes..	Laborer	60	8.10	13	105	No.
11	Yes..	Laborer	60	8.10	13	105	No.
8	No...	Laborer	60	8.10	13	105	No.
10	No...	Laborer	60	8.10	13	105	No.
9	Yes..	Railroad laborer	60	7.50	13	98	No.
5		Housewife					Miscarriage.
		At home					Pneumonia; bowlegs.
5	Yes..	Laborer	60	7.00	17	119	No.
9	Yes..	Pants finisher (b)	(a)	.54	b17	72	No.
4		Housewife					No.
4		Scholar					No.
4		Scholar					No.
14	Yes..	Laborer	48	8.25	17	140	No.
3		Housewife					Female complaint.
3		Scholar					No.
5	Yes..	Laborer	60	8.25	17	140	No.
14	Yes..	Laborer	60	9.00	26	234	No.
11		Housewife					No.
11	Yes..	No occupation					Consumption.
11		Janitor	72	4.25	35	149	No.
6	Yes.	Laborer	60	9.00	4	36	Fever, typhoid.
6	Yes..	Grinder, knife factory (c)..	(a)	9.00	c30	372	No.
1/12	No...	No occupation					No.
1/12	No...	No occupation					No.
15	Yes..	Laborer	60	9.00	26	234	No.
7	Yes..	Hod carrier	60	9.00	52	468	No.
1/7		No occupation					No.
1	No...	Tailor	60	8.00	43	344	No.
7	Yes..	Laborer	60	6.60	13	86	No.
7		Scholar and laborer	60	6.60	13	86	No.
7	Yes..	Laborer	60	6.60	13	86	No.
1	No...	No occupation					No.
1		No occupation					No.
4	No...	Laborer	60	6.60	13	86	No.
10	Yes..	Merchant, groceries	(a)	(a)	52	(a)	No.
10		Housewife					No.
		Scholar					No.
		Scholar					No.
		At home					No.
		At home					No.
1/12	No...	Peddler, fruit (d)	(a)	5.00	d4	(a)	No.
3	No...	Peddler, fruit	(a)	5.00	52	260	No.
1/12	No...	Peddler, fruit (d)	(a)	5.00	d4	(a)	No.
1/12		Peddler, fruit (d)	(a)	5.00	d4	(a)	No.
1/4	No...	Laborer (e)	(a)	6.00	e30	290	No.

d Also worked at another occupation, details not reported.
e Also worked as peddler, fruit, twenty-two weeks, at $5 per week.

TABLE **I.**—GENERAL SOCIAL AND ECONOMIC CONDITION, BY FAMILIES AND INDIVIDUALS—Continued.

Family number.	Relationship to head of family.	Sex.	Age.	Conjugal condition.	Birthplace.	Birthplace of—	
						Father.	Mother.
409	Head	M.	40	Married	Basilicata	Basilicata	Basilicata
	Wife	F.	36	Married	Basilicata	Basilicata	Basilicata
	Son	M.	12	Single	United States	Basilicata	Basilicata
	Daughter	F.	7	Single	United States	Basilicata	Basilicata
410	Head	M.	30	Married	Sicily	Sicily	Sicily
	Wife	F.	22	Married	Sicily	Sicily	Sicily
	Son	M.	2	Single	United States	Sicily	Sicily
411	Head	M.	47	Married	Campania	Campania	Campania
	Wife	F	37	Married	Campania	Campania	Campania
	Son	M.	16	Single	Campania	Campania	Campania
	Son	M.	11	Single	Campania	Campania	Campania
	Son	M.	7	Single	United States	Campania	Campania
	Daughter	F.	5	Single	United States	Campania	Campania
	Daughter	F.	2	Single	United States	Campania	Campania
	Son	M.	¹⁄₁₂	Single	United States	Campania	Campania
412	Head	M.	33	Married	Calabria	Calabria	Calabria
	Wife	F.	35	Married	Calabria	Calabria	Calabria
	Son	M.	4	Single	United States	Calabria	Calabria
	Son	M.	1	Single	United States	Calabria	Calabria
413	Head	M.	60	Married	Basilicata	Basilicata	Basilicata
	Wife	F.	60	Married	Basilicata	Basilicata	Basilicata
	Son	M.	38	Widowed	Basilicata	Basilicata	Basilicata
	Daughter	F.	29	Married	Basilicata	Basilicata	Basilicata
	Granddaughter	F.	6	Single	United States	Basilicata	Basilicata
	Grandson	M.	1	Single	United States	Basilicata	Basilicata
414	Head	M.	23	Married	Basilicata	Basilicata	Basilicata
	Wife	F.	19	Married	Campania	Campania	Campania
	Daughter	F.	¹⁄₁₂	Single	United States	Basilicata	Campania
415	Head	M.	60	Married	Basilicata	Basilicata	Basilicata
	Wife	F.	67	Married	Basilicata	Basilicata	Basilicata
416	Head	M.	39	Married	Basilicata	Basilicata	Basilicata
	Wife	F.	38	Married	Basilicata	Basilicata	Basilicata
	Son	M.	9	Single	United States	Basilicata	Basilicata
	Daughter	F.	8	Single	United States	Basilicata	Basilicata
	Daughter	F.	4	Single	United States	Basilicata	Basilicata
	Cousin	M.	33	Married	Basilicata	Basilicata	Basilicata
417	Head	M.	29	Married	Basilicata	Basilicata	Basilicata
	Wife	F.	25	Married	Basilicata	Basilicata	Basilicata
	Son	M.	3	Single	United States	Basilicata	Basilicata
	Son	M.	2	Single	United States	Basilicata	Basilicata
	Daughter	F.	¹⁄₁₂	Single	United States	Basilicata	Basilicata
	Father	M.	54	Married	Basilicata	Basilicata	Basilicata
	Mother-in-law	F.	59	Married	Basilicata	Basilicata	Basilicata
418	Head	M.	50	Married	Basilicata	Basilicata	Basilicata
	Wife	F.	47	Married	Basilicata	Basilicata	Basilicata
	Son	M.	12	Single	Basilicata	Basilicata	Basilicata
	Son	M.	9	Single	United States	Basilicata	Basilicata
	Daughter	F.	7	Single	United States	Basilicata	Basilicata
	Son	M.	4	Single	United States	Basilicata	Basilicata
419	Head	M.	40	Married	Basilicata	Basilicata	Basilicata
	Wife	F.	40	Married	Basilicata	Basilicata	Basilicata
	Daughter	F.	16	Single	Basilicata	Basilicata	Basilicata
	Son	M.	9	Single	United States	Basilicata	Basilicata
	Daughter	F.	3	Single	United States	Basilicata	Basilicata
420	Head	M.	35	Married	Basilicata	Basilicata	Basilicata
	Wife	F.	24	Married	United States	Basilicata	Ireland

a Not reported.

TABLE **I.**—GENERAL SOCIAL AND ECONOMIC CONDITION, BY FAMILIES
AND INDIVIDUALS—Continued.

Years in U. S.	Natu- ral- ized.	Profession, trade, or occupation.	Hours of work per week.	Average weekly earn- ings.	Weeks em- ploy- ed.	Total yearly earn- ings.	Sick during year, defective, maimed, or deformed.
18	Yes..	Street sweeper	60	$8.00	4	$32	No.
15		Housewife					Dyspepsia.
		Scholar					No.
		Scholar					No.
3	No...	Laborer	60	6.90	46	317	Injury by accident.
3		Housewife					No.
		At home					No.
15	Yes..	No occupation					Paralysis.
9		Housewife					Childbirth.
9		Bootblack	(a)	1.50	(a)	(a)	No.
9		Bootblack	(a)	.60	(a)	(a)	No.
		At home					Abscesses.
		At home					No.
		At home					No.
		At home					No.
6	Yes..	Laborer	60	7.50	9	68	No.
5		Housewife					No.
		At home					No.
		At home					No.
20	No...	Retired					No.
8		Housewife					No.
8	Yes..	No occupation					No.
8		Housework					No.
		Scholar					No.
		At home					No.
16	Yes..	Paver	70	8.25	17	140	No.
8		Housewife					Childbirth.
		At home					No.
20	Yes..	Retired					Bowels, inflammation of.
20		Housewife					No.
15	Yes..	Wood sawyer	24	1.00	52	52	No.
9		Housewife and merchant, wood.	18	.75	52	39	Female complaint.
		Scholar					Fever, malarial.
		At home					No.
		At home					Fever, typhoid.
4	No...	Teacher	35	2.00	52	104	Fever, not specified.
10	Yes..	Paver	48	9.00	15	135	No.
5		Housewife and merchant, wood.	24	75	26	20	Childbirth.
		At home					Dropsy, abdominal.
		At home					Dropsy, abdominal; rickets.
		At home					No.
15	No...	Wood sawyer (b)	(a)	1.00	b 26	109	No.
5		No occupation					Legs, swollen; general de- bility.
15	Yes..	Street sweeper	48	9.00	19	171	No.
10		Housewife and merchant, wood.	(a)	1.75	52	91	No.
10		Scholar and newsboy	60	1.25	34	43	No.
		Scholar					No.
		Scholar					No.
		At home					Fever, not specified.
14	Yes..	Scissors grinder	(a)	3.00	52	156	No.
10		Housewife and wood picker.	(a)	(a)	52	(a)	No.
10		Wood picker	(a)	(a)	52	(a)	No.
		Scholar					No.
		At home					No.
13	Yes..	No occupation					No.
		Housewife					No.

b Also worked as laborer eleven weeks, at $7.50 per week.

TABLE **I.**—GENERAL SOCIAL AND ECONOMIC CONDITION, BY FAMILIES AND INDIVIDUALS—Continued.

Family number.	Relationship to head of family.	Sex.	Age.	Conjugal condition.	Birthplace.	Birthplace of—	
						Father.	Mother.
421	Head	M.	36	Married...	Basilicata......	Basilicata......	Basilicata......
	Wife	F.	28	Married...	Basilicata......	Basilicata......	Basilicata......
	Son	M.	6	Single.....	United States...	Basilicata......	Basilicata......
	Son	M.	3	Single.....	United States...	Basilicata......	Basilicata......
	Daughter	F.	1	Single.....	United States...	Basilicata......	Basilicata......
422	Head	M.	45	Married...	Campania......	Campania......	Campania......
	Wife	F.	34	Married...	Basilicata......	Basilicata......	Basilicata......
	Son	M.	14	Single.....	Basilicata......	Campania......	Basilicata......
	Daughter	F.	10	Single.....	Basilicata......	Campania......	Basilicata......
	Daughter	F.	5	Single.....	Basilicata......	Campania......	Basilicata......
	Daughter	F.	3	Single.....	United States...	Campania......	Basilicata......
	Son	M.	$\frac{2}{12}$	Single.....	United States...	Campania......	Basilicata......
423	Head	M.	47	Widowed .	Basilicata......	Basilicata......	Basilicata......
	Daughter	F.	15	Single.....	Basilicata......	Basilicata......	Basilicata......
	Son	M.	13	Single.....	Basilicata......	Basilicata......	Basilicata......
	Son	M.	8	Single.....	Basilicata......	Basilicata......	Basilicata......
424	Head	M.	33	Married...	Abruzzo........	Abruzzo.......	Abruzzo........
	Wife	F.	41	Married...	Abruzzo........	Abruzzo.......	Abruzzo........
	Stepson	M.	13	Single.....	Abruzzo........	Abruzzo.......	Abruzzo........
	Stepson	M.	8	Single.....	France........	Abruzzo.......	Abruzzo........
	Son	M.	1	Single.....	United States...	Abruzzo.......	Abruzzo........
425	Head	M.	58	Married...	Abruzzo........	Abruzzo.......	Abruzzo........
	Wife	F.	50	Married...	Abruzzo........	Abruzzo.......	Abruzzo........
	Son	M.	22	Single.....	Abruzzo........	Abruzzo.......	Abruzzo........
	Son	M.	20	Single.....	Abruzzo........	Abruzzo.......	Abruzzo........
426	Head	M.	31	Married...	Abruzzo........	Abruzzo.......	Abruzzo........
	Wife	F.	27	Married...	Abruzzo........	Abruzzo.......	Abruzzo........
	Son	M.	8	Single.....	France........	Abruzzo.......	Abruzzo........
	Son	M.	3	Single.....	United States...	Abruzzo.......	Abruzzo........
	Daughter	F.	$\frac{3}{12}$	Single.....	United States...	Abruzzo.......	Abruzzo........
427	Head	M.	38	Married...	Basilicata......	Basilicata......	Basilicata......
	Wife	F.	35	Married...	Basilicata......	Basilicata......	Basilicata......
	Son	M.	13	Single.....	Basilicata......	Basilicata......	Basilicata......
	Daughter	F.	11	Single.....	Basilicata......	Basilicata......	Basilicata......
	Son	M.	9	Single.....	Basilicata......	Basilicata......	Basilicata......
	Daughter	F.	3	Single.....	United States.	Basilicata......	Basilicata......
428	Head	M.	42	Married...	Campania......	Campania......	Campania......
	Father-in-law	M.	57	Married...	Campania......	Campania......	Campania......
	Brother-in-law	M.	35	Married...	Campania......	Campania......	Campania......
	Lodger	M.	53	Married...	Campania......	Campania......	Campania......
429	Head	M.	58	Married...	Campania......	Campania...:...	Campania......
	Wife	F.	27	Married...	Basilicata......	Basilicata......	Basilicata......
	Daughter	F.	6	Single.....	Basilicata......	Campania......	Basilicata......
	Daughter	F.	3	Single.....	Basilicata......	Campania......	Basilicata......
	Son	M.	1	Single.....	United States...	Campania......	Basilicata......
430	Head	M.	30	Married...	Basilicata......	Basilicata......	Basilicata......
	Wife	F.	27	Married...	Basilicata......	Basilicata......	Basilicata......
	Son	M.	8	Single.....	Basilicata......	Basilicata......	Basilicata......
	Son	M.	6	Single.....	United States...	Basilicata......	Basilicata......
	Son	M.	4	Single.....	United States...	Basilicata......	Basilicata......
	Daughter	F.	2	Single.....	United States...	Basilicata......	Basilicata......
431	Head	M.	52	Married...	Basilicata......	Basilicata......	Basilicata......
	Wife	F.	40	Married...	Basilicata......	Basilicata......	Basilicata......
	Son	M.	17	Single.....	Basilicata......	Basilicata......	Basilicata......
	Daughter	F.	10	Single.....	United States...	Basilicata......	Basilicata......
	Daughter	F.	7	Single.....	United States...	Basilicata......	Basilicata......
	Son	M.	5	Single.....	United States...	Basilicata......	Basilicata......
	Daughter	F.	3	Single.....	United States...	Basilicata......	Basilicata......
	Daughter	F.	2	Single.....	United States...	Basilicata......	Basilicata......
	Daughter	F.	$\frac{a}{12}$	Single.....	United States...	Basilicata......	Basilicata......

a Not reported.

TABLE I.—GENERAL SOCIAL AND ECONOMIC CONDITION, BY FAMILIES AND INDIVIDUALS—Continued.

Years in U. S.	Naturalized.	Profession, trade, or occupation.	Hours of work per week.	Average weekly earnings.	Weeks employed.	Total yearly earnings.	Sick during year, defective, maimed, or deformed.
10	Yes..	Laborer......	42	$9.00	13	$117	No.
10	....	Housewife and wood picker.	(a)	1.80	(a)	(a)	No.
......	....	At home...........	....	....	....	....	No.
......	....	At home...........	....	....	....	....	Fever, typhoid.
......	....	At home...........	....	....	....	....	No.
4	No...	Laborer................	60	6.80	13	88	No.
4	....	Housewife and merchant, wood	(a)	2.00	(a)	(a)	Childbirth.
4	....	Scholar....	....	....	....	....	No.
4	....	No occupation..........	....	....	....	....	No.
4	....	At home...........	....	....	....	....	No.
......	....	At home...........	....	....	....	....	No.
......	....	At home...........	....	....	....	....	No.
8	Yes..	No occupation	....	....	....	....	No.
5	....	Housewife and wood picker.	(a)	2.70	52	140	No.
5	....	Scholar and bootblack	(a)	1.20	52	62	No.
5	....	At home	....	....	....	....	No.
10	No...	Laborer.................	60	7.50	13	98	Kidneys, disease of.
5	....	Housewife...........	....	....	....	....	No.
5	....	Scholar and newsboy	36	.60	4	2	No.
5	....	Scholar and newsboy	36	.60	4	2	Injury by accident.
......	....	At home	....	....	....	....	Fever, typhoid.
15	Yes..	No occupation	....	....	....	....	Injury by accident.
10	....	Housewife	....	....	....	....	No.
10	No...	No occupation	....	....	....	....	Injury by accident.
10	....	Newsboy ..., ...	72	5.00	52	260	No.
3	No...	Laborer..................	60	7.25	13	94	No.
3	....	Housewife	....	....	....	....	Childbirth; female com plaint.
3	....	Scholar	....	....	....	....	Eyes, inflammation of both
......	....	At home..........	....	....	....	....	No.
......	....	At home..........	....	....	....	....	No.
5	No...	No occupation...........	....	....	....	....	Rheumatism.
5	....	Housewife and coat finisher.	(a)	3.00	52	156	No.
5	....	Newsboy	(a)	1.50	52	78	No.
5	....	Housework	....	....	....	....	No.
5	....	At home	....	....	....	....	No.
......	....	At home	....	....	....	....	No.
1	No...	No occupation	....	....	....	....	No.
3	No...	Laborer..................	60	6.60	17	112	No.
7	No...	Laborer..................	60	6.60	17	112	No.
7	No...	Laborer..................	60	7.50	30	225	No..
2	No...	Teacher	(a)	3.00	52	156	No.
2	....	Housewife and merchant, wood.	(a)	1.50	(a)	(a)	No.
2	....	Scholar	....	....	....	....	No.
2	....	At home	....	....	....	....	No.
......	....	At home	....	....	....	....	No.
8	Yes..	Laborer	60	6.72	9	60	No.
8	....	Housewife and merchant, wood.	(a)	2.40	52	125	No.
8	....	Scholar	....	....	....	....	No.
......	....	Scholar	....	....	....	....	No.
......	....	At home	....	....	....	....	No.
......	....	At home	....	....	....	....	No.
15	Yes..	No occupation	....	....	....	....	Rheumatism.
15	....	Housewife..........	....	....	....	....	Childbirth.
15	....	Bicycle shop employee....	60	6.00	26	156	No.
......	....	Merchant, wood	(a)	1.20	52	62	No.
......	....	Scholar	....	....	....	....	No.
......	....	At home..........	....	....	....	....	No.
......	....	At home..........	....	....	....	....	No.
......	....	At home..........	....	....	....	....	No.
......	....	At home..........	....	....	....	....	No.

TABLE I.—GENERAL SOCIAL AND ECONOMIC CONDITION, BY FAMILIES AND INDIVIDUALS—Continued.

Family number.	Relationship to head of family.	Sex.	Age.	Conjugal condition.	Birthplace.	Birthplace of—	
						Father.	Mother.
432	Head	M.	42	Married	Basilicata	Basilicata	Basilicata
	Wife	F.	36	Married	Basilicata	Basilicata	Basilicata
	Daughter	F.	8	Single	United States	Basilicata	Basilicata
	Daughter	F.	6	Single	United States	Basilicata	Basilicata
	Son	M.	4	Single	United States	Basilicata	Basilicata
	Son	M.	2	Single	United States	Basilicata	Basilicata
433	Head	F.	56	Widowed	Campania	Campania	Campania
	Daughter	F.	18	Single	Campania	Campania	Campania
434	Head	M.	65	Married	Abruzzo	Abruzzo	Abruzzo
	Wife	F.	60	Married	Abruzzo	Abruzzo	Abruzzo
435	Cooperative	M.	45	Married	Calabria	Calabria	Calabria
	Cooperative	M.	50	Married	Calabria	Calabria	Calabria
	Cooperative	M.	55	Married	Calabria	Calabria	Calabria
	Cooperative	M.	47	Married	Calabria	Calabria	Calabria
	Cooperative	M.	25	Single	Calabria	Calabria	Calabria
436	Head	M.	30	Married	Sicily	Sicily	Sicily
	Wife	F.	37	Married	Sicily	Sicily	Sicily
	Stepson	M.	12	Single	Sicily	Sicily	Sicily
	Son	M.	4/12	Single	United States	Sicily	Sicily
437	Head	M.	34	Married	Basilicata	Basilicata	Basilicata
	Wife	F.	34	Married	Basilicata	Basilicata	Basilicata
	Son	M.	6	Single	Basilicata	Basilicata	Basilicata
	Daughter	F.	2	Single	United States	Basilicata	Basilicata
	Lodger	M.	34	Married	Basilicata	Basilicata	Basilicata
	Lodger	M.	34	Married	Basilicata	Basilicata	Basilicata
438	Head	M.	40	Married	Campania	Campania	Campania
	Wife	F.	40	Married	Campania	Campania	Campania
	Son	M.	22	Single	Campania	Campania	Campania
	Son	M.	15	Single	United States	Campania	Campania
	Son	M.	13	Single	United States	Campania	Campania
	Daughter	F.	11	Single	United States	Campania	Campania
	Daughter	F.	9	Single	United States	Campania	Campania
	Lodger	M.	26	Single	Basilicata	Basilicata	Basilicata
439	Head	M.	40	Married	Calabria	Calabria	Calabria
	Wife	F.	29	Married	Calabria	Calabria	Calabria
	Daughter	F.	2	Single	United States	Calabria	Calabria
	Daughter	F.	7/12	Single	United States	Calabria	Calabria
	Cousin	M.	29	Married	Calabria	Calabria	Calabria
440	Head	M.	41	Married	Campania	Campania	Campania
	Wife	F.	50	Married	Campania	Campania	Campania
	Son	M.	14	Single	United States	Campania	Campania
	Daughter	F.	12	Single	United States	Campania	Campania
	Son	M.	8	Single	United States	Campania	Campania
441	Head	M.	50	Married	Calabria	Calabria	Calabria
	Wife	F.	46	Married	Calabria	Calabria	Calabria
	Son	M.	16	Single	Calabria	Calabria	Calabria
	Boarder	M.	20	Single	Calabria	Calabria	Calabria
442	Head	M.	46	Married	Sicily	Sicily	Sicily
	Wife	F.	36	Married	Sicily	Sicily	Sicily
	Daughter	F.	18	Single	Sicily	Sicily	Sicily
	Daughter	F.	16	Single	Sicily	Sicily	Sicily
	Son	M.	11	Single	Sicily	Sicily	Sicily
	Daughter	F.	5	Single	United States	Sicily	Sicily
	Son	M.	4	Single	United States	Sicily	Sicily
	Son	M.	2	Single	United States	Sicily	Sicily
443	Head	M.	39	Married	Calabria	Calabria	Calabria
	Wife	F.	56	Married	Calabria	Calabria	Calabria
444	Head	M.	42	Married	Basilicata	Basilicata	Basilicata
	Wife	F.	34	Married	Basilicata	Basilicata	Basilicata
	Son	M.	17	Single	Basilicata	Basilicata	Basilicata
	Daughter	F.	7	Single	United States	Basilicata	Basilicata
	Daughter	F.	6	Single	United States	Basilicata	Basilicata
	Son	M.	2	Single	United States	Basilicata	Basilicata

a Not reported.
b Also worked as laborer nineteen weeks, at $7.50 per week.

TABLE I.—GENERAL SOCIAL AND ECONOMIC CONDITION, BY FAMILIES AND INDIVIDUALS—Continued.

Years in U.S.	Natu-ral-ized.	Profession, trade, or occupation.	Hours of work per week.	Average weekly earn-ings.	Weeks em-ploy-ed.	Total yearly earn-ings.	Sick during year, defective, maimed, or deformed.
13	Yes..	Laborer	60	$7.50	22	$165	No.
11	....	Housewife and merchant, wood.	(a)	2.40	52	125	No.
....	....	Scholar	....	....	....	....	No.
....	....	At home	....	....	....	....	Rickets.
....	....	At home	....	....	....	....	No.
....	....	At home	....	....	....	....	No.
7	....	Housewife and seamstress	60	4.00	26	104	Female complaint.
8	....	Seamstress	60	3.00	26	78	No.
1	No...	No occupation	....	....	....	....	No.
4	....	Housewife	....	....	....	....	Debility, general.
7	No...	Laborer	60	9.00	29	261	No.
3	No...	Laborer	60	(a)	15	(a)	No.
3	No...	Laborer	60	9.00	26	234	No.
3	No...	Laborer	60	9.00	26	234	No.
3	No...	Railroad laborer	60	7.50	22	165	No.
7	No...	Peddler, fruit (b)	(a)	3.00	b 33	242	No.
3	....	Housewife	....	....	....	....	Childbirth.
3	....	Scholar	....	....	....	....	Fever, typhoid.
....	....	At home	....	....	....	....	No.
5	Yes..	Ragpicker	66	1.15	52	60	No.
3	....	Housewife	....	....	....	....	No.
3	....	Scholar	....	....	....	....	No.
....	....	At home	....	....	....	....	Lungs, disease of.
5	Yes..	Laborer	60	7.50	15	113	No.
5	Yes..	Laborer	60	7.50	24	180	No.
20	Yes..	Laborer	60	7.50	9	68	Eyes, inflammation of both.
16	....	Housewife	....	....	....	....	No.
16	Yes..	Laborer	60	7.50	9	68	No.
....	....	No occupation	....	....	....	....	No.
....	....	Scholar	....	....	....	....	No.
....	....	No occupation	....	....	....	....	No.
....	....	Scholar	....	....	....	....	No.
6	No...	Laborer	60	6.60	19	125	No.
14	Yes..	Ragpicker (c)	(a)	2.50	c 48	150	Dyspepsia.
4	....	Housewife	....	....	....	....	Childbirth.
....	....	At home	....	....	....	....	Measles.
....	....	At home	....	....	....	....	No.
4	No...	Laborer	(a)	7.50	36	270	No.
17	Yes..	Carpenter	60	12.00	12	144	No.
17	....	Housewife	....	....	....	....	Rheumatism.
....	....	Knife factory employee	60	2.50	44	110	No.
....	....	Housework	....	....	....	....	No.
....	....	Scholar	....	....	....	....	No.
15	Yes..	No occupation	....	....	....	....	No.
12	....	Housewife	....	....	....	....	No.
12	....	Baker's helper	60	4.00	52	208	No.
4	....	Expressman	(a)	(a)	52	(a)	No.
10	No...	Street sweeper	60	7.50	15	113	No.
9	....	Housewife	....	....	....	....	Rheumatism.
9	....	Dressmaker	(a)	1.50	20	30	No.
9	....	Knife factory employee	48	2.40	26	62	No.
9	....	Scholar	....	....	....	....	No.
....	....	Scholar	....	....	....	....	No.
....	....	At home	....	....	....	....	Fever, not specified.
....	....	At home	....	....	....	....	No.
8	No...	Umbrella mender (d)	(a)	4.25	d 14	106	Bronchitis.
8	....	Housewife	....	....	....	....	Female complaint.
15	Yes..	Ragpicker	(a)	1.50	52	78	No.
9	....	Housewife	....	....	....	....	No.
9	....	Scholar and newsboy	30	2.50	52	130	No.
....	....	Scholar	....	....	....	....	Rickets.
....	....	Scholar	....	....	....	....	No.
....	....	At home	....	....	....	....	Rickets.

c Also worked as laborer four weeks, at $7.50 per week.
d Also worked as laborer seven weeks, at $6.60 per week.

TABLE **I.**—GENERAL SOCIAL AND ECONOMIC CONDITION, BY FAMILIES AND INDIVIDUALS—Continued.

Family number.	Relationship to head of family.	Sex.	Age.	Conjugal condition.	Birthplace.	Birthplace of— Father.	Birthplace of— Mother.
445	Head	M.	36	Married...	Basilicata.......	Basilicata.......	Basilicata......
	Wife.............	F.	26	Married..	Basilicata.......	Basilicata.......	Basilicata......
	Son	M.	6	Single.....	United States...	Basilicata.......	Basilicata......
	Daughter.........	F.	4	Single.....	United States...	Basilicata.......	Basilicata......
	Son	M.	$\frac{1}{12}$	Single.....	United States...	Basilicata.......	Basilicata......
446	Head	M.	56	Married...	Basilicata.......	Basilicata.......	Basilicata......
	Wife.............	F.	56	Married...	Basilicata.......	Basilicata.......	Basilicata......
	Son	M.	17	Single.....	Basilicata.......	Basilicata.......	Basilicata......
	Daughter.........	F.	13	Single.....	Basilicata.......	Basilicata.......	Basilicata......
447	Head	M.	37	Married...	Calabria	Calabria	Calabria ......
	Wife.............	F.	32	Married...	Calabria	Calabria	Calabria ......
	Son	M.	10	Single.....	Calabria	Calabria	Calabria ......
	Daughter.........	F.	4	Single.....	United States...	Calabria	Calabria ......
	Son	M.	3	Single.....	United States...	Calabria	Calabria ......
	Father............	M.	60	Married...	Calabria	Calabria	Calabria ......
	Mother	F.	60	Married...	Calabria	Calabria	Calabria ......
448	Head	M.	28	Married...	Basilicata.......	Basilicata.......	Basilicata......
	Wife.............	F.	22	Married...	Basilicata.......	Basilicata.......	Basilicata......
	Daughter.........	F.	2	Single.....	United States...	Basilicata.......	Basilicata......
	Son	M.	$\frac{1}{12}$	Single.....	United States...	Basilicata.......	Basilicata......
	Mother-in-law	F.	45	Widowed .	Basilicata.......	Basilicata.......	Basilicata......
449	Head	M.	46	Married...	Liguria	Liguria	Liguria ......
	Wife.............	F.	34	Married...	Liguria	Liguria	Liguria ......
	Son	M.	15	Single.....	United States...	Liguria	Liguria ......
	Son	M.	10	Single.....	United States...	Liguria	Liguria ......
	Son	M.	8	Single.....	United States...	Liguria	Liguria ......
	Daughter.........	F.	4	Single.....	United States...	Liguria	Liguria ......
	Daughter.........	F.	1	Single.....	United States...	Liguria	Liguria ......
450	Head	M.	38	Married...	Calabria	Calabria	Calabria ......
	Wife.............	F.	27	Married...	Campania......	Campania......	Campania......
	Daughter.........	F.	8	Single.....	Campania......	Calabria	Campania......
451	Head	M.	36	Married...	Basilicata.......	Basilicata.......	Basilicata......
	Wife.............	F.	30	Married...	Basilicata.......	Basilicata.......	Basilicata......
	Son	M.	9	Single.....	United States...	Basilicata.......	Basilicata......
	Son	M.	1	Single.....	United States...	Basilicata.......	Basilicata......
452	Head	M.	29	Married...	Campania......	Campania......	Campania......
	Wife.............	F.	21	Married...	Campania......	Campania......	Campania......
	Son	M.	3	Single.....	United States...	Campania......	Campania......
	Daughter.........	F.	2	Single.....	United States...	Campania......	Campania......
453	Head	M.	23	Married...	Calabria	Calabria	Calabria ......
	Wife.............	F.	20	Married...	Calabria	Calabria	Calabria ......
454	Head	M.	40	Married...	Basilicata.......	Basilicata.......	Basilicata......
	Wife.............	F.	44	Married...	Basilicata.......	Basilicata.......	Basilicata......
	Daughter.........	F.	14	Single.....	Basilicata.......	Basilicata.......	Basilicata......
	Daughter.........	F.	7	Single.....	United States...	Basilicata.......	Basilicata......
	Daughter.........	F.	4	Single.....	United States...	Basilicata.......	Basilicata......
455	Head	M.	40	Married...	Basilicata.......	Basilicata.......	Basilicata......
	Wife.............	F.	36	Married...	Basilicata.......	Basilicata.......	Basilicata......
	Daughter.........	F.	17	Single.....	Basilicata.......	Basilicata.......	Basilicata......
	Daughter.........	F.	14	Single.....	Basilicata.......	Basilicata.......	Basilicata......
	Son	M.	7	Single.....	United States...	Basilicata.......	Basilicata......
	Daughter.........	F.	6	Single.....	United States...	Basilicata.......	Basilicata......
	Daughter.........	F.	2	Single.....	United States...	Basilicata.......	Basilicata......
456	Head	M.	52	Married...	Basilicata.......	Basilicata.......	Basilicata......
	Wife.............	F.	50	Married...	Basilicata.......	Basilicata.......	Basilicata......
	Daughter.........	F.	20	Single.....	Basilicata.......	Basilicata.......	Basilicata......
	Daughter.........	F.	18	Single.....	Basilicata.......	Basilicata.......	Basilicata......
	Stepson...........	M.	18	Single.....	Basilicata.......	Basilicata.......	Basilicata......

a Not reported.
b Also worked as laborer three weeks, at $7.50 per week.
c Also worked as newsboy two weeks, at $1.50 per week.

TABLE **I.**—GENERAL SOCIAL AND ECONOMIC CONDITION, BY FAMILIES AND INDIVIDUALS—Continued.

Years in U.S.	Natu- ral- ized.	Profession, trade, or occupation.	Hours of work per week.	Average weekly earn- ings.	Weeks em- ploy- ed.	Total yearly earn- ings.	Sick during year, defective, maimed, or deformed.
10	Yes..	Driver....................	(a)	$9.00	52	$468	No.
8	......	Housewife...............					Childbirth.
......	......	Scholar					Bronchitis.
......	......	At home					No.
......	......	At home					No.
15	Yes..	Ragpicker (b)	(a)	.75	b 35	49	Fever, malarial.
8	......	Housewife					Arm, loss of one.
8	......	Laborer (c)................	60	7.50	c 3	26	Fever, malarial.
8	......	Washerwoman............	(a)	.50	52	26	No.
15	No...	Laborer....................	60	9.00	13	117	No.
5	......	Housewife					No.
5	......	Scholar					No.
......	......	At home					No.
......	......	At home					No.
3	No...	No occupation					No.
3	......	Housework					No.
13	Yes..	Brass factory employee ...	(a)	9.00	43	387	Dyspepsia.
20	......	Housewife...............					Childbirth; heart disease.
......	......	At home					Brain, congestion of.
......	......	At home					No.
20	......	Housework					No.
16	No...	Laborer....................	60	9.00	17	153	Fever, typhoid.
16	......	Housewife...............					No.
......	......	Newsboy and salesman, clothing.	64½	3.00	52	156	No.
......	......	Scholar and newsboy......	(a)	.60	52	31	Pneumonia.
......	......	Scholar and newsboy......	(a)	.60	52	31	No.
......	......	At home					No.
......	......	At home					No.
8	No...	Shoemaker (d)	(a)	4.00	d 43	237	La grippe.
4	......	Housewife....					La grippe.
4	......	Scholar					La grippe.
13	Yes..	Ragpicker	54	3.00	44	132	Fever, typhoid.
10	......	Housewife...............					No.
......	......	At home					No.
......	......	At home					No.
10	No...	Laborer....................	60	7.50	26	195	Injury by accident.
15	......	Housewife...............					Female complaint.
......	......	At home					Measles.
......	......	At home					Asthma.
12	Yes..	No occupation					Neuralgia.
4	......	Housewife					Miscarriage.
15	Yes..	Scissors grinder (e)........	(a)	3.00	e 41	131	No.
8	......	Housewife...............					Female complaint; immo- bility of one wrist.
8	......	Pants maker...............	24	.60	30	18	No.
......	......	Scholar					No.
......	......	At home					Throat, inflammation of.
14	Yes..	Street sweeper	48	9.00	26	234	Vertigo.
12	......	Housewife...............					No.
12	......	Jacket maker.............	72	3.75	23	86	No.
12	......	Jacket maker.............	57	2.50	23	58	No.
......	......	Scholar					No.
......	......	Scholar					Smallpox.
......	......	At home					Smallpox.
4	No...	Ragpicker (f)	(a)	1.00	f 45	91	No.
½	......	Housewife................					No.
½	......	No occupation					No.
½	......	No occupation					No.
½	......	Newsboy	28	1.75	(a)	(a)	No.

d Also worked as laborer nine weeks, a' $7.20 per week.
e Also worked as laborer one week, at $7.50 per week.
f Also worked as laborer seven weeks, at $6.60 per week.

TABLE I.—GENERAL SOCIAL AND ECONOMIC CONDITION, BY FAMILIES AND INDIVIDUALS—Continued.

Family number.	Relationship to head of family.	Sex.	Age.	Conjugal condition.	Birthplace.	Birthplace of—	
						Father.	Mother.
457	Head	M.	45	Married...	Campania	Campania	Campania
	Wife	F.	42	Married...	Campania	Campania	Campania
	Son	M.	21	Single	Campania	Campania	Campania
	Son	M.	14	Single	Campania	Campania	Campania
	Son	M.	3	Single	United States...	Campania	Campania
458	Head	M.	49	Married...	Basilicata	Basilicata	Basilicata
	Wife	F.	49	Married...	Basilicata	Basilicata	Basilicata
	Daughter	F.	3	Single	United States...	Basilicata	Basilicata
	Daughter	F.	1	Single	United States...	Basilicata	Basilicata
459	Head	M.	44	Married...	Basilicata	Basilicata	Basilicata
	Wife	F.	38	Married...	Sicily	Sicily	Sicily
460	Head	M.	32	Married...	Basilicata	Basilicata	Basilicata
	Wife	F.	30	Married...	Basilicata	Basilicata	Basilicata
	Daughter	F.	7	Single	Basilicata	Basilicata	Basilicata
	Daughter	F.	4	Single	United States...	Basilicata	Basilicata
	Son	M.	2	Single	United States...	Basilicata	Basilicata
	Brother-in-law	M.	35	Married...	Basilicata	Basilicata	Basilicata
	Brother-in-law	M.	24	Single	Basilicata	Basilicata	Basilicata
461	Head	M.	35	Married...	Abruzzo	Abruzzo	Abruzzo
	Wife	F.	22	Married...	Abruzzo	Abruzzo	Abruzzo
	Son	M.	4	Single	United States...	Abruzzo	Abruzzo
	Daughter	F.	2	Single	United States...	Abruzzo	Abruzzo
	Son	M.	1½	Single	United States...	Abruzzo	Abruzzo
462	Head	M.	30	Married...	Campania	Campania	Campania
	Wife	F.	27	Married...	Campania	Campania	Campania
	Son	M.	4	Single	United States...	Campania	Campania
	Daughter	F.	1	Single	United States...	Campania	Campania
	Brother-in-law	M.	30	Married	Campania	Campania	Campania
	Boarder	M.	40	Single	Campania	Campania	Campania
	Lodger	M.	35	Married	Campania	Campania	Campania
	Lodger	M.	40	Married	Campania	Campania	Campania
463	Head	M.	38	Married...	Abruzzo	Abruzzo	Abruzzo
	Wife	F.	34	Married...	Abruzzo	Abruzzo	Abruzzo
	Son	M.	10	Single	Abruzzo	Abruzzo	Abruzzo
	Son	M.	3	Single	United States...	Abruzzo	Abruzzo
	Son	M.	1	Single	United States...	Abruzzo	Abruzzo
464	Head	M.	35	Married...	Abruzzo	Abruzzo	Abruzzo
	Wife	F.	30	Married...	Abruzzo	Abruzzo	Abruzzo
	Son	M.	8	Single	United States...	Abruzzo	Abruzzo
	Son	M.	7	Single	United States...	Abruzzo	Abruzzo
	Son	M.	6	Single	United States...	Abruzzo	Abruzzo
	Son	M.	3	Single	United States...	Abruzzo	Abruzzo
	Daughter	F.	1	Single	United States...	Abruzzo	Abruzzo
465	Head	M.	42	Married...	Campania	Campania	Campania
	Wife	F.	37	Married...	Campania	Campania	Campania
	Son	M.	18	Single	Campania	Campania	Campania
	Son	M.	13	Single	United States...	Campania	Campania
	Son	M.	7	Single	United States...	Campania	Campania
	Son	M.	6	Single	United States...	Campania	Campania
	Daughter	F.	5	Single	United States...	Campania	Campania
	Daughter	F.	1	Single	United States...	Campania	Campania
466	Head	M.	45	Married...	Abruzzo	Abruzzo	Abruzzo
	Wife	F.	35	Married...	Abruzzo	Abruzzo	Abruzzo
	Son	M.	14	Single	Abruzzo	Abruzzo	Abruzzo
	Son	M.	9	Single	Abruzzo	Abruzzo	Abruzzo
	Daughter	F.	4	Single	United States...	Abruzzo	Abruzzo
	Son	M.	2	Single	United States...	Abruzzo	Abruzzo
467	Head	M.	36	Married...	Abruzzo	Abruzzo	Abruzzo
	Wife	F.	32	Married...	Abruzzo	Abruzzo	Abruzzo
	Son	M.	9	Single	Abruzzo	Abruzzo	Abruzzo
	Son	M.	½	Single	United States...	Abruzzo	Abruzzo
	Brother	M.	35	Married...	Abruzzo	Abruzzo	Abruzzo

a Not reported.   b Also worked as street sweeper nine weeks, at $7.50 per week.

TABLE I.—GENERAL SOCIAL AND ECONOMIC CONDITION, BY FAMILIES AND INDIVIDUALS—Continued.

Years in U. S.	Natu- ral- ized.	Profession, trade, or occupation.	Hours of work per week.	Average weekly earn- ings.	Weeks em- ploy- ed.	Total yearly earn- ings.	Sick during year, defective, maimed, or deformed.
14	Yes..	Laborer	60	$9.00	29	$261	No.
4	....	Housewife..............					Female complaint.
5	Yes..	Cloak maker...............	(a)	16.00	26	416	No.
4	....	Scholar					No.
......	....	At home................					No.
14	Yes..	Laborer................	60	7.50	26	195	No.
9	....	Housewife..............					No.
......	....	At home................					No.
......	....	At home................					No.
16	No...	Laborer................	60	7.20	6	43	Injury by accident.
14	....	Housewife..............					No.
6	Yes..	Laborer................	60	7.50	9	68	Rheumatism.
5	....	Housewife..............					No.
5	....	Scholar					Chicken pox.
......	....	At home................					Chicken pox.
......	....	At home................					Chicken pox.
4	No...	Street sweeper............	60	7.50	22	165	No.
5	No...	Rag sorter................	60	7.00	52	364	No.
9	Yes..	Street-car driver...........	70	11.55	39	450	No.
6	....	Housewife..............					Childbirth; female com- plaint.
......	....	At home................					No.
......	....	At home................					No.
......	....	At home................					No.
10	Yes..	Beggar					Blind.
5	....	Housewife..............					No.
......	....	At home................					No.
......	....	At home................					Bronchitis.
5	No...	Laborer................	60	8.25	17	140	No.
10	No...	Laborer................	60	7.50	17	128	No.
5	No...	Laborer................	60	8.25	17	140	No.
3	No...	Laborer................	60	9.00	13	117	No.
8	Yes..	Ragpicker (b).............	(a)	.90	b 43	106	Eyes, inflammation of both.
4	....	Housewife..............					No.
4	....	Scholar					No.
......	....	At home................					Skin, disease of.
......	....	At home................					No.
12	Yes..	No occupation					No.
10	....	Housewife..............					No.
......	....	Scholar					No.
......	....	Scholar					No.
......	....	At home................					No.
......	....	At home................					Rickets; fever, not speci- fied.
......	....	At home................					No.
16	Yes..	Ragpicker (c).............	(a)	1.00	c 30	195	No.
15	....	Housewife..............					No.
15	....	Bootblack	(a)	3.00	52	156	No.
......	....	Newsboy	(a)	.60	52	31	No.
......	....	Scholar					No.
......	....	Scholar					No.
......	....	At home................					No.
......	....	At home................					Pneumonia.
13	Yes..	Laborer................	60	7.50	13	98	No.
6	....	Housewife..............					Female complaint.
6	....	No occupation					No.
6	....	At home................					No.
......	....	At home................					Rickets.
......	....	At home................					No.
10	Yes..	Laborer................	60	9.00	22	198	No.
1	....	Housewife and pants finisher.	(a)	.90	9	8	Childbirth.
1	....	Scholar					No.
......	....	At home................					No.
10	Yes..	Laborer................	60	9.00	22	198	No.

c Also worked as street sweeper twenty-two weeks, at $7.50 per week.

TABLE **I.**—GENERAL SOCIAL AND ECONOMIC CONDITION, BY FAMILIES AND INDIVIDUALS—Continued.

Family number.	Relationship to head of family.	Sex.	Age.	Conjugal condition.	Birthplace.	Birthplace of— Father.	Birthplace of— Mother.
467	Lodger	M.	40	Married...	Abruzzo	Abruzzo	Abruzzo
	Lodger	M.	40	Married...	Abruzzo	Abruzzo	Abruzzo
	Lodger	M.	20	Single.....	Abruzzo	Abruzzo	Abruzzo
	Lodger	M.	28	Married...	Abruzzo	Abruzzo	Abruzzo
468	Head	M.	44	Married...	Abruzzo	Abruzzo	Abruzzo
	Wife	F.	42	Married...	Abruzzo	Abruzzo	Abruzzo
	Daughter	F.	13	Single.....	Abruzzo	Abruzzo	Abruzzo
	Son	M.	12	Single.....	Abruzzo	Abruzzo	Abruzzo
	Son	M.	12	Single.....	Abruzzo	Abruzzo	Abruzzo
	Daughter	F.	8	Single.....	United States	Abruzzo	Abruzzo
	Daughter	F.	5	Single.....	United States	Abruzzo	Abruzzo
	Daughter	F.	₅₁₂	Single.....	United States	Abruzzo	Abruzzo
	Boarder	M.	33	Married...	Abruzzo	Abruzzo	Abruzzo
	Boarder	M.	27	Married...	Abruzzo	Abruzzo	Abruzzo
	Lodger	M.	29	Married...	Abruzzo	Abruzzo	Abruzzo
469	Head	M.	27	Married...	Abruzzo	Abruzzo	Abruzzo
	Wife	F.	20	Married...	Abruzzo	Abruzzo	Abruzzo
	Daughter	F.	2	Single.....	United States	Abruzzo	Abruzzo
	Daughter	F.	₁₁₂	Single.....	United States	Abruzzo	Abruzzo
470	Head	M.	29	Married...	Abruzzo	Abruzzo	Abruzzo
	Wife	F.	18	Married...	Abruzzo	Abruzzo	Abruzzo
	Daughter	F.	1	Single.....	United States	Abruzzo	Abruzzo
	Cousin	M.	29	Married...	Abruzzo	Abruzzo	Abruzzo
	Boarder	M.	20	Single.....	Abruzzo	Abruzzo	Abruzzo
	Lodger	M.	42	Married...	Abruzzo	Abruzzo	Abruzzo
	Lodger	M.	10	Single.....	United States	Abruzzo	Abruzzo
471	Head	F.	31	Widowed .	Abruzzo	Abruzzo	Abruzzo
	Son	M.	12	Single.....	Abruzzo	Abruzzo	Abruzzo
	Daughter	F.	10	Single.....	Abruzzo	Abruzzo	Abruzzo
	Son	M.	5	Single.....	United States	Abruzzo	Abruzzo
472	Head	M.	35	Married...	Abruzzo	Abruzzo	Abruzzo
	Wife	F.	36	Married...	Abruzzo	Abruzzo	Abruzzo
	Daughter	F.	5	Single.....	United States	Abruzzo	Abruzzo
	Son	M.	₂₁₂	Single.....	United States	Abruzzo	Abruzzo
	Brother	M.	45	Married...	Abruzzo	Abruzzo	Abruzzo
473	Head	M.	40	Married...	Campania	Campania	Campania
	Wife	F.	35	Married...	Campania	Campania	Campania
	Daughter	F.	11	Single. ...	United States	Campania	Campania
	Son	M.	5	Single.....	United States	Campania	Campania
	Daughter	F.	3	Single.....	United States	Campania	Campania
	Daughter	F.	3	Single.....	United States	Campania	Campania
	Mother-in-law	F.	63	Widowed .	Campania	Campania	Campania
474	Cooperative	M.	50	Married...	Abruzzo	Abruzzo	Abruzzo
	Cooperative	M.	30	Single.....	Abruzzo	Abruzzo	Abruzzo
	Cooperative	M.	66	Widowed .	Abruzzo	Abruzzo	Abruzzo
	Cooperative	M.	56	Married...	Abruzzo	Abruzzo	Abruzzo
	Cooperative	M.	36	Married...	Abruzzo	Abruzzo	Abruzzo
475	Head	M.	36	Married...	Abruzzo	Abruzzo	Abruzzo
	Wife	F.	35	Married...	Abruzzo	Abruzzo	Abruzzo
	Daughter	F.	2	Single.....	United States	Abruzzo	Abruzzo
476	Head	M.	55	Married...	Abruzzo	Abruzzo	Abruzzo
	Wife	F.	55	Married...	Abruzzo	Abruzzo	Abruzzo
	Son	M.	14	Single.....	Abruzzo	Abruzzo	Abruzzo
477	Head	M.	32	Married...	Abruzzo	Abruzzo	Abruzzo
	Wife	F.	22	Married...	Abruzzo	Abruzzo	Abruzzo
	Daughter	F.	2	Single.....	United States	Abruzzo	Abruzzo
	Daughter	F.	1	Single.....	United States	Abruzzo	Abruzzo
	Mother	F.	78	Widowed .	Abruzzo	Abruzzo	Abruzzo
478	Head	M.	43	Married...	Abruzzo	Abruzzo	Abruzzo
	Wife	F.	45	Married...	Abruzzo	Abruzzo	Abruzzo
	Daughter	F.	16	Single.....	Abruzzo	Abruzzo	Abruzzo

a Not reported.

TABLE I.—GENERAL SOCIAL AND ECONOMIC CONDITION, BY FAMILIES AND INDIVIDUALS—Continued.

Years in U.S.	Naturalized.	Profession, trade, or occupation.	Hours of work per week.	Average weekly earnings.	Weeks employed.	Total yearly earnings.	Sick during year, defective, maimed, or deformed.
3	No...	Laborer	60	$9.00	13	$117	No.
8	Yes..	Laborer	60	9.00	22	198	No.
3/12		No occupation					No.
1/12	No...	No occupation					No.
11	No...	Scissors grinder	(a)	3.00	35	105	No.
11		Housewife					Childbirth.
11		Packer, knife factory (b)	60	3.00	b 22	93	No.
11		Scholar					No.
11		Scholar					No.
		Scholar					No.
		At home					No.
		At home					No.
14	Yes..	Laborer	48	13.50	26	351	No.
3	No...	Scissors grinder	(a)	8.00	35	280	No.
4	No...	Laborer	60	7.50	26	195	Pneumonia.
3	No...	Barber	81	(a)	52	(a)	No.
11		Housewife					Childbirth.
		At home					No.
		At home					No.
9	Yes.	Scissors grinder	(a)	3.00	52	156	No.
8		Housewife					No.
		At home					No.
5	No...	Laborer	60	7.50	9	68	No.
4	No...	Scissors grinder	(a)	3.00	43	129	Injury by accident.
10		Hod carrier	48	5.40	30	162	Rheumatism.
		Scholar					No.
6		Housewife and washerwoman.	(a)	1.00	52	52	Female complaint.
6		Scholar					No.
6		Scholar					No.
		At home					No.
9	No...	No occupation					No.
9		Housewife					Childbirth.
		At home					No.
		At home					No.
7	Yes..	Sewer digger	60	12.00	4	48	Rheumatism.
14	Yes..	Ragpicker	(a)	1.50	52	78	No.
14		Housewife					No.
		No occupation					No.
		At home					No.
		At home					Rickets.
		At home					Rickets.
9		No occupation					Dropsy.
6	No...	Street sweeper	60	9.00	22	198	No.
8	Yes..	Laborer	60	8.40	9	76	No.
8	No...	Laborer	60	7.50	43	323	Fever, not specified.
9	No...	Laborer	60	7.50	43	323	No.
8	Yes..	Laborer	60	8.25	22	182	No.
10	Yes..	Laborer	48	9.00	9	81	Pneumonia.
4		Housewife					Female complaint.
		At home					No.
15	No...	Scissors grinder	(a)	5.00	52	260	No.
4		Housewife					No.
4		Bootblack	(a)	3.00	(a)	(a)	No.
13	Yes..	No occupation					No.
4		Housewife					No.
		At home					No.
		At home					No.
6		No occupation					No.
18	Yes..	No occupation					Rheumatism.
8		Housewife					Childbirth.
8		Housework					No.

b Also worked as cloak finisher nine weeks, at $3 per week.

TABLE **I.**—GENERAL SOCIAL AND ECONOMIC CONDITION, BY FAMILIES
AND INDIVIDUALS—Continued.

Family number.	Relationship to head of family.	Sex.	Age.	Conjugal condition.	Birthplace.	Birthplace of—	
						Father.	Mother.
478	Son	M.	7	Single.....	United States...	Abruzzo	Abruzzo ......
	Daughter	F.	6	Single.....	United States...	Abruzzo	Abruzzo ......
	Daughter	F.	8/12	Single.....	United States...	Abruzzo.......	Abruzzo ......
479	Head	M.	23	Married...	Calabria	Calabria	Calabria ......
	Wife..............	F.	18	Married...	Basilicata........	Basilicata......	Basilicata.....
	Son	M.	7/12	Single.....	United States...	Calabria	Basilicata.....
	Father...........	M.	50	Married...	Calabria	Calabria	Calabria ......
	Mother	F.	45	Married...	Calabria	Calabria	Calabria ......
	Boarder	M.	29	Single.....	Calabria	Calabria	Calabria ......
	Boarder	M.	25	Single.....	Calabria	Calabria	Calabria ......
480	Head	M.	35	Married...	Campania........	Campania......	Campania......
	Wife..............	F.	35	Married...	Campania........	Campania......	Campania......
	Daughter...........	F.	10	Single.....	United States...	Campania......	Campania......
	Son	M.	8	Single.....	United States...	Campania......	Campania......
	Daughter...........	F.	5	Single.....	United States...	Campania......	Campania......
	Daughter...........	F.	2	Single.....	United States...	Campania......	Campania......
	Daughter...........	F.	7/12	Single.....	United States...	Campania......	Campania......
481	Head	F.	36	Widowed .	Basilicata........	Basilicata......	Basilicata.....
	Daughter...........	F.	8	Single.....	United States...	Basilicata......	Basilicata.....
	Son	M.	3	Single.....	United States...	Basilicata......	Basilicata.....
	Daughter..........	F.	1	Single.....	United States...	Basilicata......	Basilicata.....
482	Cooperative	M.	38	Single.....	Calabria	Calabria.......	Calabria ......
	Cooperative	M.	35	Married...	Calabria	Calabria	Calabria ......
	Cooperative	M.	38	Married...	Calabria	Calabria	Calabria ......
	Cooperative	M.	36	Single.....	Calabria	Calabria	Calabria ......
483	Head	M.	32	Married...	Abruzzo	Abruzzo	Abruzzo ......
	Wife..............	F.	32	Married...	Abruzzo	Abruzzo	Abruzzo ......
	Son	M.	8	Single.....	Abruzzo	Abruzzo	Abruzzo ......
	Daughter..........	F.	5	Single.....	Abruzzo	Abruzzo	Abruzzo ......
484	Head	M.	24	Married...	Calabria	Calabria	Calabria ......
	Wife..............	F.	18	Married...	Calabria	Calabria	Calabria ......
485	Head	M.	30	Married...	Calabria	Calabria	Calabria ......
	Wife..............	F.	33	Married...	Calabria	Calabria	Calabria ......
	Son	M.	10	Single.....	Calabria	Calabria	Calabria ......
	Daughter..........	F.	2	Single.....	United States...	Calabria	Calabria ......
486	Head	M.	36	Married...	Campania........	Campania......	Campania......
	Wife..............	F.	29	Married...	Campania........	Campania......	Campania......
	Daughter..........	F.	9	Single.....	United States...	Campania......	Campania......
	Son	M.	5	Single.....	United States...	Campania......	Campania......
	Daughter..........	F.	2	Single.....	United States...	Campania......	Campania......
487	Cooperative	M.	25	Single.....	Calabria	Calabria	Calabria ......
	Cooperative	M.	20	Single.....	Calabria	Calabria	Calabria ......
	Cooperative	M.	21	Single.....	Calabria	Calabria	Calabria ......
	Cooperative	M.	24	Single.....	Calabria	Calabria	Calabria ......
488	Cooperative	M.	26	Single.....	Calabria	Calabria	Calabria ......
	Cooperative	M.	36	Married...	Calabria	Calabria	Calabria ......
	Cooperative	M.	24	Single.....	Calabria	Calabria	Calabria ......
	Cooperative	M.	40	Married...	Calabria	Calabria	Calabria ......
489	Head	M.	35	Married...	Abruzzo	Abruzzo	Abruzzo ......
	Wife..............	F.	30	Married...	Abruzzo	Abruzzo	Abruzzo ......
	Daughter..........	F.	2	Single.....	United States...	Abruzzo	Abruzzo ......
	Lodger	M.	27	Single.....	Abruzzo	Abruzzo	Abruzzo ......
	Lodger	M.	30	Married...	Abruzzo	Abruzzo	Abruzzo ......
490	Head	M.	30	Single.....	Calabria	Calabria	Calabria ......
	Lodger	M.	47	Married...	Calabria	Calabria	Calabria ......
	Lodger	M.	27	Single.....	Calabria	Calabria	Calabria ......
	Lodger	M.	28	Married...	Calabria	Calabria	Calabria ......
491	Head	M.	40	Married...	Campania........	Campania......	Campania......
	Wife..............	F.	42	Married...	Campania........	Campania......	Campania......

a Not reported.

TABLE **I.**—GENERAL SOCIAL AND ECONOMIC CONDITION, BY FAMILIES AND INDIVIDUALS—Continued.

Years in U. S.	Natu- ral- ized.	Profession, trade, or occupation.	Hours of work per week.	Average weekly earn- ings.	Weeks em- ploy- ed.	Total yearly earn- ings.	Sick during year, defective, maimed, or deformed.
......	....	Scholar.................	......	....	......	....	No.
......	....	At home...............	......	....	......	....	Rickets.
......	....	At home...............	......	....	......	....	No.
7	Yes..	News dealer.............	73	$6.00	52	$312	No.
3	....	Housewife..............	......	....	......	....	Childbirth.
......	....	At home...............	......	....	......	....	No.
8	No...	Newspaper carrier........	73	7.00	52	364	Finger, deformity of one.
5	....	Housework.............	......	....	......	....	Female complaint.
7	No...	Watchman...............	63	9.00	34	306	No.
7	No...	Scholar and expressman...	54	6.00	52	312	No.
16	Yes..	Laborer.................	60	7 50	17	128	No.
14	....	Housewife..............	......	....	......	....	Childbirth.
......	....	Scholar.................	......	....	......	....	No.
......	....	At home...............	......	....	......	....	No.
......	....	At home...............	......	....	......	....	No.
......	....	At home...............	......	....	......	....	No.
......	....	At home...............	......	....	......	....	No.
15	....	Housewife and pants finisher.	72	1.80	52	94	No.
......	....	Scholar.................	......	....	......	....	No.
......	....	At home...............	......	....	......	....	No.
......	....	At home...............	......	....	......	....	No.
5	No...	Laborer.................	60	7.50	15	113	Fever, not specified.
3	No...	Laborer.................	60	7.50	15	113	No.
3	No...	Laborer.................	60	7.50	15	113	No.
5	No...	Laborer.................	60	7.50	9	68	No.
5	Yes..	Laborer.................	60	7.20	52	374	No.
3	....	Housewife..............	......	....	......	....	No.
3	....	Scholar.................	......	....	......	....	No.
3	....	At home...............	......	....	......	....	Eye, loss of one.
8	No...	Laborer.................	(a)	6.10	29	177	No.
7	....	Housewife..............	......	....	......	....	No
8	No...	Laborer.................	60	7.58	22	167	Lungs, disease of.
3	....	Housewife..............	......	....	......	....	Fever, typhoid.
3	....	Scholar.................	......	....	......	....	No.
......	....	At home...............	......	....	......	....	Debility, general.
15	No...	Stonebreaker.............	60	7.20	52	374	No.
12	....	Housewife..............	......	....	......	....	No.
......	....	At home...............	......	....	......	....	No.
......	....	At home...............	......	....	......	....	No.
......	....	At home...............	......	....	......	....	No.
6	Yes..	Laborer.................	60	6.60	26	172	No.
4	....	Laborer.................	60	6.60	26	172	No.
5	Yes..	Laborer.................	60	6.60	26	172	No.
6	Yes..	Laborer.................	60	6.60	26	172	No.
3	No...	Laborer.................	60	7.50	22	165	No.
12	Yes..	Laborer.................	60	7.50	52	390	No.
3	No...	Laborer.................	60	7.50	22	165	No.
6	No...	Laborer.................	60	7.50	52	390	No.
9	Yes..	Laborer.................	60	7.50	13	98	No.
3	....	Housewife..............	......	...	......	....	Fever, not specified.
......	....	At home...............	......	....	......	....	Bronchitis.
7	No...	Laborer.................	60	6.90	17	117	Eye, loss of one.
$\frac{3}{12}$	No...	No occupation.............	......	....	......	....	No.
13	Yes..	Padrone.................	(a)	(a)	52	(a)	No.
13	No...	Laborer.................	60	7.50	26	195	No.
6	Yes..	Railroad laborer..........	60	7.50	32	240	No.
3	No...	Laborer.................	60	7.50	52	390	No.
14	Yes..	Laborer.................	60	7.50	9	68	No.
4	....	Housewife and seamstress.	30	2.50	19	48	No.

TABLE **I.**—GENERAL SOCIAL AND ECONOMIC CONDITION, BY FAMILIES
AND INDIVIDUALS—Continued.

Family number.	Relationship to head of family.	Sex.	Age.	Conjugal condition.	Birthplace.	Birthplace of—	
						Father.	Mother.
492	Head	F.	60	Widowed	Campania	Campania	Campania
	Son	M.	26	Single	Campania	Campania	Campania
	Daughter	F.	23	Single	Campania	Campania	Campania
493	Head	M.	33	Married	Campania	Campania	Campania
	Wife	F.	32	Married	Campania	Campania	Campania
	Son	M.	10	Single	Campania	Campania	Campania
	Son	M.	5	Single	United States	Campania	Campania
	Son	M.	3	Single	United States	Campania	Campania
	Son	M.	1	Single	United States	Campania	Campania
	Boarder	M.	26	Single	Campania	Campania	Campania
494	Head	M.	41	Married	Campania	Campania	Campania
	Wife	F.	43	Married	Campania	Campania	Campania
	Daughter	F.	15	Single	Campania	Campania	Campania
	Son	M.	7	Single	United States	Campania	Campania
	Daughter	F.	6	Single	United States	Campania	Campania
	Son	M.	5	Single	United States	Campania	Campania
495	Head	M.	29	Married	Campania	Campania	Campania
	Wife	F.	23	Married	Campania	Campania	Campania
	Son	M.	3	Single	United States	Campania	Campania
	Daughter	F.	2	Single	United States	Campania	Campania
	Son	M.	$\frac{3}{12}$	Single	United States	Campania	Campania
	Father	M.	65	Married	Campania	Campania	Campania
496	Head	M.	32	Married	Campania	Campania	Campania
	Wife	F.	18	Married	Campania	Campania	Campania
	Brother	M.	25	Single	Campania	Campania	Campania
	Brother	M.	23	Single	Campania	Campania	Campania
497	Head	M.	42	Married	Abruzzo	Abruzzo	Abruzzo
	Wife	F.	32	Married	Abruzzo	Abruzzo	Abruzzo
	Daughter	F.	7	Single	United States	Abruzzo	Abruzzo
	Daughter	F.	4	Single	United States	Abruzzo	Abruzzo
	Daughter	F.	2	Single	United States	Abruzzo	Abruzzo
	Daughter	F.	1	Single	United States	Abruzzo	Abruzzo
498	Head	M.	53	Widowed	Calabria	Calabria	Calabria
	Son	M.	8	Single	Calabria	Calabria	Calabria
499	Head	M.	36	Married	Campania	Campania	Campania
	Wife	F.	32	Married	Campania	Campania	Campania
	Son	M.	11	Single	Campania	Campania	Campania
	Daughter	F.	8	Single	United States	Campania	Campania
	Son	M.	4	Single	United States	Campania	Campania
	Daughter	F.	2	Single	United States	Campania	Campania
	Son	M.	$\frac{1}{12}$	Single	United States	Campania	Campania
	Boarder	M.	32	Married	Campania	Campania	Campania
500	Head	M.	53	Married	Campania	Campania	Campania
	Wife	F.	53	Married	Campania	Campania	Campania
	Son	M.	18	Single	Campania	Campania	Campania
501	Head	M.	48	Married	Campania	Campania	Campania
	Wife	F.	59	Married	Campania	Campania	Campania
502	Head	M.	33	Married	Campania	Campania	Campania
	Wife	F.	33	Married	Campania	Campania	Campania
	Brother-in-law	M.	30	Single	Campania	Campania	Campania
503	Head	M.	35	Married	Sicily	Sicily	Sicily
	Wife	F.	25	Married	Sicily	Sicily	Sicily
504	Head	M.	36	Married	Campania	Campania	Campania
	Wife	F.	26	Married	Basilicata	Basilicata	Basilicata
	Son	M.	10	Single	Basilicata	Campania	Basilicata
	Daughter	F.	5	Single	United States	Campania	Basilicata
	Son	M.	2	Single	United States	Campania	Basilicata
505	Head	M.	36	Married	Campania	Campania	Campania
	Wife	F.	35	Married	Campania	Campania	Campania
	Son	M.	10	Single	Campania	Campania	Campania

a Not reported.
b Also worked as laborer thirteen weeks, at $7.50 per week.
c Also worked as coat finisher twenty-two weeks, at $0.75 per week.

TABLE **I.**—GENERAL SOCIAL AND ECONOMIC CONDITION, BY FAMILIES AND INDIVIDUALS—Continued.

Years in U.S.	Natu-ral-ized.	Profession, trade, or occupation.	Hours of work per week.	Average weekly earn-ings.	Weeks em-ploy-ed.	Total yearly earn-ings.	Sick during year, defective, maimed, or deformed.
2	Yes..	Housewife...............					No.
5		Laborer.................	60	$7.20	17	$122	Fever, typhoid.
2		Washerwoman	(a)	2.00	52	104	No.
10	Yes..	Ragpicker (b).............	(a)	1.50	b 30	143	Injury by accident.
8		Housewife...............					No.
8		Scholar.................					No.
		At home................					No.
		At home................					Measles.
		At home................					No.
11	Yes..	Laborer.	60	7.50	9	68	No.
14	Yes..	Street sweeper...........	56	9.75	17	166	No.
8		Housewife...............					No.
8		Servant (c)...............	(a)	2.50	c 30	92	No.
		Scholar.................					No.
		Scholar.................					Measles.
		At home................					Rickets; measles.
8	Yes..	Laborer.................	48	9.00	15	135	No.
8		Housewife...............					Childbirth; nervous affec-tion.
		At home................					Measles.
		At home................					Measles.
		At home................					No.
1	No...	No occupation					Rheumatism.
9	Yes..	Railroad laborer..........	(a)	7.50	28	210	No.
3		Housewife...............					No.
8	Yes..	Hod carrier..............	48	9.00	31	279	Fever, not specified.
6	Yes..	Hod carrier..............	48	7.50	35	263	No.
12	Yes..	Laborer.................	60	7.50	4	30	No.
7		Housewife...............					No.
		Scholar.................					Skin, disease of.
		At home................					Skin, disease of.
		At home................					Skin, disease of.
		At home................					Skin, disease of.
8	Yes..	Laborer.................	60	7.50	7	53	No.
8		At home................					No.
11	Yes..	Laborer.................	48	7.50	16	120	Fever, rheumatic.
11		Housewife					Childbirth.
11		Scholar.................					Abscesses, scrofulous.
		Scholar.................					No.
		At home................					No.
		At home................					No.
		At home................					No.
8	Yes..	Ragpicker (d).............	(a)	.75	d 47	73	No.
15	Yes..	Laborer.................	60	7.50	4	30	Blind in one eye.
8		Housewife...............					No.
8		Laborer.................	60	3.00	22	66	Fever, not specified.
16	Yes..	Laborer.................	48	9.00	15	135	No.
14		Housewife...............					No.
12	Yes..	Teamster................	60	9.00	33	297	Knee joint, immobility of one.
3		Housewife...............					Miscarriage.
7	Yes..	News dealer.............	56	4.56	52	237	No.
4	No...	Railroad laborer..........	57	7.20	52	374	No.
4		Housewife...............					No.
8	No...	Laborer	60	7.20	26	187	No.
8		Housewife and seamstress.	96	2.50	24	60	No.
8		Scholar.................					No.
		At home................					No.
		At home................					Skin, disease of.
6	No...	Ragpicker (e).............	(a)	.60	e 30	203	No.
1		Housewife...............					Childbirth.
1		No occupation					No.

d Also worked as laborer five weeks, at $7.50 per week.
e Also worked as street sweeper twenty-two weeks, at $8.40 per week.

TABLE I.—GENERAL SOCIAL AND ECONOMIC CONDITION, BY FAMILIES AND INDIVIDUALS—Continued.

Family number.	Relationship to head of family.	Sex.	Age.	Conjugal condition.	Birthplace.	Birthplace of—	
						Father.	Mother.
505	Son	M.	8	Single	Campania	Campania	Campania
	Son	M.	¾	Single	United States	Campania	Campania
	Mother	F.	80	Widowed	Campania	Campania	Campania
506	Head	M.	52	Married	Sicily	Sicily	Sicily
	Wife	F.	35	Married	Sicily	Sicily	Sicily
	Son	M.	28	Single	Sicily	Sicily	Sicily
	Son	M.	23	Single	Sicily	Sicily	Sicily
	Son	M.	22	Single	Sicily	Sicily	Sicily
	Daughter	F.	13	Single	Sicily	Sicily	Sicily
	Son	M.	10	Single	Sicily	Sicily	Sicily
507	Cooperative	M.	29	Married	Abruzzo	Abruzzo	Abruzzo
	Cooperative	M.	27	Single	Abruzzo	Abruzzo	Abruzzo
	Cooperative	M.	23	Single	Abruzzo	Abruzzo	Abruzzo
	Cooperative	M.	33	Married	Abruzzo	Abruzzo	Abruzzo
508	Head	M.	48	Married	Campania	Campania	Campania
	Wife	F.	43	Married	Campania	Campania	Campania
	Daughter	F.	17	Single	Campania	Campania	Campania
	Son	M.	14	Single	Campania	Campania	Campania
	Daughter	F.	13	Single	Campania	Campania	Campania
	Son	M.	7	Single	United States	Campania	Campania
	Son	M.	5	Single	United States	Campania	Campania
509	Head	M.	22	Married	Campania	Campania	Campania
	Wife	F.	22	Married	Campania	Campania	Campania
	Son	M.	2	Single	Campania	Campania	Campania
	Sister	F.	21	Married	Campania	Campania	Campania
	Brother-in-law	M.	38	Married	Campania	Campania	Campania
	Brother-in-law	M.	26	Married	Campania	Campania	Campania
	Niece	F.	8/12	Single	United States	Campania	Campania
510	Head	M.	30	Married	Sicily	Sicily	Sicily
	Wife	F.	18	Married	Sicily	Sicily	Sicily
	Son	M	7/12	Single	United States	Sicily	Sicily
511	Head	M.	40	Married	Sicily	Sicily	Sicily
	Wife	F.	30	Married	Sicily	Sicily	Sicily
	Daughter	F.	15	Single	Sicily	Sicily	Sicily
512	Head	M.	45	Married	Campania	Campania	Campania
	Wife	F.	45	Married	Campania	Campania	Campania
	Son	M.	14	Single	Campania	Campania	Campania
	Son	M.	7	Single	Campania	Campania	Campania
	Daughter	F.	6	Single	Campania	Campania	Campania
	Son	M.	3	Single	United States	Campania	Campania
	Nephew	M.	23	Single	Campania	Campania	Campania
513	Head	M.	48	Married	Basilicata	Basilicata	Basilicata
	Wife	F.	60	Married	Basilicata	Basilicata	Basilicata
	Daughter	F.	18	Single	Basilicata	Basilicata	Basilicata
	Daughter	F.	15	Single	Basilicata	Basilicata	Basilicata
514	Head	M.	61	Married	Campania	Campania	Campania
	Wife	F.	61	Married	Campania	Campania	Campania
	Son	M.	14	Single	Campania	Campania	Campania
	Nephew	M.	21	Single	Campania	Campania	Campania
	Nephew	M.	19	Single	Campania	Campania	Campania
	Nephew	M.	18	Single	Campania	Campania	Campania
	Lodger	M.	25	Married	Calabria	Calabria	Calabria
	Lodger	F.	18	Married	Calabria	Calabria	Calabria
515	Head	M.	30	Married	Abruzzo	Abruzzo	Abruzzo
	Wife	F.	20	Married	Abruzzo	Abruzzo	Abruzzo
	Daughter	F.	2	Single	United States	Abruzzo	Abruzzo
	Son	M.	1	Single	United States	Abruzzo	Abruzzo
516	Head	M.	29	Married	Campania	Campania	Campania
	Wife	F.	30	Married	Campania	Campania	Campania

a Also worked as laborer four weeks, at $6 per week.
b Not reported.
c Also worked as street sweeper four weeks, at $7.50 per week.

TABLE **I.**— GENERAL SOCIAL AND ECONOMIC CONDITION, BY FAMILIES AND INDIVIDUALS—Continued.

Years in U.S.	Naturalized.	Profession, trade, or occupation.	Hours of work per week.	Average weekly earnings.	Weeks employed.	Total yearly earnings.	Sick during year, defective, maimed, or deformed.
1	......	At home....................	......	......	......	......	Fever, not specified.
......	......	At home....................	......	......	......	......	No.
9	......	No occupation.............	......	......	......	......	No.
8	Yes..	No occupation.............	......	......	......	......	No.
4	......	Housewife.................	......	......	......	......	No.
6	Yes..	Peddler, fruit (a)	(b)	$1.80	a 48	$110	No.
2	No...	Peddler, fruit.............	(b)	1.80	52	94	No.
6	No...	Peddler, fruit.............	(b)	1.80	52	94	No.
4	......	Housework................	......	......	......	......	No.
4	......	Scholar...................	......	......	......	......	No.
8	Yes..	Laborer	60	9.00	9	81	Injury by accident.
10	Yes..	Laborer	60	2.16	46	99	Fever, typhoid.
8	Yes..	No occupation.............	......	......	......	......	Kidneys, disease of.
7	Yes..	Laborer	60	7.50	15	113	No.
13	Yes..	Ragpicker (c)	(b)	2.40	c 30	102	No.
9	......	Housewife.................	......	......	......	......	No.
(b)	......	Pants finisher	(b)	1.20	26	31	No.
9	......	Newsboy..................	(b)	1.50	52	78	No.
9	......	Scholar...................	......	......	......	......	No.
......	......	Scholar...................	......	......	......	......	No.
......	......	At home..................	......	......	......	......	No.
1	No...	Organ grinder.............	(b)	3.50	52	182	No.
$\frac{6}{12}$	......	Housewife.................	......	......	......	......	No.
$\frac{6}{12}$	......	At home..................	......	......	......	......	No.
1	......	Housework................	......	......	......	......	Childbirth.
$\frac{6}{12}$	No...	No occupation.............	......	......	......	......	No.
1	No...	Organ grinder.............	(b)	3.50	52	182	No.
......	......	At home..................	......	......	......	......	No.
9	No...	Laborer ....-.......	60	6.90	15	104	No.
2	......	Housewife.................	......	......	......	......	Childbirth.
......	......	At home..................	......	......	......	......	No.
15	Yes..	Tailor	48	12.00	52	624	Rheumatism.
6	......	Housewife.................	......	......	......	......	No.
11	......	Housework................	......	......	......	......	No.
5	Yes..	Merchant, groceries	(b)	(b)	52	(b)	No.
5	......	Housewife and merchant, groceries.	(b)	(b)	52	(b)	No.
5	......	Driver....................	(b)	(b)	52	(b)	No.
5	......	Scholar...................	......	......	......	......	No.
5	......	Scholar...................	......	......	......	......	No.
......	......	At home..................	......	......	......	......	No.
3	No..	Baker	72	7.00	22	154	No.
20	No...	No occupation.............	......	......	......	......	No.
20	......	Housewife and pants finisher.	(b)	1.20	26	31	No.
2	......	Musician	(b)	3.60	52	187	No.
2	......	Musician	(b)	3.60	52	187	No.
13	Yes..	No occupation.............	......	......	......	......	No.
9	......	Housewife and fortune teller.	(b)	(b)	(b)	(b)	Eyes, inflammation of both.
9	......	Barber...........,.......	81	2.00	52	104	No.
10	No...	Barber....................	81	7.00	52	364	No.
10	......	Barber....................	81	7.00	52	364	No.
6	......	Barber....................	81	5.00	52	260	No.
9	Yes..	Barber....................	81	8.00	52	416	No.
9	......	Housework................	......	......	......	......	No.
7	No...	Stonecutter (d)	48	20.00	d 9	229	No.
14	......	Housewife.................	......	......	......	......	No.
......	......	At home..................	......	......	......	......	No.
......	......	At home..................	......	......	......	......	No.
5	Yes..	Ragpicker (e).............	(b)	1.80	e 30	152	Injury by accident.
4	......	Housewife.................	......	......	......	......	No.

d Also worked as butcher seven weeks, at $7 per week.
e Also worked as laborer thirteen weeks, at $7.50 per week.

TABLE **I.**—GENERAL SOCIAL AND ECONOMIC CONDITION, BY FAMILIES AND INDIVIDUALS—Continued.

Family number.	Relationship to head of family.	Sex.	Age.	Conjugal condition.	Birthplace.	Birthplace of—	
						Father.	Mother.
516	Son	M.	7	Single	Campania	Campania	Campania
	Son	M.	5	Single	Campania	Campania	Campania
	Daughter	F.	2	Single	United States	Campania	Campania
517	Head	M.	45	Married	Campania	Campania	Campania
	Wife	F.	28	Married	Campania	Campania	Campania
518	Head	M.	40	Married	Campania	Campania	Campania
	Wife	F.	50	Married	Campania	Campania	Campania
	Son	M.	23	Single	Campania	Campania	Campania
	Daughter	F.	20	Married	Campania	Campania	Campania
	Son-in-law	M.	30	Married	Campania	Campania	Campania
	Grandson	M.	$\frac{5}{12}$	Single	United States	Campania	Campania
519	Head	M.	36	Married	Abruzzo	Abruzzo	Abruzzo
	Wife	F.	35	Married	Abruzzo	Abruzzo	Abruzzo
	Son	M.	15	Single	Abruzzo	Abruzzo	Abruzzo
	Lodger	M.	50	Married	Abruzzo	Abruzzo	Abruzzo
	Lodger	M.	40	Married	Abruzzo	Abruzzo	Abruzzo
520	Head	M.	30	Married	Basilicata	Basilicata	Basilicata
	Wife	F.	39	Married	Basilicata	Basilicata	Basilicata
	Stepdaughter	F.	13	Single	Basilicata	Basilicata	Basilicata
	Son	M.	7	Single	United States	Basilicata	Basilicata
	Daughter	F.	$\frac{5}{12}$	Single	United States	Basilicata	Basilicata
521	Head	M.	38	Married	Campania	Campania	Campania
	Wife	F.	40	Married	Campania	Campania	Campania
	Daughter	F.	8	Single	Campania	Campania	Campania
	Brother	M.	35	Widowed	Campania	Campania	Campania
	Niece	F.	8	Single	Campania	Campania	Campania
	Boarder	M.	28	Single	Campania	Campania	Campania
	Boarder	M.	22	Single	Campania	Campania	Campania
	Boarder	M.	37	Single	Campania	Campania	Campania
522	Head	M.	40	Married	Calabria	Calabria	Calabria
	Wife	F.	32	Married	Calabria	Calabria	Calabria
	Daughter	F.	9	Single	Calabria	Calabria	Calabria
	Son	M.	4	Single	United States	Calabria	Calabria
	Cousin	M.	47	Married	Calabria	Calabria	Calabria
523	Head	M.	32	Married	Liguria	Liguria	Liguria
	Wife	F.	27	Married	Liguria	Liguria	Liguria
524	Head	M.	40	Married	Basilicata	Basilicata	Basilicata
	Wife	F.	45	Married	Basilicata	Basilicata	Basilicata
	Brother	M.	39	Single	Basilicata	Basilicata	Basilicata
525	Head	M.	27	Married	Basilicata	Basilicata	Basilicata
	Wife	F.	21	Married	Basilicata	Basilicata	Basilicata
	Father-in-law	M.	40	Married	Basilicata	Basilicata	Basilicata
	Mother-in-law	F.	40	Married	Basilicata	Basilicata	Basilicata
	Brother-in-law	M.	17	Single	Basilicata	Basilicata	Basilicata
	Sister-in-law	F.	6	Single	Basilicata	Basilicata	Basilicata
	Sister-in-law	F.	4	Single	Basilicata	Basilicata	Basilicata
526	Head	M.	53	Married	Basilicata	Basilicata	Basilicata
	Wife	F.	57	Married	Basilicata	Basilicata	Basilicata
	Son	M.	27	Married	Basilicata	Basilicata	Basilicata
	Daughter-in-law	F.	20	Married	Basilicata	Basilicata	Basilicata
527	Head	M.	32	Married	Abruzzo	Abruzzo	Abruzzo
	Wife	F.	20	Married	Abruzzo	Abruzzo	Abruzzo
	Daughter	F.	3	Single	United States	Abruzzo	Abruzzo
	Daughter	F.	$\frac{1}{12}$	Single	United States	Abruzzo	Abruzzo
	Brother-in-law	M.	27	Married	Abruzzo	Abruzzo	Abruzzo
	Sister-in-law	F.	19	Married	Abruzzo	Abruzzo	Abruzzo
	Nephew	M.	$\frac{6}{12}$	Single	United States	Abruzzo	Abruzzo
528	Head	M.	42	Married	Calabria	Calabria	Calabria
	Wife	F.	33	Married	Calabria	Calabria	Calabria
	Daughter	F.	2	Single	United States	Calabria	Calabria
	Son	M.	$\frac{3}{12}$	Single	United States	Calabria	Calabria

a Not reported.
b Sick, disease not specified.
c Also worked as laborer seventeen weeks, at $6.60 per week.

TABLE **I.**—GENERAL SOCIAL AND ECONOMIC CONDITION, BY FAMILIES AND INDIVIDUALS—Continued.

Years in U. S.	Natu-ral-ized.	Profession, trade, or occupation.	Hours of work per week.	Average weekly earn-ings.	Weeks em-ploy-ed.	Total yearly earn-ings.	Sick during year, defective, maimed, or deformed.
4	......	Scholar	......	......	......	......	Measles.
4	......	At home...........	......	......	......	......	Measles.
......	......	At home...........	......	......	......	......	Measles.
1	No...	Organ grinder............	(a)	$6.00	39	$234	(b)
1	......	Housewife............	......	......	......	......	Female complaint.
8	No...	Ragpicker (c).............	(a)	1.50	c 35	165	No.
8	......	Housewife............	......	......	......	......	Bronchitis.
1	No...	Ragpicker...............	(a)	1.50	52	78	No.
8	......	Housework..........	......	......	......	......	Childbirth.
7	Yes..	Laborer (d).............	(a)	7.50	d 13	122	No.
......	......	At home......	......	......	......	......	No.
9	Yes..	Laborer...............	60	9.00	19	171	No.
3	......	Housewife............	......	......	......	......	No.
3	......	Scholar and newsboy.....	35	1.40	52	73	No.
12	Yes..	Junk picker.............	(a)	3.00	52	156	No.
6	Yes..	Laborer...............	60	9.00	17	153	Polypus.
14	No...	Janitor	60	9.25	52	481	Injury by accident.
8	......	Housewife............	......	......	......	......	Childbirth.
8	......	Scholar and candy-factory employee.	60	2.00	6	12	No.
......	......	Scholar...........	......	......	......	......	No.
......	......	At home...........	......	......	......	......	No.
6	Yes..	Laborer...............	60	9.00	26	234	No.
$\frac{1}{12}$	......	Housewife............	......	......	......	......	No.
$\frac{1}{12}$	......	At home...........	......	......	......	......	No.
6	Yes..	Laborer...............	60	6.60	26	172	No.
$\frac{1}{2}$	......	At home...........	......	......	......	......	No.
$\frac{1}{12}$	No...	No occupation	......	......	......	......	No.
$\frac{1}{12}$	No...	No occupation	......	......	......	......	No.
18	Yes..	Padrone	60	12.00	9	108	No.
5	No...	Laborer...............	60	9.00	13	117	No.
5	......	Housewife............	......	......	......	......	No.
5	......	Scholar............	......	......	......	......	No.
......	......	At home...........	......	......	......	......	No.
9	Yes..	Laborer...............	60	7.50	13	98	No.
11	No...	Macaroni maker..........	60	8.00	49	392	Boils.
10	......	Housewife............	......	......	......	......	No.
6	No...	Peddler, vegetables.......	(a)	3.00	52	156	Lame.
6	......	Housewife............	......	......	......	......	No.
24	Yes..	Peddler	(a)	3.00	52	156	No.
15	Yes..	No occupation	......	......	......	......	No.
3	......	Housewife............	......	......	......	......	No.
10	No...	Laborer...............	60	7.50	52	390	No.
3	......	Housework..........	......	......	......	......	No.
3	......	Scholar and barber's apprentice. (e)	89	1.00	e 26	52	No.
3	......	At home...........	......	......	......	......	No.
3	......	At home...........	......	......	......	......	No.
27	No...	Ragpicker	(a)	1.50	48	72	Liver, disease of.
6	......	Housewife............	......	......	......	......	Female complaint.
4	No...	Laborer...............	60	7.50	4	30	No.
7	......	Housework	......	......	......	......	No.
8	Yes..	Laborer...............	60	7.50	22	165	No.
4	......	Housewife............	......	......	......	......	Childbirth.
......	......	At home...........	......	......	......	......	Bronchitis.
......	......	At home...........	......	......	......	......	No.
6	Yes..	Laborer...............	60	7.50	22	165	Fever, not specified.
2	......	Housework	......	......	......	......	Childbirth; typhoid fever.
......	......	At home...........	......	......	......	......	No.
14	Yes..	Saloon keeper............	(a)	(a)	52	(a)	No.
8	......	Housewife............	......	......	......	......	Childbirth.
......	......	At home...........	......	......	......	......	No.
......	......	At home...........	......	......	......	......	No.

d Also worked as baker six weeks, at $4 per week.
e Also worked as bootblack twenty-six weeks, at $1 per week.

TABLE **I.**—GENERAL SOCIAL AND ECONOMIC CONDITION, BY FAMILIES AND INDIVIDUALS—Continued.

Family number.	Relationship to head of family.	Sex.	Age.	Conjugal condition.	Birthplace.	Birthplace of—	
						Father.	Mother.
529	Head	M.	48	Married	Basilicata	Basilicata	Basilicata
	Wife	F.	35	Married	Basilicata	Basilicata	Basilicata
	Daughter	F.	16	Single	United States	Basilicata	Basilicata
	Son	M.	13	Single	United States	Basilicata	Basilicata
	Son	M.	11	Single	United States	Basilicata	Basilicata
	Son	M.	9	Single	United States	Basilicata	Basilicata
	Son	M.	7	Single	United States	Basilicata	Basilicata
	Daughter	F.	5	Single	United States	Basilicata	Basilicata
	Daughter	F.	2	Single	United States	Basilicata	Basilicata
	Son	M.	$\frac{3}{12}$	Single	United States	Basilicata	Basilicata
	Aunt	F.	65	Widowed	Basilicata	Basilicata	Basilicata
530	Head	M.	38	Married	Calabria	Calabria	Calabria
	Wife	F.	40	Married	Calabria	Calabria	Calabria
	Stepson	M.	19	Single	Calabria	Calabria	Calabria
531	Head	M.	46	Married	Basilicata	Basilicata	Basilicata
	Wife	F.	46	Married	Basilicata	Basilicata	Basilicata
	Son	M.	16	Single	United States	Basilicata	Basilicata
	Daughter	F.	14	Single	United States	Basilicata	Basilicata
	Daughter	F.	12	Single	United States	Basilicata	Basilicata
532	Head	M.	42	Married	Campania	Campania	Campania
	Wife	F.	47	Married	Campania	Campania	Campania
	Daughter	F.	14	Single	Campania	Campania	Campania
	Son	M.	9	Single	Campania	Campania	Campania
	Daughter	F.	7	Single	Campania	Campania	Campania
	Son	M.	6	Single	Campania	Campania	Campania
	Son	M.	2	Single	United States	Campania	Campania
533	Head	M.	28	Married	Sicily	Sicily	Sicily
	Wife	F.	24	Married	Sicily	Sicily	Sicily
	Daughter	F.	7	Single	Sicily	Sicily	Sicily
	Son	M.	$\frac{6}{12}$	Single	United States	Sicily	Sicily
534	Head	M.	38	Married	Campania	Campania	Campania
	Wife	F.	38	Married	Campania	Campania	Campania
	Son	M.	16	Single	Campania	Campania	Campania
	Daughter	F.	2	Single	United States	Campania	Campania
535	Head	M.	26	Married	Sicily	Sicily	Sicily
	Wife	F.	23	Married	Sicily	Sicily	Sicily
	Son	M.	3	Single	United States	Sicily	Sicily
	Daughter	F.	1	Single	United States	Sicily	Sicily
	Uncle	M.	50	Married	Sicily	Sicily	Sicily
	Cousin	M.	18	Single	Sicily	Sicily	Sicily
	Lodger	M.	24	Single	Sicily	Sicily	Sicily
	Lodger	F.	22	Married	Sicily	Sicily	Sicily
536	Head	M.	35	Married	Campania	Campania	Campania
	Wife	F.	26	Married	Campania	Campania	Campania
	Daughter	F.	9	Single	United States	Campania	Campania
	Daughter	F.	7	Single	United States	Campania	Campania
	Daughter	F.	5	Single	United States	Campania	Campania
	Daughter	F.	2	Single	United States	Campania	Campania
	Son	M.	$\frac{1}{12}$	Single	United States	Campania	Campania
	Mother	F.	74	Widowed	Campania	Campania	Campania
	Lodger	M.	46	Married	Campania	Campania	Campania
537	Head	M.	27	Married	Sicily	Sicily	Sicily
	Wife	F.	23	Married	Sicily	Sicily	Sicily
	Daughter	F.	4	Single	Sicily	Sicily	Sicily
	Daughter	F.	2	Single	United States	Sicily	Sicily
	Brother-in-law	M.	27	Married	Sicily	Sicily	Sicily
	Sister-in-law	F.	21	Married	Sicily	Sicily	Sicily
538	Head	M.	33	Married	Campania	Campania	Campania
	Wife	F.	30	Married	Campania	Campania	Campania
	Son	M.	11	Single	Campania	Campania	Campania
	Daughter	F.	9	Single	Campania	Campania	Campania
	Daughter	F.	7	Single	Campania	Campania	Campania

a Not reported.
b Also worked as sewer digger three weeks, at $9 per week.
c Also worked as laborer one week, at $9 per week.

TABLE **I.**—GENERAL SOCIAL AND ECONOMIC CONDITION, BY FAMILIES
AND INDIVIDUALS—Continued.

Years in U. S.	Naturalized.	Profession, trade, or occupation.	Hours of work per week.	Average weekly earnings.	Weeks employed.	Total yearly earnings.	Sick during year, defective, maimed, or deformed.
22	Yes..	Musician	(a)	$3.00	52	$156	No.
23	......	Housewife	......	......	......	......	Childbirth.
......	......	Housework	......	......	......	......	No.
......	......	Musician	(a)	7.00	17	119	No.
......	......	Musician	(a)	1.00	17	17	No.
......	......	Scholar	......	......	......	......	No.
......	......	At home..................	......	......	......	......	No.
......	......	At home..................	......	......	......	......	No.
......	......	At home..................	......	......	......	......	No.
......	......	At home..................	......	......	......	......	No.
12	......	Housework	......	......	......	......	No.
14	No...	Laborer..................	60	6.00	9	54	No.
8	......	Housewife	......	......	......	......	No.
8	......	Barber...................	(a)	5.00	(a)	(a)	No.
21	Yes..	Street sweeper...........	60	7.50	30	225	No.
20	......	Housewife	......	......	......	......	No.
......	......	Bartender	72	4.00	52	208	No.
......	......	Housework	......	......	......	......	No.
......	......	Scholar	......	......	......	......	No.
3	No...	No occupation	......	......	......	......	No.
3	......	Housewife and wood picker.	(a)	(a)	52	(a)	No.
3	......	Wood picker.............	(a)	(a)	52	(a)	No.
3	......	Wood picker.............	(a)	(a)	52	(a)	No.
3	......	At home.................	......	......	......	......	No.
3	......	At home.................	......	......	......	......	No.
......	......	At home.................	......	......	......	......	No.
5	Yes..	Laborer..................	60	7.50	17	128	No.
2	......	Housewife	......	......	......	......	Childbirth.
2	......	Scholar	......	......	......	......	No.
......	......	At home..................	......	......	......	......	No.
15	Yes..	Teamster	(a)	18.00	19	342	No.
9	......	Housewife................	......	......	......	......	No.
9	......	Barber...................	(a)	4.50	(a)	(a)	No.
......	......	At home..................	......	......	......	......	No.
6	Yes..	Peddler, fruit (b)..........	(a)	1.80	b49	115	No.
3	......	Housewife................	......	......	......	......	No.
......	......	At home..................	......	......	......	......	No.
......	......	At home..................	......	......	......	......	No.
3	No...	Peddler, fruit (c)..........	(a)	1.80	c51	101	No.
3	...?	Peddler, fruit............	(a)	1.80	52	94	No.
5	Yes..	Peddler, fruit (d)..........	(a)	1.80	d49	94	No.
2	......	Housework	......	......	......	......	No.
12	Yes..	Street sweeper...........	48	9.00	22	198	Bronchitis.
10	......	Housewife................	......	......	......	......	Childbirth.
......	......	Scholar	......	......	......	......	No.
......	......	Scholar	......	......	......	......	No.
......	......	At home..................	......	......	......	......	Fever, typhoid.
......	......	At home..................	......	......	......	......	Fever, typhoid.
......	......	At home..................	......	......	......	......	No.
11	......	Housework	......	......	......	......	Eye, loss of one.
14	Yes..	Laborer..................	60	9.00	9	81	No.
5	Yes..	Peddler, fruit (e)..........	(a)	90	e48	73	No.
4	......	Housewife................	......	......	......	......	No.
4	......	At home.................	......	......	......	......	No.
......	......	At home.................	......	......	......	......	No.
1	No...	Peddler, fruit.............	(a)	1.80	52	94	No.
1½	......	Housework	......	......	......	......	No.
8	Yes..	Street sweeper...........	48	9.00	30	270	No.
3	......	Housewife and merchant, groceries.	(a)	(a)	(a)	(a)	Childbirth.
3	......	Scholar	......	......	......	......	No.
3	......	Scholar	......	......	......	......	No.
3	......	Scholar	......	......	......	......	No.

d Also worked as laborer one week, at $6 per week.
e Also worked as laborer four weeks, at $7.50 per week.

TABLE **I.**—GENERAL SOCIAL AND ECONOMIC CONDITION, BY FAMILIES AND INDIVIDUALS—Continued.

Family number.	Relationship to head of family.	Sex.	Age.	Conjugal condition.	Birthplace.	Birthplace of— Father.	Birthplace of— Mother.
538	Daughter	F.	5	Single	Campania	Campania	Campania
	Daughter	F.	3	Single	Campania	Campania	Campania
	Son	M.	$\frac{1}{12}$	Single	United States	Campania	Campania
	Lodger	M.	25	Single	Campania	Campania	Campania
	Lodger	M.	18	Single	Campania	Campania	Campania
539	Head	M.	32	Married	Campania	Campania	Campania
	Wife	F.	29	Married	Campania	Campania	Campania
	Lodger	M.	37	Married	Campania	Campania	Campania
	Lodger	M.	29	Single	Campania	Campania	Campania
540	Head	M.	29	Married	Abruzzo	Abruzzo	Abruzzo
	Wife	F.	19	Married	Abruzzo	Abruzzo	Abruzzo
	Brother	M.	23	Single	Abruzzo	Abruzzo	Abruzzo
541	Head	M.	40	Married	Campania	Campania	Campania
	Wife	F.	45	Married	Campania	Campania	Campania
	Daughter	F.	5	Single	Campania	Campania	Campania
	Daughter	F.	3	Single	Campania	Campania	Campania
542	Head	M.	37	Married	Calabria	Calabria	Calabria
	Wife	F.	27	Married	Basilicata	Basilicata	Basilicata
	Son	M.	6	Single	United States	Calabria	Basilicata
	Son	M.	3	Single	United States	Calabria	Basilicata
	Daughter	F.	1	Single	United States	Calabria	Basilicata
	Father-in-law	M.	75	Widowed	Basilicata	Basilicata	Basilicata
543	Head	M.	35	Married	Campania	Campania	Campania
	Wife	F.	35	Married	Campania	Campania	Campania
	Daughter	F.	7	Single	United States	Campania	Campania
	Daughter	F.	4	Single	United States	Campania	Campania
	Daughter	F.	$\frac{6}{12}$	Single	United States	Campania	Campania
544	Head	M.	25	Married	Campania	Campania	Campania
	Wife	F.	20	Married	Campania	Campania	Campania
	Son	M.	3	Single	United States	Campania	Campania
	Son	M.	1	Single	United States	Campania	Campania
	Father	M.	48	Married	Campania	Campania	Campania
	Boarder	M.	28	Single	Campania	Campania	Campania
	Boarder	M.	19	Single	Campania	Campania	Campania
545	Head	M.	47	Married	Campania	Campania	Campania
	Wife	F.	36	Married	Campania	Campania	Campania
	Daughter	F.	10	Single	Campania	Campania	Campania
	Daughter	F.	7	Single	United States	Campania	Campania
	Daughter	F.	3	Single	United States	Campania	Campania
	Son	M.	1	Single	United States	Campania	Campania
	Lodger	M.	40	Married	Campania	Campania	Campania
	Lodger	M.	44	Married	Campania	Campania	Campania
	Lodger	M.	37	Married	Campania	Campania	Campania
	Lodger	M.	26	Single	Campania	Campania	Campania
546	Head	M.	40	Married	Basilicata	Basilicata	Basilicata
	Wife	F.	39	Married	Basilicata	Basilicata	Basilicata
	Daughter	F.	10	Single	Basilicata	Basilicata	Basilicata
	Daughter	F.	4	Single	United States	Basilicata	Basilicata
	Daughter	F.	1	Single	United States	Basilicata	Basilicata
547	Head	M.	59	Married	Campania	Campania	Campania
	Wife	F.	54	Married	Campania	Campania	Campania
	Daughter	F.	14	Single	Campania	Campania	Campania
	Daughter	F.	14	Single	Campania	Campania	Campania
	Son	M.	10	Single	United States	Campania	Campania
	Son	M.	4	Single	United States	Campania	Campania
548	Head	M.	31	Married	Basilicata	Basilicata	Basilicata
	Wife	F.	30	Married	Basilicata	Basilicata	Basilicata
	Daughter	F.	4	Single	United States	Basilicata	Basilicata
	Daughter	F.	2	Single	United States	Basilicata	Basilicata
	Daughter	F.	$\frac{6}{12}$	Single	United States	Basilicata	Basilicata
549	Head	M.	39	Married	Basilicata	Basilicata	Basilicata
	Wife	F.	32	Married	Basilicata	Basilicata	Basilicata
	Daughter	F.	4	Single	United States	Basilicata	Basilicata
	Daughter	F.	$\frac{1}{12}$	Single	United States	Basilicata	Basilicata

a Also worked as laborer thirteen weeks, at $7.50 per week.
b Not reported.

TABLE **I.**—GENERAL SOCIAL AND ECONOMIC CONDITION, BY FAMILIES
AND INDIVIDUALS—Continued.

Years in U. S.	Naturalized.	Profession, trade, or occupation.	Hours of work per week.	Average weekly earnings.	Weeks employed.	Total yearly earnings.	Sick during year, defective, maimed, or deformed.
3		At home					No.
3		At home					No.
		At home					No.
5	No...	Laborer	60	$7.50	52	$390	No.
5		Candy maker	60	7.25	52	377	No.
2	No...	Street sweeper	60	9.00	52	468	No.
2		Housewife					No.
7	Yes..	Street sweeper	60	9.00	9	81	No.
5	Yes..	Laborer	60	7.50	52	390	No.
6	Yes..	Laborer	60	7.50	13	98	No.
8		Housewife					No.
9	Yes..	Laborer	60	7.50	9	68	No.
4	No...	Ragpicker (a)	(b)	1.80	a 39	168	No.
3/12		Housewife					No.
3/12		At home					Measles.
3/12		At home					Measles.
8	Yes..	No occupation					No.
8		Housewife and servant...	(b)	(b)	(b)	(b)	No.
		At home					Syphilis; rickets.
		At home					Syphilis; rickets.
		At home					Syphilis.
20	Yes..	No occupation					No.
8	Yes..	Tailor (c)	60	7.00	c 17	(b)	No.
8		Housewife					Childbirth.
		At home					No.
		At home					Skin, disease of.
		At home					No.
4	No...	Laborer	60	6.00	52	312	No.
3		Housewife					No.
		At home					No.
		At home					No.
4	No...	Laborer	60	6.00	52	312	No.
4	No...	Laborer	60	6.00	52	312	No.
(b)		Laborer	60	6.00	52	312	No.
11	Yes..	Laborer	60	9.00	22	198	No.
8		Housewife					No.
8		Scholar					No.
		At home					Rickets.
		At home					Rickets.
		At home					No.
8	Yes..	Laborer	60	9.00	26	234	No.
14	No...	Laborer	60	6.60	7	46	No.
10	Yes..	Laborer	60	9.00	26	234	No.
6	Yes..	Laborer	60	6.60	7	46	No.
8	Yes..	Packer, rags (d)	60	7.00	d 26	234	No.
6		Housewife					Female complaint.
6		Scholar					No.
		At home					No.
		At home					No.
15	No...	Wood picker	(b)	2.40	52	125	No.
10		Housewife and wood picker.	(b)	2.40	52	125	No.
10		Wood picker	(b)	2.40	52	125	No.
10		Wood picker	(b)	2.40	52	125	No.
		Scholar					Fever, typhoid.
		At home					Fever, typhoid.
6	Yes..	Scissors grinder	(b)	4.50	52	234	No.
6		Housewife					Childbirth.
		At home					No.
		At home					No.
		At home					No.
13	Yes..	No occupation					No.
7		Housewife					Childbirth.
		At home					Vaccination.
		At home					No.

c Also worked as notary public, at $1.20 per week, time not reported.
d Also worked as merchant, fruit, twenty-six weeks, at $2 per week.

TABLE I.—GENERAL SOCIAL AND ECONOMIC CONDITION, BY FAMILIES AND INDIVIDUALS—Continued.

Family number.	Relationship to head of family.	Sex.	Age.	Conjugal condition.	Birthplace.	Birthplace of—	
						Father.	Mother.
550	Head	M.	54	Married	Campania	Campania	Campania
	Wife	F.	40	Married	Campania	Campania	Campania
	Son	M.	14	Single	United States	Campania	Campania
	Son	M.	6	Single	United States	Campania	Campania
	Son	M.	5	Single	United States	Campania	Campania
	Daughter	F.	3	Single	United States	Campania	Campania
	Daughter	F.	2	Single	United States	Campania	Campania
551	Cooperative	M.	30	Single	Abruzzo	Abruzzo	Abruzzo
	Cooperative	M.	40	Married	Abruzzo	Abruzzo	Abruzzo
	Cooperative	M.	30	Single	Abruzzo	Abruzzo	Abruzzo
	Cooperative	M.	22	Single	Abruzzo	Abruzzo	Abruzzo
	Cooperative	M.	45	Married	Abruzzo	Abruzzo	Abruzzo
552	Head	M.	42	Married	Campania	Campania	Campania
	Wife	F.	42	Married	Campania	Campania	Campania
	Daughter	F.	19	Single	Campania	Campania	Campania
	Son	M.	8	Single	United States	Campania	Campania
	Daughter	F.	5	Single	United States	Campania	Campania
	Son	M.	3	Single	United States	Campania	Campania
553	Head	M.	29	Married	Abruzzo	Abruzzo	Abruzzo
	Wife	F.	24	Married	Campania	Campania	Campania
554	Head	M.	54	Married	Campania	Campania	Campania
	Wife	F.	53	Married	Campania	Campania	Campania
	Son	M.	21	Single	Campania	Campania	Campania
	Son	M.	15	Single	Campania	Campania	Campania
555	Head	M.	43	Married	Campania	Campania	Campania
	Wife	F.	46	Married	Campania	Campania	Campania
	Daughter	F.	17	Married	Campania	Campania	Campania
	Son	M.	7	Single	United States	Campania	Campania
	Son-in-law	M.	25	Married	Campania	Campania	Campania
	Boarder	M.	37	Married	Campania	Campania	Campania
556	Head	M.	33	Married	Calabria	Calabria	Calabria
	Wife	F.	37	Married	Abruzzo	Abruzzo	Abruzzo
	Stepson	M.	15	Single	Abruzzo	Abruzzo	Abruzzo
	Stepson	M.	11	Single	Abruzzo	Abruzzo	Abruzzo
557	Head	M.	63	Married	Basilicata	Basilicata	Basilicata
	Wife	F.	62	Married	Basilicata	Basilicata	Basilicata
	Son	M.	27	Single	Basilicata	Basilicata	Basilicata
558	Head	M.	38	Married	Campania	Campania	Campania
	Wife	F.	36	Married	Campania	Campania	Campania
	Son	M.	8	Single	Campania	Campania	Campania
	Daughter	F.	2	Single	United States	Campania	Campania
	Mother	F.	76	Widowed	Campania	Campania	Campania
559	Head	M.	29	Married	Campania	Campania	Campania
	Wife	F.	19	Married	Campania	Campania	Campania
	Son	M.	3	Single	United States	Campania	Campania
	Cousin	M.	22	Single	Campania	Campania	Campania
	Lodger	M.	24	Married	Campania	Campania	Campania
560	Head	M.	45	Married	Sicily	Sicily	Sicily
	Wife	F.	40	Married	Sicily	Sicily	Sicily
	Son	M.	6	Single	Sicily	Sicily	Sicily
	Son	M.	3	Single	United States	Sicily	Sicily
	Daughter	F.	$\frac{8}{12}$	Single	United States	Sicily	Sicily
561	Head	M.	50	Married	Campania	Campania	Campania
	Wife	F.	45	Married	Campania	Campania	Campania
	Daughter	F.	11	Single	Campania	Campania	Campania
	Lodger	M.	(a)	Single	Campania	Campania	Campania
	Lodger	M.	30	Single	Campania	Campania	Campania
562	Head	M.	35	Married	Abruzzo	Abruzzo	Abruzzo
	Wife	F.	36	Married	Abruzzo	Abruzzo	Abruzzo

a Not reported.

TABLE I.—GENERAL SOCIAL AND ECONOMIC CONDITION, BY FAMILIES AND INDIVIDUALS—Continued.

Years in U. S.	Naturalized.	Profession, trade, or occupation.	Hours of work per week.	Average weekly earnings.	Weeks employed.	Total yearly earnings.	Sick during year, defective, maimed, or deformed.
14	Yes..	Janitor	28	$10.50	39	$410	No.
14	....	Housewife	....	....	....	....	Miscarriage.
....	....	No occupation	....	....	....	....	Leg, loss of one.
....	....	At home......................	....	....	....	....	No.
....	....	At home......................	....	....	....	....	No.
....	....	At home......................	....	....	....	....	Rickets.
....	....	At home......................	....	....	....	....	Bronchitis.
6	Yes.	Laborer......................	60	9.00	13	117	No.
6	Yes..	Laborer......................	60	7.00	13	91	No.
4	No...	Tailor	60	8.00	52	416	No.
4	No...	Laborer......................	60	8.40	22	185	No.
5	Yes..	Laborer......................	60	6.90	35	242	No.
15	Yes..	Laborer......................	48	9.00	5	45	No.
9	....	Housewife and cloak finisher.	(a)	2.00	26	52	No.
9	....	Cloak finisher (b)..........	60	4.00	b 17	74	No.
....	....	Scholar	....	....	....	....	No.
....	....	At home	....	....	....	....	No.
....	....	At home	....	....	....	....	No.
8	No...	Laborer......................	60	7.13	52	371	No.
2	....	Housewife....................	....	....	....	....	No.
7	Yes..	Laborer......................	60	7.50	15	113	No.
4	....	Housewife and washerwoman.	(a)	.40	52	21	No.
8	Yes..	Laborer......................	60	7.50	17	128	No.
4	....	Water carrier...............	60	.75	9	7	No.
13	Yes..	Laborer......................	60	8.10	13	105	No.
9	....	Housewife....................	....	....	....	....	Female complaint.
9	....	Housework....................	....	....	....	....	No.
....	....	Scholar......................	....	....	....	....	No.
4	No...	Laborer......................	60	9.00	26	234	No.
3	No...	Laborer......................	60	8.40	52	437	No.
15	Yes..	No occupation	....	....	....	....	No.
4	....	Housewife....................	....	....	....	....	No.
4	....	No occupation	....	....	....	....	No.
4	....	Scholar	....	....	....	....	No.
5	No...	Ragpicker	(a)	.90	52	47	No.
5	....	Housewife....................	....	....	....	....	No.
5	Yes..	Street sweeper..............	60	9.00	30	270	No.
6	No...	Laborer......................	60	7.50	35	263	No.
5	....	Housewife....................	....	....	....	....	No.
5	....	Scholar	....	....	....	....	No.
....	....	At home	....	....	....	....	No.
9	....	No occupation	....	....	....	....	No.
5	No...	Organ grinder	(a)	4.00	52	208	No.
9	....	Housewife....................	....	....	....	....	Fever, typhoid.
....	....	At home	....	....	....	....	No.
$\frac{8}{12}$	No...	No occupation	....	....	....	....	No.
$\frac{7}{12}$	No...	No occupation	....	....	....	....	No.
5	No...	Laborer......................	60	7.50	10	75	No.
5	....	Housewife....................	....	....	....	....	Childbirth; nervous affection.
5	....	Scholar	....	....	....	....	No.
....	....	At home	....	....	....	....	Convulsions.
....	....	At home	....	....	....	....	No.
11	Yes..	Ragpicker	(a)	1.50	52	78	No.
10	....	Housewife and washerwoman.	(a)	.50	52	26	No.
10	....	Scholar	....	....	....	....	No.
(a)	Yes..	(a)	(a)	(a)	(a)	(a)	No.
5	Yes..	Street sweeper..............	60	7.50	22	165	No.
10	Yes..	No occupation	....	....	....	....	No.
5	....	Housewife and merchant, groceries.	(a)	(a)	52	(a)	No.

b Also worked as candy factory employee two weeks, at $3 per week.

TABLE **I.**—GENERAL SOCIAL AND ECONOMIC CONDITION, BY FAMILIES AND INDIVIDUALS—Continued.

Family number.	Relationship to head of family.	Sex.	Age.	Conjugal condition.	Birthplace.	Birthplace of—	
						Father.	Mother.
562	Son	M.	4	Single	United States	Abruzzo	Abruzzo
	Son	M.	2	Single	United States	Abruzzo	Abruzzo
	Lodger	M.	45	Married	Abruzzo	Abruzzo	Abruzzo
	Lodger	M.	43	Married	Abruzzo	Abruzzo	Abruzzo
	Lodger	M.	47	Married	Abruzzo	Abruzzo	Abruzzo
563	Head	M.	37	Married	Abruzzo	Abruzzo	Abruzzo
	Wife	F.	33	Married	Abruzzo	Abruzzo	Abruzzo
	Daughter	F.	5	Single	Abruzzo	Abruzzo	Abruzzo
	Brother	M.	40	Single	Abruzzo	Abruzzo	Abruzzo
	Brother	M.	28	Married	Abruzzo	Abruzzo	Abruzzo
564	Head	M.	32	Married	Abruzzo	Abruzzo	Abruzzo
	Wife	F.	25	Married	Abruzzo	Abruzzo	Abruzzo
	Daughter	F.	3	Single	United States	Abruzzo	Abruzzo
	Brother	M.	33	Married	Abruzzo	Abruzzo	Abruzzo
	Brother	M.	30	Married	Abruzzo	Abruzzo	Abruzzo
565	Head	M.	40	Married	Abruzzo	Abruzzo	Abruzzo
	Wife	F.	24	Married	Abruzzo	Abruzzo	Abruzzo
	Stepson	M.	5	Single	Abruzzo	Abruzzo	Abruzzo
	Stepson	M.	2	Single	United States	Abruzzo	Abruzzo
	Cousin	M.	30	Married	Abruzzo	Abruzzo	Abruzzo
	Boarder	M.	30	Married	Abruzzo	Abruzzo	Abruzzo
566	Head	M.	46	Married	Calabria	Calabria	Calabria
	Wife	F.	40	Married	Calabria	Calabria	Calabria
	Son	M.	21	Single	Calabria	Calabria	Calabria
	Son	M.	19	Single	Calabria	Calabria	Calabria
	Daughter	F.	16	Single	Calabria	Calabria	Calabria
	Daughter	F.	10	Single	Calabria	Calabria	Calabria
	Son	M.	7	Single	Calabria	Calabria	Calabria
567	Head	M.	37	Married	Campania	Campania	Campania
	Wife	F.	20	Married	Campania	Campania	Campania
	Son	M.	4	Single	United States	Campania	Campania
	Daughter	F.	3	Single	United States	Campania	Campania
	Daughter	F.	$\frac{7}{12}$	Single	United States	Campania	Campania
568	Head	M.	50	Widowed	Campania	Campania	Campania
	Son	M.	11	Single	Campania	Campania	Campania
	Daughter	F.	4	Single	United States	Campania	Campania
	Daughter	F.	3	Single	United States	Campania	Campania
569	Cooperative	M.	25	Married	Calabria	Calabria	Calabria
	Cooperative	M.	25	Married	Calabria	Calabria	Calabria
	Cooperative	M.	25	Married	Calabria	Calabria	Calabria
	Cooperative	M.	20	Single	Calabria	Calabria	Calabria
	Cooperative	M.	30	Single	Calabria	Calabria	Calabria
	Cooperative	M.	38	Widowed	Calabria	Calabria	Calabria
	Cooperative	M.	44	Married	Calabria	Calabria	Calabria
	Cooperative	M.	40	Married	Calabria	Calabria	Calabria
	Cooperative	M.	40	Married	Calabria	Calabria	Calabria
570	Head	M.	33	Married	Sicily	Sicily	Sicily
	Wife	F.	35	Married	Sicily	Sicily	Sicily
	Daughter	F.	7	Single	United States	Sicily	Sicily
	Son	M.	3	Single	United States	Sicily	Sicily
	Daughter	F.	$\frac{5}{12}$	Single	United States	Sicily	Sicily
571	Head	M.	46	Married	Sicily	Sicily	Sicily
	Wife	F.	42	Married	Sicily	Sicily	Sicily
	Son	M.	18	Single	Sicily	Sicily	Sicily
	Son	M.	16	Single	Sicily	Sicily	Sicily
	Son	M.	12	Single	Sicily	Sicily	Sicily
	Daughter	F.	10	Single	Sicily	Sicily	Sicily
572	Head	M.	38	Married	Campania	Campania	Campania
	Wife	F.	25	Married	Sicily	Sicily	Sicily
	Son	M.	8	Single	United States	Campania	Sicily
	Daughter	F.	$\frac{5}{12}$	Single	United States	Campania	Sicily
573	Head	M.	39	Married	Campania	Campania	Campania
	Wife	F.	40	Married	Campania	Campania	Campania
	Son	M.	$\frac{7}{12}$	Single	United States	Campania	Campania

a Not reported.

TABLE **I.**—GENERAL SOCIAL AND ECONOMIC CONDITION, BY FAMILIES AND INDIVIDUALS—Continued.

Years in U. S.	Natu-ral-ized.	Profession, trade, or occupation.	Hours of work per week.	Average weekly earn-ings.	Weeks em-ploy-ed.	Total yearly earn-ings.	Sick during year, defective, maimed, or deformed.
.....	......	At home	......	......	......	......	No.
.....	......	At home	......	......	......	......	No.
10	No...	Laborer......	60	$9.00	13	$117	No.
10	No...	Laborer......	60	9.00	35	315	No.
5	No...	Laborer......	60	9.00	13	117	Eyes, inflammation of both.
10	Yes..	Laborer......	60	9.00	31	279	No.
5	......	Housewife......	......	......	......	......	No.
5	......	At home......	......	......	......	......	No.
3	No...	Laborer......	60	9.00	52	468	No.
10	Yes..	Sewer digger......	60	13.50	52	702	No.
4	No...	Sewer digger......	(a)	13.50	35	473	No.
4	......	Housewife......	......	......	......	......	No.
.....	......	At home......	......	......	......	......	Measles.
4	No...	Sewer digger......	(a)	13.50	26	351	No.
4	No...	Sewer digger......	(a)	13.50	26	351	Bronchitis.
8	No...	Beggar	......	......	......	......	Deformed.
3	......	Housewife......	......	......	......	......	No.
3	......	Scholar	......	......	......	......	No.
.....	Yes..	At home......	......	......	......	......	No.
5	Yes..	Laborer......	60	9.00	30	270	No.
6	Yes..	No occupation	......	......	......	......	Rheumatism.
12	Yes..	Laborer......	60	6.60	6	40	Injury by accident.
4	......	Housewife......	......	......	......	......	No.
10	Yes..	Laborer......	48	6.60	4	26	(b)
4	......	Bootblack......	(a)	2.40	52	125	No.
4	......	Housework	......	......	......	......	No.
4	......	Scholar	......	......	......	......	No.
4	......	Scholar	......	......	......	......	No.
10	Yes..	Laborer......	60	6.75	52	351	No.
5	......	Housewife......	......	......	......	......	Childbirth.
.....	......	At home......	......	......	......	......	Fever, typhoid.
.....	......	At home......	......	......	......	......	No.
.....	......	At home......	......	......	......	......	No.
5	......	Housewife......	......	......	......	......	No.
5	......	Newsboy	(a)	.90	52	47	No.
.....	......	At home......	......	......	......	......	No.
.....	......	At home......	......	......	......	......	No.
4	No...	Laborer......	60	7.50	9	68	No.
4	No...	Laborer......	60	8.00	13	104	Rheumatism.
$\frac{7}{12}$	No...	No occupation	......	......	......	......	No.
4	......	Laborer......	60	7.50	17	128	No.
4	No...	Laborer......	60	8.25	17	140	No.
4	No...	Railroad laborer	60	7.50	13	98	No.
8	No...	Laborer......	60	7.50	17	128	No.
4	No...	Laborer......	60	7.50	17	128	No.
4	No...	Laborer......	60	7.50	17	128	No.
8	No...	Peddler, fruit......	(a)	6.00	52	312	No.
7	......	Housewife......	......	......	......	......	Childbirth.
.....	......	At home......	......	......	......	......	No.
.....	......	At home......	......	......	......	......	No.
.....	......	At home......	......	......	......	......	No.
11	No...	Laborer......	60	6.60	4	26	Rheumatism.
3	......	Housewife......	......	......	......	......	No.
3	......	Candy factory employee...	60	3.00	13	39	No.
3	......	No occupation	......	......	......	......	No.
3	......	No occupation	......	......	......	......	No.
3	......	Scholar	......	......	......	......	No.
10	No...	Flagman......	70	8.50	52	442	No.
3	......	Housewife......	......	......	......	......	Childbirth.
.....	......	Scholar	......	......	......	......	No.
.....	......	At home......	......	......	......	......	No.
5	No...	Railroad laborer	60	7.50	4	30	No.
2	......	Housewife......	......	......	......	......	Childbirth.
.....	......	At home......	......	......	......	......	No.

b Sick, disease not specified.

TABLE I.—GENERAL SOCIAL AND ECONOMIC CONDITION, BY FAMILIES
AND INDIVIDUALS—Continued.

Family number.	Relationship to head of family.	Sex.	Age.	Conjugal condition.	Birthplace.	Birthplace of—	
						Father.	Mother.
573	Brother	M.	48	Married	Campania	Campania	Campania
	Brother	M.	45	Married	Campania	Campania	Campania
	Brother	M.	36	Married	Campania	Campania	Campania
574	Head	M.	34	Married	Campania	Campania	Campania
	Wife	F.	32	Married	Sicily	Sicily	Sicily
	Daughter	F.	$\frac{9}{12}$	Single	United States	Campania	Sicily
575	Head	M.	51	Married	Campania	Campania	Campania
	Wife	F.	51	Married	Campania	Campania	Campania
	Stepson	M.	18	Single	Campania	Campania	Campania
576	Head	M.	30	Married	Campania	Campania	Campania
	Wife	F.	30	Married	Campania	Campania	Campania
	Son	M.	4	Single	United States	Campania	Campania
	Son	M.	2	Single	United States	Campania	Campania
577	Head	M.	30	Married	Campania	Campania	Campania
	Wife	F.	20	Married	Campania	Campania	Campania
	Son	M.	3	Single	United States	Campania	Campania
	Son	M.	2	Single	United States	Campania	Campania
	Daughter	F.	$\frac{3}{12}$	Single	United States	Campania	Campania
	Father-in-law	M.	60	Widowed	Campania	Campania	Campania
578	Head	M.	40	Married	Abruzzo	Abruzzo	Abruzzo
	Wife	F.	36	Married	Abruzzo	Abruzzo	Abruzzo
	Nephew	M.	22	Single	Abruzzo	Abruzzo	Abruzzo
	Lodger	M.	27	Single	Liguria	Liguria	Liguria
	Lodger	M.	50	Married	Abruzzo	Abruzzo	Abruzzo
	Lodger	M.	46	Married	Abruzzo	Abruzzo	Abruzzo
	Lodger	M.	40	Single	Basilicata	Basilicata	Basilicata
	Lodger	M.	24	Single	Abruzzo	Abruzzo	Abruzzo
	Lodger	M.	26	Single	Campania	Campania	Campania
	Lodger	M.	40	Married	Abruzzo	Abruzzo	Abruzzo
579	Head	M.	40	Married	Calabria	Calabria	Calabria
	Wife	F.	29	Married	Calabria	Calabria	Calabria
	Son	M.	1	Single	United States	Calabria	Calabria
	Brother-in-law	M.	25	Single	Calabria	Calabria	Calabria
	Brother-in-law	M.	12	Single	Calabria	Calabria	Calabria
	Boarder	M.	20	Single	Calabria	Calabria	Calabria
	Boarder	M.	20	Single	Calabria	Calabria	Calabria
580	Head	M.	33	Married	Sicily	Sicily	Sicily
	Wife	F.	25	Married	Sicily	Sicily	Sicily
	Brother	M.	25	Single	Sicily	Sicily	Sicily
	Boarder	M.	33	Single	Sicily	Sicily	Sicily
	Boarder	M.	25	Single	Sicily	Sicily	Sicily
	Boarder	M.	18	Single	Sicily	Sicily	Sicily
581	Head	M.	32	Married	Campania	Campania	Campania
	Wife	F.	30	Married	Basilicata	Basilicata	Basilicata
	Son	M.	5	Single	United States	Campania	Basilicata
	Daughter	F.	$\frac{4}{12}$	Single	United States	Campania	Basilicata
	Son	M.	$\frac{4}{12}$	Single	United States	Campania	Basilicata
	Brother	M.	18	Single	Campania	Campania	Campania
582	Head	M.	36	Married	Basilicata	Basilicata	Basilicata
	Wife	F.	35	Married	Basilicata	Basilicata	Basilicata
	Son	M.	8	Single	United States	Basilicata	Basilicata
	Daughter	F.	6	Single	United States	Basilicata	Basilicata
	Daughter	F.	1	Single	United States	Basilicata	Basilicata
	Brother	M.	25	Single	Basilicata	Basilicata	Basilicata
	Boarder	M.	26	Single	Abruzzo	Abruzzo	Abruzzo
583	Head	M.	30	Married	Calabria	Calabria	Calabria
	Wife	F.	28	Married	Calabria	Calabria	Calabria
	Daughter	F.	6	Single	United States	Calabria	Calabria
	Daughter	F.	5	Single	United States	Calabria	Calabria
	Daughter	F.	2	Single	United States	Calabria	Calabria
	Brother	M.	23	Single	Calabria	Calabria	Calabria
	Boarder	M.	29	Single	Calabria	Calabria	Calabria

a Not reported.   b Also worked as ragpicker eight weeks, at $2 per week.

TABLE I.—GENERAL SOCIAL AND ECONOMIC CONDITION, BY FAMILIES
AND INDIVIDUALS—Continued.

Years in U.S.	Natu-ral-ized.	Profession, trade, or occupation.	Hours of work per week.	Average weekly earn-ings.	Weeks em-ploy-ed.	Total yearly earn-ings.	Sick during year, defective, maimed, or deformed.
5	No...	Railroad laborer	60	$7.50	13	$98	No.
5	No...	Laborer...................	60	8.00	6	48	Dyspepsia.
5	No...	Laborer...................	60	8.00	6	48	No.
16	No...	Sewer digger	48	8.10	10	81	Rheumatism.
2	......	Housewife.................					Childbirth.
......	......	At home..................					No.
15	Yes..	Harness maker	84	(a)	52	(a)	No.
10	......	Housewife.................					No.
10	......	Harness maker	60	(a)	52	(a)	No.
10	Yes..	Street sweeper............	60	9.00	19	171	No.
8	......	Housewife.................					No.
......	......	At home..................					Rickets; convulsions.
......	......	At home..................					Rickets; rheumatism.
10	Yes..	Laborer (b)	60	7.50	b 13	114	No.
6	......	Housewife.................					Childbirth.
......	......	At home..................					No.
......	......	At home..................					No.
......	......	At home..................					No.
10	No...	Musician	24	1.80	22	40	Bowels, inflammation of.
14	Yes..	Foreman, elevated rail-road.	60	9.00	7	63	No.
4	......	Housewife.................					Bronchitis.
7	Yes..	Railroad laborer	60	7.50	7	53	No.
13	Yes..	Foreman, elevated rail-road.	60	12.00	52	624	No.
14	Yes..	Laborer...................	60	7.50	5	38	Bronchitis.
10	Yes..	Railroad laborer	60	6.60	7	46	No.
13	Yes..	Railroad laborer	60	6.90	7	48	No.
5	Yes..	Railroad laborer	60	6.60	7	46	Bronchitis.
6	Yes..	Railroad laborer	60	8.40	16	134	No.
6	Yes..	Railroad laborer (c)	60	7.50	c 10	143	No.
13	Yes..	Railroad laborer	60	7.50	22	165	Boils.
4	......	Housewife.................					Female complaint.
......	......	At home..................					No.
6	Yes..	Railroad laborer	60	6.90	22	152	Injury by accident.
4	......	Scholar					No.
7	......	Laborer...................	60	7.50	52	390	No.
7	......	Laborer...................	60	6.90	19	131	No.
5	Yes..	Peddler, fruit	(a)	(a)	52	(a)	No.
3	......	Housewife.................					No.
3	No...	Peddler, fruit	(a)	(a)	26	(a)	No.
1½	No...	Peddler, fruit	(a)	(a)	52	(a)	No.
3	No.. .	Peddler, fruit	(a)	(a)	52	(a)	No.
8	......	Peddler, fruit	(a)	(a)	52	(a)	No.
12	Yes..	Railroad laborer	60	7.50	26	195	Bronchitis.
7	......	Housewife.................					Childbirth.
......	......	At home..................					Bronchitis.
......	......	At home..................					No.
......	......	At home..................					No.
5	......	Bootblack	66	4.00	52	208	No.
17	Yes..	No occupation					Pneumonia.
10	......	Housewife.................					Female complaint.
......	......	Scholar					Fever, typhoid.
......	......	Scholar					Fever, scarlet.
......	......	At home..................					Bronchitis.
6	Yes..	Laborer...................	48	11.60	10	116	Fever, malarial.
7	No...	No occupation					Rheumatism.
15	Yes..	Laborer...................	(a)	9.00	22	198	Injury by accident.
10	......	Housewife.................					No.
......	......	Scholar					Measles.
......	......	At home..................					Measles.
......	......	At home..................					Rickets.
5	Yes..	Railroad laborer...........	48	7.69	23	177	No.
5	Yes..	Railroad laborer...........	(a)	7.77½	24	187	No.

c Also worked as street digger five weeks, at $13.50 per week.

TABLE 1.—GENERAL SOCIAL AND ECONOMIC CONDITION, BY FAMILIES AND INDIVIDUALS—Continued.

Family number.	Relationship to head of family.	Sex.	Age.	Conjugal condition.	Birthplace.	Birthplace of—	
						Father.	Mother.
584	Head	M.	36	Married	Basilicata	Basilicata	Basilicata
	Wife	F.	32	Married	Basilicata	Basilicata	Basilicata
	Son	M.	10	Single	Basilicata	Basilicata	Basilicata
	Daughter	F.	7	Single	United States	Basilicata	Basilicata
	Daughter	F.	3	Single	United States	Basilicata	Basilicata
	Son	M.	1	Single	United States	Basilicata	Basilicata
585	Cooperative	M.	32	Married	Abruzzo	Abruzzo	Abruzzo
	Cooperative	M.	46	Married	Abruzzo	Abruzzo	Abruzzo
	Cooperative	M.	45	Married	Abruzzo	Abruzzo	Abruzzo
	Cooperative	M.	51	Married	Abruzzo	Abruzzo	Abruzzo
	Cooperative	M.	45	Married	Abruzzo	Abruzzo	Abruzzo
	Cooperative	M.	40	Married	Abruzzo	Abruzzo	Abruzzo
	Cooperative	M.	40	Married	Abruzzo	Abruzzo	Abruzzo
	Cooperative	M.	45	Married	Abruzzo	Abruzzo	Abruzzo
	Cooperative	M.	46	Married	Abruzzo	Abruzzo	Abruzzo
	Cooperative	M.	51	Married	Abruzzo	Abruzzo	Abruzzo
	Cooperative	M.	45	Married	Abruzzo	Abruzzo	Abruzzo
586	Head	M.	54	Married	Basilicata	Basilicata	Basilicata
	Wife	F.	54	Married	Basilicata	Basilicata	Basilicata
	Brother-in-law	M.	47	Married	Basilicata	Basilicata	Basilicata
	Brother-in-law	M.	40	Married	Basilicata	Basilicata	Basilicata
587	Head	M.	35	Married	Campania	Campania	Campania
	Wife	F.	33	Married	Campania	Campania	Campania
	Son	M.	2	Single	United States	Campania	Campania
	Son	M.	$\frac{8}{12}$	Single	United States	Campania	Campania
588	Head	M.	40	Married	Campania	Campania	Campania
	Wife	F.	34	Married	Campania	Campania	Campania
	Son	M.	4	Single	United States	Campania	Campania
	Daughter	F.	2	Single	United States	Campania	Campania
589	Head	M.	46	Married	Abruzzo	Abruzzo	Abruzzo
	Wife	F.	31	Married	Abruzzo	Abruzzo	Abruzzo
	Son	M.	10	Single	France	Abruzzo	Abruzzo
	Son	M.	8	Single	France	Abruzzo	Abruzzo
	Son	M.	3	Single	United States	Abruzzo	Abruzzo
	Son	M.	$\frac{8}{12}$	Single	United States	Abruzzo	Abruzzo
	Brother-in-law	M.	25	Single	Abruzzo	Abruzzo	Abruzzo
	Lodger	M.	34	Married	Abruzzo	Abruzzo	Abruzzo
590	Head	M.	36	Married	Abruzzo	Abruzzo	Abruzzo
	Wife	F.	25	Married	Abruzzo	Abruzzo	Abruzzo
	Daughter	F.	$\frac{1}{12}$	Single	United States	Abruzzo	Abruzzo
591	Head	M.	35	Married	Abruzzo	Abruzzo	Abruzzo
	Wife	F.	38	Married	Abruzzo	Abruzzo	Abruzzo
	Daughter	F.	7	Single	Abruzzo	Abruzzo	Abruzzo
	Son	M.	1	Single	United States	Abruzzo	Abruzzo
	Brother-in-law	M.	27	Married	Abruzzo	Abruzzo	Abruzzo
	Cousin	M.	27	Married	Abruzzo	Abruzzo	Abruzzo
592	Head	M.	37	Married	Campania	Campania	Campania
	Wife	F.	23	Married	Campania	Campania	Campania
	Son	M.	4	Single	United States	Campania	Campania
	Daughter	F.	$\frac{5}{12}$	Single	United States	Campania	Campania
	Lodger	M.	36	Married	Campania	Campania	Campania
	Lodger	M.	28	Single	Campania	Campania	Campania
593	Head	M.	56	Married	Campania	Campania	Campania
	Wife	F.	50	Married	Campania	Campania	Campania
	Son	M.	23	Single	Campania	Campania	Campania
	Son	M.	21	Single	Campania	Campania	Campania
	Daughter	F.	14	Single	Campania	Campania	Campania
594	Head	M.	40	Married	Basilicata	Basilicata	Basilicata
	Wife	F.	28	Married	Basilicata	Basilicata	Basilicata
	Daughter	F.	7	Single	United States	Basilicata	Basilicata
	Daughter	F.	3	Single	United States	Basilicata	Basilicata
	Son	M.	1	Single	United States	Basilicata	Basilicata

a Not reported.
b Also worked as laborer one week, at $6.25 per week.
c Also worked as laborer two weeks, at $7.50 per week.

TABLE **I.**——GENERAL SOCIAL AND ECONOMIC CONDITION, BY FAMILIES AND INDIVIDUALS—Continued.

Years in U. S.	Natu- ral- ized.	Profession, trade, or occupation.	Hours of work per week.	Average weekly earn- ings.	Weeks em- ploy- ed.	Total yearly earn- ings.	Sick during year, defective, maimed, or deformed.
9	Yes..	Ragpicker	(a)	$3.00	52	$156	No.
8	......	Housewife					No.
8	......	Scholar					Rickets.
	......	Scholar					No.
......	......	At home					Rickets.
......	......	At home					No.
4	No...	Laborer	60	8.25	17	140	No.
3	No...	Laborer	60	8.25	17	140	Rheumatism.
3	No...	Laborer	60	8.25	17	140	No.
3	No...	Laborer	60	8.25	17	140	Fever, not specified.
4	No...	Laborer	60	8.25	17	140	No.
6	No...	Laborer	60	8.25	17	140	No.
3	No...	Laborer	60	8.25	17	140	No.
4	No...	Laborer	60	8.25	17	140	No.
4	No...	Laborer	60	8.25	17	140	No.
3	No...	Laborer	60	8.25	17	140	No.
3	No...	Laborer	60	8.25	17	140	No.
15	Yes..	Ragpicker (b)	(a)	.90	b 42	44	Eyes, inflammation of both.
10	......	Housewife					No.
10	No...	Ragpicker (c)	(a)	.90	c 49	59	No.
15	No...	Ragpicker (d)	(a)	.90	d 50	53	No.
4	No...	Merchant, wood (d)	(a)	1.20	d 50	68	No.
4	......	Housewife					Childbirth.
......	......	At home					Idiot.
......	......	At home					No.
16	Yes..	Rag-shop employee	60	9.00	52	468	No.
10	......	Housewife					No.
......	......	At home					No.
......	......	At home					No.
7	No...	Laborer	60	7.50	9	68	Eyes, inflammation of both.
5	......	Housewife					Childbirth.
5	......	Scholar					No.
5	......	At home					No.
	......	At home					Pneumonia.
......	......	At home					No.
3	No...	Laborer	60	9.00	17	153	No.
3	No...	Laborer	60	9.00	17	153	No.
6	No...	Laborer	60	9.00	17	153	No.
6	......	Housewife					Childbirth.
......	......	At home					No.
6	Yes..	Laborer	60	9.00	17	153	No.
3	......	Housewife					Consumption.
3	......	Scholar					Diphtheria.
......	......	At home					No.
3	No...	Laborer	60	9.00	17	153	Erysipelas.
7	Yes..	Laborer	(a)	(a)	(a)	(a)	No.
16	Yes..	Baker	(a)	12.00	52	624	No.
7	......	Housewife					Childbirth.
......	......	At home					No.
......	......	At home					No.
7	Yes..	No occupation					Rheumatism.
12	No...	Laborer	60	10.50	22	231	No.
15	No...	Laborer	60	8.25	12	99	Knee joint, inflammation of one.
3	......	Housewife					No.
3	No...	Railroad laborer (e)	60	7.50	e 15	149	No.
5	Yes..	Scholar and railroad laborer. (f)	60	7.50	f 19	179	No.
3	......	Scholar					No.
22	Yes..	Teamster, with team	60	18.00	26	468	No.
8	......	Housewife					No.
	......	Scholar					No.
......	......	At home					No.
......	......	At home					No.

d Also worked as laborer one week, at $7.50 per week.
e Also worked as newsboy nine weeks, at $4 per week.
f Also worked as newsdealer nine weeks, at $4 per week.

TABLE **I.**—GENERAL SOCIAL AND ECONOMIC CONDITION, BY FAMILIES
AND INDIVIDUALS—Continued.

Family number.	Relationship to head of family.	Sex.	Age.	Conjugal condition.	Birthplace.	Birthplace of—	
						Father.	Mother.
595	Head	M.	35	Married...	Basilicata	Basilicata	Basilicata
	Wife	F.	34	Married...	Basilicata	Basilicata	Basilicata
	Son	M.	7	Single	Basilicata	Basilicata	Basilicata
596	Cooperative	M.	25	Single	Abruzzo	Abruzzo	Abruzzo
	Cooperative	M.	54	Married...	Abruzzo	Abruzzo	Abruzzo
	Cooperative	M.	64	Married ..	Abruzzo	Abruzzo	Abruzzo
597	Head	M.	40	Married...	Abruzzo	Abruzzo	Abruzzo
	Wife	F.	32	Married...	Abruzzo	Abruzzo	Abruzzo
	Son	M.	8	Single	Belgium	Abruzzo	Abruzzo
	Daughter	F.	6	Single	Belgium	Abruzzo	Abruzzo
	Daughter	F.	4	Single	United States	Abruzzo	Abruzzo
	Daughter	F.	3	Single	United States	Abruzzo	Abruzzo
	Daughter	F.	$\frac{19}{12}$	Single	United States	Abruzzo	Abruzzo
598	Head	M.	(b)	Married...	Campania	Campania	Campania
	Wife	F.	(b)	Married...	Campania	Campania	Campania
	Daughter	F.	6	Single	United States	Campania	Campania
	Son	M.	1	Single	United States	Campania	Campania
599	Head	M.	40	Married...	Campania	Campania	Campania
	Wife	F.	40	Married...	Campania	Campania	Campania
	Son	M.	14	Single	United States	Campania	Campania
	Daughter	F.	7	Single	United States	Campania	Campania
	Son	M.	2	Single	United States	Campania	Campania
	Daughter	F.	$\frac{1}{12}$	Single	United States	Campania	Campania
600	Head	M.	30	Married...	Abruzzo	Abruzzo	Abruzzo
	Wife	F.	25	Married...	Basilicata	Basilicata	Basilicata
	Brother	M.	32	Married...	Abruzzo	Abruzzo	Abruzzo
	Lodger	M.	45	Married...	Abruzzo	Abruzzo	Abruzzo
	Lodger	M.	12	Single	Abruzzo	Abruzzo	Abruzzo
601	Head	M.	31	Married...	Calabria	Calabria	Calabria
	Wife	F.	33	Married...	Calabria	Calabria	Calabria
	Daughter	F.	6	Single	United States	Calabria	Calabria
	Daughter	F.	3	Single	United States	Calabria	Calabria
	Son	M.	$\frac{3}{12}$	Single	United States	Calabria	Calabria
602	Head	M.	42	Married...	Abruzzo	Abruzzo	Abruzzo
	Wife	F.	43	Married...	Abruzzo	Abruzzo	Abruzzo
	Daughter	F.	12	Single	Belgium	Abruzzo	Abruzzo
	Son	M.	9	Single	United States	Abruzzo	Abruzzo
	Son	M.	7	Single	United States	Abruzzo	Abruzzo
	Daughter	F.	5	Single	United States	Abruzzo	Abruzzo
	Daughter	F.	3	Single	United States	Abruzzo	Abruzzo
603	Head	M.	30	Married...	Basilicata	Basilicata	Basilicata
	Wife	F.	24	Married...	Basilicata	Basilicata	Basilicata
	Son	M.	4	Single	United States	Basilicata	Basilicata
	Son	M.	2	Single	United States	Basilicata	Basilicata
	Brother	M.	28	Single	Basilicata	Basilicata	Basilicata
604	Head	M.	46	Married...	Campania	Campania	Campania
	Wife	F.	37	Married...	Campania	Campania	Campania
605	Head	M.	30	Married...	Basilicata	Basilicata	Basilicata
	Wife	F.	30	Married...	Basilicata	Basilicata	Basilicata
	Daughter	F.	7	Single	Basilicata	Basilicata	Basilicata
	Son	M.	5	Single	United States	Basilicata	Basilicata
	Son	M.	2	Single	United States	Basilicata	Basilicata
	Daughter	F.	$\frac{3}{12}$	Single	United States	Basilicata	Basilicata
606	Head	M.	40	Married...	Basilicata	Basilicata	Basilicata
	Wife	F.	34	Married...	Basilicata	Basilicata	Basilicata
	Son	M.	17	Single	Basilicata	Basilicata	Basilicata
	Daughter	F.	13	Single	Basilicata	Basilicata	Basilicata
	Son	M.	8	Single	Basilicata	Basilicata	Basilicata
	Daughter	F.	5	Single	United States	Basilicata	Basilicata
	Son	M.	2	Single	United States	Basilicata	Basilicata

a Also worked as musician, time and wages not reported.
b Not reported.
c Also worked as laborer nine weeks, at $9 per week.

TABLE **I.**—GENERAL SOCIAL AND ECONOMIC CONDITION, BY FAMILIES AND INDIVIDUALS—Continued.

Years in U. S.	Naturalized.	Profession, trade, or occupation.	Hours of work per week.	Average weekly earnings.	Weeks employed.	Total yearly earnings.	Sick during year, defective, maimed, or deformed.
3	No...	Tinker....................	48	$3.00	52	$156	No.
$\frac{1}{3}$	......	Housewife...............					No.
$\frac{1}{2}$	......	At home.................					No.
6	No...	Laborer (a)	60	9.00	a 9	(b)	No.
5	No...	Laborer..................	60	9.00	13	117	Injury by accident.
5	No...	Peddler, ice cream (c).....	60	3.00	c 17	132	No.
6	No...	Musician	70	11.00	26	286	No.
6	......	Housewife...............					Childbirth.
6	......	Scholar					No.
6	......	Scholar					No.
......	......	At home.................					No.
......	......	At home.................					No.
......	......	At home.................					No.
14	Yes..	Ragpicker (d).............	(b)	3.00	d 43	210	No.
10	......	Housewife...............					Feeble-minded.
......	......	At home.................					No.
......	......	At home.................					No.
14	No...	Laborer..................	60	7.50	9	68	No.
14	......	Housewife...............					Childbirth.
......	......	Scholar					No.
......	......	At home.................					No.
......	......	At home.................					No.
......	......	At home.................					No.
6	Yes..	No occupation					No.
6	......	Housewife...............					No.
3	No...	Street sweeper...........	60	8.25	30	248	No.
6	No...	No occupation					No.
$\frac{1}{2}$	......	No occupation					No.
10	Yes..	Laborer..................	60	9.00	30	270	No.
8	......	Housewife...............					Childbirth.
......	......	Scholar					No.
......	......	At home.................					No.
......	......	At home.................					No.
12	No...	Laborer (e)	60	9.00	e 17	236	No.
12	......	Housewife...............					No.
12	......	Scholar					Diphtheria.
......	......	Scholar					Feeble-minded; deaf.
......	......	Scholar					Diphtheria.
......	......	At home.................					Diphtheria.
......	......	At home.................					No.
8	Yes..	Bootblack	(b)	3.00	52	156	No.
7	......	Housewife...............					No.
......	......	At home.................					No.
......	......	At home.................					No.
6	Yes..	Iron foundry employee ...	60	9.00	3	27	Fever, typhoid.
12	Yes..	Ragpicker...............	(b)	1.20	52	62	Rheumatism.
10	......	Housewife...............					No.
6	Yes..	Tinker	(b)	1.80	48	86	Fever, typhoid.
6	......	Housewife and pants finisher.	(b)	.30	9	3	Childbirth.
6	......	Scholar					No.
......	......	At home.................					No.
......	......	At home.................					No.
......	......	At home.................					No.
15	Yes..	Tinker (f)	(b)	1.80	f 51	99	No.
6	......	Housewife...............					No.
6	......	Newsboy	30	3.50	52	182	No.
6	......	Scholar.................					Eyes, inflammation of both.
6	......	Scholar.................					No.
......	......	At home.................					No.
......	......	At home.................					No.

d Also worked as street sweeper nine weeks, at $9 per week.
e Also worked as artist's model eleven weeks, at $7.50 per week.
f Also worked as laborer one week, at $7.50 per week.

Table **I.**—GENERAL SOCIAL AND ECONOMIC CONDITION, BY FAMILIES
AND INDIVIDUALS—Continued.

Family number.	Relationship to head of family.	Sex.	Age.	Conjugal condition.	Birthplace.	Birthplace of— Father.	Birthplace of— Mother.
607	Cooperative.......	M.	30	Single.....	Campania........	Campania......	Campania......
	Cooperative.......	M.	31	Married...	Basilicata........	Basilicata......	Basilicata......
	Cooperative.......	M.	47	Married...	Campania........	Campania......	Campania......
608	Cooperative.......	M.	50	Widowed .	Calabria	Calabria	Calabria ....
	Cooperative.......	M.	30	Single.....	Calabria	Calabria	Calabria ....
	Cooperative.......	M.	18	Single.....	Calabria	Calabria	Calabria ....
	Cooperative.......	M.	30	Single.....	Calabria	Calabria	Calabria ....
	Cooperative.......	M.	31	Single.....	Calabria	Calabria	Calabria ....
609	Cooperative.......	M.	31	Married...	Calabria	Calabria	Calabria ....
	Cooperative.......	M.	30	Married...	Calabria	Calabria	Calabria ....
	Cooperative.......	M.	33	Single.....	Calabria	Calabria	Calabria ....
	Cooperative.......	M.	28	Married...	Calabria	Calabria	Calabria ....
	Cooperative.......	M.	47	Married...	Calabria	Calabria	Calabria ....
	Cooperative.......	M.	25	Single.....	Calabria	Calabria	Calabria ....
610	Head	M.	46	Married....	Calabria	Calabria	Calabria ....
	Wife.............	F.	45	Married...	Calabria	Calabria	Calabria ....
	Daughter	F.	15	Single.....	Calabria	Calabria	Calabria ....
	Son	M.	12	Single.....	Calabria	Calabria	Calabria ....
	Daughter	F.	5	Single.....	United States...	Calabria	Calabria ....
	Son	M.	3	Single.....	United States...	Calabria	Calabria ....
	Son	M.	2	Single.....	United States...	Calabria	Calabria ....
	Daughter	F.	6/12	Single.....	United States...	Calabria	Calabria ....
	Lodger............	M.	30	Married...	Calabria	Calabria	Calabria ....
	Lodger............	M.	27	Single.....	Calabria	Calabria	Calabria ....
	Lodger............	M.	36	Married...	Calabria	Calabria	Calabria ....
611	Head	M.	32	Married...	Calabria	Calabria	Calabria ....
	Wife.............	F.	35	Married...	Calabria	Calabria	Calabria ....
612	Cooperative	M.	40	Married...	Calabria	Calabria	Calabria ....
	Cooperative	M.	16	Single.....	Calabria	Calabria	Calabria ....
	Cooperative	M.	47	Married...	Calabria	Calabria	Calabria ....
	Cooperative	M.	13	Single.....	Calabria	Calabria	Calabria ....
	Cooperative	M.	25	Single.....	Calabria	Calabria	Calabria ....
	Cooperative	M.	18	Single.....	Calabria	Calabria	Calabria ....
	Cooperative	M.	30	Married...	Calabria	Calabria	Calabria ....
613	Head	M.	40	Married...	Calabria	Calabria	Calabria ....
	Wife.............	F.	35	Married...	Calabria	Calabria	Calabria ....
614	Head	M.	28	Married...	Calabria	Calabria	Calabria ....
	Wife.............	F.	28	Married...	Calabria	Calabria	Calabria ....
	Lodger	M.	37	Married...	Calabria	Calabria	Calabria ....
	Lodger	M.	34	Single.....	Calabria	Calabria	Calabria ....
615	Head	M.	27	Married..	Calabria	Calabria	Calabria ....
	Wife.............	F.	23	Married...	Calabria	Calabria	Calabria ....
	Daughter	F.	2/12	Single.....	United States...	Calabria	Calabria ....
	Lodger	M.	29	Single.....	Calabria	Calabria	Calabria ....
616	Head	M.	38	Married...	Calabria	Calabria	Calabria ....
	Wife.............	F.	37	Married...	Calabria	Calabria	Calabria ....
	Son	M.	7	Single.....	United States...	Calabria	Calabria ....
	Son	M.	6	Single.....	United States...	Calabria	Calabria ....
	Son	M.	1	Single.....	United States...	Calabria	Calabria ....
	Cousin............	M.	40	Married...	Calabria	Calabria	Calabria ....
	Cousin............	M.	30	Single.....	Calabria	Calabria	Calabria ....
617	Head	M.	29	Married...	Calabria	Calabria	Calabria ....
	Wife.............	F.	26	Married...	Calabria	Calabria	Calabria ....
	Son	M.	1	Single.....	United States...	Calabria	Calabria ....
	Nephew	M.	21	Single.....	Calabria	Calabria	Calabria ....
	Cousin............	M.	30	Single.....	Calabria	Calabria	Calabria ....
618	Head	M.	(b)	Married...	Calabria	Calabria	Calabria ....
	Wife.............	F.	26	Married...	Calabria	Calabria	Calabria ....
	Daughter	F.	4	Single.....	United States...	Calabria	Calabria ....
	Cousin............	M.	30	Married...	Calabria	Calabria	Calabria ....
619	Cooperative	M.	50	Married...	Calabria	Calabria	Calabria ....
	Cooperative	M.	50	Married...	Calabria	Calabria	Calabria ....
	Cooperative	M.	30	Married...	Calabria	Calabria	Calabria ....

a Also worked as railroad laborer fifteen weeks, at $9 per week.
b Not reported.
c Also worked as laborer four weeks, at $7.50 per week.

TABLE **I.**—GENERAL SOCIAL AND ECONOMIC CONDITION, BY FAMILIES AND INDIVIDUALS—Continued.

Years in U.S.	Natu-ral-ized.	Profession, trade, or occupation.	Hours of work per week.	Average weekly earn-ings.	Weeks em-ploy-ed.	Total yearly earn-ings.	Sick during year, defective, maimed, or deformed.
11	No...	Railroad laborer	60	$7.50	11	$83	No.
4	No...	Laborer..................	60	7.50	6	45	No.
10	No...	Railroad laborer	60	7.50	11	83	No.
7	Yes..	Laborer..................	60	7.50	6	45	No.
8	Yes..	Laborer..................	60	8.10	13	105	No.
4	....	Laborer..................	60	8.10	13	105	No.
10	Yes..	Laborer..................	60	8.10	13	105	No.
10	Yes..	Laborer..................	60	7.50	13	98	No.
4	No...	Paper picker (a)	(b)	.60	a 37	157	No.
4	No...	Paper picker (a)	(b)	.60	a 37	157	No.
5	No...	Paper picker (c)	(b)	.60	c 48	59	No.
5	No...	Packer, rags	(b)	7.50	4	30	Rupture.
6	No...	Ragpicker	(b)	1.20	52	62	No.
1	No...	Ragpicker (c)	(b)	.60	c 48	59	No.
11	No...	Ragpicker	(b)	1.50	52	78	No.
6	....	Housewife................	....	....	....	....	Childbirth.
6	....	Housework	....	....	....	....	No.
6	....	Scholar and newsboy......	(b)	.30	(b)	(b)	No.
....	....	At home.................	....	....	....	....	No.
....	....	At home.................	....	....	....	....	No.
....	....	At home.................	....	....	....	....	No.
....	....	At home.................	....	....	....	....	No.
5	No...	Laborer..................	60	6.60	9	59	No.
5	No...	Railroad laborer	60	7.00	9	63	No.
3	No...	Laborer..................	60	6.60	9	59	No.
8	No...	Railroad laborer	60	6.60	26	172	**No.**
3	....	Housewife................	....	....	....	....	**No.**
4	No...	Railroad laborer	60	6.60	17	112	Injury by accident.
3	....	Bootblack and newsboy...	(b)	2.00	52	104	No.
3	No...	Ragpicker	(b)	1.50	52	78	No.
3	....	Scholar and newsboy.....	(b)	.90	52	47	No.
3	No...	Ragpicker	(b)	1.50	26	39	Rheumatism.
3	....	Newsboy	(b)	.90	52	47	No.
4	No...	Laborer..................	60	6.60	13	86	No.
14	No...	Padrone	(b)	(b)	(b)	(b)	No.
8	....	Housewife................	....	....	....	....	Bronchitis.
15	No...	Peddler, vegetables.......	(b)	3.00	44	132	Fever, not specified.
4	....	Housewife................	....	....	....	....	No.
7	Yes..	Laborer..................	60	6.60	17	112	No.
2	No...	Laborer..................	60	6.60	17	112	No.
5	No...	Laborer	60	6.60	9	59	No.
3	....	Housewife................	....	....	....	....	Childbirth.
....	No...	At home.................	....	....	....	....	No.
3	No...	Ragpicker	(b)	1.40	52	73	No.
8	No...	Ragpicker	(b)	1.40	48	67	Fever, not specified.
8	....	Housewife................	....	....	....	....	Miscarriage.
....	....	Scholar	....	....	....	....	No.
....	....	Scholar	....	....	....	....	No.
....	....	At home.................	....	....	....	....	No.
11	No...	Laborer..................	60	6.60	17	112	No.
4	No...	Laborer..................	60	6.60	17	112	No.
4	No...	Laborer..................	60	7.50	(b)	(b)	No.
2	....	Housewife................	....	....	....	....	No.
....	....	At home.................	....	....	....	....	No.
4	No...	Bootblack................	(b)	.90	(b)	(b)	Feeble-minded.
5	No...	Railroad laborer	60	7.00	9	63	No.
9	No...	Peddler..................	(b)	(b)	52	(b)	No.
5	....	Housewife................	....	....	....	....	No.
....	....	Scholar	....	....	....	....	No.
1	No...	Ragpicker (d)	(b)	1.20	d 48	84	No.
3	No...	Ragpicker (e)	(b)	1.20	e 35	161	No.
2	No...	Ragpicker (f)	(b)	1.20	f 39	133	No.
3	No...	Ragpicker (f)	(b)	1.20	f 39	133	No.

d Also worked as laborer four weeks, at $6.60 per week.
e Also worked as railroad laborer seventeen weeks, at $7 per week.
f Also worked as railroad laborer thirteen weeks, at $6.60 per week.

TABLE **I.**—GENERAL SOCIAL AND ECONOMIC CONDITION, BY FAMILIES
AND INDIVIDUALS—Continued.

Family number.	Relationship to head of family.	Sex.	Age.	Conjugal condition.	Birthplace.	Birthplace of—	
						Father.	Mother.
620	Head	M.	55	Married...	Calabria	Calabria	Calabria
	Wife	F.	25	Married..	Calabria	Calabria	Calabria
	Daughter	F.	6	Single.....	United States...	Calabria	Calabria
	Son	M.	4	Single.....	United States...	Calabria	Calabria
	Son	M.	2	Single.....	United States...	Calabria	Calabria
621	Head	M.	35	Married...	Calabria	Calabria	Calabria
	Wife	F.	25	Married...	Calabria	Calabria	Calabria
	Daughter	F.	6	Single.....	United States...	Calabria	Calabria
	Son	M.	4	Single.....	United States...	Calabria	Calabria
	Daughter	F.	1³⁄₁₂	Single.....	United States...	Calabria	Calabria
	Lodger	M.	(b)	Single.....	Calabria	Calabria	Calabria
622	Head	M.	28	Married...	Calabria	Calabria	Calabria
	Wife	F.	27	Married...	Calabria	Calabria	Calabria
	Daughter	F.	2	Single.....	United States...	Calabria	Calabria
	Cousin	M.	18	Single.....	Calabria	Calabria	Calabria
623	Head	M.	35	Married...	Campania	Campania	Campania
	Wife	F.	26	Married...	Campania	Campania	Campania
	Son	M.	15	Single.....	United States...	Campania	Campania
	Daughter	F.	11	Single.....	United States...	Campania	Campania
	Daughter	F.	8	Single.....	United States...	Campania	Campania
	Son	M.	7	Single.....	United States...	Campania	Campania
	Son	M.	4	Single.....	United States...	Campania	Campania
624	Head	M.	40	Married...	Calabria	Calabria	Calabria
	Wife	F.	30	Married...	Calabria	Calabria	Calabria
	Son	M.	4	Single....	United States...	Calabria	Calabria
	Son	M.	1	Single....	United States...	Calabria	Calabria
	Brother-in-law	M.	21	Single....	Calabria	Calabria	Calabria
	Nephew	M.	32	Single....	Calabria	Calabria	Calabria
	Lodger	M.	(b)	Widowed .	Calabria	Calabria	Calabria
	Lodger	M.	(b)	Married...	Calabria	Calabria	Calabria
625	Head	M.	60	Married...	Calabria	Calabria	Calabria
	Wife	F.	41	Married...	Calabria	Calabria	Calabria
	Daughter	F.	12	Single.....	Calabria	Calabria	Calabria
	Son	M.	7	Single.....	Calabria	Calabria	Calabria
626	Head	M.	37	Married...	Calabria	Calabria	Calabria
	Wife	F.	38	Married...	Calabria	Calabria	Calabria
	Son	M.	8	Single.....	Calabria	Calabria	Calabria
	Son	M.	6	Single.....	United States...	Calabria	Calabria
	Son	M.	2	Single.....	United States...	Calabria	Calabria
	Brother-in-law	M.	30	Married...	Calabria	Calabria	Calabria
	Sister-in-law	F.	27	Married...	Calabria	Calabria	Calabria
	Nephew	M.	³⁄₁₂	Single.....	United States...	Calabria	Calabria
627	Cooperative	M.	35	Single.....	Calabria	Calabria	Calabria
	Cooperative	M.	30	Single.....	Calabria	Calabria	Calabria
	Cooperative	M.	30	Single.....	Calabria	Calabria	Calabria
	Cooperative	M.	28	Single.....	Calabria	Calabria	Calabria
628	Head	M.	70	Married...	Calabria	Calabria	Calabria
	Wife	F.	48	Married...	Calabria	Calabria	Calabria
	Son	M.	11	Single.....	United States...	Calabria	Calabria
	Cousin	M.	40	Married...	Calabria	Calabria	Calabria
629	Head	M.	28	Married...	Calabria	Calabria	Calabria
	Brother-in-law	M.	34	Married...	Calabria	Calabria	Calabria
	Brother-in-law	M.	26	Single.....	Calabria	Calabria	Calabria
	Sister-in-law	F.	24	Married...	Calabria	Calabria	Calabria
	Nephew	M.	1	Single.....	United States...	Calabria	Calabria
630	Head	M.	48	Married...	Calabria	Calabria	Calabria
	Wife	F.	40	Married...	Calabria	Calabria	Calabria
	Daughter	F.	15	Married...	Calabria	Calabria	Calabria
	Daughter	F.	9	Single.....	Calabria	Calabria	Calabria
	Daughter	F.	2	Single.....	United States...	Calabria	Calabria
	Son	M.	1	Single.....	United States...	Calabria	Calabria
	Son-in-law	M.	26	Married...	Calabria	Calabria	Calabria
	Lodger	M.	38	Single.....	Calabria	Calabria	Calabria

a Also worked as laborer nine weeks, at $7 per week.
b Not reported.
c Also worked as laborer twelve weeks, at $7.50 per week.
d Also worked as laborer nine weeks, at $7.50 per week.

TABLE I.—GENERAL SOCIAL AND ECONOMIC CONDITION, BY FAMILIES AND INDIVIDUALS—Continued.

Years in U.S.	Natu- ral- ized.	Profession, trade, or occupation.	Hours of work per week.	Average weekly earn- ings.	Weeks em- ploy- ed.	Total yearly earn- ings.	Sick during year, defective, maimed, or deformed.
12	Yes..	Ragpicker (a)	(b)	$1.20	a 13	$79	No.
8		Housewife					No.
		Scholar					Fever, not specified.
		At home					Fever, not specified.
		At home					Fever, not specified; bow-legs.
13	Yes..	Barber	81	(b)	52	(b)	No.
10		Housewife					Childbirth.
		Scholar					No.
		At home					No.
		At home					No.
6	No...	Barber	81	(b)	52	(b)	No.
10	Yes..	Paper picker (c)	(b)	.60	c 36	112	Fever, not specified.
5		Housewife					No.
		At home					No.
7		Paper picker (c)	(b)	.60	c 36	112	No.
17	Yes..	Driver, garbage wagon	60	6.60	9	59	No.
4		Housewife					Female complaint.
		Bootblack	(b)	.50	(b)	(b)	No.
		Housework					No.
		Scholar					No.
		Scholar					No.
		At home					No.
11	Yes..	Ragpicker	(b)	1.20	52	62	No.
6		Housewife					No.
		At home					No.
		At home					No.
5	Yes..	Ragpicker (d)	(b)	.60	d 43	93	No.
11	No...	Ragpicker (e)	(b)	.60	e 43	93	No.
7	No...	Ragpicker (d)	(b)	.60	d 43	93	No.
7	No...	Newsboy	(b)	1.75	52	91	No.
9	No...	Paper picker	(b)	1.40	52	73	No.
4		Housewife					No.
4		Scholar					No.
4		At home					Feeble-minded; cross-eyed.
15	Yes..	Laborer	60	9.00	7	63	No.
8		Housewife					Female complaint.
8		Scholar					No.
		Scholar					No.
		At home					No.
9	No...	Laborer (f)	60	7.50	f 9	71	No.
5		Housework					Childbirth.
		At home					No.
4	No...	Laborer (g)	60	7.50	g 9	76	Rheumatism; deaf.
5	No...	Laborer (g)	60	7.50	g 11	91	Deaf.
5	No...	Laborer	60	7.50	11	83	No.
8	No...	No occupation					No.
12	No...	Paper picker	(b)	1.20	52	62	No.
11		Housewife					No.
		Scholar					No.
4	No...	Rag-shop employee	(b)	6.00	52	312	No.
4	No...	Railroad laborer (f)	60	6.60	f 9	63	No.
9	Yes..	No occupation					No.
5	Yes..	Railroad laborer (f)	60	6.60	f 9	63	No.
4		Housewife					No.
		At home					No.
10	No...	Railroad laborer (f)	60	6.60	f 9	63	Injury by accident.
3		Housewife					No.
3		Housework					No.
3		Scholar					No.
		At home					No.
		At home					No.
4	No...	Railroad laborer	60	5.50	9	50	No.
4	No...	Railroad laborer (h)	60	6.60	h 9	68	No.

e Also worked as railroad laborer nine weeks, at $7.50 per week.
f Also worked as ragpicker four weeks, at $0.90 per week.
g Also worked as paper picker nine weeks, at $0.90 per week.
h Also worked as ragpicker nine weeks, at $0.90 per week.

TABLE **I.**—GENERAL SOCIAL AND ECONOMIC CONDITION, BY FAMILIES
AND INDIVIDUALS—Continued.

Family number.	Relationship to head of family.	Sex.	Age.	Conjugal condition.	Birthplace.	Birthplace of—	
						Father.	Mother.
631	Head	F.	48	Widowed	Calabria	Calabria	Calabria
	Son	M.	16	Single	Calabria	Calabria	Calabria
	Son-in-law	M.	30	Married	Calabria	Calabria	Calabria
	Boarder	M.	29	Single	Calabria	Calabria	Calabria
632	Head	M.	51	Married	Campania	Campania	Campania
	Wife	F.	50	Married	Campania	Campania	Campania
	Son	M.	14	Single	United States	Campania	Campania
	Daughter	F.	12	Single	United States	Campania	Campania
	Son	M.	8	Single	United States	Campania	Campania
633	Head	M.	47	Married	Campania	Campania	Campania
	Wife	F.	45	Married	Campania	Campania	Campania
	Son	M.	18	Single	Campania	Campania	Campania
634	Head	M.	40	Married	Calabria	Calabria	Calabria
	Wife	F.	36	Married	Calabria	Calabria	Calabria
	Daughter	F.	12	Single	Calabria	Calabria	Calabria
	Son	M.	9	Single	Calabria	Calabria	Calabria
	Son	M.	5	Single	Calabria	Calabria	Calabria
	Lodger	M.	27	Single	Calabria	Calabria	Calabria
	Lodger	M.	40	Married	Calabria	Calabria	Calabria
635	Head	M.	57	Married	Calabria	Calabria	Calabria
	Wife	F.	47	Married	Calabria	Calabria	Calabria
	Son	M.	13	Single	Calabria	Calabria	Calabria
	Daughter	F.	11	Single	Calabria	Calabria	Calabria
	Brother	M.	30	Married	Calabria	Calabria	Calabria
	Cousin	M.	18	Single	Calabria	Calabria	Calabria
	Lodger	M.	30	Single	Calabria	Calabria	Calabria
	Lodger	M.	26	Single	Calabria	Calabria	Calabria
636	Head	M.	25	Married	Calabria	Calabria	Calabria
	Wife	F.	24	Married	Calabria	Calabria	Calabria
	Daughter	F.	5	Single	United States	Calabria	Calabria
	Son	M.	2	Single	United States	Calabria	Calabria
	Son	M.	$\frac{7}{12}$	Single	United States	Calabria	Calabria
	Mother	F.	56	Widowed	Calabria	Calabria	Calabria
	Lodger	M.	28	Married	Calabria	Calabria	Calabria
	Lodger	M.	22	Single	Calabria	Calabria	Calabria
	Lodger	M.	60	Widowed	Calabria	Calabria	Calabria
637	Head	M.	30	Married	Calabria	Calabria	Calabria
	Wife	F.	26	Married	Calabria	Calabria	Calabria
	Daughter	F.	1	Single	United States	Calabria	Calabria
	Uncle	M.	64	Married	Calabria	Calabria	Calabria
	Cousin	M.	43	Married	Calabria	Calabria	Calabria
	Cousin	M.	16	Single	Calabria	Calabria	Calabria
	Cousin	M.	18	Single	Calabria	Calabria	Calabria
	Cousin	M.	35	Married	Calabria	Calabria	Calabria
	Cousin	M.	19	Single	Calabria	Calabria	Calabria
638	Head	F.	36	Widowed	Calabria	Calabria	Calabria
	Son	M.	11	Single	Calabria	Calabria	Calabria
	Daughter	F.	7	Single	United States	Calabria	Calabria
	Son	M.	5	Single	United States	Calabria	Calabria
	Son	M.	3	Single	United States	Calabria	Calabria
	Lodger	M.	31	Single	Calabria	Calabria	Calabria
639	Head	M.	35	Married	Campania	Campania	Campania
	Wife	F.	32	Married	Campania	Campania	Campania
	Son	M.	5	Single	United States	Campania	Campania
640	Head	M.	46	Married	Campania	Campania	Campania
	Wife	F.	35	Married	Campania	Campania	Campania
	Daughter	F.	14	Single	Campania	Campania	Campania
	Son	M.	10	Single	United States	Campania	Campania
	Son	M.	7	Single	United States	Campania	Campania
	Son	M.	6	Single	United States	Campania	Campania
	Son	M.	2	Single	United States	Campania	Campania
	Daughter	F.	$\frac{1}{12}$	Single	United States	Campania	Campania

a Not reported.
b Also worked as laborer four weeks, at $7.50 per week.
c Also worked as railroad laborer six weeks, at $7.50 per week.

TABLE **I.**—GENERAL SOCIAL AND ECONOMIC CONDITION, BY FAMILIES AND INDIVIDUALS—Continued.

Years in U. S.	Naturalized.	Profession, trade, or occupation.	Hours of work per week.	Average weekly earnings.	Weeks employed.	Total yearly earnings.	Sick during year, defective, maimed, or deformed.
3	......	Housewife and rag-shop employee.	60	$3.50	52	$182	No.
$\frac{7}{12}$	......	Bootblack and newsboy...	28	1.40	(a)	(a)	No.
$1\frac{7}{12}$	No..	No occupation............	......	......	......	......	No.
3	No...	Railroad laborer	60	6.60	13	86	No.
16	Yes..	Laborer..................	60	7.50	9	68	Injury by accident.
15	......	Housewife................	......	......	......	......	No.
......	......	Bootblack	(a)	1.40	(a)	(a)	No.
......	......	Scholar	......	......	......	......	No.
......	......	Scholar	......	......	......	......	No.
8	Yes..	Laborer..................	60	6.90	3	21	No.
7	......	Housewife	......	......	......	......	Rheumatism.
7	......	No occupation	......	......	......	......	Consumption.
5	Yes..	Peddler, coal (b)	(a)	3.00	b 16	78	No.
3	......	Housewife	......	......	......	......	No.
3	......	Scholar	......	......	......	......	No.
3	......	Scholar	......	......	......	......	Pneumonia.
3	......	At home	......	......	......	......	Pneumonia.
10	Yes..	(a)	(a)	(a)	(a)	(a)	No.
8	No...	(a)	(a)	(a)	(a)	(a)	No.
7	No...	Ragpicker	(a)	1.80	52	94	No.
6	......	Housewife	......	......	......	......	No.
6	......	Bootblack	(a)	.90	52	47	No.
6	......	Scholar	......	......	......	......	No.
6	No...	Railroad laborer	60	6.60	4	26	No.
3	......	Newsboy	(a)	1.40	52	73	No.
9	No...	Railroad laborer	60	6.60	3	20	No.
2	No...	Railroad laborer	60	6.60	4	26	No.
9	Yes..	Laborer..................	60	6.60	4	26	No.
7	......	Housewife	......	......	......	......	Childbirth.
......	......	At home	......	......	......	......	No.
......	......	At home	......	......	......	......	No.
......	......	At home	......	......	......	......	No.
7	No...	Housework	......	......	......	......	No.
$1\frac{7}{12}$	No...	No occupation	......	......	......	......	No.
4	No...	Laborer.................	60	7.50	13	98	No.
5	No...	No occupation	......	......	......	......	No.
9	Yes..	Ragpicker (c)	(a)	.60	c 46	73	No.
3	......	Housewife	......	......	......	......	No.
......	......	At home	......	......	......	......	Bronchitis.
3	No...	Paper picker (d)	(a)	.60	d 48	58	No.
9	No...	Ragpicker (e)	(a)	.60	e 39	109	No.
3	......	Bootblack	(a)	.90	52	47	No.
3	......	Bootblack (f).............	(a)	1.50	f 42	136	No.
9	No...	Laborer.................	60	6.60	13	86	No.
2	......	Ragpicker	(a)	2.00	52	104	No.
8	......	Housewife and cigar-stub gatherer.	(a)	.30	19	6	No.
8	......	Scholar and newsboy	30	.60	52	31	No.
......	......	Scholar	......	......	......	......	No.
......	......	Scholar	......	......	......	......	No.
......	......	At home	......	......	......	......	Arm, congenital paralysis of one.
10	No...	Railroad laborer	60	6.33	19	120	No.
11	Yes..	Paver....................	(a)	7.50	19	143	Fever, not specified.
9	......	Housewife	......	......	......	......	No.
......	......	Scholar	......	......	......	......	Bronchitis.
12	Yes..	Paver....................	(a)	7.50	35	263	Rheumatism.
12	......	Housewife	......	......	......	......	Childbirth.
12	......	No occupation	......	......	......	......	No.
......	......	Scholar	......	......	......	......	No.
......	......	Scholar	......	......	......	......	Fever, not specified.
......	......	Scholar	......	......	......	......	Fever, not specified.
......	......	At home	......	......	......	......	Fever, not specified.
......	......	At home	......	......	......	......	No.

d Also worked as railroad laborer four weeks, at $7.25 per week.
e Also worked as laborer thirteen weeks, at $6.60 per week.
f Also worked as laborer ten weeks, at $7.25 per week.

TABLE I.—GENERAL SOCIAL AND ECONOMIC CONDITION, BY FAMILIES AND INDIVIDUALS—Continued.

Family number.	Relationship to head of family.	Sex.	Age.	Conjugal condition.	Birthplace.	Birthplace of— Father.	Birthplace of— Mother.
641	Head	M.	40	Married	Campania	Campania	Campania
	Wife	F.	44	Married	Campania	Campania	Campania
	Daughter	F.	15	Single	Campania	Campania	Campania
	Son	M.	10	Single	United States	Campania	Campania
	Son	M.	8	Single	United States	Campania	Campania
	Mother-in-law	F.	80	Widowed	Campania	Campania	Campania
	Boarder	M.	37	Single	Campania	Campania	Campania
642	Head	M.	47	Married	Campania	Campania	Campania
	Wife	F.	38	Married	Campania	Campania	Campania
	Daughter	F.	8	Single	United States	Campania	Campania
	Daughter	F.	6	Single	United States	Campania	Campania
	Daughter	F.	2	Single	United States	Campania	Campania
643	Head	M.	47	Married	Campania	Campania	Campania
	Wife	F.	45	Married	Campania	Campania	Campania
	Son	M.	18	Single	Campania	Campania	Campania
	Daughter	F.	6	Single	Campania	Campania	Campania
	Boarder	M.	35	Single	Campania	Campania	Campania
644	Cooperative	M.	51	Married	Campania	Campania	Campania
	Cooperative	M.	27	Married	Campania	Campania	Campania
645	Head	M.	25	Married	Campania	Campania	Campania
	Wife	F.	40	Married	Campania	Campania	Campania
646	Head	M.	35	Married	Campania	Campania	Campania
	Wife	F.	45	Married	Campania	Campania	Campania
647	Head	M.	34	Married	Campania	Campania	Campania
	Wife	F.	31	Married	Campania	Campania	Campania
	Daughter	F.	12	Single	Campania	Campania	Campania
	Son	M.	11	Single	Campania	Campania	Campania
	Son	M.	3	Single	United States	Campania	Campania
	Daughter	F.	1	Single	United States	Campania	Campania
	Cousin	M.	34	Married	Campania	Campania	Campania
648	Head	M.	30	Married	Campania	Campania	Campania
	Wife	F.	18	Married	Campania	Campania	Campania
	Son	M.	2	Single	United States	Campania	Campania
649	Head	M.	39	Married	Campania	Campania	Campania
	Wife	F.	35	Married	Campania	Campania	Campania
	Daughter	F.	14	Single	United States	Campania	Campania
	Daughter	F.	13	Single	United States	Campania	Campania
	Daughter	F.	7	Single	United States	Campania	Campania
	Son	M.	1	Single	United States	Campania	Campania
	Nephew	M.	22	Single	Campania	Campania	Campania
650	Head	M.	39	Married	Campania	Campania	Campania
	Wife	F.	34	Married	Basilicata	Basilicata	Basilicata
	Son	M.	13	Single	Basilicata	Campania	Basilicata
	Son	M.	12	Single	United States	Campania	Basilicata
	Daughter	F.	7	Single	United States	Campania	Basilicata
	Daughter	F.	5	Single	United States	Campania	Basilicata
	Daughter	F.	3	Single	United States	Campania	Basilicata
	Boarder	M.	26	Single	Campania	Campania	Campania
651	Head	M.	32	Married	Campania	Campania	Campania
	Wife	F.	28	Married	Campagna di Roma.	Campagna di Roma.	Campagna di Roma.
	Son	M.	3	Single	United States	Campania	Campagna di Roma.
	Son	M.	2	Single	United States	Campania	Campagna di Roma.
652	Head	M.	33	Married	Calabria	Calabria	Calabria
	Wife	F.	30	Married	Calabria	Calabria	Calabria
	Daughter	F.	2	Single	United States	Calabria	Calabria
	Daughter	F.	6/12	Single	United States	Calabria	Calabria
	Cousin	M.	23	Single	Calabria	Calabria	Calabria

a Not reported.
b Also worked as laborer fifteen weeks, at $7.50 per week.

TABLE **I.**—GENERAL SOCIAL AND ECONOMIC CONDITION, BY FAMILIES AND INDIVIDUALS—Continued.

Years in U. S.	Natu- ral- ized.	Profession, trade, or occupation.	Hours of work per week.	Average weekly earn- ings.	Weeks em- ploy- ed.	Total yearly earn- ings.	Sick during year, defective, maimed, or deformed.
14	Yes..	Railroad laborer	70	$7.50	39	$293	Bronchitis; one foot maimed.
14	......	Housewife...............					No.
14	......	No occupation............					No.
......	......	Scholar					No.
......	......	Scholar					No.
16	......	No occupation............					No.
(a)	Yes..	Notary public.............	(a)	(a)	52	(a)	No.
14	Yes..	Coal picker (b)............	(a)	1.00	b 33	146	No.
11	......	Housewife...............					Arm, one broken; fever, not specified.
......	......	Scholar					Rickets; typhoid fever.
......	......	Scholar					No.
......	......	At home.................					Rickets; typhoid fever.
4	No...	Wood picker (c)	(a)	1.00	c 33	176	Bronchitis.
4	......	Housewife and washer- woman.	(a)	.25	26	7	Bronchitis.
4	......	Bootblack	70	2.50	52	130	No.
4	......	Scholar					Injury by accident.
(a)	Yes..	Barber...................	88	5.00	52	260	No.
16	Yes..	Paver...................	54	7.50	15	113	Rheumatism.
16	No...	Barber's apprentice.......	92	3.00	52	156	No.
7	Yes .	Coal picker (b)	(a)	1.50	b 37	168	No.
7	......	Housewife...............					Female complaint.
15	Yes..	No occupation...........					No.
3	......	Housewife and dressmaker	(a)	1.50	26	39	Skin, disease of.
11	Yes..	No occupation...........					Pneumonia.
11	......	Housewife and dressmaker	(a)	(a)	52	(a)	No.
11	......	No occupation...........					No.
11	......	Scholar					Fever, not specified.
......	......	At home.................					No.
......	......	At home.................					No.
12	No...	No occupation...........					No.
15	Yes..	Barber...................	84½	10.00	26	260	Fever, not specified.
15	......	Housewife...............					No.
......	......	At home.................					No.
17	Yes..	Street sweeper...........	48	9.00	12	108	Rheumatism.
17	......	Housewife...............					No.
......	......	N occupation............					No.
......	......	Scholar					No.
......	......	Scholar					Measles.
......	......	At home.................					Fever, not specified.
7	Yes..	Bootblack	66	6.00	52	312	No.
13	Yes..	Laborer..................	48	9.00	15	135	No.
13	......	Housewife...............					Miscarriage.
13	......	Scholar					Knee joint, inflammation of one.
......	......	Scholar					No.
......	......	Scholar					Fever, scarlet.
......	......	Scholar					No.
......	......	At home.................					Injury by accident.
8	Yes..	Street sweeper (d)	(a)	9.00	d 13	(a)	Injury by accident.
13	Yes..	Street sweeper...........	60	7.50	11	83	No.
4	......	Housewife...............					No.
......	......	At home.................					Fever, not specified.
......	......	At home.................					Measles.
7	Yes..	Laborer..................	48	9.00	15	135	No.
3	......	Housewife...............					Childbirth; tumor of breast.
......	......	At home.................					No.
......	......	At home.................					No.
3	No...	Street railway laborer	60	7.50	22	165	No.

c Also worked as laborer nineteen weeks, at $7.50 per week.
d Also worked at other occupation, time not reported, at $7.50 per week.

TABLE I.—GENERAL SOCIAL AND ECONOMIC CONDITION, BY FAMILIES
AND INDIVIDUALS—Continued.

Family number.	Relationship to head of family.	Sex.	Age.	Conjugal condition.	Birthplace.	Birthplace of—	
						Father.	Mother.
653	Cooperative	M.	25	Single	Sicily	Sicily	Sicily
	Cooperative	M.	25	Single	Sicily	Sicily	Sicily
	Cooperative	M.	18	Single	Sicily	Sicily	Sicily
	Cooperative	M.	26	Single	Sicily	Sicily	Sicily
	Cooperative	M.	22	Single	Sicily	Sicily	Sicily
	Cooperative	M.	42	Married	Sicily	Sicily	Sicily
	Cooperative	M.	21	Single	Sicily	Sicily	Sicily
	Cooperative	M.	27	Single	Sicily	Sicily	Sicily
	Cooperative	M.	35	Widowed	Sicily	Sicily	Sicily
	Cooperative	M.	46	Married	Sicily	Sicily	Sicily
	Cooperative	M.	46	Married	Sicily	Sicily	Sicily
	Cooperative	M.	38	Married	Sicily	Sicily	Sicily
	Cooperative	M.	30	Married	Sicily	Sicily	Sicily
	Cooperative	M.	22	Single	Sicily	Sicily	Sicily
	Cooperative	M.	22	Single	Sicily	Sicily	Sicily
	Cooperative	M.	24	Single	Sicily	Sicily	Sicily
	Cooperative	M.	26	Single	Sicily	Sicily	Sicily
	Cooperative	M.	27	Single	Sicily	Sicily	Sicily
654	Head	M.	25	Single	Sicily	Sicily	Sicily
655	Cooperative	M.	40	Married	Calabria	Calabria	Calabria
	Cooperative	M.	35	Married	Calabria	Calabria	Calabria
	Cooperative	M.	19	Single	Calabria	Calabria	Calabria
	Cooperative	M.	20	Single	Calabria	Calabria	Calabria
	Cooperative	M.	50	Married	Calabria	Calabria	Calabria
	Cooperative	M.	18	Single	Calabria	Calabria	Calabria
	Cooperative	M.	21	Single	Calabria	Calabria	Calabria
	Cooperative	M.	49	Married	Calabria	Calabria	Calabria
	Cooperative	M.	27	Single	Calabria	Calabria	Calabria
	Cooperative	M.	54	Widowed	Calabria	Calabria	Calabria
	Cooperative	M.	32	Single	Calabria	Calabria	Calabria
	Cooperative	M.	34	Married	Calabria	Calabria	Calabria
	Cooperative	M.	31	Single	Calabria	Calabria	Calabria
656	Head	M.	40	Married	Basilicata	Basilicata	Basilicata
	Wife	F.	40	Married	Basilicata	Basilicata	Basilicata
	Daughter	F.	13	Single	Basilicata	Basilicata	Basilicata
	Son	M.	6	Single	United States	Basilicata	Basilicata
	Daughter	F.	4	Single	United States	Basilicata	Basilicata
	Daughter	F.	1	Single	United States	Basilicata	Basilicata
657	Head	M.	38	Married	Campania	Campania	Campania
	Wife	F.	40	Married	Campania	Campania	Campania
	Daughter	F.	15	Single	Campania	Campania	Campania
	Daughter	F.	12	Single	Campania	Campania	Campania
658	Head	M.	51	Married	Campania	Campania	Campania
	Wife	F.	45	Married	Campania	Campania	Campania
	Cousin	M.	30	Married	Campania	Campania	Campania
	Lodger	M.	45	Married	Campania	Campania	Campania
	Lodger	M.	45	Single	Campania	Campania	Campania
659	Head	M.	40	Married	Campania	Campania	Campania
	Lodger	M.	30	Married	Campania	Campania	Campania
	Lodger	M.	46	Married	Campania	Campania	Campania
	Lodger	M.	23	Married	Campania	Campania	Campania
	Lodger	M.	23	Single	Campania	Campania	Campania
660	Head	M.	30	Married	Calabria	Calabria	Calabria
	Brother	M.	25	Single	Calabria	Calabria	Calabria
661	Head	M.	60	Married	Campania	Campania	Campania
	Wife	F.	48	Married	Campania	Campania	Campania
	Daughter	F.	14	Single	Campania	Campania	Campania
	Daughter	F.	12	Single	Campania	Campania	Campania
662	Head	M.	38	Married	Campania	Campania	Campania
	Wife	F.	34	Married	Campania	Campania	Campania
	Daughter	F.	11	Single	Campania	Campania	Campania
	Daughter	F.	8	Single	United States	Campania	Campania
	Son	M.	5	Single	United States	Campania	Campania
	Son	M.	2	Single	United States	Campania	Campania
	Daughter	F.	2/12	Single	United States	Campania	Campania
	Father	M.	68	Married	Campania	Campania	Campania
	Mother	F.	69	Married	Campania	Campania	Campania

a Not reported.   b Also worked as street sweeper four weeks, at $9 per week.

TABLE **I.**—GENERAL SOCIAL AND ECONOMIC CONDITION, BY FAMILIES AND INDIVIDUALS—Continued.

Years in U.S.	Naturalized.	Profession, trade, or occupation.	Hours of work per week.	Average weekly earnings.	Weeks employed.	Total yearly earnings.	Sick during year, defective, maimed, or deformed.
3	No...	No occupation					Injury by accident.
3	No...	Laborer	84	$3.60	22	$79	No.
6	......	Salesman, grocery	72	(a)	52	(a)	No.
6	No...	Laborer	84	3.60	22	79	Fever, malarial.
5	No...	Laborer	84	3.60	26	94	No.
3	No...	Laborer	84	3.60	26	94	No.
8	No...	Railroad laborer	60	6.60	17	112	No.
6	No...	Laborer	84	3.60	13	47	No.
3	No...	Laborer	84	3.60	22	79	No.
5	No...	Laborer	84	3.60	13	47	No.
4	No...	Laborer	84	3.30	35	116	No.
4	No...	Laborer	84	3.30	22	73	Dyspepsia.
2	No...	Laborer	84	3.00	17	51	No.
3	No...	Laborer	84	3.60	17	61	No.
5	No...	Laborer	84	3.60	30	108	No.
4	No...	Laborer	84	3.60	26	94	No.
4	No...	Laborer	84	3.60	30	108	No.
5	No...	Laborer	84	3.60	17	61	No.
6	No...	Laborer	84	3.60	52	187	No.
8	Yes..	Street sweeper	60	9.00	22	198	No.
10	Yes..	Peddler	(a)	3.00	52	156	No.
3	......	Scholar and tailor	60	6.50	6	39	Injury by accident.
4	......	Scholar and candy factory employee. (b)	55	5.00	b 35	211	No.
5	No...	Laborer	60	7.50	13	98	No.
3	......	Laborer	60	6.60	9	59	No.
10	Yes..	Elevator tender	91	(a)	17	(a)	No.
9	No...	Laborer	60	7.50	13	98	No.
5	No...	Laborer	60	7.50	17	128	No.
10	No...	Laborer	60	6.60	13	86	No.
5	Yes..	Laborer	(a)	6.00	52	312	No.
8	Yes..	Laborer	60	9.00	39	351	No.
10	Yes..	Laborer	60	9.00	39	351	No.
13	Yes..	Street sweeper	60	9.00	17	153	No.
7	......	Housewife					No.
7	......	No occupation					No.
......	......	At home					Eyes, inflammation of both.
......	......	At home					Rickets.
......	......	At home					No.
13	Yes..	Laborer	60	8.00	17	136	No.
7	......	Housewife					Fever, malarial.
7	......	Scholar					No.
7	......	Scholar					Fever, typhoid.
13	Yes..	Peddler, vegetables (c)	(a)	3.00	c 50	168	No.
3	......	Housewife					Female complaint.
3	No...	Laborer	60	8.00	13	104	Fever, not specified.
15	Yes..	Laborer	60	9.00	17	153	No.
7	Yes..	Laborer	60	7.50	9	68	Rheumatism.
5	No...	Laborer	60	9.00	17	153	No.
5	Yes..	Laborer	60	7.50	13	98	No.
10	No...	Laborer	60	7.50	13	98	No.
1	No...	Laborer	60	7.50	13	98	No.
1	No...	Laborer	60	7.50	11	83	No.
8	Yes..	Peddler, vegetables	(a)	3.00	(a)	(a)	No.
8	Yes..	Laborer	60	8.10	15	122	No.
5	Yes..	Laborer	60	7.50	19	143	Injury by accident; epilepsy.
5	......	Housewife					Female complaint.
5	......	Scholar					No.
5	......	Scholar					No.
16	No...	Paver	60	9.00	22	198	No.
8	......	Housewife					Childbirth.
8	......	Scholar					No.
......	......	Scholar					No.
......	......	At home					No.
......	......	At home					No.
......	......	At home					No.
8	No...	No occupation					Injury by accident; lame.
8	......	No occupation					No.

c Also worked as laborer two weeks, at $9 per week.

TABLE I.—GENERAL SOCIAL AND ECONOMIC CONDITION, BY FAMILIES AND INDIVIDUALS—Continued.

| Family number. | Relationship to head of family. | Sex. | Age. | Conjugal condition. | Birthplace. | Birthplace of— | |
						Father.	Mother.
663	Head	M.	48	Married...	Campania	Campania	Campania
	Wife	F.	42	Married...	Campania	Campania	Campania
	Son	M.	22	Single	Campania	Campania	Campania
	Daughter	F.	13	Single	United States	Campania	Campania
	Son	M.	4	Single	United States	Campania	Campania
664	Head	M.	34	Married...	Campania	Campania	Campania
	Wife	F.	38	Married...	Campania	Campania	Campania
	Son	M.	4	Single	United States	Campania	Campania
	Daughter	F.	3	Single	United States	Campania	Campania
	Son	M	1	Single	United States	Campania	Campania
	Brother	M.	40	Married...	Campania	Campania	Campania
665	Head	M.	67	Married...	Campania	Campania	Campania
	Wife	F.	52	Married...	Campania	Campania	Campania
	Daughter	F.	4	Single	United States	Campania	Campania
666	Head	M.	34	Married...	Basilicata	Basilicata	Basilicata
	Wife	F.	37	Married...	Basilicata	Basilicata	Basilicata
	Son	M.	11	Single	Basilicata	Basilicata	Basilicata
	Daughter	F.	7	Single	Basilicata	Basilicata	Basilicata
	Lodger	M.	28	Married...	Basilicata	Basilicata	Basilicata
667	Head	M.	45	Married...	Campania	Campania	Campania
	Wife	F.	40	Married ..	Campania	Campania	Campania
	Son	M.	13	Single	Campania	Campania	Campania
	Daughter	F.	6	Single	United States	Campania	Campania
	Son	M.	2	Single	United States	Campania	Campania
668	Head	F.	54	Widowed .	Campania	Campania	Campania
	Son	M.	30	Single	Campania	Campania	Campania
	Son	M.	23	Single	Campania	Campania	Campania
669	Head	M.	38	Married...	Campania	Campania	Campania
	Wife	F.	32	Married...	Campania	Campania	Campania
	Son	M.	7	Single	France	Campania	Campania
	Daughter	F.	4	Single	United States	Campania	Campania
	Daughter	F.	2	Single	United States	Campania	Campania
670	Head	M.	50	Married...	Campania	Campania	Campania
	Wife	F.	42	Married...	Campania	Ca.. pania	Campania
	Daughter	F.	14	Single	Campania	Campania	Campania
	Daughter	F.	12	Single	United States	Campania	Campania
	Son	M.	9	Single	United States	Campania	Campania
	Daughter	F.	6	Single	United States	Campania	Campania
	Lodger	M.	64	Widowed .	Campania	Campania	Campania
671	Head	M.	52	Married...	Calabria	Calabria	Calabria
	Wife	F.	44	Married...	Calabria	Calabria	Calabria
	Daughter	F.	20	Single	Calabria	Calabria	Calabria
	Son	M.	16	Single	Calabria	Calabria	Calabria
	Daughter	F.	9	Single	United States	Calabria	Calabria
	Son	M.	8	Single	United States	Calabria	Calabria
672	Head	M.	42	Married...	Campania	Campania	Campania
	Wife	F.	52	Married...	Campania	Campania	Campania
	Son	M.	18	Single	United States	Campania	Campania
	Son	M.	17	Single	United States	Campania	Campania
	Son	M.	12	Single	United States	Campania	Campania
673	Head	M.	23	Married...	Campania	Campania	Campania
	Wife	F.	22	Married...	Campania	Campania	Campania
674	Head	M.	50	Married...	Campania	Campania	Campania
	Wife	F.	50	Married...	Campania	Campania	Campania
	Son	M.	22	Single	Campania	Campania	Campania
	Daughter	F.	15	Single	Campania	Campania	Campania
	Son	M.	10	Single	Campania	Campania	Campania
675	Head	M.	35	Married...	Sicily	Sicily	Sicily
	Wife	F.	35	Married...	Sicily	Sicily	Sicily
	Daughter	F.	1	Single	United States	Sicily	Sicily

a Not reported.   b Also worked as laborer thirteen weeks, at $7.50 per week.

TABLE I.—GENERAL SOCIAL AND ECONOMIC CONDITION, BY FAMILIES
AND INDIVIDUALS—Continued.

Years in U. S.	Natu-ral-ized.	Profession, trade, or occupation.	Hours of work per week.	Average weekly earn-ings.	Weeks em-ploy-ed.	Total yearly earn-ings.	Sick during year, defective, maimed, or deformed.
18	Yes..	Sewer digger...............	60	$13.25	39	$517	No.
15	......	Housewife and washer-woman.	(a)	2.00	52	104	No.
15	Yes..	Bootblack (b)	80	5.00	b 22	208	No.
......	......	No occupation...............	......	......	......	......	Pneumonia.
......	......	At home....................	......	......	......	......	No.
13	Yes..	Hod carrier................	60	9.00	26	234	No.
8	......	Housewife..................	......	......	......	......	No.
......	......	At home....................	......	......	......	......	No.
......	......	At home....................	......	......	......	......	No.
......	......	At home....................	......	......	......	......	No.
3	No...	Laborer....................	60	9.00	30	270	No.
11	No...	Ragpicker..................	60	1.00	52	52	No.
6	......	Housewife..................	......	......	......	......	Bronchitis.
......	......	At home....................	......	......	......	......	Tumors, bony; bowlegs.
7	Yes..	Coal miner.................	60	6.30	26	164	No.
4	......	Housewife..................	......	......	......	......	No.
4	......	Newsboy	30	(a)	52	(a)	No.
4	......	Scholar	......	......	......	......	No.
4	No...	No occupation..............	......	......	......	......	No.
13	Yes..	No occupation..............	......	......	......	......	No.
13	......	Housewife and washer-woman.	(a)	3.00	(a)	(a)	No.
13	......	No occupation..............	......	......	......	......	No.
......	......	At home....................	......	......	......	......	No.
......	......	At home....................	......	......	......	......	Rickets.
4	......	Housewife..................	......	......	......	......	Bronchitis.
9	Yes..	Paver......................	60	7.50	17	128	No.
9	Yes..	Candy factory employee...	60	6.00	26	156	No.
7	Yes..	Paver......................	54	7.50	15	113	No.
7	......	Housewife..................	......	......	......	......	No.
7	......	Scholar....................	......	......	......	......	No.
......	......	At home....................	......	......	......	......	No.
......	......	At home....................	......	......	......	......	No.
15	No...	Merchant, groceries (c) ...	(a)	(a)	c 43	(a)	No.
14	......	Housewife and merchant, groceries.	(a)	(a)	50	(a)	Fever, not specified.
14	......	No occupation..............	......	......	......	......	No.
......	......	Scholar....................	......	......	......	......	No.
......	......	Scholar....................	......	......	......	......	No.
......	......	Scholar....................	......	......	......	......	No.
12	Yes..	Street sweeper.............	44	9.50	9	86	No.
14	No...	Lamplighter................	21	5.11	52	266	No.
10	......	Housewife..................	......	......	......	......	Female complaint.
10	......	Housework..................	......	......	......	......	No.
10	......	Barber.....................	92	6.00	48	288	Not specified.
......	......	At home....................	......	......	......	......	No.
......	......	Scholar....................	......	......	......	......	No.
19	Yes..	No occupation	......	......	......	......	No.
19	......	Housewife..................	......	......	......	......	No.
......	......	Scholar and newsboy	(a)	1.25	(a)	(a)	No.
......	......	Scholar and newsboy	(a)	1.25	(a)	(a)	No.
......	......	Scholar and newsboy	(a)	1.25	(a)	(a)	No.
15	Yes..	Sewer digger	48	13.50	31	419	No.
1	......	Housewife..................	......	......	......	......	No.
8	Yes..	Paver......................	(a)	7.50	19	143	No.
1	......	Housewife..................	......	......	......	......	No.
8	Yes..	Barber.....................	92	10.00	52	520	No.
1	......	Housework..................	......	......	......	......	No.
1	......	No occupation	......	......	......	......	No.
3	No...	Peddler, fruit..............	54	4.00	52	208	No.
3	......	Housewife..................	......	......	......	......	No.
......	......	At home....................	......	......	......	......	No.

c Also worked as laborer nine weeks, at $9 per week.

TABLE I.—GENERAL SOCIAL AND ECONOMIC CONDITION, BY FAMILIES AND INDIVIDUALS—Continued.

| Family number. | Relationship to head of family. | Sex. | Age. | Conjugal condition. | Birthplace. | Birthplace of— | |
						Father.	Mother.
676	Head	M.	36	Married...	Apulia	Apulia	Apulia
	Wife	F.	32	Married...	Apulia	Apulia	Apulia
	Daughter	F.	3	Single	United States...	Apulia	Apulia
	Daughter	F.	$\frac{5}{12}$	Single	United States...	Apulia	Apulia
	Brother-in-law	M.	27	Married...	Apulia	Apulia	Apulia
	Sister-in-law	F.	26	Married...	Apulia	Apulia	Apulia
677	Cooperative	M.	33	Married...	Calabria	Calabria	Calabria
	Cooperative	M.	22	Single	Calabria	Calabria	Calabria
	Cooperative	M.	34	Married...	Calabria	Calabria	Calabria
	Cooperative	M.	37	Married...	Calabria	Calabria	Calabria
	Cooperative	M.	26	Single	Calabria	Calabria	Calabria
	Cooperative	M.	27	Married...	Calabria	Calabria	Calabria
	Cooperative	M.	35	Married...	Calabria	Calabria	Calabria
	Cooperative	M.	22	Single	Calabria	Calabria	Calabria
678	Head	M.	42	Married...	Campania	Campania	Campania
	Wife	F.	42	Married...	Campania	Campania	Campania
	Son	M.	17	Single	Campania	Campania	Campania
	Daughter	F.	14	Single	United States...	Campania	Campania
	Daughter	F.	10	Single	United States...	Campania	Campania
	Daughter	F.	7	Single	United States...	Campania	Campania
	Daughter	F.	5	Single	United States...	Campania	Campania
	Daughter	F.	2	Single	United States...	Campania	Campania
	Mother-in-law	F.	70	Widowed .	Campania	Campania	Campania
679	Head	M.	46	Married...	Campania	Campania	Campania
	Wife	M.	42	Married...	Campania	Campania	Campania
	Daughter	F.	20	Single	Campania	Campania	Campania
	Son	M.	12	Single	Campania	Campania	Campania
	Son	M.	11	Single	Campania	Campania	Campania
680	Head	M.	37	Married...	Campania	Campania	Campania
	Wife	F.	34	Married...	Campania	Campania	Campania
681	Head	M.	39	Married...	Campania	Campania	Campania
	Wife	F.	42	Married...	Campania	Campania	Campania
	Son	M.	18	Single	Campania	Campania	Campania
	Son	M.	15	Single	Campania	Campania	Campania
	Daughter	F.	12	Single	Campania	Campania	Campania
	Daughter	F.	8	Single	United States...	Campania	Campania
682	Head	M.	41	Married...	Campania	Campania	Campania
	Wife	F.	(a)	Married...	Campania	Campania	Campania
	Daughter	F.	14	Single	Campania	Campania	Campania
	Son	M.	8	Single	United States...	Campania	Campania
	Son	M.	5	Single	United States...	Campania	Campania
	Daughter	F.	3	Single	United States...	Campania	Campania
	Son	M.	$\frac{3}{12}$	Single	United States...	Campania	Campania
	Lodger	M.	24	Married...	Campania	Campania	Campania
683	Head	M.	38	Married...	Campania	Campania	Campania
	Wife	F.	42	Married...	Campania	Campania	Campania
	Son	M.	9	Single	United States...	Campania	Campania
	Daughter	F.	7	Single	United States...	Campania	Campania
	Daughter	F.	4	Single	United States...	Campania	Campania
	Son	M.	1	Single	United States...	Campania	Campania
684	Head	M.	50	Married...	Campania	Campania	Campania
	Wife	F.	48	Married...	Campania	Campania	Campania
	Son	M.	15	Single	Campania	Campania	Campania
	Daughter	F.	14	Single	Campania	Campania	Campania
	Son	M.	12	Single	Campania	Campania	Campania
	Daughter	F.	7	Single	Campania	Campania	Campania
685	Head	M.	27	Married...	Sicily	Sicily	Sicily
	Wife	F.	44	Married...	Basilicata	Basilicata	Basilicata
	Stepson	M.	11	Single	United States...	Basilicata	Basilicata
	Stepdaughter	F.	7	Single	United States...	Basilicata	Basilicata
	Stepdaughter	F.	6	Single	United States...	Basilicata	Basilicata

a Not reported.

TABLE **I.**—GENERAL SOCIAL AND ECONOMIC CONDITION, BY FAMILIES
AND INDIVIDUALS—Continued.

Years in U. S.	Naturalized.	Profession, trade, or occupation.	Hours of work per week.	Average weekly earnings.	Weeks employed.	Total yearly earnings.	Sick during year, defective, maimed, or deformed.
6	No...	Railroad laborer	60	$6.60	10	$66	No.
4	....	Housewife and pants finisher.	(a)	.90	17	15	Childbirth.
......	....	At home	......	......	......	......	No.
......	....	At home	......	......	......	......	No.
5	Yes..	Laborer	60	7.40	30	222	Rheumatism.
4	....	Pants finisher	(a)	.90	17	15	No.
3	No...	Railroad laborer	60	6.60	15	99	No.
$\frac{3}{12}$	No...	No occupation	......	......	......	......	No.
4	No...	Railroad laborer	60	6.60	15	99	No.
3	No...	Railroad laborer	60	6.60	15	99	Bronchitis.
5	No...	Railroad laborer	60	7.50	19	143	No.
4	No...	Railroad laborer	60	7.50	19	143	No.
3	No...	No occupation	......	......	......	......	No.
6	No...	Railroad laborer	60	7.50	19	143	No.
14	Yes..	Sewer digger	60	9.00	31	279	No.
14	....	Housewife	......	......	......	......	No.
14	....	Scholar and tobacco stripper.	60	4.00	52	208	No.
......	....	No occupation	......	......	......	......	No.
......	....	Scholar	......	......	......	......	No.
......	....	Scholar	......	......	......	......	No.
......	....	Scholar	......	......	......	......	No.
......	....	At home	......	......	......	......	No.
14	....	No occupation	......	......	......	......	Blind.
11	No...	Merchant, rags	72	4.50	52	234	No.
2	....	Housewife	......	......	......	......	No.
2	....	Housework	......	......	......	......	Feeble-minded.
2	....	No occupation	......	......	......	......	Fever, typhoid; feeble-minded.
2	....	No occupation	......	......	......	......	Feeble-minded.
15	Yes..	Laborer	48	9.00	11	99	Fever, not specified.
11	....	Housewife and washerwoman.	(a)	1.50	52	78	No.
11	Yes..	No occupation	......	......	......	......	Rheumatism.
9	....	Housewife	......	......	......	......	Female complaint.
9	....	Painter's apprentice	60	4.50	52	234	No.
9	....	Bootblack	(a)	1.50	52	78	No.
9	....	Scholar	......	......	......	......	No.
......	....	Scholar	......	......	......	......	Fever, typhoid.
13	Yes..	Bootblack	70	6.50	47	306	No.
13	....	Housewife and ragpicker.	(a)	2.00	42	84	Childbirth.
13	....	Ragpicker	21	1.50	52	78	No.
......	....	At home	......	......	......	......	Convulsions; feeble-minded; rickets.
......	....	At home	......	......	......	......	No.
......	....	At home	......	......	......	......	No.
......	....	At home	......	......	......	......	No.
5	No...	Bootblack	87½	7.00	52	364	No.
12	Yes..	Teamster, with team	(a)	9.00	26	234	Lame.
11	....	Housewife	......	......	......	......	No.
......	....	Scholar	......	......	......	......	No.
......	....	At home	......	......	......	......	No.
......	....	At home	......	......	......	......	Measles.
......	....	At home	......	......	......	......	No.
4	No...	Ragpicker	(a)	.50	43	22	Injury by accident.
4	....	Housewife	......	......	......	......	No.
4	....	Newsboy	(a)	1.00	52	52	No.
4	....	Ragpicker	12	.40	52	21	No.
4	....	Scholar and newsboy	(a)	.70	52	36	No.
4	....	At home	......	......	......	......	No.
7	No...	Railroad laborer	60	6.60	15	99	No.
12	....	Housewife	......	......	......	......	No.
......	....	Scholar	......	......	......	......	Measles.
......	....	Scholar	......	......	......	......	Measles.
......	....	Scholar	......	......	......	......	Measles.

TABLE I.—GENERAL SOCIAL AND ECONOMIC CONDITION, BY FAMILIES
AND INDIVIDUALS—Continued.

Family number.	Relationship to head of family.	Sex.	Age.	Conjugal condition.	Birthplace.	Birthplace of—	
						Father.	Mother.
686	Head	M.	23	Married	Campania	Campania	Campania
	Wife	F.	18	Married	Campania	Campania	Campania
	Daughter	F.	$\frac{2}{12}$	Single	United States	Campania	Campania
687	Head	M.	30	Married	Campania	Campania	Campania
	Wife	F.	29	Married	Campania	Campania	Campania
	Son	M.	8	Single	United States	Campania	Campania
	Daughter	F.	5	Single	United States	Campania	Campania
	Son	M.	3	Single	United States	Campania	Campania
688	Head	M.	50	Married	Campania	Campania	Campania
	Wife	F.	45	Married	Campania	Campania	Campania
	Son	M.	24	Married	Campania	Campania	Campania
	Son	M.	9	Single	United States	Campania	Campania
	Son	M.	5	Single	United States	Campania	Campania
	Daughter-in-law	F.	20	Married	Campania	Campania	Campania
	Lodger	M.	50	Married	Campania	Campania	Campania
	Lodger	M.	17	Single	Campania	Campania	Campania
689	Head	M.	38	Married	Campania	Campania	Campania
	Wife	F.	38	Married	Campania	Campania	Campania
	Son	M.	6	Single	United States	Campania	Campania
	Son	M.	4	Single	United States	Campania	Campania
	Daughter	F.	$\frac{1}{12}$	Single	United States	Campania	Campania
690	Head	M.	35	Married	Campania	Campania	Campania
	Wife	F.	35	Married	Campania	Campania	Campania
691	Head	M.	35	Married	Campania	Campania	Campania
	Wife	F.	33	Married	Campania	Campania	Campania
	Daughter	F.	8	Single	Campania	Campania	Campania
	Son	M.	6	Single	Campania	Campania	Campania
	Son	M.	2	Single	United States	Campania	Campania
	Daughter	F.	1	Single	United States	Campania	Campania
692	Head	M.	45	Married	Campania	Campania	Campania
	Wife	F.	40	Married	Campania	Campania	Campania
	Son	M.	18	Single	Campania	Campania	Campania
	Son	M.	15	Single	Campania	Campania	Campania
	Daughter	F.	10	Single	Campania	Campania	Campania
	Son	M.	9	Single	Campania	Campania	Campania
	Son	M.	3	Single	United States	Campania	Campania
	Daughter	F.	$\frac{9}{12}$	Single	United States	Campania	Campania
693	Head	M.	40	Married	Campania	Campania	Campania
	Wife	F.	38	Married	Campania	Campania	Campania
	Son	M.	11	Single	United States	Campania	Campania
	Daughter	F.	8	Single	United States	Campania	Campania
	Daughter	F.	1	Single	United States	Campania	Campania
	Brother	M.	20	Single	Campania	Campania	Campania
	Brother	M.	17	Single	Campania	Campania	Campania
	Boarder	M.	40	Married	Campania	Campania	Campania
694	Head	M.	45	Married	Campania	Campania	Campania
	Wife	F.	39	Married	Campania	Campania	Campania
	Son	M.	10	Single	United States	Campania	Campania
	Son	M.	9	Single	United States	Campania	Campania
	Daughter	F.	6	Single	United States	Campania	Campania
	Daughter	F.	2	Single	United States	Campania	Campania
695	Cooperative	M.	52	Married	Calabria	Calabria	Calabria
	Cooperative	M.	25	Single	Calabria	Calabria	Calabria
	Cooperative	M.	40	Married	Calabria	Calabria	Calabria
	Cooperative	M.	17	Single	Calabria	Calabria	Calabria
	Cooperative	M.	34	Married	Calabria	Calabria	Calabria
	Cooperative	M.	18	Single	Calabria	Calabria	Calabria
696	Head	M.	35	Married	Campania	Campania	Campania
	Wife	F.	30	Married	Campania	Campania	Campania
	Cousin	M.	25	Single	Campania	Campania	Campania

a Also worked as street sweeper twenty-three weeks, at $7.50 per week.
b Not reported.
c Also worked as laborer eleven weeks, at $6.90 per week.

TABLE **I.**—GENERAL SOCIAL AND ECONOMIC CONDITION, BY FAMILIES
AND INDIVIDUALS—Continued.

Years in U. S.	Naturalized.	Profession, trade, or occupation.	Hours of work per week.	Average weekly earnings.	Weeks employed.	Total yearly earnings.	Sick during year, defective, maimed, or deformed.
1	No...	Newsdealer	37	$10.00	44	$440	No.
1		Housewife					Childbirth.
		At home					Bronchitis.
11	Yes..	Laborer	60	6.00	23	138	Rheumatism.
11		Housewife					No.
		Scholar					No.
		At home					No.
		At home					No.
15	Yes..	Ragpicker (a)	(b)	2.00	a 29	231	No.
10		Housewife					No.
10	Yes..	Bootblack	85	5.00	52	260	No.
		Scholar					No.
3		Scholar					No.
		Housework					No.
16	Yes..	Quarryman	60	7.50	31	233	No.
7		Newsboy	78	2.50	52	130	No.
11	Yes..	No occupation					No.
7		Housewife					Childbirth.
		Scholar					No.
		At home					No.
		At home					No.
15	No...	Railroad laborer	60	7.20	52	374	No.
5		Housewife					No.
5	No...	Bootblack	72	4.50	31	140	Injury by accident; lame.
5		Housewife					Fever, not specified; neuralgia.
5		At home					No.
5		At home					No.
		At home					No.
		At home					Fever, malarial.
9	No...	Bootblack (c)	(b)	(b)	c 41	(b)	No.
9		Housewife					Childbirth.
9		Bootblack	72	(b)	52	(b)	No.
9		Bootblack	72	(b)	52	(b)	No.
9		Scholar					No.
9		Scholar and newsboy	(b)	.50	(b)	(b)	No.
		At home					Convulsions.
		At home					No.
16	Yes..	Railroad laborer	60	7.50	52	390	No.
15		Housewife					No.
		Scholar					No.
		At home					Rickets.
		At home					No.
6		Newsboy	78	6.00	52	312	Leg, loss of one.
6		Scholar and bootblack	72	5.00	52	260	No.
2	No...	Railroad laborer (d)	60	8.25	d 25	313	No.
14	Yes..	Railroad laborer	60	7.50	23	173	No.
14		Housewife					No.
		Scholar					No.
		Scholar					No.
		At home					No.
		At home					No.
7	No...	Elevated railroad laborer.	60	7.50	23	173	No.
5	Yes..	Elevated railroad laborer.	60	7.50	23	173	No.
8	Yes..	Peddler	60	9.00	35	315	No.
4		Scholar					No.
6	Yes..	Railroad laborer	60	6.60	19	125	No.
4		Bootblack (e)	(b)	3.00	e 47	174	No.
15	Yes..	Ragpicker (f)	(b)	(b)	f 37	(b)	No.
9		Housewife					No.
3	No...	Bootblack	85	3.00	52	156	No.

d Also worked as ragpicker seventeen weeks, at $1.40 per week.
e Also worked as railroad laborer five weeks, at $6.60 per week.
f Also worked as laborer fifteen weeks, at $7.50 per week.

TABLE **I.**—GENERAL SOCIAL AND ECONOMIC CONDITION, BY FAMILIES AND INDIVIDUALS—Continued.

Family number.	Relationship to head of family.	Sex.	Age.	Conjugal condition.	Birthplace.	Birthplace of—	
						Father.	Mother.
697	Head	M.	46	Married...	Campania	Campania	Campania
	Wife	F.	44	Married...	Campania	Campania	Campania
	Lodger	M.	22	Single	Campania	Campania	Campania
	Lodger	M.	19	Single	Campania	Campania	Campania
	Lodger	M.	15	Single	Campania	Campania	Campania
	Lodger	M.	40	Married...	Campania	Campania	Campania
698	Head	M.	50	Married...	Campania	Campania	Campania
	Wife	F.	45	Married...	Campania	Campania	Campania
	Son	M.	19	Single	Campania	Campania	Campania
	Son	M.	7	Single	Campania	Campania	Campania
	Daughter	F.	5	Single	Campania	Campania	Campania
699	Head	M.	40	Married...	Campania	Campania	Campania
	Wife	F.	(a)	Married...	Campania	Campania	Campania
	Son	M.	17	Single	Campania	Campania	Campania
	Daughter	F.	14	Single	Campania	Campania	Campania
	Daughter	F.	11	Single	Campania	Campania	Campania
	Daughter	F.	5	Single	United States..	Campania	Campania
	Son	M.	1	Single	United States...	Campania	Campania
700	Head	M.	46	Married...	Campania	Campania	Campania
	Wife	F.	43	Married...	Campania	Campania	Campania
	Son	M.	23	Single	Campania	Campania	Campania
	Daughter	F.	11	Single	Campania	Campania	Campania
	Son	M.	8	Single	United States..	Campania	Campania
	Son	M.	5	Single	United States...	Campania,	Campania
	Son	M.	1	Single	United States...	Campania	Campania
701	Head	M.	46	Married...	Campania	Campania	Campania
	Wife	F.	46	Married...	Basilicata	Basilicata	Basilicata
	Stepdaughter	F.	12	Single	United States	Campania	Basilicata
	Stepdaughter	F.	10	Single	United States...	Campania	Basilicata
	Boarder	M.	8	Single	United States...	(a)	(a)
702	Head	M.	26	Married...	Campania	Campania	Campania
	Wife	F.	22	Married...	Campania	Campania	Campania
	Daughter	F.	2	Single	United States...	Campania	Campania
703	Head	M.	43	Married...	Campania	Campania	Campania
	Wife	F.	43	Married...	Campania	Campania	Campania
	Son	M.	14	Single	United States...	Campania	Campania
	Son	M.	12	Single	United States...	Campania	Campania
	Daughter	F.	7	Single	United States...	Campania	Campania
704	Head	M.	35	Married...	Campania	Campania	Campania
	Wife	F.	40	Married...	Campania	Campania	Campania
	Daughter	F.	6	Single	Campania	Campania	Campania
	Daughter	F.	1	Single	United States...	Campania	Campania
705	Head	M.	39	Married...	Campania	Campania	Campania
	Wife	F.	31	Married...	Campania	Campania	Campania
	Son	M.	8	Single	United States...	Campania	Campania
	Daughter	F.	5	Single	United States...	Campania	Campania
	Daughter	F.	1	Single	United States...	Campania	Campania
706	Cooperative	M.	44	Married...	Campania	Campania	Campania
	Cooperative	M.	46	Single	Campania	Campania	Campania
707	Head	M.	40	Married...	Campania	Campania	Campania
	Wife	F.	37	Married...	Campania	Campania	Campania
	Daughter	F.	2	Single	United States...	Campania	Campania
708	Head	M.	32	Married...	Campania	Campania	Campania
	Wife	F.	32	Married...	Campania	Campania	Campania
	Daughter	F.	9	Single	Campania	Campania	Campania
709	Head	F.	45	Widowed .	Campania	Campania	Campania
710	Head	M.	44	Married...	Campania	Campania	Campania
	Wife	F.	39	Married...	Campania	Campania	Campania
	Daughter	F.	15	Single	Campania	Campania	Campania
	Son	M.	9	Single	United States...	Campania	Campania
	Son	M.	6	Single	United States...	Campania	Campania
	Daughter	F.	5	Single	United States...	Campania	Campania
	Daughter	F.	2	Single	United States...	Campania	Campania

a Not reported.
b Also worked as street sweeper twenty-three weeks, at $7.50 per week.

TABLE **I.**—GENERAL SOCIAL AND ECONOMIC CONDITION, BY FAMILIES AND INDIVIDUALS—Continued.

Years in U. S.	Naturalized.	Profession, trade, or occupation.	Hours of work per week.	Average weekly earnings.	Weeks employed.	Total yearly earnings.	Sick during year, defective, maimed, or deformed.
10	Yes..	Laborer..................	60	$8.40	18	$151	No.
10	......	Housewife...............	......	......	......	......	No.
5	No...	Newsdealer..............	70	5.00	52	260	No.
5	......	Newsdealer..............	70	5.00	52	260	No.
2	......	Newsdealer..............	70	5.00	52	260	No.
8	Yes..	Newsboy	70	3.00	52	156	No.
8	Yes..	Ragpicker...............	30	2.75	52	143	No
5	......	Housewife...............	......	......	......	......	No.
5	......	Candy factory employee ..	54	6.00	52	312	No.
5	......	At home................	......	......	......	......	No.
5	......	At home................	......	......	......	......	Rickets.
11	Yes..	Sewer digger............	60	9.00	15	135	Injury by accident.
6	......	Housewife...............	......	......	......	......	No.
6	......	Bootblack...............	85	5.00	23	115	No.
6	......	Ragpicker	(a)	1.50	52	78	Injury by accident.
6	......	Scholar	......	......	......	......	No.
......	......	At home................	......	......	......	......	No.
......	......	At home................	......	......	......	......	No.
10	Yes..	Street sweeper..........	60	7.50	23	173	No.
10	......	Housewife	......	......	......	......	No.
10	Yes..	Bootblack (b)...........	(a)	1.50	b 29	216	No.
10	......	Scholar	......	......	......	......	No.
......	......	Scholar	......	......	......	......	No.
......	......	At home................	......	......	......	......	No.
......	......	At home................	......	......	......	......	No.
23	Yes..	Ragpicker	(a)	1.50	52	78	No.
16	......	Housewife...............	......	......	......	......	No.
......	......	Scholar	......	......	......	......	No.
......	......	Scholar	......	......	......	......	No.
......	......	Scholar	......	......	......	......	No.
7	Yes..	Ragpicker (c)	(a)	1.50	c 37	168	No.
3	......	Housewife...............	......	......	......	......	No.
......	......	At home................	......	......	......	......	No.
17	Yes..	Ragpicker (d)...........	(a)	1.00	d 45	108	No.
16	......	Housewife...............	......	......	......	......	Female complaint.
......	......	Scholar	......	......	......	......	No.
......	......	Scholar	......	......	......	......	No.
......	......	Scholar	......	......	......	......	Arm, one crippled.
6	No...	Laborer..................	48	7.39	7	52	No.
2	......	Housewife and coal picker	(a)	.60	26	16	No.
2	......	At home................	......	......	......	......	No.
......	......	At home................	......	......	......	......	No.
15	Yes..	Street sweeper..........	60	9.00	25	225	No.
13	......	Housewife and washer-woman.	(a)	1.00	52	52	No.
......	......	Scholar	......	......	......	......	No.
......	......	At home................	......	......	......	......	Rickets.
......	......	At home................	......	......	......	......	No.
8	No...	No occupation	......	......	......	......	Rheumatism.
15	Yes..	Street sweeper..........	48	9.00	11	99	No.
10	Yes..	Paver...................	60	7.80	23	179	Bronchitis.
5	......	Housewife...............	......	......	......	......	No.
......	......	At home................	......	......	......	......	Rickets.
9	Yes..	Driver, ash wagon	72	7.50	23	173	No.
9	......	Housewife...............	......	......	......	......	Female complaint.
9	......	Scholar	......	......	......	......	No.
5	......	Ragpicker	(a)	.75	52	39	Heart, disease of.
14	Yes..	Paver...................	60	9.00	23	207	Bowels, inflammation of.
14	......	Housewife...............	......	......	......	......	Bronchitis.
14	......	Scholar	......	......	......	......	No.
......	......	Scholar and newsboy	(a)	.75	52	39	No.
......	......	At home................	......	......	......	......	No.
......	......	At home	......	......	......	......	No.
......	......	At home	......	......	......	......	No.

c Also worked as street sweeper fifteen weeks, at $7.50 per week.
d Also worked as street sweeper seven weeks, at $9 per week.

TABLE **I.**—GENERAL SOCIAL AND ECONOMIC CONDITION, BY FAMILIES AND INDIVIDUALS—Continued.

Family number.	Relationship to head of family.	Sex.	Age.	Conjugal condition.	Birthplace.	Birthplace of—	
						Father.	Mother.
711	Head	M.	20	Married	Campania	Campania	Campania
	Wife	F.	17	Married	Campania	Campania	Campania
	Daughter	F.	1	Single	United States	Campania	Campania
712	Head	M.	45	Married	Campania	Campania	Campania
	Wife	F.	42	Married	Campania	Campania	Campania
	Son	M.	15	Single	Campania	Campania	Campania
	Daughter	F.	8	Single	United States	Campania	Campania
	Son	M.	5	Single	United States	Campania	Campania
	Daughter	F.	3	Single	United States	Campania	Campania
713	Head	M.	38	Single	Calabria	Calabria	Calabria
714	Head	M.	47	Married	Basilicata	Basilicata	Basilicata
	Wife	F.	43	Married	Basilicata	Basilicata	Basilicata
	Son	M.	12	Single	Basilicata	Basilicata	Basilicata
	Daughter	F.	2	Single	United States	Basilicata	Basilicata
	Son	M.	$\frac{1}{12}$	Single	United States	Basilicata	Basilicata
	Lodger	M.	27	Married	Basilicata	Basilicata	Basilicata
	Lodger	M.	40	Married	Basilicata	Basilicata	Basilicata
715	Head	F.	38	Widowed	Basilicata	Basilicata	Basilicata
	Son	M.	13	Single	Basilicata	Basilicata	Basilicata
	Son	M.	10	Single	Basilicata	Basilicata	Basilicata
	Son	M.	4	Single	United States	Basilicata	Basilicata
	Daughter	F.	1	Single	United States	Basilicata	Basilicata
	Lodger	M.	25	Single	Basilicata	Basilicata	Basilicata
	Lodger	M.	57	Married	Basilicata	Basilicata	Basilicata
716	Head	M.	43	Married	Campania	Campania	Campania
	Wife	F.	42	Married	Campania	Campania	Campania
	Daughter	F.	18	Single	Campania	Campania	Campania
	Son	M.	15	Single	Campania	Campania	Campania
	Son	M.	8	Single	United States	Campania	Campania
	Daughter	F.	7	Single	United States	Campania	Campania
	Son	M.	$\frac{8}{12}$	Single	United States	Campania	Campania
717	Head	M.	36	Married	Basilicata	Basilicata	Basilicata
	Wife	F.	36	Married	Basilicata	Basilicata	Basilicata
	Daughter	F.	12	Single	Basilicata	Basilicata	Basilicata
	Son	M.	9	Single	United States	Basilicata	Basilicata
	Son	M.	3	Single	United States	Basilicata	Basilicata
	Son	M.	$\frac{9}{12}$	Single	United States	Basilicata	Basilicata
718	Head	M.	40	Married	Campania	Campania	Campania
	Wife	F.	60	Married	Campania	Campania	Campania
	Son	M.	20	Single	Campania	Campania	Campania
	Lodger	M.	42	Widowed	Campania	Campania	Campania
	Lodger	M.	17	Single	Campania	Campania	Campania
719	Head	M.	54	Married	Basilicata	Basilicata	Basilicata
	Wife	F.	47	Married	Basilicata	Basilicata	Basilicata
	Daughter	F.	15	Single	Basilicata	Basilicata	Basilicata
	Daughter	F.	8	Single	United States	Basilicata	Basilicata
	Nephew	M.	25	Single	Basilicata	Basilicata	Basilicata
720	Head	M.	24	Married	Basilicata	Basilicata	Basilicata
	Wife	F.	20	Married	Campania	Campania	Campania
721	Head	M.	55	Married	Campania	Campania	Campania
	Wife	F.	50	Married	Campania	Campania	Campania
	Son	M.	20	Single	Campania	Campania	Campania
	Son	M.	16	Single	Campania	Campania	Campania
722	Head	M.	49	Married	Campania	Campania	Campania
	Wife	F.	40	Married	Campania	Campania	Campania
	Daughter	F.	17	Single	Campania	Campania	Campania
	Daughter	F.	16	Single	Campania	Campania	Campania
	Son	M.	5	Single	United States	Campania	Campania
723	Head	M.	48	Married	Campania	Campania	Campania
	Wife	F.	44	Married	Campania	Campania	Campania
	Son	M.	19	Single	Campania	Campania	Campania

a Not reported.
b Also worked as laborer thirteen weeks, at $7.50 per week.

TABLE **I.**—GENERAL SOCIAL AND ECONOMIC CONDITION, BY FAMILIES AND INDIVIDUALS—Continued.

Years in U.S.	Natu ralized.	Profession, trade, or occupation.	Hours of work per week.	Average weekly earnings.	Weeks employed.	Total yearly earnings.	Sick during year, defective, maimed, or deformed.
6	No...	Railroad laborer	(a)	(a)	52	(a)	No.
6	......	Housewife	......	......	......	......	No.
......	......	At home	......	......	......	......	No.
15	Yes..	Ragpicker	84	$1.75	52	$91	Bronchitis.
10	......	Housewife	......	......	......	......	Bronchitis.
10	......	Scholar	......	......	......	......	No.
......	......	Scholar	......	......	......	......	Bronchitis.
......	......	At home	......	......	......	......	No.
......	......	At home	......	......	......	......	No.
8	No...	Railroad laborer	60	6.60	13	86	Pneumonia.
5	Yes..	Ragpicker	(a)	1.80	52	94	No.
3	......	Housewife	......	......	......	......	Childbirth.
3	......	Newsboy	66	1.40	52	73	No.
......	......	At home	......	......	......	......	Rickets.
......	......	At home	......	......	......	......	No.
3	No...	Ragpicker (b)	(a)	.90	b 39	133	No.
5	No...	Ragpicker	(a)	.90	52	47	No.
10	......	Housewife and coal picker	(a)	1.20	52	62	No.
10	......	Scholar and newsboy	·(a)	.70	(a)	(a)	No.
10	......	Scholar	......	......	......	......	No.
......	......	At home	......	......	......	......	No.
......	......	At home	......	......	......	......	No.
3	No...	Newsboy	(a)	3.50	52	182	No.
4	No...	Railroad laborer	60	7.50	9	68	No.
15	Yes..	Street sweeper	60	7.50	17	128	No.
13	......	Housewife	......	......	......	......	Childbirth; **female complaint.**
13	......	Housework	......	......	......	......	No.
13	......	Bootblack	(a)	2.10	50	105	Fever, not specified.
......	......	Scholar	......	......	......	......	No.
......	......	At home	......	......	......	......	No.
......	......	At home	......	......	......	......	No.
12	Yes..	No occupation	......	......	......	......	No.
11	......	Housewife and coal picker	(a)	1.20	(a)	(a)	Childbirth.
11	......	Scholar	......	......	......	......	No.
......	......	At home	......	......	......	......	Rickets.
......	......	At home	......	......	......	......	Rickets.
......	......	At home	......	......	......	......	No.
15	Yes..	Street sweeper	60	7.50	30	225	No.
8	......	Housewife and coal picker	(a)	1.20	52	62	No.
8	......	Newsboy	(a)	(a)	52	(a)	No.
15	Yes..	No occupation	......	......	......	......	No.
6	......	Bootblack	(a)	(a)	52	(a)	No.
15	Yes..	Coal picker	(a)	1.20	52	62	Injury by accident.
10	......	Housewife and coal picker	(a)	1.20	52	62	No.
10	......	Coal picker	(a)	1.20	52	62	No.
......	......	Scholar	......	......	......	......	No.
5	Yes..	Street sweeper (c)	60	7.50	c 9	127	No.
10	Yes..	Bootblack	(a)	5.00	52	260	No.
5	......	Housewife and coal picker	(a)	1.20	52	62	No.
15	Yes..	Paper picker	(a)	1.50	52	78	No.
10	......	Housewife and coal picker	(a)	1.20	52	62	No.
15	......	Grain elevator employee ..	60	2.00	52	104	Lame.
10	......	Bootblack	(a)	1.50	52	78	No.
15	Yes..	Railroad laborer	60	7.50	13	98	Rheumatism.
8	......	Housewife and coal picker	(a)	(a)	52	(a)	No.
8	......	Coal picker	(a)	(a)	52	(a)	No.
8	......	Coal picker	(a)	(a)	52	(a)	No.
......	......	At home	......	......	......	......	No.
6	No...	Laborer	60	10.50	52	546	No.
6	......	Housewife	......	......	......	......	No.
7	......	Bootblack	(a)	8.00	52	416	No.

c Also worked as laborer nine weeks, at $6.60 per week.

TABLE **I.**—GENERAL SOCIAL AND ECONOMIC CONDITION, BY FAMILIES AND INDIVIDUALS—Continued.

Family number.	Relationship to head of family.	Sex.	Age.	Conjugal condition.	Birthplace.	Birthplace of—	
						Father.	Mother.
723	Daughter	F.	11	Single	Campania	Campania	Campania
	Son	M.	8	Single	Campania	Campania	Campania
	Daughter	F.	5	Single	United States	Campania	Campania
	Daughter	F.	1	Single	United States	Campania	Campania
724	Head	M.	62	Married	Campania	Campania	Campania
	Wife	F.	39	Married	Campania	Campania	Campania
	Daughter	F.	8	Single	United States	Campania	Campania
	Daughter	F.	3	Single	United States	Campania	Campania
725	Head	M.	30	Married	Campania	Campania	Campania
	Wife	F.	30	Married	Campania	Campania	Campania
	Son	M.	7	Single	United States	Campania	Campania
	Daughter	F.	3	Single	United States	Campania	Campania
	Son	M.	1	Single	United States	Campania	Campania
726	Head	M.	40	Married	Campania	Campania	Campania
	Wife	F.	40	Married	Campania	Campania	Campania
	Son	M.	18	Single	Campania	Campania	Campania
	Daughter	F.	15	Single	Campania	Campania	Campania
	Son	M.	10	Single	United States	Campania	Campania
	Son	M.	7	Single	United States	Campania	Campania
	Son	M.	5	Single	United States	Campania	Campania
	Son	M.	3	Single	United States	Campania	Campania
	Son	M.	1	Single	United States	Campania	Campania
727	Head	M.	40	Married	Abruzzo	Abruzzo	Abruzzo
	Wife	F.	30	Married	Abruzzo	Abruzzo	Abruzzo
	Son	M.	9	Single	Abruzzo	Abruzzo	Abruzzo
	Daughter	F.	3	Single	Abruzzo	Abruzzo	Abruzzo
	Daughter	F.	$\frac{1}{12}$	Single	United States	Abruzzo	Abruzzo
728	Cooperative	M.	42	Married	Sicily	Sicily	Sicily
	Cooperative	M.	30	Single	Sicily	Sicily	Sicily
	Cooperative	M.	27	Single	Sicily	Sicily	Sicily
	Cooperative	M.	27	Single	United States	Sicily	Sicily
	Cooperative	M.	40	Widowed	Sicily	Sicily	Sicily
	Cooperative	M.	50	Married	Sicily	Sicily	Sicily
	Cooperative	M.	32	Married	Sicily	Sicily	Sicily
	Cooperative	M.	25	Single	Sicily	Sicily	Sicily
	Cooperative	M.	35	Married	Sicily	Sicily	Sicily
	Cooperative	M.	37	Married	Sicily	Sicily	Sicily
	Cooperative	M.	28	Married	Sicily	Sicily	Sicily
	Cooperative	M.	28	Married	Sicily	Sicily	Sicily
729	Head	M.	50	Married	Calabria	Calabria	Calabria
	Wife	F.	40	Married	Calabria	Calabria	Calabria
	Son	M.	21	Single	Calabria	Calabria	Calabria
	Daughter	F.	7	Single	United States	Calabria	Calabria
	Son	M.	6	Single	United States	Calabria	Calabria
	Son	M.	3	Single	United States	Calabria	Calabria
	Daughter	F.	1	Single	United States	Calabria	Calabria
	Brother	M.	45	Married	Calabria	Calabria	Calabria
	Brother	M.	23	Single	Calabria	Calabria	Calabria
	Nephew	M.	26	Single	Calabria	Calabria	Calabria
730	Head	M.	32	Married	Campania	Campania	Campania
	Wife	F.	32	Married	Campania	Campania	Campania
	Boarder	M.	35	Single	Campania	Campania	Campania
	Boarder	M.	28	Single	Campania	Campania	Campania
731	Head	M.	38	Married	Campania	Campania	Campania
	Wife	F.	32	Married	Campania	Campania	Campania
	Son	M.	11	Single	Campania	Campania	Campania
	Daughter	F.	9	Single	Campania	Campania	Campania
	Son	M.	7	Single	Campania	Campania	Campania
	Son	M.	1	Single	United States	Campania	Campania
732	Head	M.	37	Married	Calabria	Calabria	Calabria
	Wife	F.	35	Married	Calabria	Calabria	Calabria
	Son	M.	12	Single	Calabria	Calabria	Calabria
	Son	M.	10	Single	Calabria	Calabria	Calabria
	Daughter	F.	1	Single	United States	Calabria	Calabria
733	Head	M.	38	Married	Campania	Campania	Campania
	Wife	F.	38	Married	Campania	Campania	Campania

a Not reported.

TABLE **I.**—GENERAL SOCIAL AND ECONOMIC CONDITION, BY FAMILIES AND INDIVIDUALS—Continued.

Years in U.S.	Naturalized.	Profession, trade, or occupation.	Hours of work per week.	Average weekly earnings.	Weeks employed.	Total yearly earnings.	Sick during year, defective, maimed, or deformed.
6	......	No occupation	....	....	....	....	No.
6	......	At home.................	....	....	....	....	No.
......	......	At home...............	....	....	....	....	No.
......	......	At home...............	....	....	....	....	No.
17	Yes..	Beggar..............	....	....	....	....	Tumor, not specified.
17	......	Housewife and coal picker	(a)	$1.80	52	$94	No.
......	......	Scholar	....	....	....	....	No.
......	......	At home...............	....	....	....	....	No.
14	Yes..	Ragpicker	(a)	1.50	52	78	No.
14	......	Housewife..............	....	....	....	....	No.
......	......	Scholar	....	....	....	....	No.
......	......	At home..............	....	....	....	....	No.
......	......	At home..............	....	....	....	....	No.
14	Yes..	No occupation...........	....	....	....	....	Fever, malarial.
13	......	Housewife............	....	....	....	....	Fever, malarial.
13	......	Newsboy	60	1.20	52	62	No.
13	......	Ragpicker............	60	1.20	52	62	No.
......	......	Scholar	....	....	....	....	No.
......	......	Scholar	....	....	....	....	No.
......	......	At home..............	....	....	....	....	No.
......	......	At home..............	....	....	....	....	No.
......	......	At home..............	....	....	....	....	No.
6/12	No...	No occupation...........	....	....	....	....	No.
6/12	......	Housewife and ragpicker..	(a)	.60	(a)	(a)	Childbirth.
6/12	......	Scholar	....	....	....	....	No.
6/12	......	At home..............	....	....	....	....	No.
6/12	......	At home..............	....	....	....	....	No.
4	No...	No occupation...........	....	....	....	....	Eye, loss of one.
8	No...	No occupation...........	....	....	....	....	No.
4	No...	Laborer..............	90	3.60	13	47	No.
......	......	Laborer..............	60	10.50	17	179	No.
4	No...	Laborer..............	60	6.00	4	24	No.
7	No...	Laborer..............	90	3.60	35	126	No.
4	No...	Laborer..............	90	3.60	13	47	Fever, malarial.
4	No...	Laborer..............	90	3.60	35	126	No.
3	No...	Laborer..............	90	3.60	35	126	No.
4	No...	Laborer..............	90	3.60	35	126	No.
4	No...	No occupation...........	....	....	....	....	Injury by accident.
2	No...	Laborer..............	90	3.30	35	116	No.
13	No...	Barber..............	93	10.00	52	520	No.
9	......	Housewife............	....	....	....	....	No.
9	No...	Cashier.............	93	(a)	52	(a)	Leg, loss of one.
......	......	Scholar	....	....	....	....	No.
......	......	Scholar	....	....	....	....	No.
......	......	At home..............	....	....	....	....	No.
......	......	At home..............	....	....	....	....	No.
7	No...	Paper picker (b)	(a)	.90	b 35	144	No.
5	No...	Barber..............	93	6.00	52	312	No.
8	Yes..	Railroad laborer..........	60	6.60	17	112	No.
10	Yes..	Ragpicker	(a)	1.20	44	53	Fever, typhoid.
7	......	Housewife.............	....	....	....	....	No.
9	No...	Laborer..............	60	7.50	13	98	Rheumatism.
9	Yes..	Railroad laborer..........	60	7.50	13	98	No.
4	No...	Laborer..............	60	7.75	9	70	No.
4	......	Housewife.............	....	....	....	....	Bronchitis.
4	......	Scholar and newsboy......	(a)	.60	52	31	No.
4	......	Scholar	....	....	....	....	No.
4	......	Scholar	....	....	....	....	No.
......	......	At home..............	....	....	....	....	Bronchitis.
10	Yes..	Lodging-house keeper	(a)	(a)	(a)	(a)	No.
3	......	Housewife.............	....	....	....	....	No.
3	......	Scholar	....	....	....	....	Deaf.
3	......	Scholar	....	....	....	....	No.
......	......	At home..............	....	....	....	....	No.
14	Yes..	No occupation.............	....	....	....	....	Eyes, inflammation of both.
5	......	Housewife and seamstress	(a)	2.00	35	70	Miscarriage.

b Also worked as railroad laborer seventeen weeks, at $6.60 per week.

TABLE I.—GENERAL SOCIAL AND ECONOMIC CONDITION, BY FAMILIES AND INDIVIDUALS—Continued.

Family number.	Relationship to head of family.	Sex.	Age.	Conjugal condition.	Birthplace.	Birthplace of—	
						Father.	Mother.
734	Head	M.	40	Married...	Campania	Campania	Campania
	Wife	F.	45	Married...	Campania	Campania	Campania
	Son	M.	18	Single	Campania	Campania	Campania
	Son	M.	13	Single	United States	Campania	Campania
	Son	M.	9	Single	United States	Campania	Campania
735	Head	M.	60	Married..	Campania	Campania	Campania
	Wife	F.	60	Married...	Campania	Campania	Campania
	Stepson	M.	18	Single	Campania	Campania	Campania
736	Head	M.	45	Married...	Campania	Campania	Campania
	Wife	F.	32	Married...	Campania	Campania	Campania
	Daughter	F.	10	Single	Campania	Campania	Campania
	Son	M.	7	Single	Campania	Campania	Campania
	Daughter	F.	3	Single	United States	Campania	Campania
	Daughter	F.	1	Single	United States	Campania	Campania
737	Head	M.	43	Married...	Campania	Campania	Campania
	Wife	F.	35	Married...	Campania	Campania	Campania
	Daughter	F.	12	Single	Campania	Campania	Campania
	Son	M.	6	Single	United States	Campania	Campania
	Son	M.	4	Single	United States	Campania	Campania
	Daughter	F.	₁²₂	Single	United States	Campania	Campania
738	Head	M.	37	Married...	Campania	Campania	Campania
	Wife	F.	23	Married...	Campania	Campania	Campania
	Son	M.	9	Single	United States	Campania	Campania
	Daughter	F.	3	Single	United States	Campania	Campania
	Son	M.	₁₂	Single	United States	Campania	Campania
739	Head	M.	26	Married...	Campania	Campania	Campania
	Wife	F.	17	Married...	Campania	Campania	Campania
740	Head	M.	51	Married...	Campania	Campania	Campania
	Wife	F.	39	Married...	Campania	Campania	Campania
	Son	M.	14	Single	Campania	Campania	Campania
	Daughter	F.	3	Single	United States	Campania	Campania
	Lodger	M.	45	Married...	Campania	Campania	Campania
741	Head	M.	45	Married...	Campania	Campania	Campania
	Wife	F.	35	Married...	Campania	Campania	Campania
	Brother	M.	38	Married...	Campania	Campania	Campania
	Sister-in-law	F.	36	Married...	Campania	Campania	Campania
	Nephew	M.	18	Single	Campania	Campania	Campania
	Nephew	M.	16	Single	Campania	Campania	Campania
	Nephew	M.	4	Single	United States	Campania	Campania
	Niece	F.	3	Single	United States	Campania	Campania
	Nephew	M.	₁²₂	Single	United States	Campania	Campania
742	Head	M.	46	Widowed .	Campania	Campania	Campania
	Daughter	F.	15	Single	United States	Campania	Campania
	Daughter	F.	9	Single	United States	Campania	Campania
	Daughter	F.	3	Single	United States	Campania	Campania
	Son	M.	2	Single	United States	Campania	Campania
	Mother	F.	68	Widowed .	Campania	Campania	Campania
743	Head	M.	29	Married...	Sicily	Sicily	Sicily
	Wife	F.	32	Married...	Basilicata	Basilicata	Basilicata
	Stepson	M.	12	Single	Basilicata	Basilicata	Basilicata
	Stepson	M.	11	Single	Basilicata	Basilicata	Basilicata
	Mother	F.	55	Widowed	Sicily	Sicily	Sicily
744	Head	M.	43	Married...	Basilicata	Basilicata	Basilicata
	Wife	F.	31	Married...	Basilicata	Basilicata	Basilicata
	Daughter	F.	12	Single	Basilicata	Basilicata	Basilicata
	Daughter	F.	10	Single	United States	Basilicata	Basilicata
	Son	M.	7	Single	United States	Basilicata	Basilicata
	Son	M.	5	Single	United States	Basilicata	Basilicata
	Son	M.	3	Single	United States	Basilicata	Basilicata
	Father-in-law	M.	90	Married...	Basilicata	Basilicata	Basilicata
	Mother-in-law	F.	50	Married...	Basilicata	Basilicata	Basilicata
745	Head	M.	26	Married...	Campania	Campania	Campania
	Wife	F.	19	Married...	Campania	Campania	Campania
	Brother	M.	17	Single	Campania	Campania	Campania
	Cousin	M.	29	Married...	Campania	Campania	Campania

a Not reported.

TABLE I.—GENERAL SOCIAL AND ECONOMIC CONDITION, BY FAMILIES AND INDIVIDUALS—Continued.

Years in U. S.	Natu-ral-ized.	Profession, trade, or occupation.	Hours of work per week.	Average weekly earn-ings.	Weeks em-ploy-ed.	Total yearly earn-ings.	Sick during year, defective, maimed, or deformed.
16	No...	Laborer	60	$6.00	9	$54	No.
15		Housewife					Female complaint.
15		Bootblack	(a)	6.00	52	312	No.
		Bootblack	(a)	1.50	52	78	No.
		At home					No.
12	No...	Fruit store employee	(a)	(a)	(a)	(a)	No.
12		Housewife and coal picker	(a)	.90	(a)	(a)	No.
12		Newsboy	(a)	5.50	(a)	(a)	No.
10	Yes..	No occupation					No.
6		Housewife					No.
6		Wood picker	(a)	1.20	52	62	No.
6		Scholar					No.
		At home					Fever, gastric.
		At home					No.
10	Yes..	Street sweeper	60	9.00	17	153	No.
10		Housewife					Childbirth.
10		No occupation					No.
		At home					Idiot.
		At home					No.
		At home					No.
12	Yes..	Saloon keeper	(a)	(a)	52	(a)	No.
11		Housewife					Childbirth.
		Scholar					No.
		At home					No.
		At home					No.
3	No...	Bone picker	(a)	3.00	52	156	No.
3		Housewife					Fever, typhoid.
6	No...	Paper picker	(a)	1.20	52	62	No.
6		Housewife					Miscarriage.
6		Bootblack	(a)	1.75	(a)	(a)	No.
		At home					No.
12	No...	Railroad laborer	60	7.50	6	45	No.
15	Yes..	No occupation					No.
7/12		Housewife					No.
15	Yes..	Street sweeper	60	9.00	17	153	No.
11		Housework					Childbirth; typhoid fever.
11		Bootblack	(a)	5.00	52	260	No.
11		Bootblack	(a)	5.00	(a)	(a)	No.
		At home					No.
		At home					No.
		At home					No.
17	Yes..	Ragpicker	(a)	.90	(a)	(a)	No.
		Scholar and news girl	(a)	1.05	(a)	(a)	No.
		At home					No.
		At home					No.
		At home					No.
7		Housewife					Rheumatism.
12	Yes..	Peddler, vegetables	(a)	(a)	52	(a)	No.
5		Housewife					Bronchitis.
5		No occupation					No.
5		Scholar					No.
7/12		Housework					No.
14	Yes..	No occupation					No.
12		Housewife					No.
12		Scholar					No.
		Scholar					No.
		Scholar					No.
		At home					No.
		At home					No.
12	No...	No occupation					No.
12		No occupation					No.
7	No...	Railroad laborer	60	7.50	7	53	Injury by accident.
1		Housewife					No.
2		Bootblack	53	1.50	52	78	No.
5	Yes..	Railroad laborer	60	7.50	7	53	No.

TABLE **I.**—GENERAL SOCIAL AND ECONOMIC CONDITION, BY FAMILIES AND INDIVIDUALS—Continued.

Family number.	Relationship to head of family.	Sex.	Age.	Conjugal condition.	Birthplace.	Birthplace of—	
						Father.	Mother.
746	Head	M.	60	Married...	Basilicata......	Basilicata......	Basilicata.....
	Wife	F.	50	Married...	Basilicata......	Basilicata......	Basilicata.....
	Daughter	F.	15	Single.....	United States...	Basilicata......	Basilicata.....
747	Cooperative	M.	27	Married...	Calabria.........	Calabria	Calabria .....
	Cooperative	M.	28	Married...	Calabria.........	Calabria	Calabria .....
	Cooperative	M.	23	Single.....	Calabria.........	Calabria	Calabria .....
	Cooperative	M.	28	Single.....	Calabria.........	Calabria	Calabria .....
	Cooperative	M.	25	Single.....	Calabria.........	Calabria	Calabria .....
748	Head	M.	28	Single.....	Calabria.........	Calabria	Calabria .....
	Mother	F.	50	Widowed .	Calabria.........	Calabria	Calabria .....
749	Cooperative	M.	19	Single.....	Sicily...........	Sicily	Sicily .....
	Cooperative	M.	18	Single.....	Sicily...........	Sicily	Sicily .....
	Cooperative	M.	29	Single.....	Sicily...........	Sicily	Sicily .....
750	Cooperative	M.	48	Married...	Sicily...........	Sicily	Sicily .....
	Cooperative	M.	42	Widowed .	Sicily...........	Sicily	Sicily .....
	Cooperative	M.	40	Single.....	Sicily...........	Sicily	Sicily .....
	Cooperative	M.	55	Married...	Sicily...........	Sicily	Sicily .....
	Cooperative	M.	21	Single.....	Sicily...........	Sicily	Sicily .....
	Cooperative	M.	15	Single.....	Campania.......	Campania......	Campania.....
	Cooperative	M.	34	Married...	Campania.......	Campania......	Campania.....
	Cooperative	M.	34	Married...	Campania.......	Campania......	Campania.....
	Cooperative	M.	22	Single.....	Campania.......	Campania......	Campania.....
751	Head	M.	28	Married...	Basilicata......	Basilicata......	Basilicata.....
	Wife	F.	27	Married...	Basilicata......	Basilicata......	Basilicata.....
	Son	M.	7	Single.....	United States...	Basilicata......	Basilicata.....
	Son	M.	2	Single.....	United States...	Basilicata......	Basilicata.....
	Daughter	F.	1/12	Single.....	United States...	Basilicata......	Basilicata.....
752	Cooperative	M.	34	Single.....	Calabria.........	Calabria	Calabria .....
	Cooperative	M.	48	Married...	Calabria.........	Calabria	Calabria .....
	Cooperative	M.	41	Married...	Calabria.........	Calabria	Calabria .....
	Cooperative	M.	50	Married...	Calabria.........	Calabria	Calabria .....
	Cooperative	M.	50	Married...	Calabria.........	Calabria	Calabria .....
	Cooperative	M.	24	Single.....	Calabria.........	Calabria	Calabria .....
	Cooperative	M.	22	Single.....	Calabria.........	Calabria	Calabria .....
	Cooperative	M.	56	Married...	Calabria.........	Calabria	Calabria .....
	Cooperative	F.	50	Widowed .	Calabria.........	Calabria	Calabria .....
753	Head	M.	32	Married...	Sicily...........	Sicily	Sicily .....
	Wife	F.	28	Married...	Sicily...........	Sicily	Sicily .....
	Daughter	F.	6/12	Single	United States...	Sicily	Sicily .....
754	Head	M.	30	Married...	Calabria.........	Calabria	Calabria .....
	Wife	F.	22	Married...	Calabria.........	Calabria	Calabria .....
	Daughter	F.	5	Single.....	United States...	Calabria	Calabria .....
	Boarder	M.	19	Single.....	Calabria.........	Calabria	Calabria .....
755	Head	M.	29	Married...	Sicily...........	Sicily	Sicily .....
	Wife	F.	22	Married...	Sicily...........	Sicily	Sicily .....
	Son	M.	2/12	Single.....	United States...	Sicily	Sicily .....
	Brother-in-law	M.	26	Single.....	Sicily...........	Sicily	Sicily .....
756	Head	M.	45	Married...	Calabria.........	Calabria	Calabria .....
	Wife	F.	37	Married...	Calabria.........	Calabria	Calabria .....
	Lodger	M.	30	Single.....	Calabria.........	Calabria	Calabria .....
	Lodger	M.	44	Married...	Calabria.........	Calabria	Calabria .....
	Lodger	M.	28	Married...	Calabria.........	Calabria	Calabria .....
	Lodger	M.	42	Married...	Calabria.........	Calabria	Calabria .....
757	Head	M.	39	Married...	Sicily...........	Sicily	Sicily ....
	Wife	F.	34	Married...	Sicily...........	Sicily	Sicily ....
	Son	M.	16	Single.....	Sicily...........	Sicily	Sicily ....
	Daughter	F.	14	Single.....	Sicily...........	Sicily	Sicily ....
	Son	M.	9	Single.....	Sicily...........	Sicily	Sicily ....
	Son	M.	6	Single.....	United States...	Sicily	Sicily ....
	Daughter	F.	4	Single.....	United States...	Sicily	Sicily ....
	Son	M.	2	Single.....	United States...	Sicily	Sicily ....
	Daughter	F.	1/12	Single.....	United States...	Sicily	Sicily ....

a Not reported.　　　*b* Also worked as bootblack twenty-six weeks, at $1.75 per week.

TABLE I.—GENERAL SOCIAL AND ECONOMIC CONDITION, BY FAMILIES AND INDIVIDUALS—Continued.

Years in U. S.	Naturalized.	Profession, trade, or occupation.	Hours of work per week.	Average weekly earnings.	Weeks employed.	Total yearly earnings.	Sick during year, defective, maimed, or deformed.
17	Yes	No occupation					No.
17		Housewife					No.
		Housework					No.
7	Yes	Railroad laborer	60	$7.50	9	$68	No.
9	Yes	Railroad laborer	60	7.50	15	113	No.
3	No	Railroad laborer	60	7.50	11	83	No.
5	Yes	Railroad laborer	60	7.50	11	83	No.
8	Yes	Railroad laborer	60	7.50	11	83	No.
14	No	Biscuit factory employee	60	13.56	47	637	No.
9		Housewife					No.
4		Laborer	69½	3.60	52	187	No.
2		Laborer	69½	3.60	39	140	Fever, malarial.
6	No	Laborer	69½	3.60	52	187	No.
6	No	Laborer	69½	3.60	52	187	No.
5	No	Laborer	69½	3.60	52	187	No.
6	No	Laborer	69½	3.60	52	187	No.
3	No	Laborer	69½	3.60	52	187	No.
2	No	Laborer	69½	3.60	52	187	No.
4		Laborer	69½	3.60	52	187	No.
3	No	Laborer	69½	3.60	52	187	No.
2	No	Laborer	69½	3.60	52	187	No.
6	No	Merchant, groceries	(a)	(a)	52	(a)	No.
10	Yes	Street sweeper	48	9.00	30	270	No.
8		Housewife					Childbirth.
		Scholar					No.
		At home					No.
		At home					No.
3	No	Railroad laborer	60	7.50	15	113	No.
7	No	Railroad laborer	60	6.60	11	73	Fever, not specified.
5	No	Railroad laborer	60	6.60	11	73	No.
4	No	Laborer	60	9.00	15	135	No.
4	No	Railroad laborer	60	6.60	11	73	No.
4	No	Laborer	60	9.00	15	135	No.
5	Yes	Laborer	60	9.00	15	135	No.
4	No	Railroad laborer	60	6.60	11	73	No.
9		Ragpicker	(a)	1.00	52	52	Bronchitis.
3	No	Laborer	48	(a)	(a)	(a)	No.
3		Housewife and dressmaker	(a)	(a)	(a)	(a)	Childbirth.
		At home					No.
5	No	Gas-works employee	60	9.00	9	81	Fever, typhoid.
5		Housewife					No.
		At home					No.
5		Laborer (b)	60	3.00	b 26	124	No.
6	Yes	Laborer	(a)	9.00	16	144	No.
1		Housewife					Childbirth.
		At home					No.
6	No	Laborer	48	(a)	8	(a)	Glands, scrofulous.
10	Yes	Laborer	60	7.05	15	106	No.
4		Housewife					Dyspepsia.
10	No	Laborer	(a)	8.44	8	68	No.
10	No	Bone picker (c)	(a)	1.50	c 34	186	No.
4	No	Railroad laborer	60	7.50	5	38	No.
4	No	No occupation					Eyes, inflammation of both.
10	Yes	Watchman	56	10.50	15	158	No.
7		Housewife					Childbirth; female complaint.
7		Newsboy	30	1.40	52	73	Ear (middle), inflammation of.
7		No occupation					No.
7		Scholar					Measles; one hand crippled.
		At home					No.
		At home					Injury by accident.
		At home					No.
		At home					No.

c Also worked as laborer eighteen weeks, at $7.50 per week.

TABLE I.—GENERAL SOCIAL AND ECONOMIC CONDITION, BY FAMILIES AND INDIVIDUALS—Continued.

Family number.	Relationship to head of family.	Sex.	Age.	Conjugal condition.	Birthplace.	Birthplace of—	
						Father.	Mother.
758	Head	M.	36	Married	Sicily	Sicily	Sicily
	Wife	F.	36	Married	Sicily	Sicily	Sicily
	Son	M.	12	Single	Sicily	Sicily	Sicily
	Son	M.	2	Single	United States	Sicily	Sicily
	Son	M.	$\frac{1}{2}$	Single	United States	Sicily	Sicily
	Brother-in-law	M.	30	Single	Sicily	Sicily	Sicily
759	Head	M.	37	Married	Campania	Campania	Campania
	Wife	F.	26	Married	Campania	Campania	Campania
	Son	M.	4	Single	United States	Campania	Campania
	Son	M.	1	Single	United States	Campania	Campania
760	Head	M.	42	Married	Basilicata	Basilicata	Basilicata
	Wife	F.	37	Married	Basilicata	Basilicata	Basilicata
761	Head	M.	35	Married	Sicily	Sicily	Sicily
	Wife	F.	32	Married	Sicily	Sicily	Sicily
762	Head	M.	37	Married	Sicily	Sicily	Sicily
	Wife	F.	36	Married	Sicily	Sicily	Sicily
	Son	M.	4	Single	United States	Sicily	Sicily
	Daughter	F.	$\frac{3}{12}$	Single	United States	Sicily	Sicily
763	Head	M.	50	Married	Calabria	Calabria	Calabria
	Wife	F.	50	Married	Calabria	Calabria	Calabria
	Son	M.	18	Single	Calabria	Calabria	Calabria
	Lodger	M.	28	Married	Calabria	Calabria	Calabria
764	Cooperative	M.	29	Single	Sicily	Sicily	Sicily
	Cooperative	M.	20	Single	Sicily	Sicily	Sicily
	Cooperative	M.	48	Widowed	Sicily	Sicily	Sicily
765	Head	M.	44	Married	Sicily	Sicily	Sicily
	Wife	F.	38	Married	Sicily	Sicily	Sicily
	Son	M.	14	Single	Sicily	Sicily	Sicily
	Daughter	F.	4	Single	Sicily	Sicily	Sicily
766	Head	M.	38	Married	Sicily	Sicily	Sicily
	Wife	F.	36	Married	Sicily	Sicily	Sicily
	Son	M.	13	Single	Sicily	Sicily	Sicily
	Daughter	F.	11	Single	Sicily	Sicily	Sicily
	Son	M.	7	Single	United States	Sicily	Sicily
	Son	M.	5	Single	United States	Sicily	Sicily
	Son	M.	4	Single	United States	Sicily	Sicily
	Daughter	F.	2	Single	United States	Sicily	Sicily
767	Head	F.	44	Widowed	Liguria	Liguria	Liguria
	Daughter	F.	12	Single	United States	Liguria	Liguria
	Daughter	F.	10	Single	United States	Liguria	Liguria
	Son	M.	8	Single	United States	Liguria	Liguria
	Son	M.	6	Single	United States	Liguria	Liguria
768	Head	M.	40	Married	Campania	Campania	Campania
	Wife	F.	22	Married	Campania	Campania	Campania
	Daughter	F.	3	Single	United States	Campania	Campania
	Son	M.	$\frac{1}{2}$	Single	United States	Campania	Campania
	Brother	M.	25	Single	Campania	Campania	Campania
769	Head	M.	40	Married	Basilicata	Basilicata	Basilicata
	Wife	F.	32	Married	Basilicata	Basilicata	Basilicata
	Daughter	F.	15	Single	United States	Basilicata	Basilicata
	Daughter	F.	14	Single	United States	Basilicata	Basilicata
	Son	M.	8	Single	United States	Basilicata	Basilicata
	Son	M.	2	Single	United States	Basilicata	Basilicata
	Daughter	F.	$\frac{3}{12}$	Single	United States	Basilicata	Basilicata
770	Head	M.	38	Married	Basilicata	Basilicata	Basilicata
	Wife	F.	38	Married	Basilicata	Basilicata	Basilicata
	Sister-in-law	F.	47	Widowed	Basilicata	Basilicata	Basilicata
771	Head	M.	36	Married	Basilicata	Basilicata	Basilicata
	Wife	F.	34	Married	Basilicata	Basilicata	Basilicata

a Not reported.

TABLE **I.**—GENERAL SOCIAL AND ECONOMIC CONDITION, BY FAMILIES AND INDIVIDUALS—Continued.

Years in U.S.	Naturalized.	Profession, trade, or occupation.	Hours of work per week.	Average weekly earnings.	Weeks employed.	Total yearly earnings.	Sick during year, defective, maimed, or deformed.
9	Yes..	Laborer	(a)	(a)	15	(a)	No.
3		Housewife					Childbirth.
3		Scholar and newsboy	18	$0.60	9	$5	No.
		At home					Measles.
		At home					No.
4	No...	Laborer	(a)	(a)	25	(a)	Fever, typhoid.
12	No...	Laborer	48	(a)	23	(a)	Fever, malarial.
6		Housewife					Heart, disease of.
		At home					No.
		At home					No.
18	Yes..	Laborer	60	7.50	22	165	No.
18		Housewife					Bronchitis.
10	Yes..	Laborer	(a)	7.50	19	143	No.
5		Housewife					Female complaint.
8	No...	Laborer	(a)	7.50	15	113	No.
6		Housewife					Childbirth.
		At home					No.
		At home					No.
10	No...	Railroad laborer	60	6.00	17	102	Rheumatism.
10		Housewife					Rheumatism.
10		No occupation					No.
4	No...	Railroad laborer	60	6.60	10	66	Fever, not specified.
6	Yes..	Railroad laborer	60	6.60	10	66	No.
3		Laborer	(a)	7.00	26	182	No.
3	No...	Laborer	48	9.00	10	90	No.
6	Yes..	Laborer	48	7.50	(a)	(a)	Rheumatism.
1		Housewife					No.
6		Newsboy	36	.90	52	47	No.
1		At home					No.
7	No...	Laborer	48	7.50	(a)	(a)	Eyes, inflammation of both.
7		Housewife					Rheumatism.
7		Scholar					No.
7		No occupation					No.
		Scholar					No.
		Scholar					No.
		At home					No.
		At home					No.
16		Housewife and washerwoman.	(a)	1.50	(a)	(a)	No.
		Scholar					Mumps.
		Scholar					No.
		Scholar					No.
		At home					No.
8	Yes..	Laborer	60	7.50	13	98	Bronchitis.
9		Housewife					Childbirth.
		At home					No.
		At home					No.
7	Yes..	Laborer	60	7.50	13	98	No.
28	Yes..	Barber	81	5.00	52	260	Rheumatism.
16		Housewife and cloak finisher.	(a)	1.50	13	20	Childbirth.
		Clerk (b)	74	4.00	b 35	191	No.
		Cloak finisher	(a)	1.50	13	20	No.
		Scholar					No.
		At home					No.
		At home					No.
27	Yes..	Janitor	60	9.00	52	468	No.
22		Housewife and cloak finisher.	(a)	1.50	13	20	No.
$\frac{6}{12}$		No occupation					Crippled.
15	Yes..	Peddler, fruit	(a)	9.00	52	468	No.
15		Housewife					Childbirth.

b Also worked as seamstress seventeen weeks, at $3 per week.

TABLE **I.**—GENERAL SOCIAL AND ECONOMIC CONDITION, BY FAMILIES AND INDIVIDUALS—Continued.

Family number.	Relationship to head of family.	Sex.	Age.	Conjugal condition.	Birthplace.	Birthplace of—	
						Father.	Mother.
771	Daughter.........	F.	14	Single.....	United States...	Basilicata......	Basilicata......
	Daughter.........	F.	11	Single.....	United States...	Basilicata......	Basilicata......
	Son	M.	8	Single.....	United States...	Basilicata......	Basilicata......
	Daughter.........	F.	6	Single.....	United States...	Basilicata......	Basilicata......
	Daughter.........	F.	3	Single.....	United States...	Basilicata......	Basilicata......
	Daughter.........	F.	$\frac{5}{12}$	Single.....	United States...	Basilicata......	Basilicata......
	Mother-in-law	F.	55	Widowed .	Basilicata.......	Basilicata......	Basilicata......
772	Head	M.	31	Married...	Basilicata.......	Basilicata......	Basilicata......
	Wife.............	F.	28	Married...	Basilicata.......	Basilicata......	Basilicata......
	Brother...........	M.	20	Single.....	Basilicata.......	Basilicata......	Basilicata......
	Cousin............	M.	25	Single.....	Basilicata.......	Basilicata......	Basilicata......
773	Head	M.	60	Married...	Basilicata.......	Basilicata......	Basilicata......
	Wife.............	F.	60	Married...	Basilicata.......	Basilicata......	Basilicata......
774	Head	M.	35	Married...	Basilicata.......	Basilicata......	Basilicata......
	Wife.............	F.	30	Married...	Basilicata.	Basilicata......	Basilicata......
	Son	M.	8	Single.....	United States...	Basilicata......	Basilicata......
	Daughter.........	F.	5	Single.....	United States...	Basilicata......	Basilicata......
	Daughter.........	F.	1	Single.....	United States...	Basilicata......	Basilicata......
775	Head	M.	24	Married...	Basilicata.......	Basilicata......	Basilicata......
	Wife.............	F.	16	Married...	United States ..	Basilicata......	Basilicata......
776	Head	M.	33	Married...	Liguria.........	Liguria.......	Liguria........
	Wife.............	F.	33	Married...	Basilicata.......	Basilicata......	Basilicata.......
	Son	M.	7	Single.....	United States...	Liguria.......	Basilicata......
	Son	M.	2	Single.....	United States...	Liguria.......	Basilicata......
	Son	M.	$\frac{7}{12}$	Single.....	United States...	Liguria.......	Basilicata......
	Father-in-law.....	M.	75	Married...	Basilicata.......	Basilicata......	Basilicata......
	Mother-in-law	F.	67	Married. ..	Basilicata.......	Basilicata......	Basilicata......
777	Head	M.	31	Married...	Basilicata.......	Basilicata......	Basilicata......
	Wife.............	F.	25	Married...	Basilicata.......	Basilicata......	Basilicata......
	Daughter.........	F.	8	Single.....	United States...	Basilicata......	Basilicata......
	Son	M.	7	Single.....	United States...	Basilicata......	Basilicata......
	Daughter.........	F.	4	Single.....	United States...	Basilicata......	Basilicata......
	Son	M.	3	Single.....	United States...	Basilicata......	Basilicata......
	Daughter.........	F.	$\frac{5}{12}$	Single.....	United States...	Basilicata......	Basilicata......
778	Head	M.	42	Married...	Basilicata.......	Basilicata......	Basilicata......
	Wife.............	F.	37	Married...	Basilicata.......	Basilicata......	Basilicata......
	Son	M.	8	Single.....	United States...	Basilicata......	Basilicata......
	Son	M.	4	Single.....	United States...	Basilicata......	Basilicata......
	Son	M.	2	Single.....	United States...	Basilicata......	Basilicata......
779	Head	M.	30	Married...	Basilicata.......	Basilicata......	Basilicata......
	Wife.............	F.	27	Married...	Basilicata.......	Basilicata......	Basilicata......
	Son	M.	4	Single.....	Basilicata.......	Basilicata......	Basilicata......
	Son	M.	2	Single.....	Basilicata.......	Basilicata......	Basilicata......
780	Head	M.	45	Married...	Campania.......	Campania......	Campania......
	Wife.............	F.	40	Married...	Campania.......	Campania......	Campania......
	Son	M.	17	Single.....	Campania.......	Campania......	Campania......
	Son	M.	14	Single.....	Campania.......	Campania......	Campania......
	Daughter	F.	12	Single.....	Campania.......	Campania......	Campania......
	Son	M.	9	Single.....	Campania.......	Campania......	Campania......
781	Head	M.	26	Married...	Basilicata.......	Basilicata......	Basilicata......
	Wife.............	F.	24	Married...	Basilicata.......	Basilicata......	Basilicata......
	Daughter.........	F.	6	Single.....	Basilicata.......	Basilicata......	Basilicata......
782	Head	M.	25	Married...	Basilicata.......	Basilicata......	Basilicata......
	Wife.............	F.	23	Married...	Basilicata.......	Basilicata......	Basilicata......
	Daughter.........	F.	1	Single.....	United States...	Basilicata......	Basilicata......
	Father............	M.	57	Married...	Basilicata.......	Basilicata......	Basilicata......
	Mother	F.	59	Married...	Basilicata.......	Basilicata......	Basilicata......
783	Head	M.	35	Married...	Campania.......	Campania......	Campania......
	Wife.............	F.	31	Married...	Campania.......	Campania......	Campania......

a Not reported.

TABLE **I.**—GENERAL SOCIAL AND ECONOMIC CONDITION, BY FAMILIES AND INDIVIDUALS—Continued.

Years in U. S.	Natu- ral- ized.	Profession, trade, or occupation.	Hours of work per week.	Average weekly earn- ings.	Weeks em- ploy- ed.	Total yearly earn- ings.	Sick during year, defective, maimed, or deformed.
......	......	Housework	......	......	......	......	No.
......	......	Scholar	......	......	......	......	No.
......	......	Scholar	......	......	......	......	No.
......	......	Scholar	......	......	......	......	No.
......	......	At home	......	......	......	......	No.
......	......	At home	......	......	......	......	Abscess, scrofulous.
15	......	Housework	......	......	......	......	No.
8	Yes..	Paver	60	$7.50	17	$128	No.
6	......	Housewife	......	......	......	......	No.
7	......	No occupation	......	......	......	......	No.
6	Yes..	Paver	60	7.50	17	128	No.
24	Yes..	Retired	......	......	......	......	No.
23	......	Housewife	......	......	......	......	No.
11	Yes..	Street sweeper	60	9.00	17	153	No.
11	......	Housewife and pants fin- isher.	(a)	1.00	26	26	No.
......	......	Scholar	......	......	......	......	No.
......	......	At home	......	......	......	......	No.
......	......	At home	......	......	......	......	No.
9	Yes..	Padrone	60	(a)	43	(a)	Fever, not specified.
......	......	Housewife	......	......	......	......	No.
12	Yes..	Expressman	(a)	9.00	48	432	Bronchitis.
12	......	Housewife	......	......	......	......	Childbirth.
......	......	Scholar	......	......	......	......	Diphtheria.
......	......	At home	......	......	......	......	No.
......	......	At home	......	......	......	......	No.
25	No...	No occupation	......	......	......	......	No.
10	......	No occupation	......	......	......	......	Feeble-minded; deaf; lame.
19	Yes..	Musician	(a)	15.00	52	780	No.
20	......	Housewife	......	......	......	......	Childbirth.
......	......	Scholar	......	......	......	......	No.
......	......	Scholar	......	......	......	......	No.
......	......	At home	......	......	......	......	No.
......	......	At home	......	......	......	......	No.
......	......	At home	......	......	......	......	No.
15	Yes..	Street sweeper	60	9.00	26	234	No.
12	......	Housewife	......	......	......	......	Female complaint.
......	......	Scholar	......	......	......	......	No.
......	......	At home	......	......	......	......	No.
......	......	At home	......	......	......	......	No.
2	No..	Laborer	60	7.50	9	68	No.
1½	......	Housewife	......	......	......	......	No.
1½	......	At home	......	......	......	......	No.
1½	......	At home	......	......	......	......	No.
4	No...	No occupation	......	......	......	......	Arm, one disabled.
4	......	Housewife and pants fin- isher.	(a)	2.50	17	43	Miscarriage.
4	......	Scholar and bootblack	(a)	(a)	52	(a)	No.
4	......	Scholar and tailor's ap- prentice.	(a)	2.00	52	104	No.
4	......	Scholar	......	......	......	......	No.
4	......	Scholar	......	......	......	......	No.
2	No...	Street sweeper	60	7.50	13	98	No.
1½	......	Housewife	......	......	......	......	No.
1½	......	At home	......	......	......	......	No.
14	Yes..	Street sweeper	60	9.00	22	198	No.
9	......	Housewife and pants fin- isher.	(a)	2.00	26	52	No.
......	No...	At home	......	......	......	......	No.
14	No...	No occupation	......	......	......	......	No.
14	......	Housework	......	......	......	......	No.
9	Yes..	Street sweeper	60	7.50	26	195	Injury by accident.
9	......	Housewife and pants fin- isher.	(a)	2.50	26	65	No.

TABLE I.—GENERAL SOCIAL AND ECONOMIC CONDITION, BY FAMILIES AND INDIVIDUALS—Continued.

Family number.	Relationship to head of family.	Sex.	Age.	Conjugal condition.	Birthplace.	Birthplace of—	
						Father.	Mother.
784	Head	M.	40	Married...	Basilicata	Basilicata	Basilicata
	Wife	F.	37	Married...	Basilicata	Basilicata	Basilicata
	Nephew	M.	17	Single	Basilicata	Basilicata	Basilicata
785	Head	M.	37	Married...	Basilicata	Basilicata	Basilicata
	Wife	F.	35	Married...	Basilicata	Basilicata	Basilicata
	Daughter	F.	15	Single	Basilicata	Basilicata	Basilicata
	Daughter	F.	7	Single	Basilicata	Basilicata	Basilicata
	Brother-in-law	M.	27	Married...	Basilicata	Basilicata	Basilicata
	Sister-in-law	F.	25	Married...	Basilicata	Basilicata	Basilicata
	Niece	F.	1	Single	United States	Basilicata	Basilicata
786	Head	M.	40	Married...	Basilicata	Basilicata	Basilicata
	Wife	F.	35	Married...	Basilicata	Basilicata	Basilicata
	Son	M.	10	Single	Basilicata	Basilicata	Basilicata
	Daughter	F.	3	Single	United States	Basilicata	Basilicata
	Daughter	F.	1	Single	United States	Basilicata	Basilicata
787	Head	M.	25	Married...	Basilicata	Basilicata	Basilicata
	Wife	F.	19	Married...	Basilicata	Basilicata	Basilicata
	Son	M.	3	Single	United States	Basilicata	Basilicata
	Daughter	F.	$\frac{6}{12}$	Single	United States	Basilicata	Basilicata
788	Head	M.	30	Married...	Basilicata	Basilicata	Basilicata
	Wife	F.	33	Married...	Basilicata	Basilicata	Basilicata
	Stepson	M.	15	Single	Basilicata	Basilicata	Basilicata
	Stepdaughter	F.	12	Single	Basilicata	Basilicata	Basilicata
	Daughter	F.	6	Single	United States	Basilicata	Basilicata
	Mother	F.	60	Widowed .	Basilicata	Basilicata	Basilicata
789	Head	M.	30	Married...	Basilicata	Basilicata	Basilicata
	Wife	F.	21	Married...	Basilicata	Basilicata	Basilicata
	Daughter	F.	4	Single	United States	Basilicata	Basilicata
	Son	M.	1	Single	United States	Basilicata	Basilicata
790	Head	M.	30	Married...	Basilicata	Basilicata	Basilicata
	Wife	F.	30	Married...	Basilicata	Basilicata	Basilicata
	Daughter	F.	14	Single	Basilicata	Basilicata	Basilicata
	Daughter	F.	6	Single	United States	Basilicata	Basilicata
	Daughter	F.	3	Single	United States	Basilicata	Basilicata
	Son	M.	1	Single	United States	Basilicata	Basilicata
791	Head	M.	78	Married...	Basilicata	Basilicata	Basilicata
	Wife	F.	58	Married...	Basilicata	Basilicata	Basilicata
792	Head	M.	33	Married...	Basilicata	Basilicata	Basilicata
	Wife	F.	23	Married...	Basilicata	Basilicata	Basilicata
	Daughter	F.	$\frac{10}{12}$	Single	United States	Basilicata	Basilicata
793	Head	F.	42	Widowed .	Basilicata	Basilicata	Basilicata
	Son	M.	14	Single	Basilicata	Basilicata	Basilicata
	Son	M.	10	Single	Basilicata	Basilicata	Basilicata
	Daughter	F.	7	Single	United States	Basilicata	Basilicata
794	Head	M.	42	Married...	Calabria	Calabria	Calabria
	Wife	F.	47	Married...	Calabria	Calabria	Calabria
	Daughter	F.	12	Single	United States	Calabria	Calabria
	Son	M.	10	Single	United States	Calabria	Calabria
795	Head	M.	52	Married...	Basilicata	Basilicata	Basilicata
	Wife	F.	41	Married...	Basilicata	Basilicata	Basilicata
	Son	M.	25	Single	Basilicata	Basilicata	Basilicata
	Son	M.	24	Single	Basilicata	Basilicata	Basilicata
	Nephew	M.	20	Single	Basilicata	Basilicata	Basilicata
796	Head	M.	50	Married...	Basilicata	Basilicata	Basilicata
	Wife	F.	49	Married...	Basilicata	Basilicata	Basilicata
	Daughter	F.	17	Single	Basilicata	Basilicata	Basilicata

a Not reported.

TABLE **I.**—GENERAL SOCIAL AND ECONOMIC CONDITION, BY FAMILIES AND INDIVIDUALS—Continued.

Years in U.S.	Natu- ral- ized.	Profession, trade, or occupation.	Hours of work per week.	Average weekly earn- ings.	Weeks em- ploy- ed.	Total yearly earn- ings.	Sick during year, defective, maimed, or deformed.
10	Yes..	Barber	93	$7.00	17	$119	Abscess, scrofulous.
9	....	Housewife and dressmaker	(a)	(a)	52	(a)	No.
8	....	Barber's apprentice	93	3.00	52	156	No.
6	Yes..	Street sweeper	60	7.50	26	195	No.
3	....	Housewife and pants fin- isher.	(a)	(a)	26	(a)	No.
3	....	Pants finisher	(a)	(a)	26	(a)	No.
3	....	At home					No.
4	No...	Street sweeper	60	7.50	26	195	No.
4	....	Pants finisher	(a)	1.50	26	39	No.
....	....	At home					No.
9	Yes..	No occupation					Rheumatism.
6	....	Housewife and pants fin- isher.	(a)	2.00	26	52	No.
6	....	Scholar					No.
....	....	At home					No.
....	....	At home					No.
7	Yes..	Street sweeper	60	7.50	30	225	No.
4	....	Housewife and pants fin- isher.	(a)	1.00	26	26	Childbirth.
....	....	At home					Rickets; crippled.
....	....	At home					No.
9	Yes..	Street sweeper	60	7.50	17	128	No.
7	....	Housewife and pants fin- isher.	(a)	2.50	26	65	No.
7	....	Musician	(a)	2.00	(a)	(a)	No.
7	....	No occupation					No.
....	....	At home					No.
7	....	No occupation					No.
9	Yes..	Street sweeper	60	7.50	26	195	No.
5	....	Housewife and pants fin- isher.	(a)	1.00	4	4	Female complaint.
....	....	At home					No.
....	....	At home					No.
12	Yes..	Street sweeper	60	7.50	22	165	No.
8	....	Housewife and pants fin- isher.	(a)	(a)	26	(a)	No.
8	....	Pants finisher	(a)	(a)	(a)	(a)	No.
....	....	At home					No.
....	....	At home					No.
....	....	At home					Dyspepsia.
14	No...	No occupation					No.
9	....	Housewife					No.
15	Yes..	Gardener	60	9.00	52	468	No.
9	....	Housewife					Childbirth; dyspepsia.
....	....	At home					Measles.
9	....	Housewife and pants fin- isher.	(a)	2.00	26	52	No.
9	....	Bootblack	(a)	(a)	(a)	(a)	No.
9	....	Scholar and bootblack	(a)	(a)	(a)	(a)	No.
....	....	Scholar					No.
14	Yes..	Ragpicker	(a)	3.00	52	156	No.
13	....	Housewife					No.
....	....	Scholar					No.
....	....	Scholar					No.
20	Yes..	Retired					No.
5	....	Housewife					No.
16	Yes..	Musician	(a)	10.00	(a)	(a)	No.
10	Yes..	Barber	(a)	3.00	(a)	(a)	No.
5	....	Barber	(a)	9.00	(a)	(a)	No.
4	No...	No occupation					No.
4	....	Housewife and cloak fin- isher.	(a)	1.50	52	78	No.
4	....	Cloak finisher	(a)	1.50	52	78	No.

TABLE **I.**—GENERAL SOCIAL AND ECONOMIC CONDITION, BY FAMILIES AND INDIVIDUALS—Continued.

Family number.	Relationship to head of family.	Sex.	Age.	Conjugal condition.	Birthplace.	Birthplace of—	
						Father.	Mother.
796	Son	M.	15	Single	Basilicata	Basilicata	Basilicata
	Daughter	F.	14	Single	Basilicata	Basilicata	Basilicata
	Son	M.	10	Single	Basilicata	Basilicata	Basilicata
	Daughter	F.	8	Single	Basilicata	Basilicata	Basilicata
797	Head	M.	41	Married	Basilicata	Basilicata	Basilicata
	Wife	F.	60	Married	Basilicata	Basilicata	Basilicata
798	Head	M.	35	Married	Basilicata	Basilicata	Basilicata
	Wife	F.	34	Married	Basilicata	Basilicata	Basilicata
	Daughter	F.	10	Single	United States	Basilicata	Basilicata
	Son	M.	9	Single	United States	Basilicata	Basilicata
	Daughter	F.	6	Single	United States	Basilicata	Basilicata
	Daughter	F.	3	Single	United States	Basilicata	Basilicata
	Father	M.	70	Widowed	Basilicata	Basilicata	Basilicata
	Mother-in-law	F.	63	Widowed	Basilicata	Basilicata	Basilicata
799	Head	M.	50	Married	Basilicata	Basilicata	Basilicata
	Wife	F.	33	Married	Basilicata	Basilicata	Basilicata
	Daughter	F.	11	Single	United States	Basilicata	Basilicata
	Daughter	F.	7	Single	United States	Basilicata	Basilicata
	Son	M.	2	Single	United States	Basilicata	Basilicata
800	Head	M.	40	Married	Campania	Campania	Campania
801	Head	M.	28	Married	Calabria	Calabria	Calabria
802	Head	M.	40	Married	Campania	Campania	Campania
	Wife	F.	40	Married	Campania	Campania	Campania
	Son	M.	7	Single	United States	Campania	Campania
	Son	M.	1	Single	United States	Campania	Campania
803	Head	M.	45	Married	Campania	Campania	Campania
	Wife	F.	40	Married	Campania	Campania	Campania
804	Head	M.	35	Married	Campania	Campania	Campania
	Wife	F.	27	Married	Campania	Campania	Campania
	Daughter	F.	11	Single	Campania	Campania	Campania
	Son	M.	10	Single	Campania	Campania	Campania
	Son	M.	3	Single	United States	Campania	Campania
	Daughter	F.	$\frac{1}{12}$	Single	United States	Campania	Campania
805	Head	M.	55	Married	Campania	Campania	Campania
	Wife	F.	50	Married	Campania	Campania	Campania
	Son	M.	10	Single	Campania	Campania	Campania
806	Head	M.	37	Married	Campania	Campania	Campania
	Wife	F.	40	Married	Campania	Campania	Campania
	Son	M.	14	Single	United States	Campania	Campania
	Son	M.	13	Single	United States	Campania	Campania
	Daughter	F.	11	Single	United States	Campania	Campania
	Daughter	F.	5	Single	United States	Campania	Campania
	Daughter	F.	3	Single	United States	Campania	Campania
	Son	M.	1	Single	United States	Campania	Campania
807	Cooperative	M.	21	Single	Sicily	Sicily	Sicily
	Cooperative	M.	40	Married	Sicily	Sicily	Sicily
	Cooperative	M.	30	Single	Sicily	Sicily	Sicily
	Cooperative	M.	45	Married	Sicily	Sicily	Sicily
	Cooperative	M.	33	Single	Sicily	Sicily	Sicily
	Cooperative	M.	44	Married	Sicily	Sicily	Sicily
	Cooperative	M.	38	Single	Sicily	Sicily	Sicily
	Cooperative	M.	39	Married	Sicily	Sicily	Sicily
	Cooperative	M.	33	Married	Sicily	Sicily	Sicily
	Cooperative	M.	29	Married	Sicily	Sicily	Sicily
808	Head	M.	32	Married	Calabria	Calabria	Calabria
	Wife	F.	30	Married	Calabria	Calabria	Calabria
	Brother-in-law	M.	22	Single	Calabria	Calabria	Calabria
	Lodger	M.	20	Single	Calabria	Calabria	Calabria

a Not reported.
b Sick, disease not specified.

TABLE I.—GENERAL SOCIAL AND ECONOMIC CONDITION, BY FAMILIES AND INDIVIDUALS—Continued.

Years in U. S.	Naturalized.	Profession, trade, or occupation.	Hours of work per week.	Average weekly earnings.	Weeks employed.	Total yearly earnings.	Sick during year, defective, maimed, or deformed.
4	......	Musician	(a)	$4.00	52	$208	No.
4	......	Scholar					(b)
4	......	Scholar					Abscess, scrofulous.
4	......	Scholar					No.
16	Yes..	Laborer..................	60	7.50	22	165	No.
9	......	Housewife..............					Eye, loss of one.
11	Yes..	Laborer..................	60	7.50	13	98	No.
11	......	Housewife and washerwoman.	(a)	.60	43	26	Miscarriage.
......	......	Scholar					No.
......	......	Scholar					No.
......	......	Scholar					No.
......	......	At home..................					Rickets.
13	No..	Beggar					Blind.
9	......	Housework					No.
11	Yes..	No occupation					No.
11	......	Housewife..............					No.
......	......	Scholar					No.
......	......	Scholar					No.
......	......	At home..................					No.
13	Yes..	Laborer..................	60	7.50	3	23	No.
3	No...	Ragpicker	(a)	3.00	39	117	Injury by accident.
9	Yes..	Ragpicker (c)	(a)	2.80	c 39	207	No.
8	......	Housewife..............					No.
......	......	Scholar					No.
......	......	At home..................					No.
3	No...	Laborer	60	7.50	13	98	Rheumatism.
2	......	Housewife and washerwoman.	(a)	(a)	52	(a)	No.
3	No...	Ragpicker (d).............	(a)	1.00	d 49	72	No.
3	......	Housewife..............					Childbirth.
3	......	Scholar					No.
3	......	No occupation					No.
......	......	At home..................					Rickets.
......	......	At home..................					No.
9	Yes..	Laborer..................	60	6.60	17	112	No.
7/12	......	Housewife					No.
11/12	......	Scholar and newsboy	36	.90	(a)	(a)	No.
17	Yes..	No occupation					No.
17	......	Housewife and merchant, groceries.	(a)	(a)	(a)	(a)	No.
......	......	Scholar					No.
......	......	Scholar					No.
......	......	Scholar					No.
......	......	At home..................					No.
......	......	At home..................					No.
......	......	At home..................					No.
4	No...	Laborer..................	60	5.70	9	51	Injury by accident.
4	No...	Laborer..................	90	3.60	26	94	Fever, not specified.
5	No...	Laborer..................	90	3.30	9	30	No.
2	No...	Laborer..................	90	3.00	35	105	No.
4	No...	Laborer..................	90	3.60	17	61	No.
3	No...	Laborer..................	90	3.00	13	39	Fever, not specified.
8	No...	Laborer..................	90	3.60	13	47	Pneumonia.
3	No...	Laborer..................	90	3.00	9	27	Fever, not specified.
3	No...	Laborer..................	90	3.00	30	90	No.
2	No...	Laborer..................	90	3.60	35	126	No.
4	No...	Dishwasher..............	77	8.50	52	442	No.
3/12	......	Housewife					No.
7/12	No...	No occupation					No.
4	......	Laborer..................	60	6.60	17	112	No.

c Also worked as laborer thirteen weeks, at $7.50 per week.
d Also worked as laborer three weeks, at $7.50 per week.

TABLE **I.**--GENERAL SOCIAL AND ECONOMIC CONDITION, BY FAMILIES AND INDIVIDUALS—Continued.

Family number.	Relationship to head of family.	Sex.	Age.	Conjugal condition.	Birthplace.	Birthplace of—	
						Father.	Mother.
808	Lodger	M.	22	Single	Calabria	Calabria	Calabria
	Lodger	M.	43	Married	Calabria	Calabria	Calabria
	Lodger	M.	25	Single	Calabria	Calabria	Calabria
	Lodger	M.	32	Single	Calabria	Calabria	Calabria
	Lodger	M.	31	Married	Calabria	Calabria	Calabria
	Lodger	M.	25	Married	Calabria	Calabria	Calabria
809	Cooperative	M.	32	Married	Calabria	Calabria	Calabria
	Cooperative	M.	30	Single	Calabria	Calabria	Calabria
	Cooperative	M.	28	Single	Calabria	Calabria	Calabria
810	Head	M.	25	Married	Calabria	Calabria	Calabria
	Wife	F.	17	Married	Calabria	Calabria	Calabria
	Daughter	F.	³⁄₇	Single	United States	Calabria	Calabria
	Brother-in-law	M.	25	Single	Calabria	Calabria	Calabria
	Cousin	M.	30	Single	Calabria	Calabria	Calabria
	Cousin	M.	27	Single	Calabria	Calabria	Calabria
	Cousin	M.	27	Married	Calabria	Calabria	Calabria
	Cousin	M.	22	Single	Calabria	Calabria	Calabria
	Cousin	M.	28	Single	Calabria	Calabria	Calabria
	Cousin	M.	19	Single	Calabria	Calabria	Calabria
811	Head	M.	30	Married	Calabria	Calabria	Calabria
	Wife	F.	27	Married	Calabria	Calabria	Calabria
	Daughter	F.	4	Single	United States	Calabria	Calabria
	Son	M.	2	Single	United States	Calabria	Calabria
	Son	M.	1	Single	United States	Calabria	Calabria
812	Head	M.	44	Married	Basilicata	Basilicata	Basilicata
	Wife	F.	30	Married	Basilicata	Basilicata	Basilicata
	Daughter	F.	8	Single	United States	Basilicata	Basilicata
	Son	M.	4	Single	United States	Basilicata	Basilicata
	Son	M.	1	Single	United States	Basilicata	Basilicata
813	Head	F.	44	Married	Calabria	Calabria	Calabria
	Son	M.	23	Single	Calabria	Calabria	Calabria
	Son	M.	20	Single	Calabria	Calabria	Calabria
	Daughter	F.	14	Single	Calabria	Calabria	Calabria
814	Head	M.	38	Married	Calabria	Calabria	Calabria
815	Head	M.	50	Married	Calabria	Calabria	Calabria
	Wife	F.	45	Married	Calabria	Calabria	Calabria
	Son	M.	17	Single	Calabria	Calabria	Calabria
	Son	M.	15	Single	Calabria	Calabria	Calabria
	Niece	F.	17	Single	Calabria	Calabria	Calabria
816	Head	M.	35	Married	Calabria	Calabria	Calabria
	Wife	F.	23	Married	Calabria	Calabria	Calabria
	Son	M.	³⁄₁₂	Single	United States	Calabria	Calabria
	Father-in-law	M.	64	Married	Calabria	Calabria	Calabria
	Mother-in-law	F.	50	Married	Calabria	Calabria	Calabria
	Lodger	M.	38	Married	Calabria	Calabria	Calabria
	Lodger	M.	45	Married	Calabria	Calabria	Calabria
817	Head	F.	39	Widowed	Sicily	Sicily	Sicily
	Son	M.	21	Single	Sicily	Sicily	Sicily
	Son	M.	17	Single	Sicily	Sicily	Sicily
	Son	M.	13	Single	Sicily	Sicily	Sicily
	Son	M.	9	Single	United States	Sicily	Sicily
	Son	M.	6	Single	United States	Sicily	Sicily
	Daughter	F.	4	Single	United States	Sicily	Sicily
	Son	M.	2	Single	United States	Sicily	Sicily
	Lodger	M.	32	Married	Sicily	Sicily	Sicily
	Lodger	M.	27	Single	Sicily	Sicily	Sicily
	Lodger	M.	23	Single	Sicily	Sicily	Sicily
	Lodger	M.	21	Single	Sicily	Sicily	Sicily
	Lodger	M.	25	Single	Sicily	Sicily	Sicily
818	Head	M.	35	Married	Sicily	Sicily	Sicily
	Wife	F.	30	Married	Sicily	Sicily	Sicily
	Daughter	F.	12	Single	Sicily	Sicily	Sicily
	Son	M.	10	Single	Sicily	Sicily	Sicily
	Daughter	F.	7	Single	Sicily	Sicily	Sicily
	Son	M.	2	Single	United States	Sicily	Sicily

a Also worked at another occupation, details not reported.
b Not reported.
c Also worked as railroad laborer nine weeks, at $6.60 per week.

TABLE **I.**—GENERAL SOCIAL AND ECONOMIC CONDITION, BY FAMILIES
AND INDIVIDUALS—Continued.

Years in U. S.	Natu-ral-ized.	Profession, trade, or occupation.	Hours of work per week.	Average weekly earn-ings.	Weeks em-ploy-ed.	Total yearly earn-ings.	Sick during year, defective, maimed, or deformed.
12/12	No...	Laborer (a)	60	$8.00	a 19	(b)	No.
3	No...	Laborer................	60	6.60	17	$112	No.
4	No...	Laborer................	60	6.75	17	115	Rheumatism.
4	No...	Railroad laborer	60	6.60	17	112	No.
4	No...	Laborer................	72	8.00	26	208	No.
4	No...	Laborer................	60	6.60	17	112	No.
2	No...	Paper picker (c)	(b)	.90	c 13	71	No.
2	No...	Paper picker (c)	(b)	.90	c 13	71	No.
2	No...	Paper picker (c)	(b)	.90	c 13	71	Bronchitis.
8	Yes..	Peddler, vegetables.......	(b)	6.00	52	312	No.
5	....	Housewife...............					Childbirth.
....	....	At home					No.
8	Yes..	Railroad laborer	60	6.60	9	59	No.
7	No...	Railroad laborer	60	6.60	11	73	No.
2	No...	Railroad laborer	60	6.60	9	59	No.
1/12	No...	No occupation					No.
6	Yes..	Railroad laborer	60	6.60	13	86	No.
7	Yes..	Railroad laborer	60	6.60	13	86	No.
6	....	Railroad laborer	60	6.60	9	59	No.
10	Yes..	Saloon keeper............	(b)	(b)	52	(b)	No.
8	....	Housewife...............					No.
....	....	Scholar					No.
....	....	At home					No.
....	....	At home					No.
30	Yes..	Musician	(b)	8.00	52	416	No.
10	....	Housewife...............					No.
....	....	Scholar					No.
....	....	At home					No.
....	....	At home					No.
4	....	Rag sorter	60	3.00	52	156	No.
8	Yes..	Railroad laborer	60	6.60	13	86	No.
8	....	Railroad laborer	60	6.60	13	86	No.
4	....	Housework					No.
10	No...	Railroad laborer	60	6.60	13	86	No.
16	Yes..	Street railroad laborer	60	7.50	13	98	No.
9	....	Housewife...............					Female complaint.
9	....	Box-factory employee.....	55	4.00	52	208	No.
9	....	No occupation					No.
1/12	....	Housework					No.
9	No...	Barber..................	81	6.00	52	312	No.
2	....	Housewife...............					Childbirth; pneumonia
....	....	At home					Bronchitis.
5	No...	Paper picker	(b)	1.80	52	94	No.
2	....	Housework					No.
9	No...	No occupation					No.
3	No...	Paper picker (d)	(b)	.90	d 13	(b)	No.
10	....	Housewife...............					No.
10	No...	Newsboy (e)	(b)	1.50	e 39	104	No.
10	....	Scholar and newsboy	41	2.00	52	104	Foot, loss of one.
10	....	Scholar and newsboy	41	2.00	52	104	Eye, loss of one.
....	....	Scholar and newsboy	41	2.00	52	104	No.
....	....	Scholar					No.
....	....	At home					Rickets.
....	....	At home					No.
4	No...	Laborer................	66	3.60	23	83	No.
4	No...	Laborer................	66	3.60	23	83	No.
3	No...	Laborer................	66	3.60	23	83	No.
3	No...	Laborer................	66	3.60	23	83	No.
5	No...	Laborer................	66	3.60	23	83	No.
2	No...	Laborer................	48	7.50	15	113	Bronchitis.
2	....	Housewife...............					Debility, general.
2	....	No occupation					No.
2	....	Scholar					No.
2	....	At home					No.
....	....	At home					No.

d Also worked as laborer nine weeks, wages not reported.
e Also worked as clerk thirteen weeks, at $3.50 per week.

TABLE I.—GENERAL SOCIAL AND ECONOMIC CONDITION, BY FAMILIES
AND INDIVIDUALS—Continued.

Family number.	Relationship to head of family.	Sex.	Age.	Conjugal condition.	Birthplace.	Birthplace of—	
						Father.	Mother.
819	Head	M.	65	Married	Basilicata	Basilicata	Basilicata
	Wife	F.	71	Married	Basilicata	Basilicata	Basilicata
	Sister-in-law	F.	74	Widowed	Basilicata	Basilicata	Basilicata
820	Head	M.	26	Married	Campania	Campania	Campania
	Wife	F.	25	Married	Campania	Campania	Campania
	Daughter	F.	5	Single	Campania	Campania	Campania
	Son	M.	$\frac{3}{12}$	Single	United States	Campania	Campania
821	Head	M.	49	Married	Sicily	Sicily	Sicily
822	Head	M.	39	Married	Campania	Campania	Campania
	Wife	F.	28	Married	Campania	Campania	Campania
	Son	M.	8	Single	Argentine Rep	Campania	Campania
	Daughter	F.	2	Single	United States	Campania	Campania
	Daughter	F.	$\frac{3}{12}$	Single	United States	Campania	Campania
	Brother-in-law	M.	27	Married	Campania	Campania	Campania
	Nephew	M.	17	Single	Campania	Campania	Campania
	Nephew	M.	19	Single	Campania	Campania	Campania
823	Head	M.	45	Married	Calabria	Calabria	Calabria
	Wife	F.	38	Married	Calabria	Calabria	Calabria
	Son	M.	19	Single	Calabria	Calabria	Calabria
	Son	M.	10	Single	Calabria	Calabria	Calabria
	Daughter	F.	3	Single	United States	Calabria	Calabria
824	Head	M.	40	Married	Sicily	Sicily	Sicily
	Wife	F.	30	Married	Sicily	Sicily	Sicily
	Son	M.	10	Single	Sicily	Sicily	Sicily
	Daughter	F.	9	Single	Sicily	Sicily	Sicily
	Daughter	F.	4	Single	United States	Sicily	Sicily
	Daughter	F.	$\frac{4}{12}$	Single	United States	Sicily	Sicily
825	Head	M.	34	Married	Sicily	Sicily	Sicily
	Wife	F.	20	Married	Sicily	Sicily	Sicily
	Son	M.	1	Single	United States	Sicily	Sicily
	Brother	M.	24	Single	Sicily	Sicily	Sicily
	Lodger	M.	25	Single	Sicily	Sicily	Sicily
826	Head	M.	33	Married	Sicily	Sicily	Sicily
	Wife	F.	31	Married	Sicily	Sicily	Sicily
	Daughter	F.	3	Single	United States	Sicily	Sicily
	Daughter	F.	$\frac{1}{12}$	Single	United States	Sicily	Sicily
827	Head	M.	44	Married	Sicily	Sicily	Sicily
828	Head	M.	30	Married	Sicily	Sicily	Sicily
	Wife	F.	29	Married	Sicily	Sicily	Sicily
	Daughter	F.	5	Single	United States	Sicily	Sicily
	Son	M.	2	Single	United States	Sicily	Sicily
	Son	M.	$\frac{3}{12}$	Single	United States	Sicily	Sicily
	Cousin	M.	26	Single	Sicily	Sicily	Sicily
829	Head	M.	30	Married	Sicily	Sicily	Sicily
	Wife	F.	25	Married	Sicily	Sicily	Sicily
	Son	M.	4	Single	Sicily	Sicily	Sicily
	Daughter	F.	2	Single	United States	Sicily	Sicily
	Son	M.	$\frac{1}{12}$	Single	United States	Sicily	Sicily
830	Head	M.	37	Married	Sicily	Sicily	Sicily
	Wife	F.	34	Married	Sicily	Sicily	Sicily
	Son	M.	15	Single	Sicily	Sicily	Sicily
	Son	M.	13	Single	Sicily	Sicily	Sicily
	Daughter	F.	11	Single	Sicily	Sicily	Sicily
	Daughter	F.	10	Single	Sicily	Sicily	Sicily
	Son	M.	$\frac{7}{12}$	Single	United States	Sicily	Sicily
	Daughter	F.	$\frac{7}{12}$	Single	United States	Sicily	Sicily
831	Head	M.	26	Married	Calabria	Calabria	Calabria
	Wife	F.	27	Married	Calabria	Calabria	Calabria
	Son	M.	4	Single	United States	Calabria	Calabria
	Son	M.	2	Single	United States	Calabria	Calabria
	Daughter	F.	$\frac{1}{12}$	Single	United States	Calabria	Calabria

a Also worked as railroad laborer nineteen weeks, at $6.60 per week.
b Not reported.

TABLE **I.**—GENERAL SOCIAL AND ECONOMIC CONDITION, BY FAMILIES AND INDIVIDUALS—Continued.

Years in U.S.	Natu-ral-ized.	Profession, trade, or occupation.	Hours of work per week.	Average weekly earn-ings.	Weeks em-ploy-ed.	Total yearly earn-ings.	Sick during year, defective, maimed, or deformed.
20	Yes..	No occupation					Leg, abscess on; one hand partly paralyzed.
20		Housewife					Rheumatism.
15		No occupation					Indigestion.
5	Yes..	Ragpicker (a)	(b)	$0.90	a 33	$155	Bronchitis.
5		Housewife					Childbirth.
5		At home					Rickets.
		At home					No.
8	No...	Railroad laborer	60	6.60	15	99	Rheumatism.
9	No...	Railroad laborer	60	7.50	52	390	No.
3		Housewife					Childbirth; female complaint.
3		At home					No.
		At home					No.
		At home					No.
3	No...	No occupation					No.
1½		Newsboy (c)	72	2.75	c 4	(b)	No.
6		Newsboy	72	2.50	52	130	Leg, deformity of one.
10	Yes..	Rag picker	66	5.00	52	260	No.
4		Housewife					No.
4		Railroad laborer	66	7.50	39	293	No.
4		Scholar					No.
		At home					Rickets.
8	Yes..	Laborer	48	7.50	15	113	No.
5		Housewife					Childbirth.
5		Scholar and newsboy	(b)	.60	(b)	(b)	No.
5		Scholar					Fever, scarlet.
		At home					No.
		At home					No.
9	Yes..	Laborer	48	9.00	19	171	No.
2		Housewife					Pneumonia.
		At home					No.
1½	No...	No occupation					No.
4	No...	Railroad laborer	60	6.60	15	99	Bronchitis.
8	Yes..	Laborer	48	9.75	23	224	No.
5		Housewife					Childbirth; malarial fever.
		At home					Measles.
		At home					Measles.
8	No...	Laborer	48	8.40	16	134	Kidneys, disease of.
10	Yes..	Laborer	48	9.00	15	135	No.
6		Housewife					Childbirth.
		At home					No.
		At home					Rickets.
		At home					No.
2	No...	Laborer	48	9.00	17	153	Skin, disease of.
4	No...	Peddler, fruit	(b)	3.75	52	195	No.
3		Housewife					Childbirth.
3		At home					No.
		At home					No.
		At home					No.
8	Yes..	Laborer	(b)	9.00	11	99	No.
2		Housewife					Childbirth.
2		Newsboy	(b)	(b)	(b)	(b)	No.
2		Newsboy	(b)	(b)	(b)	(b)	No.
2		No occupation					No.
2		No occupation					No.
		At home					No.
		At home					No.
10	Yes..	Laborer	60	7.50	5	38	Indigestion.
4		Housewife					Childbirth; fever, not specified.
		At home					Fever, not specified.
		At home					Fever, not specified.
		At home					No.

c Also worked at another occupation, details not reported.

TABLE **I.**—GENERAL SOCIAL AND ECONOMIC CONDITION, BY FAMILIES AND INDIVIDUALS—Continued.

Family number.	Relationship to head of family.	Sex.	Age.	Conjugal condition.	Birthplace.	Birthplace of—	
						Father.	Mother.
832	Head	M.	44	Married...	Calabria	Calabria	Calabria
	Wife	F.	40	Married...	Calabria	Calabria	Calabria
	Son	M.	18	Single	Calabria	Calabria	Calabria
	Daughter	F.	15	Single	Calabria	Calabria	Calabria
	Son	M.	3	Single	United States	Calabria	Calabria
833	Head	M.	28	Married...	Basilicata	Basilicata	Basilicata
	Wife	F.	27	Married	Basilicata	Basilicata	Basilicata
	Son	M.	4	Single	United States	Basilicata	Basilicata
	Son	M.	2	Single	United States	Basilicata	Basilicata
834	Head	M.	25	Married...	Basilicata	Basilicata	Basilicata
	Wife	F.	17	Married...	Basilicata	Basilicata	Basilicata
835	Head	M.	42	Married...	Basilicata	Basilicata	Basilicata
	Wife	F.	41	Married..	Basilicata	Basilicata	Basilicata
	Son	M.	14	Single	Basilicata	Basilicata	Basilicata
	Daughter	F.	7	Single	United States	Basilicata	Basilicata
836	Head	M.	30	Married...	Basilicata	Basilicata	Basilicata
	Wife	F.	30	Married...	Basilicata	Basilicata	Basilicata
	Daughter	F.	6	Single	United States	Basilicata	Basilicata
	Daughter	F.	2	Single	United States	Basilicata	Basilicata
	Daughter	F.	$\frac{1}{12}$	Single	United States	Basilicata	Basilicata
837	Head	M.	38	Married...	Basilicata	Basilicata	Basilicata
	Wife	F.	33	Married...	Basilicata	Basilicata	Basilicata
	Daughter	F.	3	Single	United States	Basilicata	Basilicata
	Brother	M.	39	Married...	Basilicata	Basilicata	Basilicata
	Cousin	M.	24	Single	Basilicata	Basilicata	Basilicata
838	Head	M.	25	Married...	Tuscany	Tuscany	Tuscany
	Wife	F.	25	Married...	Tuscany	Tuscany	Tuscany
	Son	M.	$\frac{7}{12}$	Single	United States	Tuscany	Tuscany
	Lodger	M.	25	Single	Tuscany	Tuscany	Tuscany
	Lodger	M.	29	Married...	Tuscany	Tuscany	Tuscany
839	Head	M.	44	Married...	Basilicata	Basilicata	Basilicata
	Wife	F.	44	Married...	Basilicata	Basilicata	Basilicata
	Son	M.	20	Single	Basilicata	Basilicata	Basilicata
	Son	M.	18	Single	Basilicata	Basilicata	Basilicata
	Daughter	F.	12	Single	Basilicata	Basilicata	Basilicata
	Son	M.	5	Single	United States	Basilicata	Basilicata
	Son	M.	4	Single	United States	Basilicata	Basilicata
	Son	M.	3	Single	United States	Basilicata	Basilicata
	Daughter	F.	$1\frac{1}{2}$	Single	United States	Basilicata	Basilicata
840	Head	M.	24	Married...	Basilicata	Basilicata	Basilicata
	Wife	F.	18	Married...	Basilicata	Basilicata	Basilicata
	Daughter	F.	2	Single	United States	Basilicata	Basilicata
	Son	M.	$\frac{8}{12}$	Single	United States	Basilicata	Basilicata
841	Head	M.	48	Married...	Basilicata	Basilicata	Basilicata
	Wife	F.	40	Married...	Basilicata	Basilicata	Basilicata
	Son	M.	12	Single	United States	Basilicata	Basilicata
	Son	M.	10	Single	United States	Basilicata	Basilicata
	Daughter	F.	9	Single	United States	Basilicata	Basilicata
	Daughter	F.	7	Single	United States	Basilicata	Basilicata
	Son	M.	5	Single	United States	Basilicata	Basilicata
	Son	M.	$\frac{7}{12}$	Single	United States	Basilicata	Basilicata
842	Head	M.	40	Married...	Basilicata	Basilicata	Basilicata
	Wife	F.	43	Married...	Basilicata	Basilicata	Basilicata
	Son	M.	12	Single	Basilicata	Basilicata	Basilicata
843	Head	M.	30	Married...	Basilicata	Basilicata	Basilicata
	Wife	F.	29	Married...	Basilicata	Basilicata	Basilicata
	Daughter	F.	6	Single	United States	Basilicata	Basilicata
	Son	M.	1	Single	United States	Basilicata	Basilicata

a Not reported.

TABLE **I.**—GENERAL SOCIAL AND ECONOMIC CONDITION, BY FAMILIES AND INDIVIDUALS—Continued.

Years in U. S.	Natu-ral-ized.	Profession, trade, or occupation.	Hours of work per week.	Average weekly earn-ings.	Weeks em-ploy-ed.	Total yearly earn-ings.	Sick during year, defective, maimed, or deformed.
14	Yes..	Laborer	60	$8.40	13	$109	No.
8		Housewife and pants fin-isher.	(a)	1.20	52	62	No.
8		Packer, candy	60	5.00	52	260	No.
8		Pants finisher	(a)	1.20	52	62	No.
		At home					No.
10	Yes..	No occupation					Fever, typhoid.
5		Housewife and pants fin-isher.	(a)	3.50	26	91	Pneumonia.
		At home					Rickets.
		At home					Bronchitis.
7	Yes..	Shoemaker	44	15.00	52	780	No.
10		Housewife					No.
15	Yes..	No occupation					Rheumatism.
14		Housewife and pants fin-isher.	(a)	2.50	52	130	No.
14		Scholar and shoe factory employee.	55	2.50	39	98	No.
		Scholar					No.
10	Yes..	Blacksmith	55	9.00	52	468	No.
7		Housewife					Childbirth.
		Scholar					No.
		At home					No.
		At home					No.
11	Yes..	Shoemaker	50	15.00	52	780	No.
11		Housewife					No.
		At home					No.
9	Yes..	Candy factory employee	55	7.00	52	364	No.
3	No...	Hod carrier	60	9.00	35	315	No.
5	No...	Mosaic layer	48	10.50	26	273	Kidneys, disease of.
3		Housewife					Childbirth.
		At home					No.
6	No...	Expressman	(a)	(a)	52	(a)	No.
1/12	No...	No occupation					No.
9	Yes..	Paper picker	(a)	3.00	52	156	No.
7		Housewife and pants fin-isher.	(a)	2.00	(a)	(a)	Childbirth.
7		No occupation					Abscesses.
7		No occupation					No.
7		No occupation					No.
		At home					No.
		At home					No.
		At home					No.
		At home					No.
15	Yes..	Salesman, fruit	72	9.00	39	351	No.
4		Housewife					Childbirth.
		At home					No.
		At home					No.
14	No...	Newsboy	(a)	1.75	52	91	Leg, loss of one.
14		Housewife					Childbirth; heart disease.
		Newsboy	(a)	2.25	52	117	No.
		Newsboy	(a)	2.25	52	117	No.
		Scholar					No.
		Scholar					No.
		At home					No.
		At home					No.
9	Yes..	Laborer	60	7.50	9	68	No.
5		Housewife and pants fin-isher.	(a)	2.00	52	104	No.
5		No occupation					No.
8	Yes..	Street sweeper	60	9.00	22	198	No.
7		Housewife and pants fin-isher.	(a)	1.50	17	26	No.
		Scholar					No.
		At home					Pneumonia.

TABLE **I.**—GENERAL SOCIAL AND ECONOMIC CONDITION, BY FAMILIES
AND INDIVIDUALS—Continued.

Family number.	Relationship to head of family.	Sex.	Age.	Conjugal condition.	Birthplace.	Birthplace of — Father.	Birthplace of — Mother.
844	Head	F.	45	Widowed	Basilicata	Basilicata	Basilicata
	Son	M.	8	Single	United States	Basilicata	Basilicata
845	Head	F.	41	Married	Basilicata	Basilicata	Basilicata
	Son	M.	16	Single	Basilicata	Basilicata	Basilicata
	Daughter	F.	14	Single	Basilicata	Basilicata	Basilicata
	Daughter	F.	8	Single	United States	Basilicata	Basilicata
	Son	M.	6	Single	United States	Basilicata	Basilicata
846	Head	M.	38	Married	Campania	Campania	Campania
	Wife	F.	40	Married	Basilicata	Basilicata	Basilicata
	Stepson	M.	19	Single	Basilicata	Basilicata	Basilicata
	Stepson	M.	14	Single	United States	Basilicata	Basilicata
	Stepson	M.	11	Single	United States	Basilicata	Basilicata
	Son	M.	10	Single	United States	Campania	Basilicata
	Son	M.	8	Single	United States	Campania	Basilicata
	Daughter	F.	5	Single	United States	Campania	Basilicata
	Daughter	F.	3	Single	United States	Campania	Basilicata
	Son	M.	1	Single	United States	Campania	Basilicata
847	Head	M.	35	Married	Campania	Campania	Campania
	Wife	F.	29	Married	Campania	Campania	Campania
	Son	M.	10	Single	Campania	Campania	Campania
	Daughter	F.	7	Single	Campania	Campania	Campania
	Daughter	F.	3	Single	United States	Campania	Campania
	Brother-in-law	M.	27	Single	Campania	Campania	Campania
	Boarder	M.	40	Married	Abruzzo	Abruzzo	Abruzzo
	Boarder	M.	32	Married	Abruzzo	Abruzzo	Abruzzo
848	Head	M.	50	Married	Basilicata	Basilicata	Basilicata
	Wife	F.	42	Married	Basilicata	Basilicata	Basilicata
	Daughter	F.	12	Single	Basilicata	Basilicata	Basilicata
849	Head	M.	38	Married	Basilicata	Basilicata	Basilicata
	Wife	F.	30	Married	Basilicata	Basilicata	Basilicata
	Daughter	F.	9	Single	Basilicata	Basilicata	Basilicata
	Son	M.	7	Single	Basilicata	Basilicata	Basilicata
	Daughter	F.	5	Single	Basilicata	Basilicata	Basilicata
850	Head	M.	34	Married	Campania	Campania	Campania
	Wife	F.	24	Married	Basilicata	Basilicata	Basilicata
	Daughter	F.	5	Single	Basilicata	Campania	Basilicata
	Son	M.	2	Single	United States	Campania	Basilicata
851	Head	M.	37	Married	Tuscany	Tuscany	Tuscany
	Wife	F.	34	Married	Tuscany	Tuscany	Tuscany
	Son	M.	3	Single	United States	Tuscany	Tuscany
852	Head	M.	36	Married	Basilicata	Basilicata	Basilicata
	Wife	F.	34	Married	Basilicata	Basilicata	Basilicata
	Daughter	F.	6	Single	United States	Basilicata	Basilicata
	Daughter	F.	3	Single	United States	Basilicata	Basilicata
853	Head	M.	25	Married	Calabria	Calabria	Calabria
	Wife	F.	20	Married	Abruzzo	Abruzzo	Abruzzo
	Daughter	F.	3	Single	United States	Calabria	Abruzzo
	Daughter	F.	1/2	Single	United States	Calabria	Abruzzo
	Father	M.	47	Married	Calabria	Calabria	Calabria
854	Head	M.	25	Married	Abruzzo	Abruzzo	Abruzzo
	Wife	F.	25	Married	Abruzzo	Abruzzo	Abruzzo
855	Head	M.	30	Married	Abruzzo	Abruzzo	Abruzzo
	Wife	F.	25	Married	Abruzzo	Abruzzo	Abruzzo
	Son	M.	5	Single	United States	Abruzzo	Abruzzo
856	Head	M.	35	Married	Sicily	Sicily	Sicily
	Wife	F.	20	Married	Sicily	Sicily	Sicily
	Daughter	F.	4	Single	United States	Sicily	Sicily
	Son	M.	1/2	Single	United States	Sicily	Sicily

a Not reported.

TABLE **I.**—GENERAL SOCIAL AND ECONOMIC CONDITION, BY FAMILIES AND INDIVIDUALS—Continued.

Years in U. S.	Natu- ral- ized.	Profession, trade, or occupation.	Hours of work per week.	Average weekly earn- ings.	Weeks em- ploy- ed.	Total yearly earn- ings.	Sick during year, defective, maimed, or deformed.
11	......	Housewife and pants fin- isher.	(a)	$2.00	26	$52	No.
......	......	Scholar					No.
8	......	Housewife and pants fin- isher.	(a)	2.00	52	104	Consumption.
8	......	Newsboy	60	3.50	13	46	No.
8	......	Pants finisher	(a)	2.00	52	104	No.
......	......	Scholar					No.
......	......	At home					Bronchitis.
16	Yes..	Laborer	60	7.50	4	30	No.
16	......	Housewife and pants fin- isher.	(a)	1.50	26	39	No.
16	......	Laborer	60	7.50	5	38	No.
......	......	Scholar					No.
......	......	Scholar					No.
......	......	Scholar					No.
......	......	Scholar					No.
......	......	Scholar					Eyes, inflammation of both.
......	......	At home					Debility, general; arrested development.
......	......	At home					
......	......	At home					No.
6	Yes..	Laborer	60	7.00	22	154	No.
5	......	Housewife					No.
5	......	Scholar and newsboy	(a)	.30	(a)	(a)	No.
5	......	Scholar					No.
5	......	At home					No.
6	Yes..	Coal miner	60	8.00	30	240	No.
7	Yes..	Candy factory employee	55	9.00	52	468	No.
5	Yes..	Candy factory employee	55	6.60	52	343	No.
10	No...	Newsboy	60	1.20	52	62	Leg, loss of one.
5	......	Housewife					No.
(a)	......	Scholar					No.
6	Yes..	Street sweeper	60	7.50	27	203	No.
5	......	Housewife and pants fin- isher.	(a)	2.00	17	34	Female complaint.
5	......	Scholar					No.
5	......	Scholar					No.
5	......	At home					No.
5	Yes..	Street sweeper	60	7.50	17	128	No.
5	......	Housewife					No.
5	......	Scholar					No.
......	......	At home					No.
10	Yes..	Expressman	(a)	6.00	50	300	Diphtheria.
6	......	Housewife					No.
......	......	At home					Fever, scarlet.
14	Yes..	Sewer digger (b)	48	13.50	b 26	371	No.
7	......	Housewife					No.
......	......	Scholar					No.
......	......	At home					No.
9	Yes..	Sewer digger	44	13.50	13	176	No.
9	......	Housewife					Childbirth.
......	......	At home					No.
......	......	At home					No.
9	Yes..	No occupation					No.
5	Yes..	Salesman, fruit	77	8.00	52	416	No.
5	......	Housewife					No.
5	Yes..	Sewer digger	48	12.00	22	264	No.
5	......	Housewife					No.
......	......	At home					Diphtheria.
11	Yes..	Sewer digger	44	13.50	22	297	No.
5	......	Housewife					Childbirth.
......	......	At home					Idiot.
......	......	At home					No.

b Also worked as organ grinder thirteen weeks, at $1.50 per week.

TABLE **I.**—GENERAL SOCIAL AND ECONOMIC CONDITION, BY FAMILIES
AND INDIVIDUALS—Continued.

Family number.	Relationship to head of family.	Sex.	Age.	Conjugal condition.	Birthplace.	Birthplace of—	
						Father.	Mother.
857	Head	M.	40	Married...	Basilicata	Basilicata	Basilicata
	Wife	F.	40	Married...	Basilicata	Basilicata	Basilicata
	Son	M.	15	Single	Basilicata	Basilicata	Basilicata
858	Head	M.	45	Married...	Abruzzo	Abruzzo	Abruzzo
	Wife	F.	49	Married...	Abruzzo	Abruzzo	Abruzzo
	Son	M.	16	Single	France	Abruzzo	Abruzzo
	Son	M.	11	Single	France	Abruzzo	Abruzzo
	Son	M.	6	Single	United States...	Abruzzo	Abruzzo
859	Head	F.	47	Widowed	Basilicata	Basilicata	Basilicata
	Daughter	F.	14	Single	Basilicata	Basilicata	Basilicata
860	Head	M.	44	Married...	Basilicata	Basilicata	Basilicata
	Wife	F.	47	Married...	Basilicata	Basilicata	Basilicata
	Son	M.	17	Single	Basilicata	Basilicata	Basilicata
	Daughter	F.	15	Single	United States	Basilicata	Basilicata
	Daughter	F.	14	Single	United States...	Basilicata	Basilicata
	Daughter	F.	10	Single	United States...	Basilicata	Basilicata
	Daughter	F.	7	Single	United States...	Basilicata	Basilicata
	Daughter	F.	5	Single	United States...	Basilicata	Basilicata
861	Head	M.	52	Married...	Basilicata	Basilicata	Basilicata
	Wife	F.	64	Married...	Basilicata	Basilicata	Basilicata
	Son	M.	25	Single	Basilicata	Basilicata	Basilicata
862	Head	F.	57	Widowed	Basilicata	Basilicata	Basilicata
	Son	M.	24	Single	Basilicata	Basilicata	Basilicata
	Daughter-in-law..	F.	27	Married...	Basilicata	Basilicata	Basilicata
	Grandson	M.	4	Single	United States	Basilicata	Basi icata
	Grandson	M.	1/12	Single	United States...	Basilicata	Basilicata
863	Head	M.	54	Married...	Basilicata	Basilicata	Basilicata
	Wife	F.	51	Married...	Sicily	Sicily	Sicily
	Daughter	F.	17	Single	Sicily	Basilicata	Sicily
	Daughter	F.	15	Single	United States...	Basilicata	Sicily
	Daughter	F.	12	Single	United States...	Basilicata	Sicily
	Daughter	F.	7	Single	United States...	Basilicata	Sicily
	Son	M.	4	Single	United States...	Basilicata	Sicily
	Son	M.	1	Single	United States...	Basilicata	Sicily
864	Head	M.	65	Married...	Basilicata	Basilicata	Basilicata
	Wife	F.	66	Married...	Basilicata	Basilicata	Basilicata
	Nephew	M.	20	Single	Basilicata	Basilicata	Basilicata
865	Head	M.	34	Married...	Basilicata	Basilicata	Basilicata
	Wife	F.	28	Married...	Basilicata	Basilicata	Basilicata
	Daughter	F.	8	Single	United States...	Basilicata	Basilicata
	Son	M.	6	Single	United States...	Basilicata	Basilicata
	Son	M.	4	Single	United States...	Basilicata	Basilicata
	Son	M.	2	Single	United States...	Basilicata	Basilicata
	Mother	F.	80	Widowed	Basilicata	Basilicata	Basilicata
866	Head	M.	40	Married...	Basilicata	Basilicata	Basilicata
	Wife	F.	43	Married...	Basilicata	Basilicata	Basilicata
	Stepson	M.	20	Single	Basilicata	Basilicata	Basilicata
	Stepson	M.	8	Single	Basilicata	Basilicata	Basilicata
867	Head	M.	80	Married...	Basilicata	Basilicata	Basilicata
	Wife	F.	48	Married...	Basilicata	Basilicata	Basilicata
	Son	M.	24	Married...	Basilicata	Basilicata	Basilicata
	Son	M.	15	Single	Basilicata	Basilicata	Basilicata
	Daughter-in-law..	F.	19	Married...	Basilicata	Basilicata	Basilicata
	Granddaughter...	F.	1	Single	United States...	Basilicata	Basilicata
868	Head	M.	29	Married...	Sicily	Sicily	Sicily
	Wife	F.	19	Married...	Sicily	Sicily	Sicily
	Daughter	F.	2	Single	United States...	Sicily	Sicily
	Son	M.	8/12	Single	United States...	Sicily	Sicily

a Also worked as artist's model four weeks, at $4.50 per week.

TABLE **I.**—GENERAL SOCIAL AND ECONOMIC CONDITION, BY FAMILIES AND INDIVIDUALS—Continued.

Years in U. S.	Natu- ral- ized.	Profession, trade, or occupation.	Hours of work per week.	Average weekly earn- ings.	Weeks em- ploy- ed.	Total yearly earn- ings.	Sick during year, defective, maimed, or deformed.
15	Yes..	Sewer digger	48	$13.50	26	$351	No.
9	......	Housewife..................					Female complaint.
9	......	Scholar					No.
9	Yes..	No occupation					Consumption.
9	......	Housewife..................					No.
9	......	Sewer digger (a)...........	60	6.00	a 6	54	No.
9	......	Scholar......................					No.
......	......	Scholar					No.
5	......	Beggar......................					No.
5	......	Seamstress.................	(b)	4.50	39	176	No.
21	Yes..	No occupation					Rheumatism.
17	......	Housewife and pants fin- isher.	(b)	.93½	26	24	No.
17	......	Newsboy	(b)	1.50	52	78	No.
......	......	Pants finisher	(b)	.93½	26	24	No.
......	......	Pants finisher	(b)	.93½	26	24	No.
......	......	Scholar					No.
......	......	Scholar					No.
......	......	At home					Spine, weakness of.
11	Yes..	No occupation					Epilepsy.
8	......	Housewife..................					No.
11	Yes..	Musician	(b)	5.00	(b)	(b)	No.
4	......	Housewife..................					Female complaint.
8	Yes..	Laborer....................	60	8.00	22	176	No.
5	......	Pants finisher	(b)	.50	26	13	Childbirth.
......	......	At home					No.
......	......	At home					No.
17	Yes..	Musician	(b)	6.00	52	312	No.
17	......	Housewife and pants fin- isher.	(b)	1.75	(b)	(b)	No.
17	......	Pants finisher	(b)	1.75	(b)	(b)	No.
......	......	No occupation					Female complaint.
......	......	Scholar					No.
......	......	Scholar					No.
......	......	At home					No.
......	......	At home					No.
24	No...	Scissors grinder	(b)	1.50	52	78	No.
17	......	Housewife and washer- woman.	(b)	.50	(b)	(b)	No.
3	......	Tailor	(b)	7.00	26	182	No.
14	Yes..	Candy factory employee...	55	7.00	52	364	No.
9	......	Housewife and dressmaker	(b)	(b)	52	(b)	No.
......	......	Scholar					No.
......	......	At home					No.
......	......	At home					No.
......	......	At home					No.
(b)	......	No occupation					Blindness, partial.
10	Yes..	Laborer....................	(b)	(b)	(b)	(b)	No.
3	......	Housewife..................					No.
5	......	Elevated railroad laborer..	60	7.50	13	98	No.
3	......	At home....................					No.
5	No...	No occupation					No.
5	......	Housewife and pants fin- isher.	(b)	3.00	26	78	No.
10	Yes..	Musician	(b)	1.50	52	78	No.
5	......	Musician	(b)	1.50	52	78	No.
3	......	Pants finisher.............	(b)	3.00	26	78	No.
......	......	At home....................					No.
7	Yes..	Peddler, fruit.............	(b)	4.50	39	176	Lung, penetrating wound of one.
7	......	Housewife..................					Childbirth.
......	......	At home....................					No.
......	......	At home					No.

b Not reported.

TABLE **I.**—GENERAL SOCIAL AND ECONOMIC CONDITION, BY FAMILIES
AND INDIVIDUALS—Continued.

Family number.	Relationship to head of family.	Sex.	Age.	Conjugal condition.	Birthplace.	Birthplace of—	
						Father.	Mother.
869	Head	M.	32	Married	Sicily	Sicily	Sicily
	Wife	F.	28	Married	Sicily	Sicily	Sicily
	Son	M.	5	Single	Sicily	Sicily	Sicily
	Daughter	F.	3	Single	Sicily	Sicily	Sicily
870	Head	M.	27	Married	Sicily	Sicily	Sicily
	Wife	F.	27	Married	Sicily	Sicily	Sicily
	Son	M.	3	Single	United States	Sicily	Sicily
	Son	M.	2	Single	United States	Sicily	Sicily
871	Head	M.	48	Married	Apulia	Apulia	Apulia
	Wife	F.	50	Married	Apulia	Apulia	Apulia
	Lodger	M.	27	Married	Basilicata	Basilicata	Basilicata
	Lodger	F.	18	Married	Basilicata	Basilicata	Basilicata
	Lodger	M.	19	Single	United States	Basilicata	Basilicata
	Boarder	M.	21	Single	Basilicata	Basilicata	Basilicata
872	Head	F.	27	Widowed	Basilicata	Basilicata	Basilicata
	Daughter	F.	11	Single	United States	Basilicata	Basilicata
	Son	M.	7	Single	United States	Basilicata	Basilicata
	Son	M.	4	Single	United States	Basilicata	Basilicata
	Son	M.	2	Single	United States	Basilicata	Basilicata
873	Head	M.	24	Married	Basilicata	Basilicata	Basilicata
	Wife	F.	23	Married	Basilicata	Basilicata	Basilicata
	Daughter	F.	3	Single	Basilicata	Basilicata	Basilicata
874	Head	M.	60	Married	Basilicata	Basilicata	Basilicata
	Wife	F.	45	Married	Basilicata	Basilicata	Basilicata
	Son	M.	21	Married	Basilicata	Basilicata	Basilicata
	Daughter	F.	13	Single	France	Basilicata	Basilicata
	Daughter	F.	11	Single	Basilicata	Basilicata	Basilicata
	Son	M.	8	Single	Basilicata	Basilicata	Basilicata
	Daughter	F.	5	Single	Basilicata	Basilicata	Basilicata
	Daughter	F.	7/12	Single	United States	Basilicata	Basilicata
	Daughter-in-law	F.	21	Married	Basilicata	Basilicata	Basilicata
875	Head	F.	29	Married	Basilicata	Basilicata	Basilicata
	Son	M.	8	Single	Basilicata	Basilicata	Basilicata
	Daughter	F.	2	Single	United States	Basilicata	Basilicata
876	Head	M.	48	Married	Basilicata	Basilicata	Basilicata
	Wife	F.	44	Married	Basilicata	Basilicata	Basilicata
	Daughter	F.	14	Single	United States	Basilicata	Basilicata
	Son	M.	12	Single	United States	Basilicata	Basilicata
	Daughter	F.	10	Single	United States	Basilicata	Basilicata
	Daughter	F.	8	Single	United States	Basilicata	Basilicata
877	Head	M.	26	Married	Basilicata	Basilicata	Basilicata
	Wife	F.	16	Married	Basilicata	Basilicata	Basilicata
878	Head	M.	35	Married	Calabria	Calabria	Calabria
	Wife	F.	24	Married	Basilicata	Basilicata	Basilicata
	Son	M.	7	Single	United States	Calabria	Basilicata
	Daughter	F.	5	Single	United States	Calabria	Basilicata
	Mother-in-law	F.	52	Widowed	Basilicata	Basilicata	Basilicata
	Sister-in-law	F.	12	Single	United States	Basilicata	Basilicata
	Brother-in-law	M.	9	Single	United States	Basilicata	Basilicata
879	Head	M.	55	Married	Tuscany	Tuscany	Tuscany
	Wife	F.	53	Married	Tuscany	Tuscany	Tuscany
	Son	M.	23	Single	Tuscany	Tuscany	Tuscany
	Son	M.	19	Single	Tuscany	Tuscany	Tuscany
	Daughter	F.	16	Single	Tuscany	Tuscany	Tuscany
	Son	M.	12	Single	United States	Tuscany	Tuscany
	Son	M.	9	Single	United States	Tuscany	Tuscany
880	Head	F.	39	Widowed	Basilicata	Basilicata	Basilicata
	Son	M.	17	Single	Basilicata	Basilicata	Basilicata
	Daughter	F.	14	Single	Basilicata	Basilicata	Basilicata
	Sister	F.	37	Single	Basilicata	Basilicata	Basilicata

a Also worked as laborer four weeks, at $7.50 per week.
b Not reported.

TABLE **I.**—GENERAL SOCIAL AND ECONOMIC CONDITION, BY FAMILIES AND INDIVIDUALS—Continued.

Years in U.S.	Natu- ral- ized.	Profession, trade, or occupation.	Hours of work per week.	Average weekly earn- ings.	Weeks em- ploy- ed.	Total yearly earn- ings.	Sick during year, defective, maimed, or deformed.
2	No...	Peddler, fruit (a)	60	$6.00	a 43	$288	No.
☆	......	Housewife...............					No.
☆	......	At home.................					No.
☆	......	At home.................					No.
5	Yes..	Peddler, fruit..............	(b)	4.50	52	234	No.
5	......	Housewife...............					No.
......	......	At home.................					No.
......	......	At home.................					No.
10	Yes..	Tinker	(b)	4.50	52	234	No.
10	......	Housewife and pants fin- isher.	(b)	1.15	52	60	No.
17	Yes..	Laborer..................	48	12.00	26	312	No.
5	......	Pants finisher............	(b)	1.15	52	60	Childbirth.
......	......	At home.................					No.
11	No...	Printer	60	8.00	43	344	No.
20	......	Housewife and pants fin- isher. (c)	(b)	1.50	c 26	(b)	No.
......	......	Scholar					No.
......	......	Scholar					No.
......	......	At home.................					No.
......	......	At home.................					No.
9	No...	Musician	(b)	4.00	52	208	No.
☆	......	Housewife...............					No.
☆	......	At home.................					No.
2	No...	Musician	(b)	1.80	26	47	Bronchitis.
2	......	Housewife and pants fin- isher.	(b)	2.40	17	41	Childbirth.
2	No...	Musician	(b)	3.60	52	187	No.
2	......	Musician		1.80	26	47	No.
2	......	Housework...............					No.
2	......	Scholar					No.
2	......	At home.................					No.
......	......	At home.................					No.
4	......	Pants finisher............	(b)	2.40	17	41	Rheumatism.
4	......	Housewife and pants fin- isher.	(b)	2.00	26	52	No.
4	......	Scholar					No.
......	......	At home.................					No.
15	Yes..	Laborer..................	60	8.40	6	50	No.
14	......	Housewife...............					No.
......	......	Scholar and seamstress ...	(b)	3.00	26	78	Consumption
......	......	Scholar and newsboy	(b)	(b)	(b)	(b)	No.
......	......	Scholar					No.
......	......	Scholar					No.
3	No...	Elevated railroad laborer.	60	7.50	13	98	No.
3	......	Housewife and pants fin- isher.	(b)	2.50	26	65	Rheumatism.
15	Yes..	Laborer..................	60	7.50	26	195	No.
12	......	Housewife...............					No.
......	......	At home.................					No.
......	......	At home.................					No.
12	......	Housework...............					No.
......	......	Scholar					No.
......	......	Scholar					No.
17	Yes..	No occupation............					No.
16	......	Housewife...............					No.
16	No...	Tobacco factory employee.	(b)	4.00	35	140	No.
16	......	Mince-meat factory em- ployee. (d)	(b)	9.00	d 30	501	No.
16	......	Bakery employee..........	55	3.00	52	156	No.
......	......	Scholar					No.
......	......	Scholar					No.
9	......	Housewife...............					No.
9	......	Shoe cutter's apprentice..	48	3.50	52	182	No.
9	......	Scholar					No.
6	......	No occupation					Blind.

c Also worked as washerwoman, at $0.40 per week, time not reported.
d Also worked as painter twenty-two weeks, at $10.50 per week.

TABLE **I.**—GENERAL SOCIAL AND ECONOMIC CONDITION, BY FAMILIES AND INDIVIDUALS—Continued.

Family number.	Relationship to head of family.	Sex.	Age.	Conjugal condition.	Birthplace.	Birthplace of— Father.	Birthplace of— Mother.
881	Head	M.	27	Married	Basilicata	Basilicata	Basilicata
	Wife	F.	25	Married	Basilicata	Basilicata	Basilicata
	Daughter	F.	8	Single	United States	Basilicata	Basilicata
	Son	M.	6	Single	United States	Basilicata	Basilicata
	Son	M.	4	Single	United States	Basilicata	Basilicata
	Daughter	F.	2	Single	United States	Basilicata	Basilicata
	Son	M.	$\frac{1}{12}$	Single	United States	Basilicata	Basilicata
882	Head	M.	32	Married	Basilicata	Basilicata	Basilicata
	Wife	F.	24	Married	Basilicata	Basilicata	Basilicata
	Son	M.	2	Single	United States	Basilicata	Basilicata
883	Head	M.	47	Married	Basilicata	Basilicata	Basilicata
	Wife	F.	44	Married	Basilicata	Basilicata	Basilicata
	Daughter	F.	12	Single	Basilicata	Basilicata	Basilicata
	Daughter	F.	9	Single	Basilicata	Basilicata	Basilicata
	Brother	M.	40	Married	Basilicata	Basilicata	Basilicata
	Sister-in-law	F.	48	Married	Basilicata	Basilicata	Basilicata
884	Head	M.	40	Married	Basilicata	Basilicata	Basilicata
	Wife	F.	30	Married	Basilicata	Basilicata	Basilicata
	Daughter	F.	6	Single	Basilicata	Basilicata	Basilicata
	Daughter	F.	2	Single	United States	Basilicata	Basilicata
	Daughter	F.	$\frac{6}{12}$	Single	United States	Basilicata	Basilicata
885	Head	M.	40	Married	Basilicata	Basilicata	Basilicata
	Wife	F.	35	Married	Basilicata	Basilicata	Basilicata
	Daughter	F.	12	Single	Basilicata	Basilicata	Basilicata
	Son	M.	$\frac{8}{12}$	Single	United States	Basilicata	Basilicata
886	Head	M.	48	Married	Calabria	Calabria	Calabria
	Wife	F.	30	Married	Calabria	Calabria	Calabria
887	Head	M.	21	Married	Abruzzo	Abruzzo	Abruzzo
	Wife	F.	17	Married	Basilicata	Basilicata	Basilicata
888	Head	M.	24	Married	Sicily	Sicily	Sicily
	Wife	F.	27	Married	Sicily	Sicily	Sicily
	Son	M.	2	Single	United States	Sicily	Sicily
	Son	M.	$\frac{2}{12}$	Single	United States	Sicily	Sicily
889	Head	M.	31	Married	Tuscany	Tuscany	Tuscany
	Wife	F.	24	Married	Tuscany	Tuscany	Tuscany
	Daughter	F.	4	Single	United States	Tuscany	Tuscany
	Son	M.	2	Single	Tuscany	Tuscany	Tuscany
890	Head	M.	70	Married	Basilicata	Basilicata	Basilicata
	Wife	F.	56	Married	Basilicata	Basilicata	Basilicata
	Son	M.	26	Single	Basilicata	Basilicata	Basilicata
	Daughter	F.	14	Single	Basilicata	Basilicata	Basilicata
891	Head	M.	26	Married	United States	Liguria	Liguria
	Wife	F.	20	Married	Basilicata	Basilicata	Basilicata
	Daughter	F.	2	Single	United States	United States	Basilicata
892	Head	F.	54	Married	Liguria	Liguria	Liguria
	Son	M.	24	Single	United States	Liguria	Liguria
	Nephew	M.	31	Single	Liguria	Liguria	Liguria
893	Head	M.	48	Married	Sicily	Sicily	Sicily
	Wife	F.	47	Married	Sicily	Sicily	Sicily
	Daughter	F.	27	Widowed	Basilicata	Sicily	Sicily
894	Head	F.	53	Widowed	Basilicata	Basilicata	Basilicata
	Son	M.	18	Single	Basilicata	Basilicata	Basilicata
	Son	M.	15	Single	Basilicata	Basilicata	Basilicata
	Daughter	F.	14	Single	Basilicata	Basilicata	Basilicata
	Daughter	F.	10	Single	Basilicata	Basilicata	Basilicata
895	Head	M.	40	Married	Basilicata	Basilicata	Basilicata
	Wife	F.	29	Married	Basilicata	Basilicata	Basilicata
	Son	M.	4	Single	United States	Basilicata	Basilicata
	Daughter	F.	1	Single	United States	Basilicata	Basilicata

a Also worked as street sweeper four weeks, at $7.50 per week.

TABLE **I.**—GENERAL SOCIAL AND ECONOMIC CONDITION, BY FAMILIES AND INDIVIDUALS—Continued.

Years in U.S.	Naturalized.	Profession, trade, or occupation.	Hours of work per week.	Average weekly earnings.	Weeks employed.	Total yearly earnings.	Sick during year, defective, maimed, or deformed.
9	Yes..	Street sweeper............	60	$9.00	13	$117	No.
9	....	Housewife.................	......	......	......	......	Childbirth.
......	....	Scholar....................	......	......	......	......	No.
......	....	Scholar....................	......	......	......	......	No.
......	....	At home...................	......	......	......	......	No.
......	....	At home...................	......	......	......	......	No.
......	....	At home...................	......	......	......	......	No.
9	Yes..	Laborer....................	60	9.00	22	198	No.
5	....	Housewife.................	......	......	......	......	No.
......	....	At home...................	......	......	......	......	No.
8	Yes..	Laborer (a)................	60	7.50	a 13	128	No.
3	....	Housewife.................	......	......	......	......	No.
3	....	Scholar....................	......	......	......	......	No.
3	....	Scholar....................	......	......	......	......	No.
14	Yes..	Street sweeper............	60	7.50	22	165	No.
9	....	Pants finisher.............	(b)	1.00	26	26	No.
5	Yes..	Street sweeper............	60	7.50	22	165	No.
3	....	Housewife.................	......	......	......	......	Childbirth.
3	....	Scholar....................	......	......	......	......	No.
......	....	At home...................	......	......	......	......	No.
......	....	At home...................	......	......	......	......	No.
14	Yes..	Street sweeper............	60	7.50	13	98	No.
7	....	Housewife.................	......	......	......	......	Childbirth; weakness of spine.
7	....	At home...................	......	......	......	......	No.
......	....	At home...................	......	......	......	......	No.
7	Yes..	Sewer digger..............	48	10.50	9	95	No.
5	....	Housewife.................	......	......	......	......	No.
4	No...	Candy factory employee...	60	7.00	39	273	No.
16	....	Housewife and pants finisher.	(b)	1.50	26	39	No.
7	Yes..	Peddler, fruit.............	(b)	6.00	52	312	No.
7	....	Housewife.................	......	......	......	......	Childbirth.
......	....	At home...................	......	......	......	......	No.
......	....	At home...................	......	......	......	......	No.
10	Yes..	Plaster worker	48	12.00	43	516	No.
7	....	Housewife.................	......	......	......	......	No.
......	....	At home...................	......	......	......	......	No.
2	....	At home...................	......	......	......	......	Bronchitis.
14	No...	No occupation............	......	......	......	......	Injury by accident.
12	....	Housewife.................	......	......	......	......	Rheumatism.
12	Yes..	Street sweeper............	60	9.00	9	81	No.
12	....	Scholar....................	......	......	......	......	No.
......	....	Painter....................	48	2.00	13	26	No.
12	....	Housewife.................	......	......	......	......	No.
......	....	At home...................	......	......	......	......	No.
27	....	Housewife.................	......	......	......	......	No.
......	....	Bartender.................	(b)	7.50	9	68	No.
5	Yes..	Laborer	60	7.50	30	225	No.
7	No...	Peddler, fruit.........	(b)	10.50	52	546	No.
6	....	Housewife.................	......	......	......	......	No.
6	....	Housework	......	......	......	......	No.
3	....	Housewife.................	......	......	......	......	No.
3	....	Newsboy	(b)	.20	52	47	No.
3	....	Newsboy	(b)	(b)	(b)	(b)	No.
3	....	Scholar....................	......	......	......	......	No.
3	....	Scholar....................	......	......	......	......	No.
8	Yes..	Street sweeper............	60	7.50	17	128	No.
6	....	Housewife.................	......	......	......	......	No.
......	....	At home...................	......	......	......	......	Rickets.
......	....	At home...................	......	......	......	......	No.

b Not reported.

TABLE I.—GENERAL SOCIAL AND ECONOMIC CONDITION, BY FAMILIES
AND INDIVIDUALS—Continued.

Family number.	Relationship to head of family.	Sex.	Age.	Conjugal condition.	Birthplace.	Birthplace of—	
						Father.	Mother.
896	Head	M.	41	Married	Sicily	Sicily	Sicily
	Wife	F.	40	Married	Sicily	Sicily	Sicily
	Son	M.	15	Single	Sicily	Sicily	Sicily
	Daughter	F.	10	Single	United States	Sicily	Sicily
	Daughter	F.	9	Single	United States	Sicily	Sicily
	Son	M.	7	Single	United States	Sicily	Sicily
	Daughter	F.	3	Single	United States	Sicily	Sicily
	Son	M.	1	Single	United States	Sicily	Sicily
	Cousin	M.	23	Single	Sicily	Sicily	Sicily
897	Head	M.	35	Married	Basilicata	Basilicata	Basilicata
	Wife	F.	27	Married	Basilicata	Basilicata	Basilicata
	Daughter	F.	2	Single	United States	Basilicata	Basilicata
	Lodger	M.	34	Married	Basilicata	Basilicata	Basilicata
	Lodger	M.	40	Married	Basilicata	Basilicata	Basilicata
898	Head	M.	40	Married	Sicily	Sicily	Sicily
	Wife	F.	37	Married	Sicily	Sicily	Sicily
	Daughter	F.	11	Single	United States	Sicily	Sicily
	Daughter	F.	9	Single	United States	Sicily	Sicily
	Son	M.	7	Single	United States	Sicily	Sicily
899	Head	M.	28	Married	Basilicata	Basilicata	Basilicata
	Wife	F.	25	Married	Basilicata	Basilicata	Basilicata
	Daughter	F.	6	Single	United States	Basilicata	Basilicata
	Son	M.	4	Single	United States	Basilicata	Basilicata
	Daughter	F.	2	Single	United States	Basilicata	Basilicata
900	Head	M.	48	Married	Sicily	Sicily	Sicily
	Wife	F.	38	Married	Sicily	Sicily	Sicily
	Son	M.	18	Single	Sicily	Sicily	Sicily
	Son	M.	16	Single	Sicily	Sicily	Sicily
901	Cooperative	M.	24	Single	Sicily	Sicily	Sicily
	Cooperative	M.	27	Single	Sicily	Sicily	Sicily
	Cooperative	M.	36	Single	Sicily	Sicily	Sicily
	Cooperative	M.	21	Single	Sicily	Sicily	Sicily
	Cooperative	M.	28	Single	Sicily	Sicily	Sicily
	Cooperative	M.	24	Single	Sicily	Sicily	Sicily
	Cooperative	M.	47	Married	Sicily	Sicily	Sicily
902	Head	M.	48	Married	Sicily	Sicily	Sicily
	Wife	F.	48	Married	Sicily	Sicily	Sicily
	Son	M.	18	Single	Sicily	Sicily	Sicily
	Son	M.	16	Single	Sicily	Sicily	Sicily
903	Head	M.	25	Married	Calabria	Calabria	Calabria
	Wife	F.	24	Married	Calabria	Calabria	Calabria
	Stepdaughter	F.	3	Single	United States	Calabria	Calabria
	Daughter	F.	1	Single	United States	Calabria	Calabria
904	Head	M.	55	Married	Tuscany	Tuscany	Tuscany
	Wife	F.	47	Married	Tuscany	Tuscany	Tuscany
	Son	M.	20	Single	Tuscany	Tuscany	Tuscany
	Daughter	F.	5	Single	United States	Tuscany	Tuscany
905	Head	M.	40	Married	Liguria	Liguria	Liguria
	Wife	F.	30	Married	United States	Liguria	United States
	Boarder	M.	33	Single	Tuscany	Tuscany	Tuscany
906	Head	M.	35	Married	Tuscany	Tuscany	Tuscany
	Wife	F.	38	Married	Tuscany	Tuscany	Tuscany
	Son	M.	1½	Single	United States	Tuscany	Tuscany
	Brother-in-law	M.	45	Married	Tuscany	Tuscany	Tuscany
907	Head	M.	38	Married	Tuscany	Tuscany	Tuscany
	Wife	F.	25	Married	Tuscany	Tuscany	Tuscany
	Daughter	F.	5	Single	Tuscany	Tuscany	Tuscany
	Son	M.	1½	Single	United States	Tuscany	Tuscany

a Not reported.
b Also worked as paver thirteen weeks, at $9.75 per week.
c Also worked as salesman, fruit, twenty-six weeks, at $2 per week.
d Also worked as laborer nine weeks, at $4.25 per week.

TABLE **I.**—GENERAL SOCIAL AND ECONOMIC CONDITION, BY FAMILIES
AND INDIVIDUALS—Continued.

Years in U.S.	Naturalized.	Profession, trade, or occupation.	Hours of work per week.	Average weekly earnings.	Weeks employed.	Total yearly earnings.	Sick during year, defective, maimed, or deformed.
12	No...	Peddler, fruit.............	(a)	$6.00	52	$312	No.
11	......	Housewife......	......	......	......	......	No.
11	......	Scholar	......	......	......	......	No.
......	......	Scholar	......	......	......	......	No.
......	......	Scholar	......	......	......	......	No.
......	......	Scholar	......	......	......	......	No.
......	......	At home.....	......	......	......	......	No.
......	......	At home.....	......	......	......	......	No.
2	No...	Image maker	(a)	(a)	(a)	(a)	No.
13	Yes..	Laborer..............	60	9.00	30	270	No.
8	......	Housewife......	......	......	......	......	No.
......	......	At home......	......	......	......	......	No.
7	Yes..	Laborer.............	60	9.00	30	270	No.
1½	No...	No occupation	......	......	......	......	No.
12	Yes..	Peddler, fruit (b)..........	(a)	3.00	b 39	244	No.
12	......	Housewife...........	......	......	......	......	Rheumatism.
......	......	Dressmaker's apprentice..	(a)	.25	(a)	(a)	No.
......	......	Scholar	......	......	......	......	No.
......	......	At home...........	......	......	......	......	No.
6	Yes..	Laborer.............	60	7.50	17	128	No.
6	......	Housewife...........	......	......	......	......	No.
......	......	At home...........	......	......	......	......	No.
......	......	At home...........	......	......	......	......	No.
......	......	At home...........	......	......	......	......	No.
14	No...	Peddler, fruit (c)..........	(a)	1.50	c 26	91	No.
13	......	Housewife...........	......	......	......	......	Rheumatism.
13	......	Scholar and picture frame factory employee. (d)	55	5.00	d 26	168	No.
13	......	Scholar and peddler, fruit.	(a)	1.50	52	78	No.
5	No...	Laborer	72	7.50	26	195	(e)
4	No...	Laborer	72	6.00	13	78	Fever, not specified.
6	No...	Laborer	72	4.20	35	147	Fever, malarial.
6½	No...	Laborer (f)..............	72	4.50	22	(a)	Fever, malarial.
5	No...	Laborer	72	4.50	39	176	No.
4	No...	Laborer	72	4.90	43	211	No.
4	No...	Laborer	60	7.50	13	98	No.
14	No...	Peddler..............	(a)	1.50	26	39	Consumption
13	......	Housewife and merchant, groceries.	(a)	5.00	52	260	Rheumatism.
13	......	Peddler..............	(a)	1.50	52	78	No.
13	......	Peddler..............	(a)	1.50	52	78	No.
5	Yes..	Laborer (g)	60	7.50	g 5	68	No.
4	......	Housewife...........	......	......	......	......	No.
......	......	At home....	......	......	......	......	No.
......	......	At home	......	......	......	......	No.
9	No...	Peddler, fruit.............	(a)	6.00	52	312	No.
6	......	Housewife.............	......	......	......	......	Asthma.
6	......	Brass factory employee ...	(a)	6.00	52	312	No.
......	......	At home...........	......	......	......	......	No.
10	No...	Railroad laborer..........	60	9.00	52	468	No.
......	No...	Housewife.............	......	......	......	......	No.
6	No...	Peddler (h)................	(a)	(a)	h 39	(a)	No.
6	Yes..	Peddler, fruit.............	(a)	6.00	52	312	No.
6	......	Housewife.............	......	......	......	......	Childbirth.
......	......	At home...........	......	......	......	......	No.
3	No...	Peddler, fruit.............	(a)	6.00	52	312	No.
4	No...	Peddler, fruit	(a)	6.00	52	312	No.
2	......	Housewife.............	......	......	......	......	Childbirth.
2	......	At home...........	......	......	......	......	No.
......	......	At home...........	......	......	......	......	No.

e Sick, disease not specified.
f Also worked at another occupation, details not reported.
g Also worked as street sweeper four weeks, at $7.50 per week.
h Also worked as laborer thirteen weeks, at $7.50 per week.

TABLE **I.**—GENERAL SOCIAL AND ECONOMIC CONDITION, BY FAMILIES AND INDIVIDUALS—Continued.

Family number.	Relationship to head of family.	Sex.	Age.	Conjugal condition.	Birthplace.	Birthplace of—	
						Father.	Mother.
908	Head	M.	36	Married	Sicily	Sicily	Sicily
	Wife	F.	34	Married	Sicily	Sicily	Sicily
	Son	M.	5	Single	Sicily	Sicily	Sicily
	Daughter	F.	2	Single	United States	Sicily	Sicily
	Lodger	M.	28	Married	Sicily	Sicily	Sicily
	Lodger	F.	24	Married	Sicily	Sicily	Sicily
	Lodger	M.	$\frac{3}{12}$	Single	United States	Sicily	Sicily
909	Head	M.	40	Married	Sicily	Sicily	Sicily
	Wife	F.	33	Married	Sicily	Sicily	Sicily
	Daughter	F.	9	Single	United States	Sicily	Sicily
	Daughter	F.	6	Single	United States	Sicily	Sicily
	Son	M.	1	Single	United States	Sicily	Sicily
910	Head	M.	23	Married	Sicily	Sicily	Sicily
	Wife	F.	18	Married	Sicily	Sicily	Sicily
	Daughter	F.	$\frac{9}{12}$	Single	United States	Sicily	Sicily
	Father	M.	46	Married	Sicily	Sicily	Sicily
911	Head	M.	45	Married	Sicily	Sicily	Sicily
	Wife	F.	52	Married	Sicily	Sicily	Sicily
	Son	M.	27	Single	Sicily	Sicily	Sicily
	Son	M.	19	Single	Sicily	Sicily	Sicily
	Granddaughter	F.	4	Single	United States	Sicily	Sicily
912	Head	M.	46	Married	Lombardy	Lombardy	Lombardy
	Wife	F.	36	Married	Piedmont	Piedmont	Piedmont
	Daughter	F.	16	Single	United States	Lombardy	Piedmont
	Son	M.	4	Single	United States	Lombardy	Piedmont
	Daughter	F.	1	Single	United States	Lombardy	Piedmont
913	Head	M.	50	Married	Apulia	Apulia	Apulia
	Wife	F.	37	Married	Apulia	Apulia	Apulia
	Daughter	F.	15	Single	Apulia	Apulia	Apulia
	Daughter	F.	8	Single	United States	Apulia	Apulia
	Daughter	F.	$\frac{9}{12}$	Single	United States	Apulia	Apulia
914	Head	M.	34	Married	Basilicata	Basilicata	Basilicata
	Wife	F.	26	Married	Basilicata	Basilicata	Basilicata
	Daughter	F.	4	Single	United States	Basilicata	Basilicata
	Son	M.	3	Single	United States	Basilicata	Basilicata
	Daughter	F.	2	Single	United States	Basilicata	Basilicata
915	Head	M.	40	Married	Basilicata	Basilicata	Basilicata
	Wife	F.	37	Married	Basilicata	Basilicata	Basilicata
	Son	M.	10	Single	Basilicata	Basilicata	Basilicata
	Son	M.	5	Single	United States	Basilicata	Basilicata
	Son	M.	3	Single	United States	Basilicata	Basilicata
	Son	M.	$\frac{1}{12}$	Single	United States	Basilicata	Basilicata
916	Head	M.	43	Married	Tuscany	Tuscany	Tuscany
	Wife	F.	34	Married	France	France	France
	Daughter	F.	12	Single	France	Tuscany	France
	Son	M.	11	Single	France	Tuscany	France
	Son	M.	9	Single	France	Tuscany	France
	Daughter	F.	7	Single	France	Tuscany	France
	Son	M.	2	Single	United States	Tuscany	France
	Daughter	F.	1	Single	United States	Tuscany	France
917	Head	M.	36	Married	Tuscany	Tuscany	Tuscany
	Wife	F.	45	Married	France	France	France
	Son	M.	1	Single	United States	Tuscany	France
	Niece	F.	11	Single	France	Tuscany	(a)
	Boarder	M.	23	Single	France	France	France
918	Head	M.	34	Married	Campania	Campania	Campania
	Wife	F.	34	Married	Campania	Campania	Campania
	Son	M.	11	Single	Campania	Campania	Campania
	Daughter	F.	8	Single	Campania	Campania	Campania
	Son	M.	2	Single	United States	Campania	Campania
	Son	M.	1	Single	United States	Campania	Campania

a Not reported.
b Also worked as sewer digger one week, at $7.50 per week.

TABLE I.—GENERAL SOCIAL AND ECONOMIC CONDITION, BY FAMILIES
AND INDIVIDUALS—Continued.

Years in U. S.	Natu- ral- ized.	Profession, trade, or occupation.	Hours of work per week.	Average weekly earn- ings.	Weeks em- ploy- ed.	Total yearly earn- ings.	Sick during year, defective, maimed, or deformed.
5	Yes..	Peddler.....................	(a)	$4.50	52	$234	No.
4	......	Housewife................	......	......	......	......	No.
4	......	At home.................	......	......	......	......	No.
......	......	At home.................	......	......	......	......	No.
10	Yes..	Merchant, fruit............	(a)	(a)	52	(a)	No.
(a)	......	Housework...............	......	......	......	......	Childbirth.
......	......	At home.................	......	......	......	......	No.
9	No...	Peddler, fruit..............	(a)	4.50	52	234	No.
9	......	Housewife................	......	......	......	......	No.
......	......	Scholar..................	......	......	......	......	Diphtheria.
......	......	At home.................	......	......	......	......	Diphtheria.
......	......	At home.................	......	......	......	......	No.
7	No...	Laborer	72	3.75	39	146	No.
5	......	Housewife................	......	......	......	......	Childbirth.
......	......	At home.................	......	......	......	......	No.
3	No...	Laborer	72	3.75	39	146	No.
12	No...	Peddler, fruit..............	(a)	3.00	52	156	No.
8	......	Housewife................	......	......	......	......	No.
1	No...	Peddler, fruit..............	(a)	1.80	52	94	No.
8	......	Peddler, fruit..............	(a)	1.80	52	94	No.
......	......	At home.................	......	......	......	......	No.
17	Yes..	Fireman, bakery..........	60	12.00	52	624	No.
17	......	Housewife................	......	......	......	......	No.
......	......	Artificial flower maker...	47½	5.00	52	260	No.
......	......	At home.................	......	......	......	......	No.
......	......	At home.................	......	......	......	......	No.
15	Yes..	Street sweeper (b).........	60	7.50	b 22	173	No.
9	......	Housewife and pants fin- isher.	(a)	1.50	(a)	(a)	Childbirth.
9	......	Scholar and peddler, gum .	(a)	.25	52	13	No.
......	......	Scholar..................	......	......	......	......	No.
......	......	At home.................	......	......	......	......	No.
9	Yes..	Eleva'ed railroad laborer.	60	7.50	17	128	No.
6	......	Housewife................	......	......	......	......	No.
......	......	At home.................	......	......	......	......	No.
......	......	At home.................	......	......	......	......	No.
......	......	At home.................	......	......	......	......	No.
8	Yes..	Street sweeper (c).........	60	7.50	c 9	135	No.
6	......	Housewife	......	......	......	......	Childbirth.
6	......	Scholar and newsboy	35	1.05	35	37	Fever, typhoid.
......	......	At home.................	......	......	......	......	Rickets.
......	......	At home.................	......	......	......	......	No.
......	......	At home.................	......	......	......	......	No.
7	Yes	No occupation	......	......	......	......	Rheumatism.
3	......	Housewife................	......	......	......	......	No.
3	......	Scholar..................	......	......	......	......	No.
3	......	Scholar..................	......	......	......	......	No.
3	......	Scholar..................	......	......	......	......	No.
3	......	At home.................	......	......	......	......	No.
......	......	At home.................	......	......	......	......	No.
......	......	At home.................	......	......	......	......	No.
6	No...	Mosaic layer..............	60	9.00	26	234	No.
2	......	Housewife................	......	......	......	......	No.
......	......	At home.................	......	......	......	......	Rickets.
7	......	Scholar..................	......	......	......	......	No.
3	No...	Iron foundry employee....	60	9.00	52	468	No.
5	Yes..	Ragpicker	(a)	8.50	52	442	No.
4	......	Housewife................	......	......	......	......	No.
4	......	Scholar..................	......	......	......	......	No.
4	......	Scholar..................	......	......	......	......	No.
......	......	At home.................	......	......	......	......	No.
......	......	At home.................	......	......	......	......	No.

c Also worked as sewer digger nine weeks, at $7.50 per week.

TABLE **I.**—GENERAL SOCIAL AND ECONOMIC CONDITION, BY FAMILIES
AND INDIVIDUALS—Continued.

Family number.	Relationship to head of family.	Sex.	Age.	Conjugal condition.	Birthplace.	Birthplace of—	
						Father.	Mother.
919	Head	M.	33	Married	Campania	Campania	Campania
	Wife	F.	30	Married	Campania	Campania	Campania
	Daughter	F.	10	Single	Campania	Campania	Campania
	Son	M.	7	Single	United States	Campania	Campania
	Son	M.	5	Single	United States	Campania	Campania
	Son	M.	3	Single	United States	Campania	Campania
	Daughter	F.	2	Single	United States	Campania	Campania
920	Head	M.	22	Married	Campania	Campania	Campania
	Wife	F.	20	Married	Campania	Campania	Campania
	Son	M.	$\frac{1}{12}$	Single	United States	Campania	Campania
	Father	M.	53	Married	Campania	Campania	Campania
	Mother	F.	45	Married	Campania	Campania	Campania
921	Head	M.	30	Married	Campania	Campania	Campania
	Wife	F.	23	Married	Campania	Campania	Campania
	Boarder	M.	26	Single	Campania	Campania	Campania
922	Head	M.	45	Married	Campania	Campania	Campania
	Wife	F.	45	Married	Campania	Campania	Campania
	Son	M.	18	Single	Campania	Campania	Campania
	Son	M.	16	Single	Campania	Campania	Campania
	Daughter	F.	12	Single	Campania	Campania	Campania
	Son	M.	10	Single	Campania	Campania	Campania
	Daughter	F.	9	Single	Campania	Campania	Campania
	Son	M.	4	Single	United States	Campania	Campania
	Daughter	F.	$\frac{9}{12}$	Single	United States	Campania	Campania
923	Head	M.	47	Married	Campania	Campania	Campania
	Wife	F.	55	Married	Campania	Campania	Campania
924	Head	M.	58	Married	Campania	Campania	Campania
	Wife	F.	54	Married	Campania	Campania	Campania
	Son	M.	19	Single	Campania	Campania	Campania
	Son	M.	14	Single	Campania	Campania	Campania
	Daughter	F.	11	Single	Campania	Campania	Campania
925	Head	M.	50	Married	Campania	Campania	Campania
	Wife	F.	44	Married	Campania	Campania	Campania
	Son	M.	19	Single	Campania	Campania	Campania
	Son	M.	10	Single	United States	Campania	Campania
	Son	M.	7	Single	United States	Campania	Campania
	Son	M.	5	Single	United States	Campania	Campania
	Daughter	F.	3	Single	United States	Campania	Campania
	Brother	M.	46	Single	Campania	Campania	Campania
926	Head	M.	32	Married	Campania	Campania	Campania
	Wife	F.	30	Married	Campania	Campania	Campania
	Son	M.	6	Single	United States	Campania	Campania
	Daughter	F.	5	Single	United States	Campania	Campania
	Daughter	F.	3	Single	United States	Campania	Campania
	Brother-in-law	M.	40	Widowed	Campania	Campania	Campania
927	Head	M.	32	Married	Sicily	Sicily	Sicily
	Wife	F.	22	Married	Sicily	Sicily	Sicily
	Son	M.	5	Single	United States	Sicily	Sicily
	Daughter	F.	3	Single	United States	Sicily	Sicily
	Son	M.	$\frac{9}{12}$	Single	United States	Sicily	Sicily
	Lodger	M.	37	Single	Sicily	Sicily	Sicily
	Lodger	M.	25	Single	Sicily	Sicily	Sicily
928	Head	M.	46	Married	Sicily	Sicily	Sicily
	Wife	F.	38	Married	Sicily	Sicily	Sicily
	Son	M.	17	Single	Sicily	Sicily	Sicily
	Daughter	F.	13	Single	Sicily	Sicily	Sicily
	Daughter	F.	11	Single	Sicily	Sicily	Sicily
	Son	M.	9	Single	United States	Sicily	Sicily
	Son	M.	6	Single	United States	Sicily	Sicily
	Son	M.	2	Single	United States	Sicily	Sicily
929	Head	M.	40	Married	Sicily	Sicily	Sicily
	Wife	F.	38	Married	Sicily	Sicily	Sicily

a Also worked as laborer eight weeks, at $8.40 per week.   b Not reported.

TABLE **I.**—GENERAL SOCIAL AND ECONOMIC CONDITION, BY FAMILIES
AND INDIVIDUALS—Continued.

Years in U. S.	Natu- ral- ized.	Profession, trade, or occupation.	Hours of work per week.	Average weekly earn- ings.	Weeks em- ploy- ed.	Total yearly earn- ings.	Sick during year, defective, maimed, or deformed.
8	Yes..	Ragpicker (a)	(b)	$5.00	a 26	$197	Fever, typhoid.
8	......	Housewife					No.
8	......	Scholar					No.
.....	......	Scholar					No.
.....	......	At home					No.
.....	......	At home					No.
.....	......	At home					No.
19	Yes..	Ragpicker (c)	(b)	5.00	c 44	292	No.
2	......	Housewife					Miscarriage; childbirth.
.....	......	At home					No.
20	No...	Ragpicker	30	5.00	52	260	No.
19	......	No occupation					No.
6	Yes..	Ragpicker	48	3.00	52	156	No.
2	......	Housewife					No.
4	No...	Ragpicker	48	3.00	30	90	Pneumonia.
9	Yes..	Ragpicker	18	2.00	52	104	Spine, weakness of.
8	......	Housewife					Childbirth.
8	......	Ragpicker	30	2.00	52	104	No.
8	......	Ragpicker	30	2.00	52	104	No.
8	......	No occupation					Eyes, inflammation of both.
8	......	No occupation					No.
8	......	Scholar					No.
.....	......	At home					No.
.....	......	At home					No.
15	No...	Ragpicker	24	2.00	52	104	No.
7	......	Housewife					No.
7	No...	Ragpicker	18	4.00	52	208	No.
7	......	Housewife					No.
7	......	Ragpicker	42	8.00	52	416	No.
7	......	Ragpicker	30	5.00	52	260	No.
7	......	No occupation					Eyes, inflammation of both.
15	Yes..	Ragpicker	36	4.00	52	208	No.
11	......	Housewife					No.
11	......	Ragpicker	36	4.00	52	208	No.
.....	......	Scholar					No.
.....	......	At home					Rickets.
.....	......	At home					Rickets.
.....	......	At home					No.
15	Yes..	Ragpicker	42	3.00	52	156	No.
7	Yes..	Machine shop employee...	48	8.64	52	449	No.
7	......	Housewife					No.
.....	......	At home					No.
.....	......	At home					No.
.....	......	At home					No.
12	Yes..	Machine shop employee...	48	11.50	52	598	No.
12	Yes..	Laborer.....................	(b)	3.00	3	9	Fever, not specified.
9	......	Housewife					Childbirth; fever, not speci- fied.
.....	......	At home					No.
.....	......	At home					No.
.....	......	At home					No.
4	No...	Laborer.....................	(b)	3.30	50	165	Rheumatism.
5	No...	Laborer.....................	60	8.40	19	160	No.
9	Yes..	Laborer.....................	60	7.80	23	179	Indigestion.
9	......	Housewife					No.
9	......	No occupation					Convulsions; feeble-minded.
9	......	No occupation					Throat, inflammation of.
9	......	Scholar					No.
.....	......	Scholar					No.
.....	......	Scholar					No.
.....	......	At home					Pneumonia.
9	Yes..	Laborer.....................	48	8.40	9	76	Hand, penetrating wound of one.
1	......	Housewife					No.

c Also worked as laborer eight weeks, at $9 per week.

TABLE I.—GENERAL SOCIAL AND ECONOMIC CONDITION, BY FAMILIES AND INDIVIDUALS—Continued.

Family number.	Relationship to head of family.	Sex.	Age.	Conjugal condition.	Birthplace.	Birthplace of—	
						Father.	Mother.
929	Son	M.	15	Single	Sicily	Sicily	Sicily
	Daughter	F.	14	Single	Sicily	Sicily	Sicily
	Son	M.	11	Single	Sicily	Sicily	Sicily
	Son	M.	9	Single	Sicily	Sicily	Sicily
930	Head	M.	43	Married	Sicily	Sicily	Sicily
	Wife	F.	38	Married	Sicily	Sicily	Sicily
	Lodger	M.	34	Married	Sicily	Sicily	Sicily
931	Head	M.	36	Married	Campania	Campania	Campania
	Wife	F.	30	Married	Ireland	Ireland	Ireland
	Son	M.	11	Single	United States	Campania	Ireland
	Son	M.	5	Single	United States	Campania	Ireland
	Daughter	F.	4	Single	United States	Campania	Ireland
	Daughter	F.	2	Single	United States	Campania	Ireland
	Brother	M.	47	Married	Campania	Campania	Campania
932	Head	M.	60	Married	Campania	Campania	Campania
	Wife	F.	56	Married	Campania	Campania	Campania
	Son	M.	14	Single	United States	Campania	Campania
	Son	M.	10	Single	United States	Campania	Campania
	Daughter	F.	7	Single	United States	Campania	Campania
933	Head	M.	43	Married	Campania	Campania	Campania
934	Head	M.	33	Married	Campania	Campania	Campania
	Wife	F.	23	Married	Campania	Campania	Campania
	Niece	F.	9	Single	United States	Campania	Campania
	Niece	F.	7	Single	United States	Campania	Campania
935	Head	M.	28	Married	Campania	Campania	Campania
	Wife	F.	23	Married	Campania	Campania	Campania
	Daughter	F.	8	Single	United States	Campania	Campania
	Son	M.	3	Single	United States	Campania	Campania
936	Head	M.	40	Married	Campania	Campania	Campania
	Wife	F.	28	Married	Campania	Campania	Campania
937	Head	M.	31	Married	Abruzzo	Abruzzo	Abruzzo
	Wife	F.	35	Married	Abruzzo	Abruzzo	Abruzzo
	Daughter	F.	4	Single	Abruzzo	Abruzzo	Abruzzo
	Daughter	F.	$\frac{8}{12}$	Single	United States	Abruzzo	Abruzzo
938	Head	M.	36	Married	Campania	Campania	Campania
	Wife	F.	30	Married	Campania	Campania	Campania
	Son	M.	8	Single	United States	Campania	Campania
	Daughter	F.	3	Single	United States	Campania	Campania
	Daughter	F.	$\frac{5}{12}$	Single	United States	Campania	Campania
939	Head	M.	46	Married	Basilicata	Basilicata	Basilicata
	Wife	F.	45	Married	Basilicata	Basilicata	Basilicata
940	Head	M.	42	Married	Campania	Campania	Campania
	Wife	F.	38	Married	Campania	Campania	Campania
	Daughter	F.	12	Single	Campania	Campania	Campania
	Son	M.	8	Single	United States	Campania	Campania
	Son	M.	5	Single	United States	Campania	Campania
	Daughter	F.	3	Single	United States	Campania	Campania
	Son	M.	$\frac{3}{12}$	Single	United States	Campania	Campania
	Lodger	M.	19	Single	Campania	Campania	Campania
941	Head	M.	40	Married	Calabria	Calabria	Calabria
	Wife	F.	36	Married	Calabria	Calabria	Calabria
	Daughter	F.	16	Married	Calabria	Calabria	Calabria
	Son	M.	12	Single	Calabria	Calabria	Calabria
	Son	M.	1	Single	United States	Calabria	Calabria
	Son-in-law	M.	28	Married	Calabria	Calabria	Calabria
942	Head	M.	27	Married	Campania	Campania	Campania
	Wife	F.	24	Married	Campania	Campania	Campania
	Daughter	F.	2	Single	United States	Campania	Campania
	Daughter	F.	$\frac{5}{12}$	Single	United States	Campania	Campania
	Mother	F.	50	Widowed	Campania	Campania	Campania
	Brother	M.	15	Single	United States	Campania	Campania
	Sister	F.	11	Single	United States	Campania	Campania
	Lodger	M.	27	Married	Campania	Campania	Campania

a Not reported.

TABLE **I.**—GENERAL SOCIAL AND ECONOMIC CONDITION, BY FAMILIES AND INDIVIDUALS—Continued.

Years in U. S.	Naturalized.	Profession, trade, or occupation.	Hours of work per week.	Average weekly earnings.	Weeks employed.	Total yearly earnings.	Sick during year, defective, maimed, or deformed.
1	......	Newsboy	(a)	$2.50	30	$75	Fever, typhoid.
1	......	No occupation	......	......	......	......	Fever, typhoid.
1	......	Newsboy	(a)	2.50	52	130	No.
1	......	Newsboy	(a)	1.50	30	45	Fever, typhoid.
13	No...	Peddler, fruit...........	54	6.00	52	312	No.
10	......	Housewife...............	......	......	......	......	No.
3	No...	Railroad laborer	60	6.60	14	92	No.
14	Yes..	Blacksmith...............	60	9.00	52	468	No.
14	......	Housewife...............	......	......	......	......	No.
......	......	No occupation	......	......	......	......	No.
......	......	At home...............	......	......	......	......	No.
......	......	At home...............	......	......	......	......	No.
......	......	At home...............	......	......	......	......	No.
15	Yes..	No occupation	......	......	......	......	No.
15	Yes..	No occupation...........	......	......	......	......	Fever, not specified.
15	......	Housewife...............	......	......	......	......	No.
......	......	Scholar and newsboy.....	84	1.40	52	73	Leg, loss of one.
......	......	Newsboy	35	1.00	52	52	No.
......	......	At home...............	......	......	......	......	No.
3	No...	Ragpicker	42	2.50	43	108	Rheumatism.
12	No...	Railroad laborer...........	60	7.12½	52	371	Fever, not specified.
13	......	Housewife...............	......	......	......	......	Female complaint.
......	......	Scholar	......	......	......	......	No.
......	......	Scholar	......	......	......	......	No.
15	Yes..	Ragpicker...............	36	1.50	52	78	No.
10	.....	Housewife...............	......	......	......	......	No.
......	......	At home...............	......	......	......	......	No.
......	......	At home...............	......	......	......	......	Fever, not specified.
12	Yes..	Ragpicker...............	36	4.00	52	208	No.
2	......	Housewife...............	......	......	......	......	Miscarriage.
9	Yes..	Ragpicker...............	48	1.50	52	78	No.
3	......	Housewife...............	......	......	......	......	Childbirth; fever, not specified.
3	......	At home...............	......	......	......	......	No.
......	......	At home...............	......	......	......	......	Debility, general.
14	Yes..	Bone picker...............	66	6.00	52	312	No.
9	......	Housewife...............	......	......	......	......	Childbirth.
......	......	Scholar	......	......	......	......	No.
......	......	At home...............	......	......	......	......	No.
......	......	At home...............	......	......	......	......	No.
15	Yes..	Ragpicker...............	30	2.20	52	114	No.
14	......	Housewife...............	......	......	......	......	No.
11	Yes..	Paver...............	54	7.50	14	105	Kidneys, disease of.
9	......	Housewife...............	......	......	......	......	Childbirth.
9	......	No occupation	......	......	......	......	No.
......	......	Scholar	......	......	......	......	No.
......	......	At home...............	......	......	......	......	No.
......	......	At home...............	......	......	......	......	No.
......	......	At home...............	......	......	......	......	No.
3	......	Railroad laborer...........	60	6.60	14	92	No.
14	Yes..	Gas pipe layer...............	60	9.00	22	198	No.
9	......	Housewife...............	......	......	......	......	No.
9	......	No occupation...............	......	......	......	......	No.
9	......	Newsboy	(a)	.75	52	39	No.
......	......	At home...............	......	......	......	......	No.
5	Yes..	Street sweeper...............	66	9.00	31	279	No.
11	Yes..	Bootblack	(a)	6.00	52	312	No.
5	......	Housewife...............	......	......	......	......	Childbirth.
......	......	At home...............	......	......	......	......	No.
......	......	At home...............	......	......	......	......	No.
16	......	No occupation...............	......	......	......	......	No.
......	......	No occupation...............	......	......	......	......	No.
......	......	No occupation...............	......	......	......	......	No.
14	Yes..	Expressman...............	60	7.50	52	390	No.

TABLE **I.**–GENERAL SOCIAL AND ECONOMIC CONDITION, BY FAMILIES AND INDIVIDUALS—Continued.

Family number.	Relationship to head of family.	Sex.	Age.	Conjugal condition.	Birthplace.	Birthplace of—	
						Father.	Mother.
943	Head	M.	28	Married...	Sicily	Sicily	Sicily
	Wife	F.	27	Married...	Sicily	Sicily	Sicily
	Brother	M.	27	Married...	Sicily	Sicily	Sicily
	Cousin	M.	40	Married...	Sicily	Sicily	Sicily
	Cousin	M.	20	Single	Sicily	Sicily	Sicily
944	Cooperative	M.	20	Single	Sicily	Sicily	Sicily
	Cooperative	M.	30	Single	Sicily	Sicily	Sicily
	Cooperative	M.	23	Single	Sicily	Sicily	Sicily
945	Head	M.	50	Married...	Calabria	Calabria	Calabria
	Wife	F.	50	Married...	Calabria	Calabria	Calabria
946	Head	M.	32	Married...	Campania	Campania	Campania
	Wife	F.	26	Married...	Campania	Campania	Campania
	Son	M.	6	Single	United States	Campania	Campania
	Son	M.	5	Single	United States	Campania	Campania
947	Head	M.	41	Married...	Tuscany	Tuscany	Tuscany
	Wife	F.	36	Married...	Tuscany	Tuscany	Tuscany
	Daughter	F.	18	Single	Tuscany	Tuscany	Tuscany
	Son	M.	9	Single	United States	Tuscany	Tuscany
	Daughter	F.	8	Single	United States	Tuscany	Tuscany
	Son	M.	7	Single	United States	Tuscany	Tuscany
	Son	M.	5	Single	United States	Tuscany	Tuscany
	Son	M.	2	Single	United States	Tuscany	Tuscany
	Daughter	F.	$\frac{1}{2}$	Single	United States	Tuscany	Tuscany
	Nephew	M.	18	Single	Tuscany	Tuscany	Tuscany
948	Head	M.	40	Married...	Campania	Campania	Campania
	Wife	F.	39	Married...	Campania	Campania	Campania
	Daughter	F.	11	Single	United States	Campania	Campania
	Son	M.	8	Single	United States	Campania	Campania
949	Head	M.	40	Married...	Campania	Campania	Campania
	Wife	F.	38	Married...	Campania	Campania	Campania
	Son	M.	10	Single	United States	Campania	Campania
	Son	M.	7	Single	United States	Campania	Campania
	Daughter	F.	5	Single	United States	Campania	Campania
950	Head	M.	40	Married...	Campania	Campania	Campania
	Wife	F.	39	Married...	Campania	Campania	Campania
	Son	M.	18	Single	Campania	Campania	Compania
	Son	M.	7	Single	United States	Campania	Campania
	Son	M.	3	Single	United States	Campania	Campania
951	Head	M.	44	Married...	Campania	Campania	Campania
	Wife	F.	39	Married...	Campania	Campania	Campania
	Daughter	F.	13	Single	Campania	Campania	Campania
	Daughter	F.	10	Single	United States	Campania	Campania
	Son	M.	8	Single	United States	Campania	Campania
	Son	M.	7	Single	United States	Campania	Campania
	Son	M.	5	Single	United States	Campania	Campania
	Daughter	F.	2	Single	United States	Campania	Campania
952	Head	M.	28	Married...	Campania	Campania	Campania
	Wife	F.	28	Married...	Campania	Campania	Campania
	Daughter	F.	2	Single	United States	Campania	Campania
	Daughter	F.	1	Single	United States	Campania	Campania
953	Head	M.	29	Married...	Campania	Campania	Campania
	Wife	F.	20	Married...	Campania	Campania	Campania
954	Head	M.	45	Married...	Campania	Campania	Campania
	Wife	F.	44	Married...	Campania	Campania	Campania
	Daughter,adopted	F.	4	Single	United States	Campania	Campania
	Sister	F.	50	Widowed	Campania	Campania	Campania
955	Head	M.	40	Married...	Campania	Campania	Campania
	Wife	F.	35	Married...	Campania	Campania	Campania
	Daughter	F.	7	Single	United States	Campania	Campania
	Son	M.	$\frac{7}{12}$	Single	United States	Campania	Campania

a Also worked as laborer fourteen weeks, at $7.50 per week.
b Not reported.
c Also worked as laborer five weeks, at $7.50 per week.
d Also worked as laborer seven weeks, at $7.40 per week.

TABLE **I.**—GENERAL SOCIAL AND ECONOMIC CONDITION, BY FAMILIES
AND INDIVIDUALS—Continued.

Years in U. S.	Natu- ral- ized.	Profession, trade, or occupation.	Hours of work per week.	Average weekly earn- ings.	Weeks em- ploy- ed.	Total yearly earn- ings.	Sick during year, defective, maimed, or deformed.
7	Yes..	Peddler, fruit (a)..........	(b)	$4.00	a 38	$257	No.
3	......	Housewife...............	......	......	......	......	No.
4	No...	Peddler, fruit (a)..........	(b)	4.00	a 38	257	No.
9	Yes..	Peddler, fruit (a)..........	(b)	4.00	a 38	257	No.
8	......	Peddler, fruit (c)..........	(b)	4.00	c 47	226	No.
4	......	Shoemaker (d)............	(b)	3.00	d 45	187	No.
4	No...	Peddler, fruit............	24	3.00	52	156	No.
4	No...	Peddler, fruit............	24	3.50	52	182	No.
4	No...	Railroad laborer..........	60	6.00	14	84	Finger, loss of one.
4	......	Housewife...............					No.
12	Yes..	Lamplighter...............	17½	9.23	52	480	No.
8	......	Housewife...............					No.
......	......	Scholar..............					No.
......	......	Scholar......					No.
23	Yes..	Foreman, hat factory	60	20.00	51	1,020	Fever, not specified.
15	......	Housewife...............					Childbirth.
15	......	No occupation............					No.
......	......	Scholar..............					No.
......	......	Scholar..............					No.
......	......	Scholar....					No.
......	......	At home.............					No.
......	......	At home.............					No.
......	......	At home.............					No.
⁴⁄₁₂	......	Hat factory employee (e)..	60	9.00	e 17	(b)	No.
16	Yes..	Bone picker (f)............	(b)	1.00	f 32	92	Fever, typhoid.
13	......	Housewife...............					Fever, typhoid.
......	......	Scholar.............					No.
......	......	Scholar.............					No.
17	Yes..	Ragpicker...............	18	3.00	52	156	No.
14	......	Housewife...............					Female complaint.
......	......	Scholar.............					Measles.
......	......	Scholar.............					Measles.
......	......	At home.............					Measles.
15	No...	Merchant, rags	(b)	4.00	52	208	No.
15	......	Housewife...............					No.
15	......	Merchant, rags	(b)	3.00	52	156	No.
......	......	Scholar.............					No.
......	......	At home.............					No.
13	Yes..	Ragpicker...............	30	2.00	52	104	Rheumatism.
13	......	Housewife...............					No.
13	......	Scholar.............					No.
......	......	Scholar.............					No.
......	......	Scholar.............					No.
......	......	At home.............					No.
......	......	At home.............					No.
......	......	At home.............					No.
8	No...	Ragpicker...............	42	3.00	52	156	Throat, inflammation of.
4	......	Housewife... ..					No.
......	......	At home.............					Diarrhea.
......	......	At home.............					No.
13	Yes..	Ragpicker (g).............	(b)	1.00	g 47	77	Throat, inflammation of.
5	......	Housewife...............					Miscarriage; typhoid fever.
16	Yes..	Ragpicker................	36	2.50	45	113	Fever, not specified.
5	......	Housewife...............					Eyes, inflammation of both.
......	......	At home.............					Bowels, inflammation of both; rickets.
⁶⁄₁₂	......	No occupation............					Heart, disease of.
18	No...	Ragpicker................	48	3.00	52	156	No.
10	......	Housewife...............					Childbirth.
......	......	At home.............					No.
......	......	At home.............					No.

e Also worked at other occupation, details not reported.
f Also worked as laborer ten weeks, at $6 per week.
g Also worked as laborer five weeks, at $6 per week.

TABLE I.—GENERAL SOCIAL AND ECONOMIC CONDITION, BY FAMILIES AND INDIVIDUALS—Continued.

Family number.	Relationship to head of family.	Sex.	Age.	Conjugal condition.	Birthplace.	Birthplace of—	
						Father.	Mother.
956	Head	M.	32	Married	Campania	Campania	Campania
	Wife	F.	25	Married	Campania	Campania	Campania
957	Head	M.	33	Married	Campania	Campania	Campania
	Wife	F.	34	Married	Campania	Campania	Campania
	Daughter	F.	6	Single	United States	Campania	Campania
	Daughter	F.	5	Single	United States	Campania	Campania
958	Head	M.	24	Married	Campania	Campania	Campania
	Wife	F.	22	Married	Campania	Campania	Campania
	Son	M.	2	Single	United States	Campania	Campania
959	Head	F.	67	Widowed	Basilicata	Basilicata	Basilicata
960	Head	M.	30	Married	Sicily	Sicily	Sicily
	Wife	F.	28	Married	Sicily	Sicily	Sicily
	Son	M.	9	Single	United States	Sicily	Sicily
	Daughter	F.	8	Single	United States	Sicily	Sicily
	Daughter	F.	6	Single	United States	Sicily	Sicily
	Son	M.	4	Single	United States	Sicily	Sicily
	Son	M.	$\frac{a}{12}$	Single	United States	Sicily	Sicily
961	Head	M.	40	Married	Sicily	Sicily	Sicily
	Wife	F.	36	Married	Sicily	Sicily	Sicily
	Son	M.	5	Single	United States	Sicily	Sicily
962	Head	M.	40	Married	Basilicata	Basilicata	Basilicata
	Wife	F.	38	Married	Basilicata	Basilicata	Basilicata
	Son	M.	13	Single	Basilicata	Basilicata	Basilicata
	Son	M.	12	Single	Basilicata	Basilicata	Basilicata
	Son	M.	8	Single	Basilicata	Basilicata	Basilicata
	Daughter	F.	7	Single	Basilicata	Basilicata	Basilicata
	Daughter	F.	5	Single	United States	Basilicata	Basilicata
	Daughter	F.	3	Single	United States	Basilicata	Basilicata
	Son	M.	1	Single	United States	Basilicata	Basilicata
963	Head	M.	35	Married	Sicily	Sicily	Sicily
	Wife	F.	39	Married	Sicily	Sicily	Sicily
	Son	M.	10	Single	Sicily	Sicily	Sicily
	Daughter	F.	9	Single	Sicily	Sicily	Sicily
	Daughter	F.	8	Single	Sicily	Sicily	Sicily
	Son	M.	5	Single	Sicily	Sicily	Sicily
	Daughter	F.	3	Single	Sicily	Sicily	Sicily
	Daughter	F.	$\frac{6}{12}$	Single	United States	Sicily	Sicily
964	Head	M.	39	Married	Basilicata	Basilicata	Basilicata
	Wife	F.	39	Married	Basilicata	Basilicata	Basilicata
	Son	M.	11	Single	United States	Basilicata	Basilicata
	Son	M.	9	Single	United States	Basilicata	Basilicata
	Son	M.	6	Single	United States	Basilicata	Basilicata
	Daughter	F.	4	Single	United States	Basilicata	Basilicata
	Son	M.	2	Single	United States	Basilicata	Basilicata
965	Head	M.	40	Married	Basilicata	Basilicata	Basilicata
	Wife	F.	38	Married	Basilicata	Basilicata	Basilicata
	Daughter	F.	17	Single	Basilicata	Basilicata	Basilicata
	Son	M.	13	Single	Basilicata	Basilicata	Basilicata
	Daughter	F.	9	Single	United States	Basilicata	Basilicata
	Daughter	F.	7	Single	United States	Basilicata	Basilicata
	Daughter	F.	5	Single	United States	Basilicata	Basilicata
	Son	M.	3	Single	United States	Basilicata	Basilicata
966	Head	M.	26	Married	Sicily	Sicily	Sicily
	Wife	F.	20	Married	Sicily	Sicily	Sicily
	Daughter	F.	$\frac{6}{12}$	Single	United States	Sicily	Sicily
	Father	M.	50	Married	Sicily	Sicily	Sicily
	Brother-in-law	M.	26	Married	Sicily	Sicily	Sicily
	Sister-in-law	F.	20	Married	Sicily	Sicily	Sicily
967	Head	M.	33	Married	Basilicata	Basilicata	Basilicata
	Wife	F.	20	Married	Basilicata	Basilicata	Basilicata
	Son	M.	14	Single	Basilicata	Basilicata	Basilicata

a Also worked as laborer nineteen weeks, at $12 per week.

TABLE I.—GENERAL SOCIAL AND ECONOMIC CONDITION, BY FAMILIES AND INDIVIDUALS—Continued.

Years in U. S.	Naturalized.	Profession, trade, or occupation.	Hours of work per week.	Average weekly earnings.	Weeks employed.	Total yearly earnings,	Sick during year, defective, maimed, or deformed.
12	Yes..	Ragpicker (a)	(b)	$3.00	a 33	$327	No.
10	......	Housewife................					No.
8	Yes..	Ragpicker	(b)	(b)	52	(b)	No.
8	......	Housewife................					No.
......	......	At home.................					No.
......	......	At home.................					No.
14	Yes..	Ragpicker	42	(b)	52	(b)	No.
7	......	Housewife................					No.
......	......	At home.................					No.
4	......	Beggar					No.
10	No...	Candy factory employee...	55	10.50	52	546	No.
10	......	Housewife and merchant, groceries.	(b)	(b)	(b)	(b)	Childbirth.
......	......	Scholar.................					No.
......	......	Scholar.................					No.
......	......	At home.................					No.
......	......	At home.................					No.
......	......	At home.................					No.
7	No...	Peddler, fruit	(b)	3.00	52	156	No.
7	......	Housewife................					Female complaint.
......	......	At home.................					No.
6	Yes..	Sewer digger	60	12.00	9	108	No.
6	......	Housewife................					No.
6	......	Scholar.................					No.
6	......	Scholar.................					No.
6	......	Scholar.................					No.
6	......	Scholar.................					No.
......	......	At home.................					No.
......	......	At home.................					No.
......	......	At home.................					No.
2	No...	Peddler, fruit............	(b)	7.50	39	293	No.
1	......	Housewife................					Childbirth.
1	......	Driver, fruit wagon.......	(b)	(b)	(b)	(b)	No.
1	......	At home.................					No.
1	......	At home.................					No.
1	......	At home.................					No.
1	......	At home.................					No.
......	......	At home.................					No.
12	Yes..	No occupation					No.
12	......	Housewife................					No.
......	......	Scholar.................					No.
......	......	Scholar.................					No.
......	......	Scholar.................					No.
......	......	At home.................					No.
......	......	At home.................					No.
14	Yes..	Laborer..................	60	9.00	13	117	No.
11	......	Housewife................					No.
11	......	Baking powder factory employee.	(b)	4.50	52	234	No.
11	......	Scholar.................					No.
......	......	Scholar.................					No.
......	......	Scholar.................					No.
......	......	At home.................					No.
......	......	At home.................					Pneumonia.
8	No...	Peddler, fruit............	(b)	3.00	39	117	No.
3	......	Housewife................					Childbirth.
......	......	At home.................					No.
4	No...	Peddler, fruit............	(b)	3.00	52	156	No.
4	No...	Peddler, fruit............	(b)	3.00	39	117	No.
3	......	Housework...............					No.
12	No...	Laborer..................	60	10.00	35	350	No.
¾	......	Housewife................					No.
12	......	No occupation					No.

b Not reported.

TABLE I.—GENERAL SOCIAL AND ECONOMIC CONDITION, BY FAMILIES AND INDIVIDUALS—Continued.

Family number.	Relationship to head of family.	Sex.	Age.	Conjugal condition.	Birthplace.	Birthplace of—	
						Father.	Mother.
968	Head	M.	60	Married	Campania	Campania	Campania
	Wife	F.	55	Married	Campania	Campania	Campania
	Son	M.	14	Single	United States	Campania	Campania
	Daughter	F.	13	Single	United States	Campania	Campania
969	Head	M.	33	Married	Campania	Campania	Campania
	Wife	F.	30	Married	Campania	Campania	Campania
	Daughter	F.	5	Single	United States	Campania	Campania
	Daughter	F.	3	Single	United States	Campania	Campania
	Son	M.	₁²⁄₁₂	Single	United States	Campania	Campania
970	Head	M.	30	Married	Campania	Campania	Campania
	Wife	F.	30	Married	Campania	Campania	Campania
	Son	M.	4	Single	United States	Campania	Campania
971	Head	M.	39	Married	Campania	Campania	Campania
	Wife	F.	37	Married	Campania	Campania	Campania
	Daughter	F.	10	Single	United States	Campania	Campania
	Son	M.	8	Single	United States	Campania	Campania
	Daughter	F.	6	Single	United States	Campania	Campania
	Son	M.	4	Single	United States	Campania	Campania
	Son	M.	2	Single	United States	Campania	Campania
	Son	M.	₈⁄₁₂	Single	United States	Campania	Campania
972	Head	M.	38	Married	Campania	Campania	Campania
	Wife	F.	42	Married	Campania	Campania	Campania
973	Head	M.	41	Married	Campania	Campania	Campania
	Wife	F.	27	Married	Campania	Campania	Campania
	Son	M.	9	Single	United States	Campania	Campania
	Stepdaughter	F.	5	Single	United States	Campania	Campania
	Stepdaughter	F.	2	Single	United States	Campania	Campania
974	Head	M.	54	Married	Campania	Campania	Campania
	Wife	F.	54	Married	Campania	Campania	Campania
975	Head	F.	41	Widowed	Sicily	Sicily	Sicily
	Son	M.	17	Single	United States	Sicily	Sicily
	Daughter	F.	16	Single	United States	Sicily	Sicily
	Son	M.	13	Single	United States	Sicily	Sicily
	Son	M.	11	Single	United States	Sicily	Sicily
	Daughter	F.	9	Single	United States	Sicily	Sicily
	Son	M.	7	Single	United States	Sicily	Sicily
976	Head	M.	37	Married	Campania	Campania	Campania
	Wife	F.	22	Married	Campania	Campania	Campania
	Son	M.	7	Single	United States	Campania	Campania
	Daughter	F.	5	Single	United States	Campania	Campania
	Son	M.	3	Single	United States	Campania	Campania
	Son	M.	1	Single	United States	Campania	Campania
977	Head	M.	21	Married	Campania	Campania	Campania
	Wife	F.	25	Married	Campania	Campania	Campania
	Stepdaughter	F.	5	Single	United States	Campania	Campania
	Son	M.	2	Single	United States	Campania	Campania
	Mother	F.	60	Widowed	Campania	Campania	Campania
978	Head	M.	30	Married	Campania	Campania	Campania
	Wife	F.	32	Married	Campania	Campania	Campania
	Daughter	F.	9	Single	Campania	Campania	Campania
	Daughter	F.	6	Single	Campania	Campania	Campania
	Daughter	F.	4	Single	United States	Campania	Campania
	Son	M.	1	Single	United States	Campania	Campania
979	Head	M.	30	Married	Campania	Campania	Campania
	Wife	F.	30	Married	Campania	Campania	Campania
	Daughter	F.	10	Single	Campania	Campania	Campania
	Son	M.	7	Single	Campania	Campania	Campania
	Daughter	F.	₁⁄₁₂	Single	United States	Campania	Campania
980	Head	M.	33	Married	Campania	Campania	Campania
	Wife	F.	32	Married	Campania	Campania	Campania
	Son	M.	8	Single	Campania	Campania	Campania
	Son	M.	4	Single	United States	Campania	Campania

a Not reported.

TABLE **I.**—GENERAL SOCIAL AND ECONOMIC CONDITION, BY FAMILIES AND INDIVIDUALS—Continued.

Years in U.S.	Natu-ral-ized.	Profession, trade, or occupation.	Hours of work per week.	Average weekly earn-ings.	Weeks em-ploy-ed.	Total yearly earn-ings.	Sick during year, defective, maimed, or deformed.
18	Yes..	Laborer.....................	(a)	(a)	(a)	(a)	No.
17	......	Housewife..................					No.
......	......	Scholar....................					No.
......	......	Scholar....................					No.
10	Yes..	Hod carrier...............	48	$9.00	5	$45	No.
6	......	Housewife..................					Childbirth.
......	......	At home....................					No.
......	......	At home....................					No.
......	......	At home.................					No.
6	Yes..	Hod carrier...............	48	9.00	5	45	No.
5	......	Housewife..................					Miscarriage.
......	......	At home....................					No.
17	Yes..	Street sweeper............	48	9.00	22	198	No.
12	......	Housewife..................					Childbirth.
......	......	Scholar....................					No.
......	......	Scholar....................					No.
......	......	Scholar....................					No.
......	......	At home....................					No.
......	......	At home....................					No.
......	......	At home....................					No.
15	Yes..	Laborer....................	(a)	9.00	16	144	No.
10	......	Housewife..................					Rheumatism.
17	Yes..	Hod carrier...............	(a)	9.00	27	243	Injury by accident.
5	......	Housewife..................					No.
......	......	Scholar....................					No.
......	......	At home....................					No.
......	......	At home....................					No.
19	Yes..	Street sweeper............	48	9.00	18	162	No.
19	......	Housewife..................					No.
23	......	Housewife and merchant, feed.	(a)	(a)	52	(a)	No.
......	......	Barber.....................	82	4.00	(a)	(a)	No.
......	......	Housework.................					No.
......	......	Scholar....................					No.
......	......	Scholar....................					No.
......	......	Scholar....................					No.
......	......	Scholar....................					No.
13	Yes..	Stonecutter................	48	24.00	19	456	No.
10	......	Housewife..................					No.
......	......	Scholar....................					No.
......	......	At home....................					No.
......	......	At home....................					No.
......	......	At home....................					No.
9	Yes..	Sewer digger..............	48	9.00	20	180	No.
6	......	Housewife..................					No.
......	......	At home....................					No.
......	......	At home....................					No.
5	......	No occupation..............					No.
10	Yes..	Laborer	48	8.50	20	170	Fever, not specified.
5	......	Housewife..................					Female complaint.
5	......	Scholar....................					No.
5	......	At home....................					No.
......	......	At home....................					No.
......	......	At home....................					No.
6	Yes..	Hod carrier...............	48	9.00	32	288	No.
4	......	Housewife..................					Childbirth.
4	......	Scholar....................					Fever, not specified.
4	......	Scholar....................					Fever, not specified.
......	......	At home....................					No.
11	Yes..	Hod carrier...............	48	9.00	16	144	Lame.
6	......	Housewife..................					No.
6	......	Scholar....................					No.
......	......	At home....................					No.

TABLE I.—GENERAL SOCIAL AND ECONOMIC CONDITION, BY FAMILIES AND INDIVIDUALS—Continued.

Family number.	Relationship to head of family.	Sex.	Age.	Conjugal condition.	Birthplace.	Birthplace of—	
						Father.	Mother.
981	Head	M.	42	Married...	Campania.......	Campania......	Campania......
	Wife	F.	34	Married...	Campania.......	Campania......	Campania......
	Son	M.	17	Single.....	Campania.......	Campania......	Campania......
	Daughter	F.	8	Single	United States...	Campania......	Campania......
	Son	M.	6	Single.....	United States...	Campania......	Campania......
	Daughter	F.	4	Single.....	United States...	Campania......	Campania......
	Son	M.	1	Single.....	United States...	Campania......	Campania......
	Lodger	M.	(b)	Single.....	Campania.......	Campania......	Campania......
982	Head	M.	56	Married...	Campania.......	Campania......	Campania......
	Wife	F.	40	Married...	Campania.......	Campania......	Campania......
	Daughter	F.	16	Single.....	Campania.......	Campania......	Campania......
	Daughter	F.	9	Single.....	United States...	Campania......	Campania......
	Son	M.	6	Single.....	United States...	Campania......	Campania......
	Son	M.	5	Single.....	United States...	Campania......	Campania......
	Son	M.	2	Single.....	United States...	Campania......	Campania......
	Daughter	F.	$\frac{7}{12}$	Single.....	United States...	Campania......	Campania......
983	Head	M.	34	Married...	Campania.......	Campania......	Campania......
	Wife	F.	22	Married...	Campania.......	Campania......	Campania......
	Daughter	F.	5	Single.....	United States...	Campania......	Campania......
	Daughter	F.	3	Single.....	United States...	Campania......	Campania......
	Son	M.	1	Single.....	United States...	Campania......	Campania......
984	Head	M.	29	Single.....	Campania.......	Campania......	Campania......
985	Head	M.	55	Married...	Campania.......	Campania......	Campania......
	Wife	F.	61	Married ..	Campania.......	Campania......	Campania......
986	Head	M.	40	Married...	Campania.......	Campania......	Campania......
	Wife	F.	26	Married...	Campania.......	Campania......	Campania......
	Daughter	F.	10	Single.....	United States...	Campania......	Campania......
	Daughter	F.	6	Single.....	United States...	Campania......	Campania......
	Son	M.	4	Single.....	United States...	Campania......	Campania......
	Son	M.	2	Single.....	United States...	Campania......	Campania......
	Son	M.	$\frac{7}{12}$	Single.....	United States...	Campania......	Campania......
987	Head	M.	54	Married...	Campania.......	Campania......	Campania......
	Wife	F.	47	Married...	Campania.......	Campania......	Campania......
	Son	M.	21	Single.....	Campania.......	Campania......	Campania......
988	Head	M.	39	Married...	Campania.......	Campania......	Campania......
	Wife	F.	35	Married...	Campania.......	Campania......	Campania......
	Son	M.	10	Single.....	Campania.......	Campania......	Campania......
	Daughter	F.	4	Single.....	United States...	Campania......	Campania......
	Son	M.	1	Single.....	United States...	Campania......	Campania......
	Brother-in-law	M.	35	Married...	Campania.......	Campania......	Campania......
	Sister-in-law	F.	31	Married...	Campania.......	Campania......	Campania......
	Nephew	M.	7	Single.....	United States...	Campania......	Campania......
	Nephew	M.	3	Single.....	United States...	Campania......	Campania......
	Nephew	M.	1	Single.....	United States...	Campania......	Campania......
989	Head	M.	55	Married...	Campania.......	Campania......	Campania......
	Wife	F.	45	Married...	Campania.......	Campania......	Campania......
	Daughter	F.	14	Single.....	United States...	Campania......	Campania......
	Daughter	F.	5	Single.....	United States...	Campania......	Campania......
990	Head	M.	40	Married...	Campania.......	Campania......	Campania......
	Wife	F.	26	Married...	Campania.......	Campania......	Campania......
	Son	M.	10	Single.....	United States...	Campania......	Campania......
	Son	M.	9	Single.....	United States...	Campania......	Campania......
	Son	M.	6	Single.....	United States...	Campania......	Campania......
	Daughter	F.	5	Single.....	United States...	Campania......	Campania......
	Son	M.	3	Single.....	United States...	Campania......	Campania......
	Son	M.	1	Single.....	United States...	Campania......	Campania......
	Mother	F.	70	Widowed .	Campania	Campania......	Campania......
991	Head	M.	34	Married...	Campania.......	Campania......	Campania......
	Wife	F.	38	Married...	Campania.......	Campania......	Campania......
	Daughter	F.	16	Single.....	Campania.......	Campania......	Campania......
	Daughter	F.	14	Single.....	Campania.......	Campania......	Campania......
	Daughter	F.	7	Single.....	United States...	Campania......	Campania......
	Son	M.	6	Single.....	United States...	Campania......	Campania......
	Daughter	F.	4	Single.....	United States...	Campania......	Campania......
	Daughter	F.	2	Single.....	United States...	Campania......	Campania......
	Son	M.	1	Single.....	United States...	Campania......	Campania......

a Also worked as hod carrier ten weeks, at $9 per week.

TABLE I.—GENERAL SOCIAL AND ECONOMIC CONDITION, BY FAMILIES AND INDIVIDUALS—Continued.

Years in U. S.	Naturalized.	Profession, trade, or occupation.	Hours of work per week.	Average weekly earnings.	Weeks employed.	Total yearly earnings.	Sick during year, defective, maimed, or deformed.
14	Yes..	Umbrella mender (a)......	(b)	$6.00	a 42	$342	No.
10	......	Housewife.............					No.
7	......	Umbrella mender.........	(b)	6.00	52	312	No.
......	......	Scholar................					No.
......	......	Scholar................					No.
......	......	At home..............					No.
......	......	At home..............					No.
(b)	No...	Umbrella mender.........	(b)	6.00	52	312	No.
13	Yes..	Hod carrier.............	48	8.50	15	128	Fever, not specified.
13	......	Housewife.............					Childbirth.
13	......	No occupation.........					No.
......	......	Scholar................					No.
......	......	Scholar					No.
......	......	At home..............					No.
......	......	At home..............					No.
......	......	At home..............					Harelip.
14	Yes..	Hod carrier.............	48	8.50	20	170	No.
9	......	Housewife.............					Not specified.
......	......	At home..............					No.
......	......	At home..............					No.
......	......	At home..............					No.
8	Yes..	Hod carrier.............	48	8.50	22	187	No.
10	Yes..	Hod carrier.............	48	8.25	15	124	Asthma.
10	......	Housewife.............					No.
14	Yes..	Street sweeper...........	48	9.00	26	234	No.
17	......	Housewife.............					Childbirth.
......	......	Scholar................					No.
......	......	Scholar................					No.
......	......	At home..............					Rickets.
......	......	At home..............					No.
......	......	At home..............					No.
13	Yes..	Street sweeper...........	48	9.00	5	45	No.
9	......	Housewife.............					No.
9	Yes..	Hod carrier.............	48	9.00	15	135	No.
10	Yes..	Hod carrier.............	48	9.00	19	171	No.
9	......	Housewife.............					No.
9	......	Scholar................					No.
......	......	At home..............					No.
......	......	At home..............					No.
10	Yes..	Hod carrier.............	48	9.00	19	171	No.
10	......	Housework.............					No.
......	......	Scholar................					No.
......	......	At home..............					No.
......	......	At home..............					No.
15	Yes..	Artificial flower maker...	(b)	3.00	8	24	No.
15	......	Housewife.............					No.
......	......	Scholar................					Paralysis.
......	......	At home..............					No.
14	Yes..	Hod carrier	48	9.00	24	216	No.
16	......	Housewife.............					No.
......	......	Scholar................					No.
......	......	Scholar................					No.
......	......	Scholar................					No.
......	......	At home..............					No.
......	......	At home..............					No.
......	......	At home..............					No.
11	......	No occupation..........					Fever, not specified.
15	Yes..	Hod carrier.............	48	9.00	26	234	No.
14	......	Housewife.............					No.
14	......	Scholar................					No.
14	......	Scholar................					No.
......	......	Scholar................					No.
......	......	Scholar................					No.
......	......	At home..............					No.
......	......	At home..............					Fever, not specified.
......	......	At home..............					Fever, not specified.

b Not reported.

TABLE **I.**—GENERAL SOCIAL AND ECONOMIC CONDITION, BY FAMILIES AND INDIVIDUALS—Continued.

Family number.	Relationship to head of family.	Sex.	Age.	Conjugal condition.	Birthplace.	Birthplace of—	
						Father.	Mother.
992	Head	M.	40	Married...	Basilicata	Basilicata	Basilicata
	Wife	F.	40	Married...	Basilicata	Basilicata	Basilicata
	Son	M.	11	Single	United States	Basilicata	Basilicata
	Daughter	F.	9	Single	United States	Basilicata	Basilicata
	Daughter	F.	7	Single	United States	Basilicata	Basilicata
	Son	M.	5	Single	United States	Basilicata	Basilicata
	Son	M.	3	Single	United States	Basilicata	Basilicata
	Son	M.	2	Single	United States	Basilicata	Basilicata
993	Head	M.	40	Married...	Campania	Campania	Campania
	Wife	F.	39	Married...	Campania	Campania	Campania
	Daughter	F.	12	Single	United States	Campania	Campania
	Daughter	F.	10	Single	United States	Campania	Campania
	Daughter	F.	8	Single	United States	Campania	Campania
	Son	M.	5	Single	United States	Campania	Campania
	Son	M.	1	Single	United States	Campania	Campania
	Father-in-law	M.	75	Married...	Campania	Campania	Campania
	Mother-in-law	F.	60	Married...	Campania	Campania	Campania
994	Head	M.	29	Married...	Campania	Campania	Campania
	Wife	F.	20	Married...	Campania	Campania	Campania
	Son	M.	5	Single	United States	Campania	Campania
	Daughter	F.	1	Single	United States	Campania	Campania
995	Head	M.	30	Married...	Campania	Campania	Campania
	Wife	F.	26	Married...	Campania	Campania	Campania
	Daughter	F.	4	Single	United States	Campania	Campania
	Daughter	F.	2	Single	United States	Campania	Campania
996	Head	M.	38	Married...	Campania	Campania	Campania
	Wife	F.	34	Married...	Campania	Campania	Campania
	Daughter	F.	8	Single	United States	Campania	Campania
	Son	M.	6	Single	United States	Campania	Campania
	Son	M.	$\frac{7}{12}$	Single	United States	Campania	Campania
997	Head	M.	29	Married...	Campania	Campania	Campania
	Wife	F.	39	Married...	Campania	Campania	Campania
	Stepdaughter	F.	10	Single	United States	Campania	Campania
	Daughter	F.	5	Single	United States	Campania	Campania
	Son	M.	3	Single	United States	Campania	Campania
	Daughter	F.	2	Single	United States	Campania	Campania
	Son	M.	$\frac{7}{12}$	Single	United States	Campania	Campania
	Mother	F.	56	Widowed .	Campania	Campania	Campania
998	Head	M.	27	Married...	Campania	Campania	Campania
	Wife	F.	20	Married...	United States	Campania	Campania
	Son	M.	2	Single	United States	Campania	United States
999	Head	M.	40	Married...	Campania	Campania	Campania
	Wife	F.	40	Married...	Campania	Campania	Campania
	Son	M.	12	Single	Campania	Campania	Campania
	Daughter	F.	8	Single	Campania	Campania	Campania
	Son	M.	$\frac{7}{12}$	Single	United States	Campania	Campania
	Brother-in-law	M.	30	Married...	Campania	Campania	Campania
1000	Head	M.	25	Married...	Campania	Campania	Campania
	Wife	F.	18	Married...	United States	Campania	Campania
	Son	M.	a 2	Single	United States	Campania	United States
1001	Head	F.	32	Widowed .	Abruzzo	Abruzzo	Abruzzo
	Daughter	F.	3	Single	United States	Abruzzo	Abruzzo
1002	Head	M.	30	Married...	Campania	Campania	Campania
	Wife	F.	26	Married...	Campania	Campania	Campania
	Stepson	M.	7	Single	United States	Campania	Campania
	Stepdaughter	F.	5	Single	United States	Campania	Campania
	Stepson	M.	2	Single	United States	Campania	Campania
1003	Head	M.	47	Married...	Campania	Campania	Campania
	Wife	F.	50	Married...	Campania	Campania	Campania
	Brother-in-law	M.	47	Married...	Campania	Campania	Campania
	Brother-in-law	M.	47	Married...	Campania	Campania	Campania
	Sister-in-law	F.	32	Married...	Campania	Campania	Campania
	Nephew	M.	16	Single	Campania	Campania	Campania
	Niece	F.	9	Single	United States	Campania	Campania
	Niece	F.	5	Single	United States	Campania	Campania
	Boarder	M.	24	Single	Campania	Campania	Campania
	Boarder	M.	14	Single	Campania	Campania	Campania

a Not reported.

TABLE **I.**—GENERAL SOCIAL AND ECONOMIC CONDITION, BY FAMILIES AND INDIVIDUALS—Continued.

Years in U.S.	Natu- ral- ized.	Profession, trade, or occupation.	Hours of work per week.	Average weekly earn- ings.	Weeks em- ploy- ed.	Total yearly earn- ings.	Sick during year, defective, maimed, or deformed.
15	Yes..	Laborer	54	$10.50	32	$336	Injury by accident.
12		Housewife					No.
		Scholar					No.
		Scholar					No.
		At home					No.
		At home					No.
		At home					No.
		At home					No.
23	Yes..	Ragpicker	42	4.00	44	176	Kidneys, disease of.
23		Housewife					No.
		Scholar					No.
		Scholar					No.
		Scholar					No.
		At home					No.
		At home					No.
14	No...	No occupation					No.
14		No occupation					No.
9	No...	Ragpicker	36	2.00	52	104	No.
7		Housewife					No.
		At home					No.
		At home					No.
18	Yes..	Ragpicker	48	3.00	52	156	No.
9		Housewife					No.
		At home					Throat, inflammation of.
		At home					No.
14	Yes..	Ragpicker	27	2.00	44	88	Bronchitis.
9		Housewife					Childbirth.
		At home					No.
		At home					No.
		At home					No.
9	Yes..	Shoemaker	72	10.00	52	520	No.
15		Housewife					Childbirth.
		Scholar					Indigestion.
		At home					No.
		At home					No.
		At home					No.
		At home					No.
8		No occupation					No.
8	No...	Ragpicker	36	3.00	52	156	No.
		Housewife					No.
		At home					No.
13	Yes..	Ragpicker	36	2.56	31	79	Wound, gunshot.
2		Housewife					Childbirth.
2		Scholar					No.
2		Scholar					No.
		At home					No.
1	No...	Ragpicker	(a)	2.56	(a)	(a)	No.
16	Yes..	Ragpicker	48	8.00	52	416	No.
		Housewife					No.
		At home					No.
10		Housewife					No.
		At home					No.
5	Yes..	Hod carrier	48	9.00	16	144	Rheumatism.
10		Housewife					No.
		Scholar					No.
		Scholar					No.
		At home					No.
17	No...	Ragpicker	48	5.00	52	260	No.
17		Housewife					No.
14	No...	Merchant, junk	48	(a)	52	(a)	No.
17	No...	Ragpicker	42	5.00	52	260	No.
14		Housework					No.
$\frac{5}{12}$		Ragpicker	42	5.00	21	(a)	No.
		Scholar					No.
		At home					No.
4	No...	Ragpicker	42	(a)	52	(a)	No.
$\frac{1}{12}$		Ragpicker	42	(a)	4	(a)	No.

TABLE **I.**—GENERAL SOCIAL AND ECONOMIC CONDITION, BY FAMILIES AND INDIVIDUALS—Continued.

Family number.	Relationship to head of family.	Sex.	Age.	Conjugal condition.	Birthplace.	Birthplace of— Father.	Birthplace of— Mother.
1004	Head	M.	23	Single	Basilicata	Basilicata	Basilicata
	Father	M.	54	Married	Basilicata	Basilicata	Basilicata
	Mother	F.	54	Married	Basilicata	Basilicata	Basilicata
	Brother	M.	16	Single	Basilicata	Basilicata	Basilicata
1005	Head	M.	34	Married	Basilicata	Basilicata	Basilicata
	Wife	F.	30	Married	Basilicata	Basilicata	Basilicata
	Daughter	F.	8	Single	United States	Basilicata	Basilicata
	Daughter	F.	6	Single	United States	Basilicata	Basilicata
1006	Head	M.	47	Married	Sicily	Sicily	Sicily
	Wife	F.	33	Married	Sicily	Sicily	Sicily
	Daughter	F.	9	Single	United States	Sicily	Sicily
	Son	M.	7	Single	United States	Sicily	Sicily
1007	Head	M.	30	Married	Basilicata	Basilicata	Basilicata
	Wife	F.	26	Married	Basilicata	Basilicata	Basilicata
	Daughter	F.	8	Single	United States	Basilicata	Basilicata
	Daughter	F.	3	Single	United States	Basilicata	Basilicata
1008	Head	M.	29	Married	Basilicata	Basilicata	Basilicata
	Wife	F.	27	Married	Basilicata	Basilicata	Basilicata
	Son	M.	3	Single	United States	Basilicata	Basilicata
	Daughter	F.	2	Single	United States	Basilicata	Basilicata
1009	Head	M.	29	Married	Basilicata	Basilicata	Basilicata
	Wife	F.	23	Married	Basilicata	Basilicata	Basilicata
	Son	M.	8	Single	United States	Basilicata	Basilicata
	Son	M.	3	Single	United States	Basilicata	Basilicata
1010	Head	M.	32	Married	Campania	Campania	Campania
	Wife	F.	29	Married	Campania	Campania	Campania
	Daughter	F.	6	Single	United States	Campania	Campania
	Son	M.	5	Single	United States	Campania	Campania
	Son	M.	3	Single	United States	Campania	Campania
1011	Head	M.	23	Married	Abruzzo	Abruzzo	Abruzzo
	Wife	F.	17	Married	Basilicata	Basilicata	Basilicata
	Son	M.	2	Single	United States	Abruzzo	Basilicata
1012	Head	M.	30	Married	Basilicata	Basilicata	Basilicata
	Wife	F.	30	Married	Basilicata	Basilicata	Basilicata
	Daughter	F.	12	Single	United States	Basilicata	Basilicata
	Daughter	F.	9	Single	United States	Basilicata	Basilicata
1013	Head	M.	38	Married	Basilicata	Basilicata	Basilicata
	Wife	F.	33	Married	Basilicata	Basilicata	Basilicata
	Son	M.	6	Single	United States	Basilicata	Basilicata
	Son	M.	3	Single	United States	Basilicata	Basilicata
	Son	M.	9/12	Single	United States	Basilicata	Basilicata
	Brother-in-law	M.	23	Single	Basilicata	Basilicata	Basilicata
1014	Head	M.	50	Married	Campania	Campania	Campania
	Wife	F.	30	Married	Campania	Campania	Campania
	Son	M.	7	Single	Campania	Campania	Campania
	Son	M.	1	Single	United States	Campania	Campania
1015	Head	M.	32	Married	Calabria	Calabria	Calabria
	Wife	F.	29	Married	Calabria	Calabria	Calabria
	Son	M.	2	Single	Calabria	Calabria	Calabria
1016	Head	M.	30	Married	Abruzzo	Abruzzo	Abruzzo
	Wife	F.	33	Married	Abruzzo	Abruzzo	Abruzzo
	Son	M.	5	Single	United States	Abruzzo	Abruzzo
	Daughter	F.	4	Single	United States	Abruzzo	Abruzzo
	Daughter	F.	2	Single	United States	Abruzzo	Abruzzo
	Lodger	M.	23	Single	Abruzzo	Abruzzo	Abruzzo
	Lodger	M.	25	Married	Abruzzo	Abruzzo	Abruzzo
1017	Head	M.	26	Married	Campania	Campania	Campania
	Wife	F.	25	Married	Campania	Campania	Campania

a Not reported.

TABLE **I.**—GENERAL SOCIAL AND ECONOMIC CONDITION, BY FAMILIES
AND INDIVIDUALS—Continued.

Years in U.S.	Naturalized.	Profession, trade, or occupation.	Hours of work per week.	Average weekly earnings.	Weeks employed.	Total yearly earnings.	Sick during year defective, maimed, or deformed.
11	Yes..	Barber	88	$13.50	52	$702	No.
16	No...	Laborer	60	7.50	12	90	Lame.
5		Housewife					No.
5		Barber	88	7.00	52	364	No.
24	Yes..	Musician	(a)	(a)	52	(a)	No.
9		Housewife and seamstress.	(a)	3.00	(a)	(a)	No.
		Scholar					No.
		At home					No.
21	Yes..	Cigar maker	48	12.00	52	624	Lame.
13		Housewife and glove maker.	(a)	6.50	39	254	No.
		Scholar					No.
		Scholar					No.
12	Yes..	Bootblack	48	3.00	52	156	No.
17		Housewife and pants maker.	(a)	1.50	26	39	No.
		Scholar					No,
		At home					Dyspepsia.
10	No...	Sewer digger	(a)	10.50	30	315	Rheumatism.
8		Housewife					No.
		At home					No.
		At home					No.
10	Yes..	Hod carrier	(a)	10.50	30	315	No.
12		Housewife and pants maker.	(a)	1.80	22	40	No.
		Scholar					No.
		At home					No.
13	Yes..	Street sweeper	(a)	9.00	26	234	No.
8		Housewife					No.
		At home					No.
		At home					Measles.
		At home					No.
9	Yes..	No occupation					No.
6		Housewife and pants maker.	42	3.00	26	78	No.
		At home					Abscess, scrofulous.
15	Yes..	Street sweeper	60	7.50	10	75	No.
12		Housewife					No.
		Scholar					No.
		Scholar					No.
22	Yes..	Ragpicker	30	3.00	52	156	No.
18		Housewife					Childbirth.
		At home					No.
		At home					No.
		At home					Measles.
8	Yes..	Paver	48	8.40	18	151	No.
6	No...	Quarryman	60	7.50	32	240	No.
6		Housewife					No.
6		Scholar					No.
		At home					No.
9	No...	Quarryman	60	7.50	32	240	No.
1½		Housewife					No.
1½		At home					No.
10	Yes..	Quarryman	60	8.10	42	340	Throat, inflammation of.
6		Housewife					No.
		At home					No.
		At home					No.
		At home					No.
8	Yes..	Quarryman	60	8.40	42	353	Injury by accident.
2	No...	Quarryman	60	8.40	42	353	No.
4	No...	Quarryman	60	7.50	22	165	No.
4		Housewife					Childbirth.

TABLE **I.**—GENERAL SOCIAL AND ECONOMIC CONDITION, BY FAMILIES AND INDIVIDUALS—Continued.

Family number.	Relationship to head of family.	Sex.	Age.	Conjugal condition.	Birthplace.	Birthplace of— Father.	Birthplace of— Mother.
1017	Daughter	F.	5	Single	Campania	Campania	Campania
	Son	M.	3	Single	United States	Campania	Campania
	Son	M.	2	Single	United States	Campania	Campania
	Son	M.	$\frac{5}{12}$	Single	United States	Campania	Campania
1018	Head	M.	32	Married	Basilicata	Basilicata	Basilicata
	Wife	F.	32	Married	Basilicata	Basilicata	Basilicata
	Son	M.	12	Single	Basilicata	Basilicata	Basilicata
	Son	M.	7	Single	Basilicata	Basilicata	Basilicata
	Son	M.	2	Single	United States	Basilicata	Basilicata
1019	Head	M.	52	Married	Basilicata	Basilicata	Basilicata
	Wife	F.	49	Married	Basilicata	Basilicata	Basilicata
	Son-in-law	M.	34	Widowed	Basilicata	Basilicata	Basilicata
	Granddaughter	F.	5	Single	United States	Basilicata	Basilicata
1020	Head	M.	43	Widowed	Basilicata	Basilicata	Basilicata
	Mother	F.	70	Widowed	Basilicata	Basilicata	Basilicata
1021	Head	M.	56	Married	Basilicata	Basilicata	Basilicata
	Wife	F.	35	Married	Basilicata	Basilicata	Basilicata
	Daughter	F.	12	Single	United States	Basilicata	Basilicata
	Daughter	F.	5	Single	United States	Basilicata	Basilicata
	Son	M.	3	Single	United States	Basilicata	Basilicata
	Daughter	F.	$\frac{6}{12}$	Single	United States	Basilicata	Basilicata
1022	Head	M.	46	Married	Basilicata	Basilicata	Basilicata
	Wife	F.	46	Married	Basilicata	Basilicata	Basilicata
	Son	M.	20	Single	Basilicata	Basilicata	Basilicata
	Son	M.	14	Single	United States	Basilicata	Basilicata
	Son	M.	10	Single	United States	Basilicata	Basilicata
	Son	M.	7	Single	United States	Basilicata	Basilicata
	Daughter	F.	4	Single	United States	Basilicata	Basilicata
1023	Head	M.	(a)	Married	Basilicata	Basilicata	Basilicata
	Wife	F.	24	Married	Basilicata	Basilicata	Basilicata
	Daughter	F.	3	Single	United States	Basilicata	Basilicata
	Son	M.	$\frac{7}{12}$	Single	United States	Basilicata	Basilicata
1024	Head	M.	55	Married	Basilicata	Basilicata	Basilicata
	Wife	F.	46	Married	Basilicata	Basilicata	Basilicata
	Son	M.	12	Single	United States	Basilicata	Basilicata
	Son	M.	7	Single	United States	Basilicata	Basilicata
	Brother	M.	47	Married	Basilicata	Basilicata	Basilicata
	Nephew	M.	15	Single	Basilicata	Basilicata	Basilicata
1025	Head	M.	37	Married	Basilicata	Basilicata	Basilicata
	Wife	F.	30	Married	Basilicata	Basilicata	Basilicata
	Daughter	F.	9	Single	United States	Basilicata	Basilicata
	Son	M.	7	Single	United States	Basilicata	Basilicata
	Daughter	F.	4	Single	United States	Basilicata	Basilicata
	Daughter	F.	2	Single	United States	Basilicata	Basilicata
1026	Head	M.	37	Married	Basilicata	Basilicata	Basilicata
	Wife	F.	39	Married	Basilicata	Basilicata	Basilicata
	Daughter	F.	11	Single	United States	Basilicata	Basilicata
	Son	M.	10	Single	United States	Basilicata	Basilicata
	Daughter	F.	7	Single	United States	Basilicata	Basilicata
	Daughter	F.	2	Single	United States	Basilicata	Basilicata
1027	Head	M.	30	Married	Sicily	Sicily	Sicily
	Wife	F.	23	Married	Sicily	Sicily	Sicily
	Daughter	F.	3	Single	United States	Sicily	Sicily
	Son	M.	1	Single	United States	Sicily	Sicily
	Boarder	M.	27	Married	Sicily	Sicily	Sicily
	Boarder	F.	20	Single	Sicily	Sicily	Sicily
1028	Head	F.	50	Widowed	Basilicata	Basilicata	Basilicata
	Daughter	F.	22	Single	Basilicata	Basilicata	Basilicata
	Daughter	F.	16	Single	United States	Basilicata	Basilicata
	Daughter	F.	12	Single	United States	Basilicata	Basilicata
	Son	M.	8	Single	United States	Basilicata	Basilicata
1029	Head	M.	35	Married	Abruzzo	Abruzzo	Abruzzo
	Wife	F.	34	Married	Abruzzo	Abruzzo	Abruzzo
	Daughter	F.	9	Single	Abruzzo	Abruzzo	Abruzzo

a Not reported.

TABLE I.—GENERAL SOCIAL AND ECONOMIC CONDITION, BY FAMILIES AND INDIVIDUALS—Continued.

Years in U. S.	Natu-ral-ized.	Profession, trade, or occupation.	Hours of work per week.	Average weekly earn-ings.	Weeks em-ploy-ed.	Total yearly earn-ings.	Sick during year, defective, maimed, or deformed.
4	....	At home....................	....	....	....	....	Diphtheria.
....	....	At home....................	....	....	....	....	Diphtheria.
....	....	At home....................	....	....	....	....	Diphtheria.
....	....	At home....................	....	....	....	....	No.
4	No...	Quarryman	62	$7.50	20	$150	Pneumonia.
4	....	Housewife	....	....	....	....	No.
4	....	No occupation	....	....	....	....	No.
4	....	At home....................	....	....	....	....	No.
....	....	At home....................	....	....	....	....	Bronchitis.
15	Yes..	Quarryman	60	7.50	22	165	No.
10	....	Housewife	....	....	....	....	No.
12	Yes..	Quarryman	60	7.50	22	165	No.
....	....	At home....................	....	....	....	....	No.
12	Yes..	Sewer digger	60	8.40	27	227	Injury by accident.
12	....	Housewife	....	....	....	....	No.
24	Yes..	No occupation	....	....	....	....	Pneumonia.
13	....	Housewife	....	....	....	....	Childbirth.
....	....	Scholar	....	....	....	....	No.
....	....	At home....................	....	....	....	....	No.
....	....	At home....................	....	....	....	....	No.
....	....	At home....................	....	....	....	....	No.
17	Yes..	Sewer digger	48	12.00	4	48	Lame.
15	....	Housewife	....	....	....	....	No.
15	....	Sewer digger	48	12.00	6	72	No.
....	....	Scholar	....	....	....	....	No.
....	....	Scholar	....	....	....	....	No.
....	....	At home....................	....	....	....	....	No.
....	....	At home....................	....	....	....	....	No.
6	Yes..	Quarryman	54	7.50	22	165	No.
5	....	Housewife	....	....	....	....	Childbirth.
....	....	At home....................	....	....	....	....	No.
....	....	At home....................	....	....	....	....	No.
15	No...	Candy factory employee...	(a)	7.50	52	390	No.
13	....	Housewife	....	....	....	....	Rheumatism.
....	....	No occupation	....	....	....	....	No.
....	....	Scholar	....	....	....	....	No.
8	No...	Candy factory employee...	(a)	7.20	52	374	Hip-joint disease.
5	....	Scholar	....	....	....	....	No.
15	No...	No occupation	....	....	....	....	No.
10	....	Housewife	....	....	....	....	No.
....	....	Scholar	....	....	....	....	No.
....	....	At home....................	....	....	....	....	Feeble-minded.
....	....	At home....................	....	....	....	....	No.
....	....	At home....................	....	....	....	....	Measles.
15	No...	Hod carrier	54	9.00	20	180	No.
14	....	Housewife	....	....	....	....	No.
....	....	Scholar	....	....	....	....	No.
....	....	Scholar	....	....	....	....	No.
....	....	Scholar	....	....	....	....	Croup.
....	....	At home....................	....	....	....	....	No.
6	Yes..	Peddler, fruit	(a)	(a)	52	(a)	No.
6	....	Housewife	....	....	....	....	No.
....	....	At home....................	....	....	....	....	No.
....	....	At home....................	....	....	....	....	No.
9	Yes..	Peddler, fruit	(a)	(a)	52	(a)	No.
4	....	No occupation	....	....	....	....	No.
20	....	Housewife	....	....	....	....	Bronchitis.
20	....	Pants maker...............	(a)	5.00	52	260	No.
....	....	Pants maker...............	(a)	4.50	52	234	No.
....	....	Scholar	....	....	....	....	No.
....	....	Scholar	....	....	....	....	No.
11	Yes..	Quarryman	(a)	7.50	30	225	No.
7	....	Housewife	....	....	....	....	Eye, inflammation of one.
7	....	Scholar	....	....	....	....	No.

TABLE **I.**—GENERAL SOCIAL AND ECONOMIC CONDITION, BY FAMILIES
AND INDIVIDUALS—Continued.

Family number.	Relationship to head of family.	Sex.	Age.	Conjugal condition.	Birthplace.	Birthplace of— Father.	Birthplace of— Mother.
1030	Head	M.	42	Married...	Basilicata	Basilicata	Basilicata
	Wife	F.	26	Married...	Basilicata	Basilicata	Basilicata
	Daughter	F.	5	Single	United States	Basilicata	Basilicata
	Daughter	F.	3	Single	United States	Basilicata	Basilicata
	Daughter	F.	2	Single	United States	Basilicata	Basilicata
1031	Head	M.	40	Married...	Campania	Campania	Campania
	Wife	F.	38	Married...	Campania	Campania	Campania
	Daughter	F.	12	Single	United States	Campania	Campania
	Daughter	F.	10	Single	United States	Campania	Campania
	Daughter	F.	8	Single	United States	Campania	Campania
	Son	M.	3	Single	United States	Campania	Campania
	Daughter	F.	2	Single	United States	Campania	Campania
1032	Head	M.	35	Married...	Calabria	Calabria	Calabria
1033	Head	M.	28	Married...	Campania	Campania	Campania
	Wife	F.	30	Married...	Campania	Campania	Campania
	Stepdaughter	F.	9	Single	Campania	Campania	Campania
	Daughter	F.	3	Single	United States	Campania	Campania
	Son	M.	$\frac{6}{12}$	Single	United States	Campania	Campania
1034	Head	M.	39	Married...	Campania	Campania	Campania
	Wife	F.	33	Married...	Campania	Campania	Campania
	Daughter	F.	5	Single	United States	Campania	Campania
	Son	M.	2	Single	United States	Campania	Campania
1035	Head	M.	33	Married...	Campania	Campania	Campania
	Wife	F.	30	Married...	Campania	Campania	Campania
	Daughter	F.	9	Single	United States	Campania	Campania
	Daughter	F.	5	Single	United States	Campania	Campania
	Daughter	F.	3	Single	United States	Campania	Campania
	Son	M.	2	Single	United States	Campania	Campania
	Son	M.	$\frac{3}{12}$	Single	United States	Campania	Campania
	Lodger	M.	70	Single	Campania	Campania	Campania
1036	Head	M.	48	Married...	Sicily	Sicily	Sicily
	Wife	F.	38	Married...	Sicily	Sicily	Sicily
	Son	M.	14	Single	Sicily	Sicily	Sicily
	Son	M.	13	Single	Sicily	Sicily	Sicily
1037	Head	M.	44	Married...	Basilicata	Basilicata	Basilicata
	Wife	F.	44	Married...	Basilicata	Basilicata	Basilicata
	Son	M.	16	Single.	Basilicata	Basilicata	Basilicata
	Daughter	F.	5	Single	United States	Basilicata	Basilicata
1038	Head	M.	32	Married...	Basilicata	Basilicata	Basilicata
	Wife	F.	30	Married...	Basilicata	Basilicata	Basilicata
	Daughter	F.	5	Single	United States	Basilicata	Basilicata
	Daughter	F.	1	Single	United States	Basilicata	Basilicata
1039	Head	M.	28	Married...	Basilicata	Basilicata	Basilicata
	Wife	F.	25	Married...	Basilicata	Basilicata	Basilicata
	Son	M.	5	Single	United States	Basilicata	Basilicata
	Son	M.	2	Single	United States	Basilicata	Basilicata
	Daughter	F.	$\frac{1}{12}$	Single	United States	Basilicata	Basilicata
1040	Head	M.	24	Married...	Basilicata	Basilicata	Basilicata
	Wife	F.	24	Married...	Basilicata	Basilicata	Basilicata
1041	Head	M.	35	Married...	Sicily	Sicily	Sicily
	Wife	F.	30	Married...	Sicily	Sicily	Sicily
	Daughter	F.	10	Single	Sicily	Sicily	Sicily
	Son	M.	7	Single	Sicily	Sicily	Sicily
	Son	M.	4	Single	Sicily	Sicily	Sicily
1042	Head	M.	50	Married...	Basilicata	Basilicata	Basilicata
	Wife	F.	47	Married...	Basilicata	Basilicata	Basilicata
	Son	M.	23	Single	Basilicata	Basilicata	Basilicata
	Son	M.	18	Single	Basilicata	Basilicata	Basilicata
	Daughter	F.	13	Single	Basilicata	Basilicata	Basilicata
	Daughter	F.	10	Single	Basilicata	Basilicata	Basilicata

a Not reported.

TABLE **I.**—GENERAL SOCIAL AND ECONOMIC CONDITION, BY FAMILIES AND INDIVIDUALS—Continued.

Years in U. S.	Natu- ral- ized.	Profession, trade, or occupation.	Hours of work per week.	Average weekly earn- ings.	Weeks em- ploy- ed.	Total yearly earn- ings.	Sick during year, defective, maimed, or deformed.
16	Yes..	Quarryman	60	$7.50	27	$203	No.
9	......	Housewife and merchant, groceries.	(a)	(a)	20	(a)	No.
......	......	At home					No.
......	......	At home					No.
......	......	At home					Bronchitis.
15	Yes..	Quarryman	60	7.50	27	203	Vertigo.
13	......	Housewife					No.
......	......	Scholar .					No.
......	......	Scholar .					No.
......	......	Scholar .					No.
......	......	At home					Fever, not specified.
......	......	At home					Fever, not specified.
4	No...	Quarryman	60	8.00	39	312	No.
3	No...	Quarryman	(a)	7.25	36	261	No.
3	......	Housewife					Childbirth.
3	......	Scholar .					No.
......	......	At home .					No.
......	......	At home .					No.
14	Yes..	Quarryman	60	7.75	37	287	No.
10	......	Housewife					Consumption.
......	......	At home					No.
......	......	At home					No.
15	Yes..	No occupation					No.
10	......	Housewife					Childbirth; bronchitis.
......	......	Scholar					No.
......	......	At home					No.
......	......	At home					No.
......	......	At home					No.
......	......	At home					No.
17	No...	Rag picker...............	(a)	1.25	(a)	(a)	No.
13	No...	Peddler, fruit............	(a)	1.20	52	62	No.
7	......	Housewife					No.
7	......	Scholar and peddler, fruit.	(a)	6.00	13	78	No.
7	......	Scholar and peddler, fruit.	(a)	6.00	13	78	No.
12	Yes..	Street sweeper............	60	7.50	30	225	No.
9	......	Housewife and pants fin- isher.	(a)	1.25	13	16	No.
9	......	Elevator tender (b)	84	(a)	b 22	(a)	Hip-joint disease.
......	......	At home					Rickets.
8	Yes..	Shoemaker................	60	9.00	13	117	No.
7	......	Housewife					No.
......	......	At home					No.
......	......	At home					No.
10	Yes..	Shoemaker................	60	6.00	13	78	No.
6	......	Housewife					Childbirth.
......	......	At home					No.
......	......	At home					No.
......	......	At home					No.
8	Yes..	Laborer..................	60	7.50	8	60	No.
4	......	Housewife					Female complaint.
6	No...	Peddler, fruit............	(a)	9.00	52	468	No.
1	......	Housewife					No.
1	......	No occupation					No.
1	......	At home					No.
1	......	At home					No.
10	Yes..	Retired					No.
7	......	Housewife					No.
7	Yes..	Street sweeper............	60	7.50	17	128	No.
7	......	Laborer...............	(a)	(a)	52	(a)	No.
7	......	Bootblack	(a)	2.80	(a)	(a)	No.
7	......	Scholar					No.

b Also worked as spring factory employee four weeks, at $4 per week,

TABLE I.—GENERAL SOCIAL AND ECONOMIC CONDITION, BY FAMILIES
AND INDIVIDUALS—Continued.

Family number.	Relationship to head of family.	Sex.	Age.	Conjugal condition.	Birthplace.	Birthplace of—	
						Father.	Mother.
1043	Head	M.	42	Married	Campania	Campania	Campania
	Wife	F.	50	Married	Campania	Campania	Campania
	Son	M.	10	Single	Campania	Campania	Campania
1044	Head	M.	30	Married	Liguria	Liguria	Liguria
	Wife	F.	24	Married	United States	Liguria	Liguria
	Daughter	F.	13	Single	United States	Liguria	Liguria
	Son	M.	8	Single	United States	Liguria	Liguria
	Daughter	F.	$\frac{5}{12}$	Single	United States	Liguria	United States
1045	Head	F.	60	Widowed	Sicily	Sicily	Sicily
	Daughter	F.	29	Married	Sicily	Sicily	Sicily
	Son	M.	18	Single	Sicily	Sicily	Sicily
	Son-in-law	M.	34	Married	Sicily	Sicily	Sicily
1046	Head	M.	30	Married	Sicily	Sicily	Sicily
	Wife	F.	32	Married	Sicily	Sicily	Sicily
	Daughter	F.	3	Single	United States	Sicily	Sicily
	Son	M.	1	Single	United States	Sicily	Sicily
1047	Head	M.	40	Married	Sicily	Sicily	Sicily
	Wife	F.	36	Married	Sicily	Sicily	Sicily
	Son	M.	13	Single	Sicily	Sicily	Sicily
	Daughter	F.	11	Single	United States	Sicily	Sicily
	Daughter	F.	9	Single	United States	Sicily	Sicily
	Son	M.	7	Single	United States	Sicily	Sicily
	Daughter	F.	3	Single	United States	Sicily	Sicily
	Daughter	F.	$\frac{1}{12}$	Single	United States	Sicily	Sicily
1048	Head	M.	35	Married	Sicily	Sicily	Sicily
	Wife	F.	31	Married	Sicily	Sicily	Sicily
	Son	M.	10	Single	Sicily	Sicily	Sicily
	Daughter	F.	6	Single	Sicily	Sicily	Sicily
	Daughter	F.	3	Single	United States	Sicily	Sicily
	Daughter	F.	1	Single	United States	Sicily	Sicily
1049	Head	M.	34	Married	Calabria	Calabria	Calabria
	Wife	F.	22	Married	Basilicata	Basilicata	Basilicata
	Daughter	F.	6	Single	United States	Calabria	Basilicata
	Daughter	F.	4	Single	United States	Calabria	Basilicata
	Son	M.	2	Single	United States	Calabria	Basilicata
1050	Head	M.	28	Married	Calabria	Calabria	Calabria
	Wife	F.	23	Married	Calabria	Calabria	Calabria
	Daughter	F.	2	Single	United States	Calabria	Calabria
	Son	M.	$\frac{8}{12}$	Single	United States	Calabria	Calabria
1051	Head	M.	33	Married	Calabria	Calabria	Calabria
	Wife	F.	23	Married	Calabria	Calabria	Calabria
	Son	M.	3	Single	United States	Calabria	Calabria
	Daughter	F.	2	Single	United States	Calabria	Calabria
	Son	M.	1	Single	United States	Calabria	Calabria
1052	Head	M.	33	Married	Calabria	Calabria	Calabria
	Wife	F.	26	Married	Calabria	Calabria	Calabria
	Daughter	F.	$\frac{1}{12}$	Single	United States	Calabria	Calabria
1053	Head	M.	40	Married	Calabria	Calabria	Calabria
	Wife	F.	36	Married	Calabria	Calabria	Calabria
	Son	M.	15	Single	Calabria	Calabria	Calabria
	Son	M.	11	Single	Calabria	Calabria	Calabria
	Son	M.	$\frac{6}{12}$	Single	United States	Calabria	Calabria
1054	Head	M.	30	Married	Calabria	Calabria	Calabria
	Wife	F.	23	Married	Calabria	Calabria	Calabria
	Lodger	M.	30	Single	Calabria	Calabria	Calabria
1055	Head	M.	30	Married	Calabria	Calabria	Calabria
	Wife	F.	21	Married	Calabria	Calabria	Calabria
	Son	M.	6	Single	United States	Calabria	Calabria
	Daughter	F.	4	Single	United States	Calabria	Calabria
	Daughter	F.	2	Single	United States	Calabria	Calabria
	Daughter	F.	$\frac{5}{12}$	Single	United States	Calabria	Calabria

a Not reported.   b Sick, disease not specified.

TABLE **I.**—GENERAL SOCIAL AND ECONOMIC CONDITION, BY FAMILIES
AND INDIVIDUALS—Continued.

Years in U. S.	Natu-ral-ized.	Profession, trade, or occupation.	Hours of work per week.	Average weekly earnings.	Weeks employ-ed.	Total yearly earnings.	Sick during year, defective, maimed, or deformed.
6	Yes..	Barber..................	(a)	(a)	52	(a)	No.
5	....	Housewife................	....	....	....	....	Deaf.
5	....	Scholar..................	....	....	....	....	No.
25	Yes..	Merchant, fruit...........	60	$9.00	13	$117	No.
....	....	Housewife................	....	....	....	....	Childbirth.
....	....	Scholar..................	....	....	....	....	No.
....	....	Scholar..................	....	....	....	....	No.
....	....	At home.................	....	....	....	....	No.
3	....	Washerwoman	(a)	2.00	52	104	No.
7	....	Housewife................	....	....	....	....	Miscarriage.
5	....	Driver...................	(a)	(a)	(a)	(a)	No.
7	Yes..	Peddler, fruit.............	(a)	(a)	(a)	(a)	No.
11	Yes..	Painter..................	60	12.00	17	204	No.
6	....	Housewife................	....	....	....	....	Miscarriage.
....	....	At home.................	....	....	....	....	No.
....	....	At home.................	....	....	....	....	No.
12	No...	Peddler, fruit.............	(a)	6.00	39	234	(b)
12	....	Housewife................	....	....	....	....	Childbirth.
12	....	Driver...................	(a)	(a)	(a)	(a)	No.
....	....	Scholar..................	....	....	....	....	No.
....	....	Scholar..................	....	....	....	....	No.
....	....	Scholar..................	....	....	....	....	No.
....	....	At home.................	....	....	....	....	No.
....	....	At home.................	....	....	....	....	No.
7	No...	Peddler, fruit (c)	(a)	(a)	c 32	(a)	No.
5	....	Housewife................	....	....	....	....	No.
5	....	Driver...................	(a)	(a)	32	(a)	No.
5	....	At home............. ...	....	....	....	....	Glands, scrofulous; loss of one thumb.
....	....	At home.................	....	....	....	....	Rickets; loss of one eye.
....	....	At home.................	....	....	....	....	Spine, disease of; crippled.
8	Yes..	Railroad laborer..........	60	6.60	35	231	No.
16	....	Housewife................	....	....	....	....	No.
....	....	At home.................	....	....	....	....	No.
....	....	At home.................	....	....	....	....	No.
....	....	At home.................	....	....	....	....	No.
3	No...	Railroad laborer..........	60	6.60	22	145	No.
3	....	Housewife................	....	....	....	....	Childbirth.
....	....	At home.................	....	....	....	....	Dyspepsia.
....	....	At home.................	....	....	....	....	No.
10	No...	Railroad laborer..........	60	6.60	52	343	No.
6	....	Housewife................	....	....	....	....	No.
....	....	At home.................	....	....	....	....	No.
....	....	At home.................	....	....	....	....	No.
....	....	At home.................	....	....	....	....	No.
1	No...	Railroad laborer..........	60	6.60	35	231	No.
1	....	Housewife................	....	....	....	....	Childbirth.
....	....	At home.................	....	....	....	....	No.
10	No...	Railroad laborer..........	60	6.60	52	343	No.
3	....	Housewife................	....	....	....	....	Childbirth.
3	....	Scholar..................	....	....	....	....	No.
⅟₂	....	No occupation............	....	....	....	....	No.
....	....	At home.................	....	....	....	....	No.
6	No...	Railroad laborer..........	60	6.60	52	343	No.
6	....	Housewife................	....	....	....	....	No.
8	No...	Railroad laborer..........	60	6.60	52	343	No.
10	Yes..	Lamplighter..............	56	7.00	52	364	No.
10	....	Housewife................	....	....	....	....	Childbirth; female com-plaint.
....	....	At home.................	....	....	....	....	No.
....	....	At home.................	....	....	....	....	No.
....	....	At home.................	....	....	....	....	No.
....	....	At home.................	....	....	....	....	No.

c Also worked as laborer seven weeks, at $7.50 per week.

TABLE **I.**—GENERAL SOCIAL AND ECONOMIC CONDITION, BY FAMILIES AND INDIVIDUALS—Continued.

Family number.	Relationship to head of family.	Sex.	Age.	Conjugal condition.	Birthplace	Birthplace of— Father.	Birthplace of— Mother.
1056	Head	M.	32	Married	Venetia	Venetia	Venetia
	Wife	F.	23	Married	Venetia	Venetia	Venetia
	Son	M.	2	Single	United States	Venetia	Venetia
	Daughter	F.	1½	Single	United States	Venetia	Venetia
	Cousin	M.	25	Single	Venetia	Venetia	Venetia
	Lodger	M.	25	Single	Venetia	Venetia	Venetia
	Lodger	M.	40	Single	Venetia	Venetia	Venetia
	Lodger	M.	21	Single	Venetia	Venetia	Venetia
1057	Cooperative	M.	22	Single	Venetia	Venetia	Venetia
	Cooperative	M.	34	Married	Venetia	Venetia	Venetia
1058	Head	M.	44	Married	Basilicata	Basilicata	Basilicata
	Wife	F.	37	Married	Basilicata	Basilicata	Basilicata
	Son	M.	9	Single	United States	Basilicata	Basilicata
	Daughter	F.	7	Single	United States	Basilicata	Basilicata
	Son	M.	4	Single	United States	Basilicata	Basilicata
	Daughter	F.	7/12	Single	United States	Basilicata	Basilicata
1059	Head	M.	35	Married	Basilicata	Basilicata	Basilicata
	Wife	F.	27	Married	Basilicata	Basilicata	Basilicata
	Son	M.	10	Single	Basilicata	Basilicata	Basilicata
	Daughter	F.	8	Single	Basilicata	Basilicata	Basilicata
	Daughter	F.	2	Single	United States	Basilicata	Basilicata
1060	Head	M.	70	Married	Basilicata	Basilicata	Basilicata
	Wife	F.	66	Married	Basilicata	Basilicata	Basilicata
1061	Head	M.	40	Married	Basilicata	Basilicata	Basilicata
	Wife	F.	35	Married	Basilicata	Basilicata	Basilicata
	Son	M.	10	Single	United States	Basilicata	Basilicata
	Son	M.	7	Single	United States	Basilicata	Basilicata
	Daughter	F.	4	Single	United States	Basilicata	Basilicata
1062	Head	M.	34	Married	Tuscany	Tuscany	Tuscany
	Wife	F.	43	Married	Tuscany	Tuscany	Tuscany
	Son	M.	10	Single	United States	Tuscany	Tuscany
	Daughter	F.	2	Single	United States	Tuscany	Tuscany
1063	Head	M.	68	Married	Basilicata	Basilicata	Basilicata
	Wife	F.	53	Married	Basilicata	Basilicata	Basilicata
	Son	M.	14	Single	Basilicata	Basilicata	Basilicata
	Daughter	F.	10	Single	Basilicata	Basilicata	Basilicata
	Son	M.	6	Single	Basilicata	Basilicata	Basilicata
1064	Head	M.	39	Married	Basilicata	Basilicata	Basilicata
	Wife	F.	28	Married	Basilicata	Basilicata	Basilicata
	Son	M.	8/12	Single	United States	Basilicata	Basilicata
1065	Head	M.	45	Married	Basilicata	Basilicata	Basilicata
	Wife	F.	45	Married	Basilicata	Basilicata	Basilicata
	Son	M.	19	Single	Basilicata	Basilicata	Basilicata
	Son	M.	14	Single	Basilicata	Basilicata	Basilicata
	Son	M.	7	Single	Basilicata	Basilicata	Basilicata
	Daughter	F.	6	Single	Basilicata	Basilicata	Basilicata
	Daughter	F.	4	Single	United States	Basilicata	Basilicata
	Daughter	F.	2	Single	United States	Basilicata	Basilicata
1066	Head	M.	30	Married	Basilicata	Basilicata	Basilicata
	Wife	F.	21	Married	Basilicata	Basilicata	Basilicata
	Daughter	F.	2	Single	United States	Basilicata	Basilicata
	Son	M.	1/12	Single	United States	Basilicata	Basilicata
1067	Cooperative	M.	55	Married	Calabria	Calabria	Calabria
	Cooperative	M.	33	Single	Calabria	Calabria	Calabria
	Cooperative	M.	26	Single	Calabria	Calabria	Calabria
	Cooperative	M.	31	Married	Calabria	Calabria	Calabria
1068	Cooperative	M.	32	Single	Calabria	Calabria	Calabria
	Cooperative	M.	32	Single	Calabria	Calabria	Calabria
	Cooperative	M.	34	Married	Calabria	Calabria	Calabria
	Cooperative	M.	42	Married	Calabria	Calabria	Calabria
	Cooperative	M.	21	Single	Calabria	Calabria	Calabria

a Not reported.

TABLE **I.**—GENERAL SOCIAL AND ECONOMIC CONDITION, BY FAMILIES AND INDIVIDUALS—Continued.

Years in U.S.	Naturalized.	Profession, trade, or occupation.	Hours of work per week.	Average weekly earnings.	Weeks employed.	Total yearly earnings.	Sick during year, defective, maimed, or deformed.
7	No...	Greenhouse employee.....	60	$7.80	16	$125	No.
3	......	Housewife................	......	....	......	......	Childbirth.
......	......	At home.................	......	....	......	......	No.
......	......	At home.................	......	....	......	......	No.
3	No...	Iron foundry employee....	60	8.40	22	185	Injury by accident.
5	No...	Terra cotta factory employee.	60	7.80	18	140	Dyspepsia.
15	No...	Brickyard employee......	60	9.00	12	108	No.
3	No...	Iron foundry employee....	60	8.40	12	101	No.
3	No...	Sewer digger.............	60	10.50	22	231	No.
3	No...	Sewer digger.............	60	10.50	19	200	No.
13	No...	Organ grinder	66	3.00	52	156	No.
10	......	Housewife................	......	....	......	......	Childbirth.
......	......	At home.................	......	....	......	......	No.
......	......	At home.................	......	....	......	......	No.
......	......	At home.................	......	....	......	......	Measles.
......	......	At home.................	......	....	......	......	No.
5	No...	Hod carrier..............	48	9.00	12	108	No.
4	......	Housewife................	......	....	......	......	Bronchitis.
4	......	Scholar	......	....	......	......	No.
4	......	At home.................	......	....	......	......	No.
......	......	At home.................	......	....	......	......	Convulsions.
5	No...	Beggar	......	....	......	......	Rupture.
5	......	Beggar	......	....	......	......	Rheumatism.
10	No...	Musician	(a)	3.00	52	156	No.
10	......	Housewife and pants maker.	36	2.00	26	52	No.
......	......	Scholar	......	....	......	......	Fever, not specified.
......	......	Scholar	......	....	......	......	No.
......	......	At home.................	......	....	......	......	No.
11	No...	Expressman	(a)	3.00	52	156	No.
11	......	Housewife................	......	....	......	......	Pneumonia.
......	......	Scholar	......	....	......	......	No.
......	......	At home.................	......	....	......	......	No.
6	No...	Hod carrier..............	48	9.00	28	252	Bronchitis.
6	......	Housewife................	......	....	......	......	No.
6	......	Musician	18	2.00	52	104	No.
6	......	Scholar	......	....	......	......	No.
6	......	At home.................	......	....	......	......	No.
4	No...	Musician	18	(a)	52	(a)	No.
4	......	Housewife and pants maker.	(a)	1.50	(a)	(a)	Childbirth
......	......	At home.................	......	....	......	......	No.
4	No...	Organ grinder	48	2.50	52	130	No.
4	......	Housewife and pants maker.	36	1.50	26	39	No.
4	......	Musician	18	(a)	52	(a)	No.
4	......	Musician	18	(a)	52	(a)	No.
4	......	Scholar	......	....	......	......	No.
4	......	At home.................	......	....	......	......	Rickets.
......	......	At home.................	......	....	......	......	No.
12	Yes..	Lime burner..............	(a)	7.50	10	75	No.
4	......	Housewife................	......	....	......	......	Childbirth.
......	......	At home.................	......	....	......	......	No.
......	......	At home.................	......	....	......	......	No.
8	No...	Lime burner..............	84	6.00	24	144	Fever, typhoid.
8	Yes..	Lime burner..............	84	6.00	24	144	No.
8	Yes..	Lime burner..............	84	6.00	24	144	No.
1	No...	Quarryman	(a)	7.50	10	75	No.
3	No...	Lime burner..............	(a)	7.50	27	203	No.
8	Yes..	Lime burner..............	(a)	7.50	19	143	No.
6	No...	Lime burner..............	(a)	7.50	30	225	No.
3	No...	Lime burner..............	(a)	7.50	43	323	No.
5	Yes..	Lime burner..............	(a)	7.50	30	225	No.

TABLE **I.**—GENERAL SOCIAL AND ECONOMIC CONDITION, BY FAMILIES AND INDIVIDUALS—Continued.

Family number.	Relationship to head of family.	Sex.	Age.	Conjugal condition.	Birthplace.	Birthplace of—	
						Father.	Mother.
1069	Head	M.	30	Single	Sicily	Sicily	Sicily
1070	Head	M.	43	Married	Calabria	Calabria	Calabria
	Wife	F.	39	Married	Calabria	Calabria	Calabria
	Son	M.	16	Single	Calabria	Calabria	Calabria
	Daughter	F.	14	Single	Calabria	Calabria	Calabria
	Daughter	F.	8	Single	United States	Calabria	Calabria
	Son	M.	6	Single	United States	Calabria	Calabria
	Daughter	F.	1	Single	United States	Calabria	Calabria
1071	Head	M.	42	Married	Sicily	Sicily	Sicily
	Wife	F.	41	Married	Sicily	Sicily	Sicily
	Son	M.	18	Single	Sicily	Sicily	Sicily
	Son	M.	12	Single	Sicily	Sicily	Sicily
1072	Head	M.	22	Married	Sicily	Sicily	Sicily
	Wife	F.	17	Married	Sicily	Sicily	Sicily
1073	Head	M.	35	Married	Sicily	Sicily	Sicily
	Wife	F.	27	Married	Sicily	Sicily	Sicily
	Daughter	F.	5	Single	United States	Sicily	Sicily
	Son	M.	2	Single	United States	Sicily	Sicily
	Son	M.	$\frac{1}{12}$	Single	United States	Sicily	Sicily
1074	Head	M.	48	Married	Sicily	Sicily	Sicily
	Wife	F.	44	Married	Sicily	Sicily	Sicily
	Son	M.	16	Single	Sicily	Sicily	Sicily
1075	Head	M.	35	Married	Sicily	Sicily	Sicily
	Wife	F.	35	Married	Sicily	Sicily	Sicily
	Daughter	F.	9	Single	Sicily	Sicily	Sicily
	Son	M.	5	Single	United States	Sicily	Sicily
	Son	M.	3	Single	United States	Sicily	Sicily
	Daughter	F.	1	Single	United States	Sicily	Sicily
1076	Head	M.	29	Married	Calabria	Calabria	Calabria
	Wife	F.	35	Married	Calabria	Calabria	Calabria
	Daughter	F.	7	Single	Calabria	Calabria	Calabria
	Daughter	F.	5	Single	United States	Calabria	Calabria
	Daughter	F.	2	Single	United States	Calabria	Calabria
1077	Head	M.	39	Married	Campania	Campania	Campania
	Wife	F.	36	Married	Campania	Campania	Campania
	Daughter	F.	14	Single	United States	Campania	Campania
	Daughter	F.	12	Single	United States	Campania	Campania
	Son	M.	9	Single	United States	Campania	Campania
	Son	M.	7	Single	United States	Campania	Campania
	Daughter	F.	5	Single	United States	Campania	Campania
	Son	M.	2	Single	United States	Campania	Campania
1078	Head	M.	34	Married	Campania	Campania	Campania
	Wife	F.	35	Married	Campania	Campania	Campania
	Daughter	F.	7	Single	United States	Campania	Campania
	Son	M.	1	Single	United States	Campania	Campania
1079	Head	M.	37	Married	Campania	Campania	Campania
	Wife	F.	37	Married	Campania	Campania	Campania
	Son	M.	12	Single	United States	Campania	Campania
	Daughter	F.	10	Single	United States	Campania	Campania
	Daughter	F.	9	Single	United States	Campania	Campania
	Daughter	F.	6	Single	United States	Campania	Campania
	Daughter	F.	4	Single	United States	Campania	Campania
1080	Head	M.	35	Married	Basilicata	Basilicata	Basilicata
	Wife	F.	32	Married	Basilicata	Basilicata	Basilicata
	Daughter	F.	1	Single	United States	Basilicata	Basilicata
1081	Head	M.	45	Married	Basilicata	Basilicata	Basilicata
	Wife	F.	42	Married	Basilicata	Basilicata	Basilicata
	Son	M.	9	Single	United States	Basilicata	Basilicata
	Daughter	F.	7	Single	United States	Basilicata	Basilicata
	Daughter	F.	3	Single	United States	Basilicata	Basilicata
	Son	M.	2	Single	United States	Basilicata	Basilicata
	Brother-in-law	M.	32	Married	Basilicata	Basilicata	Basilicata

a Not reported.

TABLE **I.**—GENERAL SOCIAL AND ECONOMIC CONDITION, BY FAMILIES AND INDIVIDUALS—Continued.

Years in U. S.	Naturalized.	Profession, trade, or occupation.	Hours of work per week.	Average weekly earnings.	Weeks employed.	Total yearly earnings.	Sick during year, defective, maimed, or deformed.
5	No...	Peddler, fruit	(a)	$3.00	52	$156	No.
14	Yes..	Street sweeper.............	60	9.00	24	216	No.
10	......	Housewife...................	......	......	......	......	No.
10	......	Scholar and peddler, fruit.	(a)	3.00	52	156	No.
10	......	Paper factory employee...	(a)	2.00	52	104	No.
......	......	Scholar......................	......	......	......	......	No.
......	......	At home.....................	......	......	......	......	No.
......	......	At home.....................	......	......	......	......	No.
10	No...	Peddler, fruit..............	(a)	3.00	52	156	No.
5	......	Housewife..................	......	......	......	......	No.
5	......	Peddler, fruit..............	(a)	3.00	(a)	(a)	No.
5	......	Scholar and peddler, fruit.	(a)	2.00	(a)	(a)	No.
6	Yes..	Peddler, fruit..............	48	4.00	52	208	No.
4	......	Housewife..................	......	......	......	......	No.
10	No...	Peddler, fruit..............	48	4.00	52	208	No.
10	......	Housewife..................	......	......	......	......	Childbirth.
......	......	At home.....................	......	......	......	......	No.
......	......	At home.....................	......	......	......	......	No.
......	......	At home.....................	......	......	......	......	No.
15	No...	Peddler, fruit..............	(a)	3.00	52	156	No.
6	......	Housewife..................	......	......	......	......	No.
6	......	Peddler, fruit..............	(a)	3.00	52	156	No.
8	No...	Peddler, fruit..............	(a)	(a)	52	(a)	No.
6	......	Housewife..................	......	......	......	......	No.
6	......	Scholar......................	......	......	......	......	No.
......	......	At home.....................	......	......	......	......	No.
......	......	At home.....................	......	......	......	......	No.
......	......	At home.....................	......	......	......	......	No.
8	Yes..	Paver.......................	60	8.12	20	162	No.
5	......	Housewife..................	......	......	......	......	No.
5	......	At home.....................	......	......	......	......	No.
......	......	At home.....................	......	......	......	......	No.
......	......	At home.....................	......	......	......	......	No.
17	Yes..	Street sweeper.............	60	8.75	27	236	No.
16	......	Housewife..................	......	......	......	......	No.
......	......	Scholar......................	......	......	......	......	No.
......	......	Scholar......................	......	......	......	......	No.
......	......	Scholar......................	......	......	......	......	No.
......	......	Scholar......................	......	......	......	......	No.
......	......	Scholar......................	......	......	......	......	No.
......	......	At home.....................	......	......	......	......	Glands, scrofulous.
10	Yes..	Street sweeper.............	60	7.50	28	210	No.
10	......	Housewife..................	......	......	......	......	No.
......	......	Scholar......................	......	......	......	......	No.
......	......	At home.....................	......	......	......	......	Fever, not specified.
18	Yes..	Hod carrier................	48	10.00	24	240	No.
13	......	Housewife..................	......	......	......	......	No.
......	......	Scholar......................	......	......	......	......	No.
......	......	Scholar......................	......	......	......	......	No.
......	......	Scholar......................	......	......	......	......	No.
......	......	At home.....................	......	......	......	......	No.
......	......	At home.....................	......	......	......	......	No.
12	Yes..	Quarryman.................	60	7.50	28	210	No.
6	......	Housewife..................	......	......	......	......	Female complaint.
......	......	At home.....................	......	......	......	......	No.
15	No...	Quarryman.................	60	7.50	22	165	No.
9	......	Housewife..................	......	......	......	......	No.
......	......	Scholar......................	......	......	......	......	No.
......	......	At home.....................	......	......	......	......	No.
......	......	At home.....................	......	......	......	......	No.
......	......	At home.....................	......	......	......	......	No.
4	No...	Quarryman.................	60	7.50	16	120	No.

TABLE **I.**—GENERAL SOCIAL AND ECONOMIC CONDITION, BY FAMILIES
AND INDIVIDUALS—Continued.

Family number.	Relationship to head of family.	Sex.	Age.	Conjugal condition.	Birthplace.	Birthplace of—	
						Father.	Mother.
1082	Head	M.	33	Married	Calabria	Calabria	Calabria
	Wife	F.	26	Married	Basilicata	Basilicata	Basilicata
	Son	M.	4	Single	United States	Calabria	Basilicata
	Son	M.	2	Single	United States	Calabria	Basilicata
1083	Head	M.	30	Married	Basilicata	Basilicata	Basilicata
	Wife	F.	21	Married	Basilicata	Basilicata	Basilicata
	Daughter	F.	4	Single	United States	Basilicata	Basilicata
1084	Head	M.	36	Married	Basilicata	Basilicata	Basilicata
	Wife	F.	32	Married	Basilicata	Basilicata	Basilicata
	Daughter	F.	12	Single	United States	Basilicata	Basilicata
	Son	M.	11	Single	United States	Basilicata	Basilicata
	Daughter	F.	10	Single	United States	Basilicata	Basilicata
	Son	M.	8	Single	United States	Basilicata	Basilicata
	Son	M.	6	Single	United States	Basilicata	Basilicata
	Daughter	F.	5	Single	United States	Basilicata	Basilicata
	Son	M.	3	Single	United States	Basilicata	Basilicata
	Son	M.	2	Single	United States	Basilicata	Basilicata
	Daughter	F.	$\frac{6}{12}$	Single	United States	Basilicata	Basilicata
1085	Head	M.	50	Married	Basilicata	Basilicata	Basilicata
	Wife	F.	50	Married	Basilicata	Basilicata	Basilicata
1086	Head	M.	42	Married	Campania	Campania	Campania
	Wife	F.	27	Married	Basilicata	Basilicata	Basilicata
	Son	M.	8	Single	United States	Campania	Basilicata
	Daughter	F.	6	Single	United States	Campania	Basilicata
	Son	M.	2	Single	United States	Campania	Basilicata
	Son	M.	$\frac{a}{12}$	Single	United States	Campania	Basilicata
1087	Head	M.	28	Married	Calabria	Calabria	Calabria
	Wife	F.	18	Married	Calabria	Calabria	Calabria
1088	Head	M.	40	Married	Abruzzo	Abruzzo	Abruzzo
	Wife	F.	34	Married	Abruzzo	Abruzzo	Abruzzo
	Son	M.	9	Single	Abruzzo	Abruzzo	Abruzzo
	Son	M.	5	Single	United States	Abruzzo	Abruzzo
	Daughter	F.	1	Single	United States	Abruzzo	Abruzzo
1089	Head	M.	32	Married	Calabria	Calabria	Calabria
	Wife	F.	32	Married	Calabria	Calabria	Calabria
	Daughter	F.	12	Single	Calabria	Calabria	Calabria
	Daughter	F.	9	Single	Calabria	Calabria	Calabria
	Son	M.	3	Single	United States	Calabria	Calabria
	Son	M.	$\frac{1}{12}$	Single	United States	Calabria	Calabria
1090	Head	M.	39	Married	Calabria	Calabria	Calabria
	Wife	F.	30	Married	Calabria	Calabria	Calabria
	Daughter	F.	2	Single	United States	Calabria	Calabria
	Son	M.	1	Single	United States	Calabria	Calabria
1091	Head	M.	33	Married	Basilicata	Basilicata	Basilicata
	Wife	F.	25	Married	Basilicata	Basilicata	Basilicata
1092	Head	M.	36	Married	Calabria	Calabria	Calabria
	Wife	F.	28	Married	Calabria	Calabria	Calabria
	Daughter	F.	8	Single	Calabria	Calabria	Calabria
	Son	M.	5	Single	Calabria	Calabria	Calabria
	Daughter	F.	1	Single	United States	Calabria	Calabria
1093	Head	M.	27	Married	Calabria	Calabria	Calabria
	Wife	F.	18	Married	Basilicata	Basilicata	Basilicata
1094	Head	M.	44	Married	Basilicata	Basilicata	Basilicata
	Wife	F.	39	Married	Basilicata	Basilicata	Basilicata
	Son	M.	17	Single	Basilicata	Basilicata	Basilicata
	Daughter	F.	10	Single	United States	Basilicata	Basilicata
	Son	M.	7	Single	United States	Basilicata	Basilicata
	Son	M.	4	Single	United States	Basilicata	Basilicata
1095	Head	M.	35	Married	Abruzzo	Abruzzo	Abruzzo
	Wife	F.	26	Married	Abruzzo	Abruzzo	Abruzzo
	Stepdaughter	F.	9	Single	United States	Abruzzo	Abruzzo
	Son	M.	7	Single	United States	Abruzzo	Abruzzo
	Son	M.	3	Single	United States	Abruzzo	Abruzzo
	Son	M.	1	Single	United States	Abruzzo	Abruzzo

a Not reported.

TABLE **I.**—GENERAL SOCIAL AND ECONOMIC CONDITION, BY FAMILIES
AND INDIVIDUALS—Continued.

Years in U.S.	Natu- ral- ized.	Profession, trade, or occupation.	Hours of work per week.	Average weekly earn- ings.	Weeks em- ploy- ed.	Total yearly earn- ings.	Sick during year, defective, maimed, or deformed.
11	Yes..	Saloon keeper	112	(a)	36	(a)	No.
5	....	Housewife.................	....	....	....	....	No.
....	....	At home	....	....	....	....	No.
....	....	At home	....	....	....	....	No.
16	Yes..	Hod carrier...............	48	$10.00	26	$260	No.
12	....	Housewife.................	....	....	....	....	No.
....	....	At home	....	....	....	....	Fever, not specified.
22	Yes..	Saloon keeper	112	(a)	52	(a)	No.
16	....	Housewife.................	....	....	....	....	Childbirth; hysteria.
....	....	Scholar	....	....	....	....	No.
....	....	Scholar	....	....	....	....	No.
....	....	Scholar	....	....	....	....	No.
....	....	Scholar	....	....	....	....	No.
....	....	At home	....	....	....	....	No.
....	....	At home	....	....	....	....	No.
....	....	At home	....	....	....	....	No.
....	....	At home	....	....	....	....	No.
....	....	At home	....	....	....	....	No.
20	Yes..	Hod carrier...............	48	8.40	22	185	No.
16	....	Housewife.................	....	....	....	....	Female complaint.
13	Yes..	Hod carrier...............	48	9.00	32	288	No.
9	....	Housewife.................	....	....	....	....	Childbirth.
....	....	Scholar	....	....	....	....	No.
....	....	At home	....	....	....	....	No.
....	....	At home	....	....	....	....	No.
....	....	At home	....	....	....	....	No.
5	Yes..	Sewer digger...............	48	13.50	22	297	No.
15	....	Housewife.................	....	....	....	....	No.
6	Yes..	Quarryman	60	7.50	32	240	Fever, not specified.
6	....	Housewife.................	....	....	....	....	No.
6	....	Scholar	....	....	....	....	No.
....	....	At home	....	....	....	....	No.
....	....	At home	....	....	....	....	No.
10	Yes..	Quarryman.................	60	7.50	26	195	Fever, typhoid.
5	....	Housewife.................	....	....	....	....	Childbirth.
5	....	Scholar.................	....	....	....	....	Fever, typhoid.
5	....	Scholar.................	....	....	....	....	Fever, typhoid.
....	....	At home	....	....	....	....	No.
....	....	At home	....	....	....	....	No.
4	No...	Hod carrier...............	60	7.50	22	165	Injury by accident.
3	....	Housewife.................	....	....	....	....	No.
....	....	At home	....	....	....	....	No.
....	....	At home	....	....	....	....	Fever, typhoid; bronchitis.
10	Yes..	Quarryman...............	60	8.10	32	259	No.
10	....	Housewife.................	....	....	....	....	No.
6	Yes..	Laborer...................	70	7.50	52	390	No.
3	....	Housewife.................	....	....	....	....	No.
3	....	At home	....	....	....	....	No.
3	....	At home	....	....	....	....	No.
....	....	At home	....	....	....	....	No.
(a)	Yes..	Expressman...............	(a)	5.00	52	260	No.
8	....	Housewife.................	....	....	....	....	No.
25	Yes..	Saloon keeper.............	112	(a)	52	(a)	No.
10	....	Housewife.................	....	....	....	....	No.
10	....	No occupation	....	....	....	....	No.
....	....	Scholar	....	....	....	....	No.
....	....	At home	....	....	....	....	No.
....	....	At home	....	....	....	....	No.
13	Yes..	Painter and decorator	(a)	10.50	52	546	No.
11	....	Housewife.................	....	....	....	....	Female complaint.
....	....	Scholar.................	....	....	....	....	No.
....	....	Scholar	....	....	....	....	No.
....	....	At home	....	....	....	....	Bronchitis.

TABLE **I.**—GENERAL SOCIAL AND ECONOMIC CONDITION, BY FAMILIES AND INDIVIDUALS—Continued.

Family number.	Relationship to head of family.	Sex.	Age.	Conjugal condition.	Birthplace.	Birthplace of— Father.	Birthplace of— Mother.
1096	Head	M.	32	Married	Basilicata	Basilicata	Basilicata
	Wife	F.	21	Married	United States	United States	United States
1097	Head	M.	45	Married	Basilicata	Basilicata	Basilicata
	Wife	F.	52	Married	Basilicata	Basilicata	Basilicata
	Son	M.	17	Single	Basilicata	Basilicata	Basilicata
1098	Head	M.	56	Married	Basilicata	Basilicata	Basilicata
	Son	M.	22	Married	Basilicata	Basilicata	Basilicata
	Daughter	F.	13	Single	Basilicata	Basilicata	Basilicata
1099	Head	M.	28	Married	Calabria	Calabria	Calabria
	Wife	F.	27	Married	Calabria	Calabria	Calabria
	Son	M.	1½	Single	United States	Calabria	Calabria
	Brother-in-law	M.	35	Married	Calabria	Calabria	Calabria
	Boarder	M.	16	Single	Calabria	Calabria	Calabria
	Lodger	M.	27	Married	Calabria	Calabria	Calabria
1100	Head	M.	28	Married	Calabria	Calabria	Calabria
	Wife	F.	18	Married	Basilicata	Basilicata	Basilicata
	Daughter	F.	1/12	Single	United States	Calabria	Basilicata
1101	Head	M.	64	Married	Basilicata	Basilicata	Basilicata
	Wife	F.	50	Married	Basilicata	Basilicata	Basilicata
1102	Head	F.	44	Widowed	Basilicata	Basilicata	Basilicata
	Daughter	F.	9	Single	United States	Basilicata	Basilicata
	Son	M.	6	Single	United States	Basilicata	Basilicata
	Son	M.	5	Single	United States	Basilicata	Basilicata
1103	Head	M.	37	Married	Basilicata	Basilicata	Basilicata
	Wife	F.	35	Married	Basilicata	Basilicata	Basilicata
	Daughter	F.	8	Single	United States	Basilicata	Basilicata
	Son	M.	7	Single	United States	Basilicata	Basilicata
	Son	M.	5	Single	United States	Basilicata	Basilicata
	Son	M.	2	Single	United States	Basilicata	Basilicata
1104	Head	M.	33	Married	Sicily	Sicily	Sicily
	Wife	F.	28	Married	Sicily	Sicily	Sicily
	Son	M.	8	Single	Sicily	Sicily	Sicily
	Son	M.	4	Single	United States	Sicily	Sicily
	Son	M.	2	Single	United States	Sicily	Sicily
1105	Head	M.	60	Married	Sicily	Sicily	Sicily
	Wife	F.	60	Married	Sicily	Sicily	Sicily
	Son	M.	17	Single	Sicily	Sicily	Sicily
1106	Head	M.	24	Married	Sicily	Sicily	Sicily
	Wife	F.	25	Married	Sicily	Sicily	Sicily
	Son	M.	3	Single	United States	Sicily	Sicily
	Daughter	F.	1	Single	United States	Sicily	Sicily
1107	Head	M.	37	Married	Sicily	Sicily	Sicily
	Wife	F.	29	Married	Sicily	Sicily	Sicily
	Son	M.	11	Single	United States	Sicily	Sicily
	Son	M.	8	Single	United States	Sicily	Sicily
	Son	M.	3	Single	United States	Sicily	Sicily
	Daughter	F.	1/12	Single	United States	Sicily	Sicily
	Mother-in-law	F.	53	Widowed	Sicily	Sicily	Sicily
1108	Head	M.	36	Married	Sicily	Sicily	Sicily
	Wife	F.	34	Married	Sicily	Sicily	Sicily
	Daughter	F.	11	Single	United States	Sicily	Sicily
	Daughter	F.	9	Single	United States	Sicily	Sicily
	Son	M.	7	Single	United States	Sicily	Sicily
	Son	M.	5	Single	United States	Sicily	Sicily
	Son	M.	1	Single	United States	Sicily	Sicily
1109	Head	M.	30	Married	Sicily	Sicily	Sicily
	Wife	F.	20	Married	Sicily	Sicily	Sicily
	Son	M.	4	Single	United States	Sicily	Sicily
	Son	M.	1	Single	United States	Sicily	Sicily
	Mother	F.	58	Widowed	Sicily	Sicily	Sicily

a Also worked as hod carrier ten weeks, at $9 per week.　　　b Not reported.

TABLE **I.**—GENERAL SOCIAL AND ECONOMIC CONDITION, BY FAMILIES AND INDIVIDUALS—Continued.

Years in U.S.	Naturalized.	Profession, trade, or occupation.	Hours of work per week.	Average weekly earnings.	Weeks employed.	Total yearly earnings.	Sick during year, defective, maimed, or deformed.
21	Yes..	Barber	70	$14.00	50	$700	Indigestion.
.....	......	Housewife					No.
12	Yes..	No occupation					Rheumatism.
12	......	Housewife					No.
12	......	Newsboy	12	5.00	52	260	No.
3	No...	Ragpicker (a)	(b)	3.00	a 42	216	No.
2	No...	Hod carrier	48	9.00	16	144	No.
$\frac{2}{12}$	......	Housewife					No.
10	Yes..	Quarryman	(b)	7.50	28	210	Injury by accident.
4	......	Housewife					Childbirth.
.....	......	At home					No.
6	Yes..	Quarryman	(b)	7.50	26	195	No.
6	......	Bootblack	76	2.00	52	104	No.
$\frac{3}{12}$	No...	Quarryman	(b)	7.50	14	(b)	No.
4	No...	Quarryman	60	7.50	26	195	No.
12	......	Housewife					Childbirth.
.....	......	At home					No.
17	Yes..	Ragpicker (c)	(b)	(b)	c 46	(b)	No.
18	......	Housewife					Female complaint.
15	......	Housewife and pants maker.	(b)	1.50	26	39	No.
.....	......	At home					No.
.....	......	At home					No.
.....	......	At home					No.
10	No...	Hod carrier	60	9.00	15	135	No.
10	......	Housewife					No.
.....	......	At home					No.
.....	......	Scholar					No.
.....	......	At home					No.
.....	......	At home					No.
5	No...	Peddler, fruit	(b)	6.00	52	312	No.
5	......	Housewife					No.
5	......	Scholar					No.
.....	......	At home					No.
.....	......	At home					No.
14	Yes..	Peddler, fruit	(b)	(b)	52	(b)	No.
1	......	Housewife					No.
5	......	Peddler, fruit	(b)	(b)	52	(b)	No.
13	Yes..	Peddler, fruit	(b)	6.00	52	312	No.
9	......	Housewife					No.
.....	......	At home					Rickets.
.....	......	At home					No.
14	No...	Merchant, fruit	(b)	(b)	52	(b)	No.
12	......	Housewife					Childbirth.
.....	......	Scholar					No.
.....	......	At home					Idiot.
.....	......	At home					No.
.....	......	At home					No.
6	......	Housework					No.
13	Yes..	Peddler, fruit	(b)	5.00	52	260	No.
12	......	Housewife					No.
.....	......	Housework					No.
.....	......	At home					No.
.....	......	At home					No.
.....	......	At home					No.
.....	......	At home					No.
7	Yes..	Peddler, fruit	(b)	(b)	52	(b)	No.
5	......	Housewife					No.
.....	......	At home					No.
.....	......	At home					No.
11	......	Housework					No.

ç Also worked as hod carrier six weeks, at $8.40 per week.

TABLE **I.**—GENERAL SOCIAL AND ECONOMIC CONDITION, BY FAMILIES
AND INDIVIDUALS—Continued.

Family number.	Relationship to head of family.	Sex.	Age.	Conjugal condition.	Birthplace.	Birthplace of—	
						Father.	Mother.
1110	Head	M.	33	Married	Sicily	Sicily	Sicily
	Wife	F.	30	Married	Sicily	Sicily	Sicily
	Daughter	F.	6	Single	United States	Sicily	Sicily
	Son	M.	4	Single	United States	Sicily	Sicily
	Daughter	F.	3	Single	United States	Sicily	Sicily
	Daughter	F.	1/12	Single	United States	Sicily	Sicily
	Cousin	M.	30	Single	Sicily	Sicily	Sicily
	Cousin	M.	32	Single	Sicily	Sicily	Sicily
1111	Head	M.	27	Married	Sicily	Sicily	Sicily
	Wife	F.	18	Married	Sicily	Sicily	Sicily
	Daughter	F.	3	Single	United States	Sicily	Sicily
1112	Head	M.	30	Married	Sicily	Sicily	Sicily
	Wife	F.	27	Married	Sicily	Sicily	Sicily
	Son	M.	6	Single	Sicily	Sicily	Sicily
	Daughter	F.	4	Single	United States	Sicily	Sicily
	Daughter	F.	2	Single	United States	Sicily	Sicily
	Son	M.	1	Single	United States	Sicily	Sicily
1113	Head	M.	30	Married	Sicily	Sicily	Sicily
	Wife	F.	22	Married	Sicily	Sicily	Sicily
	Daughter	F.	4	Single	United States	Sicily	Sicily
	Daughter	F.	2	Single	United States	Sicily	Sicily
1114	Head	M.	53	Married	Sicily	Sicily	Sicily
	Wife	F.	40	Married	Sicily	Sicily	Sicily
	Son	M.	27	Married	Sicily	Sicily	Sicily
	Son	M.	14	Single	United States	Sicily	Sicily
	Son	M.	12	Single	United States	Sicily	Sicily
	Daughter	F.	7	Single	United States	Sicily	Sicily
	Daughter-in-law	F.	18	Married	Sicily	Sicily	Sicily
	Grandson	M.	1	Single	United States	Sicily	Sicily
1115	Head	M.	26	Married	Sicily	Sicily	Sicily
	Wife	F.	22	Married	Sicily	Sicily	Sicily
	Son	M.	1	Single	Sicily	Sicily	Sicily
1116	Head	M.	54	Widowed	Emilia	Emilia	Emilia
	Son	M.	22	Single	United States	Emilia	Emilia
	Daughter	F.	17	Single	United States	Emilia	Emilia
	Daughter	F.	14	Single	United States	Emilia	Emilia
	Son	M.	13	Single	United States	Emilia	Emilia
	Boarder	F.	42	Married	Liguria	Liguria	Liguria
1117	Head	M.	53	Married	Liguria	Liguria	Liguria
	Wife	F.	48	Married	Liguria	Liguria	Liguria
	Son	M.	26	Single	United States	Liguria	Liguria
	Son	M.	22	Single	United States	Liguria	Liguria
	Daughter	F.	20	Single	United States	Liguria	Liguria
	Daughter	F.	18	Single	United States	Liguria	Liguria
	Daughter	F.	16	Single	United States	Liguria	Liguria
	Daughter	F.	11	Single	United States	Liguria	Liguria
1118	Head	M.	34	Married	Abruzzo	Abruzzo	Abruzzo
	Wife	F.	31	Married	Abruzzo	Abruzzo	Abruzzo
	Daughter	F.	7	Single	France	Abruzzo	Abruzzo
	Daughter	F.	5	Single	United States	Abruzzo	Abruzzo
	Son	M.	2	Single	United States	Abruzzo	Abruzzo
1119	Head	M.	61	Married	Liguria	Liguria	Liguria
	Wife	F.	61	Married	Liguria	Liguria	Liguria
	Son	M.	19	Single	United States	Liguria	Liguria
1120	Head	M.	33	Married	Liguria	Liguria	Liguria
	Wife	F.	27	Married	Liguria	Liguria	Liguria
	Daughter	F.	5	Single	United States	Liguria	Liguria
	Son	M.	3	Single	United States	Liguria	Liguria
	Son	M.	1	Single	United States	Liguria	Liguria
1121	Head	M.	50	Married	Abruzzo	Abruzzo	Abruzzo
	Wife	F.	37	Married	Abruzzo	Abruzzo	Abruzzo
	Son	M.	13	Single	Abruzzo	Abruzzo	Abruzzo
	Daughter	F.	10	Single	Abruzzo	Abruzzo	Abruzzo
	Son	M.	7	Single	Abruzzo	Abruzzo	Abruzzo
	Son	M.	4	Single	United States	Abruzzo	Abruzzo

a Not reported.

TABLE **I.**—GENERAL SOCIAL AND ECONOMIC CONDITION, BY FAMILIES
AND INDIVIDUALS—Continued.

Years in U. S.	Naturalized.	Profession, trade, or occupation.	Hours of work per week.	Average weekly earnings.	Weeks employed.	Total yearly earnings.	Sick during year, defective, maimed, or deformed.
12	Yes..	Peddler, fruit..............	(a)	(a)	52	(a)	No.
9	......	Housewife.................	......	......	......	......	Childbirth.
......	......	At home...................	......	......	......	......	No.
......	......	At home...................	......	......	......	......	No.
......	......	At home...................	......	......	......	......	No.
......	......	At home...................	......	......	......	......	No.
8	Yes..	Peddler, fruit..............	(a)	$8.00	52	$416	No.
6	Yes..	Peddler, fruit..............	(a)	8.00	52	416	No.
12	No...	Peddler, fruit..............	(a)	3.50	52	182	No.
10	......	Housewife.................	......	......	......	......	No.
......	......	At home...................	......	......	......	......	No.
6	Yes..	Peddler, fruit..............	(a)	6.00	52	312	No.
5	......	Housewife.................	......	......	......	......	No.
5	......	At home...................	......	......	......	......	No.
......	......	At home...................	......	......	......	......	No.
......	......	At home...................	......	......	......	......	No.
......	......	At home...................	......	......	......	......	No.
8	Yes..	Peddler, fruit..............	(a)	5.00	39	195	No.
5	......	Housewife.................	......	......	......	......	No.
......	......	At home...................	......	......	......	......	No.
......	......	At home...................	......	......	......	......	No.
36	Yes..	No occupation.............	......	......	......	......	Rheumatism.
14	......	Housewife.................	......	......	......	......	No.
14	Yes..	Salesman, fruit............	60	18.00	17	306	No.
......	......	Scholar...................	......	......	......	......	No.
......	......	Scholar...................	......	......	......	......	No.
......	......	Scholar...................	......	......	......	......	No.
16	......	Housework................	......	......	......	......	No.
......	......	At home...................	......	......	......	......	No.
1	No...	Peddler, fruit..............	(a)	6.00	52	312	No.
$\frac{3}{12}$	......	Housewife.................	......	......	......	......	No.
$\frac{1}{12}$	......	At home...................	......	......	......	......	No.
23	No...	Mosaic layer..............	48	6.00	52	312	No.
......	......	Engineer..................	(a)	(a)	52	(a)	No.
......	......	Tin-tag factory employee.	60	4.00	52	208	No.
......	......	Tin-tag factory employee.	60	4.00	35	140	No.
......	......	No occupation.............	......	......	......	......	No.
$\frac{1}{12}$	......	Housework................	......	......	......	......	No.
27	Yes..	Mosaic layer..............	48	9.00	13	117	No.
27	......	Housewife.................	......	......	......	......	No.
......	......	Salesman..................	60	(a)	52	(a)	No.
......	......	Salesman..................	60	(a)	52	(a)	No.
......	......	Tin-tag factory employee.	60	4.00	52	208	No.
......	......	Tobacco stripper..........	60	6.00	52	312	No.
......	......	Tin-tag factory employee.	60	4.00	52	208	No.
......	......	Scholar...................	......	......	......	......	No.
7	No...	Laborer...................	60	8.00	22	176	No.
7	......	Housewife.................	......	......	......	......	No.
7	......	At home...................	......	......	......	......	No.
......	......	At home...................	......	......	......	......	No.
......	......	At home...................	......	......	......	......	No.
26	No...	Packer, fruit..............	60	11.00	52	572	No.
26	......	Housewife.................	......	......	......	......	No.
......	......	Mosaic layer..............	48	4.50	17	77	No.
12	No...	Salesman, fruit...........	60	10.00	52	520	No.
8	......	Housewife.................	......	......	......	......	No.
......	......	At home...................	......	......	......	......	No.
......	......	At home...................	......	......	......	......	No.
......	......	At home...................	......	......	......	......	No.
6	No...	Peddler, ice cream........	(a)	7.00	11	77	Injury by accident.
6	......	Housewife.................	......	......	......	......	Eyes, inflammation of both.
6	......	Newsboy..................	(a)	1.05	(a)	(a)	No.
6	......	Newsgirl..................	(a)	.50	(a)	(a)	No.
6	......	At home...................	......	......	......	......	No.
......	......	At home.................	......	......	......	......	Rickets.

TABLE **I.**—GENERAL SOCIAL AND ECONOMIC CONDITION, BY FAMILIES
AND INDIVIDUALS—Continued.

Family number.	Relationship to head of family.	Sex.	Age.	Conjugal condition.	Birthplace.	Birthplace of—	
						Father.	Mother.
1122	Head	M.	40	Married	Liguria	Liguria	Liguria
	Wife	F.	36	Married	Liguria	Liguria	Liguria
	Son	M.	12	Single	United States	Liguria	Liguria
	Daughter	F.	10	Single	United States	Liguria	Liguria
	Daughter	F.	4	Single	United States	Liguria	Liguria
	Daughter	F.	1	Single	United States	Liguria	Liguria
	Mother-in-law	F.	56	Widowed	Liguria	Liguria	Liguria
1123	Head	M.	33	Married	United States	Tuscany	Liguria
	Wife	F.	30	Married	Liguria	Liguria	Liguria
	Son	M.	9	Single	United States	United States	Liguria
	Son	M.	7	Single	United States	United States	Liguria
	Daughter	F.	6	Single	United States	United States	Liguria
	Daughter	F.	6	Single	United States	United States	Liguria
	Sister	F.	25	Single	United States	Tuscany	Liguria
1124	Head	M.	61	Married	Emilia	Emilia	Emilia
	Wife	F.	52	Married	Emilia	Emilia	Emilia
	Son	M.	22	Single	Emilia	Emilia	Emilia
	Son	M.	18	Single	United States	Emilia	Emilia
	Daughter	F.	16	Single	United States	Emilia	Emilia
	Daughter	F.	13	Single	United States	Emilia	Emilia
	Daughter	F.	9	Single	United States	Emilia	Emilia
1125	Head	M.	52	Married	Abruzzo	Abruzzo	Abruzzo
	Wife	F.	42	Married	Abruzzo	Abruzzo	Abruzzo
	Son	M.	10	Single	Abruzzo	Abruzzo	Abruzzo
	Daughter	F.	9	Single	Abruzzo	Abruzzo	Abruzzo
	Son	M.	6	Single	United States	Abruzzo	Abruzzo
	Son	M.	4	Single	United States	Abruzzo	Abruzzo
1126	Head	M.	37	Married	Liguria	Liguria	Liguria
	Wife	F.	38	Married	Liguria	Liguria	Liguria
	Son	M.	16	Single	Liguria	Liguria	Liguria
	Son	M.	13	Single	United States	Liguria	Liguria
	Daughter	F.	11	Single	United States	Liguria	Liguria
	Son	M.	9	Single	United States	Liguria	Liguria
	Son	M.	2	Single	United States	Liguria	Liguria
1127	Head	M.	45	Married	Lombardy	Lombardy	Lombardy
	Wife	F.	34	Married	Liguria	Liguria	Liguria
	Son	M.	8	Single	United States	Lombardy	Liguria
	Son	M.	5	Single	United States	Lombardy	Liguria
1128	Head	M.	33	Married	Venetia	Venetia	Venetia
	Wife	F.	31	Married	Venetia	Venetia	Venetia
	Son	M.	2	Single	United States	Venetia	Venetia
	Daughter	F.	3/12	Single	United States	Venetia	Venetia
1129	Head	M.	39	Married	Abruzzo	Abruzzo	Abruzzo
	Wife	F.	36	Married	Abruzzo	Abruzzo	Abruzzo
	Daughter	F.	13	Single	Abruzzo	Abruzzo	Abruzzo
	Daughter	F.	12	Single	Abruzzo	Abruzzo	Abruzzo
	Daughter	F.	9	Single	Abruzzo	Abruzzo	Abruzzo
	Son	M.	7	Single	France	Abruzzo	Abruzzo
	Daughter	F.	4	Single	United States	Abruzzo	Abruzzo
	Daughter	F.	2	Single	United States	Abruzzo	Abruzzo
1130	Cooperative	M.	20	Single	Venetia	Venetia	Venetia
	Cooperative	M.	25	Single	Venetia	Venetia	Venetia
	Cooperative	M.	26	Single	Venetia	Venetia	Venetia
	Cooperative	M.	27	Single	Venetia	Venetia	Venetia
1131	Head	M.	42	Married	Liguria	Liguria	Liguria
	Wife	F.	42	Married	Liguria	Liguria	Liguria
	Daughter	F.	16	Single	Liguria	Liguria	Liguria
	Daughter	F.	10	Single	Liguria	Liguria	Liguria
	Daughter	F.	3	Single	Liguria	Liguria	Liguria
	Boarder	M.	22	Single	Liguria	Liguria	Liguria
1132	Cooperative	M.	30	Married	Liguria	Liguria	Liguria
	Cooperative	M.	28	Single	Liguria	Liguria	Liguria
	Cooperative	M.	30	Married	Liguria	Liguria	Liguria

a Not reported.

TABLE **I.**—GENERAL SOCIAL AND ECONOMIC CONDITION, BY FAMILIES AND INDIVIDUALS—Continued.

Years in U.S.	Naturalized.	Profession, trade, or occupation.	Hours of work per week.	Average weekly earnings.	Weeks employed.	Total yearly earnings.	Sick during year, defective, maimed, or deformed.
18	Yes..	Merchant, fruit............	(a)	(a)	(a)	(a)	No.
17	......	Housewife.............					No.
......	......	Scholar....					No.
......	......	No occupation.............					Saint Vitus' dance.
......	......	At home.............					No.
......	......	At home					No.
17	......	Housework.............					No.
		Engineer.................	60	$15.00	52	$780	No.
(a)	......	Housewife.............					No.
......	......	Scholar....					No.
......	......	Scholar....					No.
......	......	At home....					No.
......	......	At home					Rickets.
......	......	Cracker factory employee.	60	6.00	52	312	No.
20	No...	No occupation.............					Heart, disease of.
20	......	Housewife.............					Eyes, inflammation of both.
20	Yes..	Iron foundry employee...	60	9.00	52	468	No.
......	......	Mosaic layer.............	48	4.00	22	88	No.
......	......	Tobacco stripper (b)......	60	6.00	b 35	346	No.
......	......	Scholar and dog food factory employee.	60	4.00	9	36	No.
......	......	Scholar.............					No.
7	Yes..	Laborer.................	60	9.00	9	81	No.
7	......	Housewife.............					Miscarriage.
7	......	Scholar....					No.
7	......	Scholar....					No.
......	......	Scholar....					No.
......	......	At home....					No.
16	Yes..	Packer, fruit...	60	10.00	52	520	No.
16	......	Housewife.............					No.
16	......	Glass factory employee...	60	3.00	52	156	No.
......	......	Scholar....					No.
......	......	Scholar....					No.
......	......	Scholar....					No.
......	......	At home....					No.
16	No...	Bricklayer.............	48	24.00	26	624	No.
10	......	Housewife.............					No.
......	......	Scholar....					Bronchitis.
......	......	At home....					No.
3	No...	Stonecutter.............	48	10.50	17	179	No.
3	......	Housewife.............					Childbirth.
......	......	At home....					No.
......	......	At home....					No.
5	No...	Laborer.................	60	7.50	13	98	No.
5	......	Housewife.............					No.
5	......	No occupation.............					Diphtheria.
5	......	No occupation.............					Diphtheria.
5	......	At home....					No.
5	......	At home....					Diphtheria.
......	......	At home....					Diphtheria.
......	......	At home....					No.
3	......	Mosaic layer.............	48	9.00	13	117	No.
3	No...	Laborer.................	60	9.00	9	81	No.
3	No...	Laborer.................	60	9.00	17	153	No.
3	No...	Laborer.................	60	9.00	17	153	No.
1	No...	Candy factory employee...	60	7.00	52	364	No.
1	......	Housewife.............					Rheumatism.
1	......	Macaroni factory employee.	60	3.00	52	156	No.
1	......	No occupation.............					No.
1	......	At home....					No.
1	No...	Laborer	60	7.50	17	128	No.
3	No...	Mosaic layer.............	48	10.50	43	452	No.
3	No...	Salesman	60	9.00	52	468	No.
2	No...	Salesman	60	8.00	48	384	No.

b Also worked as dog food factory employee seventeen weeks, at $8 per week.

TABLE **I.**—GENERAL SOCIAL AND ECONOMIC CONDITION, BY FAMILIES
AND INDIVIDUALS—Continued.

Family number.	Relationship to head of family.	Sex.	Age.	Conjugal condition.	Birthplace.	Birthplace of— Father.	Birthplace of— Mother.
1133	Head	M.	36	Married...	Liguria	Liguria	Liguria
	Wife	F.	35	Married...	Liguria	Liguria	Liguria
	Son	M.	13	Single	Liguria	Liguria	Liguria
	Daughter	F.	12	Single	Liguria	Liguria	Liguria
	Son	M.	9	Single	Liguria	Liguria	Liguria
	Daughter	F.	5	Single	United States...	Liguria	Liguria
	Boarder	M.	23	Single	Liguria	Liguria	Liguria
1134	Head	M.	48	Married...	Liguria	Liguria	Liguria
	Wife	F.	42	Married...	Liguria	Liguria	Liguria
	Daughter	F.	21	Single	Liguria	Liguria	Liguria
	Son	M.	19	Single	Liguria	Liguria	Liguria
	Daughter	F.	16	Single	Liguria	Liguria	Liguria
	Son	M.	15	Single	Liguria	Liguria	Liguria
	Daughter	F.	11	Single	Liguria	Liguria	Liguria
	Son	M.	10	Single	Liguria	Liguria	Liguria
	Daughter	F.	9	Single	Liguria	Liguria	Liguria
	Son	M.	7	Single	Liguria	Liguria	Liguria
1135	Head	F.	65	Widowed	Liguria	Liguria	Liguria
	Son	M.	30	Single	United States...	Liguria	Liguria
	Son	M.	27	Single	United States...	Liguria	Liguria
	Daughter	F.	25	Single	United States...	Liguria	Liguria
	Daughter	F.	23	Single	United States...	Liguria	Liguria
1136	Head	M.	31	Married...	Campagna di Roma.	Campagna di Roma.	Campagna di Roma.
	Wife	F.	29	Married...	Campagna di Roma.	Campagna di Roma.	Campagna di Roma.
	Son	M.	1	Single	United States...	Campagna di Roma.	Campagna di Roma.
1137	Head	M.	30	Married...	Tuscany	Tuscany	Tuscany
	Wife	F.	27	Married...	Tuscany	Tuscany	Tuscany
	Daughter	F.	2	Single	United States...	Tuscany	Tuscany
	Son	M.	$\frac{3}{12}$	Single	United States...	Tuscany	Tuscany
1138	Head	M.	42	Widowed	Sicily	Sicily	Sicily
	Son	M.	16	Single	Sicily	Sicily	Sicily
	Daughter	F.	9	Single	Sicily	Sicily	Sicily
1139	Head	M.	60	Married...	Basilicata	Basilicata	Basilicata
	Wife	F.	50	Married ..	Basilicata	Basilicata	Basilicata
	Daughter	F.	25	Married...	Basilicata	Basilicata	Basilicata
	Son-in-law	M.	30	Married...	Basilicata	Basilicata	Basilicata
	Grandson	M.	3	Single	Basilicata	Basilicata	Basilicata
1140	Head	M.	40	Married...	Basilicata	Basilicata	Basilicata
	Wife	F.	43	Married...	Basilicata	Basilicata	Basilicata
	Son	M.	15	Single	Basilicata	Basilicata	Basilicata
	Son	M.	4	Single	United States...	Basilicata	Basilicata
	Father	M.	77	Married...	Basilicata	Basilicata	Basilicata
	Mother	F.	76	Married...	Basilicata	Basilicata	Basilicata
	Mother-in-law	F.	80	Widowed	Basilicata	Basilicata	Basilicata
1141	Head	M.	40	Married...	Basilicata	Basilicata	Basilicata
	Wife	F.	42	Married...	Basilicata	Basilicata	Basilicata
	Daughter	F.	8	Single	Basilicata	Basilicata	Basilicata
	Son	M.	1	Single	United States...	Basilicata	Basilicata
1142	Head	M.	43	Married...	Basilicata	Basilicata	Basilicata
	Wife	F.	43	Married...	Basilicata	Basilicata	Basilicata
	Son	M.	13	Single	Basilicata	Basilicata	Basilicata
1143	Head	M.	34	Married...	Basilicata	Basilicata	Basilicata
	Wife	F.	30	Married...	Basilicata	Basilicata	Basilicata
	Daughter	F.	6	Single	United States...	Basilicata	Basilicata
	Daughter	F.	4	Single	United States...	Basilicata	Basilicata
	Daughter	F.	2	Single	United States...	Basilicata	Basilicata
1144	Head	M.	28	Married...	Basilicata	Basilicata	Basilicata
	Wife	F.	20	Married...	Basilicata	Basilicata	Basilicata
	Son	M.	2	Single	United States...	Basilicata	Basilicata
1145	Head	M.	25	Married...	Basilicata	Basilicata	Basilicata
	Wife	F.	22	Married...	Basilicata	Basilicata	Basilicata
	Mother	F.	60	Widowed .	Basilicata	Basilicata	Basilicata

a Not reported.

TABLE **I.**—GENERAL SOCIAL AND ECONOMIC CONDITION, BY FAMILIES
AND INDIVIDUALS—Continued.

Years in U. S.	Naturalized.	Profession, trade, or occupation.	Hours of work per week.	Average weekly earnings.	Weeks employed.	Total yearly earnings.	Sick during year, defective, maimed, or deformed.
6	No...	Packer, fruit...............	60	(a)	(a)	(a)	No.
6	......	Housewife...............	......	......	......	......	No.
6	......	Scholar	......	......	......	......	No.
6	......	Scholar	......	......	......	......	No.
6	......	Scholar	......	......	......	......	No.
......	......	At home	......	......	......	......	No.
17	No...	Driver...............	(a)	(a)	52	(a)	No.
5	No...	Nut cracker	60	$5.00	52	$260	No.
4	......	Housewife...............	......	......	......	......	No.
5	......	Packer, tobacco...........	(a)	6.50	52	338	No.
4	......	Mosaic layer...............	48	9.00	35	315	No.
4	......	Dog food factory employee.	60	6.50	43	280	No.
5	......	Scholar and newsboy.....	(a)	2.40	(a)	(a)	No.
4	......	Scholar...............	......	......	......	......	No.
4	......	Scholar...............	......	......	......	......	No.
4	......	Scholar...............	......	......	......	......	No.
4	......	Scholar...............	......	......	......	......	No.
40	......	Saloon keeper...............	(a)	(a)	52	(a)	No.
......	......	Saloon keeper...............	(a)	(a)	52	(a)	No.
......	......	Electric supplies employee.	60	(a)	(a)	(a)	No.
......	......	No occupation	......	......	......	......	No.
......	......	No occupation	......	......	......	......	No.
7	No...	Mosaic layer...............	60	13.50	17	230	No.
2	......	Housewife...............	......	......	......	......	No.
......	......	At home	......	......	......	......	No.
7	No...	Peddler, fruit...............	(a)	(a)	52	(a)	No.
3	......	Housewife...............	......	......	......	......	Childbirth.
......	......	At home	......	......	......	......	No.
......	......	At home	......	......	......	......	No.
7	No...	Peddler, fruit...............	(a)	(a)	52	(a)	No.
7	......	No occupation	......	......	......	......	No.
7	......	Scholar	......	......	......	......	No.
4	No...	Ragpicker...............	27	2.50	52	130	No.
2	......	Housewife...............	......	......	......	......	No.
3	......	No occupation	......	......	......	......	No.
3	No...	Hod carrier...............	60	7.50	10	75	No.
3	......	At home	......	......	......	......	No.
14	Yes..	Hod carrier...............	48	9.75	42	410	Injury by accident.
11	......	Housewife...............	......	......	......	......	No.
11	......	Scholar and tailor..........	60	2.50	28	70	No.
......	......	At home	......	......	......	......	Bronchitis.
10	No...	No occupation	......	......	......	......	No.
10	......	No occupation	......	......	......	......	No.
13	......	No occupation	......	......	......	......	No.
12	Yes..	Street sweeper	48	9.00	19	171	Neuralgia.
6	......	Housewife...............	......	......	......	......	No.
6	......	At home...............	......	......	......	......	No.
......	......	At home...............	......	......	......	......	Fever, not specified.
12	Yes..	Paver...............	60	9.00	19	171	No.
4	......	Housewife...............	......	......	......	......	Female complaint.
4	......	Scholar and tailor..........	54	2.50	32	80	No.
8	Yes..	Hod carrier...............	48	9.00	24	216	No.
8	......	Housewife...............	......	......	......	......	Injury by accident.
......	......	At home...............	......	......	......	......	No.
......	......	At home...............	......	......	......	......	No.
......	......	At home...............	......	......	......	......	No.
6	Yes..	Laborer	48	9.00	12	108	No.
5	......	Housewife...............	......	......	......	......	No.
......	......	At home...............	......	......	......	......	No.
10	Yes..	Hod carrier...............	48	9.00	12	108	No.
4	......	Housewife...............	......	......	......	......	Female complaint.
10	......	No occupation...............	......	......	......	......	No.

TABLE **I.**—GENERAL SOCIAL AND ECONOMIC CONDITION, BY FAMILIES AND INDIVIDUALS—Continued.

Family number.	Relationship to head of family.	Sex.	Age.	Conjugal condition.	Birthplace.	Birthplace of—	
						Father.	Mother.
1146	Head	M.	33	Married	Basilicata	Basilicata	Basilicata
	Wife	F.	30	Married	Basilicata	Basilicata	Basilicata
	Son	M.	11	Single	United States	Basilicata	Basilicata
	Son	M.	9	Single	United States	Basilicata	Basilicata
	Son	M.	3	Single	United States	Basilicata	Basilicata
	Daughter	F.	1	Single	United States	Basilicata	Basilicata
1147	Head	M.	31	Married	Basilicata	Basilicata	Basilicata
	Wife	F.	19	Married	Basilicata	Basilicata	Basilicata
1148	Head	M.	66	Married	Basilicata	Basilicata	Basilicata
	Wife	F.	52	Married	Basilicata	Basilicata	Basilicata
	Son	M.	21	Single	Basilicata	Basilicata	Basilicata
	Daughter	F.	19	Single	Basilicata	Basilicata	Basilicata
1149	Head	M.	47	Married	Basilicata	Basilicata	Basilicata
	Wife	F.	44	Married	Basilicata	Basilicata	Basilicata
	Son	M.	23	Single	Basilicata	Basilicata	Basilicata
	Daughter	F.	14	Single	United States	Basilicata	Basilicata
	Son	M.	11	Single	United States	Basilicata	Basilicata
	Son	M.	10	Single	United States	Basilicata	Basilicata
	Son	M.	7	Single	United States	Basilicata	Basilicata
	Daughter	F.	4	Single	United States	Basilicata	Basilicata
	Daughter	F.	3	Single	United States	Basilicata	Basilicata
1150	Head	M.	28	Married	Basilicata	Basilicata	Basilicata
	Wife	F.	25	Married	Basilicata	Basilicata	Basilicata
	Daughter	F.	6	Single	United States	Basilicata	Basilicata
	Son	M.	4	Single	United States	Basilicata	Basilicata
	Daughter	F.	$\frac{1}{12}$	Single	United States	Basilicata	Basilicata
	Aunt	F.	50	Widowed	Basilicata	Basilicata	Basilicata
1151	Head	M.	36	Married	Basilicata	Basilicata	Basilicata
	Wife	F.	33	Married	Basilicata	Basilicata	Basilicata
	Son	M.	7	Single	United States	Basilicata	Basilicata
	Daughter	F.	6	Single	United States	Basilicata	Basilicata
	Daughter	F.	3	Single	United States	Basilicata	Basilicata
	Daughter	F.	2	Single	United States	Basilicata	Basilicata
	Son	M.	$\frac{1}{12}$	Single	United States	Basilicata	Basilicata
	Brother	M.	30	Married	Basilicata	Basilicata	Basilicata
	Sister-in-law	F.	23	Married	Basilicata	Basilicata	Basilicata
	Niece	F.	1	Single	United States	Basilicata	Basilicata
1152	Head	M.	22	Married	Basilicata	Basilicata	Basilicata
	Wife	F.	16	Married	Basilicata	Basilicata	Basilicata
	Brother	M.	18	Single	Basilicata	Basilicata	Basilicata
	Sister	F.	21	Single	Basilicata	Basilicata	Basilicata
1153	Head	M.	33	Married	Basilicata	Basilicata	Basilicata
	Wife	F.	33	Married	Basilicata	Basilicata	Basilicata
	Son	M.	8	Single	United States	Basilicata	Basilicata
	Son	M.	2	Single	United States	Basilicata	Basilicata
1154	Head	F.	45	Widowed	Basilicata	Basilicata	Basilicata
	Son	M.	22	Single	Basilicata	Basilicata	Basilicata
	Son	M.	16	Single	Basilicata	Basilicata	Basilicata
1155	Head	M.	34	Married	Basilicata	Basilicata	Basilicata
	Wife	F.	32	Married	Basilicata	Basilicata	Basilicata
	Son	M.	6	Single	United States	Basilicata	Basilicata
	Daughter	F.	4	Single	United States	Basilicata	Basilicata
1156	Head	M.	32	Married	Basilicata	Basilicata	Basilicata
	Wife	F.	29	Married	Sweden	Sweden	Sweden
	Daughter	F.	7	Single	United States	Basilicata	Sweden
1157	Head	M.	39	Married	Basilicata	Basilicata	Basilicata
	Wife	F.	27	Married	Basilicata	Basilicata	Basilicata
	Daughter	F.	7	Single	Basilicata	Basilicata	Basilicata
	Daughter	F.	3	Single	United States	Basilicata	Basilicata
	Son	M.	$\frac{1}{12}$	Single	United States	Basilicata	Basilicata
1158	Head	M.	32	Married	Basilicata	Basilicata	Basilicata
	Wife	F.	24	Married	Basilicata	Basilicata	Basilicata
	Son	M.	8	Single	United States	Basilicata	Basilicata

a Not reported.

TABLE **I.**—GENERAL SOCIAL AND ECONOMIC CONDITION, BY FAMILIES AND INDIVIDUALS—Continued.

Years in U. S.	Natu ral ized.	Profession, trade, or occupation.	Hours of work per week.	Average weekly earn ings.	Weeks em ploy ed.	Total yearly earn ings.	Sick during year, defective, maimed, or deformed.
15	Yes..	Peddler, fruit	72	(a)	52	(a)	No.
12		Housewife					No.
		Scholar					No.
		Scholar					No.
		At home					No.
		At home					No.
10	Yes..	Hod carrier	60	$9.00	(a)	(a)	No.
13		Housewife					No.
15	No...	Shoemaker	(a)	2.00	52	$104	Leg, one crippled.
15		Housewife					Rheumatism.
15	No...	Musician	(a)	8.00	52	416	No.
15		Saleswoman, dry goods	80	4.00	52	208	No.
23	Yes..	Fireman	56	15.00	46	690	Rheumatism.
17		Housewife					Female complaint.
17	Yes.	Teamster	52	7.50	44	330	No.
		Scholar					No.
		Scholar					No.
		Scholar					No.
		At home					No.
		At home					No.
		At home					No.
15	Yes..	Musician	(a)	6.00	52	312	No.
7		Housewife					Childbirth.
		Scholar					No.
		At home					No.
		At home					No.
14		Washerwoman	48	4.50	52	234	No.
9	Yes..	Laborer	60	7.50	23	173	No.
8		Housewife					Childbirth.
		Scholar					No.
		At home					Rickets.
		At home					No.
		At home					Rickets.
		At home					No.
4	No...	Laborer	60	8.00	22	176	No.
4		No occupation					No.
		At home					No.
7	Yes..	Oiler, waterworks	57	16.25	52	845	No.
5		Housewife					No.
1		No occupation					No.
10		Tailoress	48	(a)	52	(a)	No.
20	Yes..	Musician	60	5.00	52	260	No.
9		Housewife					No.
		Scholar					No.
		At home					No.
2		Housewife					No.
7	Yes	Barber	66	9.00	52	468	No.
3		Barber's apprentice	66	1.50	52	78	No.
11	Yes..	Laborer	60	7.50	16	120	No.
7		Housewife					No.
		At home					No.
		At home					No.
15	Yes..	Saloon keeper	105	(a)	26	(a)	No.
15		Housewife					Diarrhea.
		At home					No.
14	No...	Baker	96	(a)	52	(a)	No.
4		Housewife					Childbirth; female com plaint.
4		Scholar					No.
		At home					No.
		At home					No.
17	Yes..	Stonecutter	44	22.00	12	264	Pneumonia.
9		Housewife					Childbirth.
		Scholar					No.

TABLE **I.**—GENERAL SOCIAL AND ECONOMIC CONDITION, BY FAMILIES AND INDIVIDUALS—Continued.

Family number.	Relationship to head of family.	Sex.	Age.	Conjugal condition.	Birthplace.	Birthplace of—	
						Father.	Mother.
1158	Daughter	F.	6	Single	United States	Basilicata	Basilicata
	Son	M.	$\frac{7}{12}$	Single	United States	Basilicata	Basilicata
	Mother	F.	70	Widowed	Basilicata	Basilicata	Basilicata
1159	Head	M.	50	Married	Basilicata	Basilicata	Basilicata
	Wife	F.	47	Married	Basilicata	Basilicata	Basilicata
	Son	M.	15	Single	Basilicata	Basilicata	Basilicata
	Son	M.	10	Single	United States	Basilicata	Basilicata
	Daughter	F.	8	Single	United States	Basilicata	Basilicata
1160	Head	M.	32	Married	Basilicata	Basilicata	Basilicata
	Wife	F.	26	Married	Basilicata	Basilicata	Basilicata
	Son	M.	4	Single	United States	Basilicata	Basilicata
	Daughter	F.	3	Single	United States	Basilicata	Basilicata
	Daughter	F.	$\frac{7}{12}$	Single	United States	Basilicata	Basilicata
	Mother	F.	70	Widowed	Basilicata	Basilicata	Basilicata
	Brother	M.	19	Single	Basilicata	Basilicata	Basilicata
1161	Head	M.	63	Married	Basilicata	Basilicata	Basilicata
	Wife	F.	53	Married	Basilicata	Basilicata	Basilicata
1162	Head	M.	41	Married	Basilicata	Basilicata	Basilicata
	Wife	F.	27	Married	Lombardy	Lombardy	Lombardy
	Son	M.	10	Single	United States	Basilicata	Lombardy
	Son	M.	8	Single	United States	Basilicata	Lombardy
	Son	M.	6	Single	United States	Basilicata	Lombardy
	Son	M.	3	Single	United States	Basilicata	Lombardy
	Son	M.	$\frac{1}{12}$	Single	United States	Basilicata	Lombardy
1163	Head	M.	47	Married	Campania	Campania	Campania
	Wife	F.	44	Married	Campania	Campania	Campania
	Daughter	F.	6	Single	United States	Campania	Campania
	Mother	F.	68	Widowed	Campania	Campania	Campania
1164	Head	M.	27	Married	Basilicata	Basilicata	Basilicata
	Wife	F.	16	Married	Basilicata	Basilicata	Basilicata
	Mother-in-law	F.	54	Widowed	Basilicata	Basilicata	Basilicata
1165	Head	M.	31	Married	Basilicata	Basilicata	Basilicata
	Wife	F.	30	Married	Basilicata	Basilicata	Basilicata
	Son	M.	7	Single	Basilicata	Basilicata	Basilicata
1166	Head	M.	35	Married	Sicily	Sicily	Sicily
	Wife	F.	33	Married	Sicily	Sicily	Sicily
	Daughter	F.	12	Single	Sicily	Sicily	Sicily
	Son	M.	2	Single	United States	Sicily	Sicily
1167	Head	M.	40	Married	Basilicata	Basilicata	Basilicata
	Wife	F.	45	Married	Basilicata	Basilicata	Basilicata
	Daughter	F.	9	Single	Basilicata	Basilicata	Basilicata
	Son	M.	3	Single	United States	Basilicata	Basilicata
	Daughter	F.	1	Single	United States	Basilicata	Basilicata
	Daughter	F.	1	Single	United States	Basilicata	Basilicata
1168	Head	M.	47	Married	Basilicata	Basilicata	Basilicata
	Wife	F.	50	Married	Basilicata	Basilicata	Basilicata
	Son	M.	10	Single	Basilicata	Basilicata	Basilicata
	Son	M.	2	Single	United States	Basilicata	Basilicata
1169	Head	M.	40	Married	Basilicata	Basilicata	Basilicata
	Wife	F.	27	Married	Basilicata	Basilicata	Basilicata
	Daughter	F.	12	Single	United States	Basilicata	Basilicata
	Son	M.	10	Single	United States	Basilicata	Basilicata
	Daughter	F.	7	Single	United States	Basilicata	Basilicata
	Daughter	F.	4	Single	United States	Basilicata	Basilicata
	Son	M.	$\frac{7}{12}$	Single	United States	Basilicata	Basilicata
1170	Head	M.	28	Married	Basilicata	Basilicata	Basilicata
	Wife	F.	20	Married	Basilicata	Basilicata	Basilicata
1171	Head	M.	34	Married	Basilicata	Basilicata	Basilicata
	Wife	F.	26	Married	Basilicata	Basilicata	Basilicata
	Son	M.	3	Single	United States	Basilicata	Basilicata
	Daughter	F.	$\frac{8}{12}$	Single	United States	Basilicata	Basilicata

a Also worked as bicycle factory employee eleven weeks, at $13 per week.

TABLE **I.**—GENERAL SOCIAL AND ECONOMIC CONDITION, BY FAMILIES AND INDIVIDUALS—Continued.

Years in U. S.	Natu- ral- ized.	Profession, trade, or occupation.	Hours of work per week.	Average weekly earn- ings.	Weeks em- ploy- ed.	Total yearly earn- ings.	Sick during year, defective, maimed, or deformed.
		Scholar					No.
		At home					No.
12		No occupation					No.
14	Yes..	Laborer	54	$8.40	16	$134	No.
12		Housewife					No.
12		Scholar					No.
		Scholar					No.
		Scholar					No.
9	Yes..	Saloon keeper (a)	(b)	(b)	a 41	(b)	No.
7		Housewife					Childbirth.
		At home					No.
		At home					No.
		At home					No.
7		Housework					No.
8		Shoe factory employee	60	6.00	52	312	No.
5	No.	Organ grinder	54	2.00	52	104	No.
5		Housewife					No.
13	Yes..	Laborer	60	9.00	32	288	No.
13		Housewife					Childbirth.
		Scholar					No.
		Scholar					No.
		At home					No.
		At home					No.
		At home					No.
13	Yes..	No occupation					No.
8		Housewife and pants maker.	(b)	2.00	52	104	No.
		Scholar					No.
8		No occupation					No.
4	No...	Street sweeper	60	7.50	16	120	No.
3		Housewife					Pneumonia.
3		No occupation					Female complaint.
5	Yes..	Candy factory employee	60	6.00	28	168	No.
4		Housewife					No.
4		Scholar					No.
6	Yes..	Street sweeper	60	7.50	20	150	No.
6		Housewife					No.
6		No occupation					No.
		At home					No.
9	Yes..	Street sweeper	60	7.30	20	146	No.
6		Housewife					No.
6		Scholar					No.
		At home					No.
		At home					Pneumonia.
		At home					Pneumonia.
10	Yes..	No occupation					Rheumatism; heart disease
5		Housewife					No.
5		Scholar					No.
		At home					Pneumonia.
18	Yes..	Foreman, street sweepers	60	9.00	32	288	No.
19		Housewife					Childbirth.
		Scholar					No.
		Scholar					No.
		Scholar					No.
		At home					No.
		At home					No.
7	Yes..	Cellar digger	60	7.50	16	120	Smallpox.
½		Housewife					No.
15	Yes..	Marble works employee	60	9.00	36	324	Rheumatism.
5		Housewife					Childbirth.
		At home					No.
		At home					No.

b Not reported.

TABLE **I.**—GENERAL SOCIAL AND ECONOMIC CONDITION, BY FAMILIES AND INDIVIDUALS—Continued.

Family number.	Relationship to head of family.	Sex.	Age.	Conjugal condition.	Birthplace.	Birthplace of—	
						Father.	Mother.
1172	Head	M.	36	Married...	Basilicata	Basilicata	Basilicata
	Wife	F.	24	Married...	Abruzzo	Abruzzo	Abruzzo
	Son	M.	7	Single	United States...	Basilicata	Abruzzo
	Daughter	F.	5	Single	United States...	Basilicata	Abruzzo
	Son	M.	3	Single	United States...	Basilicata	Abruzzo
	Daughter	F.	$\frac{9}{12}$	Single	United States...	Basilicata	Abruzzo
1173	Head	M.	32	Married...	Basilicata	Basilicata	Basilicata
	Wife	F.	32	Married...	Basilicata	Basilicata	Basilicata
	Son	M.	7	Single	Basilicata	Basilicata	Basilicata
	Son	M.	3	Single	United States...	Basilicata	Basilicata
	Daughter	F.	1	Single	United States...	Basilicata	Basilicata
1174	Head	M.	37	Married...	Basilicata	Basilicata	Basilicata
	Wife	F.	23	Married...	Basilicata	Basilicata	Basilicata
	Daughter	F.	3	Single	United States...	Basilicata	Basilicata
	Daughter	F.	2	Single	United States...	Basilicata	Basilicata
	Daughter	F.	$\frac{1}{12}$	Single	United States...	Basilicata	Basilicata
1175	Head	M.	44	Married...	Marches	Marches	Marches
	Wife	F.	47	Married...	Basilicata	Basilicata	Basilicata
	Son	M.	16	Single	Basilicata	Marches	Basilicata
	Daughter	F.	15	Single	Basilicata	Marches	Basilicata
	Son	M.	7	Single	United States...	Marches	Basilicata
1176	Head	M.	40	Married...	Basilicata	Basilicata	Basilicata
	Wife	F.	34	Married...	Basilicata	Basilicata	Basilicata
	Daughter	F.	9	Single	United States...	Basilicata	Basilicata
	Daughter	F.	4	Single	United States...	Basilicata	Basilicata
	Daughter	F.	2	Single	United States...	Basilicata	Basilicata
	Son	M.	$\frac{1}{12}$	Single	United States...	Basilicata	Basilicata
	Boarder	M.	30	Single	Calabria	Calabria	Calabria
1177	Head	M.	53	Married...	Calabria	Calabria	Calabria
	Wife	F.	44	Married...	Calabria	Calabria	Calabria
	Son	M.	22	Single	Calabria	Calabria	Calabria
	Son	M.	14	Single	United States...	Calabria	Calabria
	Daughter	F.	11	Single	United States...	Calabria	Calabria
1178	Head	M.	39	Married...	Basilicata	Basilicata	Basilicata
	Wife	F.	34	Married...	Basilicata	Basilicata	Basilicata
	Daughter	F.	13	Single	Basilicata	Basilicata	Basilicata
	Son	M.	9	Single	Basilicata	Basilicata	Basilicata
	Son	M.	7	Single	Basilicata	Basilicata	Basilicata
1179	Head	M.	50	Married...	Basilicata	Basilicata	Basilicata
	Wife	F.	50	Married...	Basilicata	Basilicata	Basilicata
1180	Head	M.	45	Married...	Basilicata	Basilicata	Basilicata
	Wife	F.	50	Married...	Basilicata	Basilicata	Basilicata
	Son	M.	19	Single	Basilicata	Basilicata	Basilicata
	Daughter	F.	14	Single	United States...	Basilicata	Basilicata
	Daughter	F.	14	Single	United States...	Basilicata	Basilicata
1181	Head	M.	43	Married...	Basilicata	Basilicata	Basilicata
	Wife	F.	39	Married...	Basilicata	Basilicata	Basilicata
	Daughter	F.	18	Single	Basilicata	Basilicata	Basilicata
	Daughter	F.	15	Single	United States...	Basilicata	Basilicata
	Son	M.	13	Single	United States...	Basilicata	Basilicata
	Son	M.	12	Single	United States...	Basilicata	Basilicata
	Son	M.	10	Single	United States...	Basilicata	Basilicata
	Son	M.	7	Single	United States...	Basilicata	Basilicata
	Son	M.	4	Single	United States...	Basilicata	Basilicata
	Son	M.	1	Single	United States...	Basilicata	Basilicata
1182	Head	M.	29	Married...	Basilicata	Basilicata	Basilicata
	Wife	F.	18	Married...	Basilicata	Basilicata	Basilicata
1183	Head	M.	42	Married...	Basilicata	Basilicata	Basilicata
	Wife	F.	37	Married...	Basilicata	Basilicata	Basilicata
	Daughter	F.	14	Single	Basilicata	Basilicata	Basilicata
	Daughter	F.	10	Single	Basilicata	Basilicata	Basilicata
	Son	M.	8	Single	United States...	Basilicata	Basilicata
	Son	M.	4	Single	United States...	Basilicata	Basilicata
	Daughter	F.	1	Single	United States...	Basilicata	Basilicata

a Not reported.

TABLE I.—GENERAL SOCIAL AND ECONOMIC CONDITION, BY FAMILIES AND INDIVIDUALS—Continued.

Years in U.S.	Natu-ral-ized.	Profession, trade, or occupation.	Hours of work per week.	Average weekly earn-ings.	Weeks em-ploy-ed.	Total yearly earn-ings.	Sick during year, defective, maimed, or deformed.
14	Yes..	Street sweeper............	60	$7.50	22	$165	No.
14	....	Housewife...............	......	....	......	......	Childbirth.
......	....	Scholar	......	....	......	....	Fever, not specified.
......	....	At home..................	......	....	......	......	No.
......	....	At home..................	......	....	......	......	No.
......	....	At home..................	......	....	......	......	No.
8	Yes..	Street sweeper............	60	7.50	24	180	No.
6	....	Housewife...............	......	....	......	......	No.
6	....	Scholar	......	....	......	......	No.
......	....	At home..................	......	....	......	......	No.
......	....	At home..................	......	....	......	......	Convulsions.
13	Yes..	Street sweeper............	60	7.50	28	210	No.
17	....	Housewife...............	......	....	......	......	Childbirth.
......	....	At home..................	......	....	......	......	No.
......	....	At home..................	......	....	......	......	No.
......	....	At home..................	......	....	......	......	No.
14	Yes..	No occupation...........	......	....	......	......	Pneumonia; injury to spine.
8	....	Housewife...............	......	....	......	......	No.
8	....	Scholar	......	....	......	......	No.
8	....	Scholar	......	....	......	......	No.
......	....	Scholar	......	....	......	......	No.
13	Yes..	Cellar digger..............	60	6.75	22	149	No.
10	....	Housewife...............	......	....	......	......	Childbirth.
......	....	Scholar	......	....	......	......	No.
......	....	At home..................	......	....	......	......	No.
......	....	At home..................	......	....	......	......	No.
......	....	At home..................	......	....	......	......	No.
14	Yes..	Laborer....................	60	9.00	17	153	No.
23	No...	Harp repairer.............	30	10.00	52	520	No.
16	....	Housewife...............	......	....	......	......	No.
16	Yes..	Musician	(a)	6.50	52	338	No.
......	....	Musician	(a)	6.50	52	338	No.
......	....	Scholar	......	....	......	......	No.
7	Yes..	Candy factory employee...	60	6.00	26	156	No.
1⅓	....	Housewife...............	......	....	......	......	No.
1⅓	....	Scholar	......	....	......	......	No.
1½	....	Scholar	......	....	......	......	No.
1½	....	Scholar	......	....	......	......	No.
18	No...	Railroad laborer	60	7.50	14	105	No.
18	....	Housewife and merchant, groceries.	(a)	(a)	52	(a)	Rheumatism.
19	Yes..	Peddler, vegetables.......	60	(a)	24	(a)	No.
13	....	Housewife...............	......	....	......	......	No.
13	....	Sign painter's apprentice..	60	8.00	24	192	No.
......	....	No occupation...........	......	....	......	......	Consumption.
......	....	Scholar	......	....	......	......	No.
17	Yes..	Stonecutter..............	52	22.00	28	616	Bronchitis.
16	....	Housewife...............	......	....	......	......	No.
16	....	No occupation	......	....	......	......	Pneumonia.
......	....	No occupation	......	....	......	......	No.
......	....	Scholar	......	....	......	......	No.
......	....	Scholar	......	....	......	......	No.
......	....	Scholar	......	....	......	......	No.
......	....	Scholar	......	....	......	......	No.
......	....	At home..................	......	....	......	......	No.
......	....	At home..................	......	....	......	......	No.
15	Yes..	Shoemaker..............	60	10.00	36	360	No.
16	....	Housewife...............	......	....	......	......	No.
10	Yes..	Street sweeper	60	7.50	23	173	No.
10	....	Housewife...............	......	....	......	......	No.
10	....	Scholar	......	....	......	......	No.
10	....	Scholar	......	....	......	......	No.
......	....	Scholar	......	....	......	......	No.
......	....	At home..................	......	....	......	......	No.
......	....	At home..................	......	....	......	......	No.

TABLE **I.**—GENERAL SOCIAL AND ECONOMIC CONDITION, BY FAMILIES
AND INDIVIDUALS—Continued.

Family number.	Relationship to head of family.	Sex.	Age.	Conjugal condition.	Birthplace.	Birthplace of—	
						Father.	Mother.
1184	Cooperative	M.	23	Single.....	Basilicata.......	Basilicata......	Basilicata......
	Cooperative	M.	30	Married...	Basilicata.......	Basilicata......	Basilicata......
1185	Head	M.	37	Married...	Basilicata.......	Basilicata......	Basilicata......
	Wife..............	F.	23	Married...	Basilicata.......	Basilicata......	Basilicata......
	Daughter.........	F.	4	Single.....	United States...	Basilicata......	Basilicata......
	Daughter.........	F.	2	Single.....	United States...	Basilicata......	Basilicata......
	Son	M.	1	Single.....	United States...	Basilicata......	Basilicata......
1186	Head	M.	24	Single.....	Basilicata.......	Basilicata......	Basilicata......
	Mother	F.	54	Widowed	Basilicata.......	Basilicata......	Basilicata......
	Brother...........	M.	18	Single.....	Basilicata.......	Basilicata......	Basilicata......
	Brother...........	M.	16	Single.....	Basilicata.......	Basilicata......	Basilicata......
1187	Head	M.	33	Married...	Basilicata.......	Basilicata......	Basilicata......
	Wife..............	F.	30	Married...	Basilicata.......	Basilicata......	Basilicata......
	Daughter.........	F.	9	Single.....	Basilicata.......	Basilicata......	Basilicata......
	Daughter.........	F.	6	Single.....	United States...	Basilicata......	Basilicata......
	Daughter...... ..	F.	4	Single.....	United States...	Basilicata......	Basilicata......
	Lodger	M.	19	Single.....	Basilicata.......	Basilicata......	Basilicata......
	Lodger	M.	22	Single.....	Basilicata.......	Basilicata......	Basilicata......
1188	Head	M.	40	Married...	Basilicata.......	Basilicata......	Basilicata......
	Wife..............	F.	29	Married. .	Basilicata.......	Basilicata......	Basilicata......
	Son	M.	10	Single.....	United States...	Basilicata......	Basilicata......
	Daughter.........	F.	2	Single.....	United States...	Basilicata......	Basilicata......
	Son	M.	$\frac{1}{12}$	Single.....	United States...	Basilicata......	Basilicata......
1189	Head	M.	23	Married...	Basilicata.......	Basilicata......	Basilicata......
	Wife..............	F.	24	Married...	Basilicata.......	Basilicata......	Basilicata......
	Son	M.	$\frac{7}{12}$	Single.....	United States...	Basilicata......	Basilicata......
	Father............	M.	56	Married...	Basilicata.......	Basilicata......	Basilicata......
1190	Head	M.	39	Married...	Campania.......	Campania......	Campania......
	Wife..............	F.	26	Married...	Basilicata.......	Basilicata......	Basilicata......
	Daughter.........	F.	13	Single.....	United States...	Campania......	Basilicata......
	Son	M.	6	Single.....	United States...	Campania......	Basilicata......
	Son	M.	3	Single.....	United States...	Campania......	Basilicata......
1191	Head	M.	34	Married...	Basilicata.......	Basilicata......	Basilicata......
	Wife..............	F.	40	Married...	Basilicata.	Basilicata......	Basilicata......
	Daughter.........	F.	2	Single.....	United States...	Basilicata......	Basilicata......
1192	Head	M.	30	Married...	Basilicata.......	Basilicata......	Basilicata......
	Wife..............	F.	26	Married...	Basilicata.......	Basilicata......	Basilicata......
	Son	M.	9	Single.....	United States...	Basilicata......	Basilicata......
	Daughter.........	F.	7	Single.....	United States...	Basilicata......	Basilicata......
	Daughter.........	F.	5	Single.....	United States...	Basilicata......	Basilicata......
	Son	M.	2	Single.....	United States...	Basilicata......	Basilicata......
1193	Head	M.	26	Married...	Basilicata.......	Basilicata......	Basilicata......
	Wife..............	F.	25	Married...	Basilicata.......	Basilicata......	Basilicata......
1194	Head	M.	36	Married...	Basilicata.......	Basilicata......	Basilicata......
	Wife..............	F.	25	Married...	Basilicata.......	Basilicata......	Basilicata......
	Daughter.........	F.	3	Single.....	United States...	Basilicata......	Basilicata......
	Daughter.........	F.	$\frac{1}{12}$	Single.....	United States...	Basilicata......	Basilicata......
1195	Head	M.	37	Married...	Basilicata.......	Basilicata......	Basilicata......
	Wife..............	F.	26	Married...	Basilicata.......	Basilicata......	Basilicata......
	Daughter	F.	7	Single.....	United States...	Basilicata......	Basilicata......
	Daughter	F.	4	Single.....	United States ..	Basilicata......	Basilicata......
1196	Head	M.	30	Married...	Basilicata.......	Basilicata......	Basilicata......
	Wife..............	F.	26	Married...	Basilicata.......	Basilicata......	Basilicata......
	Son	M.	4	Single.....	United States...	Basilicata......	Basilicata......
	Son	M.	1	Single.....	United States...	Basilicata......	Basilicata......
1197	Cooperative	M.	24	Single.....	Sicily	Sicily	Sicily ....
	Cooperative	M.	26	Single.....	Sicily	Sicily	Sicily ....
	Cooperative	M.	22	Single.....	Sicily	Sicily	Sicily ....
	Cooperative	M.	21	Single.....	Sicily	Sicily	Sicily ....

a Not reported.

TABLE I.—GENERAL SOCIAL AND ECONOMIC CONDITION, BY FAMILIES AND INDIVIDUALS—Continued.

Years in U.S.	Natu- ral- ized.	Profession, trade, or occupation.	Hours of work per week.	Average weekly earn- ings.	Weeks em- ploy- ed.	Total yearly earn- ings.	Sick during year, defective, maimed, or deformed.
4	No...	Hod carrier..............	54	$9.25	44	$407	No.
10	No...	Laborer..................	48	9.50	32	304	No.
15	Yes..	Saloon keeper............	96	(a)	52	(a)	Dyspepsia.
6	......	Housewife................					No.
......	......	At home.................					No.
......	......	At home.................					No.
......	......	At home.................					No.
11	Yes..	Paint shop employee	48	9.00	20	180	No.
3	......	Housewife...............					No.
7	......	Scholar and shoemaker's apprentice.	48	2.50	52	130	No.
4	......	Scholar and bootblack	60	2.00	52	104	No.
9	Yes..	Hod carrier..............	48	9.00	30	270	No.
8	......	Housewife................					No.
8	......	At home.................					Whooping cough.
......	......	At home.................					Whooping cough.
......	......	At home.................					Whooping cough.
7	......	Musician	(a)	8.00	52	416	No.
2	No..	Musician	(a)	8.00	52	416	No.
13	Yes..	Hod carrier..............	48	10.50	3	32	Injury by accident.
11	......	Housewife and pants maker.	(a)	2.25	24	54	Childbirth.
......	......	Scholar					No.
......	......	At home.................					No.
......	......	At home.................					No.
1	No...	Carpenter................	48	12.00	4	48	No.
1	......	Housewife and pants maker.	(a)	2.25	24	54	Childbirth.
......	......	At home.................					No.
4	No...	Mason, stone.............	48	19.20	22	422	No.
11	Yes..	Street sweeper...........	60	9.00	32	288	No.
14	......	Housewife and pants maker.	(a)	2.00	12	24	No.
......	......	No occupation					No.
......	......	At home.................					No.
......	......	At home.................					No.
10	Yes..	Candy factory employee...	60	7.00	17	119	No.
5	......	Housewife................					Eyes, inflammation of both.
......	......	At home.................					No.
15	Yes..	Railroad employee (b).....	(a)	12.00	b12	198	No.
15	......	Housewife................					No.
......	......	Scholar					No.
......	......	Scholar					No.
......	......	At home.................					No.
......	......	At home.................					No.
5	No...	Bootblack	82	7.00	52	364	No.
5	......	Housewife................					No.
10	Yes..	Paver....................	54	10.50	40	420	No.
6	......	Housewife................					Childbirth.
......	......	At home.................					No.
......	......	At home.................					No.
12	Yes..	Hod carrier..............	48	10.00	32	320	No.
10	......	Housewife................					No.
......	......	Scholar					No.
......	......	At home.................					No.
9	Yes..	Laborer..................	60	6.75	26	176	No.
5	......	Housewife................					No.
......	......	At home.................					No.
......	......	At home.................					Convulsions.
2	No...	Peddler, fruit............	36	4.50	52	234	No.
2	No...	Peddler, fruit............	36	4.50	52	234	No.
2	No...	Peddler, fruit............	36	4.50	52	234	No.
3	No...	Peddler, fruit............	36	4.50	52	234	No.

b Also worked as hydrant inspector four weeks, at $13.50 per week.

TABLE **I.**—GENERAL SOCIAL AND ECONOMIC CONDITION, BY FAMILIES
AND INDIVIDUALS—Continued.

Family number.	Relationship to head of family.	Sex.	Age.	Conjugal condition.	Birthplace.	Birthplace of—	
						Father.	Mother.
1198	Head	M.	28	Married...	Basilicata	Basilicata	Basilicata
	Wife	F.	28	Married...	Basilicata	Basilicata	Basilicata
	Daughter	F.	3	Single	United States	Basilicata	Basilicata
	Son	M.	1	Single	United States	Basilicata	Basilicata
1199	Head	M.	36	Married...	Basilicata	Basilicata	Basilicata
	Wife	F.	30	Married...	Basilicata	Basilicata	Basilicata
	Son	M.	6	Single	United States	Basilicata	Basilicata
1200	Head	M.	31	Married...	Basilicata	Basilicata	Basilicata
	Wife	F.	22	Married...	Basilicata	Basilicata	Basilicata
	Son	M.	3	Single	United States	Basilicata	Basilicata
	Son	M.	2	Single	United States	Basilicata	Basilicata
	Mother-in-law	F.	60	Widowed	Basilicata	Basilicata	Basilicata
1201	Cooperative	M.	45	Married...	Basilicata	Basilicata	Basilicata
	Cooperative	M.	20	Single	Basilicata	Basilicata	Basilicata
	Cooperative	M.	30	Married...	Basilicata	Basilicata	Basilicata
1202	Head	M.	32	Married...	Venetia	Venetia	Venetia
	Wife	F.	25	Married...	Tuscany	Tuscany	Tuscany
	Stepson	M.	7	Single	Tuscany	Tuscany	Tuscany
1203	Head	M.	31	Married...	Venetia	Venetia	Venetia
	Wife	F.	22	Married...	Venetia	Venetia	Venetia
	Brother	M.	24	Single	Venetia	Venetia	Venetia
1204	Head	M.	37	Married...	Emilia	Emilia	Emilia
	Wife	F.	26	Married...	Emilia	Emilia	Emilia
1205	Head	M.	26	Married...	Tuscany	Tuscany	Tuscany
	Wife	F.	28	Married...	Tuscany	Tuscany	Tuscany
	Son	M.	3	Single	United States	Tuscany	Tuscany
	Daughter	F.	$\frac{1}{12}$	Single	United States	Tuscany	Tuscany
1206	Head	M.	32	Married...	Lombardy	Lombardy	Lombardy
	Wife	F.	25	Married...	Lombardy	Lombardy	Lombardy
	Daughter	F.	2	Single	United States	Lombardy	Lombardy
	Son	M.	$\frac{5}{12}$	Single	United States	Lombardy	Lombardy
1207	Head	M.	37	Married...	Liguria	Liguria	Liguria
	Wife	F.	41	Married...	Liguria	Liguria	Liguria
1208	Head	M.	51	Married...	Emilia	Emilia	Emilia
	Wife	F.	45	Married...	Emilia	Emilia	Emilia
	Daughter	F.	19	Single	Emilia	Emilia	Emilia
	Daughter	F.	12	Single	Emilia	Emilia	Emilia
	Daughter	F.	10	Single	Emilia	Emilia	Emilia
	Son	M.	9	Single	Emilia	Emilia	Emilia
	Son	M.	6	Single	United States	Emilia	Emilia
	Daughter	F.	3	Single	United States	Emilia	Emilia
1209	Head	M.	60	Married...	Lombardy	Lombardy	Lombardy
	Wife	F.	50	Married...	Lombardy	Lombardy	Lombardy
1210	Head	M.	40	Married...	Liguria	Liguria	Liguria
	Wife	F.	35	Married...	Liguria	Liguria	Liguria
	Son	M.	13	Single	United States	Liguria	Liguria
	Son	M.	12	Single	United States	Liguria	Liguria
	Daughter	F.	9	Single	United States	Liguria	Liguria
	Daughter	F.	4	Single	United States	Liguria	Liguria
	Son	M.	2	Single	United States	Liguria	Liguria
	Brother-in-law	M.	23	Single	Liguria	Liguria	Liguria
1211	Head	M.	70	Married...	Liguria	Liguria	Liguria
	Wife	F.	45	Married...	Liguria	Liguria	Liguria
	Daughter	F.	25	Single	United States	Liguria	Liguria
	Son	M.	22	Single	United States	Liguria	Liguria
	Son	M.	21	Single	United States	Liguria	Liguria
	Son	M.	17	Single	United States	Liguria	Liguria
	Daughter	F.	15	Single	United States	Liguria	Liguria
	Cousin-in-law	M.	21	Single	Liguria	Liguria	Liguria

a Not reported.

TABLE **I.**—GENERAL SOCIAL AND ECONOMIC CONDITION, BY FAMILIES AND INDIVIDUALS—Continued.

Years in U. S.	Naturalized.	Profession, trade, or occupation.	Hours of work per week.	Average weekly earnings.	Weeks employed.	Total yearly earnings.	Sick during year, defective, maimed, or deformed.
6	Yes..	Hod carrier	48	$9.00	22	$198	No.
4	......	Housewife					No.
......	......	At home					No.
......	......	At home					No.
19	Yes..	Musician	(a)	8.00	52	416	No.
8	......	Housewife					No.
......	......	At home					No.
10	Yes..	Teamster, with team	48	18.00	22	396	No.
6	......	Housewife					No.
......	......	At home					No.
......	......	At home					No.
6	......	No occupation					No.
1	No...	No occupation					No.
4	......	Tailor	60	15.00	34	510	No.
4	No...	Tailor	60	12.00	34	408	No.
4	No...	Peddler, fruit	(a)	3.00	32	96	No.
6	......	Housewife					Spine, weakness of.
6	......	Scholar					No.
3	No...	Carpenter	58	9.00	22	198	No.
3	......	Housewife					No.
3	No...	Mosaic layer	53	9.00	40	360	No.
7	No...	Candy factory employee	60	7.00	27	189	No.
7	......	Housewife					No.
5	No...	Soap factory employee	59	9.00	51	459	No.
4	......	Housewife					Childbirth; loss of one leg.
......	......	At home					No.
......	......	At home					No.
13	Yes..	Stonecutter	44	27.75	20	555	No.
5	......	Housewife					Childbirth.
......	......	At home					No.
......	......	At home					Bronchitis.
7	No...	Janitor	65	9.50	52	494	No.
14	......	Housewife					No.
7	No...	Candy factory employee	44	8.00	36	288	No.
7	......	Housewife					No.
7	......	Nutcracker, candy factory	(a)	4.00	52	208	No.
7	......	Macaroni factory employee.	60	3.00	30	90	No.
7	......	Scholar					No.
7	......	Scholar					No.
......	......	Scholar					No.
......	......	At home					No.
15	No...	No occupation					No.
10	......	Housewife					No.
18	Yes..	Salesman, fruit	78	10.00	52	520	No.
15	......	Housewife					No.
......	......	Scholar					No.
......	......	Scholar					No.
......	......	Scholar					No.
......	......	At home					No.
......	......	At home					No.
4	No...	No occupation					No.
57	Yes..	Retired					No.
28	......	Housewife					No.
......	......	Tobacco stripper	54	8.00	51	408	No.
......	......	Teamster	48	9.00	36	324	No.
......	......	Teamster	48	9.00	36	324	No.
......	......	Polisher, wooden shoe forms.	48	5.00	36	180	No.
......	......	Tobacco stripper	54	5.00	52	260	No.
1	No...	Liquor store employee	48	6.00	22	132	No.

TABLE **I.**—GENERAL SOCIAL AND ECONOMIC CONDITION, BY FAMILIES AND INDIVIDUALS—Continued.

Family number.	Relationship to head of family.	Sex.	Age.	Conjugal condition.	Birthplace.	Birthplace of—	
						Father.	Mother.
1212	Head	M.	42	Married	Tuscany	Tuscany	Tuscany
	Wife	F.	44	Married	Tuscany	Tuscany	Tuscany
	Son	M.	13	Single	Tuscany	Tuscany	Tuscany
	Daughter	F.	1	Single	United States	Tuscany	Tuscany
1213	Head	M.	42	Married	Liguria	Liguria	Liguria
	Wife	F.	35	Married	United States	Liguria	Scotland
	Son	M.	12	Single	United States	Liguria	United States
	Son	M.	9	Single	United States	Liguria	United States
	Son	M.	7	Single	United States	Liguria	United States
	Daughter	F.	4	Single	United States	Liguria	United States
1214	Head	M.	34	Married	Sicily	Sicily	Sicily
	Wife	F.	28	Married	Sicily	Sicily	Sicily
	Son	M.	10	Single	Sicily	Sicily	Sicily
	Son	M.	2	Single	United States	Sicily	Sicily
	Daughter	F.	$\frac{3}{12}$	Single	United States	Sicily	Sicily
1215	Head	M.	44	Married	Sicily	Sicily	Sicily
	Wife	F.	38	Married	Sicily	Sicily	Sicily
	Son	M.	14	Single	Sicily	Sicily	Sicily
	Son	M.	10	Single	Sicily	Sicily	Sicily
	Son	M.	8	Single	Sicily	Sicily	Sicily
	Daughter	F.	3	Single	United States	Sicily	Sicily
	Daughter	F.	2	Single	United States	Sicily	Sicily
	Brother-in-law	M.	33	Single	Sicily	Sicily	Sicily
1216	Head	M.	25	Married	Tuscany	Tuscany	Tuscany
	Wife	F.	19	Married	Tuscany	Tuscany	Tuscany
	Daughter	F.	2	Single	United States	Tuscany	Tuscany
	Daughter	F.	$\frac{5}{12}$	Single	United States	Tuscany	Tuscany
	Father-in-law	M.	60	Married	Tuscany	Tuscany	Tuscany
1217	Head	M.	33	Married	Venetia	Venetia	Venetia
	Wife	F.	28	Married	Venetia	Venetia	Venetia
	Daughter	F.	8	Single	Venetia	Venetia	Venetia
	Daughter	F.	5	Single	United States	Venetia	Venetia
	Daughter	F.	2	Single	United States	Venetia	Venetia
	Daughter	F.	$\frac{1}{12}$	Single	United States	Venetia	Venetia
1218	Head	M.	48	Married	Abruzzo	Abruzzo	Abruzzo
	Wife	F.	45	Married	Abruzzo	Abruzzo	Abruzzo
	Son	M.	17	Single	Abruzzo	Abruzzo	Abruzzo
	Son	M.	15	Single	Abruzzo	Abruzzo	Abruzzo
	Son	M.	10	Single	Abruzzo	Abruzzo	Abruzzo
	Son	M.	6	Single	Abruzzo	Abruzzo	Abruzzo
1219	Head	M.	56	Married	Emilia	Emilia	Emilia
	Wife	F.	44	Married	Emilia	Emilia	Emilia
	Daughter	F.	15	Single	Emilia	Emilia	Emilia
	Son	M.	10	Single	Emilia	Emilia	Emilia
	Daughter	F.	8	Single	United States	Emilia	Emilia
1220	Head	M.	40	Married	Sicily	Sicily	Sicily
	Wife	F.	33	Married	Sicily	Sicily	Sicily
	Son	M.	13	Single	Sicily	Sicily	Sicily
	Son	M.	11	Single	Sicily	Sicily	Sicily
	Daughter	F.	7	Single	Sicily	Sicily	Sicily
	Daughter	F.	2	Single	United States	Sicily	Sicily
	Son	M.	$\frac{5}{12}$	Single	United States	Sicily	Sicily
1221	Head	M.	31	Married	Tuscany	Tuscany	Tuscany
1222	Head	M.	22	Single	Liguria	Liguria	Liguria
	Sister	F.	24	Single	Liguria	Liguria	Liguria
1223	Cooperative	M.	20	Single	Tuscany	Tuscany	Tuscany
	Cooperative	M.	17	Single	Tuscany	Tuscany	Tuscany
	Cooperative	M.	31	Married	Tuscany	Tuscany	Tuscany
	Cooperative	M.	26	Single	Tuscany	Tuscany	Tuscany
1224	Cooperative	M.	25	Single	Abruzzo	Abruzzo	Abruzzo
	Cooperative	M.	29	Married	Abruzzo	Abruzzo	Abruzzo
	Cooperative	M.	24	Single	Abruzzo	Abruzzo	Abruzzo

a Not reported.

TABLE **I.**—GENERAL SOCIAL AND ECONOMIC CONDITION, BY FAMILIES AND INDIVIDUALS—Continued.

Years in U.S.	Naturalized.	Profession, trade, or occupation.	Hours of work per week.	Average weekly earnings.	Weeks employed.	Total yearly earnings.	Sick during year, defective, maimed, or deformed.
8	Yes..	Merchant, fruit	112	(a)	52	(a)	No.
3	......	Housewife	......	......	......	......	No.
3	......	Scholar	......	......	......	......	No.
......	......	At home	......	......	......	......	No.
40	Yes..	Teamster	60	$12.00	52	$624	No.
......	......	Housewife	......	......	......	......	No.
......	......	Scholar	......	......	......	......	No.
......	......	Scholar	......	......	......	......	No.
......	......	Scholar	......	......	......	......	No.
......	......	At home	......	......	......	......	No.
6	Yes..	Hod carrier	60	7.50	16	120	No.
6	......	Housewife	......	......	......	......	Childbirth.
6	......	Scholar	......	......	......	......	No.
......	......	At home	......	......	......	......	No.
......	......	At home	......	......	......	......	No.
18	Yes..	Hod carrier	48	9.00	36	324	No.
5	......	Housewife	......	......	......	......	Leg, one swollen.
5	......	Scholar	......	......	......	......	No.
5	......	Scholar	......	......	......	......	No.
5	......	Scholar	......	......	......	......	No.
......	......	At home	......	......	......	......	Eyes, inflammation of both.
......	......	At home	......	......	......	......	No.
5	No...	Hod carrier	48	9.00	36	324	No.
5	No...	Mosaic layer	54	8.10	16	130	No.
6	......	Housewife	......	......	......	......	Childbirth.
......	......	At home	......	......	......	......	No.
......	......	At home	......	......	......	......	No.
10	No...	Expressman	(a)	(a)	36	(a)	No.
8	Yes..	Mosaic layer	53	9.00	22	198	Eye, inflammation of one.
8	......	Housewife	......	......	......	......	Childbirth.
8	......	Scholar	......	......	......	......	No.
......	......	At home	......	......	......	......	Fever, typhoid.
......	......	At home	......	......	......	......	Fever, typhoid.
......	......	At home	......	......	......	......	No.
4	No...	Hod carrier	54	9.00	22	198	No.
4	......	Housewife	......	......	......	......	Female complaint.
4	......	Scholar and hod carrier	54	9.00	22	198	No.
4	......	Scholar	......	......	......	......	No.
4	......	Scholar	......	......	......	......	No.
4	......	At home	......	......	......	......	No.
8	No...	No occupation	......	......	......	......	Sunstroke.
8	......	Housewife	......	......	......	......	No.
8	......	Scholar	......	......	......	......	No.
8	......	Scholar	......	......	......	......	No.
......	......	Scholar	......	......	......	......	No.
6	Yes..	Hod carrier	(a)	7.20	44	317	No.
5	......	Housewife	......	......	......	......	Childbirth.
5	......	Scholar	......	......	......	......	No.
5	......	Scholar and newsboy	15	.40	52	21	No.
5	......	Scholar	......	......	......	......	No.
......	......	At home	......	......	......	......	No.
......	......	At home	......	......	......	......	No.
4	No...	Scissors grinder	60	4.00	26	104	No.
$\frac{4}{12}$	No ..	No occupation	......	......	......	......	No.
$\frac{1}{12}$	......	Housewife	......	......	......	......	No.
4	......	Peddler, fruit	36	3.00	42	126	No.
3	......	No occupation	......	......	......	......	No.
1	No...	Peddler, fruit	36	3.00	28	84	No.
$\frac{1}{12}$	No...	No occupation	......	......	......	......	No.
3	No...	Railroad laborer	60	6.60	26	172	No.
2	No...	Sewer digger	(a)	8.40	12	101	No.
2	No...	Sewer digger	(a)	8.40	10	84	No.

TABLE **I.**—GENERAL SOCIAL AND ECONOMIC CONDITION, BY FAMILIES AND INDIVIDUALS—Continued.

Family number.	Relationship to head of family.	Sex.	Age.	Conjugal condition.	Birthplace.	Birthplace of—	
						Father.	Mother.
1225	Head	M.	40	Married...	Abruzzo	Abruzzo	Abruzzo
	Wife	F.	34	Married..	Abruzzo	Abruzzo	Abruzzo
	Daughter	F.	9	Single....	Abruzzo	Abruzzo	Abruzzo
	Daughter	F.	6	Single.....	United States	Abruzzo	Abruzzo
	Son	M.	4	Single.....	United States	Abruzzo	Abruzzo
	Son	M.	2	Single.....	United States	Abruzzo	Abruzzo
1226	Head	M.	34	Married...	Lombardy	Lombardy	Lombardy
	Wife	F.	33	Married..	Emilia	Emilia	Emilia
	Son	M.	5	Single.....	United States	Lombardy	Emilia
	Boarder	M.	34	Single.....	Emilia	Emilia	Emilia
1227	Head	M.	42	Married...	Venetia	Venetia	Venetia
1228	Head	M.	44	Widowed	Sicily	Sicily	Sicily
	Son	M.	8	Single.....	United States	Sicily	Sicily
	Son	M.	6	Single....	United States	Sicily	Sicily
	Housekeeper	F.	60	Single	Liguria	Liguria	Liguria
1229	Head	M.	34	Married...	Tuscany	Tuscany	Tuscany
	Wife	F.	34	Married...	Tuscany	Tuscany	Tuscany
	Son	M.	1	Single.....	United States	Tuscany	Tuscany
1230	Head	M.	30	Married...	Liguria	Liguria	Liguria
	Wife	F.	30	Married...	Liguria	Liguria	Liguria
	Daughter	F.	8	Single.....	Liguria	Liguria	Liguria
	Daughter	F.	2	Single.....	Liguria	Liguria	Liguria
1231	Head	M.	30	Married...	Tuscany	Tuscany	Tuscany
	Wife	F.	26	Married...	Tuscany	Tuscany	Tuscany
1232	Head	M.	39	Married...	Tuscany	Tuscany	Tuscany
	Wife	F.	33	Married...	Tuscany	Tuscany	Tuscany
	Daughter	F.	1	Single.....	United States	Tuscany	Tuscany
1233	Head	M.	70	Married...	Liguria	Liguria	Liguria
	Wife	F.	54	Married...	Liguria	Liguria	Liguria
1234	Head	M.	52	Married...	Sicily	Sicily	Sicily
	Wife	F.	44	Married...	Sicily	Sicily	Sicily
	Sister	F.	31	Single.....	Sicily	Sicily	Sicily
	Cousin	M.	21	Single.....	Sicily	Sicily	Sicily
1235	Head	M.	29	Married...	Venetia	Venetia	Venetia
	Wife	F.	24	Married...	Liguria	Liguria	Liguria
1236	Head	M.	24	Married...	Lombardy	Lombardy	Lombardy
	Wife	F.	21	Married...	Lombardy	Lombardy	Lombardy
1237	Head	M.	27	Married...	Piedmont	Piedmont	Piedmont
	Wife	F.	23	Married...	Piedmont	Piedmont	Piedmont
	Daughter	F.	5	Single.....	Piedmont	Piedmont	Piedmont
	Daughter	F.	$\frac{3}{7}$	Single.....	United States	Piedmont	Piedmont
	Mother-in-law	F.	61	Widowed	Piedmont	Piedmont	Piedmont
	Brother-in-law	M.	27	Married...	Piedmont	Piedmont	Piedmont
1238	Head	M.	29	Married...	Lombardy	Lombardy	Lombardy
	Wife	F.	28	Married...	Lombardy	Lombardy	Lombardy
	Son	M.	5	Single.....	United States	Lombardy	Lombardy
	Daughter	F.	2	Single.....	United States	Lombardy	Lombardy
1239	Head	M.	32	Married...	Lombardy	Lombardy	Lombardy
	Wife	F.	31	Married...	Lombardy	Lombardy	Lombardy
	Mother-in-law	F.	60	Widowed	Lombardy	Lombardy	Lombardy
	Brother-in-law	M.	22	Single.....	Lombardy	Lombardy	Lombardy
1240	Head	Sex.	35	Married...	Lombardy	Lombardy	Lombardy
	Wife	F.	36	Married...	Lombardy	Lombardy	Lombardy
	Son	M.	13	Single	Lombardy	Lombardy	Lombardy
	Daughter	F.	7	Single.....	United States	Lombardy	Lombardy
1241	Head	M.	25	Married...	Liguria	Liguria	Liguria
	Wife	F.	24	Married...	Liguria	Liguria	Liguria
	Daughter	F.	2	Single.....	United States	Liguria	Liguria
	Daughter	F.	$\frac{5}{7}$	Single.....	United States	Liguria	Liguria
	Brother-in-law	M.	29	Single.....	Liguria	Liguria	Liguria

a Not reported.

TABLE **I.**—GENERAL SOCIAL AND ECONOMIC CONDITION, BY FAMILIES AND INDIVIDUALS—Continued.

Years in U. S.	Natu-ral-ized.	Profession, trade, or occupation.	Hours of work per week.	Average weekly earn-ings.	Weeks em-ploy-ed.	Total yearly earn-ings.	Sick during year, defective, maimed, or deformed.
9	No...	Sewer digger	54	$9 00	22	$198	No.
9	......	Housewife					No.
9	......	At home					No.
......	......	At home					No.
......	......	At home					No.
......	......	At home					No.
9	Yes..	Cook	98	12 00	48	576	No.
6	......	Housewife					No.
......	......	At home					No.
(a)	Yes..	Cook	98	14. 00	48	672	No.
3	No...	Hod carrier	(a)	8. 40	20	168	No.
15	Yes..	No occupation					No.
......	......	Scholar					No.
......	......	At home					No.
14	......	Housewife					No.
5	No...	Peddler, fruit and nuts	36	9. 00	24	216	No.
3	......	Housewife					No.
......	......	At home					No.
3	No...	Salesman, fruit	72	8. 00	52	416	No.
1	......	Housewife					No.
1	......	At home					No.
1	......	At home					No.
7	No...	Candy factory employee	55	7. 00	32	224	No.
6	......	Housewife					No.
7	No...	Peddler, fruit	36	6. 00	24	144	No.
7	......	Housewife					No.
......	......	At home					Brain, congestion of.
18	Yes..	Hod carrier	48	9. 00	8	72	Sunstroke.
18	......	Housewife					No.
25	Yes..	Merchant, fruit	(a)	(a)	52	(a)	No.
25	......	Housewife					No.
2	......	No occupation					No.
5	Yes..	Barber	80	12. 00	52	624	No.
1	No...	Mosaic layer	54	9. 00	10	90	No.
1	......	Housewife					No.
6	Yes..	Mosaic layer	48	10. 50	22	231	No.
5	......	Housewife					No.
5	No...	Machinist	57½	12. 00	51	612	No.
5	......	Housewife					Childbirth.
5	......	At home					No.
......	......	At home					Female complaint.
1⅔ / 5	No...	Machinist	57½	12. 00	51	612	No.
10	Yes..	Mosaic layer	48	7. 50	17	128	No.
10	......	Housewife					No.
......	......	At home					No.
......	......	At home					No.
4	No...	Paver	54	7. 50	32	240	No.
4	......	Housewife					No.
5	......	No occupation					No.
7	Yes..	Mosaic layer	54	(a)	24	(a)	No.
13	No...	Salesman, fruit	72	9. 00	27	243	No.
13	......	Housewife					No.
13	......	Scholar					No.
......	......	Scholar					No.
6	No...	Salesman, fruit	60	10. 00	32	320	No.
6	......	Housewife					Childbirth.
......	......	At home					No.
......	......	At home					No.
4	No...	Salesman, fruit	60	(a)	52	(a)	No.

TABLE **I.**—GENERAL SOCIAL AND ECONOMIC CONDITION, BY FAMILIES AND INDIVIDUALS—Continued.

Family number.	Relationship to head of family.	Sex.	Age.	Conjugal condition.	Birthplace.	Birthplace of—	
						Father.	Mother.
1242	Head	M.	39	Married	Lombardy	Lombardy	Lombardy
	Wife	F.	38	Married	Lombardy	Lombardy	Lombardy
	Daughter	F.	12	Single	Lombardy	Lombardy	Lombardy
1243	Head	M.	32	Married	Sicily	Sicily	Sicily
	Wife	F.	25	Married	Sicily	Sicily	Sicily
	Son	M.	5	Single	United States	Sicily	Sicily
	Son	M.	2	Single	United States	Sicily	Sicily
	Son	M.	$\frac{7}{12}$	Single	United States	Sicily	Sicily
1244	Head	M.	23	Married	Liguria	Liguria	Liguria
	Wife	F.	21	Married	Liguria	Liguria	Liguria
1245	Head	M.	32	Married	Liguria	Liguria	Liguria
	Wife	F.	27	Married	Liguria	Liguria	Liguria
	Son	M.	8	Single	United States	Liguria	Liguria
	Son	M.	6	Single	United States	Liguria	Liguria
	Son	M.	4	Single	United States	Liguria	Liguria
1246	Head	M.	22	Married	Liguria	Liguria	Liguria
	Wife	F.	21	Married	Liguria	Liguria	Liguria
1247	Head	M.	50	Married	Basilicata	Basilicata	Basilicata
	Wife	F.	50	Married	Basilicata	Basilicata	Basilicata
	Daughter	F.	16	Single	Basilicata	Basilicata	Basilicata
	Daughter	F.	14	Single	United States	Basilicata	Basilicata
1248	Head	M.	28	Married	Basilicata	Basilicata	Basilicata
	Wife	F.	23	Married	Basilicata	Basilicata	Basilicata
	Daughter	F.	2	Single	United States	Basilicata	Basilicata
1249	Head	M.	37	Married	Abruzzo	Abruzzo	Abruzzo
	Wife	F.	30	Married	Abruzzo	Abruzzo	Abruzzo
	Daughter	F.	6	Single	Abruzzo	Abruzzo	Abruzzo
	Son	M.	2	Single	United States	Abruzzo	Abruzzo
1250	Head	M.	34	Married	Basilicata	Basilicata	Basilicata
	Wife	F.	29	Married	Basilicata	Basilicata	Basilicata
	Son	M.	7	Single	Basilicata	Basilicata	Basilicata
	Son	M.	3	Single	United States	Basilicata	Basilicata
	Daughter	F.	$\frac{8}{12}$	Single	United States	Basilicata	Basilicata
	Sister-in-law	F.	16	Single	Basilicata	Basilicata	Basilicata
1251	Head	M.	25	Married	Basilicata	Basilicata	Basilicata
	Wife	F.	40	Married	Basilicata	Basilicata	Basilicata
1252	Head	M.	31	Married	Basilicata	Basilicata	Basilicata
	Wife	F.	25	Married	Basilicata	Basilicata	Basilicata
	Daughter	F.	5	Single	Basilicata	Basilicata	Basilicata
	Daughter	F.	3	Single	United States	Basilicata	Basilicata
	Daughter	F.	1	Single	United States	Basilicata	Basilicata
	Son	M.	$\frac{1}{12}$	Single	United States	Basilicata	Basilicata
	Brother-in-law	M.	20	Single	Basilicata	Basilicata	Basilicata
	Lodger	M.	22	Single	Basilicata	Basilicata	Basilicata
1253	Head	M.	32	Married	Basilicata	Basilicata	Basilicata
	Wife	F.	32	Married	Basilicata	Basilicata	Basilicata
	Daughter	F.	4	Single	Basilicata	Basilicata	Basilicata
	Daughter	F.	3	Single	France	Basilicata	Basilicata
	Daughter	F.	$\frac{5}{12}$	Single	United States	Basilicata	Basilicata
1254	Head	M	39	Married	Campania	Campania	Campania
	Wife	F.	39	Married	Campania	Campania	Campania
	Nephew	M.	24	Single	Campania	Campania	Campania
1255	Head	M.	37	Married	Campania	Campania	Campania
	Wife	F.	24	Married	Basilicata	Basilicata	Basilicata
	Son	M.	5	Single	United States	Campania	Basilicata
	Daughter	F.	1	Single	United States	Campania	Basilicata
1256	Head	M.	52	Married	Basilicata	Basilicata	Basilicata
	Wife	F.	50	Married	Basilicata	Basilicata	Basilicata
	Son	M.	19	Single	United States	Basilicata	Basilicata

a Not reported.

TABLE **I.**—GENERAL SOCIAL AND ECONOMIC CONDITION, BY FAMILIES AND INDIVIDUALS—Continued.

Years in U. S.	Naturalized.	Profession, trade, or occupation.	Hours of work per week.	Average weekly earnings.	Weeks employed.	Total yearly earnings.	Sick during year, defective, maimed, or deformed.
6	No...	Cabinetmaker	(a)	$18.00	52	$936	No.
7	......	Housewife..............					No.
7	......	Scholar..............					No.
15	Yes..	Salesman, fruit	72	18.00	52	936	No.
11	......	Housewife..............					Childbirth.
......	......	At home.............					No.
......	......	At home........					No.
......	......	At home.............					No.
5	Yes..	Merchant, fruit...........	70	9.00	52	468	No.
5	......	Housewife.............					No.
11	Yes..	Saloon keeper..............	70	(a)	52	(a)	No.
11	......	Housewife.............					No.
......	......	Scholar.............					No.
......	......	At home.............					No.
......	......	At home.............					No.
5	No...	Expressman..............	(a)	(a)	52	(a)	No.
4	......	Housewife.............					No.
24	Yes..	No occupation					No.
16	......	Housewife.............					No.
16	......	No occupation					No.
......	......	Scholar.............					No.
17	Yes..	Musician..............	(a)	9.00	52	468	No.
7	......	Housewife.............					No.
......	......	At home.............					No.
6	No...	Laborer..............	60	9.00	17	153	No.
6	......	Housewife.............					No.
6	......	At home.............					Glands, scrofulous.
......	......	At home.............					No.
7	Yes..	Street sweeper............	60	8.40	12	101	No.
4	......	Housewife and pants maker.	(a)	1.00	26	26	Childbirth.
4	......	Scholar.............					No.
......	......	At home.............					No.
......	......	At home.............					No.
3	......	Pants maker..............	(a)	1.00	26	26	No.
15	Yes..	Railroad laborer............	60	7.50	12	90	Dyspepsia.
14	......	Housewife.............					Fever, not specified.
6	Yes..	Hod carrier..............	60	7.50	22	165	No.
4	......	Housewife.............					Childbirth.
4	......	At home.............					No.
......	......	At home.............					Bronchitis.
......	......	At home.............					No.
......	......	At home.............					No.
8	......	Barber..............	93	(a)	52	(a)	No.
10	Yes..	Hod carrier..............	48	7.20	14	101	No.
3	No..	News dealer	66	6.00	52	312	No.
3	......	Housewife.............					Childbirth.
3	......	At home.............					No.
3	......	At home.............					No.
......	......	At home.............					No.
11	Yes..	Candy factory employee...	60	6.00	26	156	No.
11	......	Housewife					No.
2	No...	Sewer digger	60	7.50	14	105	No.
15	Yes..	Saloon keeper..............	98	(a)	52	(a)	Bronchitis.
20	......	Housewife.............					No.
......	......	At home.............					Diphtheria.
......	......	At home.............					Bronchitis.
22	Yes...	Barber..............	86½	(a)	52	(a)	No.
20	......	Housewife.............					No.
......	......	Barber..............	86½	(a)	52	(a)	No.

TABLE **I.**—GENERAL SOCIAL AND ECONOMIC CONDITION, BY FAMILIES AND INDIVIDUALS—Continued.

Family number.	Relationship to head of family.	Sex.	Age.	Conjugal condition.	Birthplace.	Birthplace of— Father.	Birthplace of— Mother.
1257	Head	M.	28	Married...	Lombardy	Lombardy	Lombardy
	Wife	F.	24	Married...	Lombardy	Lombardy	Lombardy
	Daughter	F.	1	Single	United States...	Lombardy	Lombardy
1258	Head	M.	47	Married...	Basilicata	Basilicata	Basilicata
	Wife	F.	27	Married...	Basilicata	Basilicata	Basilicata
1259	Head	M.	25	Married...	Basilicata	Basilicata	Basilicata
	Wife	F.	23	Married...	Basilicata	Basilicata	Basilicata
1260	Head	M.	31	Single	Lombardy	Lombardy	Lombardy
	Sister	F.	45	Single	Lombardy	Lombardy	Lombardy
1261	Cooperative	M.	17	Single	Tuscany	Tuscany	Tuscany
	Cooperative	M.	47	Married...	Tuscany	Tuscany	Tuscany
	Cooperative	M.	32	Married...	Tuscany	Tuscany	Tuscany
	Cooperative	M.	26	Married...	Tuscany	Tuscany	Tuscany
1262	Head	M.	37	Married...	Basilicata	Basilicata	Basilicata
	Wife	F.	34	Married...	Basilicata	Basilicata	Basilicata
	Daughter	F.	6	Single	United States	Basilicata	Basilicata
	Daughter	F.	5	Single	United States	Basilicata	Basilicata
	Son	M.	1	Single	United States...	Basilicata	Basilicata
	Lodger	M.	50	Married...	Basilicata	Basilicata	Basilicata
	Lodger	M.	29	Married...	Abruzzo	Abruzzo	Abruzzo
	Lodger	F.	22	Married...	Abruzzo	Abruzzo	Abruzzo
1263	Head	M.	50	Married...	Lombardy	Lombardy	Lombardy
	Wife	F.	42	Married...	Basilicata	Basilicata	Basilicata
	Daughter	F.	18	Single	Basilicata	Lombardy	Basilicata
	Daughter	F.	10	Single	United States...	Lombardy	Basilicata
	Daughter	F.	7	Single	United States...	Lombardy	Basilicata
	Son	M.	5	Single	United States...	Lombardy	Basilicata
	Son	M.	3	Single	United States...	Lombardy	Basilicata
1264	Head	M.	52	Married...	Basilicata	Basilicata	Basilicata
	Wife	F.	25	Married...	Basilicata	Basilicata	Basilicata
	Daughter	F.	3	Single	United States	Basilicata	Basilicata
	Daughter	F.	2	Single	United States...	Basilicata	Basilicata
	Daughter	F.	$\frac{3}{12}$	Single	United States...	Basilicata	Basilicata
1265	Head	M.	30	Married...	Basilicata	Basilicata	Basilicata
	Wife	F.	31	Married...	Basilicata	Basilicata	Basilicata
	Stepson	M.	12	Single	Basilicata	Basilicata	Basilicata
	Stepson	M.	4	Single	United States...	Basilicata	Basilicata
	Stepson	M.	2	Single	United States...	Basilicata	Basilicata
1266	Head	M.	22	Married...	Basilicata	Basilicata	Basilicata
	Wife	F.	16	Married...	Basilicata	Basilicata	Basilicata
1267	Head	M.	60	Married...	Basilicata	Basilicata	Basilicata
	Wife	F.	50	Married...	Basilicata	Basilicata	Basilicata
	Son	M.	20	Single	Basilicata	Basilicata	Basilicata
1268	Head	M.	39	Married...	Basilicata	Basilicata	Basilicata
	Wife	F.	36	Married...	Basilicata	Basilicata	Basilicata
	Daughter	F.	12	Single	Basilicata	Basilicata	Basilicata
	Son	M.	8	Single	Basilicata	Basilicata	Basilicata
1269	Head	M.	23	Married...	Basilicata	Basilicata	Basilicata
	Wife	F.	17	Married...	Basilicata	Basilicata	Basilicata
1270	Head	M.	40	Married...	Basilicata	Basilicata	Basilicata
	Wife	F.	40	Married...	Basilicata	Basilicata	Basilicata
	Son	M.	12	Single	United States...	Basilicata	Basilicata
	Son	M.	8	Single	United States...	Basilicata	Basilicata
	Son	M.	6	Single	United States...	Basilicata	Basilicata
	Son	M.	3	Single	United States...	Basilicata	Basilicata
	Son	M.	1	Single	United States...	Basilicata	Basilicata

a Not reported.

TABLE **I.**—GENERAL SOCIAL AND ECONOMIC CONDITION, BY FAMILIES
AND INDIVIDUALS—Continued.

Years in U. S.	Naturalized.	Profession, trade, or occupation.	Hours of work per week.	Average weekly earnings.	Weeks employed.	Total yearly earnings.	Sick during year, defective, maimed, or deformed.
8	Yes..	Carpenter	48	$12.00	32	$384	No.
4		Housewife					No.
		At home					No.
16	Yes..	No occupation					No.
11		Housewife and pants maker.	60	3.50	44	154	Bronchitis.
7	Yes..	Laborer	42	8.00	52	416	No.
4		Housewife					No.
8	No...	Hod carrier	(a)	8.40	20	168	Dyspepsia.
8		Peddler, fruit	48	4.00	52	208	No.
3		Peddler, fruit	(a)	6.00	52	312	No.
4	No...	Peddler, fruit	(a)	6.00	52	312	No.
2	No...	Peddler, fruit	(a)	6.00	52	312	No.
2	No...	Peddler, fruit	(a)	6.00	52	312	No.
9	Yes..	Teamster	48	(a)	32	(a)	No.
8		Housewife					No.
		Scholar					No.
		At home					No.
		At home					No.
11	Yes..	Laborer	60	8.40	12	101	No.
8	Yes..	Laborer	60	7.50	(a)	(a)	Pneumonia.
4½		Housework					No.
12	Yes..	Saloon keeper	119	(a)	52	(a)	No.
12		Housewife and merchant, groceries.	84	(a)	52	(a)	Heart, disease of.
12		Housework					No.
		Scholar					Eye, loss of one.
		Scholar					Diphtheria.
		At home					No.
		At home					No.
9	Yes..	Baking powder factory employee.	(a)	7.50	20	150	Fever, not specified.
7		Housewife					Childbirth.
		At home					No.
		At home					No.
		At home					No.
14	Yes..	Candy factory employee	55	5.50	28	154	No.
5		Housewife					No.
5		Scholar					No.
		At home					No.
		At home					No.
6	Yes..	Candy factory employee	55	5.50	52	286	No.
5		Housewife					No.
5	Yes..	Candy factory employee	55	5.50	24	132	No.
5		Housewife					No.
6		Baking powder factory employee.	55	5.50	52	286	Sight, defective.
13	Yes..	Baking powder factory employee.	(a)	9.00	26	234	No.
6		Housewife					No.
6		Scholar					No.
6		Scholar					No.
9	Yes..	Street sweeper	60	9.00	32	288	No.
5		Housewife					No.
14	No...	Hod carrier	48	9.00	32	288	Pneumonia.
13		Housewife					No.
		Scholar					No.
		Scholar					Diphtheria.
		At home					No.
		At home					No.
		At home					No.

TABLE **I.**—GENERAL SOCIAL AND ECONOMIC CONDITION, BY FAMILIES AND INDIVIDUALS—Continued.

Family number.	Relationship to head of family.	Sex.	Age.	Conjugal condition.	Birthplace.	Birthplace of— Father.	Birthplace of— Mother.
1271	Head	M.	29	Married	Basilicata	Basilicata	Basilicata
	Wife	F.	20	Married	Basilicata	Basilicata	Basilicata
	Son	M.	1	Single	United States	Basilicata	Basilicata
1272	Cooperative	M.	24	Single	Basilicata	Basilicata	Basilicata
	Cooperative	M.	44	Married	Basilicata	Basilicata	Basilicata
	Cooperative	M.	40	Married	Basilicata	Basilicata	Basilicata
	Cooperative	M.	27	Married	Basilicata	Basilicata	Basilicata
	Cooperative	M.	45	Married	Basilicata	Basilicata	Basilicata
1273	Head	M.	33	Married	Basilicata	Basilicata	Basilicata
	Wife	F.	30	Married	Basilicata	Basilicata	Basilicata
	Son	M.	9	Single	Basilicata	Basilicata	Basilicata
	Son	M.	4	Single	United States	Basilicata	Basilicata
	Daughter	F.	1	Single	United States	Basilicata	Basilicata
1274	Head	M.	30	Married	Basilicata	Basilicata	Basilicata
	Wife	F.	23	Married	Basilicata	Basilicata	Basilicata
1275	Head	M.	30	Married	Basilicata	Basilicata	Basilicata
	Wife	F.	28	Married	Basilicata	Basilicata	Basilicata
	Daughter	F.	3	Single	United States	Basilicata	Basilicata
	Daughter	F.	1	Single	United States	Basilicata	Basilicata
1276	Head	M.	35	Married	Basilicata	Basilicata	Basilicata
	Wife	F.	32	Married	Basilicata	Basilicata	Basilicata
	Daughter	F.	14	Single	Basilicata	Basilicata	Basilicata
	Son	M.	11	Single	Basilicata	Basilicata	Basilicata
	Son	M.	6	Single	Basilicata	Basilicata	Basilicata
	Son	M.	2	Single	United States	Basilicata	Basilicata
	Son	M.	$\frac{1}{12}$	Single	United States	Basilicata	Basilicata
1277	Head	M.	32	Married	Basilicata	Basilicata	Basilicata
	Wife	F.	27	Married	Basilicata	Basilicata	Basilicata
	Son	M.	2	Single	United States	Basilicata	Basilicata
	Son	M.	$\frac{5}{12}$	Single	United States	Basilicata	Basilicata
1278	Head	M.	42	Married	Basilicata	Basilicata	Basilicata
	Wife	F.	33	Married	Basilicata	Basilicata	Basilicata
	Boarder	M.	29	Married	Basilicata	Basilicata	Basilicata
1279	Head	M.	45	Married	Basilicata	Basilicata	Basilicata
	Wife	F.	40	Married	Basilicata	Basilicata	Basilicata
	Son	M.	19	Single	Basilicata	Basilicata	Basilicata
	Daughter	F.	12	Single	Basilicata	Basilicata	Basilicata
	Son	M.	5	Single	United States	Basilicata	Basilicata
	Son	M.	4	Single	United States	Basilicata	Basilicata
	Son	M.	2	Single	United States	Basilicata	Basilicata
1280	Head	M.	45	Married	Basilicata	Basilicata	Basilicata
	Wife	F.	37	Married	Basilicata	Basilicata	Basilicata
	Daughter	F.	16	Single	Basilicata	Basilicata	Basilicata
	Daughter	F.	14	Single	United States	Basilicata	Basilicata
	Daughter	F.	13	Single	United States	Basilicata	Basilicata
	Daughter	F.	9	Single	United States	Basilicata	Basilicata
	Daughter	F.	7	Single	United States	Basilicata	Basilicata
	Daughter	F.	5	Single	United States	Basilicata	Basilicata
1281	Head	M.	28	Married	Basilicata	Basilicata	Basilicata
	Wife	F.	27	Married	Basilicata	Basilicata	Basilicata
	Son	M.	8	Single	United States	Basilicata	Basilicata
	Daughter	F.	5	Single	United States	Basilicata	Basilicata
	Daughter	F.	3	Single	United States	Basilicata	Basilicata
	Daughter	F.	$\frac{8}{12}$	Single	United States	Basilicata	Basilicata
1282	Head	M.	62	Married	Basilicata	Basilicata	Basilicata
	Wife	F.	60	Married	Basilicata	Basilicata	Basilicata
1283	Head	M.	40	Married	Lombardy	Lombardy	Lombardy
	Wife	F.	38	Married	Basilicata	Basilicata	Basilicata
	Son	M.	11	Single	United States	Lombardy	Basilicata
	Son	M.	8	Single	United States	Lombardy	Basilicata
	Son	M.	6	Single	United States	Lombardy	Basilicata
	Son	M.	4	Single	United States	Lombardy	Basilicata
	Son	M.	2	Single	United States	Lombardy	Basilicata

a Not reported.

TABLE **I.**—GENERAL SOCIAL AND ECONOMIC CONDITION, BY FAMILIES AND INDIVIDUALS—Continued.

Years in U. S.	Naturalized.	Profession, trade, or occupation.	Hours of work per week.	Average weekly earnings.	Weeks employed.	Total yearly earnings.	Sick during year, defective, maimed, or deformed.
9	Yes..	Hod carrier	48	$9.00	24	$216	No.
5		Housewife					No.
		At home					No.
5	Yes..	Hod carrier	48	8.40	16	134	No.
3	No...	Cellar digger	60	7.50	19	143	No.
5	Yes..	Cellar digger	60	7.50	7	53	No.
$\frac{2}{12}$	No...	No occupation					No.
4	No...	Laborer	(a)	(a)	(a)	(a)	No.
9	Yes..	Laborer	60	(a)	22	(a)	No.
5		Housewife					Fever, not specified.
5		Scholar					No.
		At home					No.
		At home					No.
9	Yes..	Street sweeper	60	9.00	24	216	No.
4		Housewife					Female complaint.
11	Yes..	Street sweeper	60	9.00	23	207	No.
9		Housewife					No.
		At home					No.
		At home					No.
10	Yes..	Hod carrier	(a)	8.50	16	136	No.
5		Housewife					Childbirth.
5		No occupation					No.
5		Scholar					No.
5		Scholar					No.
		At home					No.
		At home					No.
13	Yes..	Street sweeper	60	9.00	27	243	No.
4		Housewife and pants finisher.	30	1.50	27	41	Childbirth.
		At home					No.
		At home					No.
17	Yes..	Stonecutter	48	24.75	44	1,089	Rheumatism.
15		Housewife					No.
6	Yes..	Saloon keeper	126	(a)	52	(a)	No.
12	Yes..	Street sweeper	60	7.50	30	225	No.
6		Housewife					No.
6		Teamster	(a)	9.00	27	243	Injury by accident.
6		Scholar					No.
		At home					No.
		At home					No.
		At home					No.
16	Yes..	Candy factory employee	60	6.30	52	328	No.
15		Housewife					No.
15		Tailoress	48	2.50	28	70	No.
		Scholar					No.
		Scholar					No.
		Scholar					No.
		At home					No.
		At home					No.
8	Yes..	Shoemaker	44	9.00	17	153	No.
8		Housewife					Childbirth.
		Scholar					No.
		At home					No.
		At home					No.
		At home					Ear (middle), inflammation of.
16	Yes..	No occupation					Feeble-minded.
14		Housewife and washerwoman.	(a)	.50	52	26	No.
15	Yes..	Foreman, hod carriers	48	12.00	41	492	No.
15		Housewife					No.
		Scholar					No.
		Scholar					No.
		Scholar					No.
		At home					No.
		At home					No.

TABLE **I.**—GENERAL SOCIAL AND ECONOMIC CONDITION, BY FAMILIES AND INDIVIDUALS—Continued.

Family number.	Relationship to head of family.	Sex.	Age.	Conjugal condition.	Birthplace.	Birthplace of—	
						Father.	Mother.
1284	Head	M.	47	Married...	Basilicata.......	Basilicata......	Basilicata......
	Wife	F.	40	Married...	Basilicata.......	Basilicata......	Basilicata......
1285	Head	M.	36	Married...	Basilicata.......	Basilicata......	Basilicata......
	Wife	F.	31	Married...	Basilicata.......	Basilicata......	Basilicata......
	Daughter	F.	14	Single.....	Basilicata.......	Basilicata......	Basilicata......
	Son	M.	10	Single.....	United States...	Basilicata......	Basilicata......
	Daughter	F.	9	Single.....	United States...	Basilicata......	Basilicata......
	Son	M.	7	Single.....	United States...	Basilicata......	Basilicata......
	Son	M.	5	Single.....	United States...	Basilicata......	Basilicata......
	Daughter	F.	1	Single.....	United States...	Basilicata......	Basilicata......
1286	Head	M.	35	Married...	Basilicata.......	Basilicata......	Basilicata......
	Wife	F.	44	Married...	Basilicata.......	Basilicata......	Basilicata......
	Stepson	M.	13	Single.....	Basilicata.......	Basilicata......	Basilicata......
	Sister	F.	19	Single.....	Basilicata.......	Basilicata......	Basilicata......
1287	Head	M.	35	Married...	Basilicata.......	Basilicata......	Basilicata......
	Wife	F.	35	Married...	Basilicata.......	Basilicata......	Basilicata......
	Daughter	F.	9	Single.....	Basilicata.......	Basilicata......	Basilicata......
	Son	M.	$\frac{5}{12}$	Single.....	United States...	Basilicata......	Basilicata......
	Brother	M.	40	Widowed .	Basilicata.......	Basilicata......	Basilicata......
1288	Head	M.	28	Married...	Sicily...........	Sicily...........	Sicily...........
	Wife	F.	25	Married...	Sicily...........	Sicily...........	Sicily...........
	Daughter	F.	5	Single.....	United States...	Sicily...... ...	Sicily...........
	Daughter	F.	3	Single.....	United States...	Sicily...........	Sicily...........
	Son	M.	1	Single.....	United States...	Sicily...........	Sicily...........
1289	Head	M.	38	Married...	Sicily...........	Sicily...........	Sicily...........
	Wife	F.	27	Married...	Sicily...........	Sicily...........	Sicily...........
	Daughter	F.	6	Single.....	United States...	Sicily...........	Sicily...........
	Son	M.	2	Single.....	United States...	Sicily...........	Sicily...........
	Son	M.	$\frac{5}{12}$	Single.....	United States...	Sicily...........	Sicily...........
	Father-in-law	M.	55	Married...	Sicily...........	Sicily...........	Sicily...........
	Mother-in-law	F.	52	Married...	Sicily...........	Sicily...........	Sicily...........
	Brother-in-law	M.	14	Single.....	Sicily...........	Sicily...........	Sicily...........
1290	Head	M.	32	Married...	Sicily...........	Sicily...........	Sicily...........
	Wife	F.	35	Married...	Sicily...........	Sicily...........	Sicily...........
	Daughter	F.	3	Single.....	Sicily...........	Sicily...........	Sicily...........
1291	Head	M.	35	Married...	Sicily...........	Sicily...........	Sicily...........
	Wife	F.	28	Married...	Sicily...........	Sicily...........	Sicily...........
	Daughter	F.	11	Single....	Sioily...........	Sicily...........	Sicily...........
1292	Head	M.	40	Married...	Basilicata.......	Basilicata......	Basilicata......
	Wife	F.	38	Married...	Basilicata.......	Basilicata......	Basilicata......
	Daughter	F.	14	Single.....	Basilicata.......	Basilicata......	Basilicata......
	Daughter	F.	4	Single.....	United States...	Basilicata......	Basilicata......
	Son	M.	2	Single.....	United States...	Basilicata......	Basilicata......
1293	Head	M.	40	Married...	Basilicata.......	Basilicata......	Basilicata......
	Wife	F.	45	Married...	Basilicata.......	Basilicata......	Basilicata......
	Daughter	F.	10	Single.....	United States...	Basilicata......	Basilicata......
	Son	M.	6	Single.....	United States...	Basilicata......	Basilicata......
	Daughter	F.	4	Single.....	United States...	Basilicata......	Basilicata......
	Son	M.	1	Single.....	United States...	Basilicata......	Basilicata......
1294	Head	M.	25	Married...	Basilicata.......	Basilicata......	Basilicata......
	Wife	F.	17	Married...	Basilicata.......	Basilicata......	Basilicata......
	Father	M.	75	Married...	Basilicata.......	Basilicata......	Basilicata......
	Mother	F.	65	Married...	Basilicata.......	Basilicata......	Basilicata......
1295	Head	M.	41	Married...	Campania.......	Campania......	Campania......
	Wife	F.	42	Married...	Campania.......	Campania......	Campania......
	Daughter	F.	15	Single.....	Campania.......	Campania......	Campania......
	Daughter	F.	10	Single.....	United States...	Campania......	Campania......
	Daughter	F.	8	Single.....	United States...	Campania......	Campania......
	Son	M.	6	Single.....	United States...	Campania......	Campania......
	Son	M.	$1\frac{1}{2}$	Single.....	United States...	Campania......	Campania......
	Cousin	M.	28	Single.....	Campania.......	Campania......	Campania......
	Cousin	M.	30	Single.....	Campania.......	Campania......	Campania......
	Cousin	M.	42	Married...	Campania.......	Campania......	Campania......

a Not reported.

TABLE **I.**—GENERAL SOCIAL AND ECONOMIC CONDITION, BY FAMILIES AND INDIVIDUALS—Continued.

Years in U.S.	Naturalized.	Profession, trade, or occupation.	Hours of work per week.	Average weekly earnings.	Weeks employed.	Total yearly earnings.	Sick during year, defective, maimed, or deformed.
16	Yes..	No occupation............					No.
16	......	Housewife...............					No.
12	Yes..	Laborer..................	60	$9.25	36	$333	No.
12	......	Housewife...............					No.
12	......	Scholar..................					No.
......	......	Scholar..................					No.
......	......	Scholar..................					No.
......	......	Scholar..................					Measles.
......	......	At home.................					Bronchitis.
......	......	At home.................					No.
7	Yes..	Street sweeper...........	60	7.50	20	150	No.
3	......	Housewife...............					Female complaint.
7	......	Scholar..................					No.
1½	......	No occupation...........					No.
11	Yes..	No occupation...........					No.
8	......	Housewife and pants maker.	12	1.00	20	20	Childbirth.
8	......	Scholar..................					No.
......	......	At home.................					No.
14	Yes..	Shoemaker...............	30	6.00	32	192	No.
6	No...	Peddler, fruit............	54	1.50	52	78	No.
6	......	Housewife...............					No.
......	......	At home.................					No.
......	......	At home.................					No.
......	......	At home.................					No.
10	No...	Peddler, fruit............	(a)	3.00	52	156	No.
6	......	Housewife...............					Childbirth.
......	......	At home.................					No.
......	......	At home.................					No.
......	......	At home.................					No.
5	No...	Peddler, fruit............	(a)	(a)	52	(a)	No.
5	......	Housework...............					No.
5	......	Peddler, fruit............	(a)	(a)	52	(a)	No.
1	No...	Peddler, fruit............	(a)	(a)	52	(a)	No.
1	......	Housewife and merchant, groceries.	84	(a)	52	(a)	No.
1	......	At home.................					No.
7	Yes..	Laborer..................	(a)	7.50	22	165	No.
1½	......	Housewife...............					No.
1½	......	Scholar..................					No.
15	Yes..	Mason, stone.............	48	18.00	18	324	No.
10	......	Housewife and pants maker.	(a)	2.50	40	100	Female complaint.
10	......	No occupation...........					No.
......	......	At home.................					No.
......	......	At home.................					No.
13	Yes.	Street sweeper...........	60	7.50	14	105	Fever, not specified.
12	......	Housewife...............					No.
......	......	Scholar..................					No.
......	......	At home.................					No.
......	......	At home.................					No.
......	......	At home.................					No.
15	Yes..	Musician................	(a)	4.50	52	234	No.
11	......	Housewife...............					No.
15	No...	No occupation...........					No.
14	......	No occupation...........					No.
15	Yes..	Watchman...............	60	7.50	48	360	No.
12	......	Housewife...............					Childbirth.
12	......	Scholar..................					No.
......	......	Scholar..................					No.
......	......	Scholar..................					No.
......	......	At home.................					No.
......	......	At home.................					No.
3	No...	Street sweeper...........	60	9.00	30	270	No.
5	Yes..	Street sweeper...........	60	9.00	30	270	No.
4	No...	Street sweeper...........	60	7.50	10	75	No.

TABLE **I.**—GENERAL SOCIAL AND ECONOMIC CONDITION, BY FAMILIES AND INDIVIDUALS—Continued.

Family number.	Relationship to head of family.	Sex.	Age.	Conjugal condition.	Birthplace.	Birthplace of—	
						Father.	Mother.
1296	Head	M.	26	Married	Basilicata	Basilicata	Basilicata
	Wife	F.	19	Married	Basilicata	Basilicata	Basilicata
1297	Head	M.	64	Widowed	Basilicata	Basilicata	Basilicata
	Son	M.	18	Single	Basilicata	Basilicata	Basilicata
	Daughter	F.	14	Single	Basilicata	Basilicata	Basilicata
1298	Head	M.	33	Married	Basilicata	Basilicata	Basilicata
	Wife	F.	30	Married	Basilicata	Basilicata	Basilicata
	Daughter	F.	9	Single	United States	Basilicata	Basilicata
	Son	M.	7	Single	United States	Basilicata	Basilicata
	Daughter	F	4	Single	United States	Basilicata	Basilicata
	Son	M.	$\frac{5}{12}$	Single	United States	Basilicata	Basilicata
1299	Head	M.	49	Married	Basilicata	Basilicata	Basilicata
	Wife	F.	52	Married	Basilicata	Basilicata	Basilicata
	Daughter	F.	13	Single	Basilicata	Basilicata	Basilicata
	Son	M.	7	Single	United States	Basilicata	Basilicata
1300	Head	M.	34	Married	Basilicata	Basilicata	Basilicata
	Wife	F.	33	Married	Basilicata	Basilicata	Basilicata
	Son	M.	9	Single	United States	Basilicata	Basilicata
	Daughter	F.	5	Single	United States	Basilicata	Basilicata
	Daughter	F.	3	Single	United States	Basilicata	Basilicata
	Daughter	F.	2	Single	United States	Basilicata	Basilicata
1301	Head	M.	37	Married	Basilicata	Basilicata	Basilicata
	Wife	F.	30	Married	Basilicata	Basilicata	Basilicata
	Son	M.	7	Single	Basilicata	Basilicata	Basilicata
	Daughter	F.	2	Single	United States	Basilicata	Basilicata
	Son	M.	1	Single	United States	Basilicata	Basilicata
	Brother-in-law	M.	23	Single	Basilicata	Basilicata	Basilicata
1302	Head	M.	26	Married	Basilicata	Basilicata	Basilicata
	Wife	F.	26	Married	Basilicata	Basilicata	Basilicata
	Son	M.	$\frac{1}{12}$	Single	United States	Basilicata	Basilicata
1303	Head	M.	55	Married	Basilicata	Basilicata	Basilicata
	Wife	F.	60	Married	Basilicata	Basilicata	Basilicata
1304	Head	M.	35	Married	Basilicata	Basilicata	Basilicata
	Wife	F.	35	Married	Basilicata	Basilicata	Basilicata
1305	Head	M.	42	Married	Basilicata	Basilicata	Basilicata
1306	Head	M.	40	Married	Basilicata	Basilicata	Basilicata
	Wife	F.	40	Married	Basilicata	Basilicata	Basilicata
	Son	M.	12	Single	Basilicata	Basilicata	Basilicata
	Son	M.	8	Single	United States	Basilicata	Basilicata
	Son	M.	6	Single	United States	Basilicata	Basilicata
	Son	M.	4	Single	United States	Basilicata	Basilicata
1307	Head	M.	35	Married	Basilicata	Basilicata	Basilicata
	Wife	F.	28	Married	Basilicata	Basilicata	Basilicata
	Son	M.	6	Single	United States	Basilicata	Basilicata
	Daughter	F.	4	Single	United States	Basilicata	Basilicata
	Daughter	F.	2	Single	United States	Basilicata	Basilicata
1308	Head	M.	45	Married	Tuscany	Tuscany	Tuscany
	Wife	F.	39	Married	Liguria	Liguria	Liguria
	Daughter	F.	5	Single	United States	Tuscany	Liguria
	Son	M.	3	Single	United States	Tuscany	Liguria
1309	Head	M.	54	Married	Liguria	Liguria	Liguria
	Wife	F.	41	Married	Liguria	Liguria	Liguria
	Daughter	F.	22	Single	United States	Liguria	Liguria
1310	Head	M.	57	Married	Emilia	Emilia	Emilia
	Wife	F.	54	Married	Emilia	Emilia	Emilia
	Son	M.	25	Single	Emilia	Emilia	Emilia
	Son	M.	19	Single	Emilia	Emilia	Emilia
1311	Head	M.	44	Married	Emilia	Emilia	Emilia
	Wife	F.	35	Married	Emilia	Emilia	Emilia
	Daughter	F.	15	Single	Emilia	Emilia	Emilia
	Son	M.	14	Single	Emilia	Emilia	Emilia

a Not reported.

TABLE **I.**—GENERAL SOCIAL AND ECONOMIC CONDITION, BY FAMILIES AND INDIVIDUALS—Continued.

Years in U.S.	Natu-ral-ized.	Profession, trade, or occupation.	Hours of work per week.	Average weekly earn-ings.	Weeks em-ploy-ed.	Total yearly earn-ings.	Sick during year, defective, maimed, or deformed.
14	Yes..	Janitor	48	$10. 00	9	$90	No.
8	....	Housewife	......	......	......	......	No.
9	No...	Ragpicker	27	.1. 50	52	78	No.
9	....	Bootblack	54	(a)	52	(a)	No.
9	....	Housewife	......	......	......	......	No.
12	Yes..	Paver	48	9. 00	15	135	No.
12	....	Housewife	......	......	......	......	Childbirth.
......	....	Scholar	......	......	......	......	No.
......	....	Scholar	......	......	......	......	No.
......	....	At home	......	......	......	......	No.
......	....	At home	......	......	......	......	No.
10	Yes..	Hod carrier	48	9. 00	10	90	No.
9	....	Housewife	......	......	......	......	No.
9	....	Scholar	......	......	......	......	No.
......	....	Scholar	......	......	......	......	No.
16	Yes..	Paver	60	9. 00	18	162	No.
10	....	Housewife	......	......	......	......	No.
......	....	Scholar	......	......	......	......	No.
......	....	At home	......	......	......	......	No.
......	....	At home	......	......	......	......	No.
......	....	At home	......	......	......	......	No.
5	Yes..	Sewer digger	48	9. 00	42	378	No.
3	....	Housewife	......	......	......	......	No.
3	....	At home	......	......	......	......	No.
......	....	At home	......	......	......	......	No.
......	....	At home	......	......	......	......	No.
1	No...	Laborer	60	7. 50	10	75	No.
6	No...	Paver	60	7. 50	19	143	No.
4	....	Housewife	......	......	......	......	Childbirth; bronchitis.
......	....	At home	......	......	......	......	
14	Yes..	No occupation	......	......	......	......	No.
6	....	Housewife	......	......	......	......	No.
16	Yes..	Teamster, with team	60	18. 00	22	396	No.
8	....	Housewife	......	......	......	......	No.
2	No...	Paver	60	9. 00	23	207	No.
12	Yes..	Street sweeper	60	8. 40	29	244	No.
10	....	Housewife	......	......	......	......	No.
10	....	Scholar	......	......	......	......	No.
......	....	Scholar	......	......	......	......	No.
......	....	Scholar	......	......	......	......	No.
......	....	At home	......	......	......	......	No.
13	Yes..	Street sweeper	(a)	8. 40	29	244	No.
10	....	Housewife	......	......	......	......	No.
......	....	At home	......	......	......	......	No.
......	....	At home	......	......	......	......	Bronchitis.
......	....	At home	......	......	......	......	No.
13	No...	Image maker	54	12. 00	32	384	No.
14	....	Housewife	......	......	......	......	No.
......	....	At home	......	......	......	......	No.
......	....	At home	......	......	......	......	No.
24	Yes..	Merchant, fruit	(a)	(a)	52	(a)	No.
31	....	Housewife	......	......	......	......	No.
......	....	No occupation	......	......	......	......	No.
11	No...	Organ grinder	30	2. 75	52	143	Asthma.
11	....	Housewife	......	......	......	......	No.
11	Yes..	Cook	70	(a)	52	(a)	No.
11	....	Bartender	72	(a)	52	(a)	No.
8	Yes..	No occupation	......	......	......	......	No.
8	....	Housewife	......	......	......	......	No.
8	....	Scholar	......	......	......	......	No.
8	....	Scholar and newsboy	18	40	40	16	No.

TABLE **I.**—GENERAL SOCIAL AND ECONOMIC CONDITION, BY FAMILIES AND INDIVIDUALS—Continued.

Family number.	Relationship to head of family.	Sex.	Age.	Conjugal condition.	Birthplace.	Birthplace of—	
						Father.	Mother.
1311	Daughter	F.	12	Single	Emilia	Emilia	Emilia
	Daughter	F.	10	Single	Emilia	Emilia	Emilia
	Son	M.	9	Single	Emilia	Emilia	Emilia
	Daughter	F.	4	Single	United States	Emilia	Emilia
	Son	M.	1	Single	United States	Emilia	Emilia
1312	Head	M.	49	Married	Liguria	Liguria	Liguria
	Wife	F.	36	Married	Liguria	Liguria	Liguria
	Daughter	F.	15	Single	Liguria	Liguria	Liguria
	Son	M.	1	Single	United States	Liguria	Liguria
1313	Head	M.	26	Married	Tuscany	Tuscany	Tuscany
	Wife	F.	20	Married	Tuscany	Tuscany	Tuscany
	Son	M.	$\frac{1}{12}$	Single	United States	Tuscany	Tuscany
1314	Head	F.	44	Widowed	Lombardy	Lombardy	Lombardy
	Daughter	F.	15	Single	United States	Lombardy	Lombardy
	Daughter	F.	12	Single	United States	Lombardy	Lombardy
	Son	M.	11	Single	United States	Lombardy	Lombardy
	Son	M.	9	Single	United States	Lombardy	Lombardy
	Son	M.	7	Single	United States	Lombardy	Lombardy
	Daughter	F.	2	Single	United States	Lombardy	Lombardy
1315	Head	M.	28	Married	Tuscany	Tuscany	Tuscany
	Wife	F.	24	Married	United States	Germany	Germany
	Father	M.	64	Married	Tuscany	Tuscany	Tuscany
	Mother	F.	50	Married	Tuscany	Tuscany	Tuscany
	Brother	M.	15	Single	United States	Tuscany	Tuscany
	Boarder	M.	23	Single	Piedmont	Piedmont	Piedmont
	Boarder	M.	32	Married	Tuscany	Tuscany	Tuscany
	Boarder	M.	32	Married	Tuscany	Tuscany	Tuscany
1316	Head	M.	35	Married	Venetia	Venetia	Venetia
	Wife	F.	30	Married	Venetia	Venetia	Venetia
	Daughter	F.	4	Single	United States	Venetia	Venetia
	Daughter	F.	$\frac{5}{12}$	Single	United States	Venetia	Venetia
1317	Head	M.	56	Married	Tuscany	Tuscany	Tuscany
	Wife	F.	45	Married	Tuscany	Tuscany	Tuscany
	Son	M.	20	Single	Tuscany	Tuscany	Tuscany
	Daughter	F.	16	Single	United States	Tuscany	Tuscany
	Son	M.	12	Single	United States	Tuscany	Tuscany
1318	Head	F.	54	Widowed	Venetia	Venetia	Venetia
1319	Head	M.	36	Married	Venetia	Venetia	Venetia
	Wife	F.	22	Married	Venetia	Venetia	Venetia
	Daughter	F.	2	Single	United States	Venetia	Venetia
1320	Head	M.	59	Married	Liguria	Liguria	Liguria
	Wife	F.	51	Married	Liguria	Liguria	Liguria
	Son	M.	21	Single	United States	Liguria	Liguria
	Son	M.	14	Single	United States	Liguria	Liguria
1321	Head	M.	67	Married	Tuscany	Tuscany	Tuscany
	Wife	F.	57	Married	Tuscany	Tuscany	Tuscany
	Son	M.	16	Single	Tuscany	Tuscany	Tuscany
	Lodger	M.	35	Married	Tuscany	Tuscany	Tuscany
	Lodger	M.	35	Married	Tuscany	Tuscany	Tuscany
	Lodger	M.	26	Married	Tuscany	Tuscany	Tuscany
1322	Head	M.	55	Married	Lombardy	Lombardy	Lombardy
	Wife	F.	50	Married	Lombardy	Lombardy	Lombardy
	Daughter	F.	20	Single	Lombardy	Lombardy	Lombardy
	Daughter	F.	16	Single	Lombardy	Lombardy	Lombardy
	Daughter	F.	12	Single	United States	Lombardy	Lombardy
	Daughter	F.	9	Single	United States	Lombardy	Lombardy
	Daughter	F.	6	Single	United States	Lombardy	Lombardy
1323	Head	M.	28	Married	Liguria	Liguria	Liguria
	Wife	F.	28	Married	Liguria	Liguria	Liguria
	Daughter	F.	2	Single	United States	Liguria	Liguria

a Not reported.

TABLE **I.**—GENERAL SOCIAL AND ECONOMIC CONDITION, BY FAMILIES AND INDIVIDUALS—Continued.

Years in U. S.	Natu- ral- ized.	Profession, trade, or occupation.	Hours of work per week.	Average weekly earn- ings.	Weeks em- ploy- ed.	Total yearly earn- ings.	Sick during year, defective, maimed, or deformed.
8	......	Scholar and newsgirl	18	$0.40	16	$6	No.
8	......	Scholar	......	......	......	......	No.
8	......	Scholar	......	......	......	......	No.
......	......	At home	......	......	......	......	No.
......	......	At home	......	......	......	......	No.
13	Yes..	Merchant, toys	(a)	(a)	52	(a)	No.
13	......	Housewife..............	......	......	......	......	No.
13	......	Dressmaker's apprentice; no pay.	......	......	......	......	No.
......	......	At home	......	......	......	......	No.
10	No...	Cook..................	98	18.60	52	936	No.
4	......	Housewife..............	......	......	......	......	Childbirth.
......	......	At home...............	......	......	......	......	Surgical operation.
30	......	Housewife..............	......	......	......	......	No.
......	......	Macaroni factory em- ployee.	60	2.00	32	64	No.
......	......	Scholar	......	......	......	......	No.
......	......	Scholar and newsboy.....	(a)	.40	(a)	(a)	No.
......	......	Scholar and newsboy.....	(a)	.40	(a)	(a)	No.
......	......	Scholar	......	......	......	......	No.
......	......	At home...............	......	......	......	......	No.
20	Yes..	Salesman	56	(a)	52	(a)	No.
......	......	Housewife..............	......	......	......	......	No.
23	Yes..	Retired	......	......	......	......	No.
20	......	Merchant, groceries......	(a)	(a)	52	(a)	No.
......	......	Scholar	......	......	......	......	No.
3	No...	Mosaic layer............	54	9.00	27	243	Fever, typhoid.
3	No...	Elevated railroad em- ployee.	60	7.50	28	210	No.
7	Yes..	Soap factory employee....	60	9.00	32	288	No.
8	Yes..	Mosaic layer............	48	(a)	52	(a)	No.
9	......	Housewife..............	......	......	......	......	Childbirth.
......	......	At home...............	......	......	......	......	No.
......	......	At home...............	......	......	......	......	No
20	Yes..	Merchant, fruit..........	48	(a)	52	(a)	No.
20	......	Housewife..............	......	......	......	......	No.
20	......	Salesman	(a)	(a)	52	(a)	No.
......	......	Scholar	......	......	......	......	No.
......	......	Scholar	......	......	......	......	No.
8	......	Midwife	(a)	(a)	(a)	(a)	No.
4	No...	Mosaic layer............	47	12.00	28	336	Consumption.
4	......	Housewife..............	......	......	......	......	No.
......	......	At home...............	......	......	......	......	No.
23	Yes..	Candy factory employee...	55	7.00	16	112	No.
23	......	Housewife..............	......	......	......	......	Bronchitis.
......	......	Shipping clerk...........	66	(a)	52	(a)	No.
......	......	Office boy..............	(a)	3.00	52	156	No.
15	No...	Peddler, fruit...........	27	1.75	44	77	Rheumatism.
6	......	Housewife..............	......	......	......	......	No.
6	......	Nutcracker.............	36	2.50	28	70	No.
3	No...	Peddler, fruit...........	27	1.50	44	66	No.
3	No...	Peddler, fruit...........	27	1.50	44	66	No.
1	No...	Peddler, fruit...........	27	1.25	44	55	Fever, typhoid.
12	No...	Mosaic layer............	48	9.00	20	180	Bronchitis.
12	......	Housewife..............	......	......	......	......	No.
12	......	Candy factory employee...	50	6.00	30	180	No.
12	......	Scholar	......	......	......	......	Bowels, inflammation of.
......	......	Scholar	......	......	......	......	No.
......	......	Scholar	......	......	......	......	No.
......	......	Scholar	......	......	......	......	No.
7	No...	Merchant, fruit..........	105	(a)	52	(a)	No.
10	......	Housewife..............	......	......	......	......	No.
......	......	At home...............	......	......	......	......	No.

TABLE **I.**—GENERAL SOCIAL AND ECONOMIC CONDITION, BY FAMILIES AND INDIVIDUALS—Continued.

Family number.	Relationship to head of family.	Sex.	Age.	Conjugal condition.	Birthplace.	Birthplace of—	
						Father.	Mother.
1324	Head	M.	50	Married...	Liguria	Liguria	Liguria
	Wife	F.	40	Married...	Liguria	Liguria	Liguria
	Son	M.	21	Single	United States...	Liguria	Liguria
	Son	M.	19	Single	United States...	Liguria	Liguria
	Daughter	F.	17	Single	United States...	Liguria	Liguria
	Son	M.	15	Single	United States...	Liguria	Liguria
	Son	M.	11	Single	United States...	Liguria	Liguria
	Son	M.	9	Single	United States...	Liguria	Liguria
	Son	M.	4	Single	United States...	Liguria	Liguria
	Son	M.	$\frac{1}{12}$	Single	United States...	Liguria	Liguria
1325	Head	F.	55	Widowed .	Liguria	Liguria	Liguria
	Son	M.	29	Single	United States...	Liguria	Liguria
	Son	M.	24	Married...	United States...	Liguria	Liguria
	Son	M.	21	Single	United States...	Liguria	Liguria
	Daughter-in-law ..	F.	22	Married...	United States...	Venetia	Liguria
	Granddaughter ...	F.	1	Single	United States...	United States..	United States..
1326	Head	M.	47	Married...	Liguria	Liguria	Liguria
	Wife	F.	45	Married...	Liguria	Liguria	Liguria
	Son	M.	19	Single	Liguria	Liguria	Liguria
	Daughter	F.	17	Single	Liguria	Liguria	Liguria
	Son	M.	15	Single	Liguria	Liguria	Liguria
	Son	M.	14	Single	Liguria	Liguria	Liguria
	Son	M.	10	Single	Liguria	Liguria	Liguria
	Daughter	F.	8	Single	Liguria	Liguria	Liguria
	Daughter	F.	5	Single	Liguria	Liguria	Liguria
	Father	M.	81	Widowed .	Liguria	Liguria	Liguria
1327	Head	M.	42	Married...	Basilicata	Basilicata	Basilicata
	Wife	F.	46	Married...	Calabria	Calabria	Calabria
1328	Head	M.	33	Married...	Sicily	Sicily	Sicily
	Wife	F.	33	Married...	Sicily	Sicily	Sicily
	Daughter	F.	5	Single	United States...	Sicily	Sicily
	Mother-in-law	F.	60	Widowed .	Sicily	Sicily	Sicily
1329	Head	M.	27	Married...	Basilicata	Basilicata	Basilicata
	Wife	F.	25	Married...	Germany	Germany	Germany
	Daughter	F.	6	Single	United States...	Basilicata	Germany
	Son	M.	1	Single	United States .	Basilicata	Germany
1330	Head	M.	44	Married...	Basilicata	Basilicata	Basilicata
	Wife	F.	43	Married...	Basilicata	Basilicata	Basilicata
	Daughter	F.	16	Single	Basilicata	Basilicata	Basilicata
	Daughter	F.	11	Single	Basilicata	Basilicata	Basilicata
	Son	M.	7	Single	United States...	Basilicata	Basilicata
1331	Head	M.	38	Married...	Basilicata	Basilicata	Basilicata
	Wife	F.	49	Married...	Basilicata	Basilicata	Basilicata
	Daughter	F.	16	Single	United States...	Basilicata	Basilicata
	Daughter	F.	9	Single	United States...	Basilicata	Basilicata
	Daughter	F.	7	Single	United States...	Basilicata	Basilicata
	Boarder	M.	21	Single	Calabria	Calabria	Calabria
1332	Head	M.	40	Married...	Calabria	Calabria	Calabria
	Wife	F.	44	Married...	Calabria	Calabria	Calabria
	Son	M.	16	Single	Calabria	Calabria	Calabria
1333	Head	M.	30	Married...	Basilicata	Basilicata	Basilicata
	Wife	F.	19	Married...	Basilicata	Basilicata	Basilicata
	Son	M.	3	Single	United States...	Basilicata	Basilicata
1334	Head	F.	65	Widowed .	Basilicata	Basilicata	Basilicata
	Son	M.	26	Married...	Basilicata	Basilicata	Basilicata
1335	Head	M.	65	Married...	Basilicata	Basilicata	Basilicata
	Wife	F.	50	Married...	Basilicata	Basilicata	Basilicata
1336	Cooperative	M.	30	Married...	Tuscany	Tuscany	Tuscany
	Cooperative	M.	29	Married...	Tuscany	Tuscany	Tuscany
	Cooperative	M.	24	Single	Tuscany	Tuscany	Tuscany

a Not reported.

TABLE **I.**—GENERAL SOCIAL AND ECONOMIC CONDITION, BY FAMILIES
AND INDIVIDUALS—Continued.

Years in U. S.	Natu- ral- ized.	Profession, trade, or occupation.	Hours of work per week.	Average weekly earn- ings.	Weeks em- ploy- ed.	Total yearly earn- ings.	Sick during year, defective, maimed, or deformed.
25	No...	Merchant, fruit............	84	(a)	52	(a)	No.
22	......	Housewife................	......	......	......	......	Childbirth.
......	......	Teamster..................	54	(a)	28	(a)	No.
......	......	Candy factory employee...	55	$5.50	44	$242	No.
......	......	Candy factory employee...	55	3.00	44	132	No.
......	......	Scholar...................	......	......	......	......	No.
......	......	Scholar...................	......	......	......	......	No.
......	......	Scholar...................	......	......	......	......	No.
......	......	At home...................	......	......	......	......	No.
......	......	At home...................	......	......	......	......	No.
30	......	Housewife................	......	......	......	......	No.
......	......	Expressman..............	(a)	(a)	52	(a)	No.
......	......	Plumber..................	54	12.00	47	564	No.
......	......	Teamster.................	(a)	(a)	52	(a)	No.
......	......	Housework................	......	......	......	......	No.
......	......	At home...................	......	......	......	......	Bronchitis.
5	No...	Packer, fruit.............	66	9.00	52	468	No.
5	......	Housewife................	......	......	......	......	No.
5	......	Mosaic layer.............	48	6.00	26	156	No.
5	......	Tobacco stripper..........	(a)	5.00	52	260	No.
5	......	Scholar...................	......	......	......	......	No.
5	......	Scholar...................	......	......	......	......	No.
5	......	Scholar...................	......	......	......	......	No.
5	......	At home...................	......	......	......	......	No.
5	......	At home...................	......	......	......	......	No.
9	No...	No occupation	......	......	......	......	No.
12	Yes..	Street sweeper............	60	7.50	30	225	No.
9	......	Housewife................	......	......	......	......	Rheumatism.
5	Yes..	No occupation	......	......	......	......	No.
5	......	Housewife and washer- woman.	(a)	1.00	52	52	Heart, disease of.
......	......	At home...................	......	......	......	......	No.
5	......	No occupation	......	......	......	......	No.
18	Yes..	Merchant, junk............	60	(a)	52	(a)	No.
13	......	Housewife................	......	......	......	......	No.
......	......	At home...................	......	......	......	......	No.
......	......	At home...................	......	......	......	......	No.
12	Yes..	Merchant, fruit...........	98	(a)	52	(a)	No.
9	......	Housewife................	......	......	......	......	No.
9	......	Bookbinder..............	45	3.00	52	156	No.
9	......	Scholar...................	......	......	......	......	No.
......	......	Scholar...................	......	......	......	......	No.
18	Yes..	No occupation	......	......	......	......	No.
18	......	Housewife................	......	......	......	......	No.
......	......	Tailoress.................	45	3.00	26	78	No.
......	......	Scholar...................	......	......	......	......	No.
......	......	Scholar...................	......	......	......	......	No.
9	No...	Scholar and paint factory employee.	60	8.00	6	48	No.
8	Yes..	Railroad laborer..........	60	7.50	26	195	No.
8	......	Housewife................	......	......	......	......	No.
8	......	No occupation	......	......	......	......	No.
13	Yes..	Hod carrier..............	48	9.00	10	90	Neuralgia.
16	......	Housewife................	......	......	......	......	No.
......	......	At home...................	......	......	......	......	No.
5	......	Housewife................	......	......	......	......	No.
9	Yes..	Laborer, garbage dump ...	60	(a)	52	(a)	No.
16	Yes..	Rag-shop employee........	66	(a)	52	(a)	No.
16	......	Housewife................	......	......	......	......	No.
5	No...	Image maker	(a)	7.50	52	390	No.
6	Yes..	Peddler, images...........	(a)	7.50	52	390	No.
2	No...	Peddler, images...........	(a)	7.50	52	390	No.

TABLE I.—GENERAL SOCIAL AND ECONOMIC CONDITION, BY FAMILIES AND INDIVIDUALS—Concluded.

Family number.	Relationship to head of family.	Sex.	Age.	Conjugal condition.	Birthplace.	Birthplace of— Father.	Birthplace of— Mother.
1337	Head	M.	32	Married...	Basilicata.......	Basilicata......	Basilicata......
	Wife..............	F.	25	Married...	Basilicata.......	Basilicata......	Basilicata......
	Son	M.	4	Single.....	United States..	Basilicata......	Basilicata......
	Daughter	F.	3	Single.....	United States...	Basilicata......	Basilicata......
	Daughter	F.	7/12	Single.....	United States...	Basilicata......	Basilicata......
	Mother	F.	60	Widowed .	Basilicata.......	Basilicata......	Basilicata......
	Brother	M.	21	Single.....	Basilicata.......	Basilicata......	Basilicata......
1338	Head	M.	28	Married...	Basilicata.......	Basilicata......	Basilicata......
	Wife..............	F.	23	Married...	Basilicata.......	Basilicata......	Basilicata......
	Son	M.	8	Single.....	United States...	Basilicata......	Basilicata......
	Daughter	F.	3	Single.....	United States...	Basilicata......	Basilicata......
	Son	M.	2	Single.....	United States...	Basilicata......	Basilicata......
1339	Head	M.	27	Married...	Sicily	Sicily	Sicily ....
	Wife..............	F.	25	Married...	Sicily	Sicily	Sicily ....
	Son	M.	3	Single.....	United States...	Sicily	Sicily ....
	Son	M.	1	Single.....	United States...	Sicily	Sicily ......
	Lodger............	M.	40	Married...	Sicily	Sicily	Sicily ....
1340	Head	M.	30	Married...	Basilicata.......	Basilicata......	Basilicata......
	Wife..............	F.	26	Married...	Basilicata.......	Basilicata......	Basilicata......
	Daughter	F.	3/12	Single.....	United States...	Basilicata......	Basilicata......
1341	Head	M.	24	Married...	Sicily	Sicily	Sicily ....
	Wife..............	F.	20	Married...	Sicily	Sicily	Sicily ....
	Daughter	F.	3	Single.....	United States...	Sicily	Sicily ....
	Daughter	F.	8/12	Single.....	United States..	Sicily	Sicily ......
1342	Head	M.	35	Married...	Sicily	Sicily	Sicily ....
	Wife..............	F.	24	Married...	Sicily	Sicily	Sicily ....
	Daughter	F.	5	Single.....	United States...	Sicily	Sicily ....
	Daughter	F.	4	Single.....	United States...	Sicily	Sicily ....
	Daughter	F.	3	Single.....	United States...	Sicily	Sicily ....
	Sister-in-law	F.	16	Single.....	Sicily	Sicily	Sicily ......
1343	Head	M.	45	Widowed .	Campania	Campania	Campania .....
	Daughter	F.	12	Single.....	United States...	Campania	Basilicata......
	Mother-in-law	F.	69	Widowed .	Basilicata.......	Basilicata......	Basilicata......
	Sister-in-law	F.	50	Widowed .	Basilicata.......	Basilicata......	Basilicata......
	Nephew	M.	12	Single.....	United States...	Basilicata......	Basilicata......
	Nephew	M.	9	Single.....	United States...	Basilicata......	Basilicata......
1344	Head	M.	49	Married...	Basilicata.......	Basilicata......	Basilicata......
	Wife..............	F.	31	Married...	Basilicata.......	Basilicata......	Basilicata......
	Son	M.	12	Single.....	United States...	Basilicata......	Basilicata......
	Son	M.	9	Single.....	United States...	Basilicata......	Basilicata......
	Son	M.	7	Single.....	United States...	Basilicata......	Basilicata......
	Son	M.	4	Single.....	United States...	Basilicata......	Basilicata......
	Daughter	F.	2	Single.....	United States...	Basilicata.....	Basilicata......
1345	Head	M.	38	Single.....	Lombardy	Lombardy	Lombardy .....
1346	Head	M.	49	Married...	Basilicata.......	Basilicata......	Basilicata......
	Wife..............	F.	26	Married...	Basilicata.......	Basilicata......	Basilicata......
	Daughter	F.	6	Single.....	United States...	Basilicata......	Basilicata......
	Son	M.	1	Single.....	United States...	Basilicata......	Basilicata......
1347	Head	M.	36	Married...	Sicily	Sicily	Sicily ....
	Wife..............	F.	30	Married...	Sicily	Sicily	Sicily ....
1348	Head	F.	48	Widowed .	Lombardy	Lombardy	Lombardy .....
	Son	M.	22	Single.....	Lombardy	Lombardy	Lombardy .....
	Son	M.	12	Single.....	United States...	Lombardy	Lombardy .....
	Daughter	F.	9	Single.....	United States...	Lombardy	Lombardy .....

a Also worked as bicycle factory employee thirteen weeks, at $10.50 per week.

TABLE **I.**—GENERAL SOCIAL AND ECONOMIC CONDITION, BY FAMILIES AND INDIVIDUALS—Concluded.

Years in U.S.	Natural- ized.	Profession, trade, or occupation.	Hours of work per week.	Average weekly earn- ings.	Weeks em- ploy- ed.	Total yearly earn- ings.	Sick during year, defective, maimed, or deformed.
9	Yes..	Saloon keeper (a)	(b)	(b)	a 39	(b)	No.
5	....	Housewife.................					Childbirth; consumption.
......	....	At home..................					No.
......	....	At home..................					Debility, general.
......	....	At home..................					No.
6	....	Housework					No.
7	No...	Shoe factory employee....	55	$5.00	52	$260	No.
9	Yes..	Peddler, vegetables.......	(b)	7.50	39	293	Rheumatism.
19	....	Housewife.................					No.
......	....	Scholar					No.
......	....	At home..................					No.
......	....	At home..................					No.
6	No...	Peddler, fruit..............	(b)	6.00	52	312	No.
6	....	Housewife.................					No.
......	....	At home..................					No.
......	....	At home..................					Rickets.
6	No...	Peddler, fruit..............	(b)	6.00	39	234	Dyspepsia.
7	No...	Laborer...................	60	8.25	9	74	No.
3	....	Housewife.................					Childbirth.
......	....	At home..................					No.
6	Yes..	Peddler, fruit..............	(b)	6.00	39	234	No.
5	....	Housewife.................					Childbirth.
......	....	At home..................					No.
......	....	At home..................					No.
(b)	No...	Peddler, fruit..............	(b)	6.00	52	312	No.
6	....	Housewife.................					No.
......	....	At home..................					No.
......	....	At home..................					No.
......	....	At home..................					No.
1	....	Housework					No.
14	Yes..	Candy factory employee...	50	5.50	52	286	No.
......	....	Scholar					No.
11	....	Housewife.................					No.
16	....	Housework					No.
......	....	Scholar					No.
......	....	Scholar					No.
17	Yes..	Iron foundry employee....	60	9.00	5	45	Injury by accident.
15	....	Housewife.................					No.
......	....	Newsboy	(b)	1.50	52	78	No.
......	....	Scholar and newsboy......	(b)	1.25	52	65	No.
......	....	At home..................					No.
......	....	At home..................					No.
......	....	At home..................					Bronchitis.
8	No...	Saloon cleaner	(b)	(b)	52	(b)	No.
15	Yes..	Laborer...................	60	7.50	32	240	Rheumatism.
8	....	Housewife.................					Female complaint.
......	....	Scholar					No.
......	....	At home..................					Fever, not specified.
3	No...	Laborer...................	48	(b)	(b)	(b)	No.
2	....	Housewife.................					No.
19	....	Housewife.................					No.
19	No...	Teamster	60	7.00	36	252	No.
......	....	Scholar					No.
......	....	Scholar					No.

b Not reported.

TABLE **II.**—GENERAL CONDITION AS TO LITERACY AND ILLITERACY, BY
FAMILIES AND INDIVIDUALS.

[This table includes only persons 10 years of age or over.]

Family number.	Relationship to head of family.	Sex.	Age.	Birthplace.	Native language.		English language.			Years in the United States.
					Reads.	Writes.	Reads.	Writes.	Speaks.	
1	Head	M.	35	Calabria	No	No	No	No	Yes	7
	Wife	F.	28	Calabria	Yes	Yes	No	No	Yes	7
2	Head	M.	37	Basilicata	No	No	No	No	Yes	11
	Wife	F.	40	Basilicata	No	No	No	No	Yes	10
	Mother	F.	70	Basilicata	No	No	No	No	No	10
3	Head	M.	38	Campania	Yes	Yes	No	No	Yes	13
	Wife	F.	25	Campania	No	No	No	No	Yes	6
	Cousin	M.	45	Campania	Yes	Yes	No	No	No	9
	Cousin	M.	15	Campania	No	No	No	No	No	1½
	Boarder	M.	24	Apulia	Yes	Yes	No	No	Yes	6
4	Head	M.	50	Campania	No	No	No	No	Yes	13
	Wife	F.	48	Campania	No	No	No	No	No	8
	Son	M.	18	Campania	Yes	Yes	No	No	Yes	8
	Son	M.	15	Campania	Yes	Yes	Yes	Yes	Yes	8
	Sister	F.	29	Campania	No	No	No	No	No	8
	Brother-in-law	M.	30	Campania	No	No	No	No	Yes	8
5	Cooperative	M.	42	Calabria	No	No	No	No	Yes	13
	Cooperative	M.	30	Calabria	No	No	No	No	Yes	4
	Cooperative	M.	34	Calabria	No	No	No	No	No	4
	Cooperative	M.	43	Calabria	No	No	No	No	No	6
	Cooperative	M.	41	Calabria	No	No	No	No	No	5
	Cooperative	M.	40	Calabria	No	No	No	No	No	4
	Cooperative	M.	40	Calabria	No	No	No	No	Yes	7
6	Head	M.	25	Basilicata	Yes	Yes	No	No	Yes	13
	Wife	F.	20	Basilicata	No	No	No	No	Yes	12
	Mother	F.	55	Basilicata	No	No	No	No	No	4
7	Head	M.	28	Calabria	Yes	Yes	No	No	Yes	9
	Wife	F.	30	Calabria	No	No	No	No	No	7
	Boarder	M.	30	Calabria	Yes	Yes	No	No	No	7
8	Head	M.	42	Calabria	Yes	Yes	Yes	Yes	Yes	13
	Wife	F.	34	Calabria	No	No	No	No	Yes	9
9	Head	M.	52	Sicily	No	No	No	No	No	¾
	Wife	F.	49	Sicily	No	No	No	No	No	1½
	Son	M.	19	Sicily	No	No	No	No	No	1½
10	Head	M.	44	Sicily	No	No	No	No	Yes	10
	Wife	F.	34	Sicily	No	No	No	No	No	9
11	Head	M.	34	Sicily	No	No	No	No	Yes	8
	Wife	F.	29	Sicily	No	No	No	No	No	8
12	Head	M.	60	Sicily	No	No	No	No	Yes	12
	Wife	F.	50	Sicily	No	No	No	No	No	2
	Son	M.	15	Sicily	No	No	No	No	Yes	3
13	Head	M.	47	Calabria	No	No	No	No	No	4
	Wife	F.	36	Calabria	No	No	No	No	No	4
	Daughter	F.	15	Calabria	No	No	Yes	Yes	Yes	4
	Son-in-law	M.	20	Calabria	Yes	Yes	Yes	Yes	Yes	7
	Cousin	M.	29	Calabria	No	No	No	No	No	14
	Boarder	M.	26	Calabria	Yes	Yes	No	No	No	2
14	Head	M.	40	Calabria	No	No	No	No	No	12
	Wife	F.	30	Calabria	No	No	No	No	No	3
	Brother-in-law	M.	25	Calabria	Yes	No	No	No	Yes	9
	Sister-in-law	F.	21	Calabria	No	No	No	No	No	4
	Boarder	M.	37	Calabria	No	No	No	No	No	4
15	Head	M.	51	Calabria	Yes	Yes	No	No	No	11
	Wife	F.	42	Calabria	Yes	Yes	No	No	No	4
	Son	M.	22	Calabria	Yes	Yes	Yes	Yes	Yes	7
	Son	M.	17	Calabria	No	No	Yes	Yes	Yes	4
16	Head	M.	20	Marches	No	No	No	No	Yes	2
	Wife	F.	19	Marches	No	No	No	No	Yes	2
	Brother	M.	17	Marches	No	No	No	No	Yes	2
17	Head	M.	40	Venetia	Yes	Yes	No	No	Yes	11
	Wife	F.	25	United States	Yes	Yes	Yes	Yes	Yes	

TABLE **II.**—GENERAL CONDITION AS TO LITERACY AND ILLITERACY, BY
FAMILIES AND INDIVIDUALS—Continued.

[This table includes only persons 10 years of age or over.]

Family number.	Relationship to head of family.	Sex.	Age.	Birthplace.	Native language.		English language.			Years in the United States.
					Reads.	Writes.	Reads.	Writes.	Speaks.	
18	Head	M.	25	Campania	Yes..	Yes...	Yes..	Yes...	Yes...	12
	Wife	F.	20	Campania	No...	No....	No...	No....	Yes...	10
	Lodger	M.	40	Campania	No...	No....	No...	No....	No....	12
	Lodger	M.	20	Campania	No...	No....	No...	No....	No....	4
	Lodger	M.	32	Campania	No...	No....	No...	No....	No....	8
19	Head	M.	37	Campania	No...	No....	No...	No....	Yes...	11
	Wife	F.	40	Campania	No...	No....	No...	No....	No....	9
20	Head	M.	30	Calabria	Yes..	Yes...	No...	No....	Yes...	4
	Wife	F.	29	Calabria	No...	No...	No...	No....	No....	3
	Boarder	M.	18	Calabria	Yes..	Yes...	No...	No....	Yes...	3
	Boarder	M.	28	Calabria	Yes..	Yes...	No...	No....	Yes...	3
21	Head	M.	48	Calabria	No...	No....	No...	No....	Yes...	10
	Wife	F.	40	Calabria	No...	No....	No...	No....	No....	4
	Son	M.	18	Calabria	Yes..	Yes...	Yes..	Yes...	Yes...	4
	Nephew	M.	23	Calabria	Yes..	Yes...	Yes..	Yes...	Yes...	5
	Nephew	M.	15	Calabria	Yes..	Yes...	Yes..	Yes...	Yes...	4
	Lodger	M.	40	Calabria	Yes..	Yes...	No...	No....	Yes...	8
22	Head	M.	39	Campania	No...	No....	No...	No....	Yes...	13
	Wife	F.	32	Basilicata	No...	No....	No...	No....	Yes...	13
	Son	M.	12	United States	Yes..	Yes...	Yes..	Yes...	Yes...	....
23	Head	M.	31	Campania	No...	No....	No...	No....	Yes...	7
	Wife	F.	34	United States	Yes..	Yes...	Yes..	Yes...	Yes...	....
24	Head	M.	40	Campania	Yes..	Yes...	Yes..	Yes...	Yes...	14
	Wife	F.	40	Campania	Yes..	Yes...	No...	No....	Yes...	14
	Son	M.	18	Campania	Yes..	Yes...	Yes..	Yes...	Yes...	14
	Son	M.	15	Campania	Yes..	Yes...	Yes..	Yes...	Yes...	14
	Daughter	F.	14	United States	Yes..	Yes...	Yes..	Yes...	Yes...	....
	Daughter	F.	12	United States	Yes..	Yes...	Yes..	Yes...	Yes...	....
	Brother-in-law	M.	34	Campania	Yes..	Yes...	Yes..	Yes...	Yes...	(a)
	Nephew	M.	14	Campania	Yes..	Yes...	Yes..	Yes...	Yes...	(a)
25	Head	M.	34	Campania	Yes..	Yes...	No...	No....	Yes...	10
	Wife	F.	39	Basilicata	No...	No....	No...	No....	No....	10
26	Head	M.	52	Campania	No...	No....	No...	No....	No....	10
	Wife	F.	38	Campania	No...	No....	No...	No....	No....	10
	Daughter	F.	15	Campania	No...	No....	Yes..	Yes...	Yes...	10
	Son	M.	12	Campania	No...	No....	Yes..	Yes...	Yes...	10
	Son	M.	10	Campania	No...	No....	Yes..	Yes...	Yes...	10
27	Head	M.	44	Basilicata	No...	No....	No...	No....	Yes...	23
	Wife	F.	32	Basilicata	No...	No....	No...	No....	Yes...	12
	Son	M.	14	United States	Yes..	Yes...	Yes..	Yes...	Yes...	....
	Son	M.	12	Basilicata	No...	No....	Yes..	Yes...	Yes...	12
28	Head	M.	36	Abruzzo	Yes..	Yes...	No...	No....	Yes...	6
	Wife	F.	31	Abruzzo	No...	No....	No..:	No....	No....	6
29	Head	F.	44	Basilicata	No...	No....	No...	No....	No....	13
30	Head	M.	33	Calabria	No...	No....	No...	No....	Yes...	6
	Wife	F.	29	Calabria	No...	No....	No...	No....	No....	1
	Boarder	M.	38	Calabria	Yes..	Yes...	No...	No....	Yes...	16
31	Head	M.	26	Calabria	Yes..	Yes...	Yes..	Yes...	Yes...	15
	Wife	F.	29	United States	Yes..	Yes...	Yes..	Yes...	Yes...	....
	Brother	M.	24	Calabria	No...	No....	No...	No....	Yes...	5
32	Head	M.	44	Campania	No...	No....	No...	No....	Yes...	10
33	Head	M.	40	Abruzzo	No...	No....	No...	No....	Yes.:.	6
	Wife	F.	30	Abruzzo	No...	No....	No...	No....	No....	5
34	Head	M.	31	Calabria	No...	No....	No...	No....	Yes...	6
	Wife	F.	32	Calabria	No...	No....	No...	No....	No....	5
	Cousin	M.	29	Calabria	Yes..	Yes...	No...	No....	No....	2
	Cousin	M.	35	Calabria	No...	No....	No...	No....	No....	3
	Cousin	M.	36	Calabria	No...	No....	No...	No....	Yes...	7

a Not reported.

TABLE **II.**—GENERAL CONDITION AS TO LITERACY AND ILLITERACY, BY
FAMILIES AND INDIVIDUALS—Continued.

[This table includes only persons 10 years of age or over.]

Family number.	Relationship to head of family.	Sex.	Age.	Birthplace.	Native language.		English language.			Years in the United States.
					Reads.	Writes.	Reads.	Writes.	Speaks.	
35	Head	M.	30	Calabria	No...	No....	No...	No....	Yes...	5
	Wife	F.	29	Calabria	No...	No....	No...	No....	No....	4
	Boarder	M.	24	Tuscany	Yes..	Yes...	Yes..	Yes...	Yes...	8
36	Head	M.	37	Campania	No...	No....	No...	No....	Yes...	15
	Wife	F.	23	Campania	No...	No....	No...	No....	Yes...	8
37	Head	M.	34	Campania	Yes..	Yes...	Yes..	Yes...	Yes...	15
	Wife	F.	27	Campania	No...	No....	No...	No....	No....	5
38	Head	M.	30	Campania	Yes..	Yes...	Yes..	Yes...	Yes...	17
	Wife	F.	20	Campania	Yes..	Yes...	Yes..	Yes...	Yes...	18
39	Head	M.	24	Calabria	Yes..	Yes...	Yes..	Yes...	Yes...	8
	Wife	F.	15	Calabria	No...	No....	No...	No....	Yes...	3
	Boarder	M.	40	Calabria	No...	No....	No...	No....	No....	7
40	Head	M.	47	Basilicata	No...	No....	No...	No....	No....	13
	Wife	F.	35	Basilicata	No...	No....	No...	No....	No....	9
	Son	M.	13	Basilicata	Yes..	Yes...	Yes..	Yes...	Yes...	9
	Mother	F.	69	Basilicata	No...	No....	No...	No....	No....	4
41	Head	M.	36	Calabria	No...	No....	No...	No....	Yes...	13
	Wife	F.	30	Calabria	No...	No....	No...	No....	No....	3
42	Head	M.	45	Calabria	No...	No....	No...	No....	No....	14
	Wife	F.	45	Calabria	No...	No....	No...	No....	No....	8
43	Head	M.	34	Calabria	No...	No....	No...	No....	Yes...	8
	Wife	F.	38	Calabria	No...	No....	No...	No....	No....	6
	Lodger	M.	30	Calabria	Yes..	No....	No...	No....	Yes...	4
44	Head	M.	50	Campania	Yes..	Yes...	Yes..	Yes...	Yes...	18
	Wife	F.	51	Campania	Yes..	Yes...	No...	No....	No....	14
	Daughter	F.	21	Campania	Yes..	Yes...	Yes..	Yes...	Yes...	14
	Son	M.	18	Campania	Yes..	Yes...	Yes..	Yes...	Yes...	14
45	Head	M.	33	Campania	No...	No....	No...	No....	Yes...	14
	Wife	F.	29	Campania	No...	No....	No...	No....	No....	5
	Brother	M.	30	Campania	No...	No....	No...	No....	Yes...	15
46	Head	M.	36	Campania	No...	No....	No...	No....	Yes...	14
	Wife	F.	33	Campania	No...	No....	No...	No....	No....	9
47	Head	M.	45	Calabria	No...	No....	No...	No....	Yes...	12
	Son	M.	22	Calabria	Yes..	Yes...	No...	No....	No....	1½
	Cousin	M.	50	Calabria	Yes..	Yes...	No...	No....	Yes...	14
	Lodger	M.	45	Calabria	No...	No....	No...	No....	No....	14
	Lodger	M.	30	Calabria	Yes..	No....	No...	No....	Yes...	4
48	Head	M.	47	Calabria	No...	No....	No...	No....	Yes...	15
	Wife	F.	50	Calabria	No...	No....	No...	No....	No....	4
	Son	M.	16	Calabria	Yes..	Yes...	Yes..	Yes...	Yes...	4
49	Head	M.	29	Calabria	No...	No....	No...	No....	Yes...	8
	Wife	F.	27	Calabria	No...	No....	No...	No....	No....	4
50	Head	M.	40	Basilicata	Yes..	Yes...	Yes..	Yes...	Yes...	16
	Wife	F.	50	Basilicata	No...	No....	No...	No....	Yes...	23
	Stepson	M.	23	United States	Yes..	Yes...	Yes..	Yes...	Yes...	
	Boarder	M.	29	Sicily	No...	No....	No...	No....	No....	11
	Boarder	M.	23	Sicily	Yes..	No....	No...	No....	Yes...	7
	Boarder	M.	25	Sicily	No...	No....	No...	No....	Yes...	3
51	Head	M.	44	Calabria	No...	No....	No...	No....	Yes...	15
	Wife	F.	42	Calabria	No...	No....	No...	No....	No....	10
	Boarder	M.	23	Calabria	No...	No....	No...	No....	Yes...	6
	Boarder	M.	27	Calabria	No...	No....	No...	No....	No....	3
	Boarder	M.	30	Calabria	No...	No....	No...	No....	No....	5
52	Head	M.	39	Campagna di Roma	Yes..	Yes...	Yes..	Yes...	Yes...	12
	Wife	F.	35	United States	Yes..	Yes...	Yes..	Yes...	Yes...	
	Daughter	F.	11	United States	Yes..	Yes...	Yes..	Yes...	Yes...	
53	Head	M.	45	Campania	No...	No....	No...	No....	Yes...	12
	Wife	F.	36	Campania	No...	No....	No...	No....	No....	9

TABLE **II.**—GENERAL CONDITION AS TO LITERACY AND ILLITERACY, BY FAMILIES AND INDIVIDUALS—Continued.

[This table includes only persons 10 years of age or over.]

Family number.	Relationship to head of family.	Sex.	Age.	Birthplace.	Native language. Reads.	Writes.	English language. Reads.	Writes.	Speaks.	Years in the United States.
54	Head	F.	29	Campania	No	No	No	No	Yes	7
	Cousin	F.	11	Campania	No	No	No	No	No	7
55	Head	M.	32	Basilicata	No	No	No	No	Yes	13
	Wife	F.	45	Campania	No	No	No	No	No	9
56	Head	M.	36	Campania	Yes	Yes	No	No	Yes	10
	Wife	F.	39	Campania	No	No	No	No	Yes	10
	Son	M.	12	Campania	No	No	Yes	Yes	Yes	10
	Son	M.	11	Campania	No	No	Yes	Yes	Yes	10
57	Head	M.	45	Basilicata	Yes	Yes	No	No	Yes	20
	Wife	F.	34	Basilicata	No	No	No	No	No	8
	Son	M.	15	Basilicata	No	No	Yes	Yes	Yes	8
58	Head	M.	46	Basilicata	No	No	No	No	Yes	12
	Wife	F.	37	Basilicata	No	No	No	No	Yes	9
	Daughter	F.	14	Basilicata	No	No	Yes	Yes	Yes	9
	Daughter	F.	12	Basilicata	No	No	Yes	Yes	Yes	9
59	Head	M.	35	Campania	Yes	Yes	Yes	Yes	Yes	19
	Wife	F.	25	Campania	No	No	No	No	Yes	19
60	Head	M.	48	Basilicata	Yes	No	Yes	No	Yes	14
	Wife	F.	46	Basilicata	No	No	No	No	No	14
	Daughter	F.	20	Basilicata	Yes	Yes	Yes	Yes	Yes	14
	Son	M.	13	United States	Yes	Yes	Yes	Yes	Yes	......
	Daughter	F.	11	United States	Yes	Yes	Yes	Yes	Yes	......
	Son-in-law	M.	25	Campania	Yes	Yes	Yes	Yes	Yes	14
61	Head	M.	37	Basilicata	Yes	Yes	No	No	Yes	5
	Wife	F.	37	Basilicata	No	No	No	No	No	5
	Brother	M.	34	Basilicata	Yes	Yes	No	No	Yes	2
	Cousin	M.	39	Basilicata	Yes	Yes	Yes	Yes	Yes	8
62	Head	M.	50	Calabria	No	No	No	No	Yes	10
	Son	M.	18	Calabria	No	No	No	No	Yes	6
63	Head	M.	37	Abruzzo	No	No	No	No	Yes	4
	Wife	F.	37	Abruzzo	No	No	No	No	No	4
	Daughter	F.	10	Abruzzo	No	No	Yes	Yes	Yes	4
64	Head	M.	34	Abruzzo	Yes	Yes	No	No	Yes	3
	Wife	F.	24	Abruzzo	No	No	No	No	No	3
65	Head	M.	36	Basilicata	No	No	No	No	Yes	12
	Wife	F.	34	Basilicata	No	No	No	No	No	9
66	Head	M.	40	Calabria	No	No	No	No	Yes	10
	Wife	F.	38	Calabria	No	No	No	No	No	5
67	Head	F.	51	Calabria	No	No	No	No	No	5
	Son	M.	27	Calabria	Yes	Yes	No	No	Yes	3
	Son	M.	21	Calabria	Yes	Yes	No	No	Yes	5
	Daughter	F.	10	Calabria	Yes	No	Yes	Yes	Yes	5
68	Head	M.	42	Calabria	No	No	No	No	Yes	11
	Wife	F.	35	Calabria	No	No	No	No	No	8
	Son	M.	13	Calabria	No	No	Yes	Yes	Yes	8
	Daughter	F.	11	Calabria	No	No	Yes	Yes	Yes	8
69	Head	M.	52	Calabria	Yes	Yes	No	No	Yes	8
	Wife	F.	45	Calabria	No	No	No	No	No	1 2/12
	Son	M.	19	Calabria	Yes	Yes	Yes	Yes	Yes	8
	Son	M.	16	Calabria	Yes	Yes	No	No	No	1 2/12
	Son	M.	14	Calabria	Yes	Yes	No	No	No	1 2/12
	Daughter	F.	12	Calabria	Yes	Yes	No	No	No	1 2/12
	Daughter	F.	10	Calabria	No	No	No	No	No	1 2/12
	Boarder	M.	26	Calabria	Yes	Yes	Reads	No	Yes	8
	Boarder	M.	23	Calabria	Yes	Yes	No	No	Yes	3
	Boarder	M.	46	Calabria	No	No	No	No	No	3
	Boarder	M.	30	Calabria	No	No	No	No	Yes	6
	Boarder	M.	31	Calabria	No	No	No	No	Yes	8
	Boarder	M.	30	Calabria	No	No	No	No	Yes	7
	Boarder	M.	28	Calabria	Yes	Yes	No	No	Yes	7
	Boarder	M.	29	Calabria	Yes	Yes	No	No	Yes	8

TABLE **II.**—GENERAL CONDITION AS TO LITERACY AND ILLITERACY, BY FAMILIES AND INDIVIDUALS—Continued.

[This table includes only persons 10 years of age or over.]

Family number.	Relationship to head of family.	Sex.	Age.	Birthplace.	Native language. Reads.	Writes.	English language. Reads.	Writes.	Speaks.	Years in the United States.
69	Boarder	M.	34	Calabria	No	No	No	No	Yes	8
	Boarder	M.	23	Calabria	Yes	Yes	No	·No	Yes	7
70	Head	M.	39	Basilicata	No	No	No	No	Yes	12
	Wife	F.	37	Basilicata	No	No	No	No	Yes	7
	Son	M.	12	Basilicata	No	No	No	No	Yes	7
	Boarder	M.	27	Basilicata	No	No	No	No	Yes	4
	Lodger	M.	44	Calabria	No	No	No	No	No	6
	Lodger	M.	32	Calabria	Yes	Yes	No	No	Yes	8
71	Head	M.	40	Basilicata	No	No	No	No	Yes	11
	Wife	F.	30	Basilicata	No	No	No	No	No	6
	Son	M.	18	Basilicata	Yes	Yes	No	No	Yes	6
	Son	M.	11	Basilicata	No	No	Yes	Yes	Yes	6
72	Head	M.	23	Basilicata	Yes	Yes	No	No	Yes	4
	Wife	F.	37	Basilicata	No	No	No	No	Yes	7
73	Head	M.	42	Campania	Yes	No	No	No	No	10
	Wife	F.	40	Campania	No	No	No	No	No	10
	Daughter	F.	18	Campania	No	No	No	No	Yes	10
	Daughter	F.	14	Campania	No	No	Yes	Yes	Yes	10
	Son	M.	11	Campania	No	No	Yes	Yes	Yes	10
74	Head	M.	41	Campania	Yes	No	No	No	Yes	10
	Wife	F.	41	Campania	No	No	No	No	No	10
	Son	M.	20	Campania	No	No	Yes	Yes	Yes	10
	Son	M.	17	Campania	No	No	Yes	Yes	Yes	10
	Daughter	F.	15	Campania	No	No	Yes	Yes	Yes	10
	Daughter	F.	13	Campania	No	No	No	No	Yes	10
	Daughter	F.	10	United States	Yes	Yes	Yes	Yes	Yes	
75	Head	M.	40	Calabria	Yes	Yes	No	No	Yes	12
	Wife	F.	21	Campania	No	No	No	No	Yes	16
76	Head	M.	28	Abruzzo	Yes	Yes	Yes	Yes	Yes	13
	Wife	F.	28	Abruzzo	Yes	Yes	No	No	Yes	4
	Father-in-law	M.	73	Abruzzo	Yes	Yes	No	No	No	4
	Brother-in-law	M.	33	Abruzzo	Yes	Yes	Yes	Yes	Yes	13
77	Head	M.	33	Campania	Yes	Yes	Yes	No	Yes	11
	Wife	F.	25	Campania	Yes	Yes	No	No	No	4
78	Head	M.	46	Abruzzo	No	No	No	No	No	6
	Wife	F.	50	Abruzzo	No	No	No	No	No	6
	Son	M.	21	Abruzzo	Yes	Yes	No	No	Yes	6
	Son	M.	20	Abruzzo	No	No	No	No	Yes	6
	Nephew	M.	20	Abruzzo	Yes	Yes	No	No	Yes	6
79	Head	M.	40	Campania	No	No	No	No	Yes	21
80	Head	M.	30	Calabria	No	No	No	No	Yes	5
	Wife	F.	30	Calabria	No	No	No	No	No	5
	Cousin	M.	16	Calabria	Yes	Yes	No	No	No	1½
	Cousin	M.	25	Calabria	No	No	No	No	Yes	5
81	Head	M.	40	Campania	Yes	Yes	Yes	Yes	Yes	14
	Wife	F.	40	Campania	Yes	Yes	No	No	No	6
	Son	M.	17	Campania	Yes	Yes	Yes	Yes	Yes	6
	Son	M.	15	Campania	Yes	Yes	Yes	Yes	Yes	6
82	Head	M.	39	Campania	No	No	Yes	Yes	Yes	12
	Wife	F.	36	Campania	No	No	No	No	No	4
	Daughter	F.	12	Campania	No	No	Yes	Yes	Yes	4
83	Head	M.	53	Campania	No	No	No	No	Yes	13
	Wife	F.	45	Campania	No	No	No	No	Yes	12
84	Head	M.	34	Campania	Yes	Yes	Yes	Yes	Yes	24
	Wife	F.	34	Campania	Yes	Yes	No	No	Yes	12
	Son	M.	11	United States	Yes	Yes	Yes	Yes	Yes	
85	Head	M.	46	Sicily	Yes	Yes	No	No	Yes	7
	Wife	F.	36	Sicily	No	No	No	No	Yes	4
	Daughter	F.	16	Sicily	Yes	No	Yes	No	Yes	4

TABLE **II.**—GENERAL CONDITION AS TO LITERACY AND ILLITERACY, BY FAMILIES AND INDIVIDUALS—Continued.

[This table includes only persons 10 years of age or over.]

Family number.	Relationship to head of family.	Sex.	Age.	Birthplace.	Native language. Reads.	Writes.	English language. Reads.	Writes.	Speaks.	Years in the United States.
86	Head	M.	35	Calabria	No	No	No	No	Yes	11
	Wife	F.	34	Calabria	No	No	No	No	No	8
	Son	M.	18	Calabria	Yes	Yes	Yes	Yes	Yes	8
	Son	M.	13	Calabria	Yes	Yes	Yes	Yes	Yes	8
	Brother	M.	24	Calabria	Yes	Yes	No	No	Yes	3
87	Head	M.	30	Campania	Yes	No	No	No	Yes	12
	Wife	F.	29	Abruzzo	No	No	No	No	No	5
88	Head	M.	32	Campania	No	No	No	No	Yes	12
	Wife	F.	32	Campania	No	No	No	No	No	4
	Boarder	M.	40	Campania	No	No	No	No	Yes	20
	Boarder	M.	26	Campania	Yes	Yes	Yes	Yes	Yes	18
	Lodger	M.	42	Campania	No	No	No	No	No	18
	Lodger	M.	40	Campania	Yes	Yes	No	No	No	6
89	Head	M.	40	Campania	No	No	No	No	Yes	13
	Wife	F.	28	Campania	No	No	No	No	No	3
	Daughter	F.	15	Campania	No	No	No	No	Yes	3
	Son	M.	12	Campania	No	No	No	No	Yes	3
	Brother	M.	35	Campania	No	No	No	No	Yes	5
	Lodger	M.	42	Campania	No	No	No	No	Yes	5
	Lodger	M.	28	Campania	No	No	No	No	Yes	7
	Lodger	M.	27	Campania	Yes	Yes	Yes	Yes	Yes	7
	Lodger	M.	51	Campania	Yes	Yes	No	No	No	6
90	Head	M.	34	Abruzzo	No	No	No	No	Yes	8
	Wife	F.	34	Abruzzo	No	No	No	No	Yes	4
	Father	M.	60	Abruzzo	No	No	No	No	No	5
	Mother	F.	60	Abruzzo	No	No	No	No	No	5
91	Head	M.	48	Campania	Yes	Yes	No	No	Yes	13
	Wife	F.	37	Campania	No	No	No	No	No	13
	Cousin	M.	29	Campania	Yes	Yes	No	No	Yes	9
92	Head	M.	35	Campania	Yes	Yes	Yes	Yes	Yes	16
	Wife	F.	35	Campania	Yes	Yes	No	No	Yes	12
	Daughter	F.	12	Campania	Yes	No	Yes	No	No	12
	Mother	F.	82	Campania	No	No	No	No	No	16
93	Head	M.	30	Basilicata	Yes	Yes	No	No	Yes	8
	Wife	F.	25	Basilicata	No	No	No	No	No	2
	Lodger	M.	35	Basilicata	No	No	No	No	No	3
	Lodger	M.	35	Basilicata	Yes	Yes	No	No	Yes	8
	Lodger	M.	35	Basilicata	No	No	No	No	No	3
94	Head	M.	44	Basilicata	No	No	No	No	No	10
	Wife	F.	40	Basilicata	No	No	No	No	No	5
	Daughter	F.	17	Basilicata	Yes	Yes	No	No	Yes	5
	Son-in-law	M.	22	Campania	Yes	Yes	No	No	Yes	7
95	Head	M.	37	Basilicata	Yes	Yes	No	No	Yes	17
	Wife	F.	30	Basilicata	Yes	Yes	Yes	Yes	Yes	18
	Son	M.	14	United States	Yes	Yes	Yes	Yes	No	....
	Mother	F.	62	Basilicata	No	No	No	No	No	18
	Brother	M.	50	Basilicata	Yes	Yes	No	No	Yes	22
96	Head	M.	36	Calabria	Yes	Yes	No	No	Yes	6
	Wife	F.	36	Calabria	No	No	No	No	No	1½
	Son	M.	10	Calabria	No	No	No	No	No	1½
97	Head	M.	46	Campania	No	No	No	No	No	8
	Wife	F.	49	Campania	No	No	No	No	No	14
98	Head	M.	47	Campania	No	No	No	No	Yes	13
	Wife	F.	40	Campania	No	No	No	No	No	4
	Son	M.	18	Campania	Yes	Yes	Yes	Yes	Yes	4
	Son	M.	16	Campania	Yes	No	Yes	Yes	Yes	4
	Daughter	F.	14	Campania	No	No	Yes	Yes	Yes	4
	Boarder	M.	30	Calabria	Yes	Yes	No	No	Yes	6
99	Head	M.	34	Basilicata	Yes	Yes	No	No	No	4
	Wife	F.	30	Basilicata	Yes	No	No	No	No	3
	Daughter	F.	13	Basilicata	Yes	Yes	Yes	Yes	Yes	3
	Brother	M.	33	Basilicata	No	No	No	No	Yes	3
	Boarder	M.	23	Basilicata	No	No	No	No	No	3
	Boarder	M.	25	Basilicata	No	No	No	No	No	2

TABLE **II.**—GENERAL CONDITION AS TO LITERACY AND ILLITERACY, BY FAMILIES AND INDIVIDUALS—Continued.

[This table includes only persons 10 years of age or over.]

Family number.	Relationship to head of family.	Sex.	Age.	Birthplace.	Native language.		English language.			Years in the United States.
					Reads.	Writes.	Reads.	Writes.	Speaks.	
100	Head	M.	37	Campania..........	Yes..	Yes...	No...	No...	Yes...	15
	Wife..........	F.	38	Campania..........	No...	No....	No...	No....	No....	15
101	Head	M.	43	Basilicata..........	No...	No....	No...	No....	Yes...	14
102	Head	M.	34	Campania..........	Yes..	Yes...	No...	No...	Yes...	14
	Wife..........	F.	37	Calabria..........	No...	No....	No...	No...	No....	12
	Stepson.......	M.	18	Calabria..........	Yes..	Yes...	Yes..	Yes...	Yes...	6
	Stepdaughter.	F.	16	Calabria..........	Yes..	Yes...	Yes..	Yes..	Yes...	12
	Son-in-law	M.	23	Campania..........	Yes..	Yes...	Yes..	Yes..	Yes...	3
103	Head	M.	44	Campania..........	No...	No....	No...	No...	Yes...	14
	Wife..........	F.	33	Calabria..........	No...	No....	No...	No...	Yes...	16
	Son	M.	18	Campania..........	Yes..	Yes...	No...	No....	Yes...	3
104	Head	M.	60	Calabria	No...	No....	No...	No...	No....	15
	Wife..........	F.	60	Calabria	No...	No...	No...	No...	No....	5
	Son	M.	29	Calabria	No...	No....	No...	No....	No....	5
	Son	M.	19	Calabria	Yes..	Yes..	No...	No....	Yes...	5
	Nephew	M.	22	Calabria	Yes..	Yes...	No...	No....	No....	$\frac{7}{12}$
	Lodger	M.	41	Calabria	Yes..	Yes...	No...	No....	No....	$\frac{7}{12}$
105	Head	M.	30	Basilicata..........	Yes..	Yes..	No...	No....	Yes...	5
	Wife..........	F.	26	Basilicata..........	Yes..	Yes..	No...	No....	No....	4
	Father-in-law.	M.	65	Basilicata..........	No...	No...	No...	No....	No....	3
106	Head	M.	60	Campania..........	Yes..	Yes..	No...	No....	No....	6
	Son	M.	18	Campania..........	Yes..	Yes..	No...	No....	Yes...	6
	Daughter	F.	16	Campania..........	No...	No...	No...	No....	Yes...	6
	Daughter	F.	14	Campania....	No...	No...	Yes..	Yes..	Yes...	6
	Daughter	F.	12	Campania..........	No...	No...	Yes..	Yes..	Yes...	6
	Lodger	M.	57	Campania..........	No...	No...	No...	No....	No....	17
107	Head	M.	40	Calabria	No...	No....	No...	No...	No....	15
	Wife..........	F.	28	Calabria	No...	No...	No...	No....	No....	6
	Son	M.	17	Calabria	Yes..	Yes...	Yes..	No...	Yes...	10
	Brother.......	M.	38	Calabria	Yes..	Yes...	Yes..	Yes..	Yes...	17
	Brother.......	M.	30	Calabria	No...	No....	No...	No...	Yes...	10
108	Head	M.	38	Campania..........	Yes..	Yes...	No...	No...	Yes...	14
	Wife..........	F.	32	Campania..........	No...	No...	No...	No...	No....	14
	Daughter	F.	14	Campania..........	Yes..	No....	Yes..	Yes..	Yes...	14
109	Head	M.	20	Campania..........	Yes..	Yes...	No...	No....	Yes...	14
	Wife..........	F.	18	Calabria..........	Yes..	No....	Yes..	Yes..	Yes...	13
110	Head	M.	22	Campania..........	Yes..	Yes...	Yes..	No...	Yes...	12
	Wife..........	F.	18	Campania..........	No...	No...	No...	No...	Yes...	10
	Mother	F.	64	Campania..........	No...	No...	No...	No...	No....	10
111	Head	M.	55	Calabria	Yes..	Yes...	No...	No...	Yes...	20
	Wife..........	F.	42	Calabria	No...	No...	No...	No...	Yes...	28
	Son	M.	12	United States......	No(a)	No(a).	No...	No...	Yes....	......
112	Head	M.	53	Campania..........	No...	No...	No...	No...	No....	9
	Wife..........	F.	43	Campania..........	No...	No....	No...	No...	Yes...	9
	Son	M.	22	Campania..........	No...	No...	Yes..	No...	Yes...	9
	Daughter	F.	18	Campania..........	No...	No....	No...	No...	Yes...	9
	Son	M.	16	Campania..........	Yes.:	No....	Yes..	Yes..	Yes...	9
	Son	M.	12	Campania..........	No...	No....	Yes..	Yes..	Yes...	9
113	Head	M.	30	Sicily	Yes..	Yes...	No...	No...	Yes...	8
	Wife..........	F.	25	Sicily	No...	No....	No...	No...	No....	2
114	Cooperative ..	M.	47	Campania..........	No...	No....	No...	No...	Yes...	6
	Cooperative ..	M.	32	Campania..........	Yes..	Yes...	No...	No...	Yes...	4
	Cooperative ..	M.	31	Campania..........	No...	No....	No...	No...	Yes...	5
	Cooperative ..	M.	29	Campania..........	Yes..	Yes...	No...	No...	Yes...	7
115	Cooperative ..	M.	25	Sicily	Yes.	Yes...	No...	No...	No....	4
	Cooperative ..	M.	40	Sicily	Yes..	Yes...	No...	No...	No....	5
	Cooperative ..	M.	46	Sicily	No...	No....	No...	No...	No....	7
	Cooperative ..	M.	54	Sicily	Yes..	Yes...	No...	No...	No....	5
	Cooperative ..	M.	16	Sicily	No...	No....	No...	No..	Yes...	6

a Reads and writes Italian.

TABLE **II.**—GENERAL CONDITION AS TO LITERACY AND ILLITERACY, BY FAMILIES AND INDIVIDUALS—Continued.

[This table includes only persons 10 years of age or over.]

Family number.	Relationship to head of family.	Sex.	Age.	Birthplace.	Native language. Reads.	Writes.	English language. Reads.	Writes.	Speaks.	Years in the United States.
115	Cooperative ..	M.	45	Sicily	No...	No....	No...	No....	Yes...	8
	Cooperative ..	M.	40	Sicily	No...	No....	No...	No....	Yes...	4
	Cooperative ..	M.	35	Campania	Yes..	Yes...	No...	No....	Yes...	6
116	Head	M.	50	Basilicata	Yes..	Yes...	No...	No....	Yes...	8
	Wife	F.	32	Basilicata	No...	No....	No...	No....	No....	12
117	Head	M.	30	Campania	Yes..	Yes...	No...	No....	Yes...	3
	Wife	F.	27	Campania	No...	No....	No...	No....	No....	3
	Brother	M.	16	Campania	Yes..	Yes...	No...	No....	No....	2
	Brother	M.	36	Campania	No...	No....	No...	No....	No....	4
	Brother	M.	46	Campania	No...	No....	No...	No....	No....	5
118	Head	M.	48	Basilicata	No...	No....	No...	No....	Yes...	13
	Wife	F.	47	Basilicata	No...	No....	No...	No....	Yes...	9
	Son	M.	23	Basilicata	No...	No....	Yes..	Yes...	Yes...	9
	Son	M.	12	Basilicata	No...	No....	Yes..	Yes...	Yes...	9
119	Head	M.	40	Campania	Yes..	Yes...	No...	No....	Yes...	6
	Wife	F.	36	Campania	Yes..	Yes...	No...	No....	Yes...	6
120	Head	M.	46	Campania	No...	No....	No...	No....	No....	18
	Wife	F.	36	Basilicata	No...	No....	No...	No....	No....	18
	Daughter	F.	18	United States	Yes..	Yes...	Yes..	Yes..	Yes...	....
	Son	M.	10	United States	Yes..	Yes...	Yes..	Yes..	Yes...	....
	Daughter	F.	10	United States	Yes..	Yes...	Yes..	Yes..	Yes...	....
	Son-in-law	M.	28	Basilicata	Yes..	Yes...	Yes..	Yes..	Yes...	10
121	Head	M.	45	Sicily	Yes..	Yes...	No...	No....	Yes...	15
	Wife	F.	45	Sicily	No...	No....	No...	No....	Yes...	21
	Daughter	F.	13	United States	Yes..	Yes...	Yes..	Yes..	Yes...	....
122	Head	M.	53	Basilicata	No...	No....	No...	No....	No....	16
	Wife	F.	51	Basilicata	No...	No....	No...	No....	No....	15
	Son	M.	22	Basilicata	No...	No....	No .	No....	No....	15
	Daughter	F.	13	United States	Yes..	Yes...	Yes..	Yes..	Yes...	....
	Son	M.	12	United States	Yes..	Yes...	Yes..	Yes..	Yes...	....
123	Head	M.	32	Calabria	Yes..	Yes...	No...	No....	Yes...	16
	Wife	F.	32	Basilicata	No...	No....	No .	No....	No....	9
124	Head	M.	50	Basilicata	No...	No....	No...	No....	Yes...	14
	Wife	F.	42	Basilicata	No...	No....	No...	No....	No....	11
	Son	M.	22	Basilicata	Yes..	No....	No...	No....	Yes...	11
	Son	M.	18	Basilicata	Yes..	Yes...	Yes..	Yes..	Yes...	11
125	Head	M.	30	Basilicata	No...	No....	No...	No....	Yes...	9
	Wife	F.	21	Basilicata	No...	No....	No...	No....	No....	5
	Boarder	M.	30	Basilicata	Yes..	Yes...	No...	No....	Yes...	4
126	Head	M.	30	Basilicata	Yes..	No....	No...	No....	Yes...	9
	Wife	F.	32	Basilicata	Yes..	Yes...	No...	No....	No....	9
	Boarder	M.	39	Basilicata	Yes..	Yes...	Yes..	No....	Yes...	7
127	Head	M.	33	Sicily	Yes..	Yes...	No...	No....	Yes...	4
	Wife	F.	27	Sicily	No...	No....	No...	No....	No....	4
	Son	M.	10	Sicily	No...	No....	Yes..	Yes..	Yes...	4
	Lodger	M.	33	Campania	No...	No....	No...	No....	Yes	12
	Lodger	F.	28	Sicily	No...	No....	No...	No....	No....	5
128	Head	M.	40	Abruzzo	Yes..	Yes...	No...	No....	No....	5
	Wife	F.	28	Abruzzo	Yes..	Yes...	No...	No....	No....	3
	Brother	M.	23	Abruzzo	Yes..	Yes...	Yes..	No....	Yes...	6
	Uncle	M.	45	Abruzzo	Yes..	Yes...	No...	No....	No....	6
	Cousin	M.	22	Abruzzo	Yes..	Yes...	No...	No....	Yes...	5
	Cousin	M.	17	Abruzzo	Yes..	Yes...	No...	No....	Yes...	3
129	Head	M.	42	Sicily	Yes..	Yes...	No...	No....	Yes...	8
	Wife	F.	46	Sicily	No...	No....	No...	No....	No....	29
	Stepson	M.	11	United States	Yes..	Yes...	Yes..	Yes...	Yes...	....
	Lodger	M.	30	Sicily	Yes..	Yes...	No..	No....	Yes...	6
130	Head	M.	28	Campania	No...	No....	No...	No....	Yes...	6
	Wife	F.	28	Campania	No...	No....	No...	No....	No....	1

TABLE **II.**—GENERAL CONDITION AS TO LITERACY AND ILLITERACY, BY FAMILIES AND INDIVIDUALS—Continued.

[This table includes only persons 10 years of age or over.]

Family number.	Relationship to head of family.	Sex.	Age.	Birthplace.	Native language.		English language.			Years in the United States.
					Reads.	Writes.	Reads.	Writes.	Speaks.	
131	Head	M.	31	Basilicata	No	No	No	No	Yes	7
	Wife	F.	26	Basilicata	No	No	No	No	No	4
	Lodger	M.	60	Basilicata	No	No	No	No	No	20
	Lodger	M.	26	Basilicata	Yes	Yes	Yes	Yes	Yes	20
132	Cooperative	M.	34	Calabria	No	No	No	No	Yes	12
	Cooperative	M.	34	Calabria	No	No	No	No	Yes	8
	Cooperative	M.	23	Calabria	No	No	No	No	No	5
	Cooperative	M.	34	Calabria	Yes	Yes	No	No	No	5
	Cooperative	M.	30	Calabria	No	No	No	No	Yes	12
	Cooperative	M.	40	Calabria	Yes	Yes	No	No	Yes	15
	Cooperative	M.	35	Calabria	No	No	No	No	Yes	5
133	Head	M.	41	Sicily	No	No	No	No	No	9
	Wife	F.	40	Sicily	No	No	No	No	No	6
	Son	M.	17	Sicily	No	No	No	No	No	6
	Son	M.	15	Sicily	No	No	No	No	Yes	6
	Daughter	F.	12	Sicily	No	No	Yes	No	Yes	6
	Brother	M.	32	Sicily	No	No	No	No	No	3
	Cousin	M.	44	Sicily	Yes	Yes	No	No	No	3
134	Head	M.	30	Calabria	Yes	Yes	No	No	Yes	15
	Wife	F.	16	Calabria	Yes	Yes	No	No	Yes	4
135	Head	M.	35	Basilicata	Yes	Yes	Yes	Yes	Yes	23
	Wife	F.	28	Basilicata	Yes	Yes	No	No	Yes	14
	Son	M.	12	United States	Yes	Yes	Yes	Yes	Yes	
	Son	M.	10	United States	Yes	Yes	Yes	Yes	Yes	
136	Head	M.	28	Campania	No	No	No	No	Yes	7
	Wife	F.	29	Calabria	No	No	No	No	No	5
	Brother	M.	26	Campania	No	No	No	No	No	7
137	Head	M.	44	Basilicata	No	No	No	No	No	11
	Wife	F.	42	Basilicata	No	No	No	No	No	10
	Daughter	F.	16	Basilicata	No	No	Yes	Yes	Yes	10
	Son	M.	13	Basilicata	No	No	Yes	Yes	Yes	10
138	Head	M.	43	Basilicata	No	No	No	No	Yes	16
	Wife	F.	40	Basilicata	No	No	No	No	No	8
	Son	M.	21	Basilicata	Yes	Yes	Yes	Yes	Yes	8
139	Head	M.	35	Sicily	Yes	Yes	No	No	No	4
	Wife	F.	22	Sicily	Yes	Yes	No	No	No	4
	Brother	M.	23	Sicily	Yes	Yes	No	No	Yes	3
140	Head	M.	31	Calabria	Yes	Yes	No	No	Yes	8
	Wife	F.	21	Basilicata	No	No	No	No	Yes	9
	Brother-in-law	M.	37	Calabria	No	No	No	No	No	2
	Boarder	M.	37	Calabria	Yes	Yes	No	No	Yes	9
141	Head	M.	38	Campania	Yes	Yes	No	No	Yes	14
	Wife	F.	29	Basilicata	No	No	No	No	No	10
142	Head	M.	30	Abruzzo	Yes	Yes	No	No	Yes	8
	Wife	F.	30	Abruzzo	No	No	No	No	No	1
	Daughter	F.	11	Abruzzo	Yes	No	No	No	No	1
	Lodger	M.	40	Abruzzo	No	No	No	No	Yes	5
143	Head	M.	39	Campania	Yes	Yes	No	No	No	10
	Wife	F.	37	Campania	No	No	No	No	No	9
144	Head	M.	30	Basilicata	Yes	Yes	No	No	Yes	8
	Wife	F.	25	Basilicata	No	No	No	No	No	5
	Son	M.	11	Basilicata	No	No	No	No	No	8
	Sister	F.	14	Basilicata	No	No	No	No	Yes	8
145	Head	M.	60	Campania	No	No	No	No	No	14
	Son	M.	27	Campania	Yes	Yes	Yes	Yes	Yes	4
	Son	M.	24	Campania	Yes	Yes	Yes	Yes	Yes	14
	Son	M.	22	Campania	Yes	Yes	Yes	Yes	Yes	14
	Son	M.	20	Campania	Yes	Yes	Yes	Yes	Yes	14
	Daughter-in-law.	F.	20	Campania	No	No	No	No	No	4
	Daughter-in-law.	F.	20	Basilicata	Yes	Yes	No	No	Yes	12

TABLE **II.**—GENERAL CONDITION AS TO LITERACY AND ILLITERACY, BY FAMILIES AND INDIVIDUALS—Continued.

[This table includes only persons 10 years of age or over.]

Family number.	Relationship to head of family.	Sex.	Age.	Birthplace.	Native language. Reads.	Writes.	English language. Reads.	Writes.	Speaks.	Years in the United States.
146	Head	M.	47	Calabria	Yes..	Yes...	No...	No....	Yes...	13
	Wife	F.	42	Calabria	No...	No....	No...	No....	No....	4
	Son-in-law	M.	23	Calabria	No...	No....	No...	No....	No....	2
	Nephew	M.	20	Calabria	No...	No...	No...	No....	Yes...	6
147	Cooperative	M.	40	Calabria	Yes..	Yes...	No...	No....	No....	5
	Cooperative	M.	30	Calabria	Yes..	Yes...	No...	No....	No....	5
	Cooperative	M.	24	Calabria	No...	No....	No...	No....	Yes...	6
	Cooperative	M.	30	Calabria	No...	No....	No...	No....	No..,.	4
148	Cooperative	M.	25	Calabria	Yes..	Yes...	No...	No....	Yes...	3
	Cooperative	M.	26	Calabria	No...	No....	No...	No....	Yes...	4
149	Head	M.	43	Sicily	No...	No....	No..	No....	No....	10
	Wife	F.	33	Sicily	No...	No....	No...	No....	No....	9
	Daughter	F.	14	Sicily	No...	No....	Yes..	Yes...	Yes...	9
150	Cooperative	M.	47	Calabria	Yes..	Yes...	No...	No....	No....	4
	Cooperative	M.	40	Calabria	No...	No....	No...	No....	No....	3
	Cooperative	M.	20	Calabria	Yes..	Yes...	No...	No....	No....	3
	Cooperative	M.	32	Calabria	No...	No....	No...	No....	No....	3
	Cooperative	M.	50	Calabria	Yes..	Yes...	No...	No....	No....	10
151	Head	M.	40	Abruzzo	Yes..	Yes...	No...	No....	Yes...	15
	Wife	F.	38	Abruzzo	No...	No....	No...	No....	No....	9
	Son	M.	16	Abruzzo	No...	No....	Yes..	Yes...	Yes...	9
152	Head	F.	60	Emilia	Yes..	Yes...	No...	No....	No....	10
	Daughter	F.	26	Emilia	Yes..	Yes...	No...	No....	Yes.	10
	Son	M.	24	Emilia	Yes..	Yes...	Yes..	Yes...	Yes...	10
153	Head	M.	50	Sicily	Yes..	Yes...	No...	No....	No....	4
	Wife	F.	48	Sicily	Yes..	Yes...	No...	No....	No....	4
	Son	M.	27	Sicily	Yes..	Yes...	No...	No....	Yes...	5
	Son	M.	24	Sicily	Yes..	Yes...	Yes..	Yes...	Yes...	6
	Son	M.	20	Sicily	Yes..	Yes...	No...	No....	Yes...	5
	Daughter	F.	18	Sicily	Yes..	Yes...	No...	No....	Yes...	4
	Son	M.	12	Sicily	Yes..	Yes...	Yes..	Yes...	Yes...	4
	Daughter-in-law.	F.	24	Sicily	Yes..	Yes...	No..	No....	No....	4
154	Head	M.	43	Campania	Yes..	Yes...	No...	No...	Yes...	14
	Wife	F.	45	Campania	No...	No....	No...	No....	No....	10
	Daughter	F.	17	Campania	Yes..	Yes...	Yes..	No....	Yes...	10
	Son-in-law	M.	21	Campania	Yes..	Yes...	Yes..	No....	Yes...	5
	Boarder	M.	12	Campania	Yes..	Yes...	No...	No....	No....	1½
155	Head	M.	30	Calabria	No...	No....	No...	No....	Yes...	16
	Wife	F.	23	Calabria	No...	No....	No...	No....	No....	3
	Lodger	M.	25	Calabria	Yes..	No....	No...	No....	Yes...	5
156	Head	M.	29	Campania	No...	No....	No...	No....	Yes...	15
	Wife	F.	28	Calabria	Yes..	Yes...	No...	No....	Yes...	4
157	Head	M.	65	Liguria	No...	No....	No...	No....	Yes...	18
	Wife	F.	35	Liguria	No...	No....	No...	No....	Yes...	18
	Son	M.	17	United States	Yes..	Yes...	Yes..	Yes...	Yes...	....
	Daughter	F.	15	United States	Yes..	Yes...	Yes..	Yes...	Yes...	....
158	Head	M.	40	Campania	No...	No....	No...	No....	Yes...	16
	Wife	F.	43	Campania	No...	No....	No...	No....	Yes...	11
	Son	M.	21	Campania	Yes..	Yes...	Yes..	Yes...	Yes...	16
	Daughter	F.	16	Campania	No...	No....	No...	No....	Yes...	16
	Son	M.	13	United States	Yes..	Yes...	Yes..	Yes...	Yes...	....
	Son	M.	10	United States	Yes..	Yes...	Yes..	Yes...	Yes...	....
	Cousin	M.	21	Campania	Yes..	Yes...	No...	No....	No....	1½
159	Head	M.	39	Calabria	Yes..	Yes...	Yes..	Yes...	Yes...	12
	Wife	F.	39	Calabria	Yes..	Yes...	No...	No....	No....	5
	Son	M.	15	Calabria	Yes..	Yes...	Yes..	Yes...	Yes...	5
	Son	M.	13	Calabria	Yes..	Yes...	Yes..	Yes...	Yes...	5
160	Head	M.	27	Calabria	No...	No....	No...	No....	No....	6
	Wife	F.	20	Calabria	No ..	No....	No...	No....	No....	3
161	Head	M.	40	Calabria	No...	No....	No...	No....	No....	8
	Wife	F.	35	Calabria	No...	No....	No...	No....	No....	8

TABLE **II.**—GENERAL CONDITION AS TO LITERACY AND ILLITERACY, BY
FAMILIES AND INDIVIDUALS—Continued.

[This table includes only persons 10 years of age or over.]

Family number.	Relationship to head of family.	Sex.	Age.	Birthplace.	Native language. Reads.	Writes.	English language. Reads.	Writes.	Speaks.	Years in the United States.
162	Head	M.	52	Campania	No...	No...	No...	No...	No...	11
	Wife	F.	46	Campania	No...	No...	No...	No...	No...	8
	Son	M.	13	Campania	Yes...	Yes...	No...	No...	Yes...	8
163	Head	M.	36	Campania	Yes..	Yes...	No...	No...	Yes...	13
	Wife	F.	39	Campania	No...	No...	No...	No...	No...	5
	Son	M.	13	Campania	No...	No...	No...	No...	Yes...	5
	Nephew	M.	33	Campania	Yes..	Yes...	No...	No...	Yes...	3
164	Head	M.	40	Campania	No...	No...	No...	No...	Yes...	6
	Wife	F.	35	Campania	No...	No...	No...	No...	No...	3
	Son	M.	13	Campania	Yes...	No...	No...	No...	Yes...	1
165	Head	M.	25	Campania	No...	No...	No...	No...	Yes...	11
	Wife	F.	20	Campania	No...	No...	No...	No...	Yes...	8
166	Head	M.	34	Campania	No...	No...	No...	No...	Yes...	20
	Wife	F.	24	Basilicata	No...	No...	No...	No...	No...	11
167	Head	M.	43	Campania	No...	No...	No...	No...	Yes...	5
	Wife	F.	33	Campania	No...	No...	No...	No...	No...	$\frac{1}{12}$
168	Head	M.	45	Campania	Yes...	Yes..	No...	No...	Yes...	10
	Wife	F.	40	Campania	No...	No...	No...	No...	No...	4
	Boarder	M.	27	Campania	No...	No...	No...	No...	No...	3
	Lodger	M.	33	Campania	No...	No...	No...	No...	Yes...	10
	Lodger	M.	33	Campania	No...	No...	No...	No...	Yes...	6
169	Head	M.	50	Campania	No...	No...	No...	No...	No...	13
	Wife	F.	41	Campania	No...	No...	No...	No...	No...	3
	Daughter	F.	15	Campania	Yes...	Yes...	Yes...	No...	Yes...	3
170	Head	M.	27	Campania	No...	No...	No...	No...	Yes...	8
	Wife	F.	20	Campania	No...	No...	No...	No...	Yes...	10
	Lodger	M.	32	Abruzzo	No...	No...	No...	No...	Yes...	4
171	Head	M.	27	Campania	Yes..	Yes...	No...	No...	Yes...	10
	Wife	F.	25	Campania	No...	No...	No...	No...	Yes...	3
	Brother	M.	22	Campania	Yes..	Yes...	No...	No...	Yes...	6
172	Head	M.	42	Campania	Yes..	Yes...	No...	No...	Yes...	15
	Wife	F.	35	Campania	Reads..	No...	Reads..	No...	Speaks..	15
	Son	M.	14	United States	Yes...	Yes...	Yes..	Yes...	Yes...	....
	Daughter	F.	10	United States	Yes...	Yes...	Yes..	Yes...	Yes...	....
173	Head	M.	37	Basilicata	No...	No...	No...	No...	Yes...	14
	Wife	F.	34	Basilicata	No...	No...	No...	No...	No...	10
174	Head	M.	20	Calabria	Yes..	Yes...	No...	No...	No...	$\frac{7}{12}$
	Wife	F.	16	Calabria	No...	No...	No...	No...	No...	$\frac{1}{12}$
	Cousin	M.	27	Calabria	No...	No...	No...	No...	No...	4
	Boarder	M.	26	Calabria	Yes..	Yes...	No...	No...	Yes...	3
175	Head	M.	38	Calabria	Yes..	Yes...	No...	No...	Yes...	14
	Wife	F.	20	Calabria	No...	No...	No...	No...	Yes...	4
	Nephew	M.	16	Calabria	No...	No...	No...	No...	No...	$\frac{1}{12}$
	Boarder	M.	26	Calabria	Yes..	Yes...	No...	No...	Yes...	4
176	Head	M.	35	Campania	No...	No...	No...	No...	Yes...	11
	Wife	F.	32	Campania	No...	No...	No...	No...	Yes...	9
177	Head	M.	39	Basilicata	No...	No...	No...	No...	Yes...	14
	Wife	F.	37	Basilicata	No ..	No...	No...	No...	No...	9
	Daughter	F.	14	Basilicata	Yes...	Yes...	Yes..	Yes...	Yes...	9
	Lodger	M.	58	Basilicata	No...	No...	No...	No...	Yes...	14
178	Head	M.	36	Campania	No...	No...	No...	No...	Yes...	11
	Wife	F.	30	Campania	No...	No...	No ..	No...	Yes...	11
	Daughter	F.	10	United States	Yes...	Yes...	Yes..	Yes...	Yes...	....
	Stepmother	F.	60	Campania	No...	No...	No...	No...	No...	11
179	Head	M.	31	Basilicata	No...	No...	No...	No...	Yes...	13
	Wife	F.	42	Basilicata	No...	No...	No...	No...	No...	10
180	Head	M.	29	Campania	No...	No...	No...	No...	Yes...	6
	Wife	F.	20	Campania	No...	No...	No...	No...	Yes...	17

TABLE **II.**—GENERAL CONDITION AS TO LITERACY AND ILLITERACY, BY
FAMILIES AND INDIVIDUALS—Continued.

[This table includes only persons 10 years of age or over.]

Family number.	Relationship to head of family.	Sex.	Age.	Birthplace.	Native language.		English language.			Years in the United States.
					Reads.	Writes.	Reads.	Writes.	Speaks.	
181	Head	M.	35	Campania	Yes..	Yes...	Yes..	Yes...	Yes...	15
	Wife	F.	27	Campania	No...	No....	No....	No....	No....	11
182	Head	M.	26	Calabria	Yes..	Yes...	No...	No...	Yes...	7
	Wife	F.	33	Calabria	No...	No....	No...	No...	No....	2
	Stepson	M.	13	Calabria	No...	No....	No...	No...	Yes...	4
	Stepson	M.	10	Calabria	No...	No....	No...	No...	Yes...	2
	Father	M.	56	Calabria	No...	No....	No...	No...	No....	4
183	Head	M.	32	Calabria	No..	No....	No...	No....	Yes...	8
	Wife	F.	30	Calabria	No...	No....	No...	No....	No....	3
	Boarder	M.	26	Calabria	Yes.	Yes...	No...	No....	Yes...	7
184	Head	M.	48	Campania	No...	No....	No...	No....	No....	17
	Wife	F.	46	Campania	No...	No....	No...	No....	No....	15
	Son	M.	24	Campania	Yes..	Yes...	Yes..	Yes...	Yes..	15
	Son	M.	19	Campania	No...	No....	No...	No....	Yes...	15
	Daughter	F.	16	Campania	No...	No....	No...	No....	Yes...	15
	Son	M.	13	United States	Yes..	Yes...	Yes..	Yes...	Yes..	....
	Daughter	F.	12	United States	No...	No....	No...	No....	Yes...	....
185	Head	M.	30	Campania	No...	No....	No...	No....	Yes...	10
	Wife	F.	28	Campania	No...	No....	No...	No....	Yes...	10
	Nephew	M.	15	Campania	Yes..	Yes...	Yes..	Yes...	Yes..	8
186	Head	M.	47	Campania	No...	No....	No...	No....	Yes...	14
	Wife	F.	45	Campania	No...	No....	No...	No....	No....	12
	Son	M.	23	Campania	Yes..	Yes.	Yes..	Yes...	Yes...	12
	Son	M.	16	Campania	No...	No....	Yes..	Yes...	Yes...	12
	Son	M.	12	United States	Yes..	Yes...	Yes..	Yes...	Yes...	....
	Son	M.	10	United States	Yes..	Yes...	Yes..	Yes...	Yes...	....
	Daughter-in-law.	F.	21	Campania	No...	No....	No	No	Yes...	13
187	Head	M.	38	Campania	Yes..	Yes...	No...	No....	No....	10
	Wife	F.	33	Campania	No...	No....	No...	No....	No....	10
188	Head	M.	30	Campania	No...	No....	No...	No....	Yes...	11
	Wife	F.	28	Campania	No...	No....	No...	No...	No....	6
189	Head	M.	32	Campania	No...	No....	No...	No....	No....	6
	Wife	F.	36	Campania	No...	No....	No...	No....	No....	2
190	Head	M.	25	Calabria	Yes..	Yes .	Yes..	Yes...	Yes...	5
	Wife	F.	19	Calabria	No...	No....	No...	No....	Yes...	3
191	Head	M.	40	Campania	Yes..	Yes...	No...	No....	Yes...	15
	Wife	F.	35	Campania	No...	No....	No...	No....	Yes...	10
	Son	M.	13	Campania	Yes..	Yes...	No...	No....	Yes...	10
	Son	M.	11	Campania	No...	No....	No...	No....	Yes...	10
	Nephew	M.	13	Campania	Yes..	Yes...	No...	No....	Yes...	4
	Cousin	M.	19	Campania	No...	No....	No...	No....	No....	1
192	Head	M.	27	Calabria	Yes..	Yes...	No...	No....	Yes...	3
	Wife	F.	15	Calabria	Yes..	Yes...	Yes..	Yes...	Yes...	7
	Father	M.	54	Calabria	No...	No....	No...	No....	No....	3
	Brother	M.	20	Calabria	Yes..	Yes...	No...	No....	Yes..	3
	Lodger	M.	51	Calabria	No...	No....	No...	No....	No....	4
	Lodger	M.	21	Calabria	Yes..	Yes...	No...	No....	No....	4
	Lodger	M.	52	Calabria	No...	No....	No...	No....	No....	4
	Lodger	M.	22	Calabria	Yes..	Yes...	No...	No....	No....	4
	Lodger	M.	20	Calabria	Yes.	Yes...	No...	No....	No.	4
	Lodger	M.	40	Calabria	No...	No....	No...	No....	No....	14
	Lodger	M.	24	Calabria	No...	No....	No...	No....	No....	12
	Lodger	M.	26	Calabria	Yes..	Yes...	No...	No....	No....	4
193	Head	M.	30	Basilicata	No...	No....	No...	No....	Yes...	6
	Wife	F.	27	Basilicata	No...	No....	No...	No....	No....	4
194	Head	M.	32	Campania	Yes..	Yes...	No...	No....	No....	3
	Wife	F.	31	Campania	Yes..	Yes...	No...	No....	No....	3
195	Head	M.	30	Campania	Yes..	No....	No...	No....	Yes...	9
	Wife	F.	32	Campania	No...	No....	No...	No....	No....	8

TABLE **II.**—GENERAL CONDITION AS TO LITERACY AND ILLITERACY, BY
FAMILIES AND INDIVIDUALS—Continued.

[This table includes only persons 10 years of age or over.]

Family number.	Relationship to head of family.	Sex.	Age.	Birthplace.	Native language.		English language.			Years in the United States.
					Reads.	Writes.	Reads.	Writes.	Speaks.	
196	Head	M.	40	Basilicata	No	No	No	No	Yes	6
	Wife	F.	30	Basilicata	No	No	No	No	No	4
	Daughter	F.	10	Basilicata	No	No	Yes	Yes	Yes	6
197	Head	M.	29	Basilicata	No	No	No	No	Yes	10
	Wife	F.	20	Basilicata	No	No	No	No	Yes	15
	Father	M.	64	Basilicata	Yes	No	No	No	No	5
198	Head	M.	45	Basilicata	No	No	No	No	No	7
	Wife	F.	44	Basilicata	No	No	No	No	No	5
	Son	M.	15	Basilicata	Yes	Yes	Yes	Yes	Yes	5
199	Head	M.	28	Campania	No	No	No	No	Yes	7
	Wife	F.	19	Campania	Yes	Yes	No	No	Yes	5
	Lodger	M.	28	Campania	Yes	No	No	No	No	4
200	Head	M.	36	Basilicata	Yes	Yes	No	No	No	12
	Wife	F.	36	Basilicata	No	No	No	No	No	9
	Son	M.	11	Basilicata	No	No	No	No	Yes	9
201	Head	M.	31	Abruzzo	Yes	Yes	No	No	Yes	11
	Wife	F.	35	Abruzzo	No	No	No	No	Yes	6
	Stepdaughter.	F.	10	Abruzzo	No	No	No	No	Yes	6
202	Head	M.	65	Basilicata	No	No	No	No	No	14
	Wife	F.	58	Basilicata	No	No	No	No	No	10
	Son	M.	20	Basilicata	Yes	Yes	Yes	Yes	Yes	10
203	Head	M.	43	Campania	Yes	Yes	No	No	Yes	12
	Wife	F.	48	Campania	No	No	No	No	No	8
204	Head	M.	38	Basilicata	No	No	No	No	No	10
	Wife	F.	48	Basilicata	No	No	No	No	No	8
	Son	M.	13	Basilicata	No	No	Yes	Yes	Yes	10
205	Head	M.	41	Basilicata	No	No	No	No	No	10
	Wife	F.	40	Basilicata	No	No	No	No	No	5
206	Head	M.	46	Basilicata	No	No	No	No	Yes	15
	Wife	F.	45	Basilicata	No	No	No	No	No	10
	Son	M.	14	Basilicata	Yes	Yes	Yes	Yes	Yes	10
207	Head	M.	29	Abruzzo	No	No	No	No	Yes	8
	Wife	F.	20	Basilicata	No	No	No	No	Yes	11
208	Head	M.	37	Abruzzo	No	No	No	No	No	8
	Wife	F.	30	Campania	No	No	No	No	No	3
209	Head	M.	35	Calabria	No	No	No	No	No	13
	Wife	F.	30	Calabria	No	No	No	No	No	9
	Son	M.	14	Calabria	Yes	Yes	Yes	Yes	Yes	9
210	Head	M.	30	Calabria	Yes	Yes	No	No	Yes	12
	Wife	F.	23	Calabria	No	No	No	No	No	3
211	Head	M.	46	Campania	No	No	No	No	No	11
	Wife	F.	36	Campania	No	No	No	No	No	11
	Son	M.	12	Campania	Yes	Yes	Yes	Yes	Yes	12
	Lodger	M.	26	Campania	Yes	Yes	No	No	No	3
212	Head	M.	33	Calabria	No	No	No	No	No	5
	Wife	F.	34	Calabria	No	No	No	No	No	6
213	Head	M.	28	Basilicata	Yes	Yes	No	No	Yes	8
	Wife	F.	24	Basilicata	No	No	No	No	No	6
214	Head	M.	47	Basilicata	No	No	No	No	Yes	14
	Wife	F.	46	Basilicata	No	No	No	No	No	2
	Mother-in-law	F.	80	Basilicata	Reads	No	Reads	No	Speaks	3
215	Head	M.	38	Basilicata	No	No	No	No	No	8
	Wife	F.	38	Basilicata	No	No	No	No	No	7
216	Head	M.	33	Sicily	Yes	No	No	No	No	6
	Wife	F.	37	Sicily	No	No	No	No	No	6
	Daughter	F.	13	Sicily	No	No	No	No	No	6

TABLE **II.**—GENERAL CONDITION AS TO LITERACY AND ILLITERACY, BY
FAMILIES AND INDIVIDUALS—Continued.

[This table includes only persons 10 years of age or over.]

Family number.	Relationship to head of family.	Sex.	Age.	Birthplace.	Native language.		English language.			Years in the United States.
					Reads.	Writes.	Reads.	Writes.	Speaks.	
217	Head	M.	40	Campania..........	Yes..	Yes...	No...	No....	Yes...	16
	Wife..........	F.	26	Campania..........	No...	No....	No...	No....	Yes...	20
	Son	M.	11	United States......	Yes..	Yes...	Yes...	Yes...	Yes...	....
	Son	M.	10	United States......	Yes..	Yes...	Yes..	Yes...	Yes...	
218	Cooperative ..	M.	33	Campania..........	No...	No....	No...	No....	Yes...	13
	Cooperative ..	M.	40	Campania..........	Yes..	No....	No...	No....	No....	5
	Cooperative ..	M.	29	Campania..........	Yes..	Yes...	No...	No....	No....	4
219	Head	M.	39	Campania..........	No...	No...	No...	No....	Yes...	11
	Wife..........	F.	37	Campania..........	No...	No...	No...	No....	Yes...	6
	Daughter.....	F.	13	Campania..........	No...	No...	Yes...	Yes...	Yes...	6
220	Head	M.	32	Campania..........	No...	No...	No...	No....	Yes...	8
	Wife..........	F.	33	Campania..........	No...	No...	No...	No....	No....	4
	Son	M.	11	Campania..........	Yes..	Yes...	Yes...	Yes...	Yes...	4
221	Head	M.	50	Campania..........	Yes..	Yes...	No...	No....	Yes...	20
	Wife..........	F.	45	Campania..........	No...	No....	No...	No....	Yes...	20
	Son	M.	22	Campania..........	Yes..	Yes...	Yes...	Yes...	Yes...	20
	Son	M.	21	Campania..........	Yes..	Yes...	Yes...	Yes...	Yes...	20
	Son	M.	14	United States......	Yes..	Yes...	Yes..	Yes...	Yes...	....
	Daughter.....	F.	12	United States......	Yes..	Yes...	Yes..	Yes...	Yes...	....
	Daughter.....	F.	10	United States......	Yes..	Yes...	Yes..	Yes...	Yes...	
222	Head	M.	29	Campania..........	Yes..	Yes...	No...	No....	No....	4
	Wife..........	F.	29	Campania..........	No...	No...	No...	No....	No....	4
	Brother-in-law	M.	34	Campania..........	No...	No...	No...	No....	Yes ..	14
223	Head	M.	28	Campania..........	Yes..	Yes...	No...	No....	Yes...	9
	Wife..........	F.	28	Campania..........	No...	No...	No...	No....	No....	4
224	Head	M.	30	Basilicata..........	No...	No...	No...	No....	No....	8
	Wife..........	F.	27	Basilicata..........	No...	No...	No..	No....	No....	5
	Boarder.......	M.	30	Calabria	Yes..	Yes...	Yes..	Yes...	Yes...	13
225	Head	M.	50	Basilicata..........	No...	No...	No...	No....	No....	3
	Wife..........	F.	44	Basilicata..........	No...	No...	No...	No....	No....	2
	Son	M.	15	Basilicata..........	No...	No...	Yes..	Yes...	Yes...	2
	Son	M.	13	Basilicata..........	No...	No...	Yes..	Yes...	Yes...	2
226	Head	M.	25	Campania..........	No...	No...	No...	No....	Yes...	10
	Wife..........	F.	22	Basilicata..........	No...	No...	No...	No....	No....	7
227	Head	M.	26	Sicily	No...	No...	No...	No....	No....	7
	Wife..........	F.	21	Sicily	No...	No...	No...	No....	No....	3
	Brother-in-law	M.	28	Sicily	No...	No...	No...	No....	No....	5
	Sister-in-law ..	F.	26	Sicily	No...	No...	No..	No....	No....	5
228	Head	M.	24	Sicily	No...	No...	No...	No....	No....	3
	Wife..........	F.	20	Sicily	Yes..	Yes...	No...	No....	No....	3
	Father-in-law.	M.	50	Sicily	No...	No...	No...	No....	No....	4
	Brother-in-law	M.	17	Sicily	No...	No...	No...	No....	No....	¹⁄₁₂
229	Head	M.	28	Sicily	No...	No...	No...	No....	Yes...	9
	Wife..........	F.	21	Sicily	Yes..	Yes...	Yes..	Yes...	Yes...	13
230	Head	M.	55	Sicily	Yes..	Yes...	No...	No....	Yes...	8
	Wife..........	F.	35	Sicily	No...	No...	No...	No....	No....	8
	Brother.......	M.	41	Sicily	No...	No...	No...	No....	Yes...	12
	Sister-in-law ..	F.	23	Sicily	No...	No...	No...	No....	No....	6
231	Head	M.	41	Sicily	Yes..	Yes...	No...	No....	No....	9
	Wife..........	F.	35	Sicily	No...	No...	No...	No....	No....	7
	Son	M.	11	Sicily	No...	No...	Yes..	Yes...	Yes...	7
	Nephew	M.	34	Sicily	No...	No...	No...	No....	Yes...	9
	Niece.........	F.	23	Sicily	No...	No...	No...	No....	No....	3
	Uncle.........	M.	55	Sicily	No...	No...	No...	No....	No....	8
232	Head	M.	39	Basilicata..........	No...	No...	No...	No....	No....	8
	Wife..........	F.	38	Basilicata..........	No...	No...	No...	No....	No....	8
	Son	M.	15	Basilicata..........	No...	No...	Yes..	No....	Yes...	8
	Daughter.....	F.	10	Basilicata..........	No...	No....	No...	No....	Yes...	8

TABLE II.—GENERAL CONDITION AS TO LITERACY AND ILLITERACY, BY FAMILIES AND INDIVIDUALS—Continued.

[This table includes only persons 10 years of age or over.]

Family number.	Relationship to head of family.	Sex.	Age.	Birthplace.	Native language.		English language.			Years in the United States.
					Reads.	Writes.	Reads.	Writes.	Speaks.	
233	Head	M.	25	Basilicata	Yes	Yes	No	No	Yes	7
	Wife	F.	23	Basilicata	No	No	No	No	Yes	10
	Father-in-law	M.	52	Basilicata	No	No	No	No	Yes	10
234	Head	F.	45	Campania	No	No	No	No	Yes	15
	Son-in-law	M.	32	Campania	No	No	No	No	Yes	10
	Lodger	M.	38	Abruzzo	Yes	Yes	Yes	Yes	Yes	14
	Lodger	M.	25	Abruzzo	Yes	Yes	No	No	Yes	12
	Lodger	M.	52	Campania	No	No	No	No	No	9
235	Head	M.	32	Basilicata	No	No	Yes	Yes	Yes	27
	Wife	F.	32	Basilicata	No	No	No	No	Yes	11
	Son	M.	10	United States	Yes	Yes	Yes	Yes	Yes	
236	Head	M.	38	Basilicata	Yes	Yes	No	No	Yes	25
	Wife	F.	28	Basilicata	No	No	No	No	No	4
237	Head	M.	28	Calabria	Yes	Yes	No	No	Yes	9
	Wife	F.	24	Calabria	Yes	Yes	No	No	Yes	7
238	Head	M.	39	Basilicata	No	No	No	No	No	10
	Wife	F.	30	Basilicata	No	No	No	No	Yes	8
239	Head	M.	27	Calabria	Yes	Yes	No	No	Yes	5
	Wife	F.	24	Calabria	No	No	No	No	Yes	5
240	Head	M.	36	Calabria	Yes	Yes	No	No	Yes	13
	Wife	F.	24	Calabria	No	No	No	No	Yes	7
241	Head	M.	33	Calabria	No	No	No	No	Yes	6
	Wife	F.	33	Calabria	No	No	No	No	No	3
242	Head	M.	51	Calabria	Yes	Yes	No	No	Yes	22
	Wife	F.	43	Calabria	No	No	No	No	No	7
243	Head	M.	48	Calabria	No	No	No	No	Yes	11
	Wife	F.	33	Calabria	No	No	No	No	Yes	6
	Son	M.	12	Calabria	Yes	Yes	Yes	Yes	Yes	6
244	Head	M.	27	Calabria	No	No	No	No	Yes	14
	Wife	F.	19	Calabria	Yes	Yes	No	No	No	5
245	Head	M.	40	Calabria	Yes	Yes	Yes	Yes	Yes	16
	Wife	F.	35	Calabria	No	No	No	No	No	11
	Son	M.	14	Calabria	Yes	Yes	Yes	Yes	Yes	11
246	Head	M.	23	Abruzzo	No	No	No	No	Yes	13
	Wife	F.	18	Abruzzo	No	No	No	No	Yes	3
247	Head	M.	60	Abruzzo	No	No	No	No	No	3
	Wife	F.	60	Abruzzo	No	No	No	No	No	3
	Son	M.	27	Abruzzo	No	No	No	No	Yes	7
	Son	M.	15	Abruzzo	No	No	No	No	Yes	3
	Daughter-in-law.	F.	27	Abruzzo	No	No	No	No	No	3
248	Cooperative	M.	24	Calabria	Yes	Yes	No	No	Yes	3
	Cooperative	M.	25	Calabria	No	No	No	No	Yes	3
	Cooperative	M.	27	Calabria	No	No	No	No	Yes	3
	Cooperative	M.	31	Calabria	Yes	Yes	No	No	Yes	5
249	Head	M.	38	Calabria	Yes	Yes	No	No	Yes	12
	Wife	F.	36	Calabria	No	No	No	No	No	9
	Daughter	F.	13	Calabria	No	No	Yes	Yes	Yes	9
250	Head	M.	30	Sicily	Yes	Yes	No	No	Yes	9
	Wife	F.	27	Sicily	Yes	Yes	Yes	Yes	Yes	14
251	Head	M.	24	Basilicata	Yes	Yes	No	No	Yes	(a)
	Wife	F.	17	Basilicata	Yes	Yes	Yes	Yes	Yes	10
252	Head	M.	50	Basilicata	No	No	No	No	No	16
	Wife	F.	54	Basilicata	No	No	No	No	No	8
	Son	M.	22	Basilicata	Yes	Yes	Yes	Yes	Yes	8
	Daughter	F.	20	Basilicata	No	No	No	No	Yes	8

a Not reported.

TABLE **II.**—GENERAL CONDITION AS TO LITERACY AND ILLITERACY, BY FAMILIES AND INDIVIDUALS—Continued.

[This table includes only persons 10 years of age or over.]

Family number.	Relationship to head of family.	Sex.	Age.	Birthplace.	Native language. Reads.	Writes.	English language. Reads.	Writes.	Speaks.	Years in the United States.
253	Head	M.	42	Basilicata	Yes	Yes	No	No	Yes	11
	Wife	F.	38	Basilicata	No	No	No	No	No	11
	Son	M.	16	Basilicata	No	No	Yes	Yes	Yes	11
254	Head	M.	25	Campania	No	No	No	No	Yes	8
	Wife	F.	25	Campania	No	No	No	No	Yes	6
255	Head	M.	49	Basilicata	No	No	No	No	Yes	17
	Wife	F.	39	Basilicata	Yes	Yes	No	No	No	15
	Son	M.	18	Basilicata	No	No	Yes	Yes	Yes	15
	Daughter	F.	14	United States	No	No	No	No	Yes	....
	Daughter	F.	10	United States	Yes	Yes	Yes	Yes	Yes	....
256	Head	M.	47	Calabria	No	No	No	No	No	5
	Wife	F.	47	Calabria	No	No	No	No	No	5
	Nephew	M.	22	Calabria	Yes	Yes	No	No	Yes	4
257	Head	M.	27	Basilicata	No	No	No	No	Yes	8
	Wife	F.	20	Basilicata	No	No	No	No	No	8
258	Head	M.	42	Basilicata	Yes	Yes	Yes	Yes	Yes	21
	Wife	F.	32	Basilicata	No	No	No	No	Yes	8
259	Head	M.	39	Calabria	Yes	Yes	No	No	Yes	14
	Wife	F.	30	Calabria	No	No	No	No	Yes	11
	Son	M.	12	Calabria	No	No	Yes	Yes	Yes	11
260	Head	M.	30	Campania	Yes	Yes	No	No	Yes	6
	Wife	F.	31	Campania	No	No	No	No	No	6
	Father	M.	60	Campania	No	No	No	No	No	4
	Mother	F.	60	Campania	No	No	No	No	No	4
	Brother	M.	21	Campania	Yes	Yes	No	No	Yes	6
261	Head	M.	39	Abruzzo	No	No	No	No	Yes	9
	Wife	F.	32	Abruzzo	Yes	Yes	No	No	No	4
	Son	M.	10	Abruzzo	No	No	No	No	Yes	4
	Sister	F.	24	Abruzzo	Yes	Yes	No	No	No	5
	Brother	M.	32	Abruzzo	Yes	Yes	No	No	Yes	8
	Brother	M.	37	Abruzzo	Yes	Yes	No	No	Yes	8
	Brother-in-law	M.	36	Abruzzo	No	No	No	No	Yes	9
	Lodger	M.	26	Abruzzo	No	No	No	No	No	4
262	Head	M.	45	Sicily	Yes	Yes	No	No	No	6
	Wife	F.	35	Sicily	No	No	No	No	No	5
	Son	M.	17	Sicily	No	No	No	No	Yes	5
	Son	M.	11	Sicily	No	No	No	No	Yes	5
	Sister	F.	33	Sicily	Yes	Yes	No	No	No	3
	Brother-in-law	M.	28	Sicily	Yes	Yes	No	No	No	6
263	Head	M.	38	Campania	No	No	No	No	Yes	6
	Wife	F.	34	Campania	No	No	No	No	No	4
	Lodger	M.	28	Calabria	Yes	Yes	No	No	Yes	5
	Lodger	F.	17	Campania	No	No	Yes	Yes	Yes	8
264	Head	M.	43	Calabria	Yes	Yes	No	No	Yes	15
	Wife	F.	38	Calabria	No	No	No	No	No	7
	Nephew	M.	24	Calabria	Yes	Yes	No	No	Yes	5
	Lodger	M.	41	Calabria	Yes	Yes	No	No	Yes	13
	Lodger	M.	28	Calabria	No	No	No	No	No	3
265	Head	M.	23	Campania	No	No	No	No	Yes	12
	Wife	F.	16	Campania	Yes	Yes	Yes	Yes	Yes	8
266	Head	M.	26	Calabria	No	No	No	No	Yes	6
	Wife	F.	20	Calabria	No	No	No	No	No	1/2
	Cousin	M.	30	Calabria	Yes	Yes	No	No	No	4
	Cousin	M.	28	Calabria	Yes	Yes	No	No	No	6
	Boarder	M.	32	Calabria	No	No	No	No	No	6
267	Head	M.	40	Calabria	No	No	No	No	Yes	10
	Wife	F.	35	Calabria	No	No	No	No	Yes	9
	Son	M.	13	Calabria	Yes	Yes	Yes	Yes	Yes	9
	Brother	M.	45	Calabria	No	No	No	No	No	9
	Nephew	M.	25	Calabria	No	No	No	No	No	5

TABLE **II.**—GENERAL CONDITION AS TO LITERACY AND ILLITERACY, BY FAMILIES AND INDIVIDUALS—Continued.

[This table includes only persons 10 years of age or over.]

Family number.	Relationship to head of family.	Sex.	Age.	Birthplace.	Native language.		English language.			Years in the United States.
					Reads.	Writes.	Reads.	Writes.	Speaks.	
268	Head	M.	45	Calabria	No...	No...	No...	No...	No....	6
	Wife	F.	24	Calabria	No...	No...	Nó...	No...	No....	6
	Brother	M.	30	Calabria	No...	No...	No...	No...	Yes...	8
	Father-in-law	M.	50	Calabria	No...	No...	No...	No...	No....	8
	Stepmother-in-law.	F.	60	Calabria	No...	No...	No...	No...	No....	4
	Brother-in-law	M.	40	Calabria	No...	No...	No...	No...	Yes...	10
	Lodger	M.	42	Calabria	No...	No...	No...	No...	Yes...	5
	Lodger	M.	27	Calabria	No...	No...	No...	No...	No....	1
269	Head	M.	33	Calabria	Yes..	Yes...	No...	No...	No....	4
	Wife	F.	38	Calabria	No...	No...	No...	No...	No....	3
	Son	M.	14	Calabria	Yes..	Yes...	Yes...	Yes...	Yes...	3
270	Head	M.	40	Abruzzo	Yes..	Yes...	No...	No...	No....	5
	Wife	F.	41	Abruzzo	No...	No...	No...	No...	No....	5
	Daughter	F.	13	Abruzzo	Yes..	Yes...	Yes...	Yes...	Yes...	5
	Son	M.	10	Abruzzo	Yes..	Yes...	Yes...	Yes...	Yes...	5
	Brother-in-law	M.	28	Abruzzo	Yes..	Yes...	No...	No...	Yes...	5
	Lodger	M.	28	Abruzzo	Yes..	No...	No...	No...	No....	5
	Lodger	M.	45	Abruzzo	No...	No...	No...	No...	No....	4
271	Head	M.	45	Calabria	Yes..	Yes...	No...	No...	Yes...	13
	Wife	F.	43	Calabria	No...	No...	No...	No...	No....	8
	Son	M.	17	Calabria	No...	No...	Yes..	Yes...	Yes...	8
	Brother-in-law	M.	25	Calabria	Yes..	Yes...	Yes...	Yes...	Yes...	7
272	Head	M.	40	Basilicata	No...	No...	No...	No...	No....	13
	Wife	F.	38	Basilicata	No...	No...	No...	No...	Yes...	9
273	Head	M.	23	Campania	No...	No...	No...	No...	No....	3
	Wife	F.	22	Campania	No...	No...	No...	No...	No....	2
	Mother	F.	60	Campania	No...	No...	No...	No...	No....	5
274	Head	M.	48	Sicily	No...	No...	No...	No...	No....	6
	Wife	F.	40	Sicily	No...	No...	No...	No...	No....	5
	Daughter	F.	15	Sicily	No...	No...	No...	No...	No....	5
	Daughter	F.	12	Sicily	No...	No...	Yes..	Yes...	Yes...	5
275	Head	M.	38	Basilicata	No...	No...	No...	No...	Yes...	15
	Wife	F.	22	Basilicata	No...	No....	No...	No...	Yes...	15
	Cousin	M.	30	Calabria	No...	No...	No...	No...	No....	7
276	Head	M.	34	Abruzzo	Yes..	Yes...	No...	No...	No....	6
	Wife	F.	28	Abruzzo	No...	No...	No...	No...	No....	6
277	Head	M.	33	Abruzzo	Yes..	Yes...	No...	No...	Yes...	4
	Wife	F.	28	Abruzzo	No...	No...	No...	No...	No....	4
278	Head	M.	47	Basilicata	No...	No...	No...	No...	Yes...	14
	Wife	F.	41	Basilicata	No...	No...	No...	No...	No....	6
279	Head	M.	34	Basilicata	No...	No...	No...	No...	No....	13
	Wife	F.	39	Basilicata	No...	No...	No...	No...	No....	8
280	Head	M.	31	Calabria	No...	No...	No...	No...	No....	5
	Wife	F.	20	Calabria	No...	No...	No...	No...	Yes...	3
281	Head	M.	50	Calabria	No...	No...	No...	No...	No....	10
	Wife	F.	30	Calabria	No...	No...	No...	No...	No....	6
	Daughter	F.	15	Calabria	No...	No...	Yes..	Yes...	Yes...	6
	Mother-in-law	F.	48	Calabria	No...	No...	No...	No...	No....	3
	Lodger	M.	40	Calabria	No...	No...	No...	No...	No....	9
282	Head	M.	23	Basilicata	Yes..	Yes...	Yes...	Yes...	Yes...	16
	Wife	F.	26	Basilicata	No...	No...	No...	No...	No....	3
283	Head	M.	45	Campania	Yes..	Yes...	No...	No...	No....	8
	Wife	F.	32	Campania	Yes..	Yes...	No...	No...	No....	4
	Daughter	F.	14	Campania	Yes..	Yes...	Yes...	Yes...	Yes...	4
284	Head	M.	60	Basilicata	Yes..	Yes...	No...	No...	No....	10
	Wife	F.	52	Basilicata	No...	No...	No...	No...	No....	10
285	Head	M.	50	Basilicata	No...	No...	No...	No...	Yes...	20
	Wife	F.	40	Basilicata	No...	No...	No...	No...	No....	16

TABLE **II.**—GENERAL CONDITION AS TO LITERACY AND ILLITERACY, BY FAMILIES AND INDIVIDUALS—Continued.

[This table includes only persons 10 years of age or over.]

Family number.	Relationship to head of family.	Sex.	Age.	Birthplace.	Native language.		English language.			Years in the United States.
					Reads.	Writes.	Reads.	Writes.	Speaks.	
286	Cooperative ..	M.	41	Sicily	No...	No....	No...	No....	No....	1
	Cooperative ..	M.	48	Sicily	No...	No....	No...	No....	No....	6
287	Head	M.	29	Calabria	Yes..	Yes...	Yes..	Yes...	Yes...	10
	Wife..........	F.	26	Basilicata	No...	No....	No...	No....	Yes...	7
	Cousin.........	M.	33	Calabria	Yes..	Yes...	No...	No....	Yes...	6
	Cousin.........	M.	27	Calabria	Yes..	Yes...	Yes..	Yes...	Yes...	4
288	Head	M.	31	Basilicata..........	No...	No....	No...	No....	Yes...	6
	Wife..........	F.	28	Basilicata..........	No...	No....	No...	No....	No....	4
	Brother-in-law	M.	26	Basilicata..........	No...	No....	No...	No....	No....	½
	Lodger........	M.	34	Basilicata..........	No...	No....	No...	No....	No....	4
289	Head	M.	44	Calabria	Yes..	Yes..	Yes..	Yes..	Yes...	15
	Wife..........	F.	36	Calabria	No...	No....	No...	No....	No....	9
	Son	M.	18	Calabria	Yes..	Yes..	Yes..	Yes..	Yes...	9
	Daughter	F.	16	Calabria	Yes..	Yes..	No...	No....	Yes...	9
	Nephew	M.	21	Calabria	No...	No....	No...	No....	Yes...	5
	Boarder.......	M.	44	Calabria	Yes..	Yes..	No...	No....	Yes...	15
290	Head	M.	50	Calabria	No...	No....	No...	No....	No....	8
	Wife..........	F.	46	Calabria	No...	No....	No...	No....	No....	5
	Son	M.	21	Calabria	Yes..	Yes..	No...	No....	Yes...	4
291	Head	M.	30	Calabria	No...	No....	No...	No....	No....	6
	Wife..........	F.	28	Calabria	No...	No....	No...	No....	No....	½
	Brother-in-law	M.	44	Calabria	No...	No....	No...	No....	Yes..	13
292	Cooperative ..	M.	28	Calabria	Yes..	Yes..	Yes..	Yes..	Yes...	7
	Cooperative ..	M.	40	Calabria	Yes..	Yes..	No...	No....	Yes...	7
293	Cooperative ..	M.	35	Calabria	Yes..	Yes...	No...	No....	No....	7
	Cooperative ..	M.	27	Calabria	Yes..	Yes...	No...	No....	Yes...	6
	Cooperative ..	M.	21	Calabria	Yes..	Yes...	No...	No....	Yes...	5
	Cooperative ..	M.	39	Calabria	Yes..	Yes...	No...	No....	Yes...	5
294	Head	M.	35	Basilicata	No...	No....	No...	No....	No....	13
	Wife..........	F.	35	Basilicata	No...	No....	No...	No....	No....	9
	Daughter	F.	12	Basilicata	No...	No....	No...	No....	Yes...	9
295	Cooperative ..	M.	30	Calabria	No...	No....	No...	No....	Yes...	6
	Cooperative ..	M.	26	Calabria	No...	No....	No...	No....	No....	3
	Cooperative ..	M.	38	Calabria	No...	No....	No...	No....	Yes...	5
	Cooperative ..	M.	27	Calabria	Yes..	Yes..	No...	No....	Yes...	5
296	Head	M.	38	Campania	No...	No....	No...	No....	Yes...	14
	Wife..........	F.	27	Campania	No...	No....	No...	No....	No....	5
297	Head	M.	40	Calabria	Yes..	Yes..	Yes..	Yes..	Yes...	13
	Mother	F.	64	Calabria	No...	No....	No...	No....	Yes...	10
298	Head	M.	37	Campania	Yes..	Yes...	No...	No....	Yes...	9
	Wife..........	F.	40	Campania	No...	No....	No...	No....	No....	6
299	Head	M.	45	Campania	No...	No....	No...	No....	Yes...	15
	Wife..........	F.	38	Campania	Yes..	Yes..	No...	No....	Yes...	8
300	Head	M.	40	Campagna di Roma.	Yes..	Yes..	No...	No....	Yes...	18
	Wife..........	F.	36	Campagna di Roma.	No...	No....	No...	No....	Yes...	16
	Son	M.	13	United States......	Yes..	Yes..	Yes..	Yes..	Yes...	....
	Son	M.	12	United States......	Yes..	Yes..	Yes..	Yes..	Yes...	....
301	Head	M.	46	Basilicata..........	No...	No....	No...	No....	Yes...	12
	Wife..........	F.	46	Basilicata..........	No...	No....	No...	No....	No....	11
	Son	M.	10	United States......	No(a).	No(a).	No...	No....	Yes...	....
302	Head	M.	46	Campania..........	No...	No....	No...	No....	No....	16
	Wife..........	F.	36	Campania..........	No...	No....	No...	No....	Yes..	16
	Son	M.	11	United States......	Yes..	Yes..	Yes..	Yes..	Yes...	....
303	Cooperative ..	M.	41	Campania..........	Yes..	Yes..	No...	No....	No....	7
	Cooperative ..	M.	33	Campania..........	Yes..	Yes..	No...	No....	Yes...	8
	Cooperative ..	M.	32	Campania..........	No...	No....	No...	No....	No ...	6
	Cooperative ..	M.	41	Campania..........	No...	No....	No...	No....	No....	8
	Cooperative ..	M.	33	Campania..........	No...	No....	No...	No....	No....	8
	Cooperative ..	M.	22	Campania..........	Yes..	Yes..	No...	No....	No....	½

a Reads and writes Italian.

TABLE **II.**—GENERAL CONDITION AS TO LITERACY AND ILLITERACY, BY FAMILIES AND INDIVIDUALS—Continued.

[This table includes only persons 10 years of age or over.]

Family number.	Relationship to head of family.	Sex.	Age.	Birthplace.	Native language.		English language.			Years in the United States.
					Reads.	Writes.	Reads.	Writes.	Speaks.	
304	Head	M.	36	Abruzzo	Yes.	Yes.	No	No	No	9
	Wife	F.	36	Abruzzo	No.	No.	No	No	No	3
	Daughter	F.	18	Abruzzo	Yes.	Yes.	No	No	Yes.	3
	Son-in-law	M.	28	Abruzzo	No.	No.	No	No	Yes.	9
	Boarder	M.	16	Abruzzo	Yes.	Yes.	No	No	No	1/12
305	Head	M.	63	Campania	No.	No.	No	No	No	6
	Wife	F.	30	Campania	No.	No.	No	No	No	3
	Lodger	M.	25	Campania	No.	No.	No	No	No	3
	Lodger	M.	60	Abruzzo	No.	No.	No	No	No	(a)
	Lodger	M.	25	Abruzzo	No.	No.	No	No	No	(a)
306	Head	M.	44	Campania	Yes.	Yes.	No	No	No	4
	Daughter	F.	18	Campania	Yes.	Yes.	No	No	No	4
	Son-in-law	M.	24	Campania	Yes.	Yes.	No	No	Yes.	4
307	Head	M.	34	Basilicata	No.	No.	No	No	Yes.	10
	Wife	F.	24	Basilicata	No.	No.	No	No	Yes.	8
	Lodger	F.	48	Basilicata	No.	No.	No	No	No	10
308	Head	M.	45	Basilicata	No.	No.	No	No	Yes.	9
	Wife	F.	35	Basilicata	No.	No.	No	No	No	3
	Son	M.	18	Basilicata	No.	No.	No	No	Yes.	5
	Son	M.	15	Basilicata	Yes.	Yes.	Yes.	Yes.	Yes.	3
	Son	M.	11	Basilicata	No.	No.	Yes.	Yes.	Yes.	3
	Lodger	M.	27	Basilicata	No.	No.	No	No	Yes.	5
	Lodger	M.	40	Basilicata	No.	No.	No	No	Yes.	7
	Lodger	M.	42	Basilicata	No.	No.	No	No	Yes.	9
309	Head	M.	38	Abruzzo	Yes.	Yes.	No	No	Yes.	9
	Wife	F.	38	Abruzzo	No.	No.	No	No	No	1/12
	Daughter	F.	11	Abruzzo	Yes.	Yes.	No	No	No	6/12
310	Head	M.	32	Abruzzo	No.	No.	No	No	No	6
	Wife	F.	31	Abruzzo	No.	No.	No	No	No	6/12
311	Cooperative	M.	48	Campania	No.	No.	No	No	No	6
	Cooperative	M.	47	Basilicata	No.	No.	No	No	Yes.	14
312	Cooperative	M.	30	Basilicata	Yes.	Yes.	No	No	Yes.	5
	Cooperative	M.	45	Basilicata	No.	No.	No	No	Yes.	5
	Cooperative	M.	34	Basilicata	No.	No.	No	No	Yes.	14
	Cooperative	M.	38	Basilicata	No.	No.	No	No	Yes.	10
313	Head	M.	40	Basilicata	No.	No.	No	No	No	5
	Wife	F.	49	Basilicata	No.	No.	No	No	No	4
314	Cooperative	M.	73	Basilicata	Yes.	Yes.	No	No	No	10
	Cooperative	M.	52	Basilicata	Yes.	Yes.	No	No	No	10
	Cooperative	M.	45	Abruzzo	Yes.	Yes.	No	No	Yes.	15
	Cooperative	M.	48	Basilicata	No.	No.	No	No	No	5
	Cooperative	M.	30	Sicily	No	No	No	No	Yes.	4
315	Head	M.	38	Basilicata	Yes.	Yes.	Yes.	Yes.	Yes.	12
	Wife	F.	37	Basilicata	No.	No.	No	No	No	10
	Son	M.	14	Basilicata	Yes.	Yes.	Yes.	Yes.	Yes.	10
316	Head	M.	50	Campania	No.	No.	No	No	No	7
	Wife	F.	40	Campania	No.	No.	No	No	No	1 2/12
	Son	M.	19	Campania	Yes.	Yes.	No	No	Yes.	7
	Boarder	M.	50	Campania	No.	No.	No	No	No	3
317	Head	M.	32	Campania	No.	No.	No	No	Yes.	7
	Wife	F.	32	Campania	No.	No.	No	No	No	3
	Son	M.	10	Campania	No.	No.	Yes.	Yes.	Yes.	3
318	Head	M.	40	Basilicata	No.	No.	No	No	Yes.	14
	Wife	F.	27	Basilicata	No.	No.	No	No	No	2
319	Head	M.	35	Abruzzo	No.	No.	No	No	No	8
	Wife	F.	25	Abruzzo	No.	No.	No	No	No	6
320	Head	M.	26	Campania	Yes.	Yes.	Yes.	Yes.	Yes.	12
	Wife	F.	17	Campania	No.	No.	No	No	Yes.	15
	Father	M.	52	Campania	No.	No.	No	No	No	12
	Mother	F.	50	Campania	No.	No.	No	No	No	8

a Not reported.

TABLE **II.**—GENERAL CONDITION AS TO LITERACY AND ILLITERACY, BY FAMILIES AND INDIVIDUALS—Continued.

[This table includes only persons 10 years of age or over.]

Family number.	Relationship to head of family.	Sex.	Age.	Birthplace.	Native language.		English language.			Years in the United States.
					Reads.	Writes.	Reads.	Writes.	Speaks.	
321	Head	M.	30	Abruzzo	Yes..	Yes...	No...	No....	Yes...	4
322	Cooperative ..	M.	23	Campania	Yes..	Yes...	Yes..	Yes...	Yes...	6
	Cooperative ..	M.	26	Campania	Yes..	Yes...	No...	No....	Yes...	6
323	Cooperative ..	M.	32	Abruzzo	Yes..	Yes...	No...	No....	Yes...	7
	Cooperative ..	M.	36	Abruzzo	Yes..	Yes...	No...	No....	No....	17
	Cooperative ..	M.	27	Abruzzo	Yes..	Yes...	No...	No....	Yes...	7
	Cooperative ..	M.	32	Abruzzo	Yes..	Yes...	Yes..	Yes...	Yes...	5
324	Head	M.	41	Campania	Yes..	Yes...	No...	No....	No....	7
325	Head	F.	40	Sicily	Yes..	Yes...	No...	No....	No....	10
	Daughter	F.	17	Sicily	No...	No....	No...	No....	Yes...	10
	Daughter	F.	12	Sicily	No...	No....	No...	No....	Yes...	10
326	Head	M.	45	Sicily	Yes..	No....	No...	No....	No....	5
	Wife	F.	41	Sicily	No...	No....	No...	No....	Yes...	5
	Son	M.	16	Sicily	No...	No....	Yes..	Yes...	Yes...	5
327	Head	M.	28	Campania	Yes..	Yes...	No...	No....	No....	4
	Wife	F.	24	Campania	No...	No....	No...	No....	No....	3
328	Head	M.	35	Basilicata	No...	No....	No...	No....	Yes...	5
	Wife	F.	20	Basilicata	No...	No....	No...	No....	Yes...	7
	Lodger	M.	30	Basilicata	No...	No....	No...	No....	Yes...	6
	Lodger	M.	(a)	Basilicata	Yes..	Yes...	No...	No....	No....	2
329	Head	M.	50	Basilicata	Yes..	Yes...	No...	No....	No....	15
	Wife	F.	40	Basilicata	No...	No....	No...	No....	No....	9
	Son	M.	16	Basilicata	No...	No....	No...	No....	No....	9
	Daughter	F.	14	Basilicath	No...	No....	Yes..	Yes...	Yes...	9
330	Cooperative ..	M.	48	Calabria	No...	No....	No...	No....	No....	3
	Cooperative ..	M.	48	Calabria	Yes..	Yes...	No...	No....	No....	3
331	Head	M.	49	Basilicata	No...	No....	No...	No....	Yes...	15
	Wife	F.	45	Basilicata	No...	No....	No...	No....	Yes...	15
	Son	M.	19	Basilicata	Yes..	Yes...	Yes..	Yes...	Yes...	15
	Daughter	F.	14	United States	No...	No....	No...	No....	Yes...	....
	Daughter	F.	12	United States	Yes..	Yes...	Yes..	Yes...	Yes...	....
332	Head	M.	35	Calabria	Yes..	Yes...	No...	No....	Yes...	17
	Wife	F.	21	Calabria	No...	No....	No...	No....	No....	6
333	Head	M.	33	Campania	No...	No....	No...	No....	No....	7
	Wife	F.	30	Campania	No...	No....	No...	No....	Yes...	6
334	Head	M.	33	Campania	No...	No....	No...	No....	Yes...	15
	Wife	F.	33	Campania	No...	No....	No...	No....	Yes...	15
	Son	M.	11	United States	Yes..	Yes...	Yes..	Yes...	Yes...	....
335	Head	F.	34	Basilicata	No...	No...	No...	No....	Yes...	16
	Son	M.	16	Basilicata	Yes..	Yes...	Yes..	Yes...	Yes...	16
	Daughter	F.	12	United States	Yes..	Yes...	Yes..	Yes...	Yes...	....
	Son	M.	10	United States	Yes..	Yes...	Yes..	Yes...	Yes...	....
336	Head	M.	30	Basilicata	No...	No....	No...	No....	Yes...	12
	Wife	F.	32	Basilicata	No...	No....	No...	No....	No....	3
337	Head	M.	60	Campania	Yes..	Yes...	No...	No....	No....	12
	Wife	F.	37	Campania	No...	No....	No...	No....	No....	12
	Son	M.	15	Campania	Yes..	No....	Yes..	Yes...	Yes...	12
	Nephew	M.	17	Campania	No...	No....	No...	No....	Yes...	5
	Boarder	M.	(a)	Abruzzo	Yes..	Yes...	No...	No....	No....	(a)
338	Head	M.	60	Campania	No...	No....	No...	No....	No....	12
	Wife	F.	56	Campania	No...	No....	No...	No....	No....	4
	Son	M.	22	Campania	Yes .	Yes...	No...	No....	Yes...	6
	Daughter	F.	16	Campania	No...	No....	No...	No....	Yes...	4
339	Cooperative ..	M.	50	Calabria	No...	No....	No...	No....	No....	3
	Cooperative ..	M.	45	Calabria	No...	No....	No...	No....	No....	5
	Cooperative ..	M.	35	Calabria	No...	No....	No...	No....	Yes...	5

a Not reported.

TABLE **II.**—GENERAL CONDITION AS TO LITERACY AND ILLITERACY, BY FAMILIES AND INDIVIDUALS—Continued.

[This table includes only persons 10 years of age or over.]

Family number.	Relationship to head of family.	Sex.	Age.	Birthplace.	Native language. Reads.	Writes.	English language. Reads.	Writes.	Speaks.	Years in the United States.
339	Cooperative ..	M.	35	Calabria	No...	No....	No...	No....	No....	3
	Cooperative ..	M.	45	Calabria	No...	No....	No...	No....	No....	6
	Cooperative ..	M.	40	Calabria	No...	No....	No...	No....	Yes...	5
	Cooperative ..	M.	15	Calabria	Yes..	Yes...	Yes..	No....	Yes...	5
	Cooperative ..	M.	15	Calabria	Yes..	Yes...	Yes..	Yes...	Yes...	6
340	Head	M.	35	Campania	No...	No....	No...	No....	Yes...	15
	Wife	F.	25	Campania	No...	No....	No...	No....	No....	5
341	Head	M.	40	Campania	No...	No....	No...	No....	Yes...	13
	Wife	F.	30	Campania	No...	No....	No...	No....	No....	7
	Son	M.	14	Campania	Yes..	Yes...	Yes..	Yes...	Yes...	7
	Son	M.	11	Campania	No...	No....	No...	No....	Yes...	7
342	Head	M.	45	Basilicata	No...	No....	No...	No....	No....	10
	Wife	F.	36	Basilicata	No...	No....	No...	No....	No....	8
	Daughter	F.	11	Basilicata	No...	No....	Yes..	Yes...	Yes...	8
343	Head	M.	30	Sicily	No...	No....	No...	No....	Yes...	10
	Wife	F.	17	Sicily	No...	No....	No...	No....	Yes...	8
344	Head	M.	28	Sicily	Yes..	Yes...	No...	No....	Yes...	8
	Wife	F.	18	Basilicata	No...	No....	No...	No....	Yes...	12
345	Head	M.	30	Basilicata	Yes..	Yes...	Yes..	Yes...	Yes...	10
	Wife	F.	27	Basilicata	No...	No....	No...	No....	Yes...	16
346	Head	M.	39	Basilicata	No...	No....	No...	No....	Yes...	13
	Wife	F.	38	Basilicata	No...	No....	No...	No....	No....	12
	Son	M.	10	United States	Yes..	Yes...	Yes..	Yes...	Yes...	....
347	Head	M.	26	Calabria	Yes..	Yes...	Yes..	Yes...	Yes...	15
	Wife	F.	20	Calabria	No...	No....	No...	No....	Yes...	12
348	Head	M.	60	Basilicata	No...	No....	No...	No....	No....	25
	Wife	F.	45	Basilicata	No...	No....	No...	No....	Yes...	24
	Daughter	F.	13	United States	Yes..	Yes...	Yes..	Yes...	Yes...	....
349	Cooperative ..	M.	56	Calabria	No...	No....	No...	No....	No....	3
	Cooperative ..	M.	33	Calabria	Yes..	Yes...	No...	No....	Yes...	4
	Cooperative ..	M.	39	Calabria	Yes..	Yes...	No...	No....	Yes...	4
	Cooperative ..	M.	24	Calabria	Yes..	Yes...	No...	No....	Yes...	3
	Cooperative ..	M.	33	Calabria	No...	No....	No...	No....	Yes...	5
350	Head	M.	29	Basilicata	Yes..	Yes...	Yes..	Yes...	Yes...	25
	Wife	F.	22	Basilicata	No...	No....	No...	No....	No....	6
	Mother	F.	60	Basilicata	No...	No....	No...	No....	No....	(a)
351	Head	M.	40	Basilicata	Yes..	Yes...	No...	No....	Yes...	25
	Wife	F.	32	Campania	No...	No....	No...	No....	Yes...	22
	Son	M.	15	United States	Yes..	Yes...	Yes..	Yes...	Yes...	....
	Son	M.	13	United States	Yes..	Yes...	Yes..	Yes...	Yes...	....
	Son	M.	11	United States	Yes..	Yes...	Yes..	Yes...	Yes...	....
	Boarder	F.	19	Campania	No...	No....	No...	No....	Yes...	7
352	Head	M.	31	Calabria	No...	No....	No...	No....	Yes...	8
	Wife	F.	31	Calabria	No...	No....	No...	No....	No....	4
	Son	M.	13	Calabria	Yes..	Yes...	No...	No....	Yes...	4
353	Head	M.	29	Campania	Yes..	Yes...	Yes..	Yes...	Yes...	11
	Wife	F.	25	Campania	No...	No....	No...	No....	No....	4
354	Head	M.	32	Calabria	No...	No....	No...	No....	Yes...	7
	Wife	F.	32	Calabria	No...	No....	No...	No....	No....	4
355	Head	M.	28	Campania	No...	No....	No...	No....	Yes...	9
	Wife	F.	25	Campania	No...	No....	No...	No....	No....	4
	Lodger	M.	27	Campania	Yes.	Yes...	Yes..	Yes...	Yes...	5
356	Head	F.	24	Basilicata	No...	No....	No...	No....	Yes...	6
357	Head	M.	45	Calabria	No...	No....	No...	No....	No....	3
	Brother	M.	42	Calabria	No...	No....	No...	No....	No....	4
	Nephew	M.	20	Calabria	Yes..	Yes...	No...	No....	Yes...	4
	Nephew	M.	15	Calabria	Yes..	Yes...	No...	No....	Yes...	4

a Not reported.

TABLE **II.**—GENERAL CONDITION AS TO LITERACY AND ILLITERACY, BY
FAMILIES AND INDIVIDUALS—Continued.

[This table includes only persons 10 years of age or over.]

Family number.	Relationship to head of family.	Sex.	Age.	Birthplace.	Native language. Reads.	Writes.	English language. Reads.	Writes.	Speaks.	Years in the United States.
358	Head	M.	25	Calabria	No...	No....	No...	No...	Yes...	15
	Wife	F.	23	Calabria	No...	No....	No...	No...	Yes...	8
	Brother	M.	47	Calabria	Yes..	Yes..:	No...	No...	Yes...	17
	Brother	M.	23	Calabria	No...	No....	No...	No...	No....	8/12
	Sister-in-law	F.	37	Calabria	No...	No..:	No...	No...	No....	4
359	Head	M.	28	Calabria	No...	No....	No...	No...	No....	3
	Wife	F.	23	Calabria	No...	No....	No...	No...	No....	1
	Brother-in-law	M.	32	Calabria	Yes..	Yes...	No...	No...	No....	3
	Brother-in-law	M.	26	Calabria	No...	No....	No...	No...	No....	3
360	Cooperative	M.	35	Calabria	No...	No....	No...	No...	No....	3
	Cooperative	M.	50	Calabria	No...	No....	No...	No...	No....	1
	Cooperative	M.	50	Calabria	No...	No....	No...	No...	No....	2
	Cooperative	M.	50	Calabria	No...	No....	No...	No...	No....	9
	Cooperative	M.	25	Calabria	No...	No....	No...	No...	Yes...	7
	Cooperative	M.	44	Calabria	Yes..	Yes...	No...	No...	Yes..	14
	Cooperative	M.	35	Calabria	No...	No....	No...	No...	No....	4
361	Head	M.	30	Campania	No...	No....	No...	No...	No....	10
	Wife	F.	20	Campania	No...	No....	No...	No...	No....	6
362	Head	M.	50	Abruzzo	Yes..	Yes...	No...	No...	Yes...	10
	Wife	F.	42	Abruzzo	No...	No....	No...	No...	No...	5
	Daughter	F.	17	Abruzzo	Yes..	Yes...	No...	No...	Yes..	5
	Son-in-law	M.	29	Abruzzo	No...	No....	No...	No...	Yes...	8
	Lodger	M.	45	Abruzzo	No...	No....	No...	No...	Yes...	13
363	Cooperative	M.	28	Campania	Yes..	Yes...	Yes..	Yes..	Yes..	11
	Cooperative	M.	57	Campania	No...	No....	No...	No...	No....	12
	Cooperative	M.	41	Campania	No...	No....	No...	No...	No....	8
	Cooperative	M.	30	Apulia	No...	No....	No...	No...	No....	6
	Cooperative	M.	28	Apulia	No...	No....	No...	No...	No....	6
364	Head	M.	30	Campania	No...	No....	No ..	No...	Yes...	3
	Wife	F.	23	Campania	No...	No....	No...	No...	No...	1
	Brother	M.	18	Campania	Yes..	No....	Yes..	Yes..	Yes..	3
	Cousin	M.	23	Campania	No...	No....	No...	No...	No...	1
365	Head	M.	25	Basilicata	Yes..	Yes...	No...	No...	No....	3
	Wife	F.	17	Basilicata	No...	No....	No...	No...	Yes...	9
366	Head	M.	46	Campania	No...	No....	No...	No...	No....	10
	Wife	F.	48	Campania	No...	No....	No...	No...	No....	6
	Son	M.	16	Campania	No...	No....	Yes..	Yes..	Yes..	6
	Son	M.	13	Campania	No...	No....	Yes..	Yes..	Yes..	6
367	Head	M.	38	Campania	Yes..	Yes...	No...	No...	Yes...	10
	Wife	F.	32	Campania	No...	No....	No...	No...	No...	1
	Boarder	M.	30	Campania	No...	No....	No...	No...	Yes...	10
	Boarder	M.	40	Campania	No...	No....	No...	No...	No...	8
	Boarder	M.	18	Campania	Yes..	Yes...	No...	No...	Yes...	1
368	Head	M.	32	Campania	No...	No....	No...	No...	Yes...	12
	Wife	F.	28	Campania	No...	No....	No...	No...	No....	5
	Son	M.	11	Campania	No...	No....	Yes..	Yes..	Yes...	5
	Brother-in-law	M.	20	Campania	No...	No....	No...	No...	Yes..	3
369	Head	M.	44	Basilicata	No...	No....	No...	No...	Yes...	9
	Wife	F.	45	Basilicata	No...	No....	No...	No...	No....	9
	Son	M.	16	Basilicata	No...	No....	Yes..	Yes..	Yes...	9
370	Head	M.	28	Basilicata	Yes..	Yes...	Yes..	Yes..	Yes...	(a)
	Wife	F.	22	Basilicata	No...	No....	No...	No...	No....	4
371	Head	M.	48	Campania	No...	No....	No...	No...	No....	12
	Wife	F.	38	Campania	No..	No....	No...	No...	No....	8
	Son	M.	17	Campania	No...	No....	Yes..	Yes..	Yes..	8
372	Head	M.	54	Campania	Yes..	Yes...	No...	No...	Yes...	15
	Wife	F.	44	Campania	No...	No....	No...	No...	No....	15
	Son	M.	22	Campania	Yes..	Yes...	Yes..	Yes..	Yes...	15
	Daughter	F.	10	United States	Yes..	Yes...	Yes..	Yes..	Yes...	....

a Not reported.

TABLE **II.**—GENERAL CONDITION AS TO LITERACY AND ILLITERACY, BY FAMILIES AND INDIVIDUALS—Continued.

[This table includes only persons 10 years of age or over.]

Family number.	Relationship to head of family.	Sex.	Age.	Birthplace.	Native language.		English language.			Years in the United States.
					Reads.	Writes.	Reads.	Writes.	Speaks.	
373	Head	M.	35	Campania	No	No	No	No	No	8
	Wife	F.	31	Campania	No	No	No	No	No	7
374	Head	M.	22	Campania	Yes	Yes	Yes	Yes	Yes	4
	Wife	F.	16	United States	Yes	Yes	Yes	Yes	Yes	....
375	Head	M.	42	Campania	Yes	Yes	No	No	Yes	12
	Wife	F.	22	Campania	No	No	No	No	No	3
376	Head	M.	36	Campania	Yes	Yes	No	No	Yes	12
	Wife	F.	27	Campania	No	No	No	No	No	4
377	Head	M.	42	Campania	No	No	No	No	Yes	16
	Wife	F.	38	Campania	No	No	No	No	No	16
	Son	M.	18	Campania	Yes	Yes	Yes	Yes	Yes	16
	Son	M.	16	Campania	No	No	Yes	Yes	Yes	16
	Son	M.	11	United States	Yes	Yes	Yes	Yes	Yes	....
	Father	M.	87	Campania	No	No	No	No	No	9
378	Head	M.	31	Abruzzo	Yes	No	No	No	No	5
	Wife	F.	31	Abruzzo	No	No	No	No	Yes	5
379	Head	M.	40	Abruzzo	No	No	No	No	No	11
	Wife	F.	40	Abruzzo	No	No	No	No	No	6
	Mother-in-law	F.	70	Abruzzo	No	No	No	No	No	6
380	Head	M.	57	Abruzzo	No	No	No	No	No	5
	Wife	F.	54	Abruzzo	No	No	No..	No	No	5
	Son	M.	18	Abruzzo	Yes	Yes	Yes	No	Yes	5
	Son	M.	12	France	Yes	Yes	Yes	Yes	Yes	5
381	Head	M.	60	Campania	No	No	No	No	No	18
	Wife	F.	45	Campania	No	No	No	No	No	18
	Son	M.	17	United States	Yes	Yes	Yes	Yes	Yes	....
	Son	M.	15	United States	Yes	Yes	Yes	Yes	Yes	
	Son	M.	13	United States	Yes	Yes	Yes	Yes	Yes	....
382	Head	M.	33	Campania	No	No	No	No	Yes	14
	Wife	F.	20	Campania	No	No	No	No	Yes	18
383	Head	M.	30	Campania	Yes	Yes	Yes	No	Yes	12
	Wife	F.	28	Campania	No	No	No	No	No	4
384	Head	M.	50	Basilicata	No	No	No	No	No	14
	Wife	F.	45	Basilicata	No	No	No	No	No	4
	Son	M.	23	Basilicata	Yes	Yes	No	No	Yes	14
	Son	M.	14	Basilicata	Yes	Yes	Yes	Yes	Yes	4
	Boarder	M.	35	Basilicata	No	No	No	No	Yes	(a)
385	Head	M.	54	Campania	No	No	No	No	Yes	16
	Wife	F.	47	Campania	No	No	No	No	No	14
	Son	M.	23	Campania	No	No	No	No	Yes	14
	Daughter	F.	14	United States	No	No	No	No	Yes	....
	Daughter	F.	11	United States	No	No	No	No	Yes	
	Daughter-in-law	F.	17	Campania	No	No	No	No	Yes	15
386	Head	M.	35	Abruzzo	No	No	No	No	No	10
	Wife	F.	60	Abruzzo	No	No	No	No	No	10
	Mother	F.	96	Abruzzo	No	No	No	No	No	10
387	Head	M.	50	Campania	No	No	No	No	Yes	15
388	Head	M.	26	Basilicata	Yes	Yes	Yes	Yes	Yes	10
	Wife	F.	17	Basilicata	No	No	No	No	Yes	12
	Father	M.	55	Basilicata	No	No	No	No	No	9
	Mother	F.	54	Basilicata	No	No	No	No	No	9
	Sister	F.	22	Basilicata	No	No	No	No	Yes	9
	Sister	F.	14	Basilicata	No	No	No	No	Yes	9
	Brother	M.	12	Basilicata	No	No	Yes	Yes	Yes	9
	Brother-in-law	M.	32	Basilicata	No	No	No	No	Yes	8
389	Head	M.	55	Campania	Yes	Yes	No	No	Yes	17
	Wife	F.	45	Campania	No	No	No	No	Yes	16
	Son	M.	18	Campania	Yes	Yes	Yes	Yes	Yes	16

a Not reported.

TABLE **II.**—GENERAL CONDITION AS TO LITERACY AND ILLITERACY, BY FAMILIES AND INDIVIDUALS—Continued.

[This table includes only persons 10 years of age or over.]

Family number.	Relationship to head of family.	Sex.	Age.	Birthplace.	Native language.		English language.			Years in the United States.
					Reads.	Writes.	Reads.	Writes.	Speaks.	
389	Daughter	F.	12	United States	Yes	Yes	Yes	Yes	Yes	
	Lodger	M.	32	Abruzzo	No	No	No	No	Yes	13
	Lodger	M.	37	Abruzzo	Yes	Yes	No	No	No	14
	Lodger	M.	28	Basilicata	No	No	No	No	Yes	6
390	Head	M.	65	Calabria	Yes	Yes	No	No	Yes	22
	Wife	F.	60	Calabria	No	No	No	No	No	16
	Son	M.	15	United States	Yes	Yes	Yes	Yes	Yes	
	Lodger	M.	(a)	Abruzzo	No	No	No	No	No	6
	Lodger	M.	40	Calabria	No	No	No	No	No	8
391	Head	M.	39	Basilicata	Yes	Yes	No	No	No	14
	Wife	F.	40	Basilicata	No	No	No	No	No	3
	Daughter	F.	17	Basilicata	Yes	Yes	Yes	Yes	Yes	3
	Daughter	F.	13	Basilicata	No	No	Yes	Yes	Yes	3
392	Head	M.	45	Abruzzo	Yes	Yes	No	No	Yes	13
	Wife	F.	40	Abruzzo	No	No	No	No	No	7
	Son	M.	15	Abruzzo	Yes	Yes	Yes	Yes	Yes	7
393	Head	M.	41	Campania	No	No	No	No	No	12
	Wife	F.	40	Campania	No	No	No	No	No	10
	Daughter	F.	14	Campania	No	No	Yes	Yes	Yes	10
	Daughter	F.	10	United States	Yes	Yes	Yes	Yes	Yes	
	Lodger	M.	27	Campania	Yes	Yes	No	No	Yes	4
	Lodger	M.	25	Campania	Yes	Yes	No	No	No	1½
394	Head	M.	36	Campania	Yes	Yes	Yes	Yes	Yes	15
	Wife	F.	21	Campania	Yes	Yes	No	No	Yes	•10
395	Head	M.	34	Campania	No	No	No	No	No	10
	Wife	F.	21	Campania	No	No	No	No	No	6
	Boarder	M.	37	Campania	Yes	Yes	No	No	Yes	13
396	Head	M.	30	Campania	Yes	Yes	No	No	Yes	6
	Wife	F.	28	Campania	No	No	No	No	No	3
	Lodger	M.	40	Abruzzo	Yes	Yes	No	No	Yes	6
	Lodger	M.	40	Campania	Yes	Yes	No	No	Yes	5
397	Head	M.	38	Calabria	No	No	No	No	Yes	14
	Wife	F.	31	Calabria	Yes	Yes	No	No	No	8
	Son	M.	13	Calabria	Yes	Yes	Yes	Yes	Yes	8
398	Head	M.	50	•Calabria	Yes	Yes	No	No	No	18
	Wife	F.	47	Calabria	No	No	No	No	No	7
	Son	M.	19	Calabria	No	No	No	No	Yes	7
	Lodger	M.	47	Calabria	No	No	No	No	No	6
	Lodger	M.	23	Calabria	Yes	Yes	No	No	No	4
399	Head	M.	37	Calabria	No	No	No	No	Yes	13
	Lodger	M.	37	Calabria	Yes	Yes	No	No	Yes	5
	Lodger	M.	37	Calabria	Yes	Yes	No	No	Yes	13
	Lodger	M.	50	Calabria	No	No	No	No	No	4
	Lodger	M.	16	Calabria	Yes	Yes	No	No	Yes	4
	Lodger	M.	54	Calabria	No	No	No	No	No	8
	Lodger	M.	45	Calabria	No	No	No	No	No	9
400	Head	M.	28	Calabria	No	No	No	No	Yes	10
	Wife	F.	27	Calabria	No	No	No	No	No	6
	Son	M.	11	Calabria	No	No	No	No	Yes	6
	Lodger	M.	37	Calabria	Yes	Yes	No	No	No	9
	Lodger	M.	45	Calabria	No	No	No	No	Yes	14
	Lodger	M.	33	Calabria	Yes	Yes	No	No	Yes	11
	Lodger	M.	23	Calabria	Yes	Yes	No	No	Yes	8
	Lodger	M.	30	Calabria	Yes	Yes	No	No	Yes	10
401	Head	M.	31	Calabria	Yes	Yes	No	No	Yes	9
	Wife	F.	31	Calabria	No	No	No	No	No	5
	Boarder	M.	28	Basilicata	No	No	No	No	Yes	5
402	Head	M.	48	Calabria	Yes	Yes	No	No	No	9
	Wife	F.	44	Calabria	No	No	No	No	No	4
	Son	M.	11	Calabria	No	No	Yes	Yes	Yes	4
	Daughter	F.	10	Calabria	No	No	Yes	Yes	Yes	4

a Not reported.

TABLE **II.**—GENERAL CONDITION AS TO LITERACY AND ILLITERACY, BY
FAMILIES AND INDIVIDUALS—Continued.

[This table includes only persons 10 years of age or over.]

Family number.	Relationship to head of family.	Sex.	Age.	Birthplace.	Native language. Reads.	Writes.	English language. Reads.	Writes.	Speaks.	Years in the United States.
403	Head	M.	40	Calabria	No...	No...	No...	No...	Yes...	14
	Wife	F.	40	Calabria	Yes..	Yes...	No...	No...	Yes...	3
	Son	M.	14	Calabria	Yes..	Yes...	Yes..	Yes...	No....	3
	Brother-in-law	M.	33	Calabria	No...	No...	No...	No...	Yes...	5
404	Head	M.	50	Campania	Yes..	Yes...	No...	No...	Yes...	14
	Wife	F.	45	Campania	No...	No...	No...	No...	Yes...	11
	Son	M.	21	Campania	No...	No...	Yes..	Yes...	Yes...	11
	Son	M.	17	Campania	No...	No...	Yes..	Yes...	Yes...	11
405	Head	M.	48	Calabria	Yes..	Yes...	No...	No...	No....	6
	Son	M.	21	Calabria	Yes..	Yes...	No ...	No...	Yes...	6
	Cousin	M.	22	Calabria	Yes..	Yes...	No...	No...	No....	½
	Cousin	M.	21	Calabria	No...	No...	No...	No...	No....	15
	Lodger	M.	45	Calabria	Yes..	Yes...	No...	No...	Yes...	15
	Lodger	M.	45	Calabria	Yes..	Yes...	No...	No...	No ...	7
	Lodger	M.	20	Calabria	Yes..	Yes...	No...	No...	No....	7
	Lodger	M.	24	Calabria	No...	No...	No...	No...	No....	½
406	Head	M.	55	Calabria	Yes..	Yes...	Yes...	No...	Yes...	7
	Son	M.	17	Calabria	Yes..	Yes...	Yes...	Yes..	Yes...	7
	Brother	M.	44	Calabria	No...	No...	No...	No...	No....	7
	Brother	M.	51	Calabria	Yes..	Yes...	No...	No...	No....	1
	Nephew	M.	14	Calabria	No...	No...	No...	No...	No....	1
	Lodger	M.	36	Calabria	Yes..	Yes...	No...	No...	No....	4
407	Head	M.	33	Basilicata	Yes..	Yes...	No...	No...	No....	10
	Wife	F.	28	Basilicata	No...	No...	No...	No...	No....	10
	Daughter	F.	10	United States	Yes..	Yes...	Yes..	Yes...	Yes...	....
408	Head	M.	28	Sicily	Yes..	Yes...	No...	No...	No....	½
	Lodger	M.	25	Sicily	No...	No...	No...	No...	No....	3
	Lodger	M.	40	Sicily	No...	No...	No...	No...	No....	½
	Lodger	M.	20	Sicily	Yes..	Yes...	No...	No...	No....	½
	Lodger	M.	22	Sicily	No...	No...	No...	No...	No....	4
409	Head	M.	40	Basilicata	No...	No...	No...	No...	Yes...	18
	Wife	F.	36	Basilicata	No...	No...	No...	No...	No....	15
	Son	M.	12	United States	Yes..	Yes...	Yes..	Yes...	Yes...	....
410	Head	M.	30	Sicily	No...	No...	No...	No...	Yes...	3
	Wife	F.	22	Sicily	No...	No...	No...	No...	No....	3
411	Head	M.	47	Campania	No...	No...	No...	No...	No....	15
	Wife	F.	37	Campania	No...	No...	No...	No...	No....	9
	Son	M.	16	Campania	No...	No...	No...	No...	Yes...	9
	Son	M.	11	Campania	No...	No...	No...	No...	Yes...	9
412	Head	M.	33	Calabria	Yes..	Yes...	No...	No...	Yes...	6
	Wife	F.	35	Calabria	No...	No...	No...	No...	No....	5
413	Head	M.	60	Basilicata	No...	No...	No...	No...	No....	20
	Wife	F.	60	Basilicata	No...	No...	No...	No...	No....	8
	Son	M.	38	Basilicata	No...	No...	No...	No...	Yes...	8
	Daughter	F.	29	Basilicata	No	No...	No...	No...	Yes...	8
414	Head	M.	23	Basilicata	Yes..	Yes...	Yes..	Yes...	Yes...	16
	Wife	F.	19	Campania	No...	No...	No...	No...	No....	8
415	Head	M.	60	Basilicata	No...	No...	No...	No...	No....	20
	Wife	F.	67	Basilicata	No...	No...	No...	No...	No....	20
416	Head	M.	39	Basilicata	No...	No...	No...	No...	Yes...	15
	Wife	F.	38	Basilicata	No...	No...	No...	No...	No....	9
	Cousin	M.	33	Basilicata	Yes..	Yes...	No...	No...	No....	4
417	Head	M.	29	Basilicata	No...	No...	No...	No...	Yes...	10
	Wife	F.	25	Basilicata	No...	No...	No...	No...	No....	5
	Father	M.	54	Basilicata	No...	No...	No...	No...	No....	15
	Mother-in-law	F.	59	Basilicata	No...	No...	No...	No...	No....	5
418	Head	M.	50	Basilicata	No...	No...	No...	No...	Yes...	15
	Wife	F.	47	Basilicata	No...	No...	No...	No...	No....	10
	Son	M.	12	Basilicata	Yes..	Yes...	Yes..	Yes...	Yes...	10

TABLE **II.**—GENERAL CONDITION AS TO LITERACY AND ILLITERACY, BY
FAMILIES AND INDIVIDUALS—Continued.

[This table includes only persons 10 years of age or over.]

Family number.	Relationship to head of family.	Sex.	Age.	Birthplace.	Native language. Reads.	Writes.	English language. Reads.	Writes.	Speaks.	Years in the United States.
419	Head	M.	40	Basilicata	No	No	No	No	Yes	14
	Wife	F.	40	Basilicata	No	No	No	No	No	10
	Daughter	F.	16	Basilicata	Yes	Yes	No	No	Yes	10
420	Head	M.	35	Basilicata	Yes	Yes	Yes	No	Yes	13
	Wife	F.	24	United States	No	No	No	No	Yes	
421	Head	M.	36	Basilicata	No	No	No	No	Yes	10
	Wife	F.	28	Basilicata	No	No	No	No	No	10
422	Head	M.	45	Campania	No	No	No	No	No	4
	Wife	F.	34	Basilicata	No	No	No	No	No	4
	Son	M.	14	Basilicata	Yes	Yes	Yes	Yes	Yes	4
	Daughter	F.	10	Basilicata	No	No	No	No	Yes	4
423	Head	M.	47	Basilicata	No	No	No	No	No	8
	Daughter	F.	15	Basilicata	No	No	No	No	Yes	5
	Son	M.	13	Basilicata	No	No	No	No	Yes	5
424	Head	M.	33	Abruzzo	Yes	No	No	No	No	10
	Wife	F.	41	Abruzzo	No	No	No	No	No	5
	Stepson	M.	13	Abruzzo	Yes	Yes	Yes	Yes	Yes	5
425	Head	M.	58	Abruzzo	No	No	No	No	Yes	15
	Wife	F.	50	Abruzzo	No	No	No	No	No	10
	Son	M.	22	Abruzzo	Yes	Yes	Yes	Yes	Yes	10
	Son	M.	20	Abruzzo	Yes	Yes	Yes	Yes	Yes	10
426	Head	M.	31	Abruzzo	No	No	No	No	No	3
	Wife	F.	27	Abruzzo	No	No	No	No	No	3
427	Head	M.	38	Basilicata	No	No	No	No	No	5
	Wife	F.	35	Basilicata	No	No	No	No	No	5
	Son	M.	13	Basilicata	Yes	Yes	No	No	Yes	5
	Daughter	F.	11	Basilicata	No	No	No	No	Yes	5
428	Head	M.	42	Campania	Yes	Yes	No	No	No	1
	Father-in-law.	M.	57	Campania	Yes	Yes	No	No	Yes	3
	Brother-in-law	M.	35	Campania	Yes	Yes	No	No	Yes	7
	Lodger	M.	53	Campania	No	No	No	No	Yes	7
429	Head	M.	58	Campania	Yes	Yes	No	No	No	2
	Wife	F.	27	Basilicata	No	No	No	No	No	2
430	Head	M.	30	Basilicata	No	No	No	No	Yes	8
	Wife	F.	27	Basilicata	No	No	No	No	No	8
431	Head	M.	52	Basilicata	Yes	Yes	No	No	No	15
	Wife	F.	40	Basilicata	No	No	No	No	No	15
	Son	M.	17	Basilicata	Yes	Yes	Yes	Yes	Yes	15
	Daughter	F.	10	United States	No	No	No	No	Yes	
432	Head	M.	42	Basilicata	Yes	Yes	No	No	Yes	13
	Wife	F.	36	Basilicata	No	No	No	No	Yes	11
433	Head	F.	56	Campania	No	No	No	No	No	7
	Daughter	F.	18	Campania	No	No	Yes	Yes	Yes	8
434	Head	M.	65	Abruzzo	No	No	No	No	No	1
	Wife	F.	60	Abruzzo	No	No	No	No	No	4
435	Cooperative	M.	45	Calabria	No	No	No	No	No	7
	Cooperative	M.	50	Calabria	No	No	No	No	No	3
	Cooperative	M.	55	Calabria	Yes	Yes	No	No	No	3
	Cooperative	M.	47	Calabria	No	No	No	No	No	3
	Cooperative	M.	25	Calabria	Yes	Yes	No	No	Yes	3
436	Head	M.	30	Sicily	Yes	Yes	No	No	Yes	7
	Wife	F.	37	Sicily	No	No	No	No	No	3
	Stepson	M.	12	Sicily	No	No	No	No	Yes	3
437	Head	M.	34	Basilicata	No	No	No	No	No	5
	Wife	F.	34	Basilicata	No	No	No	No	No	3
	Lodger	M.	34	Basilicata	No	No	No	No	Yes	5
	Lodger	M.	34	Basilicata	No	No	No	No	Yes	5

TABLE **II.**—GENERAL CONDITION AS TO LITERACY AND ILLITERACY, BY FAMILIES AND INDIVIDUALS—Continued.

[This table includes only persons 10 years of age or over.]

Family number.	Relationship to head of family.	Sex.	Age.	Birthplace.	Native language.		English language.			Years in the United States.
					Reads.	Writes.	Reads.	Writes.	Speaks.	
438	Head	M.	40	Campania	No	No	No	No	No	20
	Wife	F.	40	Campania	No	No	No	No	No	16
	Son	M.	22	Campania	Yes	Yes	Yes	Yes	Yes	16
	Son	M.	15	United States	No	No	No	No	Yes	
	Son	M.	13	United States	Yes	Yes	Yes	Yes	Yes	
	Daughter	F.	11	United States	Yes	Yes	Yes	Yes	Yes	
	Lodger	M.	26	Basilicata	Yes	Yes	No	No	No	6
439	Head	M.	40	Calabria	No	No	No	No	No	14
	Wife	F.	29	Calabria	No	No	No	No	No	4
	Cousin	M.	29	Calabria	No	No	No	No	Yes	4
440	Head	M.	41	Campania	Yes	Yes	Yes	No	Yes	17
	Wife	F.	50	Campania	No	No	No	No	No	17
	Son	M.	14	United States	Yes	Yes	Yes	Yes	Yes	
	Daughter	F.	12	United States	Yes	Yes	Yes	Yes	Yes	
441	Head	M.	50	Calabria	No	No	No	No	Yes	15
	Wife	F.	46	Calabria	No	No	No	No	Yes	12
	Son	M.	16	Calabria	No	No	Yes	Yes	Yes	12
	Boarder	M.	20	Calabria	Yes	Yes	No	No	Yes	4
442	Head	M.	46	Sicily	No	No	No	No	No	10
	Wife	F.	36	Sicily	No	No	No	No	No	9
	Daughter	F.	18	Sicily	Yes	Yes	Yes	Yes	Yes	9
	Daughter	F.	16	Sicily	No	No	Yes	Yes	Yes	9
	Son	M.	11	Sicily	No	No	No	No	Yes	9
443	Head	M.	39	Calabria	No	No	No	No	No	8
	Wife	F.	56	Calabria	No	No	No	No	No	8
444	Head	M.	42	Basilicata	No	No	No	No	Yes	15
	Wife	F.	34	Basilicata	No	No	No	No	No	9
	Son	M.	17	Basilicata	No	No	Yes	Yes	Yes	9
445	Head	M.	36	Basilicata	Yes	Yes	No	No	Yes	10
	Wife	F.	26	Basilicata	No	No	No	No	No	8
446	Head	M.	56	Basilicata	No	No	No	No	No	15
	Wife	F.	56	Basilicata	No	No	No	No	No	8
	Son	M.	17	Basilicata	No	No	No	No	Yes	8
	Daughter	F.	13	Basilicata	No	No	No	No	Yes	8
447	Head	M.	37	Calabria	No	No	No	No	No	15
	Wife	F.	32	Calabria	No	No	No	No	No	5
	Son	M.	10	Calabria	Yes	Yes	No	No	Yes	5
	Father	M.	60	Calabria	No	No	No	No	Yes	3
	Mother	F.	60	Calabria	No	No	No	No	No	3
448	Head	M.	28	Basilicata	Yes	Yes	No	No	Yes	13
	Wife	F.	22	Basilicata	No	No	Yes	Yes	Yes	20
	Mother-in-law	F.	45	Basilicata	No	No	No	No	Yes	20
449	Head	M.	46	Liguria	Yes	Yes	No	No	Yes	16
	Wife	F.	34	Liguria	Yes	Yes	Yes	No	Yes	16
	Son	M.	15	United States	Yes	Yes	Yes	Yes	Yes	
	Son	M.	10	United States	Yes	Yes	Yes	Yes	Yes	
450	Head	M.	38	Calabria	Yes	Yes	No	No	Yes	8
	Wife	F.	27	Campania	No	No	No	No	No	4
451	Head	M.	36	Basilicata	Yes	Yes	No	No	Yes	13
	Wife	F.	30	Basilicata	No	No	No	No	No	10
452	Head	M.	29	Campania	No	No	No	No	Yes	10
	Wife	F.	21	Campania	No	No	Yes	No	Yes	15
453	Head	M.	23	Calabria	No	No	No	No	Yes	12
	Wife	F.	20	Calabria	Yes	Yes	No	No	Yes	4
454	Head	M.	40	Basilicata	No	No	No	No	Yes	15
	Wife	F.	44	Basilicata	No	No	No	No	No	8
	Daughter	F.	14	Basilicata	No	No	No	No	Yes	8
455	Head	M.	40	Basilicata	Yes	Yes	No	No	Yes	14
	Wife	F.	36	Basilicata	No	No	No	No	No	12

TABLE **II.**—GENERAL CONDITION AS TO LITERACY AND ILLITERACY, BY FAMILIES AND INDIVIDUALS—Continued.

[This table includes only persons 10 years of age or over.]

Family number.	Relationship to head of family.	Sex.	Age.	Birthplace.	Native language.		English language.			Years in the United States.
					Reads.	Writes.	Reads.	Writes.	Speaks.	
455	Daughter	F.	17	Basilicata	Yes	Yes	Yes	Yes	Yes	12
	Daughter	F.	14	Basilicata	No	No	No	No	Yes	12
456	Head	M.	52	Basilicata	No	No	No	No	No	4
	Wife	F.	50	Basilicata	No	No	No	No	No	1½
	Daughter	F.	20	Basilicata	No	No	No	No	No	1½
	Daughter	F.	18	Basilicata	No	No	No	No	No	1½
	Stepson	M.	18	Basilicata	Yes	Yes	Yes	No	Yes	1½
457	Head	M.	45	Campania	Yes	Yes	No	No	Yes	14
	Wife	F.	42	Campania	Yes	Yes	No	No	No	4
	Son	M.	21	Campania	Yes	Yes	Yes	Yes	Yes	5
	Son	M.	14	Campania	Yes	Yes	Yes	Yes	Yes	4
458	Head	M.	49	Basilicata	No	No	No	No	Yes	14
	Wife	F.	49	Basilicata	No	No	No	No	No	9
459	Head	M.	44	Basilicata	No	No	No	No	No	16
	Wife	F.	38	Sicily	No	No	No	No	Yes	14
460	Head	M.	32	Basilicata	No	No	No	No	Yes	6
	Wife	F.	30	Basilicata	No	No	No	No	No	5
	Brother-in-law	M.	35	Basilicata	Yes	Yes	No	No	Yes	4
	Brother-in-law	M.	24	Basilicata	Yes	Yes	No	No	Yes	5
461	Head	M.	35	Abruzzo	Yes	Yes	Yes	Yes	Yes	9
	Wife	F.	22	Abruzzo	No	No	No	No	Yes	6
462	Head	M.	30	Campania	No	No	No	No	Yes	10
	Wife	F.	27	Campania	No	No	No	No	No	5
	Brother-in-law	M.	30	Campania	No	No	No	No	No	5
	Boarder	M.	40	Campania	No	No	No	No	Yes	10
	Lodger	M.	35	Campania	No	No	No	No	No	5
	Lodger	M.	40	Campania	No	No	No	No	No	3
463	Head	M.	38	Abruzzo	No	No	No	No	No	8
	Wife	F.	34	Abruzzo	No	No	No	No	No	4
	Son	M.	10	Abruzzo	Yes	Yes	Yes	Yes	Yes	4
464	Head	M.	35	Abruzzo	Yes	Yes	Yes	Yes	Yes	12
	Wife	F.	30	Abruzzo	Yes	Yes	No	No	No	10
465	Head	M.	42	Campania	Yes	Yes	No	No	Yes	16
	Wife	F.	37	Campania	No	No	No	No	No	15
	Son	M.	18	Campania	No	No	No	No	Yes	15
	Son	M.	13	United States	Yes	Yes	Yes	Yes	Yes	
466	Head	M.	45	Abruzzo	Yes	Yes	No	No	Yes	13
	Wife	F.	35	Abruzzo	No	No	No	No	No	6
	Son	M.	14	Abruzzo	No	No	No	No	Yes	6
467	Head	M.	36	Abruzzo	Yes	Yes	Yes	Yes	Yes	10
	Wife	F.	32	Abruzzo	No	No	No	No	No	1
	Brother	M.	35	Abruzzo	No	No	No	No	Yes	10
	Lodger	M.	40	Abruzzo	Yes	Yes	No	No	Yes	3
	Lodger	M.	40	Abruzzo	Yes	Yes	No	No	Yes	8
	Lodger	M.	20	Abruzzo	Yes	Yes	No	No	No	1½
	Lodger	M.	28	Abruzzo	Yes	Yes	No	No	No	1½
468	Head	M.	44	Abruzzo	No	No	No	No	Yes	11
	Wife	F.	42	Abruzzo	No	No	No	No	No	11
	Daughter	F.	13	Abruzzo	No	No	Yes	Yes	Yes	11
	Son	M.	12	Abruzzo	No	No	Yes	Yes	Yes	11
	Son	M.	12	Abruzzo	No	No	Yes	Yes	Yes	11
	Boarder	M.	33	Abruzzo	Yes	Yes	No	No	Yes	14
	Boarder	M.	27	Abruzzo	No	No	No	No	No	3
	Lodger	M.	29	Abruzzo	No	No	No	No	No	4
469	Head	M.	27	Abruzzo	Yes	Yes	No	No	No	3
	Wife	F.	20	Abruzzo	No	No	Yes	Yes	Yes	11
470	Head	M.	29	Abruzzo	No	No	No	No	Yes	9
	Wife	F.	18	Abruzzo	Yes	No	No	No	Yes	8
	Cousin	M.	29	Abruzzo	Yes	Yes	No	No	Yes	5
	Boarder	M.	20	Abruzzo	Yes	Yes	No	No	Yes	4
	Lodger	M.	42	Abruzzo	No	No	No	No	Yes	10
	Lodger	M.	10	United States	Yes	Yes	Yes	Yes	Yes	

TABLE **II.**—GENERAL CONDITION AS TO LITERACY AND ILLITERACY, BY FAMILIES AND INDIVIDUALS—Continued.

[This table includes only persons 10 years of age or over.]

Family number.	Relationship to head of family.	Sex.	Age.	Birthplace.	Native language. Reads.	Writes.	English language. Reads.	Writes.	Speaks.	Years in the United States.
471	Head	F.	31	Abruzzo	No	No	No	No	No	6
	Son	M.	12	Abruzzo	Yes	Yes	Yes	Yes	Yes	6
	Daughter	F.	10	Abruzzo	No	No	Yes	Yes	Yes	6
472	Head	M.	35	Abruzzo	Yes	Yes	No	No	Yes	9
	Wife	F.	36	Abruzzo	No	No	No	No	No	9
	Brother	M.	45	Abruzzo	No	No	No	No	No	7
473	Head	M.	40	Campania	No	No	No	No	No	14
	Wife	F.	35	Campania	No	No	No	No	No	14
	Daughter	F.	11	United States	No	No	No	No	No	....
	Mother-in-law	F.	63	Campania	No	No	No	No	No	9
474	Cooperative	M.	50	Abruzzo	No	No	No	No	No	6
	Cooperative	M.	30	Abruzzo	No	No	No	No	Yes	8
	Cooperative	M.	66	Abruzzo	Yes	Yes	No	No	No	8
	Cooperative	M.	56	Abruzzo	No	No	No	No	No	9
	Cooperative	M.	36	Abruzzo	Yes	Yes	No	No	No	8
475	Head	M.	36	Abruzzo	No	No	No	No	Yes	10
	Wife	F.	35	Abruzzo	No	No	No	No	No	4
476	Head	M.	55	Abruzzo	No	No	No	No	Yes	15
	Wife	F.	55	Abruzzo	No	No	No	No	No	4
	Son	M.	14	Abruzzo	Yes	Yes	No	No	Yes	4
477	Head	M.	32	Abruzzo	Yes	Yes	No	No	Yes	13
	Wife	F.	22	Abruzzo	No	No	No	No	No	4
	Mother	F.	78	Abruzzo	No	No	No	No	No	6
478	Head	M.	43	Abruzzo	Yes	Yes	No	No	Yes	18
	Wife	F.	45	Abruzzo	No	No	No	No	No	8
	Daughter	F.	16	Abruzzo	No	No	Yes	Yes	Yes	8
479	Head	M.	23	Calabria	Yes	Yes	Yes	Yes	Yes	7
	Wife	F.	18	Basilicata	Yes	Yes	Yes	No	No	3
	Father	M.	50	Calabria	Yes	Yes	No	No	Yes	8
	Mother	F.	45	Calabria	No	No	No	No	Yes	5
	Boarder	M.	29	Calabria	No	No	No	No	Yes	7
	Boarder	M.	25	Calabria	Yes	Yes	Yes	Yes	Yes	7
480	Head	M.	35	Campania	No	No	No	No	No	16
	Wife	F.	35	Campania	No	No	No	No	No	14
	Daughter	F.	10	United States	Yes	Yes	Yes	Yes	Yes	....
481	Head	F.	36	Basilicata	No	No	No	No	Yes	15
482	Cooperative	M.	38	Calabria	Yes	Yes	No	No	No	5
	Cooperative	M.	35	Calabria	Yes	Yes	No	No	No	3
	Cooperative	M.	38	Calabria	Yes	Yes	No	No	No	3
	Cooperative	M.	36	Calabria	No	No	No	No	No	5
483	Head	M.	32	Abruzzo	Yes	Yes	Yes	Yes	Yes	5
	Wife	F.	32	Abruzzo	No	No	No	No	No	3
484	Head	M.	24	Calabria	No	No	No	No	Yes	8
	Wife	F.	18	Calabria	Yes	Yes	No	Yes	Yes	7
485	Head	M.	30	Calabria	No	No	No	No	Yes	8
	Wife	F.	33	Calabria	No	No	No	No	No	3
	Son	M.	10	Calabria	No	No	Yes	Yes	Yes	3
486	Head	M.	36	Campania	No	No	No	No	No	15
	Wife	F.	29	Campania	No	No	No	No	No	12
487	Cooperative	M.	25	Calabria	Yes	Yes	No	No	Yes	6
	Cooperative	M.	20	Calabria	No	No	No	No	No	4
	Cooperative	M.	21	Calabria	No	No	No	No	No	5
	Cooperative	M.	24	Calabria	Yes	Yes	No	No	No	6
488	Cooperative	M.	26	Calabria	No	No	No	No	Yes	3
	Cooperative	M.	36	Calabria	No	No	No	No	Yes	12
	Cooperative	M.	24	Calabria	No	No	No	No	Yes	3
	Cooperative	M.	40	Calabria	No	No	No	No	Yes	6
489	Head	M.	35	Abruzzo	No	No	No	No	Yes	9
	Wife	F.	30	Abruzzo	No	No	No	No	No	3

TABLE **II.**—GENERAL CONDITION AS TO LITERACY AND ILLITERACY, BY FAMILIES AND INDIVIDUALS—Continued.

[This table includes only persons 10 years of age or over.]

Family number.	Relationship to head of family.	Sex.	Age.	Birthplace.	Native language. Reads.	Native language. Writes.	English language. Reads.	English language. Writes.	English language. Speaks.	Years in the United States.
489	Lodger	M.	27	Abruzzo	Yes..	Yes...	No...	No....	Yes...	7
	Lodger	M.	30	Abruzzo	No...	No....	No...	No....	No....	12
490	Head	M.	30	Calabria	Yes..	Yes...	No...	No....	Yes...	13
	Lodger	M.	47	Calabria	No...	No....	No...	No....	Yes...	13
	Lodger	M.	27	Calabria	Yes..	Yes...	No...	No....	Yes...	6
	Lodger	M.	28	Calabria	Yes..	Yes...	No...	No....	Yes...	3
491	Head	M.	40	Campania	Yes..	Yes...	No...	No....	Yes...	14
	Wife	F.	42	Campania	No...	No....	No...	No....	No....	4
492	Head	F.	60	Campania	No...	No....	No...	No....	No....	2
	Son	M.	26	Campania	Yes..	Yes...	No...	No....	Yes...	5
	Daughter	F.	23	Campania	No...	No....	No...	No....	Yes...	2
493	Head	M.	33	Campania	·Yes..	Yes...	Yes..	Yes..	Yes...	10
	Wife	F.	32	Campania	No...	No....	No...	No....	No....	8
	Son	M.	10	Campania	No...	No....	Yes..	Yes..	Yes...	8
	Boarder	M.	26	Campania	Yes..	Yes...	Yes..	No....	Yes...	11
494	Head	M.	41	Campania	Yes..	Yes..	Yes..	Yes..	Yes...	14
	Wife	F.	43	Campania	No...	No....	No...	No....	No....	8
	Daughter	F.	15	Campania	No...	No....	No...	No....	Yes...	8
495	Head	M.	29	Campania	Yes..	Yes...	Yes..	No....	Yes...	8
	Wife	F.	23	Campania	No...	No....	No...	No....	Yes...	8
	Father	M.	65	Campania	No...	No....	No...	No....	No....	1
496	Head	M.	32	Campania	Yes..	Yes...	No...	No....	Yes...	9
	Wife	F.	18	Campania	No...	No....	No...	No....	Yes...	3
	Brother	M.	25	Campania	Yes..	Yes...	No...	No....	Yes...	8
	Brother	M.	23	Campania	Yes..	Yes...	Yes..	Yes..	Yes...	6
497	Head	M.	42	Abruzzo	Yes..	Yes...	No...	No....	Yes...	12
	Wife	F.	32	Abruzzo	No...	No....	No...	No....	No....	7
498	Head	M.	53	Calabria	Yes..	Yes...	No...	No....	No ..	8
499	Head	M.	36	Campania	No...	No....	No...	No....	Yes...	11
	Wife	F.	32	Campania	No...	No....	No...	No....	Yes...	11
	Son	M.	11	Campania	Yes..	Yes...	Yes..	Yes..	Yes...	11
	Boarder	M.	32	Campania	No...	No....	No...	No....	No....	8
500	Head	M.	53	Campania	Yes..	Yes...	No...	No....	No....	15
	Wife	F.	53	Campania	No...	No....	No...	No....	No....	8
	Son	M.	18	Campania	Yes..	Yes...	No...	No....	Yes...	8
501	Head	M.	48	Campania	No...	No....	No...	No....	Yes ..	16
	Wife	F.	59	Campania	No...	No....	No...	No....	Yes...	14
502	Head	M.	33	Campania	No...	No....	No...	No....	Yes...	12
	Wife	F.	33	Campania	No...	No....	No...	No....	No....	3
	Brother-in-law	M.	30	Campania	No...	No....	No...	No....	Yes...	7
503	Head	M.	35	Sicily	Yes..	Yes.	No...	No....	No....	4
	Wife	F.	25	Sicily	No...	No....	No...	No....	No....	4
504	Head	M.	36	Campania	Yes..	Yes...	No...	No....	No....	8
	Wife	F.	26	Basilicata	Yes..	Yes...	No...	No....	Yes...	8
	Son	M.	10	Basilicata	No...	No....	Yes..	Yes..	Yes...	8
505	Head	M.	36	Campania	No...	No.	No...	No....	Yes...	6
	Wife	F.	35	Campania	No...	No....	No...	No....	No....	1
	Son	M.	10	Campania	No...	No....	No...	No....	No....	1
	Mother	F.	80	Campania	No...	No....	No...	No....	No....	9
506	Head	M.	52	Sicily	Yes..	Yes...	No...	No....	No....	8
	Wife	F.	35	Sicily	No...	No....	No...	No....	No....	4
	Son	M.	28	Sicily	No...	No....	No...	No....	Yes...	6
	Son	M.	23	Sicily	No...	No....	No...	No....	No....	2
	Son	M.	22	Sicily	No...	No....	No...	No....	Yes...	6
	Daughter	F.	13	Sicily	No...	No....	Yes..	Yes..	Yes...	4
	Son	M.	10	Sicily	Yes..	Yes...	Yes..	Yes..	Yes...	4
507	Cooperative	M.	29	Abruzzo	Yes..	Yes...	No...	No....	Yes...	8
	Cooperative	M.	27	Abruzzo	Yes..	Yes...	No...	No....	Yes...	10

TABLE **II.**—GENERAL CONDITION AS TO LITERACY AND ILLITERACY, BY FAMILIES AND INDIVIDUALS—Continued.

[This table includes only persons 10 years of age or over.]

Family number.	Relationship to head of family.	Sex.	Age.	Birthplace.	Native language. Reads.	Writes.	English language. Reads.	Writes.	Speaks.	Years in the United States.
507	Cooperative ..	M.	23	Abruzzo	Yes..	Yes...	No...	No....	Yes...	8
	Cooperative ..	M.	33	Abruzzo	Yes..	Yes...	No...	No....	No....	7
508	Head	M.	48	Campania	Yes..	Yes...	No...	No....	Yes...	13
	Wife	F.	43	Campania	No...	No....	No...	No....	No....	9
	Daughter	F.	17	Campania	No...	No....	Yes..	Yes...	Yes...	(a)
	Son	M.	14	Campania	No...	No....	Yes..	Yes...	Yes...	9
	Daughter	F.	13	Campania	No...	No....	Yes..	Yes...	Yes...	9
509	Head	M.	22	Campania	Yes..	Yes...	No...	No....	Yes...	1
	Wife	F.	22	Campania	No...	No....	No...	No....	No....	$\frac{8}{12}$
	Sister	F.	21	Campania	Yes..	Yes...	No...	No....	No....	1
	Brother-in-law	M.	26	Campania	Yes..	Yes...	No...	No....	No....	1
	Brother-in-law	M.	38	Campania	Yes..	Yes...	No...	No....	No....	$\frac{6}{12}$
510	Head	M.	30	Sicily	No...	No....	No...	No....	Yes...	9
	Wife	F.	18	Sicily	No...	No....	No...	No....	No....	2
511	Head	M.	40	Sicily	Yes..	Yes ..	No...	No....	Yes...	15
	Wife	F.	30	Sicily	No...	No....	No...	No....	No....	6
	Daughter	F.	15	Sicily	Yes..	Yes...	Yes..	Yes...	Yes...	11
512	Head	M.	45	Campania	No...	No....	No...	No....	No....	5
	Wife	F.	45	Campania	No...	No....	No...	No....	No....	5
	Son	M.	14	Campania	No...	No....	No...	No....	Yes...	5
	Nephew	M.	23	Campania	Yes..	Yes...	No...	No....	Yes...	3
513	Head	M.	48	Basilicata	Yes..	Yes...	No...	No....	No....	20
	Wife	F.	60	Basilicata	No...	No....	No...	No....	No....	20
	Daughter	F.	18	Basilicata	No...	No....	No...	No....	No....	2
	Daughter	F.	15	Basilicata	Yes..	Yes...	No...	No....	Yes...	2
514	Head	M.	61	Campania	No...	No....	No...	Nc...	No....	13
	Wife	F.	61	Campania	No...	No....	No...	No....	No....	9
	Son	M.	14	Campania	Yes..	Yes...	Yes..	Yes	Yes...	9
	Nephew	M.	21	Campania	Yes..	Yes...	Yes..	Yes...	Yes...	10
	Nephew	M.	19	Campania	Yes..	Yes...	Yes..	Yes...	Yes...	10
	Nephew	M.	18	Campania	Yes..	Yes...	Yes..	Yes...	Yes...	6
	Lodger	M.	25	Calabria	Yes..	Yes...	Yes..	Yes...	Yes...	9
	Lodger	F.	18	Calabria	Yes..	Yes...	Yes..	Yes...	Yes...	9
515	Head	M.	30	Abruzzo	Yes..	Yes...	Yes..	Yes...	Yes...	7
	Wife	F.	20	Abruzzo	Yes..	Yes...	Yes..	Yes...	Yes...	14
516	Head	M.	29	Campania	No...	No....	No...	No....	No....	5
	Wife	F.	30	Campania	No...	No....	No...	No....	No....	4
517	Head	M.	45	Campania	Yes..	Yes...	No...	No....	No....	1
	Wife	F.	28	Campania	No...	No....	No...	No....	No....	1
518	Head	M.	40	Campania	No...	No....	No...	No....	No....	8
	Wife	F.	50	Campania	No...	No....	No...	No....	No....	8
	Son	M.	23	Campania	Yes..	Yes...	No...	No....	No....	1
	Daughter	F.	20	Campania	Yes..	Yes...	No...	No....	No....	8
	Son-in-law	M.	30	Campania	No...	No....	No...	No....	Yes...	7
519	Head	M.	36	Abruzzo	No...	No....	No...	No....	No....	9
	Wife	F.	35	Abruzzo	Yes..	Yes...	No...	No....	No....	3
	Son	M.	15	Abruzzo	Yes..	Yes...	No...	No....	Yes...	3
	Lodger	M.	50	Abruzzo	No...	No....	No...	No....	No....	12
	Lodger	M.	40	Abruzzo	No...	No....	No...	No....	No....	6
520	Head	M.	30	Basilicata	No...	No....	No...	No....	Yes...	14
	Wife	F.	39	Basilicata	No...	No....	No...	No....	No....	8
	Stepdaughter.	F.	13	Basilicata	Yes..	Yes...	Yes..	Yes...	Yes...	8
521	Head	M.	38	Campania	No...	No....	No...	No....	Yes...	6
	Wife	F.	40	Campania	No...	No....	No...	No....	No....	$\frac{1}{12}$
	Brother	M.	35	Campania	Reads.	No....	No...	No....	Yes...	6
	Boarder	M.	28	Campania	No...	No....	No...	No....	No....	$\frac{1}{12}$
	Boarder	M.	22	Campania	Yes..	Yes...	No...	No....	No....	$\frac{4}{12}$
	Boarder	M.	37	Campania	Yes..	Yes...	Yes..	Yes...	Yes...	18
522	Head	M.	40	Calabria	No...	No....	No...	No....	No....	5
	Wife	F.	32	Calabria	No...	No....	No...	No....	No....	5
	Cousin	M.	47	Calabria	Yes..	Yes...	No...	No....	Yes...	9

a Not reported.

TABLE **II.**—GENERAL CONDITION AS TO LITERACY AND ILLITERACY, BY FAMILIES AND INDIVIDUALS—Continued.

[This table includes only persons 10 years of age or over.]

Family number.	Relationship to head of family.	Sex.	Age.	Birthplace.	Native language. Reads.	Writes.	English language. Reads.	Writes.	Speaks.	Years in the United States.
523	Head	M.	32	Liguria	Yes..	Yes...	No...	No....	Yes...	11
	Wife	F.	27	Liguria	No...	No...	No...	No....	Yes...	10
524	Head	M.	40	Basilicata	No...	No...	No...	No....	No....	6
	Wife	F.	45	Basilicata	No...	No....	No...	No....	No....	6
	Brother	M.	39	Basilicata	No...	No....	No...	No....	Yes...	24
525	Head	M.	27	Basilicata	No...	No...	No...	No....	Yes...	15
	Wife	F.	21	Basilicata	No...	No...	No...	No....	No...	3
	Father-in-law	M.	40	Basilicata	Yes..	Yes...	No...	No....	Yes...	10
	Mother-in-law	F.	40	Basilicata	No...	No....	No...	No....	No...	3
	Brother-in-law	M.	17	Basilicata	Yes..	Yes...	No...	No....	Yes...	3
526	Head	M.	53	Basilicata	No...	No...	No...	No....	Yes...	27
	Wife	F.	57	Basilicata	No...	No...	No...	No....	No...	6
	Son	M.	27	Basilicata	Yes..	Yes...	No...	No....	Yes...	4
	Daughter-in-law.	F.	20	Basilicata	No...	No...	No...	No.٨..	Yes...	7
527	Head	M.	32	Abruzzo	No...	No...	No...	No....	Yes...	8
	Wife	F.	20	Abruzzo	No...	No...	No...	No....	Yes...	4
	Brother-in-law	M.	27	Abruzzo	No...	No...	No...	No....	Yes...	6
	Sister-in law..	F.	19	Abruzzo	No...	No...	No...	No....	No ...	2
528	Head	M.	42	Calabria	Yes..	Yes...	No...	No....	Yes...	14
	Wife	F.	33	Calabria	No...	No...	No...	No....	No....	8
529	Head	M.	48	Basilicata	No...	No...	No...	No....	Yes...	22
	Wife	F.	35	Basilicata	Yes..	Yes...	No...	No....	No...	23
	Daughter	F.	16	United States	Yes..	Yes...	Yes...	Yes...	Yes...	....
	Son	M.	13	United States	Yes..	Yes...	Yes..	Yes...	Yes...	
	Son	M.	11	United States	Yes..	Yes...	Yes..	Yes...	Yes...	
	Aunt	F.	65	Basilicata	No...	No...	No...	No....	No....	12
530	Head	M.	38	Calabria	No...	No...	No...	No....	Yes...	14
	Wife	F.	40	Calabria	No...	No...	No...	No....	No...	8
	Stepson	M.	19	Calabria	No...	No...	No...	No....	Yes...	8
531	Head	M.	46	Basilicata	No...	No...	No...	No....	Yes...	21
	Wife	F.	46	Basilicata	No...	No...	No...	No....	Yes...	20
	Son	M.	16	United States	Yes..	Yes...	Yes..	Yes...	Yes...	....
	Daughter	F.	14	United States	Yes..	Yes...	Yes..	Yes...	Yes...	
	Daughter	F.	12	United States	Yes..	Yes...	Yes..	Yes...	Yes...	....
532	Head	M.	42	Campania	No...	No...	No....	No....	No....	3
	Wife	F.	47	Campania	No...	No...	No....	No....	No....	3
	Daughter	F.	14	Campania	No...	No...	No....	No....	Yes...	3
533	Head	M.	28	Sicily	No...	No...	No...	No....	Yes...	5
	Wife	F.	24	Sicily	No...	No...	No...	No....	No....	2
534	Head	M.	38	Campania	No...	No...	No...	No....	Yes...	15
	Wife	F.	38	Campania	No...	No...	No...	No....	No....	9
	Son	M.	16	Campania	Yes..	Yes...	Yes..	Yes...	Yes...	9
535	Head	M.	26	Sicily	Yes..	Yes...	No...	No....	Yes...	6
	Wife	F.	23	Sicily	No...	No...	No...	No....	No...	3
	Uncle	M.	50	Sicily	Yes..	Yes...	No...	No....	No...	3
	Cousin	M.	18	Sicily	Yes..	Yes...	No...	No....	Yes...	3
	Lodger	M.	24	Sicily	No...	No...	No...	No....	Yes...	5
	Lodger	F.	22	Sicily	No...	No...	No...	No....	No...	2
536	Head	M.	35	Campania	Yes..	Yes...	No...	No....	Yes...	12
	Wife	F.	26	Campania	No...	No...	No...	No....	No...	10
	Mother	F.	74	Campania	No...	No...	No...	No....	No...	11
	Lodger	M.	46	Campania	No...	No...	No...	No....	Yes ...	14
537	Head	M.	27	Sicily	Yes..	Yes...	No...	No....	Yes...	5
	Wife	F.	23	Sicily	No...	No...	No...	No....	No...	4
	Brother-in-law	M.	27	Sicily	No...	No...	No...	No....	No...	1
	Sister-in-law.	F.	21	Sicily	No...	No...	No...	No....	No...	₁⁄₂
538	Head	M.	33	Campania	No...	No...	No...	No....	Yes...	8
	Wife	F.	30	Campania	No...	No...	No...	No....	No...	3
	Son	M.	11	Campania	No...	No...	Yes..	Yes...	Yes...	3
	Lodger	M.	25	Campania	Yes..	Yes...	Yes..	Yes...	Yes...	5
	Lodger	M.	18	Campania	No...	No...	No...	No....	Yes...	5

TABLE **II.**—GENERAL CONDITION AS TO LITERACY AND ILLITERACY, BY
FAMILIES AND INDIVIDUALS—Continued.

[This table includes only persons 10 years of age or over.]

Family number.	Relationship to head of family.	Sex.	Age.	Birthplace.	Native-language.		English language.			Years in the United States.
					Reads.	Writes.	Reads.	Writes.	Speaks.	
539	Head	M.	32	Campania	No	No	No	No	No	2
	Wife	F.	29	Campania	No	No	No	No	No	2
	Lodger	M.	37	Campania	No	No	No	No	Yes	7
	Lodger	M.	29	Campania	Yes	Yes	No	No	No	5
540	Head	M.	29	Abruzzo	No	No	No	No	Yes	6
	Wife	F.	19	Abruzzo	No	No	No	No	Yes	8
	Brother	M.	23	Abruzzo	No	No	No	No	Yes	9
541	Head	M.	40	Campania	No	No	No	No	No	4
	Wife	F.	45	Campania	No	No	No	No	No	1½
542	Head	M.	37	Calabria	No	No	No	No	Yes	8
	Wife	F.	27	Basilicata	No	No	No	No	Yes	8
	Father-in-law	M.	75	Basilicata	No	No	No	No	No	20
543	Head	M.	35	Campania	Yes	Yes	No	No	Yes	8
	Wife	F.	35	Campania	No	No	No	No	No	8
544	Head	M.	25	Campania	Yes	Yes	No	No	Yes	4
	Wife	F.	20	Campania	No	No	No	No	No	3
	Father	M.	48	Campania	No	No	No	No	No	4
	Boarder	M.	28	Campania	Yes	Yes	No	No	Yes	4
	Boarder	M.	19	Campania	Yes	Yes	No	No	Yes	(a)
545	Head	M.	47	Campania	No	No	No	No	No	11
	Wife	F.	36	Campania	No	No	No	No	No	8
	Daughter	F.	10	Campania	No	No	Yes	Yes	Yes	8
	Lodger	M.	40	Campania	No	No	No	No	No	8
	Lodger	M.	44	Campania	No	No	No	No	Yes	14
	Lodger	M.	37	Campania	No	No	No	No	No	10
	Lodger	M.	26	Campania	No	No	No	No	Yes	6
546	Head	M.	40	Basilicata	Yes	Yes	No	No	Yes	8
	Wife	F.	39	Basilicata	No	No	No	No	No	6
	Daughter	F.	10	Basilicata	No	No	Yes	Yes	Yes	6
547	Head	M.	59	Campania	No	No	No	No	Yes	15
	Wife	F.	54	Campania	No	No	No	No	No	10
	Daughter	F.	14	Campania	No	No	No	No	Yes	10
	Daughter	F.	14	Campania	No	No	Yes	Yes	Yes	10
	Son	M.	10	United States	Yes	Yes	Yes	Yes	Yes	....
548	Head	M.	31	Basilicata	Yes	Yes	No	No	No	6
	Wife	F.	30	Basilicata	No	No	No	No	No	6
549	Head	M.	39	Basilicata	Yes	Yes	No	No	Yes	13
	Wife	F.	32	Basilicata	No	No	No	No	No	7
550	Head	M.	54	Campania	Yes	Yes	No	No	Yes	14
	Wife	F.	40	Campania	No	No	No	No	No	14
	Son	M.	14	United States	Yes	Yes	Yes	Yes	Yes	....
551	Cooperative	M.	30	Abruzzo	Yes	Yes	No	No	No	6
	Cooperative	M.	40	Abruzzo	No	No	No	No	No	6
	Cooperative	M.	30	Abruzzo	Yes	Yes	No	No	Yes	4
	Cooperative	M.	22	Abruzzo	No	No	No	No	Yes	4
	Cooperative	M.	45	Abruzzo	No	No	No	No	No	5
552	Head	M.	42	Campania	No	No	No	No	No	15
	Wife	F.	42	Campania	No	No	No	No	No	9
	Daughter	F.	19	Campania	Yes	Yes	Yes	Yes	Yes	9
553	Head	M.	29	Abruzzo	Yes	Yes	No	No	Yes	8
	Wife	F.	24	Campania	Yes	No	No	No	Yes	2
554	Head	M.	54	Campania	No	No	No	No	No	7
	Wife	F.	53	Campania	No	No	No	No	No	4
	Son	M.	21	Campania	No	No	No	No	Yes	8
	Son	M.	15	Campania	Yes	Yes	No	No	Yes	4
555	Head	M.	43	Campania	Yes	Yes	No	No	Yes	13
	Wife	F.	46	Campania	No	No	No	No	No	9
	Daughter	F.	17	Campania	No	No	No	No	Yes	9

a Not reported

TABLE **II.**—GENERAL CONDITION AS TO LITERACY AND ILLITERACY, BY FAMILIES AND INDIVIDUALS—Continued.

[This table includes only persons 10 years of age or over.]

Family number.	Relationship to head of family.	Sex.	Age.	Birthplace.	Native language. Reads.	Native language. Writes.	English language. Reads.	English language. Writes.	English language. Speaks.	Years in the United States.
555	Son-in-law	M.	25	Campania...........	No...	No....	No...	No....	Yes...	4
	Boarder........	M.	37	Campania...........	Yes..	Yes...	No...	No....	Yes...	3
556	Head	M.	33	Calabria	Yes..	Yes...	No...	No....	Yes...	15
	Wife..........	F.	37	Abruzzo	No...	No....	No...	No....	No....	4
	Stepson.......	M.	15	Abruzzo	Yes..	Yes...	No...	No....	Yes...	4
	Stepson.......	M.	11	Abruzzo	Yes..	Yes...	Yes..	Yes..	Yes...	4
557	Head	M.	63	Basilicata..........	No...	No....	No...	No....	No....	5
	Wife..........	F.	62	Basilicata..........	No...	No....	No...	No....	No....	5
	Son	M.	27	Basilicata..........	No...	No....	No...	No....	No....	5
558	Head	M.	38	Campania...........	No...	No....	No...	No....	No....	6
	Wife..........	F.	36	Campania...........	No...	No....	No...	No....	No....	5
	Mother	F.	76	Campania...........	No...	No....	No...	No....	No....	9
559	Head	M.	29	Campania...........	Yes..	Yes...	Yes..	Yes..	Yes...	5
	Wife..........	F.	19	Campania...........	Yes..	Yes...	Yes..	Yes..	Yes...	9
	Cousin........	M.	22	Campania...........	Yes..	Yes...	No...	No....	No....	$\frac{6}{12}$
	Lodger	M.	24	Campania...........	No...	No	No...	No....	No....	$\frac{1}{12}$
560	Head	M.	45	Sicily	No...	No....	No...	No....	No....	5
	Wife..........	F.	40	Sicily	No...	No....	No...	No....	Yes...	5
561	Head	M.	50	Campania...........	Yes..	Yes...	No...	No....	Yes...	11
	Wife..........	F.	45	Campania...........	No...	No....	No...	No....	No....	10
	Daughter	F.	11	Campania...........	Yes..	Yes...	Yes..	Yes..	Yes...	10
	Lodger	M.	(a)	Campania...........	No...	No....	No...	No....	Yes...	(a)
	Lodger	M.	30	Campania...........	No...	No....	No...	No....	Yes...	5
562	Head	M.	35	Abruzzo	Yes..	Yes...	No...	No....	Yes...	10
	Wife..........	F.	36	Abruzzo	No...	No....	No...	No....	No....	5
	Lodger	M.	45	Abruzzo	No...	No....	No...	No....	No....	10
	Lodger	M.	43	Abruzzo	No...	No....	No...	No....	No....	10
	Lodger	M.	47	Abruzzo	No...	No....	No...	No....	No....	5
563	Head	M.	37	Abruzzo	Yes..	Yes...	No...	No....	Yes...	10
	Wife..........	F.	33	Abruzzo	No...	No....	No...	No....	No....	5
	Brother.......	M.	40	Abruzzo	Yes..	Yes...	No...	No....	No....	3
	Brother.......	M.	28	Abruzzo	Yes..	Yes...	No...	No....	Yes...	10
564	Head	M.	32	Abruzzo	No...	No....	No...	No....	No....	4
	Wife..........	F.	25	Abruzzo	No...	No....	No...	No....	No....	4
	Brother.......	M.	33	Abruzzo	Yes..	Yes...	No...	No....	Yes...	4
	Brother.......	M.	30	Abruzzo	Yes..	Yes...	No...	No....	Yes...	4
565	Head	M.	40	Abruzzo	No...	No....	No...	No....	Yes...	8
	Wife..........	F.	24	Abruzzo	No...	No....	No...	No....	No....	3
	Cousin........	M.	30	Abruzzo	Yes..	Yes...	No...	No....	Yes...	5
	Boarder.......	M.	30	Abruzzo	Yes..	Yes...	No...	No....	Yes...	6
566	Head	M.	46	Calabria	No...	No....	No...	No....	No....	12
	Wife..........	F.	40	Calabria	No...	No....	No...	No....	No....	4
	Son	M.	21	Calabria	No...	No....	Yes..	Yes..	Yes...	10
	Son	M.	19	Calabria	No...	No....	No...	No....	Yes...	4
	Daughter	F.	16	Calabria	No...	No....	No...	No....	No....	4
	Daughter	F.	10	Calabria	No...	No....	Yes..	Yes..	Yes...	4
567	Head	M.	37	Campania...........	No...	No....	No...	No....	Yes...	10
	Wife..........	F.	20	Campania...........	No...	No....	No...	No....	No....	5
568	Head	F.	50	Campania...........	No...	No....	No...	No....	Yes...	5
	Son	M.	11	Campania...........	No...	No....	No...	No....	Yes...	5
569	Cooperative ..	M.	25	Calabria	No...	No....	No...	No....	No....	4
	Cooperative ..	M.	25	Calabria	Yes..	Yes...	No...	No....	Yes...	4
	Cooperative ..	M.	25	Calabria	No...	No....	No...	No....	No....	$\frac{1}{12}$
	Cooperative ..	M.	20	Calabria	Yes..	Yes...	No...	No....	Yes...	4
	Cooperative ..	M.	30	Calabria	Yes..	Yes...	No...	No....	Yes...	4
	Cooperative ..	M.	38	Calabria	No...	No....	No...	No....	No....	4
	Cooperative ..	M.	44	Calabria	No...	No....	No...	No....	Yes...	8
	Cooperative ..	M.	40	Calabria	No...	No....	No...	No....	No....	4
	Cooperative ..	M.	40	Calabria	No...	No....	No...	No....	No....	4
570	Head	M.	33	Sicily	No...	No....	No...	No....	No....	8
	Wife..........	F.	35	Sicily	No...	No....	No...	No....	No....	7

a Not reported.

TABLE **II.**—GENERAL CONDITION AS TO LITERACY AND ILLITERACY, BY FAMILIES AND INDIVIDUALS—Continued.

[This table includes only persons 10 years of age or over.]

Family number.	Relationship to head of family.	Sex.	Age.	Birthplace.	Native language.		English language.			Years in the United States.
					Reads.	Writes.	Reads.	Writes.	Speaks.	
571	Head	M.	46	Sicily	No	No	No	No	No	11
	Wife	F.	42	Sicily	No	No	No	No	No	3
	Son	M.	18	Sicily	Yes	Yes	Yes	Yes	Yes	3
	Son	M.	16	Sicily	No	No	No	No	Yes	3
	Son	M.	12	Sicily	No	No	No	No	Yes	3
	Daughter	F.	10	Sicily	No	No	Yes	Yes	Yes	3
572	Head	M.	38	Campania	Yes	Yes	No	No	Yes	10
	Wife	F.	25	Sicily	Yes	Yes	No	No	No	3
573	Head	M.	39	Campania	No	No	No	No	Yes	5
	Wife	F.	40	Campania	No	No	No	No	No	2
	Brother	M.	48	Campania	No	No	No	No	No	5
	Brother	M.	45	Campania	No	No	No	No	No	5
	Brother	M.	36	Campania	No	No	No	No	No	5
574	Head	M.	34	Campania	No	No	No	No	Yes	16
	Wife	F.	32	Sicily	No	No	No	No	No	2
575	Head	M.	51	Campania	No	No	No	No	Yes	15
	Wife	F.	51	Campania	No	No	No	No	Yes	10
	Stepson	M.	18	Campania	Yes	No	Yes	Yes	Yes	10
576	Head	M.	30	Campania	Yes	No	No	No	Yes	10
	Wife	F.	30	Campania	No	No	No	No	No	8
577	Head	M.	30	Campania	No	No	No	No	Yes	10
	Wife	F.	20	Campania	No	No	No	No	No	6
	Father-in-law	M.	60	Campania	Yes	Yes	No	No	No	10
578	Head	M.	40	Abruzzo	Yes	Yes	No	No	Yes	14
	Wife	F.	36	Abruzzo	No	No	No	No	No	4
	Nephew	M.	22	Abruzzo	Yes	Yes	No	No	Yes	7
	Lodger	M.	27	Liguria	Yes	Yes	Yes	Yes	Yes	13
	Lodger	M.	50	Abruzzo	Yes	Yes	No	No	No	14
	Lodger	M.	46	Abruzzo	No	No	No	No	Yes	10
	Lodger	M.	40	Basilicata	No	No	No	No	No	13
	Lodger	M.	24	Abruzzo	No	No	No	No	Yes	5
	Lodger	M.	26	Campania	No	No	No	No	Yes	6
	Lodger	M.	40	Abruzzo	No	No	No	No	No	6
579	Head	M.	40	Calabria	No	No	No	No	Yes	13
	Wife	F.	29	Calabria	No	No	No	No	No	4
	Brother-in-law	M.	25	Calabria	Yes	No	No	No	Yes	6
	Brother-in-law	M.	12	Calabria	No	No	No	No	Yes	4
	Boarder	M.	20	Calabria	No	No	No	No	Yes	7
	Boarder	M.	20	Calabria	Yes	Yes	No	No	Yes	7
580	Head	M.	33	Sicily	No	No	No	No	Yes	5
	Wife	F.	25	Sicily	No	No	No	No	No	3
	Brother	M.	25	Sicily	No	No	No	No	No	7
	Boarder	M.	33	Sicily	No	No	No	No	No	3
	Boarder	M.	25	Sicily	No	No	No	No	No	3
	Boarder	M.	18	Sicily	Yes	Yes	No	No	Yes	8
581	Head	M.	32	Campania	No	No	No	No	Yes	12
	Wife	F.	30	Basilicata	No	No	No	No	Yes	7
	Brother	M.	18	Campania	No	No	No	No	Yes	5
582	Head	M.	36	Basilicata	No	No	No	No	Yes	17
	Wife	F.	35	Basilicata	No	No	No	No	No	10
	Brother	M.	25	Basilicata	No	No	No	No	No	6
	Boarder	M.	26	Abruzzo	Yes	Yes	No	No	Yes	7
583	Head	M.	30	Calabria	No	No	No	No	Yes	15
	Wife	F.	28	Calabria	No	No	No	No	No	10
	Brother	M.	23	Calabria	No	No	No	No	No	5
	Boarder	M.	29	Calabria	No	No	No	No	Yes	5
584	Head	M.	36	Basilicata	Yes	Yes	No	No	Yes	9
	Wife	F.	32	Basilicata	No	No	No	No	No	8
	Son	M.	10	Basilicata	Yes	Yes	Yes	Yes	Yes	8
585	Cooperative	M.	32	Abruzzo	Yes	Yes	No	No	Yes	4
	Cooperative	M.	46	Abruzzo	No	No	No	No	No	3
	Cooperative	M.	45	Abruzzo	No	No	No	No	No	3

TABLE **II.**—GENERAL CONDITION AS TO LITERACY AND ILLITERACY, BY FAMILIES AND INDIVIDUALS—Continued.

[This table includes only persons 10 years of age or over.]

Family number.	Relationship to head of family.	Sex.	Age.	Birthplace.	Native language. Reads.	Writes.	English language. Reads.	Writes.	Speaks.	Years in the United States.
585	Cooperative ..	M.	51	Abruzzo	No...	No....	No...	No....	No....	3
	Cooperative ..	M.	45	Abruzzo	No...	No....	No...	No....	No....	4
	Cooperative ..	M.	40	Abruzzo	No...	No....	No...	No....	No....	6
	Cooperative ..	M.	40	Abruzzo	Yes..	Yes...	No...	No....	No....	3
	Cooperative ..	M.	45	Abruzzo	Yes..	Yes...	No...	No....	Yes...	4
	Cooperative ..	M.	46	Abruzzo	No...	No....	No...	No....	No....	4
	Cooperative ..	M.	51	Abruzzo	No...	No....	No...	No....	No....	3
	Cooperative ..	M.	45	Abruzzo	Yes..	Yes...	No...	No....	No....	3
586	Head	M.	54	Basilicata	Yes..	Yes...	No...	No....	Yes...	15
	Wife	F.	54	Basilicata	No...	No....	No...	No....	No....	10
	Brother-in-law	M.	47	Basilicata	No...	No....	No...	No....	No....	10
	Brother-in-law	M.	40	Basilicata	No...	No....	No...	No....	No....	15
587	Head	M.	35	Campania	No...	No....	No...	No....	No....	4
	Wife	F.	33	Campania	No...	No....	No...	No....	No....	4
588	Head	M.	40	Campania	No...	No....	No...	No....	Yes...	16
	Wife	F.	34	Campania	No...	No....	No...	No....	No....	10
589	Head	M.	46	Abruzzo	Yes..	Yes...	No...	No....	Yes...	7
	Wife	F.	31	Abruzzo	No...	No....	No...	No....	No....	5
	Son	M.	10	France	No...	No....	Yes..	Yes...	Yes...	5
	Brother-in-law	M.	25	Abruzzo	Yes..	Yes...	No...	No....	No....	3
	Lodger	M.	34	Abruzzo	Yes..	Yes...	No...	No....	No....	3
590	Head	M.	36	Abruzzo	Yes..	Yes...	No...	No....	Yes...	6
	Wife	F.	25	Abruzzo	No...	No....	No...	No....	No....	6
591	Head	M.	35	Abruzzo	Yes..	Yes...	No...	No....	No....	6
	Wife	F.	38	Abruzzo	No...	No....	No...	No....	No....	3
	Brother-in-law	M.	27	Abruzzo	No...	No....	No...	No....	No....	3
	Cousin	M.	27	Abruzzo	Yes..	Yes...	No...	No....	No....	7
592	Head	M.	37	Campania	No...	No....	No...	No....	Yes...	16
	Wife	F.	23	Campania	Yes..	Yes...	No...	No....	Yes...	7
	Lodger	M.	36	Campania	Yes..	Yes...	No...	No....	Yes...	7
	Lodger	M.	28	Campania	No...	No....	No...	No....	Yes...	12
593	Head	M.	56	Campania	No...	No....	No...	No....	Yes...	15
	Wife	F.	50	Campania	No...	No....	No...	No....	No....	3
	Son	M.	23	Campania	Yes..	Yes...	No...	No....	Yes...	3
	Son	M.	21	Campania	Yes..	Yes...	Yes..	Yes...	Yes...	5
	Daughter	F.	14	Campania	No...	No....	Yes..	Yes...	Yes...	3
594	Head	M.	40	Basilicata	Yes..	Yes...	Yes..	Yes...	Yes...	22
	Wife	F.	28	Basilicata	No...	No....	No...	No....	Yes...	8
595	Head	M.	35	Basilicata	No...	No....	No...	No....	No....	3
	Wife	F.	34	Basilicata	No...	No....	No...	No....	No....	₁⁄₁₂
596	Cooperative ..	M.	25	Abruzzo	Yes..	Yes...	No...	No....	Yes...	6
	Cooperative ..	M.	54	Abruzzo	No...	No....	No...	No....	No....	5
	Cooperative ..	M.	64	Abruzzo	No...	No....	No...	No....	No....	5
597	Head	M.	40	Abruzzo	Yes..	Yes...	No...	No....	Yes...	6
	Wife	F.	32	Abruzzo	No...	No....	No...	No....	No....	6
598	Head	M.	(a)	Campania	No...	No....	No...	No....	No....	14
	Wife	F.	(a)	Campania	No...	No....	No...	No....	No....	10
599	Head	M.	40	Campania	No...	No....	No...	No....	Yes...	14
	Wife	F.	40	Campania	No...	No....	No...	No....	No....	14
	Son	M.	14	United States	Yes..	Yes...	Yes..	Yes...	Yes...	....
600	Head	M.	30	Abruzzo	No...	No....	No...	No....	No....	6
	Wife	F.	25	Basilicata	No...	No....	No...	No....	Yes...	6
	Brother	M.	32	Abruzzo	No..	No....	No...	No....	No....	3
	Lodger	M.	45	Abruzzo	No...	No....	No...	No....	No....	6
	Lodger	M.	12	Abruzzo	No...	No....	No...	No....	No....	₁⁄₁₂
601	Head	M.	31	Calabria	Yes..	Yes.	Yes..	Yes...	Yes...	10
	Wife	F.	33	Calabria	No...	No....	No...	No....	Yes...	8

a Not reported.

TABLE **II.**—GENERAL CONDITION AS TO LITERACY AND ILLITERACY, BY FAMILIES AND INDIVIDUALS—Continued.

[This table includes only persons 10 years of age or over.]

Family number.	Relationship to head of family.	Sex.	Age.	Birthplace.	Native language. Reads.	Writes.	English language. Reads.	Writes.	Speaks.	Years in the United States.
602	Head	M.	42	Abruzzo	Yes.	Yes...	No...	No...	Yes...	12
	Wife	F.	43	Abruzzo	No...	No...	No...	No...	No...	12
	Daughter	F.	12	Belgium	No...	No...	Yes.	Yes.	Yes...	12
603	Head	M.	30	Basilicata	No...	No...	No...	No...	Yes...	8
	Wife	F.	24	Basilicata	No...	No...	No...	No...	Yes...	7
	Brother	M.	28	Basilicata	No...	No...	No...	No...	Yes...	6
604	Head	M.	46	Campania	No...	No...	No...	No...	No...	12
	Wife	F.	37	Campania	No...	No...	No...	No...	Yes...	10
605	Head	M.	30	Basilicata	No...	No...	No...	No...	No...	6
	Wife	F.	30	Basilicata	No...	No...	No...	No...	No...	6
606	Head	M.	40	Basilicata	Yes.	Yes...	No...	No...	Yes...	15
	Wife	F.	34	Basilicata	No...	No...	No...	No...	Yes...	6
	Son	M.	17	Basilicata	Yes.	Yes...	Yes.	Yes...	Yes...	6
	Daughter	F.	13	Basilicata	Yes.	Yes...	Yes.	Yes...	Yes...	6
607	Cooperative	M.	30	Campania	No...	No...	No...	No...	Yes...	11
	Cooperative	M.	31	Basilicata	No...	No...	No...	No...	Yes...	4
	Cooperative	M.	47	Campania	No...	No...	No...	No...	Yes...	10
608	Cooperative	M.	50	Calabria	No...	No...	No...	No...	No...	7
	Cooperative	M.	30	Calabria	No...	No...	No...	No...	Yes...	8
	Cooperative	M.	18	Calabria	Yes.	Yes...	No...	No...	Yes...	4
	Cooperative	M.	30	Calabria	No...	No...	No...	No...	Yes...	10
	Cooperative	M.	31	Calabria	No...	No...	No...	No...	Yes...	10
609	Cooperative	M.	31	Calabria	No...	No...	No...	No...	No...	4
	Cooperative	M.	30	Calabria	No...	No...	No...	No...	No...	4
	Cooperative	M.	33	Calabria	No...	No...	No...	No...	No...	5
	Cooperative	M.	28	Calabria	No...	No...	No...	No...	No...	5
	Cooperative	M.	47	Calabria	No...	No...	No...	No...	No...	6
	Cooperative	M.	25	Calabria	No...	No...	No...	No...	No...	1
610	Head	M.	46	Calabria	No...	No...	No...	No...	No...	11
	Wife	F.	45	Calabria	No...	No...	No...	No...	No...	6
	Daughter	F.	15	Calabria	Yes.	Yes...	No...	No...	No...	6
	Son	M.	12	Calabria	Yes.	Yes...	Yes.	Yes...	Yes...	6
	Lodger	M.	30	Calabria	Yes.	Yes...	No...	No...	No...	5
	Lodger	M.	27	Calabria	Yes.	Yes...	No...	No...	No...	5
	Lodger	M.	36	Calabria	No...	No...	No...	No...	No...	3
611	Head	M.	32	Calabria	No...	No...	No...	No...	Yes...	8
	Wife	F.	35	Calabria	No...	No...	No...	No...	No...	3
612	Cooperative	M.	40	Calabria	No...	No...	No...	No...	No...	4
	Cooperative	M.	16	Calabria	No...	No...	No...	No...	Yes...	3
	Cooperative	M.	47	Calabria	No...	No...	No...	No...	No...	3
	Cooperative	M.	13	Calabria	Yes.	Yes...	No...	No...	Yes...	3
	Cooperative	M.	25	Calabria	Yes.	Yes...	No...	No...	Yes...	3
	Cooperative	M.	18	Calabria	Yes.	Yes...	No...	No...	No...	3
	Cooperative	M.	30	Calabria	No...	No...	No...	No...	No...	4
613	Head	M.	40	Calabria	No...	No...	No...	No...	Yes...	14
	Wife	F.	25	Calabria	No...	No...	No...	No...	No...	8
614	Head	M.	28	Calabria	No...	No...	No...	No...	Yes...	15
	Wife	F.	28	Calabria	No...	No...	No...	No...	No...	4
	Lodger	M.	37	Calabria	Yes.	Yes...	No...	No...	Yes...	7
	Lodger	M.	34	Calabria	Yes.	Yes...	No...	No...	No...	2
615	Head	M.	27	Calabria	No...	No...	No...	No...	Yes...	5
	Wife	F.	23	Calabria	No...	No...	No...	No...	No...	3
	Lodger	M.	29	Calabria	No...	No...	No...	No...	Yes...	3
616	Head	M.	38	Calabria	No...	No...	No...	No...	Yes...	8
	Wife	F.	37	Calabria	Reads.	Writes.	Reads.	No...	No...	8
	Cousin	M.	40	Calabria	No...	No...	No...	No...	No...	11
	Cousin	M.	30	Calabria	Yes.	Yes...	No...	No...	Yes...	4
617	Head	M.	29	Calabria	No...	No...	No...	No...	No...	4
	Wife	F.	26	Calabria	No...	No...	No...	No...	No...	2
	Nephew	M.	21	Calabria	No...	No...	No...	No...	No...	4
	Cousin	M.	30	Calabria	No...	No...	No...	No...	No...	5

TABLE **II.**—GENERAL CONDITION AS TO LITERACY AND ILLITERACY, BY FAMILIES AND INDIVIDUALS—Continued.

[This table includes only persons 10 years of age or over.]

Family number.	Relationship to head of family.	Sex.	Age.	Birthplace.	Native language. Reads.	Writes.	English language. Reads.	Writes.	Speaks.	Years in the United States.
618	Head	M.	(a)	Calabria	No...	No....	No...	No....	Yes...	9
	Wife	F.	26	Calabria	No...	No....	No...	No....	No...	5
	Cousin	M.	30	Calabria	No...	No....	No...	No....	No....	1
619	Cooperative	M.	50	Calabria	Yes...	Yes...	No...	No....	No....	3
	Cooperative	M.	50	Calabria	No...	No....	No...	No....	No....	2
	Cooperative	M.	30	Calabria	No...	No....	No...	No....	No....	3
620	Head	M.	55	Calabria	Yes...	Yes...	No...	No....	Yes...	12
	Wife	F.	25	Calabria	No...	No....	No...	No....	No....	8
621	Head	M.	35	Calabria	Yes...	Yes...	No...	No....	Yes...	13
	Wife	F.	25	Calabria	No...	No....	No...	No....	No....	10
	Lodger	M.	(a)	Calabria	No...	No....	No...	No....	Yes...	6
622	Head	M.	28	Calabria	No...	No....	No...	No....	Yes...	10
	Wife	F.	27	Calabria	No...	No....	No...	No....	No....	5
	Cousin	M.	18	Calabria	No...	No....	No...	No....	Yes...	7
623	Head	M.	35	Campania	Yes...	Yes...	Yes..	Yes...	Yes...	17
	Wife	F.	26	Campania	No...	No....	No...	No....	No....	4
	Son	M.	15	United States	Yes...	Yes...	Yes..	Yes...	Yes...	....
	Daughter	F.	11	United States	No...	No....	No...	No....	Yes...	....
624	Head	M.	40	Calabria	No...	No....	No...	No....	No....	11
	Wife	F.	30	Calabria	No...	No....	No...	No....	No....	6
	Brother-in-law	M.	21	Calabria	No...	No....	No...	No....	Yes...	5
	Nephew	M.	32	Calabria	No...	No....	No...	No....	No....	11
	Lodger	M.	(a)	Calabria	No...	No....	No...	No....	Yes...	7
	Lodger	M.	(a)	Calabria	No...	No....	No...	No....	Yes...	7
625	Head	M.	60	Calabria	No...	No....	No...	No....	No....	9
	Wife	F.	41	Calabria	No...	No....	No...	No....	No....	4
	Daughter	F.	12	Calabria	Yes..	No....	No...	No....	No....	4
626	Head	M.	37	Calabria	Yes..	Yes...	Yes...	Yes...	Yes...	15
	Wife	F.	38	Calabria	No...	No....	No...	No....	No....	8
	Brother-in-law	M.	30	Calabria	No...	No....	No...	No....	No....	9
	Sister-in-law	F.	27	Calabria	No...	No....	No...	No....	No....	5
627	Cooperative	M.	35	Calabria	Yes..	Yes...	No...	No....	No....	4
	Cooperative	M.	30	Calabria	Yes..	Yes...	No...	No....	No....	5
	Cooperative	M.	30	Calabria	Yes..	Yes...	No...	No....	Yes...	5
	Cooperative	M.	28	Calabria	Yes..	Yes...	No...	No....	Yes...	8
628	Head	M.	70	Calabria	No...	No....	No...	No....	No....	12
	Wife	F.	48	Calabria	No...	No....	No...	No....	No....	11
	Son	M.	11	United States	Yes..	Yes...	Yes..	Yes...	Yes...	....
	Cousin	M.	40	Calabria	Yes..	Yes...	No...	No....	No....	4
629	Head	M.	28	Calabria	No...	No....	No...	No....	No....	4
	Brother-in-law	M.	34	Calabria	No...	No....	No...	No....	Yes...	9
	Brother-in-law	M.	26	Calabria	No...	No....	No...	No....	No....	5
	Sister-in-law	F.	24	Calabria	No...	No....	No...	No....	No....	4
630	Head	M.	48	Calabria	No...	No....	No...	No....	No....	10
	Wife	F.	40	Calabria	No...	No....	No...	No....	No....	3
	Daughter	F.	15	Calabria	Yes..	No....	No...	No....	No....	3
	Son-in-law	M.	26	Calabria	Yes..	Yes...	No...	No....	No....	4
	Lodger	M.	38	Calabria	No...	No....	No...	No....	No....	4
631	Head	F.	48	Calabria	No...	No....	No...	No....	No....	3
	Son	M.	16	Calabria	Yes..	Yes...	No...	No	No....	1½
	Son-in-law	M.	30	Calabria	No...	No....	No...	No....	No....	1½
	Boarder	M.	29	Calabria	No...	No....	No...	No....	No....	3
632	Head	M.	51	Campania	No...	No....	No...	No....	No....	16
	Wife	F.	50	Campania	No...	No....	No...	No....	No....	15
	Son	M.	14	United States	No...	No....	No...	No....	Yes...	....
	Daughter	F.	12	United States	Yes..	Yes...	Yes..	Yes...	Yes...	....
633	Head	M.	47	Campania	Yes..	Yes...	No...	No....	Yes...	8
	Wife	F.	45	Campania	No...	No....	No...	No....	No....	7
	Son	M.	18	Campania	No...	No....	Yes..	Yes...	Yes...	7

a Not reported.

TABLE **II.**—GENERAL CONDITION AS TO LITERACY AND ILLITERACY, BY FAMILIES AND INDIVIDUALS—Continued.

[This table includes only persons 10 years of age or over.]

Family number.	Relationship to head of family.	Sex.	Age.	Birthplace.	Native language. Reads.	Writes.	English language. Reads.	Writes.	Speaks.	Years in the United States.
634	Head	M.	40	Calabria	No...	No....	No...	No....	Yes...	5
	Wife	F.	36	Calabria	No...	No....	No...	No....	No....	3
	Daughter	F.	12	Calabria	No...	No....	Yes..	Yes..	Yes...	3
	Lodger	M.	27	Calabria	Yes..	Yes..	Yes..	Yes..	Yes...	10
	Lodger	M.	40	Calabria	No...	No....	No...	No....	No....	8
635	Head	M.	57	Calabria	No...	No....	No...	No....	No....	7
	Wife	F.	47	Calabria	No...	No....	No...	No....	No....	6
	Son	M.	13	Calabria	Yes..	Yes..	Yes..	Yes..	Yes...	6
	Daughter	F.	11	Calabria	Yes..	Yes..	Yes..	Yes..	Yes...	6
	Brother	M.	30	Calabria	No...	No....	No...	No....	No....	6
	Cousin	M.	18	Calabria	Yes..	Yes..	No...	No....	No....	3
	Lodger	M.	30	Calabria	Yes..	Yes..	No...	No....	No....	9
	Lodger	M.	26	Calabria	Yes..	Yes..	No...	No....	No....	2
636	Head	M.	25	Calabria	Yes..	Yes..	No...	No....	Yes...	9
	Wife	F.	24	Calabria	No...	No....	No...	No....	No....	7
	Mother	F.	56	Calabria	No...	No....	No...	No....	No....	7
	Lodger	M.	28	Calabria	No...	No....	No...	No....	No....	1½
	Lodger	M.	22	Calabria	Yes..	Yes..	No...	No....	Yes...	4
	Lodger	M.	60	Calabria	No...	No....	No...	No....	No....	5
637	Head	M.	30	Calabria	No...	No....	No...	No....	Yes...	9
	Wife	F.	26	Calabria	No...	No....	No...	No....	No....	3
	Uncle	M.	64	Calabria	No...	No....	No...	No....	No....	3
	Cousin	M.	43	Calabria	No...	No....	No...	No....	No....	9
	Cousin	M.	16	Calabria	No...	No....	No...	No....	Yes...	3
	Cousin	M.	18	Calabria	Yes..	Yes..	No...	No....	Yes...	3
	Cousin	M.	35	Calabria	No...	No....	No...	No....	Yes...	9
	Cousin	M.	19	Calabria	No...	No....	No...	No....	No....	2
638	Head	F.	36	Calabria	No...	No....	No...	No....	Yes...	8
	Son	M.	11	Calabria	Yes..	Yes..	Yes..	Yes..	Yes...	8
	Lodger	M.	31	Calabria	No...	No....	No...	No....	No....	10
639	Head	M.	35	Campania	No...	No....	No...	No....	Yes...	11
	Wife	F.	32	Campania	No...	No....	No...	No....	No....	9
640	Head	M.	46	Campania	No...	No....	No...	No....	Yes...	12
	Wife	F.	35	Campania	No...	No....	No...	No....	No....	12
	Daughter	F.	14	Campania	No...	No....	No...	No....	Yes...	12
	Son	M.	10	United States	No...	No....	No...	No....	Yes...	....
641	Head	M.	40	Campania	Yes..	Yes..	No...	No....	No....	14
	Wife	F.	44	Campania	No...	No....	No...	No....	No....	14
	Daughter	F.	15	Campania	Yes..	Yes..	Yes..	Yes..	Yes...	14
	Son	M.	10	United States	Yes..	Yes..	Yes..	Yes..	Yes...	....
	Mother-in-law	F.	80	Campania	No...	No....	No...	No....	No....	16
	Boarder	M.	37	Campania	Yes..	Yes..	Yes..	Yes..	Yes...	(a)
642	Head	M.	47	Campania	No...	No....	No...	No....	Yes...	14
	Wife	F.	38	Campania	No...	No....	No...	No....	No....	11
643	Head	M.	47	Campania	No...	No....	No...	No....	Yes...	4
	Wife	F.	45	Campania	No...	No....	No...	No....	No....	4
	Son	M.	18	Campania	Yes..	Yes..	No...	No....	Yes...	4
	Boarder	M.	35	Campania	No...	No....	No...	No....	Yes...	(a)
644	Cooperative	M.	51	Campania	No.:.	No....	No...	No....	No....	16
	Cooperative	M.	27	Campania	Yes..	Yes..	No...	No....	Yes...	16
645	Head	M.	25	Campania	No...	No.	No...	No....	Yes...	7
	Wife	F.	40	Campania	No...	No....	No...	No....	No....	7
646	Head	M.	35	Campania	No...	No....	No...	No....	Yes...	15
	Wife	F.	45	Campania	No...	No....	No...	No....	No....	3
647	Head	M.	34	Campania	Yes..	Yes..	No...	No....	Yes...	11
	Wife	F.	31	Campania	Yes..	Yes..	No...	No....	Yes...	11
	Daughter	F.	12	Campania	Yes..	Yes..	Yes..	Yes..	Yes...	11
	Son	M.	11	Campania	No...	No....	Yes..	Yes..	Yes...	11
	Cousin	M.	34	Campania	No...	No....	No...	No....	No....	1½
648	Head	M.	30	Campania	Yes..	Yes...	Yes..	Yes..	Yes...	15
	Wife	F.	18	Campania	No...	No....	Yes..	Yes..	Yes...	15

a Not reported.

TABLE **II.**—GENERAL CONDITION AS TO LITERACY AND ILLITERACY, BY
FAMILIES AND INDIVIDUALS—Continued.

[This table includes only persons 10 years of age or over.]

Family number.	Relationship to head of family.	Sex.	Age.	Birthplace.	Native language. Reads.	Writes.	English language. Reads.	Writes.	Speaks.	Years in the United States.
649	Head	M.	39	Campania	No	No	No	No	Yes	17
	Wife	F.	35	Campania	No	No	No	No	No	17
	Daughter	F.	14	United States	Yes	Yes	Yes	Yes	Yes	
	Daughter	F.	13	United States	Yes	Yes	Yes	Yes	Yes	
	Nephew	M.	22	Campania	Yes	Yes	Yes	Yes	Yes	7
650	Head	M.	39	Campania	No	No	No	No	Yes	13
	Wife	F.	34	Basilicata	No	No	No	No	Yes	13
	Son	M.	13	Basilicata	Yes	Yes	Yes	Yes	Yes	13
	Son	M.	12	United States	Yes	Yes	Yes	Yes	Yes	
	Boarder	M.	26	Campania	No	No	No	No	Yes	8
651	Head	M.	32	Campania	No	No	No	No	Yes	13
	Wife	F.	28	Campagna di Roma	No	No	No	No	No	4
652	Head	M.	33	Calabria	No	No	No	No	Yes	7
	Wife	F.	30	Calabria	No	No	No	No	No	3
	Cousin	M.	23	Calabria	No	No	No	No	No	3
653	Cooperative	M.	25	Sicily	No	No	No	No	No	3
	Cooperative	M.	25	Sicily	Yes	Yes	No	No	Yes	3
	Cooperative	M.	18	Sicily	No	No	No	No	Yes	6
	Cooperative	M.	26	Sicily	No	No	No	No	Yes	6
	Cooperative	M.	22	Sicily	Yes	Yes	No	No	Yes	5
	Cooperative	M.	42	Sicily	Yes	Yes	No	No	No	3
	Cooperative	M.	21	Sicily	Yes	Yes	No	No	Yes	8
	Cooperative	M.	27	Sicily	No	No	No	No	Yes	6
	Cooperative	M.	35	Sicily	Yes	Yes	No	No	Yes	3
	Cooperative	M.	46	Sicily	No	No	No	No	Yes	5
	Cooperative	M.	46	Sicily	No	No	No	No	No	4
	Cooperative	M.	38	Sicily	Yes	Yes	No	No	No	4
	Cooperative	M.	30	Sicily	No	No	No	No	No	2
	Cooperative	M.	22	Sicily	No	No	No	No	Yes	3
	Cooperative	M.	22	Sicily	No	No	No	No	Yes	5
	Cooperative	M.	24	Sicily	No	No	No	No	No	4
	Cooperative	M.	26	Sicily	Yes	Yes	No	No	Yes	4
	Cooperative	M.	27	Sicily	Yes	Yes	No	No	Yes	5
654	Head	M.	25	Sicily	No	No	No	No	Yes	6
655	Cooperative	M.	40	Calabria	Yes	Yes	No	No	No	8
	Cooperative	M.	35	Calabria	No	No	No	No	Yes	10
	Cooperative	M.	19	Calabria	Yes	Yes	Yes	Yes	Yes	3
	Cooperative	M.	20	Calabria	Yes	Yes	Yes	Yes	Yes	4
	Cooperative	M.	50	Calabria	Yes	Yes	No	No	No	5
	Cooperative	M.	18	Calabria	No	No	No	No	Yes	3
	Cooperative	M.	21	Calabria	No	No	No	No	Yes	10
	Cooperative	M.	49	Calabria	Yes	Yes	No	No	No	9
	Cooperative	M.	27	Calabria	No	No	No	No	No	5
	Cooperative	M.	54	Calabria	No	No	No	No	No	10
	Cooperative	M.	32	Calabria	Yes	Yes	No	No	Yes	5
	Cooperative	M.	34	Calabria	No	No	No	No	Yes	8
	Cooperative	M.	31	Calabria	Yes	Yes	No	No	No	10
656	Head	M.	40	Basilicata	No	No	No	No	Yes	13
	Wife	F.	40	Basilicata	No	No	No	No	No	7
	Daughter	F.	13	Basilicata	No	No	No	No	Yes	7
657	Head	M.	38	Campania	No	No	No	No	Yes	13
	Wife	F.	40	Campania	No	No	No	No	No	7
	Daughter	F.	15	Campania	Yes	Yes	Yes	Yes	Yes	7
	Daughter	F.	12	Campania	No	No	No	No	Yes	7
658	Head	M.	51	Campania	Yes	Yes	No	No	No	13
	Wife	F.	45	Campania	No	No	No	No	No	3
	Cousin	M.	30	Campania	No	No	No	No	No	3
	Lodger	M.	45	Campania	Yes	Yes	No	No	No	15
	Lodger	M.	45	Campania	Yes	Yes	No	No	Yes	7
659	Head	M.	40	Campania	Yes	Yes	No	No	Yes	5
	Lodger	M.	30	Campania	No	No	No	No	Yes	5
	Lodger	M.	46	Campania	Yes	Yes	No	No	Yes	10
	Lodger	M.	23	Campania	Yes	Yes	No	No	Yes	1
	Lodger	M.	23	Campania	No	No	No	No	Yes	1

TABLE **II.**—GENERAL CONDITION AS TO LITERACY AND ILLITERACY, BY FAMILIES AND INDIVIDUALS—Continued.

[This table includes only persons 10 years of age or over.]

Family number.	Relationship to head of family.	Sex.	Age.	Birthplace.	Native language. Reads.	Native language. Writes.	English language. Reads.	English language. Writes.	English language. Speaks.	Years in the United States.
660	Head	M.	30	Calabria	No...	No...	No....	No...	Yes...	8
	Brother	M.	25	Calabria	No...	No...	No....	No...	Yes...	8
661	Head	M.	60	Campania	No...	No...	No....	No...	No....	5
	Wife	F.	48	Campania	No...	No...	No....	No...	No....	5
	Daughter	F.	14	Campania	Yes..	Yes..	Yes..	Yes..	Yes...	5
	Daughter	F.	12	Campania	No...	No...	Yes..	Yes..	Yes...	5
662	Head	M.	38	Campania	No...	No...	No....	No...	Yes...	16
	Wife	F.	34	Campania	No...	No...	No....	No...	No....	8
	Daughter	F.	11	Campania	Yes..	Yes..	Yes..	Yes..	Yes...	8
	Father	M.	68	Campania	No...	No...	No....	No...	No....	8
	Mother	F.	69	Campania	No...	No...	No....	No...	No....	8
663	Head	M.	48	Campania	Yes..	Yes..	No....	No...	No....	18
	Wife	F.	42	Campania	No...	No...	No....	No...	No....	15
	Son	M.	22	Campania	No...	No...	Yes..	Yes..	Yes...	15
	Daughter	F.	13	United States	No...	No...	No....	No...	Yes...	
664	Head	M.	34	Campania	No...	No...	No....	No...	Yes...	13
	Wife	F.	38	Campania	No...	No...	No....	No...	No....	8
	Brother	M.	40	Campania	No...	No...	No....	No...	No....	3
665	Head	M.	67	Campania	No...	No...	No....	No...	No....	11
	Wife	F.	52	Campania	No...	No...	No....	No...	No....	6
666	Head	M.	34	Basilicata	Yes..	Yes..	No....	No...	Yes...	7
	Wife	F.	37	Basilicata	No...	No...	No....	No...	No....	4
	Son	M.	11	Basilicata	No...	No...	No....	No...	Yes...	4
	Lodger	M.	28	Basilicata	Yes..	Yes..	No....	No...	Yes...	4
667	Head	M.	45	Campania	Yes..	Yes..	No....	No...	Yes...	13
	Wife	F.	40	Campania	No...	No...	No....	No...	Yes...	13
	Son	M.	13	Campania	No...	No...	No....	No...	Yes...	13
668	Head	F.	54	Campania	No...	No...	No....	No...	No....	4
	Son	M.	30	Campania	No...	No...	No....	No...	Yes...	9
	Son	M.	23	Campania	No...	No...	No....	No...	Yes...	9
669	Head	M.	38	Campania	No...	No...	No....	No...	Yes...	7
	Wife	F.	32	Campania	No...	No...	No....	No...	No....	7
670	Head	M.	50	Campania	Yes..	Yes..	No....	No...	Yes...	15
	Wife	F.	42	Campania	No...	No...	No....	No...	No....	14
	Daughter	F.	14	Campania	No...	No...	Yes..	Yes..	Yes...	14
	Daughter	F.	12	United States	Yes..	Yes..	Yes..	Yes..	Yes...	
	Lodger	M.	64	Campania	No...	No...	No....	No...	Yes...	12
671	Head	M.	52	Calabria	Yes..	Yes..	No....	No...	Yes...	14
	Wife	F.	44	Calabria	No...	No...	No....	No...	No....	10
	Daughter	F.	20	Calabria	Yes..	Yes..	No....	No...	No....	4
	Son	M.	16	Calabria	Yes..	Yes..	Yes..	Yes..	Yes...	10
672	Head	M.	42	Campania	Yes..	Yes..	Yes..	Yes..	Yes...	19
	Wife	F.	52	Campania	No...	No...	No....	No...	Yes...	19
	Son	M.	18	United States	Yes..	Yes..	Yes..	Yes..	Yes...	
	Son	M.	17	United States	Yes..	Yes..	Yes..	Yes..	Yes...	
	Son	M.	12	United States	Yes..	Yes..	Yes..	Yes..	Yes...	
673	Head	M.	23	Campania	Yes..	Yes..	Yes..	Yes..	Yes...	15
	Wife	F.	22	Campania	Yes..	Yes..	No....	No...	No....	1
674	Head	M.	50	Campania	Yes..	Yes..	No...	No...	No....	8
	Wife	F.	50	Campania	No...	No...	No...	No...	No....	1
	Son	M.	22	Campania	Yes..	Yes..	Yes..	Yes..	Yes...	8
	Daughter	F.	15	Campania	Yes..	Yes..	No...	No...	No....	1
	Son	M.	10	Campania	Yes..	Yes..	No...	No...	No....	1
675	Head	M.	35	Sicily	No...	No...	No....	No...	Yes...	3
	Wife	F.	35	Sicily	No...	No...	No....	No...	No....	3
676	Head	M.	36	Apulia	Yes..	Yes..	No...	No...	No....	6
	Wife	F.	32	Apulia	No...	No...	No...	No...	Yes...	4
	Brother-in-law	M.	27	Apulia	No...	No...	No...	No...	Yes...	5
	Sister-in-law	F.	26	Apulia	No...	No...	No...	No...	Yes...	4

TABLE **II.**—GENERAL CONDITION AS TO LITERACY AND ILLITERACY, BY FAMILIES AND INDIVIDUALS—Continued.

[This table includes only persons 10 years of age or over.]

Family number.	Relationship to head of family.	Sex.	Age.	Birthplace.	Native language.		English language.			Years in the United States.
					Reads.	Writes.	Reads.	Writes.	Speaks.	
677	Cooperative...	M.	33	Calabria	No...	No....	No...	No....	Yes...	3
	Cooperative...	M.	22	Calabria	No...	No....	No...	No....	No....	7
	Cooperative...	M.	34	Calabria	Yes...	Yes...	No...	No....	Yes...	4
	Cooperative...	M.	37	Calabria	No...	No....	No...	No....	No....	3
	Cooperative...	M.	26	Calabria	No...	No....	No...	No....	No....	5
	Cooperative...	M.	27	Calabria	No...	No....	No...	No....	No....	4
	Cooperative...	M.	35	Calabria	No...	No....	No...	No....	No....	3
	Cooperative...	M.	22	Calabria	No...	No....	No...	No....	Yes...	6
678	Head	M.	42	Campania..........	No...	No....	No...	No....	Yes...	14
	Wife.........	F.	42	Campania..........	No...	No....	No...	No....	Yes...	14
	Son	M.	17	Campania..........	Yes..	Yes...	Yes..	Yes..	Yes...	14
	Daughter	F.	14	United States......	Yes..	Yes...	Yes..	Yes..	Yes...	....
	Daughter	F.	10	United States......	Yes..	Yes...	Yes..	Yes..	Yes...	....
	Mother-in-law.	F.	70	Campania..........	No...	No....	No...	No....	No....	14
679	Head	M.	46	Campania..........	No...	No....	No...	No....	No....	11
	Wife.........	F.	42	Campania..........	No...	No....	No...	No....	No....	2
	Daughter	F.	20	Campania..........	No...	No....	No...	No....	No....	2
	Son ..,......	M.	12	Campania..........	No...	No....	No...	No...	No....	2
	Son	M.	11	Campania..........	No...	No....	No...	No....	No....	2
680	Head	M.	37	Campania..........	No...	No....	No...	No....	Yes...	15
	Wife.........	F.	34	Campania..........	No...	No....	No...	No....	Yes...	11
681	Head	M.	39	Campania..........	No...	No....	No...	No....	Yes...	11
	Wife.........	F.	42	Campania..........	No...	No....	No...	No....	Yes...	9
	Son	M.	18	Campania..........	Yes..	Yes...	Yes..	Yes...	Yes...	9
	Son	M.	15	Campania..........	No...	No....	Yes..	Yes...	Yes...	9
	Daughter	F.	12	Campania..........	No...	No....	Yes..	Yes...	Yes...	9
682	Head	M.	41	Campania..........	No...	No....	No...	No....	Yes...	13
	Wife.........	F.	(a)	Campania..........	No...	No....	No...	No....	Yes...	13
	Daughter	F.	14	Campania..........	No...	No....	No...	No....	Yes...	13
	Lodger	M.	24	Campania..........	No...	No....	No...	No....	Yes...	5
683	Head	M.	38	Campania..........	No...	No....	No...	No....	Yes...	12
	Wife.........	F.	42	Campania..........	No...	No....	No...	No....	No....	11
684	Head	M.	50	Campania..........	No...	No....	No...	No....	No....	4
	Wife.........	F.	48	Campania..........	No...	No....	No...	No....	No....	4
	Son	M.	15	Campania..........	No...	No....	No...	No....	Yes...	4
	Daughter	F.	14	Campania..........	No...	No....	No...	No....	Yes...	4
	Son	M.	12	Campania..........	No...	No....	No...	No....	Yes...	4
685	Head	M.	27	Sicily	No...	No....	No...	No....	No....	7
	Wife.........	F.	44	Basilicata..........	No...	No....	No...	No....	No....	12
	Stepson.......	M.	11	United States......	Yes..	Yes..	Yes..	Yes..	Yes...	....
686	Head	M.	23	Campania..........	Yes..	Yes...	No...	No....	Yes...	1
	Wife.........	F.	18	Campania..........	No...	No....	No...	No....	No....	1
687	Head	M.	30	Campania..........	Yes..	Yes...	No...	No....	Yes...	11
	Wife.........	F.	29	Campania..........	No...	No....	No...	No....	No....	11
688	Head	M.	50	Campania..........	No...	No....	No...	No....	Yes...	15
	Wife.........	F.	45	Campania..........	No...	No....	No...	No....	No....	10
	Son	M.	24	Campania..........	Yes..	Yes...	No...	No....	Yes...	10
	Daughter-in-law.	F.	20	Campania..........	No...	No....	No...	No....	No....	3
	Lodger	M.	50	Campania..........	Yes..	Yes...	No...	No....	Yes...	16
	Lodger	M.	17	Campania..........	Yes..	Yes...	No...	No....	Yes...	7
689	Head	M.	38	Campania..........	No...	No....	No...	No....	Yes...	11
	Wife.........	F.	38	Campania..........	No...	No....	No...	No....	No....	7
690	Head	M.	35	Campania..........	No...	No....	No...	No....	Yes...	15
	Wife.........	F.	35	Campania..........	No...	No....	No...	No....	No....	5
691	Head	M.	35	Campania..........	No...	No....	No...	No....	No....	5
	Wife.........	F.	33	Campania..........	No...	No....	No...	No....	No....	5
692	Head	M.	45	Campania..........	No...	No....	No...	No....	No....	9
	Wife.........	F.	40	Campania..........	No...	No....	No...	No....	No....	9

a Not reported.

TABLE **II.**—GENERAL CONDITION AS TO LITERACY AND ILLITERACY, BY FAMILIES AND INDIVIDUALS—Continued.

[This table includes only persons 10 years of age or over.]

Family number.	Relationship to head of family.	Sex.	Age.	Birthplace.	Native language.		English language.			Years in the United States.
					Reads.	Writes.	Reads.	Writes.	Speaks.	
692	Son	M.	18	Campania	No...	No....	No...	No....	Yes...	9
	Son	M.	15	Campania	Yes...	Yes...	No...	No....	Yes...	9
	Daughter	F.	10	Campania	No...	No....	No...	No....	Yes...	9
693	Head	M.	40	Campania	No...	No....	No...	No....	Yes...	16
	Wife	F.	38	Campania	No...	No....	No...	No....	No....	15
	Son	M.	11	United States	No(a)	No(a).	No...	No....	Yes...	....
	Brother	M.	20	Campania	Yes...	Yes...	No...	No....	Yes...	6
	Brother	M.	17	Campania	No...	No....	No...	No....	Yes...	6
	Boarder	M.	40	Campania	No...	No....	No...	No....	No....	2
694	Head	M.	45	Campania	No...	No....	No...	No....	No....	14
	Wife	F.	39	Campania	No...	No....	No...	No....	No....	14
	Son	M.	10	United States	Yes...	Yes...	Yes...	Yes...	Yes...	....
695	Cooperative	M.	52	Calabria	No...	No....	No...	No....	No....	7
	Cooperative	M.	25	Calabria	No...	No....	No...	No....	Yes...	5
	Cooperative	M.	40	Calabria	Yes...	Yes...	No...	No....	No....	8
	Cooperative	M.	17	Calabria	Yes...	Yes...	Yes...	Yes...	Yes...	4
	Cooperative	M.	34	Calabria	Yes...	Yes...	No...	No....	Yes...	6
	Cooperative	M.	18	Calabria	Yes...	Yes...	No...	No....	Yes...	4
696	Head	M.	35	Campania	Yes...	Yes...	No...	No....	Yes...	15
	Wife	F.	30	Campania	No...	No....	No...	No....	No....	9
	Cousin	M.	25	Campania	Yes...	Yes...	No...	No....	Yes...	3
697	Head	M.	46	Campania	No...	No....	No...	No....	Yes...	10
	Wife	F.	44	Campania	No...	No....	No...	No....	No....	10
	Lodger	M.	22	Campania	Yes...	Yes...	No...	No....	Yes...	5
	Lodger	M.	19	Campania	Yes...	Yes...	No...	No....	Yes...	5
	Lodger	M.	15	Campania	No...	No....	No...	No....	Yes...	2
	Lodger	M.	40	Campania	No...	No....	No...	No....	No....	8
698	Head	M.	50	Campania	No...	No....	No...	No....	No....	8
	Wife	F.	45	Campania	No...	No....	No...	No....	No....	5
	Son	M.	19	Campania	No...	No....	No...	No....	Yes...	5
699	Head	M.	40	Campania	No...	No....	No...	No....	Yes...	11
	Wife	F.	(b)	Campania	No...	No....	No...	No....	No....	6
	Son	M.	17	Campania	Yes...	Yes...	No...	No....	Yes...	6
	Daughter	F.	14	Campania	No...	No....	No...	No....	Yes...	6
	Daughter	F.	11	Campania	No...	No....	No...	No....	Yes...	6
700	Head	M.	46	Campania	No...	No....	No...	No....	Yes...	10
	Wife	F.	43	Campania	No...	No....	No...	No....	Yes...	10
	Son	M.	23	Campania	No...	No....	No...	No....	Yes...	10
	Daughter	F.	11	Campania	Yes...	Yes...	No...	No....	Yes...	10
701	Head	M.	46	Campania	No...	No....	No...	No....	Yes...	23
	Wife	F.	46	Basilicata	No...	No....	No...	No....	No...	16
	Stepdaughter	F.	12	United States	Yes...	Yes...	Yes...	Yes...	Yes...	....
	Stepdaughter	F.	10	United States	Yes...	Yes...	Yes...	Yes...	Yes...	....
702	Head	M.	26	Campania	Yes...	Yes...	No...	No....	Yes...	7
	Wife	F.	22	Campania	No...	No....	No...	No....	Yes...	3
703	Head	M.	43	Campania	No...	No....	No...	No....	No....	17
	Wife	F.	43	Campania	No...	No....	No...	No....	No....	16
	Son	M.	14	United States	Yes...	Yes...	Yes...	Yes...	Yes...	....
	Son	M.	12	United States	No...	No....	No...	No....	Yes...	....
704	Head	M.	35	Campania	No...	No....	No...	No....	Yes...	6
	Wife	F.	40	Campania	No...	No....	No...	No....	No....	2
705	Head	M.	39	Campania	Yes...	Yes...	No...	No....	Yes...	15
	Wife	F.	31	Campania	No...	No....	No...	No....	No....	13
706	Cooperative	M.	44	Campania	Yes...	Yes...	Reads...	No...	Yes...	8
	Cooperative	M.	46	Campania	No...	No....	No...	No....	Yes...	15
707	Head	M.	40	Campania	No...	No....	No...	No....	Yes...	10
	Wife	F.	37	Campania	No...	No....	No...	No....	Yes...	5

a Reads and writes Italian.   b Not reported.

TABLE **II.**—GENERAL CONDITION AS TO LITERACY AND ILLITERACY, BY
FAMILIES AND INDIVIDUALS—Continued.

[This table includes only persons 10 years of age or over.]

Family number.	Relationship to head of family.	Sex.	Age.	Birthplace.	Native language.		English language.			Years in the United States.
					Reads.	Writes.	Reads.	Writes.	Speaks.	
708	Head	M.	32	Campania	No	No	No	No	Yes	9
	Wife	F.	32	Campania	No	No	No	No	Yes	9
709	Head	F.	45	Campania	No	No	No	No	No	5
710	Head	M.	44	Campania	No	No	No	No	Yes	14
	Wife	F.	39	Campania	No	No	No	No	No	14
	Daughter	F.	15	Campania	Yes	Yes	No	No	Yes	14
711	Head	M.	20	Campania	Yes	Yes	No	No	Yes	6
	Wife	F.	17	Campania	No	No	No	No	Yes	6
712	Head	M.	45	Campania	No	No	No	No	Yes	15
	Wife	F.	42	Campania	No	No	No	No	No	10
	Son	M.	15	Campania	Yes	Yes	Yes	Yes	Yes	10
713	Head	M.	38	Calabria	No	No	No	No	Yes	8
714	Head	M.	47	Basilicata	Yes	Yes	No	No	No	5
	Wife	F.	43	Basilicata	No	No	No	No	No	3
	Son	M.	12	Basilicata	No	No	No	No	Yes	3
	Lodger	M.	27	Basilicata	No	No	No	No	No	3
	Lodger	M.	40	Basilicata	No	No	No	No	No	5
715	Head	F.	38	Basilicata	No	No	No	No	No	10
	Son	M.	13	Basilicata	Yes	Yes	No	No	Yes	10
	Son	M.	10	Basilicata	No	No	No	No	Yes	10
	Lodger	M.	25	Basilicata	No	No	No	No	Yes	3
	Lodger	M.	57	Basilicata	No	No	No	No	No	4
716	Head	M.	43	Campania	No	No	No	No	Yes	15
	Wife	F.	42	Campania	No	No	No	No	No	13
	Daughter	F.	18	Campania	No	No	No	No	Yes	13
	Son	M.	15	Campania	Yes	Yes	No	No	Yes	13
717	Head	M.	36	Basilicata	Yes	Yes	Yes	Yes	Yes	12
	Wife	F.	36	Basilicata	No	No	No	No	No	11
	Daughter	F.	12	Basilicata	Yes	Yes	Yes	Yes	Yes	11
718	Head	M.	40	Campania	No	No	No	No	No	15
	Wife	F.	60	Campania	No	No	No	No	No	8
	Son	M.	20	Campania	Yes	Yes	Yes	Yes	Yes	8
	Lodger	M.	42	Campania	No	No	No	No	No	15
	Lodger	M.	17	Campania	Yes	Yes	No	No	Yes	6
719	Head	M.	54	Basilicata	No	No	No	No	No	15
	Wife	F.	47	Basilicata	No	No	No	No	No	10
	Daughter	F.	15	Basilicata	No	No	No	No	Yes	10
	Nephew	M.	25	Basilicata	Yes	Yes	No	No	Yes	5
720	Head	M.	24	Basilicata	Yes	Yes	No	No	Yes	10
	Wife	F.	20	Campania	No	No	No	No	Yes	5
721	Head	M.	55	Campania	No	No	No	No	No	15
	Wife	F.	50	Campania	No	No	No	No	No	10
	Son	M.	20	Campania	No	No	Yes	Yes	Yes	15
	Son	M.	16	Campania	Yes	Yes	Yes	Yes	Yes	10
722	Head	M.	49	Campania	No	No	No	No	Yes	15
	Wife	F.	40	Campania	No	No	No	No	No	8
	Daughter	F.	17	Campania	No	No	No	No	Yes	8
	Daughter	F.	16	Campania	No	No	No	No	Yes	8
723	Head	M.	48	Campania	No	No	No	No	Yes	6
	Wife	F.	44	Campania	No	No	No	No	No	6
	Son	M.	19	Campania	No	No	No	No	Yes	7
	Daughter	F.	11	Campania	No	No	No	No	Yes	6
724	Head	M.	62	Campania	Yes	Yes	No	No	No	17
	Wife	F.	39	Campania	No	No	No	No	Yes	17
725	Head	M.	30	Campania	Yes	Yes	No	No	Yes	14
	Wife	F.	30	Campania	No	No	No	No	Yes	14
726	Head	M.	40	Campania	No	No	No	No	Yes	14
	Wife	F.	40	Campania	No	No	No	No	No	13

TABLE **II.**—GENERAL CONDITION AS TO LITERACY AND ILLITERACY, BY FAMILIES AND INDIVIDUALS—Continued.

[This table includes only persons 10 years of age or over.]

Family number.	Relationship to head of family.	Sex.	Age.	Birthplace.	Native language. Reads.	Writes.	English language. Reads.	Writes.	Speaks.	Years in the United States.
726	Son	M.	18	Campania	Yes.	Yes	Yes.	Yes.	Yes	13
	Daughter	F.	15	Campania	No.	No	No	No	Yes	13
	Son	M.	10	United States	Yes.	Yes	Yes.	Yes.	Yes	
727	Head	M.	40	Abruzzo	Yes.	Yes	No	No	No	6/12
	Wife	F.	30	Abruzzo	No.	No	No	No	No	1/12
728	Cooperative	M.	42	Sicily	Yes.	Yes	No	No	Yes	4
	Cooperative	M.	30	Sicily	No.	No	No	No	No	8
	Cooperative	M.	27	Sicily	No.	No	No	No	Yes	4
	Cooperative	M.	27	United States	Yes.	Yes	Yes.	Yes.	Yes	
	Cooperative	M.	40	Sicily	No.	No	No	No	No	4
	Cooperative	M.	50	Sicily	No.	No	No	No	No	7
	Cooperative	M.	32	Sicily	No.	No	No	No	No	4
	Cooperative	M.	25	Sicily	No.	No	No	No	Yes	4
	Cooperative	M.	35	Sicily	Yes.	Yes	No	No	Yes	3
	Cooperative	M.	37	Sicily	No.	No	No	No	Yes	4
	Cooperative	M.	28	Sicily	Yes.	Yes	No	No	Yes	4
	Cooperative	M.	28	Sicily	No.	No	No	No	No	2
729	Head	M.	50	Calabria	Yes.	Yes	No	No	Yes	13
	Wife	F.	40	Calabria	No.	No	No	No	No	9
	Son	M.	21	Calabria	Yes.	No	No	No	Yes	9
	Brother	M.	45	Calabria	No.	No	No	No	Yes	7
	Brother	M.	23	Calabria	Yes.	Yes	No	No	Yes	5
	Nephew	M.	26	Calabria	No.	No	No	No	Yes	8
730	Head	M.	32	Campania	No.	No	No	No	No	10
	Wife	F.	32	Campania	No.	No	No	No	No	7
	Boarder	M.	35	Campania	Yes.	Yes	No	No	Yes	9
	Boarder	M.	28	Campania	Yes.	Yes	No	No	Yes	9
731	Head	M.	38	Campania	No.	No	No	No	No	4
	Wife	F.	32	Campania	No.	No	No	No	No	4
	Son	M.	11	Campania	Yes.	Yes	No	No	Yes	4
732	Head	M.	37	Calabria	Yes.	Yes	No	No	Yes	10
	Wife	F.	35	Calabria	No.	No	No	No	No	3
	Son	M.	12	Calabria	No.	No	Yes.	Yes.	Yes	3
	Son	M.	10	Calabria	No.	No	Yes.	Yes.	Yes	3
733	Head	M.	38	Campania	No.	No	No	No	Yes	14
	Wife	F.	38	Campania	No.	No	No	No	No	5
734	Head	M.	40	Campania	No.	No	No	No	No	16
	Wife	F.	45	Campania	No.	No	No	No	No	15
	Son	M.	18	Campania	Yes.	Yes	Yes.	Yes.	Yes	15
	Son	M.	13	United States	No.	No	No	No	Yes	
735	Head	M.	60	Campania	No.	No	No	No	Yes	12
	Wife	F.	60	Campania	No.	No	No	No	Yes	12
	Stepson	M.	18	Campania	Yes.	Yes	Yes.	Yes.	Yes	12
736	Head	M.	45	Campania	No.	No	No	No	No	10
	Wife	F.	32	Campania	No.	No	No	No	No	6
	Daughter	F.	10	Campania	No.	No	No	No	Yes	6
737	Head	M.	43	Campania	No.	No	No	No	Yes	10
	Wife	F.	35	Campania	No.	No	No	No	No	10
	Daughter	F.	12	Campania	No.	No	No	No	Yes	10
738	Head	M.	37	Campania	Yes.	Yes	No	No	Yes	12
	Wife	F.	23	Campania	Yes.	Yes	No	No	No	11
739	Head	M.	26	Campania	Yes.	Yes	No	No	Yes	3
	Wife	F.	17	Campania	No.	No	No	No	No	3
740	Head	M.	51	Campania	No.	No	No	No	No	6
	Wife	F.	39	Campania	No.	No	No	No	No	6
	Son	M.	14	Campania	No.	No	No	No	Yes	6
	Lodger	M.	45	Campania	No.	No	No	No	Yes	12
741	Head	M.	45	Campania	No.	No	No	No	Yes	15
	Wife	F.	35	Campania	No.	No	No	No	No	15
	Brother	M.	38	Campania	No.	No	No	No	No	1/12
	Sister-in-law	F.	36	Campania	No.	No	No	No	No	11

TABLE **II.**—GENERAL CONDITION AS TO LITERACY AND ILLITERACY, BY FAMILIES AND INDIVIDUALS—Continued.

[This table includes only persons 10 years of age or over.]

Family number.	Relationship to head of family.	Sex.	Age.	Birthplace.	Native language. Reads.	Writes.	English language. Reads.	Writes.	Speaks.	Years in the United States.
741	Nephew	M..	18	Campania..........	Yes..	Yes...	Yes..	Yes...	Yes...	11
	Nephew	M..	16	Campania..........	No....	No....	Yes..	Yes...	Yes...	11
742	Head	M..	46	Campania..........	No....	No....	No....	No....	Yes...	17
	Daughter.....	F.	15	United States......	Yes..	Yes...	Yes..	Yes...	Yes...	....
	Mother	F.	68	Campania..........	No?..	No....	No....	No....	No....	7
743	Head	M..	29	Sicily..........	No....	No....	No....	No....	Yes...	12
	Wife..........	F.	32	Basilicata	No....	No....	No....	No....	No....	5
	Stepson.......	M..	12	Basilicata	No....	No....	Yes..	Yes...	Yes...	5
	Stepson.......	M..	11	Basilicata	No....	No....	Yes..	Yes...	Yes...	5
	Mother	F.	55	Sicily..........	No....	No....	No....	No....	No....	$\frac{7}{12}$
744	Head	M..	43	Basilicata..........	No....	No....	No....	No....	Yes...	14
	Wife..........	F.	31	Basilicata	Yes..	Yes...	No....	No....	Yes...	12
	Daughter.....	F.	12	Basilicata	Yes..	Yes...	Yes..	Yes...	Yes...	12
	Daughter.....	F.	10	United States.......	Yes..	Yes...	Yes..	Yes...	Yes...	....
	Father-in-law.	M..	90	Basilicata	Yes..	Yes...	No....	No....	No....	12
	Mother-in-law	F.	50	Basilicata	No....	No....	No....	No....	No....	12
745	Head	M..	26	Campania..........	No....	No....	No....	No....	Yes...	7
	Wife..........	F.	19	Campania..........	Yes..	No....	No....	No....	Yes...	1
	Brother.......	M..	17	Campania..........	No....	No....	No....	No....	Yes...	2
	Cousin........	M..	29	Campania..........	Yes..	Yes...	No....	No....	Yes...	5
746	Head	M..	60	Basilicata..........	No....	No....	Nd...	No....	No....	17
	Wife..........	F.	50	Basilicata..........	No....	No....	No....	No....	No....	17
	Daughter.....	F.	15	United States......	No....	No....	No....	No....	Yes...	....
747	Cooperative ..	M..	27	Calabria	No....	No....	No....	No....	Yes...	7
	Cooperative ..	M..	28	Calabria	No....	No....	No....	No....	Yes...	9
	Cooperative ..	M..	23	Calabria	No....	No....	No....	No....	No....	3
	Cooperative ..	M..	28	Calabria	No....	No....	No....	No....	No....	5
	Cooperative ..	M..	25	Calabria	Yes..	Yes...	No....	No....	Yes...	8
748	Head	M..	28	Calabria	Yes..	Yes...	Yes..	Yes...	Yes...	14
	Mother	F.	50	Calabria	No....	No....	No....	No....	No....	9
749	Cooperative ..	M..	19	Sicily	No....	No....	No....	No....	Yes...	4
	Cooperative ..	M..	18	Sicily	Yes..	Yes...	No....	No....	No....	2
	Cooperative ..	M..	29	Sicily	No....	No....	No....	No....	No....	6
750	Cooperative ..	M..	48	Sicily	Yes..	Yes...	No....	No....	No....	6
	Cooperative ..	M..	42	Sicily	Yes..	Yes...	No....	No....	No....	5
	Cooperative ..	M..	40	Sicily	Yes..	Yes...	No....	No....	No....	6
	Cooperative ..	M..	55	Sicily	No....	No....	No....	No....	No....	3
	Cooperative ..	M..	21	Sicily	No....	No....	No....	No....	No....	2
	Cooperative ..	M..	15	Campania	Yes..	Yes...	No....	No....	Yes...	4
	Cooperative ..	M..	34	Campania	No....	No....	No....	No....	No....	3
	Cooperative ..	M..	34	Campania	No....	No....	No....	No....	No....	2
	Cooperative ..	M..	22	Campania	Yes..	Yes...	No....	No....	No....	6
751	Head	M..	28	Basilicata..........	Yes..	Yes...	No....	No....	Yes...	10
	Wife..........	F.	27	Basilicata..........	No....	No....	No....	No....	No....	8
752	Cooperative ..	M..	34	Calabria	Yes..	Yes...	No....	No....	Yes...	3
	Cooperative ..	M..	48	Calabria	No....	No....	No....	No....	Yes...	7
	Cooperative ..	M..	41	Calabria	No....	No....	No....	No....	Yes...	5
	Cooperative ..	M..	50	Calabria	No....	No....	No....	No....	No....	4
	Cooperative ..	M..	50	Calabria	No....	No....	No....	No....	No....	4
	Cooperative ..	M..	24	Calabria	No....	No....	No....	No....	Yes...	4
	Cooperative ..	M..	22	Calabria	Yes..	Yes...	Yes..	Yes...	Yes...	5
	Cooperative ..	M..	56	Calabria	No....	No....	No....	No....	No....	4
	Cooperative ..	F.	50	Calabria	No....	No....	No....	No....	No....	9
753	Head	M..	32	Sicily	Yes..	Yes...	No....	No....	Yes...	3
	Wife..........	F.	28	Sicily	No....	No....	No....	No....	No....	3
754	Head	M..	30	Calabria	No....	No....	No....	No....	Yes...	5
	Wife..........	F.	22	Calabria	No....	No....	No....	No....	No....	5
	Boarder.......	M..	19	Calabria	No....	No....	No....	No....	Yes...	5
755	Head	M..	29	Sicily	No....	No....	No....	No....	Yes...	6
	Wife..........	F.	22	Sicily	No....	No....	No....	No....	No....	1
	Brother-in-law	M..	26	Sicily	Yes..	Yes...	No....	No....	Yes...	6

TABLE **II.**—GENERAL CONDITION AS TO LITERACY AND ILLITERACY, BY FAMILIES AND INDIVIDUALS—Continued.

[This table includes only persons 10 years of age or over.]

Family number.	Relationship to head of family.	Sex.	Age.	Birthplace.	Native language. Reads.	Writes.	English language. Reads.	Writes.	Speaks.	Years in the United States.
756	Head	M.	45	Calabria	Yes..	Yes...	No...	No....	Yes...	10
	Wife	F.	37	Calabria	No...	No....	No...	No....	No....	4
	Lodger	M.	30	Calabria	Yes..	No....	No...	No....	Yes...	10
	Lodger	M.	44	Calabria	No...	No....	No...	No....	Yes...	10
	Lodger	M.	28	Calabria	No...	No....	No...	No....	Yes...	4
	Lodger	M.	43	Calabria	No...	No....	No...	No....	No....	4
757	Head	M.	39	Sicily	No...	No....	No...	No....	Yes...	10
	Wife	F.	34	Sicily	No...	No....	No...	No....	No....	7
	Son	M.	16	Sicily	No...	No....	No...	No....	Yes...	7
	Daughter	F.	14	Sicily	No...	No....	Yes..	Yes..	Yes...	7
758	Head	M.	36	Sicily	No...	No....	No...	No....	Yes...	9
	Wife	F.	36	Sicily	No...	No....	No...	No....	No....	3
	Son	M.	12	Sicily	Yes..	Yes...	Yes..	Yes..	Yes...	3
	Brother-in-law	M.	30	Sicily	Yes..	Yes...	No...	No....	Yes...	4
759	Head	M.	37	Campania	No...	No....	No...	No....	Yes...	12
	Wife	F.	26	Campania	No...	No....	No...	No....	No....	6
760	Head	M.	42	Basilicata	No...	No....	No...	No....	Yes...	18
	Wife	F.	37	Basilicata	No...	No....	No...	No....	No....	18
761	Head	M.	35	Sicily	Yes..	Yes...	No...	No....	Yes...	10
	Wife	F.	32	Sicily	No...	No....	No...	No....	No....	5
762	Head	M.	37	Sicily	Yes..	Yes...	No...	No....	No....	8
	Wife	F.	36	Sicily	No...	No....	No...	No....	No....	6
763	Head	M.	50	Calabria	No...	No....	No...	No....	No....	10
	Wife	F.	50	Calabria	No...	No....	No...	No....	No....	10
	Son	M.	18	Calabria	Yes..	Yes...	Yes..	Yes..	Yes...	10
	Lodger	M.	28	Calabria	No...	No....	No...	No....	No....	4
764	Cooperative...	M.	29	Sicily	No...	No....	No...	No....	Yes...	6
	Cooperative...	M.	20	Sicily	No...	No....	No...	No....	Yes...	3
	Cooperative...	M.	48	Sicily	Yes..	Yes...	No...	No....	No....	3
765	Head	M.	44	Sicily	Yes..	Yes...	No...	No....	Yes...	6
	Wife	F.	38	Sicily	No...	No....	No...	No....	No....	1
	Son	M.	14	Sicily	No...	No....	No...	No....	Yes..	6
766	Head	M.	38	Sicily	No...	No....	No...	No....	No....	7
	Wife	F.	36	Sicily	No...	No....	No...	No....	No....	7
	Son	M.	13	Sicily	Yes..	Yes...	Yes..	Yes..	Yes...	7
	Daughter	F.	11	Sicily	No...	No....	Yes..	Yes..	Yes..	7
767	Head	F.	44	Liguria	No...	No....	No...	No....	Yes...	16
	Daughter	F.	12	United States	Yes..	Yes...	Yes..	Yes..	Yes...	....
	Daughter	F.	10	United States	Yes..	Yes...	Yes..	Yes..	Yes...	....
768	Head	M.	40	Campania	Yes..	Yes...	No...	No....	Yes...	8
	Wife	F.	22	Campania	No...	No....	No...	No....	No....	9
	Brother	M.	25	Campania	No...	No....	No...	No....	Yes...	7
769	Head	M.	40	Basilicata	No...	No....	Yes..	No....	Yes...	28
	Wife	F.	32	Basilicata	No...	No....	No...	No....	No....	16
	Daughter	F.	15	United States	Yes..	Yes...	Yes..	Yes..	Yes...	....
	Daughter	F.	14	United States	Yes..	Yes...	Yes..	Yes..	Yes...	....
770	Head	M.	38	Basilicata	No...	No....	No...	No....	Yes...	27
	Wife	F.	38	Basilicata	No...	No....	No...	No....	Yes...	22
	Sister-in-law	F.	47	Basilicata	No...	No....	No...	No....	No....	2/12
771	Head	M.	36	Basilicata	No...	No....	No...	No....	Yes...	15
	Wife	F.	34	Basilicata	No...	No....	No...	No....	Yes...	15
	Daughter	F.	14	United States	Yes..	Yes...	Yes..	Yes..	Yes...	....
	Daughter	F.	11	United States	Yes..	Yes...	Yes..	Yes..	Yes...	....
	Mother-in-law	F.	55	Basilicata	No...	No....	No...	No....	No....	15
772	Head	M.	31	Basilicata	No...	No....	No...	No....	Yes...	8
	Wife	F.	28	Basilicata	No...	No....	No...	No....	No....	6
	Brother	M.	20	Basilicata	No...	No....	No...	No....	Yes...	7
	Cousin	M.	25	Basilicata	No...	No....	No...	No....	No....	6
773	Head	M.	60	Basilicata	No...	No....	No...	No....	Yes...	24
	Wife	F.	60	Basilicata	No...	No....	No...	No....	No....	23

TABLE **II.**—GENERAL CONDITION AS TO LITERACY AND ILLITERACY, BY FAMILIES AND INDIVIDUALS—Continued.

[This table includes only persons 10 years of age or over.]

Family number.	Relationship to head of family.	Sex.	Age.	Birthplace.	Native language.		English language.			Years in the United States.
					Reads.	Writes.	Reads.	Writes.	Speaks.	
774	Head	M.	35	Basilicata	Yes	Yes	No	No	Yes	11
	Wife	F.	30	Basilicata	No	No	No	No	No	11
775	Head	M.	24	Basilicata	Yes	Yes	Yes	Yes	Yes	9
	Wife	F.	16	United States	Yes	Yes	Yes	Yes	Yes	
776	Head	M.	33	Liguria	No	No	No	No	Yes	12
	Wife	F.	33	Basilicata	No	No	No	No	Yes	12
	Father-in-law	M.	75	Basilicata	Yes	Yes	No	No	Yes	25
	Mother-in-law	F.	67	Basilicata	No	No	No	No	No	10
777	Head	M.	31	Basilicata	Yes	Yes	Yes	Yes	Yes	19
	Wife	F.	25	Basilicata	No	No	No	No	Yes	20
778	Head	M.	42	Basilicata	No	No	No	No	Yes	15
	Wife	F.	37	Basilicata	No	No	No	No	Yes	12
779	Head	M.	30	Basilicata	No	No	No	No	No	2
	Wife	F.	27	Basilicata	No	No	No	No	No	$\frac{4}{12}$
780	Head	M.	45	Campania	No	No	No	No	No	4
	Wife	F.	40	Campania	No	No	No	No	No	4
	Son	M.	17	Campania	Yes	Yes	No	No	Yes	4
	Son	M.	14	Campania	Yes	Yes	Yes	Yes	Yes	4
	Daughter	F.	12	Campania	No	No	Yes	Yes	Yes	4
781	Head	M.	26	Basilicata	Yes	No	No	No	Yes	2
	Wife	F.	24	Basilicata	No	No	No	No	No	$\frac{4}{12}$
782	Head	M.	25	Basilicata	No	No	No	No	Yes	14
	Wife	F.	23	Basilicata	No	No	No	No	Yes	9
	Father	M.	57	Basilicata	No	No	No	No	No	14
	Mother	F.	59	Basilicata	No	No	No	No	No	14
783	Head	M.	35	Campania	No	No	No	No	No	9
	Wife	F.	31	Campania	No	No	No	No	No	9
784	Head	M.	40	Basilicata	Yes	Yes	No	No	Yes	10
	Wife	F.	37	Basilicata	No	No	No	No	No	9
	Nephew	M.	17	Basilicata	No	No	Yes	Yes	Yes	8
785	Head	M.	37	Basilicata	No	No	No	No	No	6
	Wife	F.	35	Basilicata	No	No	No	No	Yes	3
	Daughter	F.	15	Basilicata	No	No	No	No	No	3
	Brother-in-law	M.	27	Basilicata	Yes	Yes	No	No	Yes	4
	Sister-in-law	F.	25	Basilicata	No	No	No	No	No	4
786	Head	M.	40	Basilicata	Yes	Yes	No	No	Yes	9
	Wife	F.	35	Basilicata	No	No	No	No	No	6
	Son	M.	10	Basilicata	No	No	Yes	Yes	Yes	6
787	Head	M.	25	Basilicata	No	No	No	No	Yes	7
	Wife	F.	19	Basilicata	No	No	No	No	No	4
788	Head	M.	30	Basilicata	No	No	No	No	Yes	9
	Wife	F.	33	Basilicata	No	No	No	No	No	7
	Stepson	M.	15	Basilicata	No	No	No	No	Yes	7
	Stepdaughter	F.	12	Basilicata	No	No	No	No	Yes	7
	Mother	F.	60	Basilicata	No	No	No	No	No	7
789	Head	M.	30	Basilicata	No	No	No	No	Yes	9
	Wife	F.	21	Basilicata	Yes	Yes	No	No	No	5
790	Head	M.	30	Basilicata	No	No	No	No	Yes	12
	Wife	F.	30	Basilicata	No	No	No	No	No	8
	Daughter	F.	14	Basilicata	No	No	No	No	Yes	8
791	Head	M.	78	Basilicata	No	No	No	No	No	14
	Wife	F.	58	Basilicata	No	No	No	No	No	9
792	Head	M.	33	Basilicata	Yes	Yes	No	No	Yes	15
	Wife	F.	23	Basilicata	Yes	Yes	No	No	Yes	9
793	Head	F.	42	Basilicata	No	No	No	No	No	9
	Son	M.	14	Basilicata	No	No	No	No	Yes	9
	Son	M.	10	Basilicata	No	No	Yes	Yes	Yes	9

TABLE **II.**—GENERAL CONDITION AS TO LITERACY AND ILLITERACY, BY FAMILIES AND INDIVIDUALS—Continued.

[This table includes only persons 10 years of age or over.]

Family number.	Relationship to head of family.	Sex.	Age.	Birthplace.	Native language. Reads.	Writes.	English language. Reads.	Writes.	Speaks.	Years in the United States.
794	Head	M.	42	Calabria	No	No	No	No	Yes	14
	Wife	F.	47	Calabria	No	No	No	No	No	13
	Daughter	F.	12	United States	Yes	Yes	Yes	Yes	Yes	
	Son	M.	10	United States	Yes	Yes	Yes	Yes	Yes	
795	Head	M.	52	Basilicata	No	No	No	No	No	20
	Wife	F.	41	Basilicata	No	No	No	No	Yes	5
	Son	M.	25	Basilicata	Yes	Yes	Yes	Yes	Yes	16
	Son	M.	24	Basilicata	Yes	Yes	Yes	Yes	Yes	10
	Nephew	M.	20	Basilicata	Yes	Yes	No	No	Yes	5
796	Head	M.	50	Basilicata	Yes	Yes	No	No	No	4
	Wife	F.	49	Basilicata	Yes	Yes	No	No	No	4
	Daughter	F.	17	Basilicata	Yes	Yes	No	No	Yes	4
	Son	M.	15	Basilicata	Yes	Yes	No	No	Yes	4
	Daughter	F.	14	Basilicata	No	No	Yes	Yes	Yes	4
	Son	M.	10	Basilicata	Yes	Yes	No	No	Yes	4
797	Head	M.	41	Basilicata	No	No	No	No	Yes	16
	Wife	F.	60	Basilicata	No	No	No	No	No	9
798	Head	M.	35	Basilicata	No	No	No	No	No	11
	Wife	F.	34	Basilicata	No	No	No	No	Yes	11
	Daughter	F.	10	United States	Yes	Yes	Yes	Yes	Yes	
	Father	M.	70	Basilicata	No	No	No	No	No	13
	Mother-in-law	F.	63	Basilicata	No	No	No	No	No	9
799	Head	M.	50	Basilicata	No	No	No	No	Yes	11
	Wife	F.	33	Basilicata	No	No	No	No	Yes	11
	Daughter	F.	11	United States	Yes	Yes	Yes	Yes	Yes	
800	Head	M.	40	Campania	Yes	Yes	No	No	Yes	13
801	Head	M.	28	Calabria	No	No	No	No	No	3
802	Head	M.	40	Campania	No	No	No	No	No	9
	Wife	F.	40	Campania	No	No	No	No	No	8
803	Head	M.	45	Campania	No	No	No	No	No	3
	Wife	F.	40	Campania	No	No	No	No	No	2
804	Head	M.	35	Campania	Yes	Yes	No	No	No	3
	Wife	F.	27	Campania	No	No	No	No	No	3
	Daughter	F.	11	Campania	No	No	Yes	Yes	Yes	3
	Son	M.	10	Campania	No	No	No	No	Yes	3
805	Head	M.	55	Campania	No	No	No	No	Yes	9
	Wife	F.	50	Campania	No	No	No	No	No	$\frac{4}{12}$
	Son	M.	10	Campania	Yes	Yes	No	No	No	$\frac{4}{12}$
806	Head	M.	37	Campania	No	No	No	No	Yes	17
	Wife	F.	40	Campania	Yes	Yes	Yes	Yes	Yes	17
	Son	M.	14	United States	Yes	Yes	Yes	Yes	Yes	
	Son	M.	13	United States	Yes	Yes	Yes	Yes	Yes	
	Daughter	F.	11	United States	Yes	Yes	Yes	Yes	Yes	
807	Cooperative	M.	21	Sicily	Yes	Yes	No	No	Yes	4
	Cooperative	M.	40	Sicily	No	No	No	No	Yes	4
	Cooperative	M.	30	Sicily	Yes	Yes	No	No	Yes	5
	Cooperative	M.	45	Sicily	No	No	No	No	No	2
	Cooperative	M.	33	Sicily	No	No	No	No	No	4
	Cooperative	M.	44	Sicily	No	No	No	No	No	3
	Cooperative	M.	38	Sicily	Yes	Yes	No	No	Yes	8
	Cooperative	M.	39	Sicily	Yes	Yes	No	No	No	3
	Cooperative	M.	33	Sicily	No	No	No	No	Yes	3
	Cooperative	M.	29	Sicily	Yes	Yes	No	No	Yes	2
808	Head	M.	32	Calabria	No	No	No	No	No	4
	Wife	F.	30	Calabria	No	No	No	No	No	$\frac{4}{12}$
	Brother-in-law	M.	22	Calabria	Yes	Yes	No	No	No	$\frac{4}{12}$
	Lodger	M.	20	Calabria	No	No	No	No	No	4
	Lodger	M.	22	Calabria	No	No	No	No	No	$\frac{10}{12}$
	Lodger	M.	43	Calabria	No	No	No	No	No	3
	Lodger	M.	25	Calabria	No	No	No	No	Yes	4
	Lodger	M.	32	Calabria	No	No	No	No	No	4
	Lodger	M.	31	Calabria	No	No	No	No	No	4
	Lodger	M.	25	Calabria	Yes	Yes	No	No	No	4

TABLE **II.**—GENERAL CONDITION AS TO LITERACY AND ILLITERACY, BY
FAMILIES AND INDIVIDUALS—Continued.

[This table includes only persons 10 years of age or over.]

Family number.	Relationship to head of family.	Sex.	Age.	Birthplace.	Native language.		English language.			Years in the United States.
					Reads.	Writes.	Reads.	Writes.	Speaks.	
809	Cooperative ..	M.	32	Calabria	No...	No....	No...	No....	Yes...	2
	Cooperative ..	M.	30	Calabria	No...	No....	No...	No....	No....	2
	Cooperative ..	M.	28	Calabria	No...	No....	No...	No....	No....	2
810	Head	M.	25	Calabria	No...	No....	No...	No....	Yes...	8
	Wife..........	F.	17	Calabria	No...	No....	No...	No....	No....	5
	Brother-in-law	M.	25	Calabria	No...	No....	No...	No....	Yes...	8
	Cousin........	M.	30	Calabria	No...	No....	No...	No....	No....	7
	Cousin........	M.	27	Calabria	No...	No....	No...	No....	No....	2
	Cousin........	M.	27	Calabria	No...	No....	No...	No....	No....	$\frac{1}{12}$
	Cousin........	M.	22	Calabria	Yes..	Yes...	No...	No....	Yes...	6
	Cousin........	M.	28	Calabria	No...	No....	No...	No....	Yes...	7
	Cousin........	M.	19	Calabria	No...	No....	No...	No....	Yes...	6
811	Head	M.	30	Calabria............	No...	No....	No...	No....	Yes...	10
	Wife..........	F.	27	Calabria............	Yes..	Yes...	No...	No....	Yes...	8
812	Head	M.	44	Basilicata	Yes..	Yes...	Yes..	Yes...	Yes...	30
	Wife..........	F.	30	Basilicata	No...	No....	No...	No....	No....	10
813	Head	F.	44	Calabria	No...	No....	No...	No....	No....	4
	Son	M.	23	Calabria	No...	No....	No...	No....	Yes...	8
	Son	M.	20	Calabria	No...	No....	No...	No....	Yes..:	8
	Daughter	F.	14	Calabria	Yes..	Yes...	No...	No....	Yes...	4
814	Head	M.	38	Calabria	No...	No....	No...	No....	Yes...	10
815	Head	M.	50	Calabria	No...	No....	No...	No....	Yes...	16
	Wife..........	F.	45	Calabria	No...	No....	No...	No....	No....	9
	Son	M.	17	Calabria	Yes..	Yes...	Yes..	Yes...	Yes...	9
	Son	M.	15	Calabria	No...	No....	No...	No....	Yes...	9
	Niece	F.	17	Calabria	No...	No....	No...	No....	No....	$\frac{4}{12}$
816	Head	M.	35	Calabria	No...	No....	No...	No....	Yes...	9
	Wife..........	F.	23	Calabria	No...	No....	No...	No....	No....	2
	Father-in-law.	M.	64	Calabria	No...	No....	No...	No....	No....	5
	Mother-in-law	F.	50	Calabria	No...	No....	No...	No....	No....	2
	Lodger	M.	38	Calabria	Yes..	Yes...	No...	No....	Yes...	9
	Lodger	M.	45	Calabria	No...	No....	No...	No....	No....	3
817	Head	F.	39	Sicily	Yes..	Yes...	No...	No....	Yes...	10
	Son	M.	21	Sicily	Yes..	Yes...	Yes..	Yes...	Yes...	10
	Son	M.	17	Sicily	No...	No....	Yes..	Yes...	Yes...	10
	Son	M.	13	Sicily	No...	No....	Yes..	Yes...	Yes...	10
	Lodger	M.	32	Sicily	No...	No....	No...	No....	No....	4
	Lodger	M.	27	Sicily	No...	No....	No...	No....	No....	4
	Lodger	M.	23	Sicily	Yes..	Yes...	No..	No....	No....	3
	Lodger	M.	21	Sicily	No...	No....	No...	No....	Yes...	3
	Lodger	M.	25	Sicily	No...	No....	No...	No....	No....	5
818	Head	M.	35	Sicily	No...	No....	No...	No....	Yes...	2
	Wife..........	F.	30	Sicily	No...	No....	No...	No....	No....	2
	Daughter	F.	12	Sicily	Yes..	Yes...	Yes..	Yes...	Yes...	2
	Son	M.	10	Sicily	No...	No....	No...	No....	Yes...	2
819	Head	M.	65	Basilicata..........	Yes..	Yes...	No...	No....	No....	20
	Wife..........	F.	71	Basilicata..........	No...	No....	No...	No....	No....	20
	Sister-in-law..	F.	74	Basilicata..........	No...	No....	No...	No....	No....	15
820	Head	M.	26	Campania..........	No...	No....	No...	No....	Yes...	5
	Wife..........	F.	25	Campania..........	No...	No....	No...	No....	No....	5
821	Head	M.	49	Sicily	No...	No....	No...	No....	Yes...	8
822	Head	M.	39	Campania..........	No...	No....	No...	No....	Yes...	9
	Wife..........	F.	28	Campania..........	Yes..	Yes...	No...	No....	No....	3
	Brother-in-law	M.	27	Campania..........	No...	No....	No...	No....	No....	3
	Nephew	M.	19	Campania..........	No...	No....	No...	No....	No....	$\frac{1}{12}$
	Nephew	M.	17	Campania..........	No...	No....	No...	No....	Yes...	$\frac{6}{}$
823	Head	M.	45	Calabria	No...	No....	No...	No....	No....	10
	Wife..........	F.	38	Calabria	No...	No....	No...	No....	No....	4
	Son	M.	19	Calabria	Yes..	Yes...	No...	No....	Yes...	4
	Son	M.	10	Calabria	No...	No....	Yes..	Yes...	Yes...	4

TABLE **II.**—GENERAL CONDITION AS TO LITERACY AND ILLITERACY, BY FAMILIES AND INDIVIDUALS—Continued.

[This table includes only persons 10 years of age or over.]

Family number.	Relationship to head of family.	Sex.	Age.	Birthplace.	Native language. Reads.	Writes.	English language. Reads.	Writes.	Speaks.	Years in the United States.
824	Head	M.	40	Sicily	No...	No...	No...	No...	Yes...	8
	Wife	F.	30	Sicily	No...	No...	No...	No...	No...	5
	Son	M.	10	Sicily	Yes..	Yes..	Yes..	Yes...	Yes...	5
825	Head	M.	34	Sicily	No...	No...	No...	No...	Yes...	9
	Wife	F.	20	Sicily	No...	No...	No...	No...	No...	2
	Brother	M.	24	Sicily	Yes..	Yes..	No...	No...	No...	1½
	Lodger	M.	25	Sicily	No...	No...	No...	No...	Yes...	4
826	Head	M.	33	Sicily	Yes..	Yes..	No...	No...	Yes...	8
	Wife	F.	31	Sicily	No...	No...	No...	No...	No...	5
827	Head	M.	44	Sicily	No...	No...	No...	No...	Yes...	8
828	Head	M.	30	Sicily	No...	No...	No...	No...	Yes...	10
	Wife	F.	29	Sicily	No...	No...	No...	No...	No...	6
	Cousin	M.	26	Sicily	No...	No...	No...	No...	No...	2
829	Head	M.	30	Sicily	No...	No...	No...	No...	Yes...	4
	Wife	F.	25	Sicily	No...	No...	No...	No...	No...	3
830	Head	M.	37	Sicily	No...	No...	No...	No...	Yes...	8
	Wife	F.	34	Sicily	No...	No...	No...	No...	No...	2
	Son	M.	15	Sicily	No...	No...	No...	No...	Yes...	2
	Son	M.	13	Sicily	No...	No...	No...	No...	Yes...	2
	Daughter	F.	11	Sicily	No...	No...	No...	No...	Yes...	2
	Daughter	F.	10	Sicily	No...	No...	No...	No...	No...	2
831	Head	M.	26	Calabria	No...	No...	No...	No...	No...	10
	Wife	F.	27	Calabria	No...	No...	No...	No...	No...	4
832	Head	M.	44	Calabria	No...	No...	No...	No...	Yes...	14
	Wife	F.	40	Calabria	No...	No...	No...	No...	Yes...	8
	Son	M.	18	Calabria	No...	No...	No...	No...	Yes...	8
	Daughter	F.	15	Calabria	No...	No...	No...	No...	Yes...	8
833	Head	M.	28	Basilicata	No...	No...	No...	No...	Yes...	10
	Wife	F.	27	Basilicata	No...	No...	No...	No...	No...	5
834	Head	M.	25	Basilicata	Yes..	Yes...	Yes..	No...	Yes...	7
	Wife	F.	17	Basilicata	No...	No...	No...	No...	Yes...	10
835	Head	M.	42	Basilicata	No...	No...	No...	No...	Yes...	15
	Wife	F.	41	Basilicata	No...	No...	No...	No...	Yes...	14
	Son	M.	14	Basilicata	No...	No...	Yes..	Yes..	Yes...	14
836	Head	M.	30	Basilicata	No...	No...	No...	No...	Yes...	10
	Wife	F.	30	Basilicata	No...	No...	No...	No...	No...	7
837	Head	M.	38	Basilicata	Yes..	Yes...	No...	No...	Yes...	11
	Wife	F.	33	Basilicata	Yes..	Yes...	No...	No...	Yes...	11
	Brother	M.	39	Basilicata	Yes..	Yes...	No...	No...	Yes...	9
	Cousin	M.	24	Basilicata	No...	No...	No...	No...	Yes...	3
838	Head	M.	25	Tuscany	Yes..	Yes...	No...	No...	Yes...	5
	Wife	F.	25	Tuscany	No...	No...	No...	No...	No...	3
	Lodger	M.	25	Tuscany	Yes..	Yes...	No...	No...	Yes...	6
	Lodger	M.	29	Tuscany	Yes..	Yes...	No...	No...	No...	1½
839	Head	M.	44	Basilicata	No...	No...	No...	No...	Yes...	9
	Wife	F.	44	Basilicata	No...	No...	No...	No...	Yes...	7
	Son	M.	20	Basilicata	No...	No...	No...	No...	Yes...	7
	Son	M.	18	Basilicata	No...	No...	No...	No...	Yes...	7
	Daughter	F.	12	Basilicata	No...	No...	No...	No...	Yes...	7
840	Head	M.	24	Basilicata	Yes..	Yes...	Yes..	Yes...	Yes...	15
	Wife	F.	18	Basilicata	No...	No...	No...	No...	Yes...	4
841	Head	M.	48	Basilicata	No...	No...	No...	No...	No...	14
	Wife	F.	40	Basilicata	No...	No...	No...	No...	No...	14
	Son	M.	12	United States	No...	No...	No...	No...	Yes...	
	Son	M.	10	United States	No...	No...	No...	No...	Yes...	
842	Head	M.	40	Basilicata	No...	No...	No...	No...	No...	9
	Wife	F.	43	Basilicata	No...	No...	No...	No...	No...	5
	Son	M.	12	Basilicata	No...	No...	Yes..	Yes..	Yes...	5

TABLE **II.**—GENERAL CONDITION AS TO LITERACY AND ILLITERACY, BY
FAMILIES AND INDIVIDUALS—Continued.

[This table includes only persons 10 years of age or over.]

Family number.	Relationship to head of family.	Sex.	Age.	Birthplace.	Native language.		English language.			Years in the United States.
					Reads.	Writes.	Reads.	Writes.	Speaks.	
843	Head	M.	30	Basilicata	No	No	No	No	Yes	8
	Wife	F.	29	Basilicata	No	No	No	No	Yes	7
844	Head	F.	45	Basilicata	No	No	No	No	No	11
845	Head	F.	41	Basilicata	No	No	No	No	No	8
	Son	M.	16	Basilicata	No	No	Yes	Yes	Yes	8
	Daughter	F.	14	Basilicata	No	No	No	No	Yes	8
846	Head	M.	38	Campania	No	No	No	No	Yes	16
	Wife	F.	40	Basilicata	No	No	No	No	No	16
	Stepson	M.	19	Basilicata	No	No	Yes	Yes	Yes	16
	Stepson	M.	14	United States	Yes	Yes	Yes	Yes	Yes	
	Stepson	M.	11	United States	Yes	Yes	Yes	Yes	Yes	
	Son	M.	10	United States	Yes	Yes	Yes	Yes	Yes	
847	Head	M.	35	Campania	No	No	No	No	Yes	6
	Wife	F.	29	Campania	No	No	No	No	Yes	5
	Son	M.	10	Campania	No	No	Yes	Yes	Yes	5
	Brother-in-law	M.	27	Campania	Yes	Yes	No	No	Yes	6
	Boarder	M.	40	Abruzzo	Yes	Yes	No	No	Yes	7
	Boarder	M.	32	Abruzzo	Yes	Yes	No	No	Yes	5
848	Head	M.	50	Basilicata	No	No	No	No	No	10
	Wife	F.	42	Basilicata	No	No	No	No	No	5
	Daughter	F.	12	Basilicata	No	No	Yes	Yes	Yes	(a)
849	Head	M.	38	Basilicata	No	No	No	No	No	6
	Wife	F.	30	Basilicata	No	No	No	No	No	5
850	Head	M.	34	Campania	No	No	No	No	No	5
	Wife	F.	24	Basilicata	No	No	No	No	No	5
851	Head	M.	37	Tuscany	Yes	Yes	No	No	Yes	10
	Wife	F.	34	Tuscany	Yes	Yes	No	No	Yes	6
852	Head	M.	36	Basilicata	No	No	No	No	Yes	14
	Wife	F.	34	Basilicata	No	No	No	No	Yes	7
853	Head	M.	25	Calabria	Yes	Yes	Yes	Yes	Yes	9
	Wife	F.	20	Abruzzo	No	No	No	No	Yes	9
	Father	M.	47	Calabria	No	No	No	No	Yes	9
854	Head	M.	25	Abruzzo	Yes	Yes	Yes	Yes	Yes	5
	Wife	F.	25	Abruzzo	Yes	Yes	No	No	Yes	5
855	Head	M.	30	Abruzzo	No	No	No	No	Yes	5
	Wife	F.	25	Abruzzo	No	No	No	No	No	5
856	Head	M.	35	Sicily	Yes	Yes	No	No	Yes	11
	Wife	F.	20	Sicily	No	No	No	No	No	5
857	Head	M.	40	Basilicata	No	No	No	No	Yes	15
	Wife	F.	40	Basilicata	No	No	No	No	No	9
	Son	M.	15	Basilicata	No	No	Yes	Yes	Yes	9
858	Head	M.	45	Abruzzo	No	No	No	No	Yes	9
	Wife	F.	49	Abruzzo	No	No	No	No	No	9
	Son	M.	16	France	Yes	Yes	No	No	Yes	9
	Son	M.	11	France	No	No	Yes	Yes	Yes	9
859	Head	F.	47	Basilicata	No	No	No	No	No	5
	Daughter	F.	14	Basilicata	No	No	No	No	Yes	5
860	Head	M.	44	Basilicata	No	No	No	No	Yes	21
	Wife	F.	47	Basilicata	No	No	No	No	No	17
	Son	M.	17	Basilicata	Yes	Yes	Yes	Yes	Yes	17
	Daughter	F.	15	United States	No	No	No	No	Yes	
	Daughter	F.	14	United States	Yes	Yes	Yes	Yes	Yes	
	Daughter	F.	10	United States	Yes	Yes	Yes	Yes	Yes	
861	Head	M.	52	Basilicata	No	No	No	No	No	11
	Wife	F.	64	Basilicata	No	No	No	No	No	8
	Son	M.	25	Basilicata	Yes	Yes	No	No	Yes	11

a Not reported.

TABLE **II.**—GENERAL CONDITION AS TO LITERACY AND ILLITERACY, BY FAMILIES AND INDIVIDUALS—Continued.

[This table includes only persons 10 years of age or over.]

Family number.	Relationship to head of family.	Sex.	Age.	Birthplace.	Native language. Reads.	Writes.	English language. Reads.	Writes.	Speaks.	Years in the United States.
862	Head	F.	57	Basilicata	No	No	No	No	No	4
	Son	M.	24	Basilicata	Yes	Yes	Yes	Yes	Yes	8
	Daughter-in-law.	F.	27	Basilicata	No	No	No	No	No	5
863	Head	M.	54	Basilicata	Yes	Yes	No	No	Yes	17
	Wife	F.	37	Sicily	No	No	No	No	Yes	17
	Daughter	F.	17	Sicily	No	No	Yes	Yes	Yes	17
	Daughter	F.	15	United States	Yes	Yes	Yes	Yes	Yes	
	Daughter	F.	12	United States	Yes	Yes	Yes	Yes	Yes	
864	Head	M.	65	Basilicata	No	No	No	No	Yes	24
	Wife	F.	66	Basilicata	No	No	No	No	No	17
	Nephew	M.	20	Basilicata	Yes	Yes	No	No	Yes	3
865	Head	M.	34	Basilicata	Yes	Yes	Yes	Yes	Yes	14
	Wife	F.	28	Basilicata	Yes	Yes	No	No	Yes	9
	Mother	F.	80	Basilicata	Yes	No	No	No	No	(a)
866	Head	M.	40	Basilicata	No	No	No	No	Yes	10
	Wife	F.	43	Basilicata	No	No	No	No	No	3
	Stepson	M.	20	Basilicata	No	No	No	No	Yes	5
867	Head	M.	80	Basilicata	No	No	No	No	No	5
	Wife	F.	48	Basilicata	No	No	No	No	No	5
	Son	M.	24	Basilicata	Yes	Yes	Yes	Yes	Yes	10
	Son	M.	15	Basilicata	No	No	No	No	Yes	5
	Daughter-in-law.	F.	19	Basilicata	No	No	No	No	No	3
868	Head	M.	29	Sicily	No	No	No	No	Yes	7
	Wife	F.	19	Sicily	No	No	No	No	Yes	7
869	Head	M.	32	Sicily	Yes	Yes	No	No	Yes	2
	Wife	F.	28	Sicily	No	No	No	No	No	1/12
870	Head	M.	27	Sicily	No	No	No	No	No	5
	Wife	F.	27	Sicily	No	No	No	No	No	5
871	Head	M.	48	Apulia	No	No	No	No	Yes	10
	Wife	F.	50	Apulia	No	No	No	No	No	10
	Boarder	M.	21	Basilicata	No	No	Yes	Yes	Yes	11
	Lodger	M.	27	Basilicata	Yes	Yes	Yes	Yes	Yes	17
	Lodger	F.	18	Basilicata	No	No	No	No	Yes	5
872	Head	F.	27	Basilicata	No	No	No	No	Yes	20
	Daughter	F.	11	United States	Yes	Yes	Yes	Yes	Yes	
873	Head	M.	24	Basilicata	Yes	Yes	No	No	Yes	9
	Wife	F.	23	Basilicata	Yes	Yes	No	No	No	1/12
874	Head	M.	60	Basilicata	No	No	No	No	No	2
	Wife	F.	45	Basilicata	Yes	No	No	No	No	2
	Son	M.	21	Basilicata	Yes	Yes	No	No	No	2
	Daughter	F.	13	France	Yes	Yes	No	No	No	2
	Daughter	F.	11	Basilicata	Yes	No	No	No	No	2
	Daughter-in-law.	F.	21	Basilicata	Yes	Yes	No	No	No	4
875	Head	F.	29	Basilicata	No	No	No	No	No	4
876	Head	M.	48	Basilicata	Yes	Yes	No	No	Yes	15
	Wife	F.	44	Basilicata	No	No	No	No	Yes	14
	Daughter	F.	14	United States	Yes	Yes	Yes	Yes	Yes	
	Son	M.	12	United States	Yes	Yes	Yes	Yes	Yes	
	Daughter	F.	10	United States	Yes	Yes	Yes	Yes	Yes	
877	Head	M.	26	Basilicata	Yes	Yes	No	No	Yes	3
	Wife	F.	16	Basilicata	No	No	No	No	Yes	3
878	Head	M.	35	Calabria	No	No	No	No	Yes	15
	Wife	F.	24	Basilicata	No	No	No	No	Yes	12
	Mother-in-law	F.	52	Basilicata	No	No	No	No	No	12
	Sister-in-law	F.	12	United States	Yes	Yes	Yes	Yes	Yes	

a Not reported.

TABLE **II.**—GENERAL CONDITION AS TO LITERACY AND ILLITERACY, BY FAMILIES AND INDIVIDUALS—Continued.

[This table includes only persons 10 years of age or over.]

Family number.	Relationship to head of family.	Sex.	Age.	Birthplace.	Native language.		English language.			Years in the United States.
					Reads.	Writes.	Reads.	Writes.	Speaks.	
879	Head	M.	55	Tuscany	No...	No....	No...	No....	Yes...	17
	Wife	F.	53	Tuscany	No...	No....	No...	No....	Yes...	16
	Son	M.	23	Tuscany	No...	No....	No...	No....	Yes...	16
	Son	M.	19	Tuscany	No...	No....	Yes...	Yes...	Yes...	16
	Daughter	F.	16	Tuscany	No...	No....	Yes...	Yes...	Yes...	16
	Son	M.	12	United States	Yes..	Yes..	Yes..	Yes..	Yes...	....
880	Head	F.	39	Basilicata	No...	No....	No...	No....	Yes...	9
	Son	M.	17	Basilicata	Yes..	No....	Yes..	Yes...	Yes...	9
	Daughter	F.	14	Basilicata	No...	No....	Yes..	Yes..	Yes...	9
	Sister	F.	37	Basilicata	No...	No....	No...	No....	No....	6
881	Head	M.	27	Basilicata	No...	No....	No...	No....	Yes...	9
	Wife	F.	25	Basilicata	No...	No....	No...	No....	Yes...	9
882	Head	M.	32	Basilicata	Yes..	Yes...	No...	No....	Yes...	9
	Wife	F.	24	Basilicata	No...	No....	No...	No....	No....	5
883	Head	M.	47	Basilicata	No...	No....	No...	No....	No....	8
	Wife	F.	44	Basilicata	No...	No....	No...	No....	No....	3
	Daughter	F.	12	Basilicata	No...	No....	No...	No....	Yes...	3
	Brother	M.	40	Basilicata	No...	No....	No...	No....	Yes...	14
	Sister-in-law	F.	48	Basilicata	No...	No....	No...	No....	No....	9
884	Head	M.	40	Basilicata	Yes..	Yes..	No...	No....	No....	5
	Wife	F.	30	Basilicata	No...	No....	No...	No....	No....	3
885	Head	M.	40	Basilicata	No...	No....	No...	No....	No....	14
	Wife	F.	35	Basilicata	No...	No....	No...	No....	No....	7
	Daughter	F.	12	Basilicata	No...	No....	No...	No....	Yes...	7
886	Head	M.	48	Calabria	Yes..	Yes...	No...	No....	Yes...	7
	Wife	F.	30	Calabria	No...	No....	No...	No....	No....	5
887	Head	M.	21	Abruzzo	Yes..	Yes...	Yes...	Yes...	Yes...	4
	Wife	F.	17	Basilicata	No...	No....	No...	No....	Yes...	16
888	Head	M.	24	Sicily	Yes..	Yes...	No...	No....	Yes...	7
	Wife	F.	27	Sicily	No...	No....	No...	No....	No....	7
889	Head	M.	31	Tuscany	No...	No....	No...	No....	Yes...	10
	Wife	F.	24	Tuscany	Yes..	Yes...	No...	No....	Yes...	7
890	Head	M.	70	Basilicata	No...	No....	No...	No....	No....	14
	Wife	F.	56	Basilicata	No...	No....	No...	No....	No....	12
	Son	M.	26	Basilicata	No...	No....	Yes..	Yes...	Yes...	12
	Daughter	F.	14	Basilicata	No...	No....	Yes..	Yes...	Yes...	12
891	Head	M.	26	United States	Yes..	Yes...	Yes..	Yes...	Yes...	....
	Wife	F.	20	Basilicata	No...	No....	No...	No....	Yes...	12
892	Head	F.	54	Liguria	No...	No....	No...	No....	Yes...	27
	Son	M.	24	United States	Yes..	Yes...	Yes..	Yes...	Yes...	....
	Nephew	M.	31	Liguria	Yes..	Yes...	No...	No....	Yes...	5
893	Head	M.	48	Sicily	No...	No....	No...	No....	Yes...	7
	Wife	F.	47	Sicily	No...	No....	No...	No....	No....	6
	Daughter	F.	27	Basilicata	No...	No....	No...	No....	No....	6
894	Head	F.	53	Basilicata	No...	No....	No...	No....	No....	3
	Son	M.	18	Basilicata	No...	No....	No...	No....	No....	3
	Son	M.	16	Basilicata	No...	No....	No...	No....	No....	3
	Daughter	F.	14	Basilicata	No...	No....	No...	No....	Yes...	3
	Daughter	F.	10	Basilicata	No...	No....	Yes..	Yes...	Yes...	3
895	Head	M.	40	Basilicata	No...	No....	No...	No....	No....	8
	Wife	F.	29	Basilicata	No...	No....	No...	No....	No....	6
896	Head	M.	41	Sicily	Yes..	No....	No...	No....	Yes...	12
	Wife	F.	40	Sicily	No...	No....	No...	No....	No....	11
	Son	M.	15	Sicily	No...	No....	Yes..	Yes...	Yes...	11
	Daughter	F.	10	United States	Yes..	Yes...	Yes..	Yes...	Yes...	....
	Cousin	M.	23	Sicily	No...	No....	No...	No....	No....	2
897	Head	M.	35	Basilicata	Yes..	No....	No...	No....	Yes...	13
	Wife	F.	27	Basilicata	Yes..	No....	No...	No....	No....	8

TABLE **II.**—GENERAL CONDITION AS TO LITERACY AND ILLITERACY, BY
FAMILIES AND INDIVIDUALS—Continued.

[This table includes only persons 10 years of age or over.]

Family number.	Relationship to head of family.	Sex.	Age.	Birthplace	Native language.		English language.			Years in the United States.
					Reads.	Writes.	Reads.	Writes.	Speaks.	
897	Lodger	M.	34	Basilicata	Yes..	Yes...	No...	No....	Yes...	7
	Lodger	M.	40	Basilicata	No...	No....	No...	No....	No....	$\frac{1}{12}$
898	Head	M.	40	Sicily	No...	No....	No...	No....	Yes...	12
	Wife	F.	37	Sicily	No...	No....	No...	No....	No....	12
	Daughter	F.	11	United States	No...	No....	No...	No....	Yes...	....
899	Head	M.	28	Basilicata	Yes:.	Yes...	No...	No....	Yes...	6
	Wife	F.	25	Basilicata	No...	No....	No...	No....	No....	6
900	Head	M.	48	Sicily	No...	No....	No...	No....	Yes...	14
	Wife	F.	38	Sicily	No...	No....	No...	No....	Yes...	13
	Son	M.	18	Sicily	Yes..	Yes...	Yes..	No....	Yes...	13
	Son	M.	16	Sicily	No...	No....	Yes..	Yes...	Yes...	13
901	Cooperative	M.	24	Sicily	Yes..	Yes...	No...	No....	Yes...	5
	Cooperative	M.	27	Sicily	Yes..	Yes...	No...	No....	Yes...	4
	Cooperative	M.	36	Sicily	No...	No....	No...	No....	Yes...	6
	Cooperative	M.	21	Sicily	Yes..	Yes...	No...	No....	Yes...	$1\frac{8}{12}$
	Cooperative	M.	28	Sicily	Yes..	Yes...	No...	No....	Yes...	5
	Cooperative	M.	24	Sicily	Yes..	Yes...	Yes..	No....	Yes...	4
	Cooperative	M.	47	Sicily	No...	No....	No...	No....	Yes...	4
902	Head	M.	48	Sicily	No...	No....	No...	No....	Yes...	14
	Wife	F.	48	Sicily	No...	No....	No...	No....	No....	13
	Son	M.	18	Sicily	Yes..	Yes...	No...	No....	Yes...	13
	Son	M.	16	Sicily	Yes..	Yes...	No...	No....	Yes...	13
903	Head	M.	25	Calabria	Yes..	No....	No...	No....	Yes...	5
	Wife	F.	24	Calabria	No...	No....	No...	No....	No....	4
904	Head	M.	55	Tuscany	No...	No....	No...	No....	No....	9
	Wife	F.	47	Tuscany	No...	No....	No...	No....	No....	6
	Son	M.	20	Tuscany	Yes..	Yes...	No...	No....	Yes...	6
905	Head	M.	40	Liguria	Yes..	Yes...	No...	No....	Yes...	10
	Wife	F.	30	United States	Yes..	Yes...	Yes..	Yes...	Yes...	....
	Boarder	M.	33	Tuscany	Yes..	Yes...	Yes..	Yes...	Yes...	6
906	Head	M.	35	Tuscany	Yes..	Yes...	No...	No....	No....	6
	Wife	F.	38	Tuscany	Yes..	Yes...	No...	No....	No....	6
	Brother-in-law	M.	45	Tuscany	No...	No....	No...	No....	No....	3
907	Head	M.	38	Tuscany	Yes..	Yes...	No...	No....	Yes...	4
	Wife	F.	25	Tuscany	No...	No....	No...	No....	No....	2
908	Head	M.	36	Sicily	Yes..	Yes...	No...	No....	Yes...	5
	Wife	F.	34	Sicily	No...	No....	No...	No....	No....	4
	Lodger	M.	28	Sicily	Yes..	Yes...	Yes..	Yes...	Yes...	10
	Lodger	F.	24	Sicily	No...	No....	No...	No....	Yes...	(a)
909	Head	M.	40	Sicily	No...	No....	No...	No....	No....	9
	Wife	F.	33	Sicily	Yes..	No....	No...	No....	No....	9
910	Head	M.	23	Sicily	Yes..	Yes...	No...	No....	Yes...	7
	Wife	F.	18	Sicily	No...	No....	No...	No....	No....	5
	Father	M.	46	Sicily	No...	No....	No...	No....	No....	3
911	Head	M.	45	Sicily	No...	No....	No...	No....	No....	12
	Wife	F.	52	Sicily	No...	No....	No...	No....	No....	8
	Son	M.	27	Sicily	No...	No....	No...	No....	No....	1
	Son	M.	19	Sicily	No...	No....	No...	No....	Yes...	8
912	Head	M.	46	Lombardy	Yes..	Yes...	Yes..	Yes...	Yes...	17
	Wife	F.	36	Piedmont	Yes..	Yes...	Yes..	Yes...	Yes...	17
	Daughter	F.	16	United States	Yes..	Yes...	Yes..	Yes...	Yes...	....
913	Head	M.	50	Apulia	No...	No....	No...	No....	Yes...	15
	Wife	F.	37	Apulia	Reads.	No....	No...	No....	Yes...	9
	Daughter	F.	15	Apulia	No...	No....	Yes..	Yes...	Yes...	9
914	Head	M.	34	Basilicata	No...	No....	No...	No....	Yes...	9
	Wife	F.	26	Basilicata	No...	No....	No...	No....	Yes...	6

a Not reported.

TABLE **II.**—GENERAL CONDITION AS TO LITERACY AND ILLITERACY, BY
FAMILIES AND INDIVIDUALS—Continued.

[This table includes only persons 10 years of age or over.]

Family number.	Relationship to head of family.	Sex.	Age.	Birthplace.	Native language.		English language.			Years in the United States.
					Reads.	Writes.	Reads.	Writes.	Speaks.	
915	Head	M.	40	Basilicata..........	No...	No....	No...	No....	Yes...	8
	Wife...........	F.	37	Basilicata..........	No....	No....	No...	No....	No...	6
	Son	M.	10	Basilicata..........	No...	No...	Yes..	Yes..	Yes...	6
916	Head	M.	43	Tuscany	Yes..	Yes...	No...	No....	Yes...	7
	Wife...........	F.	34	France.............	No...	No...	No...	No....	No...	3
	Daughter.....	F.	12	France.............	No...	No...	Yes..	Yes..	Yes...	3
	Son	M.	11	France.............	No...	No...	Yes..	Yes..	Yes...	3
917	Head	M.	36	Tuscany	No...	No...	No...	No....	No....	6
	Wife...........	F.	45	France.............	No...	No...	No...	No....	No....	2
	Niece	F.	11	France.............	No...	No...	Yes..	Yes..	Yes...	7
	Boarder.......	M.	23	France.............	No...	No...	No...	No....	Yes...	3
918	Head	M.	34	Campania..........	No...	No...	No...	No....	No....	5
	Wife...........	F.	34	Campania..........	No...	No...	No...	No....	No....	4
	Son	M.	11	Campania..........	No...	No...	Yes..	Yes..	Yes...	4
919	Head	M.	33	Campania..........	No...	No...	No...	No....	Yes...	8
	Wife...........	F.	30	Campania..........	No...	No...	No...	No....	Yes...	8
	Daughter.....	F.	10	Campania..........	No...	No...	Yes..	Yes..	Yes...	8
920	Head	M.	22	Campania..........	No...	No...	No...	No....	Yes...	19
	Wife...........	F.	20	Campania..........	No...	No...	No...	No....	No....	2
	Father........	M.	53	Campania..........	No...	No...	No...	No....	Yes...	20
	Mother	F.	45	Campania..........	No...	No...	No...	No....	No....	19
921	Head	M.	30	Campania..........	No...	No...	No...	No....	No....	6
	Wife...........	F.	23	Campania..........	No...	No...	No...	No....	No....	2
	Boarder.......	M.	26	Campania..........	No...	No...	No...	No....	Yes...	4
922	Head	M.	45	Campania..........	No...	No....	No...	No....	No....	9
	Wife...........	F.	45	Campania..........	No...	No...	No...	No....	No....	8
	Son	M.	18	Campania..........	No...	No...	No...	No....	Yes...	8
	Son	M.	16	Campania..........	No...	No...	No...	No....	Yes...	8
	Daughter.....	F.	12	Campania..........	No...	No...	No...	No....	Yes...	8
	Son	M.	10	Campania..........	No...	No...	No...	No....	Yes...	8
923	Head	M.	47	Campania..........	No...	No...	No...	No....	No....	15
	Wife...........	F.	55	Campania..........	No...	No...	No...	No....	No....	7
924	Head	M.	58	Campania..........	No...	No....	No...	No....	No....	7
	Wife...........	F.	54	Campania..........	No...	No....	No...	No....	No....	7
	Son	M.	19	Campania..........	No...	No...	No...	No....	Yes...	7
	Son	M.	14	Campania..........	No...	No...	No...	No....	Yes...	7
	Daughter......	F.	11	Campania..........	No...	No...	Yes..	Yes..	Yes...	7
925	Head	M.	50	Campania..........	No...	No...	No...	No....	No....	15
	Wife...........	F.	44	Campania..........	No...	No...	No...	No....	No....	11
	Son	M.	19	Campania..........	No...	No...	No...	No....	Yes...	11
	Son	M.	10	United States.......	Yes..	Yes..	Yes..	Yes..	Yes...	....
	Brother.......	M.	46	Campania..........	No...	No...	No...	No....	No....	15
926	Head	M.	32	Campania..........	No...	No...	No...	No....	Yes...	7
	Wife...........	F.	30	Campania..........	No...	No...	No...	No....	Yes...	7
	Brother-in-law	M.	40	Campania..........	Yes..	Yes..	No...	No....	No....	12
927	Head	M.	32	Sicily	No...	No...	No...	No....	Yes...	12
	Wife...........	F.	22	Sicily	No...	No...	No...	No....	Yes...	9
	Lodger	M.	37	Sicily	Yes..	Yes..	No...	No....	Yes...	4
	Lodger	M.	25	Sicily	No...	No...	No...	No....	Yes...	5
928	Head	M.	46	Sicily	No...	No....	No...	No....	Yes...	9
	Wife...........	F.	38	Sicily	No...	No...	No...	No...	Yes...	9
	Son	M.	17	Sicily	No...	No...	No...	No....	Yes...	9
	Daughter.....	F.	13	Sicily	Yes..	Yes..	Yes..	Yes..	Yes...	9
	Daughter.....	F.	11	Sicily	No...	No...	Yes..	Yes..	Yes...	9
929	Head	M.	40	Sicily	No...	No....	No...	No....	Yes...	9
	Wife...........	F.	38	Sicily	No...	No...	No...	No....	No....	1
	Son	M.	15	Sicily	Yes..	Yes..	No...	No....	Yes...	1
	Daughter.....	F.	14	Sicily	Yes..	Yes..	No...	No....	No....	1
	Son	M.	11	Sicily	Yes..	Yes..	No...	No....	Yes...	1
930	Head	M.	43	Sicily	No...	No...	No...	No....	Yes...	13
	Wife...........	F.	38	Sicily	No...	No...	No...	No....	Yes...	10
	Lodger	M.	34	Sicily	No...	No...	No..	No....	No....	3

TABLE II.—GENERAL CONDITION AS TO LITERACY AND ILLITERACY, BY FAMILIES AND INDIVIDUALS—Continued.

[This table includes only persons 10 years of age or over.]

Family number.	Relationship to head of family.	Sex.	Age.	Birthplace.	Native language. Reads.	Writes.	English language. Reads.	Writes.	Speaks.	Years in the United States.
931	Head	M.	36	Campania	Yes	Yes	No	No	Yes	14
	Wife	F.	30	Ireland	No	No	No	No	Yes	14
	Son	M.	11	United States	No	No	No	No	Yes	
	Brother	M.	47	Campania	No	No	No	No	Yes	15
932	Head	M.	60	Campania	No	No	No	No	Yes	15
	Wife	F.	56	Campania	No	No	No	No	Yes	15
	Son	M.	14	United States	Yes	Yes	Yes	Yes	Yes	
	Son	M.	10	United States	No	No	No	No	Yes	
933	Head	M.	43	Campania	No	No	No	No	No	3
934	Head	M.	33	Campania	Yes	Yes	Yes	Yes	Yes	12
	Wife	F.	23	Campania	No	No	No	No	Yes	13
935	Head	M.	28	Campania	No	No	No	No	Yes	15
	Wife	F.	23	Campania	Yes	Yes	No	No	Yes	10
936	Head	M.	40	Campania	No	No	No	No	No	12
	Wife	F.	28	Campania	No	No	No	No	No	2
937	Head	M.	31	Abruzzo	No	No	No	No	Yes	9
	Wife	F.	35	Abruzzo	No	No	No	No	No	3
938	Head	M.	36	Campania	No	No	No	No	Yes	14
	Wife	F.	30	Campania	No	No	No	No	No	9
939	Head	M.	46	Basilicata	No	No	No	No	No	15
	Wife	F.	45	Basilicata	No	No	No	No	No	14
940	Head	M.	42	Campania	No	No	No	No	No	11
	Wife	F.	38	Campania	No	No	No	No	No	9
	Daughter	F.	12	Campania	No	No	No	No	Yes	9
	Lodger	M.	19	Campania	No	No	No	No	No	3
941	Head	M.	40	Calabria	Yes	Yes	No	No	Yes	14
	Wife	F.	36	Calabria	No	No	No	No	No	9
	Daughter	F.	16	Calabria	No	No	Yes	Yes	Yes	9
	Son	M.	12	Calabria	No	No	Yes	Yes	Yes	9
	Son-in-law	M.	28	Calabria	Yes	Yes	No	No	Yes	5
942	Head	M.	27	Campania	Yes	Yes	Yes	Yes	Yes	11
	Wife	F.	24	Campania	No	No	No	No	No	5
	Mother	F.	50	Campania	No	No	No	No	No	16
	Brother	M.	15	United States	No	No	No	No	Yes	
	Sister	F.	11	United States	No	No	No	No	Yes	
	Lodger	M.	27	Campania	Yes	Yes	Yes	Yes	Yes	14
943	Head	M.	28	Sicily	No	No	No	No	Yes	7
	Wife	F.	27	Sicily	No	No	No	No	No	3
	Brother	M.	27	Sicily	No	No	No	No	No	4
	Cousin	M.	40	Sicily	No	No	No	No	No	9
	Cousin	M.	20	Sicily	Yes	Yes	Yes	Yes	Yes	8
944	Cooperative	M.	20	Sicily	Yes	Yes	Yes	Yes	Yes	4
	Cooperative	M.	30	Sicily	No	No	No	No	Yes	4
	Cooperative	M.	23	Sicily	No	No	No	No	Yes	4
945	Head	M.	50	Calabria	Yes	Yes	No	No	No	4
	Wife	F.	50	Calabria	No	No	No	No	No	4
946	Head	M.	32	Campania	Yes	Yes	Yes	Yes	Yes	12
	Wife	F.	26	Campania	No	No	No	No	Yes	8
947	Head	M.	41	Tuscany	Yes	Yes	Yes	Yes	Yes	23
	Wife	F.	36	Tuscany	Yes	Yes	Yes	Yes	Yes	15
	Daughter	F.	18	Tuscany	No	No	Yes	Yes	Yes	15
	Nephew	M.	18	Tuscany	Yes	Yes	No	No	No	1½
948	Head	M.	40	Campania	No	No	No	No	Yes	16
	Wife	F.	39	Campania	Yes	No	No	No	Yes	13
	Daughter	F.	11	United States	Yes	Yes	Yes	Yes	Yes	
949	Head	M.	40	Campania	No	No	No	No	Yes	17
	Wife	F.	38	Campania	No	No	No	No	Yes	14
	Son	M.	10	United States	Yes	Yes	Yes	Yes	Yes	

TABLE **II.**—GENERAL CONDITION AS TO LITERACY AND ILLITERACY, BY FAMILIES AND INDIVIDUALS—Continued.

[This table includes only persons 10 years of age or over.]

Family number.	Relationship to head of family.	Sex.	Age.	Birthplace.	Native language. Reads.	Writes.	English language. Reads.	Writes.	Speaks.	Years in the United States.
950	Head	M.	40	Campania	No	No	No	No	No	15
	Wife	F.	39	Campania	No	No	No	No	No	15
	Son	M.	18	Campania	No	No	Yes	Yes	Yes	15
951	Head	M.	44	Campania	Yes	Yes	No	No	Yes	13
	Wife	F.	39	Campania	No	No	No	No	No	13
	Daughter	F.	13	Campania	No	No	Yes	Yes	Yes	13
	Daughter	F.	10	United States	Yes	Yes	Yes	Yes	Yes	....
952	Head	M.	28	Campania	No	No	No	No	Yes	8
	Wife	F.	28	Campania	No	No	No	No	No	4
953	Head	M.	29	Campania	No	No	No	No	Yes	13
	Wife	F.	20	Campania	No	No	No	No	No	5
954	Head	M.	45	Campania	Yes	Yes	No	No	Yes	16
	Wife	F.	44	Campania	No	No	No	No	No	5
	Sister	F.	50	Campania	No	No	No	No	No	12
955	Head	M.	40	Campania	No	No	No	No	Yes	18
	Wife	F.	35	Campania	No	No	No	No	No	10
956	Head	M.	32	Campania	No	No	No	No	Yes	12
	Wife	F.	25	Campania	No	No	No	No	No	10
957	Head	M.	33	Campania	No	No	No	No	Yes	8
	Wife	F.	34	Campania	No	No	No	No	No	8
958	Head	M.	24	Campania	No	No	No	No	No	14
	Wife	F.	22	Campania	Yes	Yes	No	No	No	7
959	Head	F.	67	Basilicata	No	No	No	No	No	4
960	Head	M.	30	Sicily	Yes	Yes	No	No	Yes	10
	Wife	F.	28	Sicily	No	No	No	No	Yes	10
961	Head	M.	40	Sicily	No	No	No	No	Yes	7
	Wife	F.	36	Sicily	No	No	No	No	No	7
962	Head	M.	40	Basilicata	No	No	No	No	Yes	6
	Wife	F.	38	Basilicata	No	No	No	No	No	6
	Son	M.	13	Basilicata	No	No	Yes	Yes	Yes	6
	Son	M.	12	Basilicata	No	No	Yes	Yes	Yes	6
963	Head	M.	35	Sicily	No	No	No	No	Yes	2
	Wife	F.	39	Sicily	No	No	No	No	No	1
	Son	M.	10	Sicily	No	No	No	No	Yes	1
964	Head	M.	39	Basilicata	No	No	No	No	Yes	12
	Wife	F.	39	Basilicata	No	No	No	No	No	12
	Son	M.	11	United States	Yes	Yes	Yes	Yes	Yes	....
965	Head	M.	40	Basilicata	Yes	No	No	No	Yes	14
	Wife	F.	38	Basilicata	No	No	No	No	Yes	11
	Daughter	F.	17	Basilicata	Yes	Yes	No	No	Yes	11
	Son	M.	13	Basilicata	No	No	Yes	Yes	Yes	11
966	Head	M.	26	Sicily	No	No	No	No	Yes	8
	Wife	F.	20	Sicily	No	No	No	No	No	3
	Father	M.	50	Sicily	No	No	No	No	No	4
	Brother-in-law	M.	26	Sicily	No	No	No	No	Yes	4
	Sister-in-law	F.	20	Sicily	No	No	No	No	No	3
967	Head	M.	33	Basilicata	No	No	No	No	Yes	12
	Wife	F.	20	Basilicata	Yes	Yes	No	No	No	12
	Son	M.	14	Basilicata	No	No	No	No	Yes	12
968	Head	M.	60	Campania	No	No	No	No	No	18
	Wife	F.	55	Campania	No	No	No	No	No	17
	Son	M.	14	United States	Yes	Yes	Yes	Yes	Yes	....
	Daughter	F.	13	United States	Yes	Yes	Yes	Yes	Yes	....
969	Head	M.	33	Campania	Yes	Yes	No	No	Yes	10
	Wife	F.	30	Campania	No	No	No	No	No	6

TABLE II.—GENERAL CONDITION AS TO LITERACY AND ILLITERACY, BY FAMILIES AND INDIVIDUALS—Continued.

[This table includes only persons 10 years of age or over.]

Family number.	Relationship to head of family.	Sex.	Age.	Birthplace.	Native language.		English language.			Years in the United States.
					Reads.	Writes.	Reads.	Writes.	Speaks.	
970	Head	M.	30	Campania	No	No	No	No	Yes	6
	Wife	F.	30	Campania	No	No	No	No	No	5
971	Head	M.	39	Campania	No	No	No	No	Yes	17
	Wife	F.	37	Campania	No	No	No	No	No	12
	Daughter	F.	10	United States	Yes	Yes	Yes	Yes	Yes	
972	Head	M.	38	Campania	No	No	No	No	Yes	15
	Wife	F.	42	Campania	No	No	No	No	No	10
973	Head	M.	41	Campania	Yes	Yes	No	No	Yes	17
	Wife	F.	27	Campania	No	No	No	No	No	5
974	Head	M.	54	Campania	No	No	No	No	Yes	19
	Wife	F.	54	Campania	No	No	No	No	No	19
975	Head	F.	41	Sicily	Yes	Yes	No	No	Yes	23
	Son	M.	17	United States	Yes	Yes	Yes	Yes	Yes	
	Daughter	F.	16	United States	Yes	Yes	Yes	Yes	Yes	
	Son	M.	13	United States	Yes	Yes	Yes	Yes	Yes	
	Son	M.	11	United States	Yes	Yes	Yes	Yes	Yes	
976	Head	M.	37	Campania	Yes	Yes	No	No	Yes	13
	Wife	F.	22	Campania	Yes	Yes	No	No	Yes	10
977	Head	M.	21	Campania	Yes	Yes	No	No	Yes	9
	Wife	F.	25	Campania	No	No	No	No	No	6
	Mother	F.	60	Campania	No	No	No	No	No	5
978	Head	M.	30	Campania	No	No	No	No	Yes	10
	Wife	F.	32	Campania	No	No	No	No	No	5
979	Head	M.	30	Campania	Yes	Yes	No	No	Yes	6
	Wife	F.	30	Campania	No	No	No	No	No	4
	Daughter	F.	10	Campania	No	No	Yes	Yes	Yes	4
980	Head	M.	33	Campania	Yes	Yes	No	No	Yes	11
	Wife	F.	32	Campania	No	No	No	No	Yes	6
981	Head	M.	42	Campania	No	No	No	No	Yes	14
	Wife	F.	34	Campania	No	No	No	No	Yes	10
	Son	M.	17	Campania	No	No	No	No	Yes	7
	Lodger	M.	(a)	Campania	Yes	No	No	No	Yes	(a)
982	Head	M.	56	Campania	No	No	No	No	Yes	13
	Wife	F.	40	Campania	No	No	No	No	Yes	13
	Daughter	F.	16	Campania	Yes	Yes	Yes	Yes	Yes	13
983	Head	M.	34	Campania	No	No	No	No	Yes	14
	Wife	F.	22	Campania	No	No	No	No	Yes	9
984	Head	M.	29	Campania	No	No	No	No	Yes	8
985	Head	M.	55	Campania	No	No	No	No	No	10
	Wife	F.	61	Campania	No	No	No	No	No	10
986	Head	M.	40	Campania	No	No	No	No	Yes	14
	Wife	F.	26	Campania	No	No	No	No	Yes	17
	Daughter	F.	10	United States	Yes	Yes	Yes	Yes	Yes	
987	Head	M.	54	Campania	No	No	No	No	Yes	13
	Wife	F.	47	Campania	No	No	No	No	No	9
	Son	M.	21	Campania	No	No	No	No	Yes	9
988	Head	M.	39	Campania	Yes	Yes	No	No	Yes	10
	Wife	F.	35	Campania	No	No	No	No	Yes	9
	Son	M.	10	Campania	Yes	Yes	Yes	Yes	Yes	9
	Brother-in-law	M.	35	Campania	No	No	No	No	Yes	10
	Sister-in-law	F.	31	Campania	No	No	No	No	Yes	10
989	Head	M.	55	Campania	Yes	Yes	No	No	Yes	15
	Wife	F.	45	Campania	No	No	No	No	Yes	15
	Daughter	F.	14	United States	Yes	Yes	Yes	Yes	Yes	

a Not reported.

TABLE **II.**—GENERAL CONDITION AS TO LITERACY AND ILLITERACY, BY
FAMILIES AND INDIVIDUALS—Continued.

[This table includes only persons 10 years of age or over.]

Family number.	Relationship to head of family.	Sex.	Age.	Birthplace.	Native language. Reads.	Writes.	English language. Reads.	Writes.	Speaks.	Years in the United States.
990	Head	M.	40	Campania	Yes..	Yes...	No...	No....	Yes...	14
	Wife	F.	26	Campania	No...	No...	No...	No....	Yes...	16
	Son	M.	10	United States	Yes..	Yes...	Yes..	Yes...	Yes...	
	Mother	F.	70	Campania	No...	No...	No...	No....	No....	11
991	Head	M.	34	Campania	No...	No...	No...	No....	Yes...	15
	Wife	F.	38	Campania	Yes..	Yes...	No...	No....	No...	14
	Daughter	F.	16	Campania	Yes..	Yes...	Yes..	Yes...	Yes...	14
	Daughter	F.	14	Campania	Yes..	Yes...	Yes..	Yes...	Yes...	14
992	Head	M.	40	Basilicata	No...	No...	No...	No....	Yes...	15
	Wife	F.	40	Basilicata	No...	No...	No...	No....	Yes...	12
	Son	M.	11	United States	Yes..	Yes...	Yes..	Yes...	Yes...	
993	Head	M.	40	Campania	Yes..	Yes...	No...	No....	Yes...	23
	Wife	F.	39	Campania	No...	No...	No...	No....	No....	23
	Daughter	F.	12	United States	Yes..	Yes...	Yes..	Yes...	Yes..	
	Daughter	F.	10	United States	Yes..	Yes...	Yes..	Yes...	Yes..	
	Father-in-law	M.	75	Campania	No...	No...	No...	No....	No....	14
	Mother-in-law	F.	60	Campania	No...	No...	No...	No....	No....	14
994	Head	M.	29	Campania	No...	No...	No...	No....	Yes...	9
	Wife	F.	20	Campania	No...	No...	No...	No....	Yes...	7
995	Head	M.	30	Campania	No...	No...	No...	No....	Yes...	18
	Wife	F.	26	Campania	No...	No...	No...	No....	No....	9
996	Head	M.	38	Campania	No...	No...	No...	No....	No....	14
	Wife	F.	34	Campania	No...	No...	No...	No....	No....	9
997	Head	M.	29	Campania	No...	No...	No...	No....	Yes...	9
	Wife	F.	39	Campania	No...	No...	No...	No....	No....	15
	Stepdaughter	F.	10	United States	No...	No...	No...	No....	Yes...	
	Mother	F.	56	Campania	No...	No...	No...	No....	No....	8
998	Head	M.	27	Campania	No...	No...	No...	No....	Yes...	8
	Wife	F.	20	United States	No...	No...	No...	No....	No...	
999	Head	M.	40	Campania	No...	No...	No...	No....	Yes...	13
	Wife	F.	40	Campania	No...	No...	No...	No....	No....	2
	Son	M.	12	Campania	Yes..	Yes...	Yes..	Yes...	Yes...	2
	Brother-in-law	M.	30	Campania	No...	No...	No...	No....	No....	1
1000	Head	M.	25	Campania	Yes..	Yes...	Yes..	Yes...	Yes...	16
	Wife	F.	18	United States	Yes..	Yes...	Yes..	Yes...	Yes...	
1001	Head	F.	32	Abruzzo	No...	No...	No...	No....	No....	10
1002	Head	M.	30	Campania	No...	No...	No...	No....	Yes...	5
	Wife	F.	26	Campania	No...	No...	No...	No....	Yes...	10
1003	Head	M.	47	Campania	No...	No...	No...	No....	Yes...	17
	Wife	F.	50	Campania	No...	No...	No...	No....	No...	17
	Brother-in-law	M.	47	Campania	No...	No...	No...	No....	No...	17
	Brother-in-law	M.	47	Campania	No...	No...	No...	No....	Yes..	14
	Sister-in-law	F.	32	Campania	No...	No...	No...	No....	Yes...	14
	Nephew	M.	16	Campania	No...	No...	No...	No....	No...	$\frac{5}{12}$
	Boarder	M.	24	Campania	No...	No...	No...	No....	Yes..	4
	Boarder	M.	14	Campania	No...	No...	No...	No....	No...	$\frac{1}{12}$
1004	Head	M.	23	Basilicata	No...	No...	No...	No....	Yes...	11
	Father	M.	54	Basilicata	No...	No...	No...	No....	Yes...	16
	Mother	F.	54	Basilicata	No...	No...	No...	No....	No...	5
	Brother	M.	16	Basilicata	Yes..	Yes...	Yes..	Yes...	Yes...	5
1005	Head	M.	34	Basilicata	Yes..	Yes...	No...	No....	Yes...	24
	Wife	F.	30	Basilicata	No...	No...	No...	No....	Yes...	9
1006	Head	M.	47	Sicily	Yes..	Yes...	Reads.	Yes...	Yes...	21
	Wife	F.	33	Sicily	Yes..	Yes...	No...	No....	Yes...	13
1007	Head	M.	30	Basilicata	No...	No...	Yes..	Yes...	Yes...	12
	Wife	F.	26	Basilicata	No...	No...	Yes..	Yes...	Yes...	17
1008	Head	M.	29	Basilicata	No...	No...	No...	No....	Yes...	10
	Wife	F.	27	Basilicata	No...	No...	No...	No....	No....	8

TABLE **II.**—GENERAL CONDITION AS TO LITERACY AND ILLITERACY, BY FAMILIES AND INDIVIDUALS—Continued.

[This table includes only persons 10 years of age or over.]

Family number.	Relationship to head of family.	Sex.	Age.	Birthplace.	Native language.		English language.			Years in the United States.
					Reads.	Writes.	Reads.	Writes.	Speaks.	
1009	Head	M.	29	Basilicata	No	No	No	No	Yes	10
	Wife	F.	23	Basilicata	No	No	No	No	Yes	12
1010	Head	M.	32	Campania	Yes	Yes	No	No	Yes	13
	Wife	F.	29	Campania	No	No	No	No	No	8
1011	Head	M.	23	Abruzzo	Yes	Yes	Yes	Yes	Yes	9
	Wife	F.	17	Basilicata	Yes	No	No	No	No	6
1012	Head	M.	30	Basilicata	No	No	No	No	Yes	15
	Wife	F.	30	Basilicata	No	No	No	No	No	12
	Daughter	F.	12	United States	Yes	Yes	Yes	Yes	Yes	
1013	Head	M.	38	Basilicata	No	No	No	No	Yes	22
	Wife	F.	33	Basilicata	No	No	No	No	Yes	18
	Brother-in-law	M.	23	Basilicata	Yes	Yes	Yes	No	Yes	8
1014	Head	M.	50	Campania	No	No	No	No	Yes	6
	Wife	F.	30	Campania	No	No	No	No	Yes	6
1015	Head	M.	32	Calabria	Yes	Yes	No	No	Yes	9
	Wife	F.	29	Calabria	No	No	No	No	No	½
1016	Head	M.	30	Abruzzo	Yes	No	No	No	Yes	10
	Wife	F.	33	Abruzzo	No	No	No	No	Yes	6
	Lodger	M.	23	Abruzzo	No	No	No	No	Yes	8
	Lodger	M.	25	Abruzzo	No	No	No	No	No	2
1017	Head	M.	26	Campania	No	No	No	No	Yes	4
	Wife	F.	25	Campania	No	No	No	No	No	4
1018	Head	M.	32	Basilicata	No	No	No	No	No	4
	Wife	F.	32	Basilicata	No	No	No	No	No	4
	Son	M.	12	Basilicata	No	No	No	No	No	4
1019	Head	M.	52	Basilicata	No	No	No	No	Yes	15
	Wife	F.	49	Basilicata	No	No	No	No	No	10
	Son-in-law	M.	34	Basilicata	Yes	Yes	No	No	Yes	12
1020	Head	M.	43	Basilicata	No	No	No	No	Yes	12
	Mother	F.	70	Basilicata	No	No	No	No	No	12
1021	Head	M.	56	Basilicata	No	No	No	No	Yes	24
	Wife	F.	35	Basilicata	No	No	No	No	No	13
	Daughter	F.	12	United States	Yes	Yes	Yes	Yes	Yes	
1022	Head	M.	46	Basilicata	No	No	No	No	Yes	17
	Wife	F.	46	Basilicata	No	No	No	No	No	15
	Son	M.	20	Basilicata	No	No	No	No	Yes	15
	Son	M.	14	United States	Yes	Yes	Yes	Yes	Yes	
	Son	M.	10	United States	Yes	Yes	Yes	Yes	Yes	
1023	Head	M.	(a)	Basilicata	Yes	Yes	No	No	Yes	6
	Wife	F.	24	Basilicata	No	No	No	No	No	5
1024	Head	M.	55	Basilicata	No	No	No	No	No	15
	Wife	F.	46	Basilicata	No	No	No	No	No	13
	Son	M.	12	United States	Yes	Yes	Yes	Yes	Yes	
	Brother	M.	47	Basilicata	Yes	Yes	Yes	Yes	Yes	8
	Nephew	M.	15	Basilicata	Yes	Yes	Yes	Yes	Yes	5
1025	Head	M.	37	Basilicata	No	No	No	No	Yes	15
	Wife	F.	30	Basilicata	No	No	No	No	No	10
1026	Head	M.	37	Basilicata	No	No	No	No	Yes	15
	Wife	F.	39	Basilicata	No	No	No	No	No	14
	Daughter	F.	11	United States	Yes	Yes	Yes	Yes	Yes	
	Son	M.	10	United States	Yes	Yes	Yes	Yes	Yes	
1027	Head	M.	30	Sicily	No	No	No	No	Yes	6
	Wife	F.	23	Sicily	Yes	Yes	No	No	No	6
	Boarder	M.	27	Sicily	No	No	No	No	Yes	9
	Boarder	F.	20	Sicily	Yes	Yes	No	No	No	4

a Not reported.

TABLE II.—GENERAL CONDITION AS TO LITERACY AND ILLITERACY, BY FAMILIES AND INDIVIDUALS—Continued.

[This table includes only persons 10 years of age or over.]

Family number.	Relationship to head of family.	Sex.	Age.	Birthplace.	Native language. Reads.	Writes.	English language. Reads.	Writes.	Speaks.	Years in the United States.
1028	Head	F.	50	Basilicata	No	No	No	No	No	20
	Daughter	F.	22	Basilicata	No	No	No	No	Yes	20
	Daughter	F.	16	United States	Yes	Yes	Yes	Yes	Yes	
	Daughter	F.	12	United States	Yes	Yes	Yes	Yes	Yes	
1029	Head	M.	35	Abruzzo	No	No	No	No	Yes	11
	Wife	F.	34	Abruzzo	Yes	Yes	No	No	Yes	7
1030	Head	M.	42	Basilicata	No	No	No	No	Yes	16
	Wife	F.	26	Basilicata	Yes	Yes	No	No	No	9
1031	Head	M.	40	Campania	No	No	No	No	No	15
	Wife	F.	38	Campania	No	No	No	No	No	13
	Daughter	F.	12	United States	Yes	Yes	Yes	Yes	Yes	
	Daughter	F.	10	United States	Yes	Yes	Yes	Yes	Yes	
1032	Head	M.	35	Calabria	No	No	No	No	No	4
1033	Head	M.	28	Campania	Yes	Yes	No	No	Yes	3
	Wife	F.	30	Campania	No	No	No	No	No	3
1034	Head	M.	39	Campania	Yes	Yes	No	No	Yes	14
	Wife	F.	33	Campania	Yes	Yes	No	No	No	10
1035	Head	M.	33	Campania	Yes	Yes	No	No	Yes	15
	Wife	F.	30	Campania	No	No	No	No	No	10
	Lodger	M:	70	Campania	No	No	No	No	No	17
1036	Head	M.	48	Sicily	No	No	No	No	No	13
	Wife	F.	38	Sicily	No	No	No	No	Yes	7
	Son	M.	14	Sicily	No	No	No	No	Yes	7
	Son	M.	13	Sicily	No	No	No	No	Yes	7
1037	Head	M.	44	Basilicata	No	No	No	No	Yes	12
	Wife	F.	44	Basilicata	No	No	No	No	No	9
	Son	M.	16	Basilicata	Yes	Yes	Yes	Yes	Yes	9
1038	Head	M.	32	Basilicata	Yes	Yes	No	No	Yes	8
	Wife	F.	30	Basilicata	No	No	No	No	No	7
1039	Head	M.	28	Basilicata	Yes	Yes	Yes	Yes	Yes	10
	Wife	F.	25	Basilicata	No	No	No	No	Yes	6
1040	Head	M.	24	Basilicata	Yes	Yes	Yes	No	Yes	8
	Wife	F.	24	Basilicata	No	No	No	No	No	4
1041	Head	M.	35	Sicily	No	No	No	No	Yes	6
	Wife	F.	30	Sicily	No	No	No	No	No	1
	Daughter	F.	10	Sicily	Yes	Yes	No	No	Yes	1
1042	Head	M.	50	Basilicata	No	No	No	No	Yes	10
	Wife	F.	47	Basilicata	No	No	No	No	No	7
	Son	M.	23	Basilicata	Yes	Yes	No	No	Yes	7
	Son	M.	18	Basilicata	Yes	Yes	No	No	Yes	7
	Daughter	F.	13	Basilicata	No	No	No	No	Yes	7
	Daughter	F.	10	Basilicata	No	No	Yes	Yes	Yes	7
1043	Head	M.	42	Campania	Yes	Yes	No	No	Yes	6
	Wife	F.	50	Campania	No	No	No	No	No	5
	Son	M.	10	Campania	Yes	Yes	Yes	Yes	Yes	5
1044	Head	M.	30	Liguria	Yes	Yes	Yes	Yes	Yes	25
	Wife	F.	24	United States	Yes	Yes	Yes	Yes	Yes	
	Daughter	F.	13	United States	Yes	Yes	Yes	Yes	Yes	
1045	Head	F.	60	Sicily	No	No	No	No	No	3
	Daughter	F.	29	Sicily	No	No	No	No	No	7
	Son	M.	18	Sicily	No	No	No	No	Yes	5
	Son-in-law	M.	34	Sicily	No	No	No	No	No	7
1046	Head	M.	30	Sicily	Yes	Yes	No	Yes	Yes	11
	Wife	F.	32	Sicily	No	No	No	No	No	6
1047	Head	M.	40	Sicily	Yes	No	No	No	Yes	12
	Wife	F.	36	Sicily	No	No	No	No	No	12

TABLE **II.**—GENERAL CONDITION AS TO LITERACY AND ILLITERACY, BY FAMILIES AND INDIVIDUALS—Continued.

[This table includes only persons 10 years of age or over.]

Family number.	Relationship to head of family.	Sex.	Age.	Birthplace.	Native language. Reads.	Writes.	English language. Reads.	Writes.	Speaks.	Years in the United States.
1047	Son	M.	13	Sicily	No	No	Yes	Yes	Yes	12
	Daughter	F.	11	United States	Yes	Yes	Yes	Yes	Yes	
1048	Head	M.	35	Sicily	No	No	No	No	Yes	7
	Wife	F.	31	Sicily	Yes	Yes	No	No	No	5
	Son	M.	10	Sicily	No	No	No	No	Yes	5
1049	Head	M.	34	Calabria	Yes	Yes	No	No	Yes	8
	Wife	F.	22	Basilicata	No	No	No	No	Yes	16
1050	Head	M.	28	Calabria	No	No	No	No	Yes	3
	Wife	F.	23	Calabria	No	No	No	No	No	3
1051	Head	M.	33	Calabria	No	No	No	No	Yes	10
	Wife	F.	23	Calabria	No	No	No	No	No	6
1052	Head	M.	33	Calabria	No	No	No	No	Yes	1
	Wife	F.	26	Calabria	No	No	No	No	No	1
1053	Head	M.	40	Calabria	No	No	No	No	Yes	10
	Wife	F.	36	Calabria	No	No	No	No	No	3
	Son	M.	15	Calabria	Yes	Yes	Yes	Yes	Yes	3
	Son	M.	11	Calabria	No	No	No	No	No	1/12
1054	Head	M.	30	Calabria	No	No	No	No	Yes	6
	Wife	F.	23	Calabria	No	No	No	No	No	6
	Lodger	M.	30	Calabria	No	No	No	No	Yes	8
1055	Head	M.	30	Calabria	No	No	No	No	Yes	10
	Wife	F.	21	Calabria	No	No	No	No	Yes	10
1056	Head	M.	32	Venetia	No	No	No	No	Yes	7
	Wife	F.	23	Venetia	No	No	No	No	Yes	3
	Cousin	M.	25	Venetia	No	No	No	No	Yes	3
	Lodger	M.	25	Venetia	Yes	Yes	No	No	Yes	5
	Lodger	M.	40	Venetia	Yes	Yes	No	No	Yes	15
	Lodger	M.	21	Venetia	Yes	Yes	No	No	Yes	3
1057	Cooperative	M.	22	Venetia	Yes	Yes	No	No	Yes	3
	Cooperative	M.	34	Venetia	Yes	Yes	No	No	Yes	3
1058	Head	M.	44	Basilicata	No	No	No	No	Yes	13
	Wife	F.	37	Basilicata	No	No	No	No	No	10
1059	Head	M.	35	Basilicata	No	No	No	No	Yes	5
	Wife	F.	27	Basilicata	No	No	No	No	No	4
	Son	M.	10	Basilicata	No	No	No	No	Yes	4
1060	Head	M.	70	Basilicata	No	No	No	No	No	5
	Wife	F.	66	Basilicata	No	No	No	No	No	5
1061	Head	M.	40	Basilicata	No	No	No	No	Yes	10
	Wife	F.	35	Basilicata	No	No	No	No	No	10
	Son	M.	10	United States	Yes	Yes	Yes	Yes	Yes	
1062	Head	M.	34	Tuscany	Yes	Yes	No	No	Yes	11
	Wife	F.	43	Tuscany	Yes	Yes	No	No	No	11
	Son	M.	10	United States	Yes	Yes	Yes	Yes	Yes	
1063	Head	M.	68	Basilicata	No	No	No	No	No	6
	Wife	F.	53	Basilicata	No	No	No	No	No	6
	Son	M.	14	Basilicata	No	No	No	No	Yes	6
	Daughter	F.	10	Basilicata	No	No	Yes	Yes	Yes	6
1064	Head	M.	39	Basilicata	Yes	Yes	No	No	Yes	4
	Wife	F.	28	Basilicata	No	No	No	No	No	4
1065	Head	M.	45	Basilicata	No	No	No	No	No	4
	Wife	F.	45	Basilicata	No	No	No	No	No	4
	Son	M.	19	Basilicata	Yes	Yes	No	No	Yes	4
	Son	M.	14	Basilicata	Yes	Yes	No	No	Yes	4
1066	Head	M.	30	Basilicata	No	No	No	No	Yes	12
	Wife	F.	21	Basilicata	No	No	No	No	No	4
1067	Cooperative	M.	55	Calabria	No	No	No	No	Yes	8
	Cooperative	M.	33	Calabria	No	No	No	No	Yes	8

TABLE **II.**—GENERAL CONDITION AS TO LITERACY AND ILLITERACY, BY FAMILIES AND INDIVIDUALS—Continued.

[This table includes only persons 10 years of age or over.]

Family number.	Relationship to head of family.	Sex.	Age.	Birthplace.	Native language.		English language.			Years in the United States.
					Reads.	Writes.	Reads.	Writes.	Speaks.	
1067	Cooperative ..	M.	26	Calabria	No...	No....	No...	No....	Yes...	8
	Cooperative ..	M.	31	Calabria	Yes..	Yes...	No...	No....	No....	1
1068	Cooperative ..	M.	32	Calabria	Yes..	Yes...	No...	No....	Yes...	3
	Cooperative ..	M.	32	Calabria	No...	No....	No...	No...	Yes...	8
	Cooperative ..	M.	34	Calabria	Yes..	Yes...	No...	No....	Yes...	6
	Cooperative ..	M.	42	Calabria	No...	No....	No...	No....	Yes...	3
	Cooperative ..	M.	21	Calabria	No...	No....	No...	No....	Yes...	5
1069	Head	M.	30	Sicily	No...	No....	No...	No....	No....	5
1070	Head	M.	43	Calabria	No...	No....	No...	No....	Yes...	14
	Wife..........	F.	39	Calabria	No...	No....	No...	No....	Yes...	10
	Son	M.	16	Calabria	Yes..	Yes...	Yes..	Yes...	Yes...	10
	Daughter	F.	14	Calabria	Yes..	Yes...	Yes..	Yes...	Yes...	10
1071	Head	M.	42	Sicily	No...	No....	No...	No....	Yes...	10
	Wife..........	F.	41	Sicily	No...	No....	No...	No....	No....	5
	Son	M.	18	Sicily	No...	No....	No...	No....	Yes...	5
	Son	M.	12	Sicily	No...	No....	No...	No....	Yes...	5
1072	Head	M.	22	Sicily	Yes..	Yes...	No...	No....	Yes...	6
	Wife..........	F.	17	Sicily	No...	No....	No...	No....	No....	4
1073	Head	M.	35	Sicily	No...	No....	No...	No....	Yes...	10
	Wife..........	F.	27	Sicily	No...	No....	No...	No....	Yes...	10
1074	Head	M.	48	Sicily	No...	No....	No...	No....	Yes.	15
	Wife..........	F.	44	Sicily	No...	No....	No...	No....	No....	6
	Son	M.	16	Sicily	No...	No....	No...	No....	Yes...	6
1075	Head	M.	35	Sicily	Yes..	Yes...	No...	No....	Yes...	8
	Wife..........	F.	35	Sicily.	No...	No....	No...	No....	No....	6
1076	Head	M.	29	Calabria	No...	No....	No...	No....	Yes...	8
	Wife..........	F.	35	Calabria	No...	No....	No...	No....	Yes...	5
1077	Head	M.	39	Campania..........	No...	No....	No...	No....	Yes...	17
	Wife..........	F.	36	Campania..........	No...	No....	No...	No....	Yes...	16
	Daughter	F.	14	United States......	Yes..	Yes...	Yes..	Yes...	Yes...	....
	Daughter	F.	12	United States......	Yes..	Yes...	Yes..	Yes...	Yes...	....
1078	Head	M.	34	Campania..........	Yes..	Yes...	No...	No....	Yes...	10
	Wife..........	F.	35	Campania..........	No...	No....	No...	No....	No....	10
1079	Head	M.	37	Campania..........	Yes..	Yes...	Yes..	Yes...	Yes...	18
	Wife..........	F.	37	Campania..........	No...	No....	No...	No....	Yes...	13
	Son	M.	12	United States......	Yes..	Yes...	Yes..	Yes...	Yes...	....
	Daughter	F.	10	United States......	Yes..	Yes...	Yes..	Yes...	Yes...	....
1080	Head	M.	35	Basilicata..........	Yes..	Yes...	No...	No....	Yes...	12
	Wife..........	F.	32	Basilicata..........	No...	No....	No...	No....	No....	6
1081	Head	M.	45	Basilicata..........	Yes..	Yes...	No...	No....	Yes...	15
	Wife..........	F.	42	Basilicata..........	No...	No....	No...	No....	No....	9
	Brother-in-law	M.	32	Basilicata..........	Yes..	Yes...	No...	No....	Yes...	4
1082	Head	M.	33	Calabria	Yes..	Yes...	No...	No....	Yes...	11
	Wife..........	F.	26	Basilicata..........	No...	No....	No...	No....	No....	5
1083	Head	M.	30	Basilicata..........	No...	No....	No...	No....	Yes...	16
	Wife..........	F.	21	Basilicata..........	No...	No....	No...	No....	Yes...	12
1084	Head	M.	36	Basilicata..........	Yes..	Yes...	Yes..	Yes...	Yes...	22
	Wife..........	F.	32	Basilicata..........	No...	No....	No...	No....	No....	16
	Daughter	F.	12	United States......	Yes..	Yes...	Yes..	Yes...	Yes...	....
	Son	M.	11	United States......	Yes..	Yes...	Yes..	Yes...	Yes...	....
	Daughter	F.	10	United States......	Yes..	Yes...	Yes..	Yes...	Yes	....
1085	Head	M.	50	Basilicata..........	No...	No....	No...	No....	Yes...	20
	Wife..........	F.	50	Basilicata..........	No...	No....	No...	No....	No....	16
1086	Head	M.	42	Campania..........	Yes..	Yes...	No...	No....	Yes...	13
	Wife..........	F.	27	Basilicata..........	No...	No....	No...	No....	Yes...	9
1087	Head	M.	28	Calabria	No...	No....	No...	No....	Yes...	5
	Wife..........	F.	18	Calabria	No...	No....	No...	No....	Yes...	15

TABLE **II.**—GENERAL CONDITION AS TO LITERACY AND ILLITERACY, BY FAMILIES AND INDIVIDUALS—Continued.

[This table includes only persons 10 years of age or over.]

Family number.	Relationship to head of family.	Sex.	Age.	Birthplace.	Native language. Reads.	Writes.	English language. Reads.	Writes.	Speaks.	Years in the United States.
1088	Head	M.	40	Abruzzo	No...	No....	No...	No....	Yes...	6
	Wife	F.	34	Abruzzo	No...	No....	No...	No....	No....	6
1089	Head	M.	32	Calabria	No...	No....	No...	No....	Yes...	10
	Wife	F.	32	Calabria	No...	No....	No...	No....	No....	5
	Daughter	F.	12	Calabria	Yes..	Yes...	No...	No....	Yes...	5
1090	Head	M.	39	Calabria	No...	No....	No...	No....	No....	4
	Wife	F.	30	Calabria	No...	No....	No...	No....	No....	3
1091	Head	M.	33	Basilicata	Yes..	Yes...	No...	No....	Yes...	10
	Wife	F.	25	Basilicata	Yes..	Yes...	No...	No....	No....	10
1092	Head	M.	36	Calabria	No...	No....	No...	No....	Yes...	6
	Wife	F.	28	Calabria	No...	No....	No...	No....	Yes...	3
1093	Head	M.	27	Calabria	Yes..	Yes...	No...	No....	Yes...	(a)
	Wife	F.	18	Basilicata	Yes..	Yes...	No...	No....	Yes...	8
1094	Head	M.	44	Basilicata	Yes.	Yes...	No...	No....	Yes...	25
	Wife	F.	39	Basilicata	No...	No....	No...	No....	No....	10
	Son	M.	17	Basilicata	No...	No....	No...	No....	Yes...	10
	Daughter	F.	10	United States	Yes..	No....	Yes...	No....	Yes...	....
1095	Head	M.	35	Abruzzo	Yes..	Yes...	Yes...	Yes...	Yes...	13
	Wife	F.	26	Abruzzo	No...	No....	No...	No....	Yes...	11
1096	Head	M.	32	Basilicata	No...	No....	No...	No....	Yes...	21
	Wife	F.	21	United States	Yes..	Yes...	Yes...	Yes...	Yes...	....
1097	Head	M.	45	Basilicata	No...	No....	No...	No....	Yes...	12
	Wife	F.	52	Basilicata	No...	No....	No...	No....	Yes...	12
	Son	M.	17	Basilicata	No...	No....	Yes...	Yes...	Yes...	12
1098	Head	M.	56	Basilicata	No...	No....	No...	No....	No....	3
	Son	M.	22	Basilicata	No...	No....	No...	No....	Yes...	2
	Daughter	F.	13	Basilicata	No...	No....	No...	No....	No....	$\frac{2}{12}$
1099	Head	M.	28	Calabria	Yes..	Yes...	No...	No....	Yes...	10
	Wife	F.	27	Calabria	No...	No....	No...	No....	No....	4
	Brother-in-law	M.	35	Calabria	Yes..	Yes...	No...	No....	Yes...	6
	Boarder	M.	16	Calabria	Yes..	Yes...	Yes..	Yes...	Yes...	6
	Lodger	M.	27	Calabria	No...	No....	No...	No....	No....	$\frac{2}{12}$
1100	Head	M.	28	Calabria	Yes..	Yes...	No...	No....	Yes...	4
	Wife	F.	18	Basilicata	No...	No....	No...	No....	Yes...	12
1101	Head	M.	64	Basilicata	No...	No....	No...	No....	No....	17
	Wife	F.	50	Basilicata	No...	No....	No...	No....	Yes...	18
1102	Head	F.	44	Basilicata	No...	No....	No...	No....	No....	15
1103	Head	M.	37	Basilicata	No...	No....	No...	No....	Yes...	10
	Wife	F.	35	Basilicata	No...	No....	No...	No....	No....	10
1104	Head	M.	33	Sicily	No...	No....	No...	No....	Yes...	5
	Wife	F.	28	Sicily	No...	No....	No...	No....	No....	5
1105	Head	M.	60	Sicily	No...	No....	No...	No....	Yes...	14
	Wife	F.	60	Sicily	No...	No....	No...	No....	No....	1
	Son	M.	17	Sicily	Yes..	Yes...	No...	No....	Yes...	5
1106	Head	M.	24	Sicily	No...	No....	No...	No....	Yes...	13
	Wife	F.	25	Sicily	No...	No....	No...	No....	No....	9
1107	Head	M.	37	Sicily	Yes..	Yes...	No...	No....	Yes...	14
	Wife	F.	29	Sicily	Yes..	Yes...	No...	No....	Yes...	12
	Son	M.	11	United States	Yes..	Yes...	Yes..	Yes...	Yes...	....
	Mother-in-law	F.	53	Sicily	No...	No....	No...	No....	No....	6
1108	Head	M.	36	Sicily	No...	No....	No...	No....	Yes...	13
	Wife	F.	34	Sicily	No...	No....	No...	No....	No....	12
	Daughter	F.	11	United States	No...	No....	No...	No....	Yes...	....

a Not reported.

TABLE **II.**—GENERAL CONDITION AS TO LITERACY AND ILLITERACY, BY FAMILIES AND INDIVIDUALS—Continued.

[This table includes only persons 10 years of age or over.]

Family number.	Relationship to head of family.	Sex.	Age.	Birthplace.	Native language.		English language.			Years in the United States.
					Reads.	Writes.	Reads.	Writes.	Speaks.	
1109	Head	M.	30	Sicily	Yes..	Yes...	No...	No....	Yes...	7
	Wife	F.	20	Sicily	Yes..	Yes...	No...	No....	No....	5
	Mother	F.	58	Sicily	No...	No....	No...	No....	No....	11
1110	Head	M.	33	Sicily	Yes..	Yes...	No...	No....	Yes...	12
	Wife	F.	30	Sicily	No...	No....	No...	No....	No....	9
	Cousin	M.	30	Sicily	No...	No....	No...	No....	No....	8
	Cousin	M.	32	Sicily	Yes..	Yes...	No...	No....	No....	6
1111	Head	M.	27	Sicily	No...	No....	No...	No....	Yes...	12
	Wife	F.	18	Sicily	No...	No....	No...	No....	Yes...	10
1112	Head	M.	30	Sicily	Yes..	Yes...	No...	No....	Yes...	6
	Wife	F.	27	Sicily	Yes..	Yes...	No...	No....	Yes...	5
1113	Head	M.	30	Sicily	Yes..	Yes...	No...	No....	Yes...	8
	Wife	F.	22	Sicily	Yes..	Yes...	No...	No....	No....	5
1114	Head	M.	53	Sicily	Yes..	No....	No...	No....	Yes..	36
	Wife	F.	40	Sicily	No...	No....	No...	No....	No....	14
	Son	M.	27	Sicily	Yes..	Yes...	Yes..	Yes...	Yes...	14
	Son	M.	14	United States	Yes..	Yes..	Yes..	Yes..	Yes...	....
	Son	M.	12	United States	Yes..	Yes...	Yes..	Yes..	Yes...	....
	Daughter-in-law.	F.	18	Sicily	No...	No....	Yes..	Yes...	Yes...	16
1115	Head	M.	26	Sicily	Yes..	Yes...	No...	No....	No....	1
	Wife	F.	22	Sicily	No...	No....	No...	No....	No....	₁⁄₂
1116	Head	M.	54	Emilia	No...	No....	No...	No....	Yes...	23
	Son	M.	22	United States	Yes..	Yes...	Yes..	Yes...	Yes...	....
	Daughter	F.	17	United States	Yes..	Yes...	Yes..	Yes...	Yes...	....
	Daughter	F.	14	United States	Yes..	Yes...	Yes..	Yes...	Yes...	....
	Son	M.	13	United States	Yes..	Yes...	Yes..	Yes...	Yes...	....
	Boarder	F.	42	Liguria	No...	No....	No...	No....	No....	₁⁄₂
1117	Head	M.	53	Liguria	Yes..	Yes...	Yes..	No....	Yes...	27
	Wife	F.	48	Liguria	No...	No....	No...	No....	Yes...	27
	Son	M.	26	United States	Yes..	Yes...	Yes..	Yes...	Yes...	.....
	Son	M.	22	United States	Yes..	Yes...	Yes..	Yes...	Yes...	.....
	Daughter	F.	20	United States	Yes..	Yes...	Yes..	Yes...	Yes...	.....
	Daughter	F.	18	United States	Yes..	Yes...	Yes..	Yes...	Yes...	.....
	Daughter	F.	16	United States	Yes..	Yes...	Yes..	Yes...	Yes...	.....
	Daughter	F.	11	United States	Yes..	Yes...	Yes..	Yes...	Yes...	.....
1118	Head	M.	34	Abruzzo	Yes..	Yes...	No...	No....	Yes...	7
	Wife	F.	31	Abruzzo	No...	No....	No...	No....	No....	7
1119	Head	M.	61	Liguria	No...	No....	No...	No....	Yes..	26
	Wife	F.	61	Liguria	No...	No....	No...	No....	Yes...	26
	Son	M.	19	United States	Yes..	Yes...	Yes..	Yes...	Yes...	....
1120	Head	M.	33	Liguria	No...	No....	No...	No....	Yes...	12
	Wife	F.	27	Liguria	Yes..	Yes...	No...	No....	No....	8
1121	Head	M.	50	Abruzzo	No...	No....	No...	No....	No....	6
	Wife	F.	37	Abruzzo	No...	No....	No...	No....	No....	6
	Son	M.	13	Abruzzo	No...	No....	No...	No....	Yes...	6
	Daughter	F.	10	Abruzzo	No...	No....	No...	No....	Yes. .	6
1122	Head	M.	40	Liguria	No...	No....	No...	No....	Yes...	18
	Wife	F.	36	Liguria	Yes..	Yes...	No...	No....	Yes...	17
	Son	M.	12	United States	Yes..	Yes...	Yes..	Yes...	Yes...	.....
	Daughter	F.	10	United States	No...	No....	No...	No....	Yes...	.....
	Mother-in law	F.	56	Liguria	No...	No....	No...	No....	No....	17
1123	Head	M.	33	United States	Yes..	Yes...	Yes..	Yes...	Yes...	.....
	Wife	F.	30	Liguria	Yes..	Yes...	Yes..	Yes...	Yes...	(a)
	Sister	F.	25	United States	Yes..	Yes...	Yes..	Yes...	Yes...	.....
1124	Head	M.	61	Emilia	No...	No....	No...	No....	Yes...	20
	Wife	F.	52	Emilia	No...	No....	No...	No....	No...	20
	Son	M.	22	Emilia	Yes..	Yes...	Yes..	Yes...	Yes...	20
	Son	M.	18	United States	Yes..	Yes...	Yes..	Yes...	Yes...	....

a Not reported.

TABLE **II.**—GENERAL CONDITION AS TO LITERACY AND ILLITERACY, BY FAMILIES AND INDIVIDUALS—Continued.

[This table includes only persons 10 years of age or over.]

Family number.	Relationship to head of family.	Sex.	Age.	Birthplace.	Native language. Reads.	Native language. Writes.	English language. Reads.	English language. Writes.	English language. Speaks.	Years in the United States.
1124	Daughter.....	F.	16	United States......	Yes..	Yes...	Yes...	Yes...	Yes...	....
	Daughter.....	F.	13	United States......	Yes..	Yes...	Yes..	Yes...	Yes...	....
1125	Head	M.	52	Abruzzo	Yes..	Yes...	No...	No....	Yes...	7
	Wife..........	F.	42	Abruzzo	Yes..	Yes...	No...	No....	No....	7
	Son	M.	10	Abruzzo	No...	No....	Yes..	Yes...	Yes...	7
1126	Head	M.	37	Liguria	No...	No....	No...	No....	Yes...	16
	Wife..........	F.	38	Liguria	No...	No....	No...	No....	No....	16
	Son	M.	16	Liguria	No...	No....	Yes..	Yes...	Yes...	16
	Son	M.	13	United States......	Yes..	Yes...	Yes..	Yes...	Yes...	....
	Daughter.....	F.	11	United States......	Yes..	Yes...	Yes..	Yes...	Yes...	....
1127	Head	M.	45	Lombardy	Yes..	Yes...	No...	No....	Yes...	16
	Wife..........	F.	34	Liguria	No...	No....	No...	No....	No....	10
1128	Head	M.	33	Venetia.............	Yes..	Yes...	No...	No....	No....	3
	Wife..........	F.	31	Venetia.............	Yes..	Yes...	No...	No....	No....	3
1129	Head	M.	39	Abruzzo	Yes..	Yes...	No...	No....	Yes...	5
	Wife..........	F.	36	Abruzzo	No...	No....	No...	No....	Yes...	5
	Daughter.....	F.	13	Abruzzo	No...	No....	No...	No....	Yes...	5
	Daughter.....	F.	12	Abruzzo	No...	No....	No...	No....	Yes...	5
1130	Cooperative ..	M.	20	Venetia.............	Yes..	Yes...	No...	No....	Yes...	3
	Cooperative ..	M.	25	Venetia.............	Yes..	Yes...	No...	No....	No....	3
	Cooperative ..	M.	26	Venetia.............	Yes..	Yes...	No...	No....	No....	3
	Cooperative ..	M.	27	Venetia.............	No...	No....	No...	No....	No....	3
1131	Head	M.	42	Liguria	No...	No....	No...	No....	Yes...	1
	Wife..........	F.	42	Liguria	No...	No....	No...	No....	No....	1
	Daughter.....	F.	16	Liguria	Yes..	Yes...	No...	No....	Yes...	1
	Daughter.....	F.	10	Liguria	No...	No....	No...	No....	Yes...	1
	Boarder	M.	22	Liguria	Yes..	Yes...	No...	No....	No....	1
1132	Cooperative ..	M.	30	Liguria	Yes..	Yes...	No...	No....	Yes...	3
	Cooperative ..	M.	28	Liguria	Yes..	Yes...	No...	No....	Yes...	3
	Cooperative ..	M.	30	Liguria	Yes..	Yes...	No...	No....	Yes...	2
1133	Head	M.	36	Liguria	Yes..	Yes...	No...	No....	No....	6
	Wife..........	F.	35	Liguria	No...	No....	No...	No....	No....	6
	Son	M.	13	Liguria	No...	No....	Yes..	Yes...	Yes...	6
	Daughter.....	F.	12	Liguria	No...	No....	Yes..	Yes...	Yes...	6
	Boarder	M.	23	Liguria	No...	No....	No...	No....	Yes...	17
1134	Head	M.	48	Liguria	Yes..	Yes...	No...	No....	No....	5
	Wife..........	F.	42	Liguria	No...	No....	No...	No....	No....	4
	Daughter.....	F.	21	Liguria	Yes..	Yes...	No...	No....	Yes...	5
	Son	M.	19	Liguria	No...	No....	No...	No....	Yes...	4
	Daughter.....	F.	16	Liguria	No...	No....	No...	No....	Yes...	4
	Son	M.	15	Liguria	No...	No....	Yes..	Yes...	Yes...	5
	Daughter.....	F.	11	Liguria	No...	No....	Yes..	Yes...	Yes...	4
	Son	M.	10	Liguria	No...	No....	Yes..	Yes...	Yes...	4
1135	Head	F.	65	Liguria	No...	No....	No...	No....	Yes...	40
	Son	M.	30	United States......	Yes..	Yes...	Yes..	Yes...	Yes...	....
	Son	M.	27	United States......	Yes..	Yes...	Yes..	Yes...	Yes...	....
	Daughter.....	F.	25	United States......	Yes..	Yes...	Yes..	Yes...	Yes...	....
	Daughter.....	F.	23	United States......	Yes..	Yes...	Yes..	Yes...	Yes...	....
1136	Head	M.	31	Campagna di Roma.	No...	No....	No...	No....	Yes...	7
	Wife..........	F.	29	Campagna di Roma.	No...	No....	No...	No....	No....	2
1137	Head	M.	30	Tuscany............	Yes..	Yes...	No...	No....	Yes...	7
	Wife..........	F.	27	Tuscany............	No...	No....	No...	No....	No....	3
1138	Head	M.	42	Sicily .-	No...	No....	No...	No...	No....	7
	Son	M.	16	Sicily	No...	No....	No...	No....	Yes...	7
1139	Head	M.	60	Basilicata	No...	No....	No...	No....	No....	4
	Wife..........	F.	50	Basilicata	No...	No....	No...	No....	No....	2
	Daughter.....	F.	25	Basilicata	No...	No....	No .	No....	No....	3
	Son-in-law	M.	30	Basilicata	Yes..	Yes...	No...	No....	No....	3
1140	Head	M.	40	Basilicata	No...	No....	No...	No....	Yes...	14
	Wife..........	F.	43	Basilicata	No...	No....	No...	No....	No....	11
	Son	M.	15	Basilicata	No...	No....	Yes..	Yes...	Yes...	11

TABLE **II.**—GENERAL CONDITION AS TO LITERACY AND ILLITERACY, BY FAMILIES AND INDIVIDUALS—Continued.

[This table includes only persons 10 years of age or over.]

Family number.	Relationship to head of family.	Sex.	Age.	Birthplace.	Native language. Reads.	Writes.	English language. Reads.	Writes.	Speaks.	Years in the United States.
1140	Father........	M.	77	Basilicata	No...	No....	No...	No....	No....	10
	Mother	F.	76	Basilicata	No...	No....	No...	No....	No....	10
	Mother-in-law	F.	80	Basilicata	No...	No....	No...	No....	No....	13
1141	Head	M.	40	Basilicata..........	No...	No....	No...	No....	Yes...	12
	Wife..........	F.	42	Basilicata..........	No...	No....	No...	No....	No....	6
1142	Head	M.	43	Basilicata..........	No...	No....	No...	No....	Yes...	12
	Wife..........	F.	43	Basilicata..........	No...	No....	No...	No....	No....	4
	Son	M.	13	Basilicata..........	Yes..	Yes..	Yes..	Yes...	Yes..	4
1143	Head	M.	34	Basilicata..........	Yes..	Yes..	No...	No....	No....	8
	Wife..........	F.	30	Basilicata..........	No...	No....	No...	No....	No....	8
1144	Head	M.	28	Basilicata..........	No...	No....	No...	No....	Yes...	6
	Wife..........	F.	20	Basilicata..........	No...	No....	No...	No....	No....	5
1145	Head	M.	25	Basilicata..........	No...	No....	No...	No....	Yes...	10
	Wife..........	F.	22	Basilicata..........	No...	No....	No...	No....	Yes...	4
	Mother	F.	60	Basilicata..........	No...	No....	No ..	No....	No....	10
1146	Head	M.	33	Basilicata..........	Yes..	Yes..	Yes..	Yes..	Yes...	15
	Wife..........	F.	30	Basilicata..........	No...	No....	No...	No....	Yes...	12
	Son	M.	11	United States......	Yes..	Yes..	Yes..	Yes..	Yes...	....
1147	Head	M.	31	Basilicata..........	No...	No....	No...	No....	Yes...	10
	Wife..........	F.	19	Basilicata..........	No...	No....	No...	No....	Yes...	13
1148	Head	M.	66	Basilicata..........	No...	No....	No...	No....	Yes...	15
	Wife..........	F.	52	Basilicata..........	No...	No....	No...	No....	No....	15
	Son	M.	21	Basilicata..........	Yes..	Yes..	Yes..	Yes..	Yes...	15
	Daughter	F.	19	Basilicata..........	Yes..	Yes..	Yes..	Yes..	Yes...	15
1149	Head	M.	47	Basilicata..........	Yes..	Yes..	No...	No....	Yes..	23
	Wife..........	F.	44	Basilicata..........	No...	No....	No...	No....	Yes...	17
	Son	M.	23	Basilicata..........	No...	No....	No...	No....	Yes...	17
	Daughter	F.	14	United States......	Yes..	Yes..	Yes..	Yes..	Yes...	....
	Son	M.	11	United States......	Yes..	Yes..	Yes..	Yes..	Yes...	....
	Son	M.	10	United States......	Yes..	Yes..	Yes..	Yes..	Yes...	....
1150	Head	M.	28	Basilicata..........	Yes..	Yes..	Yes..	Yes..	Yes...	15
	Wife..........	F.	25	Basilicata..........	No...	No....	No...	No....	No....	7
	Aunt	F.	50	Basilicata..........	No...	No....	No...	No....	Yes...	14
1151	Head	M.	36	Basilicata..........	No...	No....	No...	No....	Yes...	9
	Wife..........	F.	33	Basilicata..........	No...	No....	No...	No....	No....	8
	Brother	M.	30	Basilicata..........	Yes..	Yes..	No...	No....	Yes...	4
	Sister-in-law..	F.	23	Basilicata..........	No...	No....	No...	No....	No....	4
1152	Head	M.	22	Basilicata..........	No...	No....	No...	No....	Yes...	7
	Wife	F.	16	Basilicata..........	No...	No....	No...	No....	No....	5
	Brother	M.	18	Basilicata..........	No...	No....	No...	No....	No....	1
	Sister	F.	21	Basilicata	No...	No....	No...	No....	Yes...	10
1153	Head	M.	33	Basilicata..........	No...	No....	No...	No....	Yes...	20
	Wife..........	F.	33	Basilicata..........	No...	No....	No...	No....	No....	9
1154	Head	F.	45	Basilicata..........	No...	No....	No...	No....	No....	2
	Son	M.	22	Basilicata..........	Yes..	Yes..	No...	No....	Yes...	7
	Son	M.	16	Basilicata..........	Yes..	Yes..	No...	No....	Yes...	3
1155	Head	M.	34	Basilicata..........	No...	No....	No...	No....	Yes...	11
	Wife..........	F.	32	Basilicata..........	No...	No....	No...	No....	No....	7
1156	Head	M.	32	Basilicata..........	Yes..	Yes..	No...	No....	Yes...	15
	Wife..........	F.	29	Sweden	Yes..	Yes..	Yes..	Yes..	Yes...	15
1157	Head	M.	39	Basilicata..........	Yes..	Yes..	No...	No....	Yes...	14
	Wife..........	F.	27	Basilicata..........	Yes..	Yes..	No...	No....	No....	4
1158	Head	M.	32	Basilicata..........	Yes..	Yes..	Yes..	Yes..	Yes...	17
	Wife..........	F.	24	Basilicata..........	No...	No....	No...	No....	Yes...	9
	Mother	F.	70	Basilicata..........	No...	No....	No...	No....	No....	12
1159	Head	M.	50	Basilicata..........	No...	No....	No...	No....	Yes...	14
	Wife..........	F.	47	Basilicata..........	No...	No....	No...	No....	No....	12

TABLE **II.**—GENERAL CONDITION AS TO LITERACY AND ILLITERACY, BY FAMILIES AND INDIVIDUALS—Continued.

[This table includes only persons 10 years of age or over.]

Family number.	Relationship to head of family.	Sex.	Age.	Birthplace.	Native language. Reads.	Native language. Writes.	English language. Reads.	English language. Writes.	English language. Speaks.	Years in the United States.
1159	Son	M.	15	Basilicata	No	No	Yes	Yes	Yes	12
	Son	M.	10	United States	Yes	Yes	Yes	Yes	Yes	
1160	Head	M.	32	Basilicata	Yes	Yes	Yes	No	Yes	9
	Wife	F.	26	Basilicata	Yes	Yes	No	No	Yes	7
	Mother	F.	70	Basilicata	No	No	No	No	No	7
	Brother	M.	19	Basilicata	Yes	Yes	Yes	Yes	Yes	8
1161	Head	M.	63	Basilicata	Yes	Yes	No	No	No	5
	Wife	F.	53	Basilicata	No	No	No	No	No	5
1162	Head	M.	41	Basilicata	Yes	Yes	Yes	No	Yes	13
	Wife	F.	27	Lombardy	Yes	Yes	No	No	Yes	13
	Son	M.	10	United States	Yes	Yes	Yes	Yes	Yes	
1163	Head	M.	47	Campania	No	No	No	No	Yes	13
	Wife	F.	44	Campania	No	No	No	No	No	8
	Mother	F.	68	Campania	No	No	No	No	No	8
1164	Head	M.	27	Basilicata	No	No	No	No	Yes	4
	Wife	F.	16	Basilicata	No	No	No	No	No	3
	Mother-in-law	F.	54	Basilicata	No	No	No	No	No	3
1165	Head	M.	31	Basilicata	No	No	No	No	Yes	5
	Wife	F.	30	Basilicata	No	No	No	No	No	4
1166	Head	M.	35	Sicily	Yes	Yes	No	No	Yes	6
	Wife	F.	33	Sicily	No	No	No	No	No	6
	Daughter	F.	12	Sicily	No	No	Yes	Yes	Yes	6
1167	Head	M.	40	Basilicata	No	No	No	No	Yes	9
	Wife	F.	45	Basilicata	No	No	No	No	No	6
1168	Head	M.	47	Basilicata	No	No	No	No	Yes	10
	Wife	F.	50	Basilicata	No	No	No	No	No	5
	Son	M.	10	Basilicata	No	No	Yes	Yes	Yes	5
1169	Head	M.	40	Basilicata	Yes	Yes	No	No	Yes	18
	Wife	F.	27	Basilicata	No	No	No	No	Yes	19
	Daughter	F.	12	United States	Yes	Yes	Yes	Yes	Yes	
	Son	M.	10	United States	Yes	Yes	Yes	Yes	Yes	
1170	Head	M.	28	Basilicata	Yes	Yes	No	No	Yes	7
	Wife	F.	20	Basilicata	No	No	No	No	No	1/2
1171	Head	M.	34	Basilicata	No	No	No	No	Yes	15
	Wife	F.	26	Basilicata	No	No	No	No	No	5
1172	Head	M.	36	Basilicata	No	No	No	No	Yes	14
	Wife	F.	24	Abruzzo	No	No	No	No	No	14
1173	Head	M.	32	Basilicata	No	No	No	No	Yes	8
	Wife	F.	32	Basilicata	No	No	No	No	No	6
1174	Head	M.	37	Basilicata	No	No	No	No	Yes	13
	Wife	F.	23	Basilicata	No	No	No	No	Yes	17
1175	Head	M.	44	Marches	No	No	No	No	Yes	14
	Wife	F.	47	Basilicata	No	No	No	No	No	8
	Son	M.	16	Basilicata	No	No	Yes	Yes	Yes	8
	Daughter	F.	15	Basilicata	No	No	Yes	Yes	Yes	8
1176	Head	M.	40	Basilicata	No	No	No	No	Yes	13
	Wife	F.	34	Basilicata	No	No	No	No	Yes	10
	Boarder	M.	30	Calabria	No	No	No	No	No	14
1177	Head	M.	53	Calabria	Yes	Yes	No	No	Yes	23
	Wife	F.	44	Calabria	No	No	No	No	No	16
	Son	M.	22	Calabria	Yes	Yes	No	No	Yes	16
	Son	M.	14	United States	Yes	Yes	Yes	Yes	Yes	
	Daughter	F.	11	United States	Yes	Yes	Yes	Yes	Yes	
1178	Head	M.	39	Basilicata	Yes	Yes	No	No	Yes	7
	Wife	F.	34	Basilicata	No	No	No	No	No	1/2
	Daughter	F.	13	Basilicata	Yes	Yes	No	No	No	1/2

TABLE **II.**—GENERAL CONDITION AS TO LITERACY AND ILLITERACY, BY
FAMILIES AND INDIVIDUALS—Continued.

[This table includes only persons 10 years of age or over.]

Family number.	Relationship to head of family.	Sex.	Age.	Birthplace.	Native language. Reads.	Writes.	English language. Reads.	Writes.	Speaks.	Years in the United States.
1179	Head	M.	50	Basilicata	No...	No....	No...	No....	Yes...	18
	Wife	F.	50	Basilicata	No...	No....	No...	No....	Yes...	18
1180	Head	M.	45	Basilicata	No...	No....	No...	No....	Yes...	19
	Wife	F.	50	Basilicata	No...	No....	No...	No....	No....	13
	Son	M.	19	Basilicata	Yes...	Yes...	Yes.	Yes	Yes...	13
	Daughter	F.	14	United States	Yes...	Yes...	Yes.	Yes.	Yes...	
	Daughter	F.	14	United States	Yes...	Yes...	Yes.	Yes.	Yes	
1181	Head	M.	43	Basilicata	Yes...	Yes...	No...	No....	Yes...	17
	Wife	F.	39	Basilicata	Yes...	Yes...	No...	No....	Yes...	16
	Daughter	F.	18	Basilicata	No...	No....	Yes.	Yes.	Yes...	16
	Daughter	F.	15	United States	Yes..	Yes...	Yes.	Yes..	Yes...	
	Son	M.	13	United States	Yes..	Yes...	Yes.	Yes..	Yes...	
	Son	M.	12	United States	Yes..	Yes...	Yes.	Yes..	Yes...	
	Son	M.	10	United States	Yes..	Yes...	Yes.	Yes..	Yes...	
1182	Head	M.	29	Basilicata	Yes..	Yes...	Yes..	Yes..	Yes...	15
	Wife	F.	18	Basilicata	Yes..	Yes...	Yes..	Yes..	Yes...	16
1183	Head	M.	42	Basilicata	No...	No....	No...	No....	Yes...	10
	Wife	F.	37	Basilicata	No...	No....	No...	No....	Yes...	10
	Daughter	F.	14	Basilicata	No...	No....	Yes..	Yes..	Yes...	10
	Daughter	F.	10	Basilicata	No...	No....	No ..	No....	Yes...	10
1184	Cooperative	M.	23	Basilicata	Yes..	Yes...	No...	No....	Yes...	4
	Cooperative	M.	30	Basilicata	No...	No....	No...	No....	Yes...	10
1185	Head	M.	37	Basilicata	Yes..	Yes...	No..	No....	Yes...	15
	Wife	F.	23	Basilicata	Yes..	Yes...	No...	No....	No....	6
1186	Head	M.	24	Basilicata	No...	No....	No...	No....	Yes...	11
	Mother	F.	54	Basilicata	No...	No....	No...	No....	No ...	3
	Brother	M.	18	Basilicata	No...	No....	Yes.	Yes..	Yes...	7
	Brother	M.	16	Basilicata	No...	No....	No...	No....	Yes...	4
1187	Head	M.	33	Basilicata	Yes..	Yes...	No...	No....	Yes...	9
	Wife	F.	30	Basilicata	No...	No....	No...	No....	No....	8
	Lodger	M.	19	Basilicata	No...	No....	No...	No....	Yes...	7
	Lodger	M.	22	Basilicata	Yes..	Yes...	No...	No....	No....	2
1188	Head	M.	40	Basilicata	No...	No....	No...	No....	Yes...	13
	Wife	F.	29	Basilicata	No...	No....	No...	No....	No....	11
	Son	M.	10	United States	Yes..	Yes...	Yes..	Yes..	Yes...	
1189	Head	M.	23	Basilicata	Yes..	Yes...	No...	No....	No....	1
	Wife	F.	24	Basilicata	Yes..	Yes...	No...	No....	No....	1
	Father	M.	56	Basilicata	No...	No....	No...	No....	No....	4
1190	Head	M.	39	Campania	No...	No....	No...	No....	Yes...	11
	Wife	F.	26	Basilicata	Yes..	Yes...	No...	No....	Yes...	14
	Daughter	F.	13	United States	No...	No....	No...	No....	Yes...	
1191	Head	M.	34	Basilicata	No...	No....	No...	No....	Yes...	10
	Wife	F.	40	Basilicata	No...	No....	No...	No....	No....	5
1192	Head	M.	30	Basilicata	No...	No....	No...	No....	Yes...	15
	Wife	F.	26	Basilicata	No...	No....	No...	No....	Yes...	15
1193	Head	M.	26	Basilicata	No...	No....	No...	No....	Yes...	5
	Wife	F	25	Basilicata	No...	No....	No...	No....	Yes...	5
1194	Head	M.	36	Basilicata	No...	No....	No...	No....	Yes...	10
	Wife	F.	25	Basilicata	No...	No....	No...	No....	No....	6
1195	Head	M.	37	Basilicata	No...	No....	No...	No....	Yes...	12
	Wife	F.	26	Basilicata	No...	No....	No...	No....	No....	10
1196	Head	M.	30	Basilicata	Reads.	No....	Reads.	No....	Yes...	9
	Wife	F.	26	Basilicata	No...	No....	No...	No....	Yes...	5
1197	Cooperative	M.	24	Sicily	No...	No....	No...	No....	Yes...	2
	Cooperative	M.	26	Sicily	No...	No....	No...	No....	Yes...	2
	Cooperative	M.	22	Sicily	No...	No....	No...	No....	Yes...	2
	Cooperative	M.	21	Sicily	Yes..	Yes...	No...	No....	Yes...	3

TABLE **II.**—GENERAL CONDITION AS TO LITERACY AND ILLITERACY, BY FAMILIES AND INDIVIDUALS—Continued.

[This table includes only persons 10 years of age or over.]

Family number.	Relationship to head of family.	Sex.	Age.	Birthplace.	Native language.		English language.			Years in the United States.
					Reads.	Writes.	Reads.	Writes.	Speaks.	
1198	Head	M.	28	Basilicata	No	No	No	No	Yes	6
	Wife	F.	28	Basilicata	No	No	No	No	No	4
1199	Head	M.	36	Basilicata	Yes	Yes	No	No	Yes	19
	Wife	F.	30	Basilicata	No	No	No	No	Yes	8
1200	Head	M.	31	Basilicata	No	No	No	No	Yes	10
	Wife	F.	22	Basilicata	No	No	No	No	No	6
	Mother-in-law	F.	60	Basilicata	No	No	No	No	No	6
1201	Cooperative	M.	45	Basilicata	No	No	No	No	No	1
	Cooperative	M.	20	Basilicata	Yes	Yes	Yes	No	Yes	4
	Cooperative	M.	30	Basilicata	Yes	Yes	No	No	Yes	4
1202	Head	M.	32	Venetia	Yes	Yes	No	No	Yes	4
	Wife	F.	25	Tuscany	No	No	No	No	Yes	6
1203	Head	M.	31	Venetia	Yes	Yes	No	No	Yes	3
	Wife	F.	22	Venetia	Yes	Yes	No	No	Yes	3
	Brother	M.	24	Venetia	Yes	Yes	No	No	Yes	3
1204	Head	M.	37	Emilia	No	No	No	No	Yes	7
	Wife	F.	26	Emilia	No	No	No	No	No	7
1205	Head	M.	26	Tuscany	Yes	Yes	No	No	No	5
	Wife	F.	28	Tuscany	Yes	Yes	No	No	No	4
1206	Head	M.	32	Lombardy	Yes	Yes	No	No	Yes	13
	Wife	F.	25	Lombardy	Yes	Yes	Yes	No	Yes	5
1207	Head	M.	37	Liguria	Yes	Yes	Yes	No	Yes	7
	Wife	F.	41	Liguria	Yes	Yes	No	No	Yes	14
1208	Head	M.	51	Emilia	No	No	No	No	No	7
	Wife	F.	45	Emilia	No	No	No	No	No	7
	Daughter	F.	19	Emilia	No	No	No	No	Yes	7
	Daughter	F.	12	Emilia	No	No	No	No	Yes	7
	Daughter	F.	10	Emilia	No	No	Yes	Yes	Yes	7
1209	Head	M.	60	Lombardy	Yes	Yes	No	No	Yes	15
	Wife	F.	50	Lombardy	Yes	Yes	No	No	Yes	10
1210	Head	M.	40	Liguria	Yes	Yes	Yes	No	Yes	18
	Wife	F.	35	Liguria	No	No	No	No	No	15
	Son	M.	13	United States	Yes	Yes	Yes	Yes	Yes	
	Son	M.	12	United States	Yes	Yes	Yes	Yes	Yes	
	Brother-in-law	M.	23	Liguria	No	No	No	No	No	4
1211	Head	M.	70	Liguria	Yes	Yes	Yes	No	Yes	57
	Wife	F.	45	Liguria	No	No	No	No	Yes	28
	Daughter	F.	25	United States	Yes	Yes	Yes	Yes	Yes	
	Son	M.	22	United States	Yes	Yes	Yes	Yes	Yes	
	Son	M.	21	United States	Yes	Yes	Yes	Yes	Yes	
	Son	M.	17	United States	Yes	Yes	Yes	Yes	Yes	
	Daughter	F.	15	United States	Yes	Yes	Yes	Yes	Yes	
	Cousin-in-law	M.	21	Liguria	Yes	Yes	No	No	No	1
1212	Head	M.	42	Tuscany	Yes	Yes	No	No	Yes	8
	Wife	F.	44	Tuscany	Yes	Yes	No	No	No	3
	Son	M.	13	Tuscany	Yes	Yes	Yes	Yes	Yes	8
1213	Head	M.	42	Liguria	No	No	Yes	Yes	Yes	40
	Wife	F.	35	United States	Yes	Yes	Yes	Yes	Yes	
	Son	M.	12	United States	Yes	Yes	Yes	Yes	Yes	
1214	Head	M.	34	Sicily	Yes	Yes	No	No	Yes	6
	Wife	F.	28	Sicily	No	No	No	No	No	6
	Son	M.	10	Sicily	No	No	No	No	Yes	6
1215	Head	M.	44	Sicily	No	No	No	No	Yes	18
	Wife	F.	38	Sicily	No	No	No	No	No	5
	Son	M.	14	Sicily	Yes	Yes	Yes	Yes	Yes	5
	Son	M.	10	Sicily	No	No	Yes	Yes	Yes	5
	Brother-in-law	M.	33	Sicily	No	No	No	No	Yes	5

TABLE **II.**—GENERAL CONDITION AS TO LITERACY AND ILLITERACY, BY FAMILIES AND INDIVIDUALS—Continued.

[This table includes only persons 10 years of age or over.]

Family number.	Relationship to head of family.	Sex.	Age.	Birthplace.	Native language.		English language.			Years in the United States.
					Reads.	Writes.	Reads.	Writes.	Speaks.	
1216	Head	M.	25	Tuscany	No...	No....	No...	No....	Yes...	5
	Wife	F.	19	Tuscany	Yes..	Yes...	No...	No....	No....	6
	Father-in-law.	M.	60	Tuscany	No...	No....	No...	No....	No....	10
1217	Head	M.	33	Venetia	Yes..	Yes...	Yes...	No....	Yes...	8
	Wife	F.	28	Venetia	No...	No....	No...	No....	Yes...	8
1218	Head	M.	48	Abruzzo	Yes..	Yes...	No...	No....	No....	4
	Wife	F.	45	Abruzzo	Yes..	No....	No...	No....	No....	4
	Son	M.	17	Abruzzo	Yes..	Yes...	Yes..	Yes..	Yes...	4
	Son	M.	15	Abruzzo	No...	No....	Yes..	Yes..	Yes...	4
	Son	M.	10	Abruzzo	No...	No....	Yes..	Yes..	Yes...	4
1219	Head	M.	56	Emilia	Yes..	Yes...	Yes..	Yes..	Yes...	8
	Wife	F.	44	Emilia	No...	No....	No...	No....	No....	8
	Daughter	F.	15	Emilia	No...	No....	Yes..	Yes..	Yes...	8
	Son	M.	10	Emilia	No...	No....	Yes..	Yes..	Yes...	8
1220	Head	M.	40	Sicily	No...	No....	No...	No....	No....	6
	Wife	F.	33	Sicily	No...	No....	No...	No....	No....	5
	Son	M.	13	Sicily	No...	No....	Yes..	Yes..	Yes...	5
	Son	M.	11	Sicily	No...	No....	Yes..	Yes..	Yes...	5
1221	Head	M.	31	Tuscany	No...	No....	No...	No...	Yes...	4
1222	Head	M.	22	Liguria	Yes..	Yes...	No...	No....	No....	$\frac{1}{12}$
	Sister	F.	24	Liguria	Yes..	Yes...	No...	No....	No....	$\frac{1}{12}$
1223	Cooperative...	M.	20	Tuscany	Yes..	Yes...	No...	No....	Yes...	4
	Cooperative...	M.	17	Tuscany	Yes..	Yes...	No...	No....	Yes...	3
	Cooperative...	M.	31	Tuscany	No...	No....	No...	No....	No....	1
	Cooperative...	M.	26	Tuscany	No...	No....	No...	No....	No....	$\frac{1}{12}$
1224	Cooperative...	M.	25	Abruzzo	Yes..	Yes...	No...	No....	No....	3
	Cooperative...	M.	29	Abruzzo	Yes..	Yes...	No...	No....	Yes..	2
	Cooperative...	M.	24	Abruzzo	Yes..	Yes...	No...	No....	Yes...	2
1225	Head	M.	40	Abruzzo	Yes..	Yes...	Yes..	Yes..	Yes...	9
	Wife	F.	34	Abruzzo	No...	No....	No...	No....	No....	9
1226	Head	M.	34	Lombardy	Yes..	Yes...	No...	No....	Yes...	9
	Wife	F.	33	Emilia	Yes..	Yes...	No...	No....	Yes...	6
	Boarder	M.	34	Emilia	Yes..	Yes...	Yes..	No....	Yes...	(a)
1227	Head	M.	42	Venetia	No...	No....	No...	No....	No....	3
1228	Head	M.	44	Sicily	Yes..	Yes...	Yes..	Yes..	Yes...	15
	Housekeeper..	F.	60	Liguria	No	No....	No...	No....	No....	14
1229	Head	M.	34	Tuscany	Yes..	Yes...	No...	No....	Yes...	5
	Wife	F.	34	Tuscany	No...	No....	No...	No....	No....	3
1230	Head	M.	30	Liguria	Yes..	Yes...	No...	No....	Yes...	3
	Wife	F.	30	Liguria	Yes..	Yes...	No...	No....	No....	1
1231	Head	M.	30	Tuscany	No...	No....	No...	No....	Yes...	7
	Wife	F.	26	Tuscany	No...	No....	No...	No....	Yes...	6
1232	Head	M.	39	Tuscany	Yes..	Yes...	No...	No....	Yes...	7
	Wife	F.	33	Tuscany	No...	No....	No...	No....	Yes...	7
1233	Head	M.	70	Liguria	No...	No....	No...	No....	Yes...	18
	Wife	F.	54	Liguria	No...	No....	No...	No....	Yes...	18
1234	Head	M.	52	Sicily	Yes..	Yes...	No...	No....	Yes...	25
	Wife	F.	44	Sicily	No...	No....	No...	No....	Yes...	25
	Sister	F.	31	Sicily	Yes..	Yes...	No...	No....	No....	2
	Cousin	M.	21	Sicily	Yes..	Yes...	Yes..	Yes..	Yes...	5
1235	Head	M.	29	Venetia	Yes..	Yes...	No...	No....	No....	1
	Wife	F.	24	Liguria	Yes..	Yes...	No...	No....	No....	1
1236	Head	M.	24	Lombardy	No...	No....	No...	No....	Yes...	6
	Wife	F.	21	Lombardy	Yes..	No....	No...	No....	Yes...	5

a Not reported.

TABLE **II.**—GENERAL CONDITION AS TO LITERACY AND ILLITERACY, BY FAMILIES AND INDIVIDUALS—Continued.

[This table includes only persons 10 years of age or over.]

Family number.	Relationship to head of family.	Sex.	Age.	Birthplace.	Native language. Reads.	Writes.	English language. Reads.	Writes.	Speaks.	Years in the United States.
1237	Head	M.	27	Piedmont	Yes..	Yes...	Yes...	No...	Yes...	5
	Wife	F.	23	Piedmont	Yes..	Yes...	No...	No...	Yes...	5
	Mother-in-law	F.	61	Piedmont	Yes..	Yes...	No...	No...	No....	1½
	Brother-in-law	M.	27	Piedmont	Yes..	Yes...	No...	No...	Yes...	5
1238	Head	M.	29	Lombardy	No...	No....	No...	No...	Yes...	10
	Wife	F.	28	Lombardy	Yes..	Yes...	No...	No...	No....	10
1239	Head	M.	32	Lombardy	No...	No....	No...	No...	Yes...	4
	Wife	F.	31	Lombardy	No...	No....	No ..	No...	Yes...	4
	Mother-in-law	F.	60	Lombardy	No...	No....	No...	No...	No....	5
	Brother-in-law	M.	22	Lombardy	Yes..	Yes...	Yes..	Yes..	Yes...	7
1240	Head	M.	35	Lombardy	No...	No....	No...	No...	Yes...	13
	Wife	F.	36	Lombardy	Yes..	Yes...	No...	No...	Yes...	13
	Son	M.	13	Lombardy	No...	No....	Yes..	Yes..	Yes...	13
1241	Head	M.	25	Liguria	Yes..	Yes...	No..	No...	Yes...	6
	Wife	F.	24	Liguria	Yes..	Yes...	No...	No...	Yes...	6
	Brother-in-law	M.	29	Liguria	Yes..	Yes...	No...	No...	Yes...	4
1242	Head	M.	39	Lombardy	Yes..	Yes...	Yes..	No...	Yes...	6
	Wife	F.	38	Lombardy	Yes..	Yes...	No...	No...	Yes...	7
	Daughter	F.	12	Lombardy	No...	No....	Yes..	Yes..	Yes...	7
1243	Head	M.	32	Sicily	Yes..	Yes...	Yes..	Yes..	Yes...	15
	Wife	F.	25	Sicily	Yes..	Yes...	Yes..	Yes..	Yes...	11
1244	Head	M.	23	Liguria	Yes..	Yes...	Yes..	Yes..	Yes...	5
	Wife	F.	21	Liguria	Yes..	Yes...	Yes..	Yes..	Yes...	5
1245	Head	M.	32	Liguria	Yes..	Yes...	No...	No...	Yes...	11
	Wife	F.	27	Liguria	Yes..	Yes...	No...	No...	Yes...	11
1246	Head	M.	22	Liguria	Yes..	Yes...	No...	No...	Yes...	5
	Wife	F.	21	Liguria	Yes..	Yes...	No...	No...	Yes...	4
1247	Head	M.	50	Basilicata	No...	No....	No...	No...	No....	24
	Wife	F.	50	Basilicata	No...	No....	No...	No...	No....	16
	Daughter	F.	16	Basilicata	No...	No....	Yes..	Yes..	Yes...	16
	Daughter	F.	14	United States	Yes..	Yes...	Yes..	Yes..	Yes...	....
1248	Head	M.	28	Basilicata	Yes..	Yes...	Yes..	Yes..	Yes...	17
	Wife	F.	23	Basilicata	Yes..	Yes...	No...	No...	Yes...	7
1249	Head	M.	37	Abruzzo	Yes..	Yes...	No...	No...	Yes...	6
	Wife	F.	30	Abruzzo	No...	No....	No...	No...	No....	6
1250	Head	M.	34	Basilicata	No...	No....	No...	No...	Yes...	7
	Wife	F.	29	Basilicata	No...	No....	No...	No...	No....	4
	Sister-in-law	F.	16	Basilicata	Yes..	Yes...	No...	No...	Yes...	3
1251	Head	M.	25	Basilicata	No...	No....	No...	No...	Yes...	15
	Wife	F.	40	Basilicata	No...	No....	No...	No...	No....	14
1252	Head	M.	31	Basilicata	Yes..	Yes...	No...	No...	Yes...	6
	Wife	F.	25	Basilicata	No...	No....	No...	No...	No....	4
	Brother-in-law	M.	20	Basilicata	Yes..	Yes...	No...	No...	Yes...	8
	Lodger	M.	22	Basilicata	No...	No....	No...	No...	Yes...	10
1253	Head	M.	32	Basilicata	No...	No....	No...	No...	No....	3
	Wife	F.	32	Basilicata	No...	No....	No...	No...	No....	3
1254	Head	M.	39	Campania	No...	No....	No...	No...	Yes...	11
	Wife	F.	39	Campania	No...	No....	No...	No...	No....	11
	Nephew	M.	24	Campania	Yes..	Yes...	No...	No...	No....	2
1255	Head	M.	37	Campania	Yes..	Yes...	Yes..	Yes..	Yes...	15
	Wife	F.	24	Basilicata	No...	No....	No...	No...	Yes...	20
1256	Head	M.	52	Basilicata	No...	No....	No...	No...	Yes...	22
	Wife	F.	50	Basilicata	No...	No....	No...	No...	No....	20
	Son	M.	19	United States	Yes..	Yes...	Yes..	Yes..	Yes...	....
1257	Head	M.	28	Lombardy	Yes..	Yes...	No...	No...	Yes...	8
	Wife	F.	24	Lombardy	Yes..	Yes...	No...	No...	No....	4

TABLE **II.**—GENERAL CONDITION AS TO LITERACY AND ILLITERACY, BY FAMILIES AND INDIVIDUALS—Continued.

[This table includes only persons 10 years of age or over.]

Family number.	Relationship to head of family.	Sex.	Age.	Birthplace.	Native language.		English language.			Years in the United States.
					Reads.	Writes.	Reads.	Writes.	Speaks.	
1258	Head	M.	47	Basilicata	Yes..	Yes...	No...	No....	Yes...	16
	Wife	F.	27	Basilicata	No...	No....	No...	No....	Yes...	11
1259	Head	M.	25	Basilicata	No...	No....	No...	No....	Yes...	7
	Wife	F.	23	Basilicata	No...	No....	No...	No....	No....	4
1260	Head	M.	31	Lombardy	Yes..	Yes...	No...	No....	Yes...	8
	Sister	F.	45	Lombardy	No...	No....	No...	No....	Yes...	8
1261	Cooperative ..	M.	17	Tuscany	Yes..	Yes...	No...	No....	Yes...	3
	Cooperative ..	M.	47	Tuscany	Yes..	Yes...	No...	No....	No....	4
	Cooperative ..	M.	32	Tuscany	Yes..	Yes...	No...	No....	No....	2
	Cooperative ..	M.	26	Tuscany	Yes..	Yes...	No...	No....	No....	2
1262	Head	M.	37	Basilicata	No...	No....	No...	No....	Yes...	9
	Wife	F.	34	Basilicata	No...	No....	No...	No....	No....	8
	Lodger	M.	50	Basilicata	No...	No....	No...	No....	Yes...	11
	Lodger	M.	29	Abruzzo	Yes..	Yes...	No...	No....	Yes...	8
	Lodger	F.	22	Abruzzo	Yes..	Yes...	No...	No....	No....	$\frac{4}{12}$
1263	Head	M	50	Lombardy	Yes..	Yes...	No...	No....	Yes...	12
	Wife	F.	42	Basilicata	Yes..	Yes...	No...	No....	Yes...	12
	Daughter	F.	18	Basilicata	Yes..	Yes...	Yes..	Yes...	Yes...	12
	Daughter	F.	10	United States	Yes..	Yes...	Yes...	Yes...	Yes...	....
1264	Head	M.	52	Basilicata	No...	No....	No...	No....	Yes...	9
	Wife	F.	25	Basilicata	No...	No....	No...	No....	Yes...	7
1265	Head	M.	30	Basilicata	Yes..	Yes...	No. .	No....	Yes...	14
	Wife	F.	31	Basilicata	No...	No....	No...	No....	No....	5
	Stepson	M.	12	Basilicata	No...	No....	Yes...	Yes...	Yes...	5
1266	Head	M.	22	Basilicata	No...	No....	No...	No....	Yes...	6
	Wife	F.	16	Basilicata	No...	No....	No...	No....	Yes...	5
1267	Head	M.	60	Basilicata	No...	No....	No...	No....	No....	5
	Wife	F.	50	Basilicata	No...	No....	No...	No....	No....	5
	Son	M.	20	Basilicata	No...	No. .	No...	No....	Yes...	6
1268	Head	M.	39	Basilicata	No...	No....	No...	No....	Yes...	13
	Wife	F.	36	Basilicata	No...	No....	No...	No....	No...	6
	Daughter	F.	12	Basilicata	No...	No....	Yes..	Yes...	Yes...	6
1269	Head	M.	23	Basilicata	No...	No....	No...	No....	Yes...	9
	Wife	F.	17	Basilicata	No...	No....	No...	No....	No....	5
1270	Head	M.	40	Basilicata	No...	No....	No...	No....	Yes...	14
	Wife	F.	40	Basilicata	No...	No....	No...	No....	No....	13
	Son	M.	12	United States	Yes..	Yes...	Yes...	Yes...	Yes...	....
1271	Head	M.	29	Basilicata	No...	No....	No...	No....	Yes...	9
	Wife	F.	20	Basilicata	No...	No....	No...	No....	No....	5
1272	Cooperative ..	M.	24	Basilicata	No...	No....	No...	No....	Yes...	5
	Cooperative ..	M.	44	Basilicata	No...	No....	No...	No....	No....	3
	Cooperative ..	M.	40	Basilicata	No...	No....	No...	No....	Yes...	5
	Cooperative ..	M.	27	Basilicata	No...	No....	No...	No....	No....	$\frac{2}{12}$
	Cooperative ..	M.	45	Basilicata	No...	No....	No...	No....	No....	4
1273	Head	M.	33	Basilicata	No...	No....	No...	No....	Yes...	9
	Wife	F.	30	Basilicata	No...	No....	No...	No....	No....	5
1274	Head	M.	30	Basilicata	No...	No....	No...	No....	Yes...	9
	Wife	F.	23	Basilicata	No...	No....	No...	No....	No....	4
1275	Head	M.	30	Basilicata	No...	No....	No...	No....	Yes...	11
	Wife	F.	28	Basilicata	No...	No....	No...	No....	No....	9
1276	Head	M.	35	Basilicata	Reads.	No....	No...	No....	Yes...	10
	Wife	F.	32	Basilicata	No...	No....	No...	No....	Yes...	5
	Daughter	F.	14	Basilicata	Yes..	No....	Yes..	Yes...	Yes...	5
	Son	M.	11	Basilicata	No...	No....	Yes..	Yes...	Yes...	5
1277	Head	M.	32	Basilicata	No...	No....	No...	No....	Yes...	13
	Wife	F.	27	Basilicata	No...	No....	No...	No....	Yes...	4

TABLE **II.**—GENERAL CONDITION AS TO LITERACY AND ILLITERACY, BY FAMILIES AND INDIVIDUALS—Continued.

[This table includes only persons 10 years of age or over.]

Family number.	Relationship to head of family.	Sex.	Age.	Birthplace.	Native language. Reads.	Writes.	English language. Reads.	Writes.	Speaks.	Years in the United States.
1278	Head	M.	42	Basilicata	No	No	No	No	Yes	17
	Wife	F.	33	Basilicata	No	No	No	No	Yes	15
	Boarder	M.	29	Basilicata	No	No	No	No	Yes	6
1279	Head	M.	45	Basilicata	No	No	No	No	Yes	12
	Wife	F.	40	Basilicata	No	No	No	No	No	6
	Son	M.	19	Basilicata	Yes	Yes	Yes	Yes	Yes	6
	Daughter	F.	12	Basilicata	No	No	Yes	Yes	Yes	6
1280	Head	M.	45	Basilicata	Yes	Yes	Yes	No	Yes	16
	Wife	F.	37	Basilicata	No	No	No	No	No	15
	Daughter	F.	16	Basilicata	Yes	Yes	Yes	Yes	Yes	15
	Daughter	F.	14	United States	Yes	Yes	Yes	Yes	Yes	....
	Daughter	F.	13	United States	Yes	Yes	Yes	Yes	Yes	....
1281	Head	M.	28	Basilicata	Yes	Yes	No	No	Yes	8
	Wife	F.	27	Basilicata	No	No	No	No	No	8
1282	Head	M.	62	Basilicata	No	No	No	No	No	16
	Wife	F.	60	Basilicata	No	No	No	No	No	14
1283	Head	M.	40	Lombardy	Yes	Yes	Yes	No	Yes	15
	Wife	F.	38	Basilicata	Yes	Yes	No	No	Yes	15
	Son	M.	11	United States	Yes	Yes	Yes	Yes	Yes	....
1284	Head	M.	47	Basilicata	Yes	Yes	No	No	Yes	16
	Wife	F.	40	Basilicata	No	No	No	No	No	16
1285	Head	M.	36	Basilicata	No	No	No	No	Yes	12
	Wife	F.	31	Basilicata	No	No	No	No	No	12
	Daughter	F.	14	Basilicata	Yes	Yes	Yes	Yes	Yes	12
	Son	M.	10	United States	Yes	Yes	Yes	Yes	Yes	....
1286	Head	M.	35	Basilicata	No	No	No	No	Yes	7
	Wife	F.	44	Basilicata	No	No	No	No	No	3
	Stepson	M.	13	Basilicata	No	No	Yes	Yes	Yes	7
	Sister	F.	19	Basilicata	No	No	No	No	No	$\frac{1}{12}$
1287	Head	M.	35	Basilicata	Yes	Yes	No	No	Yes	11
	Wife	F.	35	Basilicata	No	No	No	No	Yes	8
	Brother	M.	40	Basilicata	No	No	No	No	Yes	14
1288	Head	M.	28	Sicily	Yes	Yes	No	No	Yes	6
	Wife	F.	25	Sicily	No	No	No	No	No	6
1289	Head	M.	38	Sicily	No	No	No	No	Yes	10
	Wife	F.	27	Sicily	No	No	No	No	No	6
	Father-in-law	M.	55	Sicily	No	No	No	No	No	5
	Mother-in-law	F.	52	Sicily	No	No	No	No	No	5
	Brother-in-law	M.	14	Sicily	No	No	No	No	Yes	5
1290	Head	M.	32	Sicily	No	No	No	No	No	1
	Wife	F.	35	Sicily	No	No	No	No	No	1
1291	Head	M.	35	Sicily	Yes	Yes	No	No	Yes	7
	Wife	F.	28	Sicily	Yes	Yes	No	No	No	$\frac{5}{12}$
	Daughter	F.	11	Sicily	Yes	Yes	No	No	No	$\frac{5}{12}$
1292	Head	M.	40	Basilicata	Yes	Yes	No	No	Yes	15
	Wife	F.	38	Basilicata	Yes	Yes	No	No	No	10
	Daughter	F.	14	Basilicata	No	No	Yes	Yes	Yes	10
1293	Head	M.	40	Basilicata	No	No	No	No	Yes	13
	Wife	F.	45	Basilicata	No	No	No	No	No	12
	Daughter	F.	10	United States	Yes	Yes	Yes	Yes	Yes	....
1294	Head	M.	25	Basilicata	Yes	Yes	No	No	Yes	15
	Wife	F.	17	Basilicata	Yes	Yes	No	No	Yes	11
	Father	M.	75	Basilicata	No	No	No	No	No	15
	Mother	F.	65	Basilicata	No	No	No	No	No	14
1295	Head	M.	41	Campania	Yes	Yes	Yes	Yes	Yes	15
	Wife	F.	42	Campania	No	No	No	No	No	12
	Daughter	F.	15	Campania	No	No	No	No	Yes	12
	Daughter	F.	10	United States	No	No	No	No	Yes	....
	Cousin	M.	28	Campania	No	No	No	No	Yes	3

TABLE **II.**—GENERAL CONDITION AS TO LITERACY AND ILLITERACY, BY
FAMILIES AND INDIVIDUALS—Continued.

[This table includes only persons 10 years of age or over.]

Family number.	Relationship to head of family.	Sex.	Age.	Birthplace.	Native language.		English language.			Years in the United States.
					Reads.	Writes.	Reads.	Writes.	Speaks.	
1295	Cousin........	M.	30	Campania..........	No...	No....	No...	No....	No....	5
	Cousin........	M.	42	Campania..........	No...	No....	No...	No....	No....	4
1296	Head	M.	26	Basilicata..........	Yes..	Yes...	Yes..	Yes...	Yes...	14
	Wife..........	F.	19	Basilicata..........	No...	No....	No...	No....	Yes...	8
1297	Head	M.	64	Basilicata..........	No...	No....	No...	No....	No....	9
	Son	M.	18	Basilicata..........	No...	No....	No...	No....	Yes...	9
	Daughter.....	F.	14	Basilicata..........	No...	No....	No...	No....	Yes...	9
1298	Head	M.	33	Basilicata..........	No...	No....	No...	No....	Yes...	12
	Wife..........	F.	30	Basilicata..........	No...	No....	No...	No....	Yes...	12
1299	Head	M.	49	Basilicata..........	No...	No....	No...	No....	Yes...	10
	Wife..........	F.	52	Basilicata..........	No...	No....	No...	No....	No....	9
	Daughter.....	F.	13	Basilicata..........	No...	No....	Yes..	Yes...	Yes...	9
1300	Head	M.	34	Basilicata..........	Yes..	No....	No...	No....	Yes...	16
	Wife..........	F.	33	Basilicata..........	Yes..	Yes...	No...	No....	Yes...	10
1301	Head	M.	37	Basilicata..........	No...	No....	No...	No....	Yes...	5
	Wife..........	F.	30	Basilicata..........	No...	No....	No...	No....	No....	3
	Brother-in-law	M.	23	Basilicata..........	Yes..	Yes...	No...	No....	No....	1
1302	Head	M.	26	Basilicata..........	No...	No....	No...	No....	Yes...	6
	Wife..........	F.	26	Basilicata..........	No...	No....	No...	No....	No....	4
1303	Head	M.	55	Basilicata..........	No...	No	No...	No....	No....	14
	Wife..........	F.	60	Basilicata..........	No...	No....	No...	No....	No....	6
1304	Head	M.	35	Basilicata..........	No...	No....	No...	No....	Yes...	16
	Wife..........	F.	35	Basilicata..........	No...	No....	No...	No....	Yes...	8
1305	Head	M.	42	Basilicata..........	Yes..	Yes...	No...	No....	Yes...	2
1306	Head	M.	40	Basilicata..........	No...	No....	No...	No....	Yes...	12
	Wife..........	F.	40	Basilicata..........	No...	No....	No...	No....	No....	10
	Son	M.	12	Basilicata..........	No...	No....	Yes..	Yes...	Yes...	10
1307	Head	M.	35	Basilicata..........	Yes..	Yes...	No...	No....	Yes...	13
	Wife..........	F.	28	Basilicata..........	No...	No....	No...	No....	No....	10
1308	Head	M.	45	Tuscany..........	Yes..	Yes...	No...	No....	Yes...	13
	Wife..........	F.	39	Liguria	No...	No....	No...	No....	Yes...	14
1309	Head	M.	54	Liguria	Yes..	Yes...	No...	No....	Yes...	24
	Wife..........	F.	41	Liguria	No...	No....	No...	No....	Yes...	31
	Daughter.....	F.	22	United States.......	Yes..	Yes...	Yes..	Yes...	Yes...	....
1310	Head	M.	57	Emilia	No...	No....	No...	No....	No....	11
	Wife..........	F.	54	Emilia	No...	No....	No...	No....	No....	11
	Son	M.	25	Emilia	Yes..	Yes...	Yes..	Yes...	Yes...	11
	Son	M.	19	Emilia	No...	No....	Yes..	Yes...	Yes...	11
1311	Head	M.	44	Emilia	No...	No....	No...	No....	Yes...	8
	Wife..........	F.	35	Emilia	No...	No....	No...	No....	No....	8
	Daughter.....	F.	15	Emilia	No...	No....	Yes..	Yes...	Yes...	8
	Son	M.	14	Emilia	No...	No....	Yes..	Yes...	Yes...	8
	Daughter.....	F.	12	Emilia	No...	No....	Yes..	Yes...	Yes...	8
	Daughter.....	F.	10	Emilia	No...	No....	Yes..	Yes...	Yes...	8
1312	Head	M.	49	Liguria	Yes..	Yes...	No...	No....	Yes...	13
	Wife..........	F.	36	Liguria	Yes..	Yes...	Yes..	Yes...	Yes...	13
	Daughter.....	F.	15	Liguria	Yes..	No....	Yes..	Yes...	Yes...	13
1313	Head	M.	26	Tuscany..........	Yes..	Yes...	No...	No....	Yes...	10
	Wife..........	F.	20	Tuscany..........	Yes..	Yes...	No...	No....	No....	4
1314	Head	F.	44	Lombardy..........	No...	No....	No...	No....	Yes...	30
	Daughter.....	F.	15	United States.......	Yes..	Yes...	Yes..	Yes...	Yes...	....
	Daughter.....	F.	12	United States.......	Yes..	Yes...	Yes..	Yes...	Yes...	....
	Son	M.	11	United States.......	Yes..	Yes...	Yes..	Yes...	Yes...	....
1315	Head	M.	28	Tuscany..........	Yes..	Yes...	Yes..	Yes...	Yes...	20
	Wife..........	F.	24	United States.......	Yes..	Yes...	Yes..	Yes...	Yes...	....
	Father........	M.	64	Tuscany..........	Yes..	Yes...	No...	No....	Yes...	23

TABLE **II.**—GENERAL CONDITION AS TO LITERACY AND ILLITERACY, BY FAMILIES AND INDIVIDUALS—Continued.

[This table includes only persons 10 years of age or over.]

Family number.	Relationship to head of family.	Sex.	Age.	Birthplace.	Native language. Reads.	Native language. Writes.	English language. Reads.	English language. Writes.	English language. Speaks.	Years in the United States.
1315	Mother	F.	50	Tuscany	Yes..	No....	No...	No....	Yes...	20
	Brother	M.	15	United States	Yes..	Yes...	Yes..	Yes...	Yes...	
	Boarder	M.	23	Piedmont	Yes..	Yes...	No...	No....	Yes...	3
	Boarder	M.	32	Tuscany	Yes..	Yes...	No...	No....	Yes...	3
	Boarder	M.	32	Tuscany	Yes..	Yes...	No...	No....	Yes...	7
1316	Head	M.	35	Venetia	Yes..	Yes...	No...	No....	Yes...	8
	Wife	F.	30	Venetia	Yes..	Yes...	No...	No....	Yes...	9
1317	Head	M.	56	Tuscany	No...	No....	Yes..	Yes...	Yes...	20
	Wife	F.	45	Tuscany	No...	No....	No...	No....	Yes...	20
	Son	M.	20	Tuscany	Yes..	Yes...	Yes..	Yes...	Yes...	20
	Daughter	F.	16	United States	Yes..	Yes...	Yes..	Yes...	Yes...	
	Son	M.	12	United States	Yes..	Yes...	Yes..	Yes...	Yes...	
1318	Head	F.	54	Venetia	Yes..	Yes...	No...	No....	Yes...	8
1319	Head	M.	36	Venetia	Yes..	Yes...	No...	No....	Yes...	4
	Wife	F.	22	Venetia	Yes..	Yes...	No...	No....	No....	4
1320	Head	M.	59	Liguria	Yes..	Yes...	Yes..	No....	Yes...	23
	Wife	F.	51	Liguria	Yes..	No....	Yes..	No....	No....	23
	Son	M.	21	United States	Yes..	Yes...	Yes..	Yes...	Yes...	
	Son	M.	14	United States	Yes..	Yes...	Yes..	Yes...	Yes...	
1321	Head	M.	67	Tuscany	No...	No....	No...	No....	Yes...	15
	Wife	F.	57	Tuscany	No...	No....	No...	No....	No....	6
	Son	M.	16	Tuscany	No...	No....	No...	No....	Yes...	6
	Lodger	M.	35	Tuscany	Yes..	No....	No...	No....	Yes...	3
	Lodger	M.	35	Tuscany	No...	No....	No...	No....	Yes...	3
	Lodger	M.	26	Tuscany	No...	No....	No...	No....	No....	1
1322	Head	M.	55	Lombardy	No...	No....	No...	No....	Yes...	12
	Wife	F.	50	Lombardy	Yes..	Yes...	No...	No....	Yes...	12
	Daughter	F.	20	Lombardy	Yes..	Yes...	Yes..	Yes...	Yes...	12
	Daughter	F.	16	Lombardy	No...	No....	Yes..	Yes...	Yes...	12
	Daughter	F.	12	United States	Yes..	Yes...	Yes..	Yes...	Yes...	
1323	Head	M.	28	Liguria	Yes..	Yes...	No...	No....	Yes...	7
	Wife	F.	28	Liguria	No...	No....	No...	No....	Yes...	10
1324	Head	M.	50	Liguria	No...	No....	No...	No....	Yes...	25
	Wife	F.	40	Liguria	No...	No....	No...	No....	No....	22
	Son	M.	21	United States	Yes..	Yes...	Yes	Yes...	Yes...	
	Son	M.	19	United States	Yes..	Yes...	Yes..	Yes...	Yes...	
	Daughter	F.	17	United States	Yes..	Yes...	Yes..	Yes...	Yes...	
	Son	M.	15	United States	Yes..	Yes...	Yes..	Yes...	Yes...	
	Son	M.	11	United States	Yes..	Yes...	Yes..	Yes...	Yes...	
1325	Head	F.	55	Liguria	No...	No....	No...	No....	No....	30
	Son	M.	29	United States	Yes..	No....	Yes..	No....	Yes...	
	Son	M.	24	United States	Yes..	Yes...	Yes..	Yes...	Yes...	
	Son	M.	21	United States	Yes..	Yes...	Yes..	Yes...	Yes...	
	Daughter-in-law.	F.	22	United States	Yes..	Yes...	Yes..	Yes...	Yes...	
1326	Head	M.	47	Liguria	Yes..	Yes...	No...	No....	Yes...	5
	Wife	F.	45	Liguria	No...	No....	No...	No....	No....	5
	Son	M.	19	Liguria	Yes..	Yes...	Yes..	Yes...	Yes...	5
	Daughter	F.	17	Liguria	Yes..	Yes...	No...	No....	Yes...	5
	Son	M.	15	Liguria	No...	No....	Yes..	Yes...	Yes...	5
	Son	M.	14	Liguria	No...	No....	Yes..	Yes...	Yes...	5
	Son	M.	10	Liguria	No...	No....	Yes..	Yes...	Yes...	5
	Father	M.	81	Liguria	No...	No....	No...	No....	No....	9
1327	Head	M.	42	Basilicata	No...	No....	No...	No....	Yes...	12
	Wife	F.	46	Calabria	No...	No....	No...	No....	Yes...	9
1328	Head	M.	33	Sicily	No...	No....	No...	No....	Yes...	5
	Wife	F.	33	Sicily	No...	No....	No...	No....	Yes...	5
	Mother-in-law	F.	60	Sicily	No...	No....	No...	No....	No....	5
1329	Head	M.	27	Basilicata	No...	No....	No...	No....	Yes...	18
	Wife	F.	25	Germany	No...	No....	No...	No....	Yes...	13
1330	Head	M.	44	Basilicata	No...	No....	No...	No....	Yes...	12
	Wife	F.	43	Basilicata	No...	No....	No...	No....	No....	9

TABLE **II.**—GENERAL CONDITION AS TO LITERACY AND ILLITERACY, BY FAMILIES AND INDIVIDUALS—Concluded.

[This tables includes only persons 10 years of age or over.]

Family number.	Relationship to head of family.	Sex.	Age.	Birthplace.	Native language. Reads.	Writes.	English language. Reads.	Writes.	Speaks.	Years in the United States.
1330	Daughter	F.	16	Basilicata	No	No	Yes	Yes	Yes	9
	Daughter	F.	11	Basilicata	No	No	Yes	Yes	Yes	9
1331	Head	M.	38	Basilicata	No	No	No	No	Yes	18
	Wife	F.	49	Basilicata	No	No	No	No	No	18
	Daughter	F.	16	United States	Yes	Yes	Yes	Yes	Yes	
	Boarder	M.	21	Calabria	Yes	Yes	Yes	Yes	Yes	9
1332	Head	M.	40	Calabria	No	No	No	No	Yes	8
	Wife	F.	44	Calabria	No	No	No	No	Yes	8
	Son	M.	16	Calabria	No	No	No	No	Yes	8
1333	Head	M.	30	Basilicata	No	No	No	No	Yes	13
	Wife	F.	19	Basilicata	No	No	Yes	Yes	Yes	16
1334	Head	F.	65	Basilicata	No	No	No	No	No	5
	Son	M.	26	Basilicata	No	No	No	No	Yes	9
1335	Head	M.	65	Basilicata	No	No	No	No	No	16
	Wife	F.	50	Basilicata	No	No	No	No	No	16
1336	Cooperative	M.	30	Tuscany	Yes	Yes	No	No	Yes	5
	Cooperative	M.	29	Tuscany	Yes	Yes	No	No	Yes	6
	Cooperative	M.	24	Tuscany	Yes	Yes	No	No	Yes	2
1337	Head	M.	32	Basilicata	Yes	Yes	Yes	Yes	Yes	9
	Wife	F.	25	Basilicata	Yes	Yes	No	No	No	5
	Mother	F.	60	Basilicata	No	No	No	No	No	6
	Brother	M.	21	Basilicata	Yes	Yes	Yes	Yes	Yes	7
1338	Head	M.	28	Basilicata	No	No	No	No	Yes	9
	Wife	F.	23	Basilicata	Yes	Yes	Yes	Yes	Yes	19
1339	Head	M.	27	Sicily	No	No	No	No	Yes	6
	Wife	F.	25	Sicily	No	No	No	No	No	6
	Lodger	M.	40	Sicily	No	No	No	No	Yes	6
1340	Head	M.	30	Basilicata	No	No	No	No	Yes	7
	Wife	F.	26	Basilicata	Yes	Yes	No	No	Yes	3
1341	Head	M.	24	Sicily	No	No	No	No	Yes	6
	Wife	F.	20	Sicily	Yes	Yes	No	No	Yes	5
1342	Head	M.	35	Sicily	Yes	Yes	No	No	Yes	(a)
	Wife	F.	24	Sicily	Yes	Yes	No	No	No	6
	Sister-in-law	F.	16	Sicily	No	No	No	No	No	1
1343	Head	M.	45	Campania	No	No	No	No	No	14
	Daughter	F.	12	United States	Yes	Yes	Yes	Yes	Yes	
	Mother-in-law	F.	69	Basilicata	No	No	No	No	No	11
	Sister-in-law	F.	50	Basilicata	No	No	No	No	Yes	16
	Nephew	M.	12	United States	Yes	Yes	Yes	Yes	Yes	
1344	Head	M.	49	Basilicata	No	No	No	No	No	17
	Wife	F.	31	Basilicata	No	No	No	No	Yes	15
	Son	M.	12	United States	Yes	Yes	Yes	Yes	Yes	
1345	Head	M.	38	Lombardy	Yes	Yes	No	No	No	8
1346	Head	M.	49	Basilicata	No	No	No	No	Yes	15
	Wife	F.	26	Basilicata	Yes	Yes	No	No	Yes	8
1347	Head	M.	36	Sicily	No	No	No	No	No	3
	Wife	F.	30	Sicily	No	No	No	No	No	2
1348	Head	F.	48	Lombardy	No	No	No	No	No	19
	Son	M.	22	Lombardy	Yes	Yes	Yes	Yes	Yes	19
	Son	M.	12	United States	Yes	Yes	Yes	Yes	Yes	

a Not reported.

TABLE **III.**—SCHOOL ATTENDANCE, BY FAMILIES AND INDIVIDUALS.

[This table includes all persons from 5 to 17 years of age, inclusive, and 13 persons below or above these ages reported as scholars.]

Family number.	Relationship to head of family.	Age.	School.		Family number.	Relationship to head of family.	Age.	School.	
			Mos.	Kind.				Mos.	Kind.
1	Daughter.....	5	None.		40	Son...........	13	3	Public, night.
						Son...........	7	None.	
2	Daughter.....	9	10	Public.		Son...........	7	None.	
3	Cousin.........	15	None.		43	Daughter.....	8	10	Public.
4	Son...........	15	3	Public, night.	44	Grandson.....	6	None.	
	Son...........	6	7	Public.	45	Son...........	5	None.	
	Nephew	7	None.		46	Son...........	8	10	Public.
7	Daughter.....	9	7	Public.		Son...........	5	None.	
8	Son	9	10	Public.	48	Son...........	16	3	Public.
	Daughter.....	8	10	Public.	49	Daughter.....	5	None.	
9	Son	9	None.		51	Son...........	5	7	Public.
10	Daughter.....	9	10	Public.	52	Daughter.....	11	10	Public.
	Daughter.....	7	10	Public.	53	Son...........	6	None.	
	Son...........	6	5	Public.	54	Son...........	5	2	Public.
11	Daughter.....	5	None.			Cousin.........	11	None.	
12	Son	15	6	Public, night.	56	Son	12	10	Public.
13	Daughter.....	15	None.			Son	11	10	Public.
14	Daughter.....	9	None.			Son	7	10	Public.
15	Son	17	None.		57	Son...........	15	9	Public.
16	Brother	17	None.			Daughter.....	7	10	Public.
17	Daughter.....	5	10	Private, kindergarten.		Daughter.....	5	None.	
					58	Daughter.....	14	None.	
21	Nephew	15	None.			Daughter.....	12	9	Public.
22	Son	12	10	Public.		Daughter.....	7	10	Public.
	Daughter.....	8	10	Public.		Daughter.....	5	None.	
	Son...........	5	None.		59	Daughter.....	8	10	Parochial.
24	Son	15	None.			Daughter.....	6	10	Parochial.
	Daughter.....	14	4	Public.		Son...........	5	None.	
	Daughter.....	12	10	Public.	60	Son	13	6	Parochial.
	Daughter.....	9	10	Public.		Daughter.....	11	10	Public.
	Nephew	14	None.			Daughter.....	9	10	Public.
25	Daughter.....	9	10	Public.	63	Daughter.....	10	8	Public.
26	Daughter.....	15	None.			Daughter.....	6	None.	
	Son...........	12	None.		65	Daughter.....	7	None.	
	Son...........	10	10	Public.	66	Daughter.....	9	10	Public.
27	Son	14	5	Public, night.		Son...........	6	10	Public.
	Son	12	None.		67	Daughter.....	10	None.	
	Daughter.....	9	10	Public.		Son...........	9	10	Public.
	Son...........	5	None.		68	Son...........	13	10	Public.
28	Daughter.....	7	None.			Daughter.....	11	10	Public.
29	Son	9	10	Public.		Daughter.....	7	None.	
	Son...........	7	10	Public.		Daughter.....	5	None.	
	Daughter.....	6	None.		69	Son...........	16	None.	
	Daughter.....	5	None.			Son...........	14	None.	
30	Son...........	7	7	Public.		Daughter.....	12	4	Public.
31	Son...........	5	None.			Daughter.....	10	4	Public.
33	Son...........	5	None.		70	Son...........	12	None.	
35	Daughter.....	7	4	Public.		Daughter.....	6	7	Public.
39	Wife..........	15	None.		71	Son...........	11	10	Public.
						Son...........	9	10	Public.
					73	Daughter.....	14	None.	
						Son...........	11	10	Public.

TABLE **III.**—SCHOOL ATTENDANCE, BY FAMILIES AND INDIVIDUALS—
Continued.

[This table includes all persons from 5 to 17 years of age, inclusive, and 13 persons below or above these ages reported as scholars.]

Family number.	Relationship to head of family.	Age.	School. Mos.	School. Kind.	Family number.	Relationship to head of family.	Age.	School. Mos.	School. Kind.
74	Son	17	6	Public.	115	Cooperative ..	16	None.	
	Daughter	15	None.		116	Son	8	10	Public.
	Daughter	13	None.			Son	6	None.	
	Daughter	10	10	Public.	117	Daughter	5	None.	
	Daughter	8	10	Public.		Brother	16	None.	
80	Cousin	16	None.		118	Son	12	10	Parochial.
81	Son	17	6	Public, night.		Daughter	8	10	Parochial.
	Son	15	6	Public, night.		Daughter	6	10	Parochial.
82	Daughter	12	10	Public.		Son	4	10	Parochial.
83	Son	5	None.		119	Son	7	None.	
84	Son	11	9	Public.	120	Son	10	10	Parochial.
	Daughter	9	6	Public.		Daughter	10	10	Parochial.
	Son	8	9	Public.		Son	5	10	Parochial.
	Son	6	None.		121	Daughter	13	10	Public.
85	Daughter	16	None.			Daughter	9	None.	
	Son	7	10	Public.	122	Daughter	13	None.	
86	Son	13	6	Public, night.		Son	12	10	Public.
	Brother	24	6	Public, night.		Daughter	8	10	Public.
88	Son	7	10	Public.	124	Son	9	10	Public.
89	Daughter	15	5	Public.	127	Son	10	10	Public.
	Son	12	None.			Daughter	8	10	Public.
90	Daughter	7	10	Public.	128	Son	7	3	Public.
92	Daughter	12	None.			Son	6	None.	
94	Daughter	17	None.			Son	5	None.	
95	Son	14	10	Public.		Cousin	17	6	Parochial, night.
	Son	7	10	Public.	129	Stepson	11	10	Public.
96	Son	10	None.		133	Son	17	None.	
	Son	7	None.			Son	15	3	Public, night.
98	Son	16	3	Public.		Daughter	12	None.	
	Daughter	14	6	Public.		Son	5	None.	
99	Daughter	13	4	Public.	134	Wife	16	None.	
100	Daughter	7	10	Public.	135	Son	12	10	Public.
102	Stepdaughter	16	None.			Son	10	10	Public.
103	Daughter	9	10	Public.		Son	9	10	Public.
105	Son	7	7	Public.		Daughter	7	None.	
106	Daughter	16	None.		137	Daughter	16	None.	
	Daughter	14	6	Public, night.		Son	13	10	Parochial.
	Daughter	12	10	Public.		Son	7	10	Parochial.
107	Son	17	None.		138	Daughter	6	10	Parochial.
108	Daughter	14	6	Public, night.	141	Nephew	7	10	Parochial.
	Daughter	8	10	Public.		Nephew	5	1	Parochial.
	Daughter	7	10	Public.	142	Daughter	11	None.	
	Daughter	5	None.		143	Son	7	10	Public.
111	Son	12	None.		144	Son	11	None.	
	Daughter	9	None.			Sister	14	None.	
	Daughter	7	None.		149	Daughter	14	None.	
112	Son	16	None.			Son	9	10	Public.
	Son	12	3	Public.		Daughter	7	10	Public.
	Daughter	9	10	Public.	151	Son	16	6	Public, night.
	Son	6	10	Public.		Son	8	10	Public.
						Son	7	10	Public.

TABLE **III.**—SCHOOL ATTENDANCE, BY FAMILIES AND INDIVIDUALS—
Continued.

[This table includes all persons from 5 to 17 years of age, inclusive, and 13 persons below or above these ages reported as scholars.]

| Family number. | Relationship to head of family. | Age. | School. | | Family number. | Relationship to head of family. | Age. | School. | |
			Mos.	Kind.				Mos.	Kind.
152	Grandson	7	10	Public.	184	Daughter.....	16	None.	
153	Son	12	6	Public, night.		Son	13	None.	
	Daughter.....	8	10	Public.		Daughter.....	12	None.	
154	Daughter.....	17	None.			Daughter.....	7	10	Public.
	Boarder.......	12	None.		185	Daughter.....	8	10	Public.
157	Son	17	None.			Daughter.....	5	None.	
	Daughter.....	15	10	Public.		Nephew	15	6	Public, night.
	Daughter.....	8	10	Public.	186	Son	16	10	Public.
158	Daughter.....	16	None.			Son	12	4	Public.
	Son	13	10	Public.		Son	10	10	Public.
	Son	10	10	Public.		Grandson.....	5	None.	
	Son	8	10	Public.	187	Son	9	10	Public.
	Daughter.....	6	10	Parochial.		Son	5	None.	
159	Son	15	None.		188	Son	5	None.	
	Son	13	None.		191	Son	13	None.	
161	Daughter.....	7	10	Public.		Son	11	None.	
	Daughter.....	6	7	Public.		Son	8	10	Public.
162	Son	13	10	Parochial.		Nephew	13	None.	
	Daughter, adopted.	5	None.		192	Wife..........	15	None.	
163	Son	13	None.			Lodger	9	10	Public.
	Son	7	10	Public.	194	Daughter.....	8	7	Public.
164	Son	13	9	Parochial.	195	Daughter.....	5	None.	
	Daughter.....	9	None.		196	Daughter.....	10	10	Public.
	Daughter.....	6	None.		198	Son	15	10	Public.
166	Son	8	None.		200	Son	11	7	Public.
	Son	6	10	Public.		Son	8	10	Public.
168	Daughter.....	6	10	Public.	201	Stepdaughter.	10	None.	
169	Daughter.....	15	None.		203	Son	8	3	Public.
	Son	9	10	Public.		Son	5	None.	
172	Son	14	10	Public.	204	Son	13	10	Public.
	Daughter.....	10	10	Public.		Daughter.....	8	8	Public.
	Daughter.....	7	10	Public.	205	Daughter	6	None.	
173	Son	6	None.			Stepdaughter.	5	None.	
174	Wife..........	16	None.		206	Son	14	None.	
175	Nephew	16	None.			Son	9	10	Public.
176	Daughter.....	9	None.		208	Son	7	None.	
	Son	5	None.		209	Son	14	3	Public, night.
177	Daughter.....	14	3	Public.	211	Son	12	None.	
178	Daughter.....	10	10	Public.		Daughter.....	8	10	Public.
	Daughter.....	8	None.			Son	7	10	Public.
	Son	6	1	Public.	212	Son	8	10	Public.
179	Son	9	10	Public.	214	Daughter.....	8	10	Public.
	Daughter.....	5	None.			Son	6	10	Public.
181	Son	7	10	Parochial.	216	Daughter.....	13	None.	
	Son	5	None.			Son	9	10	Parochial.
182	Stepson.......	13	None.		217	Son	11	10	Public.
	Stepson.......	10	None.			Son	10	10	Public.
183	Daughter.....	9	3	Public.		Daughter.....	8	10	Public.
	Son	6	None.		219	Daughter.....	13	6	Public, night.
	Son	6	None.			Daughter.....	6	2	Parochial.

TABLE **III.**—SCHOOL ATTENDANCE, BY FAMILIES AND INDIVIDUALS—
Continued.

[This table includes all persons from 5 to 17 years of age, inclusive, and 13 persons below or above
these ages reported as scholars.]

Family number.	Relationship to head of family.	Age.	School.		Family number.	Relationship to head of family.	Age.	School.	
			Mos.	Kind.				Mos.	Kind.
220	Son	11	10	Public.	262	Son	5	None.	
	Daughter	8	10	Public.		Niece	6	None.	
221	Son	14	10	Public.	263	Daughter	8	None.	
	Daughter	12	10	Parochial.		Daughter	5	None.	
	Daughter	10	10	Parochial.		Lodger	17	None.	
225	Son	15	6	Public, night.	264	Son	6	3	Parochial.
	Son	13	6	Public, night.		Daughter	5	None.	
	Daughter	8	10	Parochial.	265	Wife	16	None.	
	Son	7	10	Public.	267	Son	13	6	Public, night.
226	Son	6	6	Public.		Daughter	7	10	Public.
228	Brother-in-law	17	None.		269	Son	14	9	Public.
230	Niece	5	None.			Daughter	9	10	Public.
231	Son	11	10	Public.	270	Daughter	13	8	Parochial.
	Daughter	9	10	Public.		Son	10	10	Parochial.
	Daughter	6	None.			Son	6	10	Public.
232	Son	15	4	Public, night.	271	Son	17	None.	
	Daughter	10	10	Public.		Daughter	5	None.	
	Son	8	10	Parochial.	272	Son	8	10	Parochial.
	Son	5	None.			Daughter	6	1	Public.
233	Stepdaughter .	8	10	Public.	274	Daughter	15	None.	
235	Son	10	7	Parochial.		Daughter	12	None.	
	Son	7	7	Parochial.		Daughter	9	10	Public.
	Daughter	5	4	Parochial.		Daughter	6	None.	
236	Daughter	5	None.			Son	5	6	Public.
238	Son	7	8	Public.	275	Daughter	6	10	Public.
241	Son	9	10	Public.	276	Son	9	10	Public.
	Daughter	8	None.		277	Daughter	8	10	Public.
243	Son	12	10	Public.	281	Daughter	15	5	Public.
245	Son	14	6	Public, night.	283	Daughter	14	10	Public.
	Daughter	7	2	Public.		Daughter	8	10	Public.
247	Son	15	None.		288	Daughter	6	None.	
249	Daughter	13	10	Public.	289	Daughter	16	None.	
	Son	8	10	Public.	291	Daughter	6	None.	
250	Daughter	5	None.		294	Daughter	12	None.	
251	Wife	17	None.			Daughter	7	None.	
253	Son	16	None.		296	Daughter	5	None.	
	Daughter	6	10	Public.	299	Son	7	10	Public.
255	Daughter	14	None.		300	Son	13	10	Public.
	Daughter	10	10	Parochial.		Son	12	10	Public.
	Son	8	10	Parochial.	301	Son	10	10	Parochial.
	Son	7	10	Parochial.		Son	9	10	Parochial.
258	Son	6	None.		302	Son	11	8	Public.
259	Son	12	10	Public.		Son	8	8	Public.
	Daughter	9	10	Parochial.		Daughter	6	8	Public.
	Son	6	4	Parochial.	304	Boarder	16	None.	
260	Son	5	None.		305	Son	7	10	Public.
261	Son	10	10	Public.	307	Daughter	7	10	Public.
262	Son	17	None.			Son	5	6	Public.
	Son	11	None.						

TABLE **III.**—SCHOOL ATTENDANCE, BY FAMILIES AND INDIVIDUALS—
Continued.

[This table includes all persons from 5 to 17 years of age, inclusive, and 13 persons below or above these ages reported as scholars.]

Family number.	Relationship to head of family.	Age.	School. Mos.	School. Kind.	Family number.	Relationship to head of family.	Age.	School. Mos.	School. Kind.
308	Son	15	6	Public, night.	346	Son	10	10	Public.
	Son	11	10	Public.	348	Daughter	13	(a)	Public.
309	Daughter	11	None.			Daughter	9	(a)	Public.
313	Son	5	10	Private, kindergarten.		Daughter	6	None.	
					350	Son	5	None.	
315	Son	14	9	Public.	351	Son	15	5	Public.
	Son	5	8	Public.		Son	13	6	Public.
316	Daughter	9	None.			Son	11	10	Public.
317	Son	10	10	Public.		Son	8	None.	
	Daughter	7	4	Public.		Son	6	10	Public.
319	Son	5	None.		352	Son	13	10	Public.
320	Wife	17	None.			Son	8	10	Public.
325	Daughter	17	None.		354	Daughter	6	3	Public.
	Daughter	12	None.		357	Nephew	20	6	Public, night.
	Son	9	10	Parochial.		Nephew	15	6	Public, night.
326	Son	16	None.		362	Daughter	17	None.	
	Daughter	7	8	Public.	365	Wife	17	None.	
	Son	5	None.		366	Son	16	6	Public.
329	Son	16	None.			Son	13	8	Public.
	Daughter	14	None.			Son	5	None.	
	Son	8	10	Public.	368	Son	11	9	Public.
	Daughter	5	None.		369	Son	16	None.	
331	Daughter	14	None.			Son	8	10	Public.
	Daughter	12	10	Public.	371	Son	17	None.	
	Daughter	9	None.			Son	7	None.	
	Daughter	7	10	Public.		Son	5	None.	
333	Son	8	3	Public.	372	Daughter	10	10	Public.
334	Son	11	7	Public.		Son	9	10	Public.
	Daughter	7	10	Public.		Son	6	10	Public.
	Daughter	5	None.		373	Daughter	5	6	Private, kindergarten.
335	Son	16	None.		374	Wife	16	None.	
	Daughter	12	8	Public.	376	Son	7	10	Parochial.
	Son	10	10	Public.	377	Son	16	6	Public, night.
	Son	7	10	Public.		Son	11	10	Parochial.
337	Son	15	None.			Daughter	9	10	Parochial.
	Daughter	6	10	Public.		Son	7	10	Public.
	Nephew	17	None.		378	Daughter	7	10	Public.
338	Daughter	16	None.		379	Son	5	None.	
339	Cooperative	15	6	Public, day and night.	380	Son	12	10	Public.
	Cooperative	15	6	Public, day and night.	381	Son	17	7	Public.
341	Son	14	None.			Son	15	10	Public.
	Son	11	None.			Son	13	8	Public.
	Son	5	None.		384	Son	14	3	Public.
342	Daughter	11	10	Public.	385	Daughter	14	None.	
	Son	7	10	Public.		Daughter	11	None.	
	Daughter	5	None.			Son	8	10	Public.
343	Wife	17	None.			Daughter	8	10	Public.
345	Son	8	10	Public.		Daughter	5	None.	
	Daughter	6	None.			Daughter-in-law	17	None.	
	Daughter	5	None.						

a Not reported.

TABLE **III.**—SCHOOL ATTENDANCE, BY FAMILIES AND INDIVIDUALS—
Continued.

[This table includes all persons from 5 to 17 years of age, inclusive, and 13 persons below or above these ages reported as scholars.]

Family number.	Relationship to head of family.	Age.	School. Mos.	School. Kind.	Family number.	Relationship to head of family.	Age.	School. Mos.	School. Kind.
388	Wife	17	None.		426	Son	8	7	Parochial.
	Brother	12	10	Parochial;	427	Son	13	None.	
	Sister	9	10	Public.		Daughter	11	None.	
	Sister	14	None.			Son	9	None.	
389	Daughter	12	None.		429	Daughter	6	10	Public.
390	Son	15	10	Public.	430	Son	8	10	Parochial.
391	Daughter	17	None.			Son	6	10	Public.
	Daughter	13	10	Public.	431	Son	17	None.	
	Son	7	10	Public.		Daughter	10	None.	
392	Son	15	10	Public.		Daughter	7	7	Public.
	Daughter	7	10	Public.		Son	5	None.	
393	Daughter	14	10	Parochial.	432	Daughter	8	2	Public.
	Daughter	10	10	Public.		Daughter	6	None.	
	Daughter	5	None.		436	Stepson	12	4	Public.
394	Daughter	5	None.		437	Son	6	5	Public.
397	Son	13	9	Public.	438	Son	15	None.	
399	Lodger	16	None.			Son	13	10	Parochial.
400	Son	11	9	Parochial.		Daughter	11	None.	
	Son	6	6	Public.		Daughter	9	9	Public.
402	Son	11	10	Public.	440	Son	14	None.	
	Daughter	10	10	Public.		Daughter	12	None.	
403	Son	14	10	Public.		Son	8	10	Public.
404	Son	17	None.		441	Son	16	None.	
406	Son	17	4	Public.	442	Daughter	16	None.	
	Nephew	14	None.			Son	11	8	Public.
407	Daughter	10	10	Parochial.		Daughter	5	2	Public.
	Daughter	6	10	Parochial.	444	Son	17	6	Public, night.
409	Son	12	10	Public.		Daughter	7	10	Public.
	Daughter	7	10	Public.		Daughter	6	10	Public.
411	Son	16	None.		445	Son	6	4	Public.
	Son	11	None.		446	Son	17	None.	
	Son	7	None.			Daughter	13	None.	
	Daughter	5	None.		447	Son	10	10	Private, Italian.
413	Granddaughter.	6	4	Public.	449	Son	15	None.	
416	Son	9	7	Public.		Son	10	5	Public.
	Daughter	8	None.			Son	8	5	Public.
418	Son	12	4	Public.	450	Daughter	8	8	Public.
	Son	9	10	Public.	451	Son	9	None.	
	Daughter	7	8	Public.	454	Daughter	14	None.	
419	Daughter	16	None.			Daughter	7	10	Public.
	Son	9	10	Parochial.	455	Daughter	17	None.	
421	Son	6	None.			Daughter	14	None.	
422	Son	14	10	Public.		Son	7	10	Public.
	Daughter	10	None.			Daughter	6	9	Private, kindergarten.
	Daughter	5	None.		457	Son	14	9	Public.
423	Daughter	15	None.		460	Daughter	7	10	Public.
	Son	13	6	Public, night.	463	Son	10	10	Public.
	Son	8	None.		464	Son	8	4	Public.
424	Stepson	13	9	Public.		Son	7	4	Public.
	Stepson	8	9	Public.		Son	6	None.	

TABLE **III.**—SCHOOL ATTENDANCE, BY FAMILIES AND INDIVIDUALS—
Continued.

[This table includes all persons from 5 to 17 years of age, inclusive, and 13 persons below or above
these ages reported as scholars.]

Family number.	Relationship to head of family.	Age.	School.		Family number.	Relationship to head of family.	Age.	School.	
			Mos.	Kind.				Mos.	Kind.
465	Son	13	None.		508	Daughter	13	10	Public.
	Son	7	10	Public.		Son	7	10	Public.
	Son	6	10	Public.		Son	5	None.	
	Daughter	5	None.		511	Daughter	15	None.	
466	Son	14	None.		512	Son	14	None.	
	Son	9	None.			Son	7	10	Public.
467	Son	9	4	Public.		Daughter	6	10	Public.
468	Daughter	13	None.		513	Daughter	15	None.	
	Son	12	10	Parochial.	514	Son	14	None.	
	Son	12	10	Parochial.	516	Son	7	10	Public.
	Daughter	8	10	Parochial.		Son	5	None.	
	Daughter	5	None.		519	Son	15	10	Private, Italian.
470	Lodger	10	10	Parochial.	520	Stepdaughter .	13	8	Public.
471	Son	12	10	Public.		Son	7	10	Public.
	Daughter	10	10	Public.	521	Daughter	8	None.	
	Son	5	None.			Niece	8	None.	
472	Daughter	5	None.		522	Daughter	9	10	Public.
473	Daughter	11	None.		525	Brother-in-law	17	6	Public, night.
	Son	5	None.			Sister-in-law ..	6	None.	
476	Son	14	None.		529	Daughter	16	None.	
478	Daughter	16	None.			Son	13	None.	
	Son	7	10	Public.		Son	11	None.	
	Daughter	6	None.			Son	9	10	Public.
479	Boarder........	25	6	Public, night.		Son	7	None.	
480	Daughter	10	10	Public.		Daughter	5	None.	
	Son	8	None.		531	Son	16	None.	
	Daughter	5	None.			Daughter	14	None.	
481	Daughter	8	10	Public.		Daughter	12	10	Public.
483	Son	8	10	Public.	532	Daughter	14	None.	
	Daughter	5	None.			Son	9	None.	
485	Son	10	10	Public.		Daughter	7	None.	
486	Daughter	9	None.			Son	6	None.	
	Son	5	None.		533	Daughter	7	10	Public.
493	Son	10	10	Public.	534	Son	16	None.	
	Son	5	None.		536	Daughter	9	10	Public.
494	Daughter	15	None.			Daughter	7	10	Public.
	Son	7	10	Public.		Daughter	5	None.	
	Daughter	6	10	Public.	538	Son	11	10	Public.
	Son	5	None.			Daughter	9	10	Public.
497	Daughter	7	3	Public.		Daughter	7	10	Public.
498	Son	8	None.			Daughter	5	None.	
499	Son	11	8	Private, Italian.	541	Daughter	5	None.	
	Daughter	8	4	Public.	542	Son	6	None.	
504	Son	10	10	Public.	543	Daughter	7	None.	
	Daughter	5	None.		545	Daughter	10	10	Public.
505	Son	10	None.			Daughter	7	None.	
	Son	8	None.		546	Daughter	10	10	Public.
506	Daughter	13	None.		547	Daughter	14	None.	
	Son	10	10	Public.		Daughter	14	None.	
508	Daughter	17	None.			Son	10	9	Public.
	Son	14	None.		550	Son	14	None.	
						Son	6	None.	
						Son	5	None.	

TABLE **III.**—SCHOOL ATTENDANCE, BY FAMILIES AND INDIVIDUALS—
Continued.

[This table includes all persons from 5 to 17 years of age, inclusive, and 13 persons below or above
these ages reported as scholars.]

Family number.	Relationship to head of family.	Age.	School.		Family number.	Relationship to head of family.	Age.	School.	
			Mos.	Kind.				Mos.	Kind.
552	Son	8	10	Public.	602	Son	7	10	Public.
	Daughter	5	None.			Daughter	5	None.	
554	Son	15	None.		605	Daughter	7	10	Public.
555	Daughter	17	None.			Son	5	None.	
	Son	7	10	Public.	606	Son	17	None.	
556	Stepson	15	None.			Daughter	13	6	Public.
	Stepson	11	10	Public.		Son	8	10	Public.
						Daughter	5	None.	
558	Son	8	10	Private, Italian.	610	Daughter	15	None.	
						Son	12	10	Public.
560	Son	6	6	Public.		Daughter	5	None.	
561	Daughter	11	10	Public.	612	Cooperative	16	None.	
						Cooperative	13	4	Parochial.
563	Daughter	5	None.		616	Son	7	10	Public.
565	Stepson	5	7	Public.		Son	6	10	Public.
566	Daughter	16	None.		618	Daughter	4	6	Public.
	Daughter	10	10	Public.	620	Daughter	6	2	Public.
	Son	7	10	Public.					
568	Son	11	None.		621	Daughter	6	6	Public.
570	Daughter	7	None.		623	Son	15	None.	
571	Son	16	None.			Daughter	11	None.	
	Son	12	None.			Daughter	8	10	Public.
	Daughter	10	10	Public.		Son	7	10	Public.
572	Son	8	10	Public.	625	Daughter	12	10	Private, Italian.
579	Brother-in-law	12	10	Public.		Son	7	None.	
581	Son	5	None.		626	Son	8	10	Public.
582	Son	8	7	Public.		Son	6	10	Public.
	Daughter	6	3	Public.	628	Son	11	10	Public.
583	Daughter	6	10	Public.	630	Daughter	15	None.	
	Daughter	5	None.			Daughter	9	10	Public.
584	Son	10	10	Public.	631	Son	16	None.	
	Daughter	7	10	Public.	632	Son	14	None.	
589	Son	10	10	Public.		Daughter	12	10	Public.
	Son	8	None.			Son	8	10	Public.
591	Daughter	7	10	Public.	634	Daughter	12	10	Public.
593	Son	21	2	Public, night.		Son	9	10	Public.
	Daughter	14	3	Public.		Son	5	None	
594	Daughter	7	7	Public.	635	Son	13	None.	
595	Son	7	None.			Daughter	11	2	Public.
597	Son	8	10	Public.	636	Daughter	5	None.	
	Daughter	6	2	Public.	637	Cousin	16	None.	
598	Daughter	6	None.		638	Son	11	9	Public.
599	Son	14	10	Private, Italian, night.		Daughter	7	7	Public.
						Son	5	7	Public.
	Daughter	7	None.		639	Son	5	7	Public.
600	Lodger	12	None.		640	Daughter	14	None.	
601	Daughter	6	6	Public.		Son	10	10	Public.
602	Daughter	12	10	Public.		Son	7	10	Public.
	Son	9	4	Public.		Son	6	10	Public.
					641	Daughter	15	None.	
						Son	10	10	Public.
						Son	8	10	Public.

TABLE **III.**—SCHOOL ATTENDANCE, BY FAMILIES AND INDIVIDUALS—
Continued.

[This table includes all persons from 5 to 17 years of age, inclusive, and 13 persons below or above these ages reported as scholars.]

Family number.	Relationship to head of family.	Age.	School.		Family number.	Relationship to head of family.	Age.	School.	
			Mos.	Kind.				Mos.	Kind.
642	Daughter.....	8	5	Public.	683	Son	9	10	Public.
	Daughter.....	6	10	Public.		Daughter	7	None.	
643	Daughter.....	6	10	Public.	684	Son	15	None.	
						Daughter	14	None.	
647	Daughter.....	12	None.			Son	12	4	Public.
	Son	11	10	Parochial.		Daughter	7	None.	
649	Daughter.....	14	None.		685	Stepson.......	11	10	Public.
	Daughter.....	13	3	Public.		Stepdaughter.	7	10	Public.
	Daughter.....	7	10	Public.		Stepdaughter.	6	10	Public.
650	Son	13	10	Public.	687	Son	8	5	Private, Italian.
	Son	12	10	Public.					
	Daughter.....	7	10	Public.		Daughter	5	None.	
	Daughter.....	5	6	Public.	688	Son	9	10	Private, Italian.
655	Cooperative...	19	3	Public, night.					
	Cooperative...	20	9	Public.		Son	5	10	Private, Italian.
656	Daughter.....	13	None.			Lodger	17	None.	
	Son	6	None.		689	Son	6	2	Public.
657	Daughter	15	10	Public.	691	Daughter	8	None.	
	Daughter	12	7	Public.		Son..........	6	None.	
661	Daughter	14	10	Public.	692	Son	15	None.	
	Daughter	12	10	Public.		Daughter	10	3	Private, Italian.
662	Daughter	11	10	Private, Italian.		Son	9	10	Public.
	Daughter	8	10	Public.	693	Son	11	10	Private, Italian.
	Son	5	None.			Daughter	8	None.	
663	Daughter	13	None.			Brother.......	17	10	Private, Italian.
666	Son	11	None.		694	Son	10	10	Public.
	Daughter	7	3	Public.		Son	9	10	Public.
667	Son	13	None.			Daughter	6	None.	
	Daughter	6	None.		695	Cooperative...	17	10	Public.
669	Son	7	10	Public.	697	Lodger	15	None.	
670	Daughter	14	None.		698	Son	7	None.	
	Daughter	12	10	Public.		Daughter	5	None.	
	Son	9	10	Public.	699	Son	17	None.	
	Daughter	6	10	Public.		Daughter	14	None.	
671	Son	16	None.			Daughter	11	5	Public.
	Daughter	9	None.			Daughter	5	None.	
	Son	8	10	Public.	700	Daughter	11	10	Private, Italian.
672	Son	18	10	Public.		Son	8	10	Public.
	Son	17	10	Public.		Son	5	None.	
	Son	12	10	Public.	701	Stepdaughter.	12	10	Public.
674	Daughter	15	None.			Stepdaughter.	10	8	Public.
	Son	10	None.			Boarder.......	8	5	Public.
678	Son	17	6	Public, night.	703	Son	14	7	Public.
	Daughter.....	14	None.			Son	12	10	Public.
	Daughter.....	10	10	Public.		Daughter	7	10	Public.
	Daughter.....	7	10	Public.	704	Daughter	6	None.	
	Daughter.....	5	10	Public.	705	Son	8	10	Public.
679	Son	12	None.			Daughter	5	None.	
	Son	11	None.		708	Daughter	9	5	Public.
681	Son	15	None.		710	Daughter	15	10	Private.
	Daughter.....	12	10	Public.		Son	9	10	Private.
	Daughter.....	8	10	Public.					
682	Daughter.....	14	None.						
	Son	8	None.						
	Son	5	None.						

TABLE **III.**—SCHOOL ATTENDANCE, BY FAMILIES AND INDIVIDUALS—
Continued.

[This table includes all persons from 5 to 17 years of age, inclusive, and 13 persons below or above these ages reported as scholars.]

Family number.	Relationship to head of family.	Age.	School.		Family number.	Relationship to head of family.	Age.	School.	
			Mos.	Kind.				Mos.	Kind.
710	Son	6	None.		742	Daughter	15	10	Private.
	Daughter	5	None.			Daughter	9	None.	
711	Wife	17	None.		743	Stepson	12	None.	
						Stepson	11	10	Public.
712	Son	15	10	Public.	744	Daughter	12	10	Public.
	Daughter	8	6	Public.		Daughter	10	10	Public.
	Son	5	None.			Son	7	10	Public.
714	Son	12	None.			Son	5	None.	
715	Son	13	10	Private.	745	Brother	17	None.	
	Son	10	(a)	Public.	746	Daughter	15	None.	
716	Son	15	None.		750	Cooperative...	15	None.	
	Son	8	10	Private.	751	Son	7	10	Public.
	Daughter	7	None.		754	Daughter	5	None.	
717	Daughter	12	10	Public.	757	Son	16	None.	
	Son	9	None.			Daughter	14	None.	
718	Lodger	17	None.			Son	9	7	Public.
719	Daughter	15	None.			Son	6	None.	
	Daughter	8	10	Private.	758	Son	12	10	Public.
721	Son	16	None.		765	Son	14	None.	
722	Daughter	17	None.		766	Son	13	10	Public.
	Daughter	16	None.			Daughter	11	None.	
	Son	5	None.			Son	7	10	Public.
723	Daughter	11	None.			Son	5	10	Public.
	Son	8	None.		767	Daughter	12	10	Public.
	Daughter	5	None.			Daughter	10	10	Public.
724	Daughter	8	10	Public.		Son	8	10	Public.
725	Son	7	6	Public.		Son	6	None.	
726	Daughter	15	None		769	Daughter	15	None.	
	Son	10	10	Public.		Daughter	14	None.	
	Son	7	10	Public.		Son	8	10	Public.
	Son	5	None.		771	Daughter	14	None.	
727	Son	9	6	Private.		Daughter	11	10	Public.
729	Daughter	7	10	Public.		Son	8	10	Public.
	Son	6	10	Public.		Daughter	6	3	Public.
731	Son	11	10	Private,night.	774	Son	8	10	Public.
	Daughter	9	10	Public.		Daughter	5	None.	
	Son	7	10	Public.	775	Wife	16	None.	
732	Son	12	6	Public.	776	Son	7	7	Public.
	Son	10	10	Public.	777	Daughter	8	10	Public.
734	Son	13	None.			Son	7	10	Public.
	Son	9	None.		778	Son	8	10	Public.
736	Daughter	10	None.		780	Son	17	(a)	Public.
	Son	7	(a)	Public.		Son	14	6	Public, night.
737	Daughter	12	None.			Daughter	12	10	Public.
	Son	6	None.			Son	9	10	Public.
738	Son	9	10	Public.	781	Daughter	6	None.	
739	Wife	17	None.		784	Nephew	17	None.	
740	Son	14	None.		785	Daughter	15	None.	
						Daughter	7	None.	
741	Nephew	16	None.		786	Son	10	10	Public.

a Not reported.

TABLE **III.**—SCHOOL ATTENDANCE, BY FAMILIES AND INDIVIDUALS—
Continued.

[This table includes all persons from 5 to 17 years of age, inclusive, and 13 persons below or above
these ages reported as scholars.]

Family number.	Relationship to head of family.	Age.	School.		Family number.	Relationship to head of family.	Age.	School.	
			Mos.	Kind.				Mos.	Kind.
788	Stepson	15	None.		830	Daughter	11	None.	
	Stepdaughter	12	None.			Daughter	10	None.	
	Daughter	6	None.		832	Daughter	15	None.	
790	Daughter	14	None.		834	Wife	17	None.	
	Daughter	6	None.		825	Son	14	6	Public, night
793	Son	14	None.			Daughter	7	10	Public.
	Son	10	10	Public.	836	Daughter	6	10	Public.
	Daughter	7	10	Public.	839	Daughter	12	None.	
794	Daughter	12	10	Public.		Son	5	None.	
	Son	10	10	Public.	841	Son	12	None.	
796	Daughter	17	None.			Son	10	None.	
	Son	15	None.			Daughter	9	10	Public.
	Daughter	14	9	Public.		Daughter	7	10	Public.
	Son	10	10	Public.		Son	5	None.	
	Daughter	8	10	Public.	842	Son	12	None.	
798	Daughter	10	10	Public.	843	Daughter	6	4	Public.
	Son	9	10	Public.	844	Son	8	10	Public.
	Daughter	6	10	Public.	845	Son	16	None.	
799	Daughter	11	10	Public.		Daughter	14	None.	
	Daughter	7	10	Public.		Daughter	8	10	Public.
802	Son	7	10	Public.		Son	6	None.	
804	Daughter	11	10	Public.	846	Stepson	14	4	Public.
	Son	10	None.			Stepson	11	10	Public.
805	Son	10	3	Public.		Son	10	10	Public.
806	Son	14	10	Public.		Son	8	10	Public.
	Son	13	10	Public.		Daughter	5	None.	
	Daughter	11	10	Public.	847	Son	10	10	Public.
	Daughter	5	None.			Daughter	7	4	Public.
810	Wife	17	None.		848	Daughter	12	10	Public.
811	Daughter	4	6	Public, kindergarten.	849	Daughter	9	10	Public.
						Son	7	10	Public.
812	Daughter	8	7	Public.		Daughter	5	None.	
813	Daughter	14	None.		850	Daughter	5	2	Public.
815	Son	17	None.		852	Daughter	6	10	Public.
	Son	15	None.		855	Son	5	None.	
	Niece	17	None.		857	Son	15	10	Public.
817	Son	17	10	Public.	858	Son	16	None.	
	Son	13	10	Public.		Son	11	10	Public.
	Son	9	10	Public.		Son	6	1	Public.
	Son	6	10	Public.	859	Daughter	14	None.	
818	Daughter	12	None.		860	Son	17	None.	
	Son	10	7	Public.		Daughter	15	None.	
	Daughter	7	None.			Daughter	14	None.	
820	Daughter	5	None.			Daughter	10	10	Public.
822	Son	8	None.			Daughter	7	10	Public.
	Nephew	17	None.			Daughter	5	None.	
823	Son	10	10	Public.	863	Daughter	17	None.	
824	Son	10	10	Public.		Daughter	15	None.	
	Daughter	9	4	Public.		Daughter	12	10	Public.
828	Daughter	5	None.			Daughter	7	10	Public.
830	Son	15	None.		865	Daughter	8	10	Public.
	Son	13	None.			Son	6	None.	

TABLE **III.**—SCHOOL ATTENDANCE, BY FAMILIES AND INDIVIDUALS—Continued.

[This table includes all persons from 5 to 17 years of age, inclusive, and 13 persons below or above these ages reported as scholars.]

Family number.	Relationship to head of family.	Age.	School. Mos.	School. Kind.	Family number.	Relationship to head of family.	Age.	School. Mos.	School. Kind.
866	Stepson	8	None.		909	Daughter	9	10	Public.
						Daughter	6	None.	
867	Son	15	None.		912	Daughter	16	None.	
869	Son	5	None.		913	Daughter	15	10	Public.
872	Daughter	11	10	Public.		Daughter	8	10	Public.
	Son	7	10	Public.	915	Son	10	7	Public.
874	Daughter	13	None.			Son	5	None.	
	Daughter	11	None.		916	Daughter	12	10	Public.
	Son	8	10	Public.		Son	11	10	Public.
	Daughter	5	None			Son	9	10	Public.
875	Son	8	10	Public.		Daughter	7	None.	
876	Daughter	14	3	Public.	917	Niece	11	10	Public.
	Son	12	10	Public.	918	Son	11	10	Public.
	Daughter	10	10	Public.		Daughter	8	10	Public.
	Daughter	8	10	Public.	919	Daughter	10	10	Public.
877	Wife	16	None.			Son	7	10	Public
878	Son	7	None.			Son	5	None.	
	Daughter	5	None.		922	Son	16	None.	
	Sister-in-law	12	10	Public.		Daughter	12	None.	
	Brother-in-law	9	10	Public.		Son	10	None.	
879	Daughter	16	None.			Daughter	9	4	Public.
	Son	12	10	Public.	924	Son	14	None.	
	Son	9	10	Public.		Daughter	11	None.	
880	Son	17	None.		925	Son	10	10	Public.
	Daughter	14	10	Public.		Son	7	None.	
881	Daughter	8	10	Public.		Son	5	None.	
	Son	6	10	Public.	926	Son	6	None.	
883	Daughter	12	10	Public.		Daughter	5	None.	
	Daughter	9	10	Public.	927	Son	5	None.	
884	Daughter	6	10	Public.	928	Son	17	None.	
885	Daughter	12	None.			Daughter	13	None.	
887	Wife	17	None.			Daughter	11	10	Public.
890	Daughter	14	10	Public.		Son	9	10	Public.
894	Son	16	None.			Son	6	4	Public.
	Daughter	14	1	Public.	929	Son	15	None.	
	Daughter	10	10	Public.		Daughter	14	None.	
896	Son	15	10	Public.		Son	11	None.	
	Daughter	10	10	Public.		Son	9	None.	
	Daughter	9	10	Public.	931	Son	11	None.	
	Son	7	10	Private, kindergarten.		Son	5	None.	
898	Daughter	11	None.		932	Son	14	3	Public.
	Daughter	9	10	Private.		Son	10	None.	
	Son	7	None.			Daughter	7	None.	
899	Daughter	6	None.		934	Niece	9	10	Public.
900	Son	18	6	Public, night.		Niece	7	10	Public.
	Son	16	6	Public, night.	935	Daughter	8	None.	
902	Son	16	None.		938	Son	8	8	Private.
904	Daughter	5	None.		940	Daughter	12	None.	
907	Daughter	5	None.			Son	8	10	Public.
908	Son	5	None.			Son	5	None.	
					941	Daughter	16	None.	
						Son	12	None.	
					942	Brother	15	None.	
						Sister	11	None.	

TABLE **III.**—SCHOOL ATTENDANCE, BY FAMILIES AND INDIVIDUALS—
Continued.

[This table includes all persons from 5 to 17 years of age, inclusive, and 13 persons below or above these ages reported as scholars.]

Family number.	Relationship to head of family.	Age.	School Mos.	School Kind.	Family number.	Relationship to head of family.	Age.	School Mos.	School Kind.
946	Son	6	10	Parochial.	976	Son	7	10	Public.
	Son	5	4	Parochial.		Daughter	5		None.
947	Son	9	10	Parochial.	977	Stepdaughter.	5		None.
	Daughter	8	10	Parochial.	978	Daughter	9	10	Public.
	Son	7	10	Parochial.		Daughter	6		None.
	Son	5		None.	979	Daughter	10	10	Public.
948	Daughter	11	10	Public.		Son	7	10	Public.
	Son	8	10	Public.	980	Son	8	10	Public.
949	Son	10	10	Parochial.	981	Son	17		None.
	Son	7	10	Parochial.		Daughter	8	10	Public.
	Daughter	5		None.		Son	6	10	Public.
950	Son	7	10	Parochial.	982	Daughter	16		None.
951	Daughter	13	10	Parochial.		Daughter	9	10	Public.
	Daughter	10	10	Parochial.		Son	6	10	Public.
	Son	8	8	Parochial.		Son	5		None.
	Son	7		None.	983	Daughter	5		None.
	Son	5		None.	986	Daughter	10	10	Public.
955	Daughter	7		None.		Daughter	6	10	Public.
957	Daughter	6		None.	988	Son	10	10	Public.
	Daughter	5		None.		Nephew	7	10	Public.
960	Son	9	10	Public.	989	Daughter	14	10	Public.
	Daughter	8	10	Public.		Daughter	5		None.
	Daughter	6		None.	990	Son	10	10	Public.
961	Son	5		None.		Son	9	10	Public.
962	Son	13	10	Public.		Son	6	10	Public.
	Son	12	10	Public.		Daughter	5		None.
	Son	8	10	Public.	991	Daughter	16	10	Public.
	Daughter	7	10	Public.		Daughter	14	10	Public.
	Daughter	5		None.		Daughter	7	10	Public.
963	Son	10		None.		Son	6	10	Public.
	Daughter	9		None.	992	Son	11	10	Public.
	Daughter	8		None.		Daughter	9	10	Public.
	Son	5		None.		Daughter	7		None.
964	Son	11	10	Public.		Son	5		None.
	Son	9	10	Public.	993	Daughter	12	4	Public.
	Son	6	6	Public.		Daughter	10	4	Public.
965	Daughter	17		None.		Daughter	8	4	Public.
	Son	13	10	Public.		Son	5		None.
	Daughter	9	10	Public.	994	Son	5		None.
	Daughter	7	10	Public.	996	Daughter	8		None.
	Daughter	5		None.		Son	6		None.
967	Son	14		None.	997	Stepdaughter.	10	4	Public.
968	Son	14	10	Public.		Daughter	5		None.
	Daughter	13	10	Public.	999	Son	12	7	Private.
969	Daughter	5		None.		Daughter	8	10	Public.
971	Daughter	10	10	Public.	1002	Stepson	7	10	Public.
	Son	8	10	Public.		Stepdaughter.	5	3	Public.
	Daughter	6	10	Public.	1003	Nephew	16		None.
973	Son	9	10	Public.		Niece	9	10	Public.
	Stepdaughter.	5		None.		Niece	5		None.
975	Son	17		None.		Boarder	14		None.
	Daughter	16		None.	1004	Brother	16		None.
	Son	13	10	Public.	1005	Daughter	8	10	Public.
	Son	11	10	Public.		Daughter	6		None.
	Daughter	9	10	Public.					
	Son	7	10	Public.					

TABLE **III.**—SCHOOL ATTENDANCE, BY FAMILIES AND INDIVIDUALS—
Continued.

[This table includes all persons from 5 to 17 years of age, inclusive, and 13 persons below or above
these ages reported as scholars.]

Family number.	Relationship to head of family.	Age	School.		Family number.	Relationship to head of family.	Age	School.	
			Mos.	Kind.				Mos.	Kind.
1006	Daughter.....	9	10	Public.	1041	Daughter.....	10	None.	
	Son...........	7	10	Public.		Son...........	7	None.	
1007	Daughter.....	8	10	Public.	1042	Daughter.....	13	None.	
						Daughter.....	10	10	Public.
1009	Son...........	8	10	Public.	1043	Son...........	10	10	Public.
1010	Daughter.....	6	None.						
	Son...........	5	None.		1044	Daughter.....	13	3	Public.
						Son...........	8	10	Public.
1011	Wife.........	17	None.						
					1047	Son...........	13	None.	
1012	Daughter.....	12	10	Public.		Daughter.....	11	10	Public.
	Daughter.....	9	10	Public.		Daughter.....	9	10	Public.
						Son...........	7	10	Public.
1013	Son...........	6	None.		1048	Son...........	10	None.	
1014	Son...........	7	10	Public.		Daughter.....	6	None.	
1016	Son...........	5	None.		1049	Daughter.....	6	None.	
1017	Daughter.....	5	None.		1053	Son...........	15	10	Public.
1018	Son...........	12	None.			Son...........	11	None.	
	Son...........	7	None.		1055	Son...........	6	None.	
1019	Granddaughter	5	None.		1058	Son...........	9	None.	
						Daughter.....	7	None.	
1021	Daughter.....	12	10	Public.	1059	Son...........	10	10	Public.
	Daughter.....	5	None.			Daughter.. ...	8	None.	
1022	Son...........	14	10	Public.	1061	Son...........	10	10	Public.
	Son...........	10	10	Public.		Son...........	7	3	Public.
	Son...........	7	None.		1062	Son...........	10	10	Public.
1024	Son...........	12	None.		1063	Son...........	14	None.	
	Son...........	7	7	Public.		Daughter.....	10	10	Public.
	Nephew.......	15	10	Public.		Son...........	6	None.	
1025	Daughter.....	9	10	Public.	1065	Son...........	14	None.	
	Son...........	7	None.			Son...........	7	7	Public.
1026	Son...........	10	10	Public.		Daughter.....	6	None.	
	Daughter.....	11	10	Public.	1070	Son...........	16	10	Public, night.
	Daughter.....	7	10	Public.		Daughter.....	14	None.	
1028	Daughter.....	16	None.			Daughter.....	8	7	Public.
	Daughter.....	12	10	Public.		Son...........	6	None.	
	Son...........	8	10	Public.	1071	Son...........	12	2	Public.
1029	Daughter.....	9	10	Public.	1072	Wife.........	17	None.	
1030	Daughter.....	5	None.		1073	Daughter.....	5	None.	
1031	Daughter.....	12	10	Public.	1074	Son...........	16	None.	
	Daughter.....	10	10	Public.	1075	Daughter.....	9	10	Public.
	Daughter.....	8	10	Public.		Son...........	5	None.	
1033	Stepdaughter.	9	10	Public.	1076	Daughter.....	7	None.	
1034	Daughter....	5	None.			Daughter.....	5	None.	
1035	Daughter.....	9	10	Public.	1077	Daughter.....	14	10	Public.
	Daughter.....	5	None.			Daughter.....	12	10	Public.
1036	Son...........	14	10	Public.		Son...........	9	10	Public.
	Son...........	13	10	Public.		Son...........	7	7	Public.
1037	Son...........	16	None.			Daughter.....	5	7	Public.
	Daughter.....	5	None.		1078	Daughter.....	7	10	Public.
1038	Daughter.....	5	None.		1079	Son...........	12	10	Public.
1039	Son...........	5	None.			Daughter.....	10	10	Public.

TABLE **III.**—SCHOOL ATTENDANCE, BY FAMILIES AND INDIVIDUALS—
Continued.

[This table includes all persons from 5 to 17 years of age, inclusive, and 13 persons below or above these ages reported as scholars.]

Family number.	Relationship to head of family.	Age.	School.		Family number.	Relationship to head of family.	Age.	School.	
			Mos.	Kind.				Mos.	Kind.
1079	Daughter	9	7	Public.	1120	Daughter	5	None.	
	Daughter	6	None.		1121	Son	13	None.	
1081	Son	9	10	Public.		Daughter	10	None.	
	Daughter	7	None.			Son	7	None.	
1084	Daughter	12	10	Public.	1122	Son	12	10	Public.
	Son	11	10	Public.		Daughter	10	None.	
	Daughter	10	10	Public.	1123	Son	9	10	Public.
	Son	8	10	Public.		Son	7	10	Public.
	Son	6	None.			Daughter	6	None.	
	Daughter	5	None.			Daughter	6	None.	
1086	Son	8	10	Public.	1124	Daughter	16	None.	
	Daughter	6	None.			Daughter	13	3	Public.
1088	Son	9	10	Public.		Daughter	9	10	Public.
	Son	5	None.		1125	Son	10	10	Public.
1089	Daughter	12	10	Public.		Daughter	9	10	Public.
	Daughter	9	2	Public.		Son	6	10	Public.
1092	Daughter	8	None.		1126	Son	16	None.	
	Son	5	None.			Son	13	10	Public.
1094	Son	17	None.			Daughter	11	10	Public.
	Daughter	10	10	Public.		Son	9	10	Public.
	Son	7	None.		1127	Son	8	9	Public.
1095	Stepdaughter	9	10	Public.		Son	5	None.	
	Son	7	10	Public.	1129	Daughter	13	None.	
1097	Son	17	None.			Daughter	12	None.	
1098	Daughter	13	None.			Daughter	9	None.	
1099	Son	16	None.			Son	7	None.	
1102	Daughter	9	None.		1131	Daughter	16	None.	
	Son	6	None.			Daughter	10	None.	
	Son	5	None.		1133	Son	13	10	Public.
1103	Daughter	8	None.			Daughter	12	10	Public.
	Son	7	10	Public.		Son	9	10	Public.
	Son	5	None.			Daughter	5	None.	
1104	Son	8	10	Public.	1134	Daughter	16	None.	
1105	Son	17	None.			Son	15	10	Public.
1107	Son	11	10	Public.		Daughter	11	10	Public.
	Son	8	None.			Son	10	10	Public.
1108	Daughter	11	None.			Daughter	9	10	Public.
	Daughter	9	None.			Son	7	10	Public.
	Son	7	None.		1138	Son	16	None.	
	Son	5	None.			Daughter	9	1	Public.
1110	Daughter	6	None.		1140	Son	15	4	Public.
1112	Son	6	None.		1141	Daughter	8	None.	
1114	Son	14	10	Public.	1142	Son	13	4	Public.
	Son	12	10	Public.	1143	Daughter	6	None.	
	Daughter	7	10	Public.	1146	Son	11	10	Public.
1116	Daughter	17	None.			Son	9	10	Public.
	Daughter	14	None		1149	Daughter	14	10	Public.
	Son	13	None.			Son	11	10	Public.
1117	Daughter	16	None.			Son	10	10	Public.
	Daughter	11	10	Public.		Son	7	None.	
1118	Daughter	7	None.		1150	Daughter	6	7	Public.
	Daughter	5	None.		1151	Son	7	10	Public.
						Daughter	6	None.	
					1152	Wife	16	None.	

TABLE **III.**—SCHOOL ATTENDANCE, BY FAMILIES AND INDIVIDUALS—
Continued.

[This table includes all persons from 5 to 17 years of age, inclusive, and 13 persons below or above
these ages reported as scholars.]

Family number.	Relationship to head of family.	Age.	School.		Family number.	Relationship to head of family.	Age.	School.	
			Mos.	Kind.				Mos.	Kind.
1153	Son	8	7	Public.	1188	Son	10	10	Public.
1154	Son	16	None.		1190	Daughter	13	None.	
1155	Son	6	None.			Son	6	None.	
1156	Daughter	7	None.		1192	Son	9	10	Public.
1157	Daughter	7	4	Public.		Daughter	7	2	Public.
1158	Son	8	10	Public.		Daughter	5	None.	
	Daughter	6	7	Public.	1195	Daughter	7	10	Public.
1159	Son	15	10	Public.	1199	Son	6	None.	
	Son	10	10	Public.	1202	Stepson........	7	7	Public.
	Daughter	8	10	Public.	1208	Daughter	12	None.	
1162	Son	10	10	Public.		Daughter	10	10	Public.
	Son	8	10	Public.		Son	9	10	Public.
	Son	6	None.			Son	6	7	Public.
1163	Daughter	6	10	Public.	1210	Son	13	10	Public.
1164	Wife..........	16	None.			Son	12	10	Public.
1165	Son	7	7	Public.		Daughter	9	10	Public.
1166	Daughter	12	None.		1211	Son	17	None.	
1167	Daughter	9	10	Public.		Daughter	15	None.	
1168	Son	10	10	Public.	1212	Son	13	10	Public.
1169	Daughter	12	10	Public.	1213	Son	12	10	Public.
	Son	10	10	Public.		Son	9	10	Public.
	Daughter	7	7	Public.		Son	7	7	Public.
1172	Son	7	10	Public.	1214	Son	10	10	Public.
	Daughter	5	None.		1215	Son	14	3	Public.
1173	Son	7	10	Public.		Son	10	10	Public.
1175	Son	16	4	Public.		Son	8	10	Public.
	Daughter	15	10	Public.	1217	Daughter	8	10	Public.
	Son	7	10	Public.		Daughter	5	None.	
1176	Daughter	9	10	Public.	1218	Son	17	4	Public, night.
1177	Son	14	None.			Son	15	7	Public.
	Daughter	11	10	Public.		Son	10	10	Public.
1178	Daughter	13	10	Private.		Son	6	None.	
	Son	9	10	Private.	1219	Daughter	15	10	Public.
	Son	7	10	Private.		Son	10	10	Public.
1180	Daughter	14	None.			Daughter	8	10	Public.
	Daughter	14	10	Public.	1220	Son	13	10	Public.
1181	Daughter	15	None.			Son	11	10	Public.
	Son	13	10	Public.		Daughter	7	7	Public.
	Son	12	10	Public.	1223	Cooperative...	17	None.	
	Son	10	10	Public.	1225	Daughter	9	None.	
	Son	7	7	Public.		Daughter	6	None.	
1183	Daughter	14	10	Public.	1226	Son	5	None.	
	Daughter	10	10	Public.	1228	Son	8	10	Public.
	Son	8	10	Public.		Son	6	None.	
1186	Brother........	18	5	Public, night.	1230	Daughter	8	None.	
	Brother........	16	4	Public, night.	1237	Daughter	5	None.	
1187	Daughter	9	None.		1238	Son	5	None.	
	Daughter	6	None.		1240	Son	13	10	Public.
						Daughter	7	7	Public.

TABLE **III.**—SCHOOL ATTENDANCE, BY FAMILIES AND INDIVIDUALS—
Continued.

[This table includes all persons from 5 to 17 years of age, inclusive, and 13 persons below or above
these ages reported as scholars.]

Family number.	Relationship to head of family.	Age.	School. Mos.	School. Kind.	Family number.	Relationship to head of family.	Age.	School. Mos.	School. Kind.
1242	Daughter	12	10	Public.	1288	Daughter	5	None.	
1243	Son	5	None.		1289	Daughter	6	None.	
1245	Son	8	10	Public.		Brother-in law	14	None.	
	Son	6	None.		1291	Daughter	11	5	Public.
1247	Daughter	16	None.		1292	Daughter	14	None.	
	Daughter	14	10	Public.	1293	Daughter	10	10	Public.
1249	Daughter	6	None.			Son	6	None.	
1250	Son	7	7	Public.	1294	Wife..........	17	None.	
	Sister-in-law..	16	None.		1295	Daughter	15	7	Public.
1252	Daughter	5	None.			Daughter	10	(a)	Public.
						Daughter	8	10	Public.
1255	Son	5	None.			Son	6	None.	
1261	Cooperative...	17	None.		1297	Daughter	14	None.	
1262	Daughter	6	7	Public.	1298	Daughter	9	10	Public.
	Daughter	5	None.			Son	7	7	Public.
1263	Daughter	10	10	Public.	1299	Daughter	13	10	Public.
	Daughter	7	10	Public.		Son	7	7	Public.
	Son	5	None.		1300	Son	9	10	Public.
1265	Stepson	12	10	Public.		Daughter	5	None.	
1266	Wife..........	16	None.		1301	Son	7	None.	
1268	Daughter	12	10	Public.	1306	Son	12	10	Public.
	Son	8	10	Public.		Son	8	10	Public.
1269	Wife..........	17	None.			Son	6	7	Public.
1270	Son	12	10	Public.	1307	Son	6	None.	
	Son	8	10	Public.	1308	Daughter	5	None.	
	Son	6	None.		1311	Daughter	15	10	Public.
1273	Son	9	10	Public.		Son	14	10	Public.
1276	Daughter	14	None.			Daughter	12	10	Public.
	Son	11	10	Public.		Daughter	10	10	Public.
	Son	6	7	Public.		Son	9	10	Public.
1279	Daughter	12	10	Public.	1312	Daughter	15	None.	
	Son	5	None.		1314	Daughter	15	None.	
1280	Daughter	16	None.			Daughter	12	10	Public.
	Daughter	14	10	Public.		Son	11	10	Public.
	Daughter	13	10	Public.		Son	9	10	Public.
	Daughter	9	10	Public.		Son	7	10	Public.
	Daughter	7	None.		1315	Brother........	15	10	Public.
	Daughter	5	None.		1317	Daughter	16	10	Public.
1281	Son	8	10	Public.		Son	12	10	Public.
	Daughter	5	None.		1320	Son	14	None.	
1283	Son	11	10	Public.	1321	Son	16	None.	
	Son	8	10	Public.	1322	Daughter	16	2	Public, night.
	Son	6	7	Public.		Daughter	12	10	Public.
1285	Daughter	14	10	Public.		Daughter	9	10	Public.
	Son	10	10	Public.		Daughter	6	7	Public.
	Daughter	9	10	Public.	1324	Daughter	17	None.	
	Son	7	10	Public.		Son	15	10	Public.
	Son	5	None.			Son	11	10	Public.
1286	Stepson	13	10	Public.		Son	9	10	Public.
1287	Daughter	9	10	Public.					

a Not reported.

TABLE **III.**—SCHOOL ATTENDANCE, BY FAMILIES AND INDIVIDUALS—
Concluded.

[This table includes all persons from 5 to 17 years of age, inclusive, and 13 persons below or above these ages reported as scholars.]

Family number.	Relationship to head of family.	Age.	School.		Family number.	Relationship to head of family.	Age.	School.	
			Mos.	Kind.				Mos.	Kind.
1326	Daughter	17	None.		1332	Son	16	None.	
	Son	15	10	Public.					
	Son	14	10	Public.	1338	Son	8	10	Public.
	Son	10	10	Public.					
	Daughter	8	None.		1342	Daughter	5	None.	
	Daughter	5	None.			Sister-in-law	16	None.	
1328	Daughter	5	None.		1343	Daughter	12	10	Public.
						Nephew	12	10	Public.
1329	Daughter	6	None.			Nephew	9	10	Public.
1330	Daughter	16	None.		1344	Son	12	None.	
	Daughter	11	10	Public.		Son	9	10	Public.
	Son	7	7	Public.		Son	7	None.	
1331	Daughter	16	None.		1346	Daughter	6	8	Public.
	Daughter	9	10	Public.					
	Daughter	7	7	Public.	1348	Son	12	10	Public.
	Boarder	21	3	Public.		Daughter	9	10	Public.

TABLE **IV.**—CONJUGAL CONDITION, BY SEX, NATIVITY, AND AGE.

Nativity and age.	Single.			Married.			Widowed.			Aggregate.		
	Male.	Female.	Total.	Male.	Female.	Total.	Male.	Female.	Total.	Male.	Female.	Total.
NATIVE BORN.												
Under 1 year	156	148	304							156	148	304
1 year	130	93	223							130	93	223
2 years	146	165	311							146	165	311
3 years	114	128	242							114	128	242
4 years	102	97	199							102	97	199
5 years	84	96	180							84	96	180
6 years	68	66	134							68	66	134
7 years	80	67	147							80	67	147
8 years	64	50	114							64	50	114
9 years	48	47	95							48	47	95
10 years	34	32	66							34	32	66
11 years	23	19	42							23	19	42
12 years	25	26	51							25	26	51
13 years	16	10	26							16	10	26
14 years	17	19	36							17	19	36
15 years	9	9	18							9	9	18
16 years	1	8	9		2	2				1	10	11
17 years	5	2	7							5	2	7
18 years	2	1	3		2	2				2	3	5
19 years	3		3							3		3
20 years		1	1		1	1					2	2
21 years	4		4		1	1				4	1	5
22 years	3	1	4		1	1				3	2	5
23 years	1	1	2							1	1	2
24 years	1		1	1	3	4				2	3	5
25 years		3	3		1	1					4	4
26 years	1		1	1		1				2		2
27 years	2		2							2		2
29 years	1		1		1	1				1	1	2
30 years	1		1		1	1				1	1	2
33 years				1		1				1		1
34 years					1	1					1	1
35 years					2	2					2	2
Total	1,141	1,089	2,230	3	16	19				1,144	1,105	2,249
FOREIGN BORN.												
Under 1 year												
1 year	1		1							1		1
2 years	4	2	6							4	2	6
3 years	3	10	13							3	10	13
4 years	6	8	14							6	8	14
5 years	11	20	31							11	20	31
6 years	13	22	35							13	22	35
7 years	38	23	61							38	23	61

TABLE **IV.**—CONJUGAL CONDITION, BY SEX, NATIVITY, AND AGE—Cont'd.

Nativity and age.	Single.			Married.			Widowed.			Aggregate.		
	Male.	Female.	Total.	Male.	Female.	Total.	Male.	Female.	Total.	Male.	Female.	Total.
FOREIGN BORN—con'd.												
8 years	26	24	50							26	24	50
9 years	25	35	60							25	35	60
10 years	43	27	70							43	27	70
11 years	33	22	55							33	22	55
12 years	37	38	75							37	38	75
13 years	39	22	61							39	22	61
14 years	33	41	74							33	41	74
15 years	45	26	71		3	3				45	29	74
16 years	49	22	71		10	10				49	32	81
17 years	41	10	51		20	20				41	30	71
18 years	63	11	74		23	23				63	34	97
19 years	36	4	40		17	17				36	21	57
20 years	45	6	51	5	48	53				50	54	104
21 years	40	2	42	4	22	26		1	1	44	25	69
22 years	50	1	51	11	31	42				61	32	93
23 years	44	1	45	22	36	58				66	37	103
24 years	30	1	31	24	35	59		1	1	54	37	91
25 years	49		49	40	51	91				89	51	140
26 years	31		31	36	37	73		1	1	67	38	105
27 years	23		23	55	51	106		2	2	78	53	131
28 years	22		22	68	47	115				90	47	137
29 years	15		15	45	30	75				60	30	90
30 years	39		39	133	77	210				172	77	249
31 years	5	1	6	33	23	56		1	1	38	25	63
32 years	11		11	73	52	125	1	1	2	85	53	138
33 years	9		9	63	36	99	1		1	73	36	109
34 years	5		5	64	42	106	1	1	2	70	43	113
35 years	4		4	95	55	150	2		2	101	55	156
36 years	2		2	56	43	99		2	2	58	45	103
37 years	6	1	7	55	36	91				61	37	98
38 years	6		6	52	45	97	3	1	4	61	46	107
39 years	2		2	44	25	69		2	2	46	27	73
40 years	12		12	169	63	232	4	1	5	185	64	249
41 years				24	13	37		1	1	24	14	38
42 years	1		1	47	31	78	4	1	5	52	32	84
43 years				23	16	39	2		2	25	16	41
44 years	1		1	37	26	63	2	4	6	40	30	70
45 years	2	1	3	77	46	123	1	4	5	80	51	131
46 years	2		2	38	14	52	1		1	41	14	55
47 years				44	16	60	2	2	4	46	18	64
48 years	1		1	36	14	50	1	2	3	38	16	54
49 years				10	8	18				10	8	18
50 years	1		1	70	35	105	2	8	10	73	43	116
51 years	1		1	12	4	16		1	1	13	5	18
52 years	1		1	19	9	28	1	1	2	21	10	31
53 years				10	5	15	1	2	3	11	7	18
54 years				15	10	25	3	5	8	18	15	33
55 years				20	3	23	1	4	5	21	7	28
56 years				12	5	17		4	4	12	9	21
57 years				7	2	9	1	1	2	8	3	11
58 years				4	2	6		1	1	4	3	7
59 years				2	3	5				2	3	5
60 years		1	1	28	19	47	4	13	17	32	33	65
61 years				3	3	6		1	1	3	4	7
62 years				2	1	3		1	1	2	2	4
63 years				3		3		2	2	3	2	5
64 years				5	1	6	3	2	5	8	3	11
65 years				9	1	10		3	3	9	4	13
66 years				1	2	3	1		1	2	2	4
67 years				2	2	4		1	1	2	3	5
68 years				2		2		2	2	2	2	4
69 years					1	1		2	2		3	3
70 years	1		1	5		5	1	7	8	7	7	14
71 years					1	1					1	1
73 years							2		2	2		2
74 years								2	2		2	2
75 years				3		3	1		1	4		4
76 years					1	1		1	1		2	2
77 years				1		1				1		1
78 years				1		1		1	1	1	1	2
80 years				1		1		5	5	1	5	6
81 years							1		1	1		1
82 years								1	1		1	1
87 years							1		1	1		1
90 years				1		1				1		1
96 years								1	1		1	1
Not reported	5		5	5	3	8	1		1	11	3	14
Total	1,012	382	1,394	1,726	1,255	2,981	49	100	149	2,787	1,737	4,524

TABLE **IV.**—CONJUGAL CONDITION, BY SEX, NATIVITY, AND AGE—Cont'd.

Nativity and age.	Single.			Married.			Widowed.			Aggregate.		
	Male.	Female.	Total.	Male.	Female.	Total.	Male.	Female.	Total.	Male.	Female.	Total.
NATIVE AND FOREIGN BORN.												
Under 1 year	156	148	304							156	148	304
1 year	131	93	224							131	93	224
2 years	150	167	317							150	167	317
3 years	117	138	255							117	138	255
4 years	108	105	213							108	105	213
5 years	95	116	211							95	116	211
6 years	81	88	169							81	88	169
7 years	118	90	208							118	90	208
8 years	90	74	164							90	74	164
9 years	73	82	155							73	82	155
10 years	77	59	136							77	59	136
11 years	56	41	97							56	41	97
12 years	62	64	126							62	64	126
13 years	55	32	87							55	32	87
14 years	50	60	110							50	60	110
15 years	54	35	89		3	3				54	38	92
16 years	50	30	80		12	12				50	42	92
17 years	46	12	58		20	20				46	32	78
18 years	65	12	77		25	25				65	37	102
19 years	39	4	43		17	17				39	21	60
20 years	45	7	52	5	49	54				50	56	106
21 years	44	2	46	4	23	27		1	1	48	26	74
22 years	53	2	55	11	32	43				64	34	98
23 years	45	2	47	22	36	58				67	38	105
24 years	31	1	32	25	38	63		1	1	56	40	96
25 years	49	3	52	40	52	92				89	55	144
26 years	32		32	37	37	74		1	1	69	38	107
27 years	25		25	55	51	106		2	2	80	53	133
28 years	22		22	68	47	115				90	47	137
29 years	16		16	45	31	76				61	31	92
30 years	40		40	133	78	211				173	78	251
31 years	5	1	6	33	23	56		1	1	38	25	63
32 years	11		11	73	52	125	1	1	2	85	53	138
33 years	9		9	64	36	100	1		1	74	36	110
34 years	5		5	64	43	107	1	1	2	70	44	114
35 years	4		4	95	57	152	2		2	101	57	158
36 years	2		2	56	43	99		2	2	58	45	103
37 years	6	1	7	55	36	91				61	37	98
38 years	6		6	52	45	97	3	1	4	61	46	107
39 years	2		2	44	25	69		2	2	46	27	73
40 years	12		12	169	63	232	4	1	5	185	64	249
41 years				24	13	37		1	1	24	14	38
42 years	1		1	47	31	78	4	1	5	52	32	84
43 years				23	16	39	2		2	25	16	41
44 years	1		1	37	26	63	2	4	6	40	30	70
45 years	2	1	3	77	46	123	1	4	5	80	51	131
46 years	2		2	38	14	52	1		1	41	14	55
47 years				44	16	60	2	2	4	46	18	64
48 years	1		1	36	14	50	1	2	3	38	16	54
49 years				10	8	18				10	8	18
50 years	1		1	70	35	105	2	8	10	73	43	116
51 years	1		1	12	4	16		1	1	13	5	18
52 years	1		1	19	9	28	1	1	2	21	10	31
53 years				10	5	15	1	2	3	11	7	18
54 years				15	10	25	3	5	8	18	15	33
55 years				20	3	23	1	4	5	21	7	28
56 years				12	5	17		4	4	12	9	21
57 years				7	2		1	1	2	8	3	11
58 years				4	2	6		1	1	4	3	7
59 years				2	3	5				2	3	5
60 years		1	1	28	19	47	4	13	17	32	33	65
61 years				3	3	6		1	1	3	4	7
62 years				2	1	3		1	1	2	2	4
63 years				3		3		2	2	3	2	5
64 years				5	1	6	3	2	5	8	3	11
65 years				9	1	10		3	3	9	4	13
66 years				1	2	3	1		1	2	2	4
67 years				2	2	4		1	1	2	3	5
68 years				2		2		2	2	2	2	4
69 years					1	1		2	2		3	3
70 years	1		1	5		5	1	7	8	7	7	14
71 years					1	1					1	1
73 years							2		2	2		2
74 years								2	2		2	2
75 years				3		3	1		1	4		4
76 years					1	1		1	1		2	2
77 years				1		1				1		1
78 years				1		1		1	1	1	1	2
80 years				1		1		5	5	1	5	6

TABLE **IV.**—CONJUGAL CONDITION, BY SEX, NATIVITY, AND AGE—Conc'd.

Nativity and age.	Single.			Married.			Widowed.			Aggregate.		
	Male.	Fe-male.	Total.	Male.	Fe-male.	Total.	Male.	Fe-male.	Total.	Male.	Fe-male.	Total.
NATIVE AND FOREIGN BORN—concluded.												
81 years							1		1	1		1
82 years								1	1		1	1
87 years							1		1	1		1
90 years				1		1				1		1
96 years								1	1		1	1
Not reported	5		5	5	3	8	1		1	11	3	14
Total	2,153	1,471	3,624	1,729	1,271	3,000	49	100	149	3,931	2,842	6,773

TABLE **V.**—PLACE OF BIRTH, BY SEX.

Place of birth.	Males.		Females.		Total.	
	Number.	Per cent.	Number.	Per cent.	Number.	Per cent.
United States	1,144	29.10	1,105	38.88	2,249	33.20
Italy:						
Abruzzo	233	5.93	118	4.15	351	5.18
Apulia	7	.18	5	.18	12	.18
Basilicata	635	16.15	569	20.02	1,204	17.78
Calabria	646	16.43	213	7.49	859	12.68
Campagna di Roma	3	.08	3	.11	6	.09
Campania	740	18.82	498	17.52	1,238	18.28
Emilia	16	.41	16	.56	32	.47
Liguria	53	1.35	52	1.83	105	1.55
Lombardy	19	.48	17	.60	36	.53
Marches	3	.08	1	.04	4	.05
Piedmont	3	.08	4	.14	7	.10
Sicily	336	8.55	194	6.83	530	7.83
Tuscany	56	1.42	24	.84	80	1.18
Venetia	21	.53	8	.28	29	.43
Total for Italy	2,771	70.49	1,722	60.59	4,493	66.33
Argentine Republic	1	.03			1	.02
Belgium	2	.05	2	.07	4	.05
Canada			1	.04	1	.02
England	1	.03			1	.02
France	12	.30	9	.30	21	.30
Germany			1	.04	1	.02
Ireland			1	.04	1	.02
Sweden			1	.04	1	.02
Total	3,931	100.00	2,842	100.00	6,773	100.00

TABLE **VI.**—NUMBER AND SIZE OF FAMILIES, BY KIND OF FAMILY.

Families of—	Private families.		Cooperative.		Boarding and lodging houses.		Total.	
	Number.	Per cent.	Number.	Per cent.	Number.	Per cent.	Number.	Per cent.
1 person	24	1.90					24	1.78
2 persons	123	9.72	9	13.24			132	9.79
3 persons	150	11.86	12	17.65			162	12.02
4 persons	259	20.47	17	25.00	1	6.67	277	20.55
5 persons	249	19.68	11	16.18	3	20.00	263	19.51
6 persons	174	13.75	3	4.41	4	26.65	181	13.43
7 persons	140	11.07	5	7.35	1	6.67	146	10.83
8 persons	79	6.25	3	4.41	1	6.67	83	6.16
9 persons	31	2.45	3	4.41			34	2.52
10 persons	25	1.98	1	1.47	3	20.00	29	2.15
11 persons	9	.71	1	1.47			10	.74
12 persons	1	.08	1	1.47			2	.15
13 persons	1	.08	1	1.47	1	6.67	3	.23
17 persons					1	6.67	1	.07
18 persons			1	1.47			1	.07
Total families	1,265	100.00	68	100.00	15	100.00	1,348	100.00
Total individuals	6,310		345		118		6,773	
Average size of family	4.99		5.07		7.87		5.02	

TABLE **VII.**—NATIVITY OF PARENTS.

Birthplace of—		Native born.		Foreign born.		Total per-
Father.	Mother.	Male.	Female.	Male.	Female.	sons.
United States	United States		3			3
United States	Basilicata		1			1
United States	Liguria	2	2			4
Abruzzo	Abruzzo	59	58	243	122	482
Abruzzo	Basilicata	1	1			2
Abruzzo	Campania			1		1
Apulia	Apulia		4	7	5	16
Basilicata	Abruzzo	2	2			4
Basilicata	Basilicata	347	368	631	564	1,910
Basilicata	Campania	7	1			8
Basilicata	Lombardy	5				5
Basilicata	Sicily	2	3		1	6
Basilicata	Germany	1	1			2
Basilicata	Ireland		1			1
Basilicata	Sweden		1			1
Calabria	United States	1	1			2
Calabria	Abruzzo		2			2
Calabria	Basilicata	8	6			14
Calabria	Calabria	109	91	646	213	1,059
Calabria	Campania	1			1	2
Campagna di Roma	United States		1			1
Campagna di Roma	Campagna di Roma	3		3	3	9
Campania	United States	3				3
Campania	Abruzzo		2			2
Campania	Basilicata	26	26	3	5	60
Campania	Calabria	2	4	1		7
Campania	Campagna di Roma	2				2
Campania	Campania	351	327	741	497	1,916
Campania	Sicily	2	5			7
Campania	Ireland	2	2			4
Emilia	Emilia	6	8	16	16	46
Liguria	United States	3	3			6
Liguria	Basilicata	3				3
Liguria	Liguria	43	30	53	52	178
Liguria	Scotland		1			1
Lombardy	Basilicata	7	2		1	10
Lombardy	Emilia	1				1
Lombardy	Liguria	2				2
Lombardy	Lombardy	6	11	19	17	53
Lombardy	Piedmont	1	2			3
Marches	Basilicata	1		1	1	3
Marches	Marches			3	1	4
Piedmont	Piedmont	1	1	3	4	8
Sicily	Basilicata	1	1			2
Sicily	Sicily	109	104	336	194	743
Tuscany	Liguria	2	2			4
Tuscany	Tuscany	17	12	56	24	109
Tuscany	France	2	1	2	2	7
Tuscany	Not specified				1	1
Venetia	United States	1	1			2
Venetia	Liguria		1			1
Venetia	Venetia	2	8	21	8	39
France	France			1	2	3
Germany	Germany		2		1	3
Ireland	United States		1			1
Ireland	Ireland				1	1
Sweden	Sweden				1	1
Not specified	Campania		1			1
Not specified	Not specified	1				1
Total		1,144	1,105	2,787	1,737	6,773

TABLE **VIII.**—RELATIONSHIP TO HEAD OF FAMILY, BY NATIVITY AND SEX.

Relationship to head of family.	Number.			Per cent.		
	Male.	Female.	Total.	Male.	Female.	Total.
NATIVE BORN.						
Heads of families	2	....	2	0.17	....	0.09
Wives	....	14	14	....	1.27	.62
Sons and daughters	1,093	1,044	2,137	95.54	94.48	95.02
Stepsons and stepdaughters	10	13	23	.87	1.18	1.02
Sons and daughters, adopted	1	2	3	.09	.18	.13
Sons-in-law and daughters-in-law	....	1	1	....	.09	.05
Grandsons and granddaughters	13	10	23	1.14	.90	1.02
Brothers and sisters	2	2	4	.17	.18	.17
Brothers-in-law and sisters-in-law	1	1	2	.09	.09	.09
Nephews and nieces	14	15	29	1.22	1.36	1.29
Boarders	1	....	1	.09	....	.05
Lodgers	6	3	9	.53	.27	.40
Cooperative	1	....	1	.09	....	.05
Total	1,144	1,105	2,249	100.00	100.00	100.00
FOREIGN BORN.						
Heads of families	1,233	44	1,277	44.24	2.53	28.23
Wives	....	1,169	1,169	....	67.30	25.84
Sons and daughters	533	375	908	19.12	21.59	20.07
Stepsons and stepdaughters	22	5	27	.79	.29	.60
Sons and daughters, adopted	....	1	1	....	.06	.02
Sons-in-law and daughters-in-law	19	12	31	.68	.69	.68
Grandsons and granddaughters	1	....	1	.04	....	.02
Fathers and mothers	26	45	71	.93	2.59	1.57
Stepfathers and stepmothers	....	1	1	....	.06	.02
Fathers-in-law and mothers-in-law	15	26	41	.54	1.50	.91
Stepfathers-in-law and stepmothers-in-law	....	1	1	....	.06	.02
Brothers and sisters	79	14	93	2.83	.80	2.06
Brothers-in-law and sisters-in-law	66	23	89	2.37	1.32	1.97
Nephews and nieces	42	5	47	1.51	.29	1.04
Uncles and aunts	4	2	6	.14	.11	.13
Cousins	69	1	70	2.48	.06	1.55
Cousins-in-law	1	....	1	.04	....	.02
Boarders	101	3	104	3.62	.17	2.30
Lodgers	231	8	239	8.29	.46	5.28
Cooperative	345	1	346	12.38	.06	7.65
Housekeepers	....	1	1	....	.06	.02
Total	2,787	1,737	4,524	100.00	100.00	100.00
NATIVE AND FOREIGN BORN.						
Heads of families	1,235	44	1,279	31.42	1.55	18.88
Wives	....	1,183	1,183	....	41.63	17.47
Sons and daughters	1,626	1,419	3,045	41.36	49.93	44.96
Stepsons and stepdaughters	32	18	50	.81	.63	.74
Sons and daughters, adopted	1	3	4	.03	.10	.06
Sons-in-law and daughters-in-law	19	13	32	.48	.46	.47
Grandsons and granddaughters	14	10	24	.36	.35	.35
Fathers and mothers	26	45	71	.66	1.58	1.05
Stepfathers and stepmothers	....	1	1	....	.04	.02
Fathers-in-law and mothers-in-law	15	26	41	.38	.91	.60
Stepfathers-in-law and stepmothers-in-law	....	1	1	....	.04	.02
Brothers and sisters	81	16	97	2.06	.56	1.43
Brothers-in-law and sisters-in-law	67	24	91	1.70	.84	1.34
Nephews and nieces	56	20	76	1.42	.70	1.12
Uncles and aunts	4	2	6	.10	.07	.09
Cousins	69	1	70	1.76	.04	1.03
Cousins-in-law	1	....	1	.03	....	.02
Boarders	102	3	105	2.60	.10	1.55
Lodgers	237	11	248	6.03	.39	3.66
Cooperative	346	1	347	8.80	.04	5.12
Housekeepers	....	1	1	....	.04	.02
Total	3,931	2,842	6,773	100.00	100.00	100.00

TABLE **IX.**—FOREIGN-BORN VOTERS AND ALIENS, BY YEARS IN THE UNITED STATES.

[All males of foreign birth 21 years of age or over, not naturalized, have been termed aliens. A residence of five years in the United States is necessary to become naturalized and a voter.]

Years in the United States.	Foreign-born males 21 years of age or over.			Per cent.	
	Voters.	Aliens.	Total.	Voters.	Aliens.
Under 1		39	39		100.00
1		34	34		100.00
2		48	48		100.00
3		169	169		100.00
4		185	185		100.00
5	90	110	200	45.00	55.00
6	108	70	178	60.67	39.33
7	79	52	131	60.31	39.69
8	114	57	171	66.67	33.33
9	86	37	123	69.92	30.08
10	110	59	169	65.09	34.91
11	53	19	72	73.61	26.39
12	76	25	101	75.25	24.75
13	85	12	97	87.63	12.37
14	95	27	122	77.87	22.13
15	108	30	138	78.26	21.74
16	44	10	54	81.48	18.52
17	33	6	39	84.62	15.38
18	21	3	24	87.50	12.50
19	7	1	8	87.50	12.50
20	18	6	24	75.00	25.00
21	6		6	100.00	
22	7	1	8	87.50	12.50
23	8	2	10	80.00	20.00
24	7	1	8	87.50	12.50
25	6	3	9	66.67	33.33
26		1	1		100.00
27	3	1	4	75.00	25.00
28	1		1	100.00	
30	1		1	100.00	
36	1		1	100.00	
40	1		1	100.00	
57	1		1	100.00	
Not reported	10	4	14	71.43	28.57
Total	1,179	1,012	2,191	53.81	46.19

TABLE **X.**—WEEKLY EARNINGS AND HOURS OF WORK, BY OCCUPATION AND SEX.

Occupation.	Number of persons.	Sex.	Average hours of work per week.	Weekly earnings.		
				Highest.	Lowest.	Average.
AGRICULTURE, FISHERIES, AND MINING.						
Coal miners	2	M.	60	$8.00	$6.30	$7.15
Gardeners	1	M.	60	9.00	9.00	9.00
Greenhouse employees	1	M.	60	7.80	7.80	7.80
Quarrymen	28	M.	a 59.8	8.40	7.25	7.62¼
PROFESSIONAL.						
Electricians	1	M.	48	(b)	(b)	(b)
Musicians	42	M.	c 35.5	d 15.00	d 1.00	d 5.79
Do	3	F.	(b)	3.60	1.80	3.00
Notaries public	1	M.	(b)	(b)	(b)	(b)
Organ grinders	17	M.	e 67.5	f 6.00	f 2.00	f 3.81½
Teachers	2	M.	g 35	3.00	2.00	2.50
DOMESTIC AND PERSONAL SERVICE.						
Barbers	45	M.	h 83.8	i 17.50	i 2.00	i 7.26
Barbers' apprentices	5	M.	g 83	3.00	1.50	2.30
Bartenders	4	M.	j 72	f 7.50	f 4.00	f 5.75
Boarding-house keepers	1	M.	(b)	(b)	(b)	(b)
Boiler washers	1	M.	70	10.50	10.50	10.50
Bootblacks	64	M.	c 76	k 13.00	k .50	k 3.33
Do	1	F.	(b)	2.80	2.80	2.80
Bootblacks and newsboys	8	M.	l 62	6.00	.90	2.47½
Cooks	4	M.	91	m 18.00	m 12.00	m 14.66⅔
Dishwashers	1	M.	77	8.50	8.50	8.50
Drivers, garbage wagon	1	M.	60	6.60	6.60	6.60
Elevator tenders	3	M.	g 87.5	f 9.00	f 9.00	f 9.00
Engineers	2	M.	g 60	m 15.00	m 15.00	m 15.00
Firemen	2	M.	58	15.00	4.20	9.60
Foremen, laborers	1	M.	60	10.50	10.50	10.50
Foremen, sewer diggers	1	M.	48	11.00	11.00	11.00
Foremen, street sweepers	1	M.	60	9.00	9.00	9.00
Helpers in saloons	1	M.	(b)	(b)	(b)	(b)
Hospital employees	1	M.	(b)	(b)	(b)	(b)
Janitors	10	M.	55.7	10.50	4.25	8.47⅓
Laborers	796	M.	n 60.7	o 13.50	o 2.00	o 7.27½
Laborers, garbage dump	1	M.	60	(b)	(b)	(b)
Lamplighters	3	M.	31.5	9.23	5.11	7.11½
Lodging-house keepers	1	M.	(b)	(b)	(b)	(b)
Midwives	1	F.	(b)	(b)	(b)	(b)
Oilers, waterworks	1	M.	57	16.25	16.25	16.25
Padrones	6	M.	l 60	p 15.75	p 12.00	p 13.87½
Pavers	23	M.	l 57.2	10.50	7.50	8.20
Porters	2	M.	g 60	9.00	6.00	7.50
Saloon cleaners	1	M.	(b)	(b)	(b)	(b)
Saloon keepers	20	M.	q 108.6	(b)	(b)	(b)
Do	1	F.	(b)	(b)	(b)	(b)
Saloon keepers and interpreters	1	M.	(b)	11.25	11.25	11.25
Scissors grinders	18	M.	r 60	9.00	1.50	4.23⅓
Scrubbers	1	M.	(b)	6.00	6.00	6.00
Servants	1	F.	(b)	2.50	2.50	2.50
Sewer diggers	32	M.	s 53.2	m 13.50	m 6.00	m 11.03½
Street sweepers	126	M.	q 58	9.75	4.50	8.19
Washerwomen	6	F.	t 39	4.50	.50	2.16½
Watchmen	4	M.	g 59.7	14.00	7.50	10.25
Water carriers	2	M.	60	3.00	.75	1.87½
TRADE AND TRANSPORTATION.						
Bone pickers	4	M.	l 66	6.00	1.00	2.87¼
Cash girls	1	F.	57	2.00	2.00	2.00
Cashiers	1	M.	93	(b)	(b)	(b)
Clerks	1	F.	74	4.00	4.00	4.00
Coal pickers	3	M.	(b)	1.50	1.00	1.23½
Do	3	F.	(b)	f 1.20	f 1.20	f 1.20
Draymen	1	M.	(b)	2.00	2.00	2.00

a Hours of 6 not reported.	h Hours of 8 not reported.	o Wages of 22 not reported.
b Not reported.	i Wages of 12 not reported.	p Wages of 4 not reported.
c Hours of 32 not reported.	j Hours of 2 not reported.	q Hours of 9 not reported.
d Wages of 7 not reported.	k Wages of 8 not reported.	r Hours of 12 not reported.
e Hours of 5 not reported.	l Hours of 3 not reported.	s Hours of 7 not reported.
f Wages of 2 not reported.	m Wages of 1 not reported.	t Hours of 4 not reported.
g Hours of 1 not reported.	n Hours of 70 not reported.	

TABLE **X.**—WEEKLY EARNINGS AND HOURS OF WORK, BY OCCUPATION AND SEX—Continued.

Occupation.	Number of persons.	Sex.	Average hours of work per week.	Weekly earnings.		
				Highest.	Lowest.	Average.
TRADE AND TRANSPORTATION—continued.						
Drivers	7	M.	a 72	b $9.00	b $8.00	b $8.50
Drivers, ash wagon	1	M.	72	7.50	7.50	7.50
Drivers, fruit wagon	1	M.	(c)	(c)	(c)	(c)
Drivers, milk wagon	1	M.	52	3.00	3.00	3.00
Drivers, rag shop	1	M.	60	(c)	(c)	(c)
Electric supplies employees	1	M.	60	(c)	(c)	(c)
Elevated railroad employees	1	M.	60	7.50	7.50	7.50
Elevated railroad laborers	5	M.	60	7.50	7.50	7.50
Expressmen	10	M.	d 60	b 9.00	b 3.00	b 6.10
Flagmen	1	M.	70	8.50	8.50	8.50
Foremen, elevated railroad	2	M.	60	12.00	9.00	10.50
Fruit store employees	1	M.	(c)	(c)	(c)	(c)
Grain elevator employees	1	M.	60	2.00	2.00	2.00
Grain elevator laborers	1	M.	60	9.00	9.00	9.00
Hill boys	1	M.	70	7.50	7.50	7.50
Junk pickers	1	M.	(c)	3.00	3.00	3.00
Liquor store employees	1	M.	48	6.00	6.00	6.00
Lumber shovers	1	M.	60	7.50	7.50	7.50
Merchants, fruit	12	M.	e 82.4	f 9.00	f 9.00	f 9.00
Merchants, groceries	7	M.	(c)	(c)	(c)	(c)
Do	1	F.	(c)	(c)	(c)	(c)
Merchants, junk	2	M.	54	(c)	(c)	(c)
Merchants, rag	7	M.	g 73.2	h 6.00	h 3.00	h 4.30
Merchants, toys	1	M.	(c)	(c)	(c)	(c)
Merchants, wood	1	M.	(c)	1.20	1.20	1.20
Do	1	F.	(c)	1.20	1.20	1.20
Messengers	1	M.	42	3.00	3.00	3.00
Newsboys	68	M.	i 55.9	j 7.50	j .60	j 2.28½
Newsboys and salesmen, clothing	1	M.	64.5	3.00	3.00	3.00
Newsdealers	7	M.	63.1	10.00	4.56	5.93½
Newsgirls	1	F.	(c)	.50	.50	.50
Newspaper carriers	1	M.	73	7.00	7.00	7.00
Nutcrackers	2	M.	48	5.00	2.50	3.75
Office boys	1	M.	(c)	3.00	3.00	3.00
Packers, fruit	5	M.	60	k 11.00	k 7.50	k 9.37½
Packers, rag	4	M.	l 64	k 7.50	k 3.50	k 6.00
Packers, tobacco	1	F.	(c)	6.50	6.50	6.50
Paper pickers	17	M.	(c)	3.00	.60	1.07
Peddlers	10	M.	d 60	h 9.00	h 1.50	h 3.30
Peddlers, coal	1	M.	(c)	3.00	3.00	3.00
Peddlers, cottage cheese	1	M.	(c)	5.25	5.25	5.25
Peddlers, eggs	1	M.	30	1.50	1.50	1.50
Peddlers, fruit	124	M.	m 48	n 14.00	n .90	n 4.33
Do	1	F.	48	4.00	4.00	4.00
Peddlers, fruit and nuts	1	M.	36	9.00	9.00	9.00
Peddlers, fruit and vegetables	2	M.	l 60	9.00	1.50	5.25
Peddlers, ice cream	2	M.	l 60	7.00	3.00	5.00
Peddlers, images	2	M.	(c)	7.50	7.50	7.50
Peddlers, vegetables	8	M.	o 60	h 7.50	h 3.00	h 4.25
Peddlers, wood	1	F.	36	1.80	1.80	1.80
Ragpickers	155	M.	p 42.4	q 8.50	q .40	q 2.14
Do	8	F.	r 33	2.50	.40	1.25½
Rag shop employees	3	M.	l 63	k 9.00	k 6.00	k 7.50
Rag sorters	1	M.	60	7.00	7.00	7.00
Do	2	F.	60	3.00	3.00	3.00
Railroad employees	1	M.	(c)	12.00	12.00	12.00
Railroad laborers	112	M.	r 60.1	k 9.00	k 5.50	k 7.06½
Salesmen	6	M.	l 59.2	s 9.00	s 8.00	s 8.50
Salesmen, fruit	10	M.	68.3	k 18.00	k 8.00	k 11.11
Salesmen, groceries	2	M.	72	k 7.50	k 7.50	k 7.50
Saleswomen, bakery	1	F.	72	(c)	(c)	(c)
Saleswomen, dry goods	1	F.	80	4.00	4.00	4.00
Shipping clerks	1	M.	66	(c)	(c)	(c)
Street car conductors	1	M.	63	16.00	16.00	16.00
Street car drivers	1	M.	70	11.55	11.55	11.55
Street railroad laborers	2	M.	60	7.50	7.50	7.50
Teamsters	11	M.	r 53.8	t 18.00	t 7.00	t 10.06½

a Hours of 6 not reported.
b Wages of 5 not reported.
c Not reported.
d Hours of 9 not reported.
e Hours of 5 not reported.
f Wages of 10 not reported.
g Hours of 2 not reported.

h Wages of 2 not reported.
i Hours of 32 not reported.
j Wages of 8 not reported.
k Wages of 1 not reported.
l Hours of 1 not reported.
m Hours of 93 not reported.
n Wages of 21 not reported.

o Hours of 7 not reported.
p Hours of 97 not reported.
q Wages of 7 not reported.
r Hours of 3 not reported.
s Wages of 4 not reported.
t Wages of 3 not reported.

TABLE **X.**—WEEKLY EARNINGS AND HOURS OF WORK, BY OCCUPATION AND SEX—Continued.

Occupation.	Number of persons.	Sex.	Average hours of work per week.	Weekly earnings.		
				Highest.	Lowest.	Average.
TRADE AND TRANSPORTATION—concluded.						
Teamsters, with team	4	M.	a 56	$18. 00	$9. 00	$15. 75
Wood pickers	5	M.	(b)	c 6. 00	c. 75	c 2. 65
Do	9	F.	d 19. 5	e 3. 50	e. 75	e 2. 09½
Wood sawyers	4	M.	f 24	c 1. 00	c. 75	c. 91½
MANUFACTURES AND MECHANICAL INDUSTRIES.						
Accordion makers	1	M.	60	5. 00	5. 00	5. 00
Artificial flower makers	1	M.	(b)	3. 00	3. 00	3. 00
Do	1	F.	47. 5	5. 00	5. 00	5. 00
Bakers	8	M.	a 69. 4	e 12. 00	e 5. 00	e 7. 50
Bakers' helpers	5	M.	60	5. 50	4. 00	4. 50
Bakery employees	1	F.	55	3. 00	3. 00	3. 00
Baking powder factory employees	3	M.	g 55	9. 00	5. 50	7. 33⅓
Do	1	F.	(b)	4. 50	4. 50	4. 50
Bicycle shop employees	1	M.	60	6. 00	6. 00	6. 00
Biscuit factory employees	1	M.	60	13. 56	13. 56	13. 56
Blacksmiths	2	M.	57. 5	9. 00	9. 00	9. 00
Bookbinders	1	F.	45	3. 00	3. 00	3. 00
Box factory employees	1	M.	55	4. 00	4. 00	4. 00
Brass factory employees	2	M.	(b)	9. 00	6. 00	7. 50
Bricklayers	2	M.	48	24. 00	12. 00	18. 00
Brickyard employees	1	M.	60	9. 00	9. 00	9. 00
Cabinetmakers	1	M.	(b)	18. 00	18. 00	18. 00
Candy factory employees	30	M.	g 56. 9	10. 50	3. 00	6. 45½
Do	3	F.	55	6. 00	2. 00	3. 66½
Candy makers	4	M.	a 60	7. 25	3. 00	5. 81¼
Carpenters	6	M.	53. 7	12. 00	9. 00	11. 25
Cellar diggers	4	M.	60	7. 50	6. 75	7. 31¼
Cigar makers	2	M.	42	12. 00	6. 00	9. 00
Cloak finishers	3	F.	g 60	4. 00	1. 50	2. 33⅓
Cloak makers	1	M.	(b)	16. 00	16. 00	16. 00
Do	1	F.	(b)	9. 00	9. 00	9. 00
Compositors	1	M.	72	4. 75	4. 75	4. 75
Cracker factory employees	1	M.	60	6. 00	6. 00	6. 00
Do	1	F.	60	6. 00	6. 00	6. 00
Dog food factory employees	1	F.	60	6. 50	6. 50	6. 50
Dressmakers	1	M.	(b)	. 75	. 75	. 75
Do	1	F.	(b)	1. 50	1. 50	1. 50
Dressmakers' apprentices	1	F.	(b)	. 25	. 25	. 25
Drivers, brewery	1	M.	(b)	9. 00	9. 00	9. 00
Firemen, bakery	1	M.	60	12. 00	12. 00	12. 00
Foremen, hat factory	1	M.	60	20. 00	20. 00	20. 00
Foremen, hod carriers	1	M.	48	12. 00	12. 00	12. 00
Frame factory employees	1	M.	60	4. 00	4. 00	4. 00
Furniture finishers	1	M.	60	5. 00	5 00	5. 00
Furniture polishers	3	M.	56	6. 00	4. 00	5. 33⅓
Gas pipe layers	1	M.	60	9. 00	9. 00	9. 00
Gas works employees	1	M.	60	9. 00	9. 00	9. 00
Glass factory employees	1	M.	60	3. 00	3. 00	3. 00
Grinders, knife factory	1	M.	(b)	9. 00	9. 00	9. 00
Harness makers	2	M.	72	(b)	(b)	(b)
Harp repairers	1	M.	30	10. 00	10. 00	10. 00
Hat factory employees	1	M.	60	9. 00	9. 00	9. 00
Hod carriers	60	M.	h 50. 7	14. 00	5. 40	8. 87
Image makers	3	M.	g 54	c 12. 00	c 7. 50	c 9. 75
Iron foundry employees	6	M.	60	9. 00	8. 40	8. 80
Jacket makers	2	F.	64. 5	3. 75	2. 50	3. 12½
Knife factory employees	1	M.	60	2. 50	2. 50	2. 50
Do	1	F.	48	2. 40	2. 40	2. 40
Lime burners	9	M.	h 84	7. 50	6. 00	7. 00
Macaroni factory employees	3	F.	60	3. 00	2. 00	2. 66½
Macaroni makers	2	M.	a 60	8. 00	8. 00	8. 00
Do	3	F.	a 60	3. 50	3. 00	3. 16½
Machine shop employees	2	M.	48	11. 50	8. 64	10. 07
Machinists	2	M.	57. 5	12. 00	12. 00	12. 00
Marble polishers	1	M.	(b)	(b)	(b)	(b)
Marble works employees	1	M.	60	9. 00	9. 00	9. 00
Masons' helpers	1	M.	48	7. 50	7. 50	7. 50
Masons, stone	5	M.	48	24. 00	18. 00	20. 74
Mince-meat factory employees	1	M.	(b)	9. 00	9. 00	9. 00

a Hours of 1 not reported.
b Not reported.
c Wages of 1 not reported.
d Hours of 7 not reported.
e Wages of 2 not reported.
f Hours of 3 not reported.
g Hours of 2 not reported.
h Hours of 6 not reported.

TABLE **X.**—WEEKLY EARNINGS AND HOURS OF WORK, BY OCCUPATION AND SEX—Continued.

Occupation.	Number of persons.	Sex.	Average hours of work per week.	Weekly earnings.		
				Highest.	Lowest.	Average.
MANUFACTURES AND MECHANICAL INDUSTRIES—concluded.						
Mosaic layers	22	M.	50.6	*a* $13.50	*a* $4.00	*a* $8.70½
Nutcrackers, candy factory	1	F.	(*b*)	4.00	4.00	4.00
Packers, candy	1	M.	60	5.00	5.00	5.00
Packers, knife factory	1	F.	60	3.00	3.00	3.00
Packing house employees	1	M.	(*b*)	9.00	9.00	9.00
Painters	3	M.	56	12.00	2.00	7.00
Painters and decorators	1	M.	(*b*)	10.50	10.50	10.50
Painters' apprentices	1	M.	60	4.50	4.50	4.50
Paint shop employees	1	M.	48	9.00	9.00	9.00
Pants finishers	4	M.	*c* 96	*d* 1.80	*d* .54	*d* 1.03
Do	18	F.	(*b*)	*e* 3.00	*e* .50	*e* 1.40½
Pants makers	4	F.	*c* 24	5.00	.60	2.77⅞
Paper factory employees	1	F.	(*b*)	2.00	2.00	2.00
Paper sorters	1	F.	48	3.00	3.00	3.00
Plaster cast makers	1	M.	54	9.00	9.00	9.00
Plasterers	1	M.	48	9.00	9.00	9.00
Plaster workers	1	M.	48	12.00	12.00	12.00
Plumbers	1	M.	54	12.00	12.00	12.00
Polishers, wooden shoe forms	1	M.	48	5.00	5.00	5.00
Porters, bakery	1	M.	60	7.00	7.00	7.00
Press feeders	1	M.	59	6.25	6.25	6.25
Printers	1	M.	60	8.00	8.00	8.00
Seamstresses	4	F.	*f* 42	4.50	.25	2.43½
Shoe cutters' apprentices	1	M.	48	3.50	3.50	3.50
Shoe factory employees	2	M.	57.5	6.00	5.00	5.50
Shoemakers	16	M.	*g* 60.5	15.00	2.00	6.87¼
Sign painters' apprentices	1	M.	60	8.00	8.00	8.00
Skirt finishers	1	F.	(*b*)	1.25	1.25	1.25
Soap factory employees	2	M.	59.5	9.00	9.00	9.00
Stonebreakers	4	M.	61.3	8.00	6.50	7.30
Stonecutters	10	M.	47.8	27.75	6.00	20.05
Tailoresses	4	F.	50.3	*d* 3.60	*d* 2.50	*d* 3.03½
Tailors	15	M.	*c* 59	15.00	3.00	7.93½
Terra cotta factory employees	1	M.	60	7.80	7.80	7.80
Tinkers	14	M.	*h* 51	4.50	1.40	2.57
Tin tag factory employees	4	F.	60	4.00	4.00	4.00
Tobacco factory employees	1	M.	(*b*)	4.00	4.00	4.00
Tobacco strippers	5	F.	*i* 57	8.00	5.00	6.00
Trunk factory employees	1	M.	48	4.00	4.00	4.00
Umbrella menders	5	M.	*j* 72	6.00	3.00	5.05
Watchmakers	1	M.	(*b*)	9.00	9.00	9.00
NONPRODUCTIVE.						
At home	830	M.				
Do	859	F.				
Beggars	5	M.				
Do	5	F.				
Dressmakers' apprentices (no pay)	1	F.				
Housewives	1,044	F.				
Houseworkers	113	F.				
Masons', stone, apprentices (no pay)	1	M.				
No occupation	259	M.				
Do	102	F.				
Retired	10	M.				
Scholars	471	M.				
Do	405	F.				
Not reported	5	M.				
HOUSEWIVES AND AT WORK.						
Housewives and boarding-house keepers	2	F.	(*b*)	10.00	4.00	7.00
Housewives and button sewers	1	F.	60	.40	.40	.40
Housewives and cigar makers	1	F.	(*b*)	(*b*)	(*b*)	(*b*)
Housewives and cigar-stub gatherers	1	F.	(*b*)	.30	.30	.30
Housewives and cloak finishers	6	F.	*g* 42	2.00	.75	1.40½
Housewives and coal pickers	10	F.	(*b*)	*d* 1.80	*d* .60	*d* 1.16½
Housewives and coat finishers	3	F.	*i* 60	3.00	1.50	2.30
Housewives and dress finishers	3	F.	*f* 36	1.50	.45	.90
Housewives and dressmakers	10	F.	(*b*)	*k* 1.50	*k* .60	*k* .96½

a Wages of 2 not reported.
b Not reported.
c Hours of 3 not reported.
d Wages of 1 not reported.
e Wages of 3 not reported.
f Hours of 2 not reported.
g Hours of 5 not reported.
h Hours of 8 not reported.
i Hours of 1 not reported.
j Hours of 4 not reported
k Wages of 7 not reported.

TABLE **X.**—WEEKLY EARNINGS AND HOURS OF WORK, BY OCCUPATION AND SEX—Concluded.

Occupation.	Number of persons.	Sex.	Average hours of work per week.	Weekly earnings.		
				Highest.	Lowest.	Average.
HOUSEWIVES AND AT WORK—concluded.						
Housewives and fortune tellers	1	F.	(a)	(a)	(a)	(a)
Housewives and glove makers	1	F.	(a)	$6.50	$6.50	$6.50
Housewives and jacket finishers	1	F.	72	3.00	3.00	3.00
Housewives and laundresses	1	F.	84	(a)	(a)	(a)
Housewives and macaroni makers	1	F.	60	3.00	3.00	3.00
Housewives and merchants, feed	1	F.	(a)	(a)	(a)	(a)
Housewives and merchants, groceries	14	F.	b 84	c 5.00	c 3.50	c 4.25
Housewives and merchants, wood	8	F.	d 21	2.40	.75	1.59¼
Housewives and nurses	2	F.	(a)	2.25	.75	1.50
Housewives and organ grinders	1	F.	60	(a)	(a)	(a)
Housewives and pants finishers	54	F.	e 60.8	f 3.50	f .30	f 1.57½
Housewives and pants makers	15	F.	g 37.2	3.50	1.00	1.95¼
Housewives and paper sorters	1	F.	48	1.00	1.00	1.00
Housewives and ragpickers	6	F.	h 24	2.40	.60	1.56
Housewives and rag shop employees	1	F.	60	3.50	3.50	3.50
Housewives and saloon keepers	1	F.	(a)	(a)	(a)	(a)
Housewives and seamstresses	13	F.	h 50.3	4.00	.25	1.71½
Housewives and servants	1	F.	(a)	(a)	(a)	(a)
Housewives and skirt finishers	1	F.	(a)	1.25	1.25	1.25
Housewives and tailoresses	2	F.	i 60	6.00	1.75	3.87½
Housewives and waist finishers	1	F.	(a)	.40	.40	.40
Housewives and washerwomen	16	F.	j 48	k 3.00	k .25	k 1.16¼
Housewives and wetnurses	1	F.	(a)	1.50	1.50	1.50
Housewives and wood pickers	7	F.	d 24	l 2.70	l .55	l 1.85
SCHOLARS AND AT WORK.						
Scholars and barbers' apprentices	1	M.	89	1.00	1.00	1.00
Scholars and bartenders	1	M.	72	3.00	3.00	3.00
Scholars and bootblacks	12	M.	d 46.7	l 5.00	l .30	l 2.21
Scholars and candy factory employees	1	M.	55	5.00	5.00	5.00
Do	1	F.	60	2.00	2.00	2.00
Scholars and compositors	1	M.	72	2.75	2.75	2.75
Scholars and dog food factory employees	1	F.	60	4.00	4.00	4.00
Scholars and expressmen	1	M.	54	6.00	6.00	6.00
Scholars and hod carriers	1	M.	54	9.00	9.00	9.00
Scholars and knife factory employees	2	M.	60	3.00	3.00	3.00
Scholars and laborers	4	M.	60	7.50	6.60	7.27½
Scholars and macaroni makers	1	F.	60	1.50	1.50	1.50
Scholars and musicians	1	F.	(a)	1.20	1.20	1.20
Scholars and newsboys	53	M.	m 44.4	k 2.50	k .15	k 1.02
Scholars and newsgirls	2	F.	i 18	1.05	.40	.72¼
Scholars and packers, knife factory	1	F.	60	2.50	2.50	2.50
Scholars and paint factory employees	1	M.	60	8.00	8.00	8.00
Scholars and pants finishers	1	F.	36	1.50	1.50	1.50
Scholars and peddlers	1	M.	(a)	1.25	1.25	1.25
Scholars and peddlers, fruit	7	M.	d 60	6.00	1.50	3.28¼
Scholars and peddlers, gum	1	F.	(a)	.25	.25	.25
Scholars and picture frame factory employees	1	M.	55	5.00	5.00	5.00
Scholars and picture frame joiners	2	M.	60	4.00	3.50	3.75
Scholars and ragpickers	1	M.	(a)	(a)	(a)	(a)
Scholars and railroad laborers	1	M.	60	7.50	7.50	7.50
Scholars and salesmen, groceries	1	M.	72	2.00	2.00	2.00
Scholars and saleswomen, dry goods	1	F.	18	3.50	3.50	3.50
Scholars and seamstresses	2	F.	i 47.5	3.00	2.50	2.75
Scholars and shoe factory employees	1	M.	55	2.50	2.50	2.50
Scholars and shoemakers' apprentices	1	M.	48	2.50	2.50	2.50
Scholars and tailors	3	M.	58	6.50	2.50	3.83½
Scholars and tailors' apprentices	1	M.	(a)	2.00	2.00	2.00
Scholars and tobacco strippers	1	M.	60	4.00	4.00	4.00
Scholars and water carriers	1	M.	60	6.00	6.00	6.00

a Not reported.
b Hours of 12 not reported.
c Wages of 12 not reported.
d Hours of 6 not reported.
e Hours of 46 not reported.

f Wages of 5 not reported.
g Hours of 10 not reported.
h Hours of 5 not reported.
i Hours of 1 not reported.

j Hours of 15 not reported.
k Wages of 1 not reported.
l Wages of 2 not reported.
m Hours of 19 not reported.

TABLE **XI.**—PERSONS UNEMPLOYED, BY MONTHS UNEMPLOYED, SEX, AND AGE.

[This table includes all persons 15 years of age or over engaged in remunerative occupations who were unemployed during any part of the year.]

Sex and age.	Persons unemployed.											Total.
	1 mo.	2 mos.	3 mos.	4 mos.	5 mos.	6 mos.	7 mos.	8 mos.	9 mos.	10 mos.	11 mos.	
MALES.												
15 years					1	1	1			1	1	5
16 years	2				1	4	1	1	1	2		12
17 years				2		4	2	2	2		1	13
18 years	3		2			2	2	1	2	3		16
19 years		2	2	1		3	2	1	2	1	2	16
20 years		2	2	1		3	3	3	7	1	1	23
21 years	1	1	1	1	1	5	4	3	3	1	2	23
22 years		1		3	2	3	2	5	7	2		25
23 years		4	3	6	4	4	6	5	7	5	1	42
24 years	2	4	4	1	1	3	4	2	5	5	1	32
25 years		3		2	4	6	9	10	12	6	1	53
26 years		1	3		4	2	4	10	10	10	3	47
27 years	2	1		1	5	9	2	11	9	7	1	48
28 years	4	2	3	5	7	8	9	8	9	3	3	61
29 years		1	1	4	4	5	4	2	11	6		38
30 years	4	3	2	1	6	13	15	18	21	21	5	109
31 years		1	2		2	4	5	5	6	2	2	29
32 years	3	1	1	2	6	13	10	6	10	4	2	58
33 years	1	2		8	6	3	4	8	9	2	4	47
34 years	2		2	2	2	8	4	15	10	4	2	51
35 years	1	2	6	1	6	10	10	15	11	3	1	66
36 years		1	3	3		6	8	4	5	5	1	36
37 years		1		2	4	6	5	7	11	6		42
38 years	3	1		1		5	4	8	12	3	1	38
39 years			1		2	8	5	4	6	4	1	31
40 years	2	6	4	2	9	13	17	18	25	12	5	113
41 years	2					1	1	3	6	2	1	17
42 years	1	2		4		6	5	2	7	1		28
43 years		1		2			5		7		1	16
44 years				2		1	3	4	4	6	2	22
45 years	2	2	1	2	5	7	5	7	16	3	3	53
46 years				1		4	6	5	7	3	4	30
47 years	2			1		4	1		9	4	1	22
48 years	2				3		4	1	9	4	1	24
49 years					1	1		1	3	1	1	8
50 years	1	1		1	2	6	3	5	15	3	3	40
51 years				1				2	2	1		6
52 years							3			1	2	6
53 years	1				1			1	2	1	1	7
54 years		1	2				2		5	2		12
55 years		1	1			2	2	1	3			10
56 years			1				1	1	3	2		8
57 years							1	2		2		5
58 years						1						1
59 years									1			1
60 years				1		2	1	1	2	1	1	9
Over 60 years		2				2			1	2		7
Age not reported						1	1					2
Total	39	51	46	62	96	197	175	219	303	156	64	1,408
FEMALES.												
15 years					1	3		1				5
16 years		1				5						6
17 years		1				3	1				1	6
18 years						2	1					3
19 years						2		1				3
20 years					1			1				2
21 years						1		1			1	3
23 years						1	1					2
24 years						1			1	1		3
25 years						2						2
26 years						2	1	1	1			5
27 years		1				4						5
29 years						3		2			1	6
30 years			1	1		2		1		1		6
31 years						1						1
32 years								1	1	1	1	4
33 years		1				2						3
34 years				1								1
35 years						3	1				1	5
36 years					1		1	1	1			4

TABLE **XI.**—PERSONS UNEMPLOYED, BY MONTHS UNEMPLOYED, SEX, AND AGE—Concluded.

[This table includes all persons 15 years of age or over engaged in remunerative occupations who were unemployed during any part of the year.]

Sex and age.	Persons unemployed.											Total.
	1 mo.	2 mos.	3 mos.	4 mos.	5 mos.	6 mos.	7 mos.	8 mos.	9 mos.	10 mos.	11 mos.	
FEMALES—concluded.												
37 years	1					1						2
38 years			1	1					1	1		4
39 years				1								1
40 years					2	2		2				6
42 years						2		1				3
44 years						1			1			2
45 years				1		4	1	1				7
46 years									1			1
47 years						1						1
48 years						2	1					3
56 years						1						1
60 years						1				1		2
Age not reported		1										1
Total	1	5	3	4	6	53	8	13	7	5	4	109
MALES AND FEMALES.												
15 years					2	4	1	1		1	1	10
16 years	2	1			1	9	1	1	1	2	1	18
17 years		1		2	1	7	3	2	2		1	19
18 years	3		2	1		4	3	1	2	3		19
19 years		2	2	1		5	2	2	2	1	2	19
20 years		2	2	1	1	4	3	3	7	1	1	25
21 years	1	1	1	1	1	6	4	4	3	1	3	26
22 years		1		3	2	3	2	5	7	2		25
23 years		4	1	3	6	5	7	5	7	5	1	44
24 years	2	4	4	1	1	4	4	2	6	6	1	35
25 years		3		2	4	8	9	10	12	6	1	55
26 years		1	3		4	4	5	11	11	10	3	52
27 years	2	2		1	5	13	2	11	9	7	1	53
28 years	4	2	3	5	7	8	9	8	9	3	3	61
29 years		1	1	4	4	8	4	4	11	6	1	44
30 years	4	3	3	2	6	15	15	19	21	22	5	115
31 years		1	2		2	5	5	5	6	2	2	30
32 years	3	1	1	2	6	13	10	7	11	5	3	62
33 years	1	2	1	8	6	5	4	8	9	3	4	50
34 years	2	1	2	2	2	8	4	15	10	4	2	52
35 years	1	2	6	1	6	13	11	15	11	3	1	71
36 years		1	3	3	1	6	9	5	6	5	1	40
37 years	1	1		2	4	7	5	7	11	6		44
38 years	3	1	1	2		5	4	8	13	4	1	42
39 years			1	1	2	8	5	4	4	4	1	32
40 years	2	6	4	2	11	15	17	20	25	12	5	119
41 years	2				1	1	1	3	6	2	1	17
42 years	1	2			4	8	5	3	4	1	3	31
43 years		1		2		5		7	1			16
44 years				2	1	4	1	4	7	3	2	24
45 years	2	2	1	3	5	11	6	8	16	3	3	60
46 years		1	1	3	2	1	6	4	5	5	3	31
47 years	2					5	2	3	7	3	1	23
48 years			1	3		6	2		9	4	2	27
49 years					1	1	1		3	1	1	8
50 years	1	1		1	2	6	3	5	15	3	3	40
51 years				1				2	2	1		6
52 years							3		2	1		6
53 years	1				1			1	1	1	2	7
54 years		1	2					2	5	1	1	12
55 years						2	2	1	3	2		10
56 years			1	1		1	1	1	3	1		9
57 years							1	2		2		5
58 years						1						1
59 years								1				1
60 years				1		3	1	1	2	2	1	11
Over 60 years		2				2			1	2		7
Age not reported		1				1	1					3
Total	40	56	49	66	102	250	183	232	310	161	68	1,517

TABLE **XII.**—ILLITERATES, BY SEX, AGE PERIODS, AND DEGREE OF ILLITERACY.

[This table includes all persons 10 years of age or over who can not read and write and who can not write.]

Age periods.	Unable to read and write.						Unable to write.					
	Male.			Female.			Male.			Female.		
	Native born.	Foreign born.	Total.	Native born.	Foreign born.	Total.	Native born.	Foreign born.	Total.	Native born.	Foreign born.	Total.
10 to 14 years	8	53	61	16	49	65	......	3	3	1	5	6
15 to 20 years	2	89	91	3	107	110	......	1	1	......	5	5
21 to 30 years	......	378	378	1	344	345	1	19	20	......	5	5
31 to 50 years	......	739	739	......	611	611	......	18	18	......	5	5
51 years or over	......	140	140	......	134	134	......	2	2	......	2	2
Age not reported	......	7	7	......	3	3	......	1	1	......	......	......
Total	10	1,406	1,416	20	1,248	1,268	1	44	45	1	22	23

TABLE **XIII.**—LITERATES, BY SEX, AGE PERIODS, AND LANGUAGE.

[This table includes all persons 10 years of age or over who can read and write the language specified.]

Age periods.	Males.						Females.					
	Native born.			Foreign born.			Native born.			Foreign born.		
	English only.	Italian only.	Both English and Italian.	English only.	Italian only.	Both English and Italian.	English only.	Italian only.	Both English and Italian.	English only.	Italian only.	Both English and Italian.
10 to 14 years	104	3	....	67	18	44	89	....	....	68	10	18
15 to 20 years	18	....	....	45	81	68	23	....	....	28	35	25
21 to 30 years	15	....	....	7	277	100	12	....	....	2	67	9
31 to 50 years	1	....	....	3	389	58	3	....	....	....	53	4
51 years or over	....	....	....	1	47	2	....	....	....	....	4	....
Age not reported	....	....	....	....	3	....	....	....	....	....	....	....
Total	138	3	....	123	815	272	127	....	....	98	169	56

TABLE **XIV.**—LITERATES AND ILLITERATES, BY SEX.

[This table includes all persons 10 years of age or over.]

Literates and illiterates.	Males.		Females.		Total.	
	Number.	Per cent.	Number.	Per cent.	Number.	Per cent.
Read and write English only	261	19.32	225	50.00	486	26.99
Read and write Italian only	818	60.55	169	37.56	987	54.80
Read and write English and Italian	272	20.13	56	12.44	328	18.21
Total literates	1,351	48.04	450	25.85	1,801	39.56
Total illiterates	1,461	51.96	1,291	74.15	2,752	60.44
Aggregate	2,812	100.00	1,741	100.00	4,553	100.00

TABLE **XV.**—SCHOOL ATTENDANCE, BY NATIVITY, AGE, KIND OF SCHOOL, AND SEX.

Nativity and age.	Public schools.			Private schools.			Aggregate.		
	Male.	Female.	Total.	Male.	Female.	Total.	Male	Female.	Total.
NATIVE BORN.									
Under 5 years		2	2	1		1	1	2	3
5 years	8	5	13	4	3	7	12	8	20
6 years	31	30	61	3	7	10	34	37	71
7 years	56	49	105	9		9	65	49	114
8 years	53	39	92	6	5	11	59	44	103
9 years	38	36	74	6	3	9	44	39	83
10 years	27	25	52	5	5	10	32	30	62
11 years	19	12	31	2		2	21	12	33
12 years	21	22	43		1	1	21	23	44
13 years	9	7	16	2		2	11	7	18
14 years	11	8	19	1		1	12	8	20
15 years	5	1	6		1	1	5	2	7
16 years		1	1					1	1
17 years	2		2				2		2
18 years	1		1				1		1
Total	281	237	518	39	25	64	320	262	582
FOREIGN BORN.									
Under 5 years									
5 years	1	1	2	1		1	2	1	3
6 years	5	8	13				5	8	13
7 years	24	15	39	2		2	26	15	41
8 years	15	12	27	4	1	5	19	13	32
9 years	17	27	44	3		3	20	27	47
10 years	33	18	51	2	1	3	35	19	54
11 years	19	11	30	4	2	6	23	13	36
12 years	18	21	39	5	1	6	23	22	45
13 years	23	8	31	5	3	8	28	11	39
14 years	14	14	28		1	1	14	15	29
15 years	24	8	32	1	1	2	25	9	34
16 years	10	2	12				10	2	12
17 years	10		10	2		2	12		12
18 years	2		2				2		2
19 years	1		1				1		1
20 years	2		2				2		2
21 years	2		2				2		2
24 years	1		1				1		1
25 years	1		1				1		1
Total	222	145	367	29	10	39	251	155	406
NATIVE AND FOREIGN BORN.									
Under 5 years		2	2	1		1	1	2	3
5 years	9	6	15	5	3	8	14	9	23
6 years	36	38	74	3	7	10	39	45	84
7 years	80	64	144	11		11	91	64	155
8 years	68	51	119	10	6	16	78	57	135
9 years	55	63	118	9	3	12	64	66	130
10 years	60	43	103	7	6	13	67	49	116
11 years	38	23	61	6	2	8	44	25	69
12 years	39	43	82	5	2	7	44	45	89
13 years	32	15	47	7	3	10	39	18	57
14 years	25	22	47	1	1	2	26	23	49
15 years	29	9	38	1	2	3	30	11	41
16 years	10	3	13				10	3	13
17 years	12		12	2		2	14		14
18 years	3		3				3		3
19 years	1		1				1		1
20 years	2		2				2		2
21 years	2		2				2		2
24 years	1		1				1		1
25 years	1		1				1		1
Total	503	382	885	68	35	103	571	417	988

TABLE **XVI.**—CONDITION OF ALL CHILDREN FROM 5 TO 14 YEARS OF AGE, INCLUSIVE, BY NATIVITY AND SEX.

Nativity and age.	At home.			At work.			At school.			At work and at school.			Aggregate.		
	M.	F.	Total.	M.	F.	Total.	M.	F.	Total.	M.	F.	Total.	M.	F.	Total.
NATIVE BORN.															
5 years	72	88	160	....	....	....	12	8	20	....	....	....	84	96	180
6 years	34	29	63				34	37	71				68	66	134
7 years	15	18	33				65	49	114				80	67	147
8 years	5	6	11				58	44	102	1	....	1	64	50	114
9 years	4	8	12				40	39	79	4	....	4	48	47	95
10 years	....	1	1	2	1	3	30	30	60	2	....	2	34	32	66
11 years	1	5	6	1	2	3	18	12	30	3	....	3	23	19	42
12 years	2	2	4	2	1	3	17	22	39	4	1	5	25	26	51
13 years	1	2	3	4	1	5	10	6	16	1	1	2	16	10	26
14 years	1	7	8	4	4	8	10	7	17	2	1	3	17	19	36
Total	135	166	301	13	9	22	294	254	548	17	3	20	459	432	891
FOREIGN BORN.															
5 years	9	19	28				2	1	3				11	20	31
6 years	8	14	22				5	8	13				13	22	35
7 years	12	8	20				26	15	41				38	23	61
8 years	7	11	18				18	13	31	1	....	1	26	24	50
9 years	3	8	11	2	....	2	19	27	46	1	....	1	25	35	60
10 years	6	4	10	2	4	6	30	19	49	5	....	5	43	27	70
11 years	5	9	14	5	....	5	19	13	32	4	....	4	33	22	55
12 years	7	14	21	7	2	9	16	21	37	7	1	8	37	38	75
13 years	2	7	9	9	4	13	15	9	24	13	2	15	39	22	61
14 years	5	11	16	14	15	29	6	14	20	8	1	9	33	41	74
Total	64	105	169	39	25	64	156	140	296	39	4	43	298	274	572
NATIVE AND FOREIGN BORN.															
5 years	81	107	188				14	9	23				95	116	211
6 years	42	43	85				39	45	84				81	88	169
7 years	27	26	53				91	64	155				118	90	208
8 years	12	17	29				76	57	133	2	....	2	90	74	164
9 years	7	16	23	2	....	2	59	66	125	5	....	5	73	82	155
10 years	6	5	11	4	5	9	60	49	109	7	....	7	77	59	136
11 years	6	14	20	6	2	8	37	25	62	7	....	7	56	41	97
12 years	9	16	25	9	3	12	33	43	76	11	2	13	62	64	126
13 years	3	9	12	13	5	18	25	15	40	14	3	17	55	32	87
14 years	6	18	24	18	19	37	16	21	37	10	2	12	50	60	110
Total	199	271	470	52	34	86	450	394	844	56	7	63	757	706	1,463

TABLE **XVII.**—MARRIED WOMEN HAVING A SPECIFIED NUMBER OF ITALIAN-BORN CHILDREN LIVING, BY NUMBER OF CHILDREN BORN TO EACH IN ITALY AND YEARS OF MARRIED LIFE IN ITALY.

[In this table married women include also widowed women.]

Children born in Italy and children living.	Married women having spent specified number of years of married life in Italy.										
	Under 1.	1.	2.	3.	4.	5.	6.	7.	8.	9.	10.
No children	2	32	16	5	2	3	5	5	2	4	1
1 child:											
None living		5	15	7	11	8	3	1		1	
1 living	1	14	12	24	17	12	7	3	8	3	1
Total	1	19	27	31	28	20	10	4	8	4	1
2 children:											
None living				1	2	6	3	3	3	3	1
1 living		1	3	3	4	7	10	9	3	3	8
2 living			4	4	2	2	6	8	9	4	4
Total		1	7	8	8	15	19	20	15	10	13
3 children:											
None living											
1 living				1	1		2	2	1	1	1
2 living			2		1	3	3	3	3	8	5
3 living					3	2	1	4	8	2	4
Not specified											
Total			2	1	5	6	8	9	14	11	14
4 children:											
None living					1		1	2	1	1	
1 living							1	2	2	2	1
2 living					1	1	1	2	3	3	3
3 living							1	2	1	2	3
4 living										1	1
Total					2	1	4	8	7	9	8
5 children:											
None living								1	1	1	
1 living									1		1
2 living											
3 living								1		1	1
4 living								1			
5 living										2	1
Total								3	2	4	3
6 children:											
None living											
1 living											
2 living											
3 living										1	1
4 living											
5 living											
Total										1	1
7 children:											
None living										1	1
1 living											
2 living											
3 living											
4 living											
5 living											
6 living											
7 living											
Total										1	1

a One married 26 years and one married 31 years.
b Married 26 years.
c Married 29 years.
d One married 27 years and one married 32 years.
e Married 30 years.
f Married 34 years.

TABLE **XVII.**—MARRIED WOMEN HAVING A SPECIFIED NUMBER OF ITALIAN-BORN CHILDREN LIVING, BY NUMBER OF CHILDREN BORN TO EACH IN ITALY AND YEARS OF MARRIED LIFE IN ITALY.

[In this table married women include also widowed women.]

	Married women having spent specified number of years of married life in Italy.																	Total.
	11.	12.	13.	14.	15.	16.	17.	18.	19.	20.	21.	22.	23.	24.	25.	Over 25.	Not reported.	
	1		1		2		1	1	2	1		1				a 2	7	96
	2											1					3	57
	3	2	2	1	1					1		1		1			4	118
	5	2	2	1	1					1		2		1			7	175
	3	2				1				1						b 1		30
	2	2	3	1	1					1						c 1		62
	3	4	2	1		2	1	3			1	1		1			1	63
	8	8	5	2	1	3	1	3		2	1	1		1		2	1	155
	1	1	2			1											1	14
	3	1	1		1					1							1	36
			3	3	2			3			2	1				d 2	2	40
	2	1	2	2			3		1				1			c 1	2	26
																e 1		1
	6	6	8	4	1	4	3	1		3	1	1				4	5	117
				1													1	8
	3	1	4	1	2											b 1	1	21
	2		4	3	1		2	1	1					1			1	30
	2	1	4		1								1				2	20
	1	1		1		1		1	1	1					1	f 1	3	14
	8	3	12	5	5	1	2	2	2	1			1	1	1	2	8	93
			1	2	1											g 1		8
	2		2	1	1		1				1	1		1	1	h 1	1	11
		1	2	1	1			2		1		2		1		i 2	1	11
			3	1	1	1			2									14
		2	1	1		1	1	1	2	2	1					c 1	1	15
	1																	4
	3	3	7	6	4	2	2	1	4	2	3	3		2	1	5	3	63
		1								1		1					1	6
	2	1				1		1				1					1	9
	1	2	1		2			1	1			1			1	j 1	1	10
			1		1	1		1	1		1					k 1	1	5
				1	1			1						1			1	6
	3	5	2	3	2	3		3	3		2	1		2	2	4	37
		1								1		1			1	f 1	1	4
	1	1				1					1			1		c 1	1	7
							1	3			1						1	9
					1		1	1		3						e 1	1	3
		1		1			1	1		3				1		h 1	3	11
										1							1	2
										1								2
										1								1
	1	3		1	1		3	6		6	1	1		2		4	8	39

g Married 27 years.
h Married 31 years.
i One married 36 years and one married 38 years.
j Married 37 years.
k Married 35 years.

TABLE **XVII.**—MARRIED WOMEN HAVING A SPECIFIED NUMBER OF ITALIAN-BORN CHILDREN LIVING, BY NUMBER OF CHILDREN BORN TO EACH IN ITALY AND YEARS OF MARRIED LIFE IN ITALY—Continued.

[In this table married women include also widowed women.]

Children born in Italy and children living.	Married women having spent specified number of years of married life in Italy.										
	Under 1.	1.	2.	3.	4.	5.	6.	7.	8.	9.	10.
8 children:											
1 living											
2 living											
3 living											
4 living											
5 living											
6 living											
7 living											
8 living											
Total											
9 children:											
None living											
1 living											
2 living											
3 living											
4 living											
6 living											
8 living											
Total											
10 children:											
2 living											
3 living											
5 living											
6 living											
8 living											
9 living											
Total											
11 children:											
1 living											
2 living											
3 living											
5 living											
7 living											
Total											
12 children:											
4 living											
9 living											
Total											
13 children:											
2 living											
Total											
14 children:											
1 living											
7 living											
Total											
15 children:											
2 living											
Total											

a One married 31 years and one married 45 years.
b One married 27 years and one married 34 years.
c Married 32 years.
d Married 26 years.
e Married 30 years.
f One married 27 years, one married 36 years, and one married 38 years.
g One married 30 years and one married 32 years.

TABLE **XVII.**—MARRIED WOMEN HAVING A SPECIFIED NUMBER OF
ITALIAN-BORN CHILDREN LIVING, BY NUMBER OF CHILDREN BORN
TO EACH IN ITALY AND YEARS OF MARRIED LIFE IN ITALY—Continued.

[In this table married women include also widowed women.]

	Married women having spent specified number of years of married life in Italy.																	Total.
11.	12.	13.	14.	15.	16.	17.	18.	19.	20.	21.	22.	23.	24.	25.	Over 25.	Not reported.	
.....	.....	.....	.....	.....	1	.....	.....	1	.....	.....	.....	.....	.....	.....	.....	1	3
.....	2	1	1	.....	1	.....	.....	.....	.....	.....	.....	.....	1	.....	.....	2	5
.....	2	2	.....	.....	1	1	1	.....	.....	.....	1	1	.....	.....	a2	.....	11
.....	.....	1	.....	.....	.....	.....	.....	1	.....	.....	.....	.....	.....	.....	b2	.....	4
.....	.....	.....	.....	.....	.....	.....	.....	.....	1	.....	.....	.....	.....	.....	c1	.....	2
.....	.....	.....	.....	.....	.....	.....	.....	.....	.....	.....	.....	1	.....	.....	.....	.....	1
.....	.....	.....	.....	.....	.....	.....	.....	.....	.....	.....	.....	.....	.....	.....	d1	.....	1
.....	.....	.....	.....	.....	.....	1	.....	.....	.....	.....	.....	.....	.....	.....	.....	.....	1
.....	2	4	1	.....	2	2	1	2	.....	1	1	2	1	.....	6	3	28
.....	.....	.....	.....	.....	1	.....	.....	.....	.....	.....	.....	.....	.....	.....	.....	.....	1
.....	.....	.....	.....	.....	.....	.....	1	.....	.....	.....	1	.....	.....	.....	.....	.....	2
.....	.....	1	.....	.....	.....	.....	.....	.....	1	1	.....	.....	.....	.....	e1	.....	4
.....	.....	.....	.....	.....	.....	2	.....	.....	.....	1	.....	.....	.....	.....	c1	1	5
.....	.....	.....	.....	.....	1	.....	.....	.....	.....	.....	1	.....	.....	.....	f3	.....	5
.....	.....	.....	.....	.....	.....	.....	.....	.....	.....	.....	.....	.....	.....	.....	g2	.....	2
.....	.....	.....	.....	.....	.....	.....	.....	.....	.....	.....	.....	.....	.....	.....	h1	.....	1
.....	.....	1	.....	.....	2	2	1	.....	1	2	2	.....	.....	.....	8	1	20
.....	.....	.....	.....	.....	.....	.....	.....	.....	.....	.....	.....	.....	.....	.....	d1	1	2
.....	.....	.....	.....	.....	.....	.....	.....	.....	.....	.....	.....	1	.....	.....	d1	.....	2
.....	.....	.....	.....	.....	.....	.....	.....	.....	.....	.....	.....	1	1	.....	i3	.....	3
.....	.....	.....	.....	.....	.....	1	.....	.....	.....	.....	.....	.....	.....	.....	.....	.....	2
.....	.....	.....	.....	.....	.....	.....	.....	.....	.....	.....	.....	.....	.....	.....	.....	.....	1
.....	.....	.....	.....	.....	.....	.....	.....	.....	.....	.....	.....	.....	.....	.....	.....	1	1
.....	.....	.....	.....	.....	.....	.....	1	.....	.....	.....	.....	2	1	.....	5	2	11
.....	.....	.....	.....	.....	1	.....	.....	.....	.....	.....	.....	.....	.....	.....	.....	.....	1
.....	.....	.....	.....	.....	.....	1	.....	.....	.....	.....	.....	.....	.....	.....	j2	1	3
.....	.....	.....	.....	.....	1	.....	.....	.....	.....	.....	.....	.....	1	.....	.....	.....	2
.....	.....	.....	1	.....	.....	.....	.....	.....	.....	.....	.....	.....	.....	.....	.....	.....	1
.....	.....	.....	.....	.....	.....	.....	.....	.....	.....	.....	.....	.....	.....	.....	k1	.....	1
.....	.....	.....	.....	1	2	.....	.....	.....	.....	.....	.....	.....	1	.....	3	1	8
.....	.....	.....	.....	.....	.....	.....	1	.....	.....	.....	.....	.....	.....	.....	.....	.....	1
.....	.....	.....	.....	.....	.....	.....	.....	.....	.....	.....	.....	.....	.....	.....	l1	.....	1
.....	.....	.....	.....	.....	.....	.....	1	.....	.....	.....	.....	.....	.....	.....	1	.....	2
.....	.....	.....	.....	.....	.....	.....	.....	.....	.....	.....	.....	.....	.....	.....	.....	1	1
.....	.....	.....	.....	.....	.....	.....	.....	.....	.....	.....	.....	.....	.....	.....	.....	1	1
.....	.....	.....	.....	.....	.....	.....	.....	1	.....	.....	.....	.....	.....	.....	m1	.....	1
.....	.....	.....	.....	.....	1	.....	.....	.....	.....	.....	.....	.....	.....	.....	.....	1	3
.....	.....	.....	.....	.....	1	.....	.....	1	.....	.....	.....	.....	.....	.....	1	1	4
.....	.....	.....	.....	.....	.....	.....	.....	1	.....	.....	.....	.....	.....	.....	.....	.....	1
.....	.....	.....	.....	.....	.....	.....	.....	1	.....	.....	.....	.....	.....	.....	.....	.....	1

h Married 42 years.
i One married 33 years, one married 37 years, and one married 40 years.
j One married 26 years and one married 34 years.
k Married 28 years.
l Married 33 years.
m Married 27 years.

TABLE **XVII.**—MARRIED WOMEN HAVING A SPECIFIED NUMBER OF
ITALIAN-BORN CHILDREN LIVING, BY NUMBER OF CHILDREN BORN
TO EACH IN ITALY AND YEARS OF MARRIED LIFE IN ITALY—Concluded.

[In this table married women include also widowed women.]

Children born in Italy and children living.	Married women having spent specified number of years of married life in Italy.										
	Un-der 1.	1.	2.	3.	4.	5.	6.	7.	8.	9.	10.
17 children:											
4 living	.....	.....	.....	.....	.....	.....	.....	.....	.....	.....	.....
Total	.....	.....	.....	.....	.....	.....	.....	.....	.....	.....	.....
19 children:											
3 living	.....	.....	.....	.....	.....	.....	.....	.....	.....	.....	.....
Total	.....	.....	.....	.....	.....	.....	.....	.....	.....	.....	.....
Not specified:											
None living	.....	.....	.....	.....	.....	.....	.....	.....	.....	.....	.....
1 living	.....	.....	.....	.....	.....	1	.....	.....	.....	.....	.....
2 living	.....	.....	.....	.....	.....	1	.....	.....	.....	.....	.....
Not specified	.....	.....	.....	.....	.....	.....	.....	1	.....	.....	.....
Total	.....	.....	.....	.....	.....	2	.....	1	.....	.....	.....
Total who have had children	1	20	36	40	43	44	41	45	47	39	41
Aggregate	3	52	52	45	45	47	46	50	49	43	42

a Married 39 years.

TABLE **XVII.**—MARRIED WOMEN HAVING A SPECIFIED NUMBER OF ITALIAN-BORN CHILDREN LIVING, BY NUMBER OF CHILDREN BORN TO EACH IN ITALY AND YEARS OF MARRIED LIFE IN ITALY—Concluded.

[In this table married women include also widowed women.]

| Married women having spent specified number of years of married life in Italy. | | | | | | | | | | | | | | | | | Total. |
11.	12.	13.	14.	15.	16.	17.	18.	19.	20.	21.	22.	23.	24.	25.	Over 25.	Not reported.	
																1	1
																1	1
															a 1		1
															1		1
																1	1
																	1
			1												b 1		2
			1													19	21
			1													20	25
34	32	41	24	16	19	16	19	11	19	9	13	6	10	4	45	66	781
35	32	42	24	18	19	17	20	13	20	9	14	6	10	4	47	73	877

b Married 31 years.

TABLE **XVIII.**—MARRIED WOMEN HAVING A SPECIFIED NUMBER OF NATIVE-BORN CHILDREN LIVING, BY NUMBER OF CHILDREN BORN TO EACH IN THE UNITED STATES AND YEARS OF MARRIED LIFE IN THE UNITED STATES.

[In this table married women include also widowed women.]

Children born in the United States and children living.	Married women having spent specified number of years of married life in the United States.										
	Under 1.	1.	2.	3.	4.	5.	6.	7.	8.	9.	10.
No children	58	36	17	23	34	29	12	12	22	14	16
1 child:											
None living		3	6	9	2	3	1	3		1	2
1 living	2	15	32	32	21	11	11	1	5	5	
Total	2	18	38	41	23	14	12	4	5	6	2
2 children:											
None living			2	2	4	3		1	1	2	1
1 living			5	19	21	16	5	1	2	4	1
2 living			2	36	31	26	14	8	6	4	2
Total			9	57	56	45	19	10	9	10	4
3 children:											
None living			1	4	1	2	1		1	1	2
1 living			1	1	6	7	4	2	2	1	1
2 living			1	2	14	17	14	3	8	4	4
3 living					6	14	17	6	13	4	2
Total			3	7	27	40	36	11	24	10	9
4 children:											
None living						1					
1 living						1	3	1	3	1	
2 living						5	5	5	7	3	4
3 living						3	5	9	10	9	10
4 living						1	3	3	6	8	2
Total						11	16	18	26	21	16
5 children:											
None living							1				
1 living							1	1	1	2	1
2 living							1	2	4	2	5
3 living							2	3	3	6	6
4 living								2	4	5	6
5 living									1	3	2
Total							5	8	13	18	20
6 children:											
None living							1				
1 living									1	1	1
2 living							1	1		2	2
3 living							1	1	1	3	
4 living											4
5 living										3	3
6 living											
Total							3	2	2	9	10
7 children:											
None living											
1 living											
2 living											
3 living											1
4 living									3	2	2
5 living											
6 living											1
7 living											1
Total									3	2	5

a Married 27 years.   b Married 26 years.

TABLE **XVIII**.—MARRIED WOMEN HAVING A SPECIFIED NUMBER OF NATIVE-BORN CHILDREN LIVING, BY NUMBER OF CHILDREN BORN TO EACH IN THE UNITED STATES AND YEARS OF MARRIED LIFE IN THE UNITED STATES.

[In this table married women include also widowed women.]

| Married women having spent specified number of years of married life in the United States. | | | | | | | | | | | | | | | | | Total. |
11.	12.	13.	14.	15.	16.	17.	18.	19.	20.	21.	22.	23.	24.	25.	Over 25.	Not reported.	
3	5	1	8	4	3	3		1	2	1						27	331
									1								31
1		1			1	1						1				3	143
1		1			1	1			1			1				3	174
1	1		1				2										20
1																1	77
1	1	2			1	1			1						a1	2	139
3	2	2	1		1	1	2		1						1	3	236
1									1						b1		15
					1											1	27
		2							1			1					72
	1	1	1	1		1											67
1	1	3	1	1	1	1			2			1			1	1	181
		1															1
	2	1		1	1												10
5	3	1	1	1			1		1						c1	1	35
												1				1	61
4	5		2	1			1		1								37
9	10	3	3	3	1		2		2			1			1	2	144
		2															3
1																	7
		1		1												1	17
1	3	1	2									1					26
3	1	1	2	1					2								27
1	2	1	4		1												15
6	6	5	7	2	1				2			1				1	95
			1														1
				1		1										2	4
4	2							1									11
2	3		3	1	2				1								13
	4	4	1	2	1					1							19
				1	1										1		16
																	3
6	9	4	5	5	5	1		1	1	1					1	2	67
		1															1
	1																1
2			1	1		1											5
3	1			3	2		1										17
		2	2		1	2	1										4
3		2		1	2	1									a1		10
	2												1				4
				1													2
8	4	4	4	5	5	1	1					1			1		44

c Married 30 years.

TABLE **XVIII.**—MARRIED WOMEN HAVING A SPECIFIED NUMBER OF NATIVE-BORN CHILDREN LIVING, BY NUMBER OF CHILDREN BORN TO EACH IN THE UNITED STATES AND YEARS OF MARRIED LIFE IN THE UNITED STATES—Concluded.

[In this table married women include also widowed women.]

Children born in the United States and children living.	Married women having spent specified number of years of married life in the United States.										
	Under 1.	1.	2.	3.	4.	5.	6.	l.	8.	9.	10.
8 children:											
1 living											
2 living											
3 living												1
4 living										1	
5 living											
6 living											
7 living										1	
Total										2	1
9 children:											
2 living											
3 living											
5 living											
6 living											
7 living											
8 living											
9 living											
Total											
10 children:											
None living											
1 living											
5 living											
6 living											
7 living											
Total											
11 children:											
3 living											
4 living											
5 living											
8 living											
Total											
12 children:											
3 living											
Total											
Not specified:											
None living											
2 living						1					
3 living											1
Not specified										1	
Total						1			1		1
Total who have had children	2	18	50	105	106	111	91	53	83	78	68
Aggregate	60	54	67	128	140	140	103	65	105	92	84

TABLE **XVIII.**—MARRIED WOMEN HAVING A SPECIFIED NUMBER OF NATIVE-BORN CHILDREN LIVING, BY NUMBER OF CHILDREN BORN TO EACH IN THE UNITED STATES AND YEARS OF MARRIED LIFE IN THE UNITED STATES—Concluded.

[In this table married women include also widowed women.]

| Married women having spent specified number of years of married life in the United States. | | | | | | | | | | | | | | | | | Total. |
11.	12.	13.	14.	15.	16.	17.	18.	19.	20.	21.	22.	23.	24.	25.	Over 25.	Not reported.	
		1			1												1
	1		1			1											2
	1	1	1				1										5
	1	1	1	2			1					1					6
		1		2			1										4
	2		1														3
				1													2
	4	**3**	**3**	**5**	**1**	**1**	**2**					**1**					**23**
				1													1
		1				1											2
	1			2			1										3
			1	2		1	1										5
					1												1
								1									1
		1															1
	1	**2**	**1**	**5**	**1**	**2**	**1**	**1**									**14**
						1											1
												1					1
	1																1
				1													1
						1											1
	1			**1**		**1**	**1**					**1**					**5**
													1				1
				1													1
						1											1
											1						1
				1		**1**					**1**		**1**				**4**
				1													1
				1													1
																1	1
																	1
1							1									20	23
1							1									21	26
35	38	27	25	28	18	10	9	3	9	1	1	6	1	1	4	33	1,014
38	43	28	33	32	21	13	9	4	11	2	1	6	1	1	4	60	1,345

TABLE **XIX.**—MARRIED WOMEN HAVING A SPECIFIED NUMBER OF CHILDREN LIVING, BY NUMBER OF CHILDREN BORN TO EACH AND YEARS OF MARRIED LIFE.

[In this table married women include also widowed women.]

Children born and children living.	Married women having spent specified number of years of married life.										
	Under 1.	1.	2.	3.	4.	5.	6.	7.	8.	9.	10.
No children	31	21	9	7	6	3	5	4	5	4	4
1 child:											
None living		1	5	4	....	1	....	3	2	2	....
1 living		8	26	19	11	4	4	2	1	2	2
Total		9	31	23	11	5	4	5	3	4	2
2 children:											
None living				2	4	....	1	1	2	1	....
1 living			2	8	8	10	2	2	1	2	1
2 living			1	15	17	17	4	5	3	4	....
Total			3	25	29	27	7	8	6	7	1
3 children:											
None living				2	1	1	....	....	....	....	2
1 living				....	3	4	4	4	1	3	3
2 living			1	....	9	8	9	5	7	5	1
3 living					2	12	13	6	6	4	3
Not specified											
Total			1	2	15	25	26	15	14	12	9
4 children:											
None living						2	....		1	....	....
1 living						1	2	....	2	1	1
2 living						1	2	5	5	2	4
3 living						4	1	5	5	6	13
4 living							3	2	3	3	1
Total						8	8	12	16	12	19
5 children:											
None living									1	....	1
1 living								2	....	1	1
2 living									2	3	4
3 living							2	1	3	6	7
4 living								1	3	3	3
5 living									1	3	2
Total							2	4	10	16	18
6 children:											
None living											
1 living										1	....
2 living										1	2
3 living							1	1	1	3	1
4 living										3	4
5 living											3
6 living											
Total							1	1	1	8	10

a Two married 26 years, one married 30 years, and one married 43 years.
b Married 28 years.
c Married 31 years.
d Married 26 years.
e One married 28 years and one married 34 years.
f One married 26 years and two married 28 years.
g Married 33 years.
h Married 32 years.
i Two married 28 years, one married 33 years, and one married 36 years.
j Married 38 years.
k Married 35 years.
l One married 30 years and one married 40 years.
m Two married 28 years and one married 30 years.

TABLE **XIX.**—MARRIED WOMEN HAVING A SPECIFIED NUMBER OF CHILDREN LIVING, BY NUMBER OF CHILDREN BORN TO EACH AND YEARS OF MARRIED LIFE.

[In this table married women include also widowed women.]

Married women having spent specified number of years of married life.																	Total.
11.	12.	13.	14.	15.	16.	17.	18.	19.	20.	21.	22.	23.	24.	25.	Over 25.	Not reported.	
1	1	1		3		1	1	1	2	1	1		3		*a* 4	3	122
															b 1		19
	1	2		1								1	1	1	*c* 1	2	89
	1	2		1								1	1	1	2	2	108
			1			1		1		1				1	*d* 1		17
	1		1	1	2		2					1			*e* 2		46
1	2	1	3	2	1	1		1					1	1	*f* 3	2	85
1	**3**	**1**	**4**	**4**	**3**	**1**	**3**	**1**	**1**		**1**	**1**	**1**	**2**	**6**	**2**	**148**
	1			1	1		1							1	*g* 1		11
		2		1			1		1		1			1	*h* 1		30
2	1	1	1			3			1					1	*i* 4	3	62
3	1		2	1	1	1			1	1					*j* 1	4	62
															k 1		1
5	**3**	**3**	**3**	**2**	**2**	**5**		**2**	**3**	**1**	**1**			**2**	**8**	**7**	**166**
							1		1						*l* 2	1	6
	1		1			1		1							*e* 2	1	14
7	2	1	2		1		2		1			1	1		*m* 3	1	40
4	3	6	1	2	2		2	1	1		2	3		1	*n* 6	1	59
5	2	1	6	1	1		2	1	1		2	3		1		3	47
16	**8**	**8**	**10**	**3**	**4**	**1**	**6**	**2**	**4**		**3**	**3**	**1**	**2**	**13**	**7**	**166**
			1	1			1								*o* 1		6
2															*p* 2	1	9
	3	2	1		1	2	1		1	1	1			2	*q* 2	1	27
3	7	3	2	1	3	2	1	3	3	1		2			*r* 6	1	57
5	3	2	3	1	1	1	1		1	1		1	3		*s* 4	2	39
2	2	2	1	2	3	2		2	1								23
12	**15**	**9**	**8**	**5**	**8**	**7**	**4**	**5**	**6**	**3**	**1**	**3**	**3**	**2**	**15**	**5**	**161**
	1																1
								1	1						*t* 2		5
2			2	2	1		1	1	1			1	1		*u* 3	2	20
1	2	3		4	1	1	2	1	3			2			*v* 6		33
1	5	2	4	3	2	3	1	3				2			*w* 2		37
	2		3	2		2	5		3					1	*x* 3	1	30
	2		1	3	1	1		1			1						11
4	**12**	**9**	**10**	**14**	**5**	**7**	**9**	**6**	**8**	**1**	**3**	**6**	**2**	**1**	**16**	**3**	**137**

n One married 27 years, one married 28 years, two married 30 years, one married 35 years, and one married 36 years.
o Married 27 years.
p One married 27 years and one married 28 years.
q One married 30 years and one married 39 years.
r Three married 30 years, two married 36 years, and one married 38 years.
s One married 27 years, one married 28 years, one married 30 years, and one married 39 years.
t Married 30 years.
u One married 26 years, one married 28 years, and one married 31 years.
v Two married 30 years, one married 35 years, one married 36 years, one married 40 years, and one married 44 years.
w One married 27 years and one married 40 years.
x One married 27 years and two married 40 years.

TABLE **XIX.**—MARRIED WOMEN HAVING A SPECIFIED NUMBER OF CHILDREN LIVING, BY NUMBER OF CHILDREN BORN TO EACH AND YEARS OF MARRIED LIFE—Continued.

[In this table married women include also widowed women.]

Children born and children living.	Married women having spent specified number of years of married life.										
	Under 1.	1.	2.	3.	4.	5.	6.	7.	8.	9.	10.
7 children:											
None living											
1 living											
2 living											
3 living										2		
4 living												
5 living												3
6 living												
7 living												
Total										2		3
8 children:											
None living												
1 living												
2 living												
3 living												
4 living												
5 living												
6 living												
7 living												
8 living												
Total												
9 children:											
1 living												
2 living												
3 living												
4 living												
5 living												
6 living												
7 living												
8 living												
9 living												
Total												
10 children:											
None living												
1 living												
2 living												
3 living												
4 living												
5 living												
6 living												
7 living												
8 living												
9 living												
Total												

a Married 30 years.
b Married 26 years.
c One married 26 years and one married 34 years.
d One married 28 years, one married 30 years, one married 32 years, and one married 34 years.
e Married 31 years.
f Married 37 years.
g One married 28 years and one married 30 years.
h Married 39 years.
i One married 26 years, one married 28 years, one married 30 years, one married 38 years, and one married 59 years.
j One married 27 years and one married 43 years.

TABLE **XIX.**—MARRIED WOMEN HAVING A SPECIFIED NUMBER OF CHILDREN LIVING, BY NUMBER OF CHILDREN BORN TO EACH AND YEARS OF MARRIED LIFE—Continued.

[In this table married women include also widowed women.]

11.	12.	13.	14.	15.	16.	17.	18.	19.	20.	21.	22.	23.	24.	25.	Over 25.	Not reported.	Total.
															a 1		1
	1												1		b 1		4
3		2	1	2		1	2	1	1	2					c 2	2	17
2	2	2			1					2	2						14
1	3	1	1	2	2	1	1		2		1			1	d 4	3	23
1		1		1	1	4			1		3			1	e 1	1	18
	2		2	1			2	1	1		1		1	1	f 1	1	13
									2		1		1	1	f 1		5
7	**8**	**4**	**4**	**7**	**3**	**8**	**5**	**2**	**7**	**4**	**6**		**3**	**3**	**11**	**8**	**95**
1																1	1
			1		1								2		g 2	1	7
		1	1		1			1			2		2		h 1	2	11
		2	2	1		1	2	1			2				i 5		18
	2	2	3	1		1	2								j 2		12
		1			3	1	1	3	2					1	k 2	1	18
	2		1	1	2	2		1			1			4		1	14
			1	1		4		1									7
							1	1			1						2
1	**4**	**4**	**7**	**5**	**7**	**11**	**6**	**10**	**4**		**5**		**4**	**5**	**12**	**5**	**90**
								1							l 1	1	3
			1		1			2				1			m 2		7
		1	1		2	2	1	2		2	2				n 4	2	16
					2			4	1	1	1				o 5		14
		1	1	1	1	1	1	3	1	3	1	1	1		p 4		15
						1	1	1		1	1						10
			1				1				1						3
							1				1						2
		1															1
		2	**2**	**3**	**5**	**4**	**3**	**4**	**12**	**3**	**5**	**6**	**2**	**1**	**16**	**3**	**71**
															f 1		1
										1		1					2
						1					1				e 2	1	3
												1			g 2		3
			1		1						1				b 1		4
			1		1										r 6		8
		1				1	1				1				a 1		5
				1		1						1			a 1		3
				1							2						4
																1	1
		1	**2**	**1**	**3**		**2**	**1**	**1**	**3**	**3**	**1**			**14**	**2**	**34**

k One married 29 years and one married 35 years.
l Married 52 years.
m One married 39 years and one married 41 years.
n One married 28 years, one married 32 years, one married 33 years, and one married 40 years.
o One married 30 years, one married 32 years, one married 35 years, one married 36 years, and one married 40 years.
p One married 29 years, one married 30 years, one married 35 years, and one married 38 years.
q One married 26 years and one married 30 years.
r One married 27 years, two married 30 years, one married 35 years, one married 40 years, and one married 47 years.

TABLE **XIX.**—MARRIED WOMEN HAVING A SPECIFIED NUMBER OF CHILDREN LIVING, BY NUMBER OF CHILDREN BORN TO EACH AND YEARS OF MARRIED LIFE—Concluded.

[In this table married women include also widowed women.]

Children born and children living.	Married women having spent specified number of years of married life.										
	Under 1.	1.	2.	3.	4.	5.	6.	7.	8.	9.	10.
11 children:											
2 living											
3 living											
4 living											
5 living											
6 living											
7 living											
8 living											
Not specified											
Total											
12 children:											
None living											
2 living											
3 living											
5 living											
6 living											
7 living											
9 living											
Total											
13 children:											
2 living											
3 living											
5 living											
6 living											
Total											
14 children:											
1 living											
2 living											
7 living											
Total											
17 children:											
4 living											
Total											
18 children:											
2 living											
Total											
19 children:											
3 living											
Total											
Not specified:											
None living											
2 living											
Not specified											
Total											
Total who have had children		9	35	50	55	65	48	45	52	59	62
Aggregate	31	30	44	57	61	68	53	49	57	63	66

a One married 34 years and one married 40 years.
b Married 29 years.
c One married 26 years and one married 31 years.
d One married 32 years and one married 33 years.

TABLE **XIX.**—MARRIED WOMEN HAVING A SPECIFIED NUMBER OF CHILDREN LIVING, BY NUMBER OF CHILDREN BORN TO EACH AND YEARS OF MARRIED LIFE—Concluded.

[In this table married women include also widowed women.]

Married women having spent specified number of years of married life.

11.	12.	13.	14.	15.	16.	17.	18.	19.	20.	21.	22.	23.	24.	25.	Over 25.	Not reported.	Total.
															2[a]	1	3
				1								1			1[b]		3
				1							2						3
									2						2[c]		4
									2	1				1			4
									1				1		2[d]		4
										1	1						2
															1[e]		1
				2					**5**	**2**	**3**	**1**	**1**	**1**	**8**	**1**	**24**
											1						1
														1			1
											1		1	1			3
													1		1[f]		2
															1[g]		1
											1						1
									1						1[h]		2
									1		**3**		**2**	**2**	**3**		**11**
															1[i]		1
											1		1				2
									1								1
																1	1
									1		**1**		**1**		**1**	**1**	**5**
											1				1[i]		2
									1								1
											1		1		1[j]	1	3
									1		**1**		**1**		**2**	**1**	**6**
																1	1
																1	1
															1[g]		1
															1		1
															1[g]		1
															1		1
																1	1
															1[k]		1
1											1					20	22
1											1				1	21	24
47	54	42	49	48	38	47	36	34	54	15	36	25	22	23	130	69	1,249
48	55	43	49	51	38	48	37	35	56	16	37	25	25	23	134	72	1,371

e Married 26 years.
f Married 32 years.
g Married 40 years.
h Married 33 years.

i Married 28 years.
j Married 27 years.
k Married 35 years.

TABLE **XX.**—PERSONS SICK OR PHYSICALLY DEFECTIVE, BY KIND OF AILMENT OR DEFECT AND SEX.

Ailment or defect.	Male.	Female.	Total.	Ailment or defect.	Male.	Female.	Total.
Abscesses	2	....	2	Dropsy	....	1	1
Abscesses, scrofulous	5	1	6	Dropsy, abdominal	1	....	1
Arm, congenital paralysis of one	1	....	1	Dropsy, abdominal; rickets	1	....	1
Arm, loss of one	2	1	3	Dyspepsia	16	6	22
Arm, one broken; fever, not specified	....	1	1	Ear (middle), inflammation of	1	2	3
Arm, one crippled	....	1	1	Elbow joint, immobility of one	1	....	1
Arm, one disabled	1	....	1	Epilepsy	4	2	6
Asthma	4	4	8	Erysipelas	2	2	4
Bladder, inflammation of	....	1	1	Erysipelas; loss of one leg	1	....	1
Blind	2	4	6	Eye, inflammation of one	1	1	2
Blind in one eye	1	....	1	Eye, loss of one	8	6	14
Blindness, partial	....	1	1	Eyes, inflammation of both	14	10	24
Blood poisoning	....	1	1	Eyes, weakness of	2	....	2
Boils	4	....	4	Feeble-minded	7	3	10
Bowels, inflammation of	4	2	6	Feeble-minded; cross-eyed	1	....	1
Bowels, inflammation of; rickets	....	1	1	Feeble-minded; deaf	1	....	1
Bowlegs	1	....	1	Feeble-minded; deaf; lame	....	1	1
Brain, congestion of	....	2	2	Female complaint	....	62	62
Bronchitis	60	42	102	Female complaint; immobility of one wrist	....	1	1
Bronchitis; fever, not specified	1	....	1	Fever, gastric	1	1	2
Bronchitis; one foot maimed	1	....	1	Fever, malarial	16	6	22
Catarrh, chronic	....	1	1	Fever, not specified	62	20	82
Chicken pox	1	2	3	Fever, not specified; bowlegs	1	....	1
Childbirth	....	263	263	Fever, not specified; lame	....	1	1
Childbirth; abscess	....	1	1	Fever, not specified; neuralgia	....	1	1
Childbirth; bronchitis	....	2	2	Fever, puerperal	....	1	1
Childbirth; congestion of liver	....	1	1	Fever, rheumatic	1	....	1
Childbirth; consumption	....	1	1	Fever, scarlet	1	3	4
Childbirth; cross-eyed	....	1	1	Fever, typhoid	45	23	68
Childbirth; dyspepsia	....	1	1	Fever, typhoid; bronchitis	1	1	2
Childbirth; female complaint	....	10	10	Fever, typhoid; consumption	1	....	1
Childbirth; fever, not specified	....	3	3	Fever, typhoid; feeble-minded	1	....	1
Childbirth; heart disease	....	2	2	Finger, deformity of one	1	....	1
Childbirth; hysteria	....	1	1	Finger, loss of one	1	....	1
Childbirth; loss of one leg	....	1	1	Fingers, loss of two	1	....	1
Childbirth; malarial fever	....	1	1	Fingers, loss of three	1	....	1
Childbirth; miscarriage	....	1	1	Foot, loss of one	2	....	2
Childbirth; nervous affection	....	2	2	Glands, scrofulous	3	1	4
Childbirth; pneumonia	....	1	1	Glands, scrofulous; loss of one thumb	....	1	1
Childbirth; puerperal fever	....	1	1	Goiter	....	1	1
Childbirth; rheumatism	....	2	2	Hand, one crippled	1	....	1
Childbirth; syphilis	....	1	1	Hand, penetrating wound of one	1	....	1
Childbirth; tumor of breast	....	1	1	Harelip	1	1	2
Childbirth; typhoid fever	....	2	2	Hay fever	1	....	1
Childbirth; varicose veins	....	1	1	Heart, disease of	1	7	8
Childbirth; weakness of spine	....	1	1	Hip-joint disease	2	2	4
Consumption	11	6	17	Humpback	1	....	1
Convulsions	4	2	6	Idiot	7	3	10
Convulsions; feeble-minded	1	....	1	Idiot; malarial fever	....	1	1
Convulsions; feeble-minded; rickets	1	....	1	Indigestion	4	2	6
Crippled	....	1	1	Injury by accident	67	8	75
Cross-eyed	....	4	4	Injury by accident; epilepsy	1	....	1
Croup	....	1	1	Injury by accident; lame	2	....	2
Deaf	3	1	4	Injury by accident; loss of one eye	1	....	1
Deafness, partial	2	....	2	Injury by accident; rickets	1	....	1
Debility, general	1	7	8	Insane	....	1	1
Debility, general; arrested development	....	1	1	Insane; dropsy	1	....	1
Debility, general; deformity of one hand	1	....	1	Kidneys, disease of	10	1	11
Deformed	1	....	1	Knee joint, immobility of one	1	....	1
Diarrhea	1	2	3	Knee joint, inflammation of one	2	....	2
Diarrhea, chronic	....	1	1				
Diphtheria	16	12	28				

TABLE **XX.**—PERSONS SICK OR PHYSICALLY DEFECTIVE, BY KIND OF AILMENT OR DEFECT AND SEX—Concluded.

Ailment or defect.	Number.			Ailment or defect.	Number.		
	Male.	Female.	Total.		Male.	Female.	Total.
La grippe	2	2	4	Rheumatism; heart disease	1	....	1
Lame	11	3	14	Rickets	43	46	89
Leg, abscess on; one hand partly paralyzed	1	....	1	Rickets; bronchitis	4	2	6
Leg, deformity of one	1	....	1	Rickets; convulsions	1	1	2
Leg, loss of one	13	1	14	Rickets; crippled	1	....	1
Leg, one broken	1	....	1	Rickets; fever, not specified	2	....	2
Leg, one crippled	1	....	1	Rickets; loss of one eye	....	1	1
Leg, one swollen	....	1	1	Rickets; measles	1	....	1
Legs, swollen; general debility	....	1	1	Rickets; rheumatism	1	....	1
Liver, disease of	1	....	1	Rickets; typhoid fever	1	2	3
Lung, penetrating wound of one	1	....	1	Rupture	2	1	3
Lungs, disease of	1	1	2	Saint Vitus' dance	....	1	1
Measles	18	21	39	Sight defective	1	....	1
Measles; one hand crippled	1	....	1	Skin, disease of	4	10	14
Miscarriage	....	16	16	Smallpox	1	2	3
Miscarriage; typhoid fever	....	1	1	Spine, disease of; crippled	....	1	1
Mumps	....	1	1	Spine, weakness of	1	2	3
Neuralgia	4	2	6	Sunstroke	2	....	2
Operation, surgical	1	....	1	Syphilis	1	4	5
Palsy	1	....	1	Syphilis; loss of one eye	....	1	1
Paralysis	2	1	3	Syphilis; rickets	2	....	2
Pleurisy	1	....	1	Throat, inflammation of	4	3	7
Pneumonia	28	11	39	Toe, loss of one	1	....	1
Pneumonia; bowlegs	1	....	1	Tumor, not specified	1	....	1
Pneumonia; injury to spine	1	....	1	Tumors, bony; bowlegs	....	1	1
Polypus	1	....	1	Vaccination	....	1	1
Rheumatism	71	24	95	Vertigo	2	....	2
Rheumatism; deaf	1	....	1	Whooping cough	....	4	4
				Wound, gunshot	1	....	1
				Not specified	7	6	13
				Total	686	762	1,448

INDEX.